Large Herbivore Ecology, Ecosystem Dy

The major drivers forming the shape and function of terrestrial ecosystems are large herbivores. These animals modify primary production, nutrient cycles, soil properties and fire regimes, which all have an impact on the ecology of other organisms. Most large herbivores require some type of management within their habitats, as some species populations are at the brink of extinction, and others already occur in dense populations causing conflicts with other land uses. Due to the huge importance of herbivores in shaping a wide variety of ecosystems worldwide, it is important to understand how and why these communities function the way they do, and what implications this has not only for the conservation of the herbivores themselves but also for the conservation of the habitats as a whole. This book deals with the scientific basis for the management of these systems.

KJELL DANELL is Professor of Animal Ecology at the Swedish University of Agricultural Sciences, Umeå, Sweden. His main research interests are basic and applied plant–animal interactions, community ecology, invasive species and macro-ecology.

ROGER BERGSTRÖM is Senior Researcher at The Forestry Research Institute of Uppsala, Sweden and Associate Professor at the Swedish University of Agricultural Sciences.

PATRICK DUNCAN is Director of the Centre d'Etudes Biologiques de Chizé, Centre National de la Recherche Scientifique 79 360 Beauvoir-sur-Noirt, France.

JOHN PASTOR is Professor of the Department of Biology and The Natural Resources Research Institute, University of Minnesota, Duluth, USA.

Conservation Biology

Conservation biology is a flourishing field, but there is still enormous potential for making further use of the science that underpins it. This new series aims to present internationally significant contributions from leading researchers in particularly active areas of conservation biology. It will focus on topics where basic theory is strong and where there are pressing problems for practical conservation. The series will include both single-authored and edited volumes and will adopt a direct and accessible style targeted at interested undergraduates, postgraduates, researchers and university teachers. Books and chapters will be rounded, authoritative accounts of particular areas with the emphasis on review rather than original data papers. The series is the result of a collaboration between the Zoological Society of London and Cambridge University Press. The series editor is Professor Morris Gosling, Professor of Animal Behaviour at the University of Newcastle upon Tyne. The series ethos is that there are unexploited areas of basic science that can help define conservation biology and bring a radical new agenda to the solution of pressing conservation problems.

Published Titles

1. *Conservation in a Changing World*, edited by Georgina Mace, Andrew Balmford and Joshua Ginsberg 0 521 63270 6 (hardcover), 0 521 63445 8 (paperback)
2. *Behaviour and Conservation*, edited by Morris Gosling and William Sutherland 0 521 66230 3 (hardcover), 0 521 66539 6 (paperback)
3. *Priorities for the Conservation of Mammalian Diversity*, edited by Abigail Entwistle and Nigel Dunstone 0 521 77279 6 (hardcover), 0 521 77536 1 (paperback)
4. *Genetics, Demography and Viability of Fragmented Populations*, edited by Andrew G. Young and Geoffrey M. Clarke 0 521 782074 (hardcover), 0 521 794218 (paperback)
5. *Carnivore Conservation* Edited by Gittleman *et al*. 0 521 66232 X (hardcover), 0 521 66537 X (paperback)
6. *Conservation of Exploited Species* Edited by Reynolds *et al*. 0 521 78216 3 (hardcover), 0 521 78733 5 (paperback)
7. *Conserving Bird Biodiversity* Edited by Ken Norris, Deborah J. Pain 0 521 78340 2 (hardcover), 0 521 78949 4 (paperback)
8. *Reproductive Science and Integrated Conservation* Edited by Holt *et al*. 0 521 81215 1 (hardcover), 0 521 01110 8 (paperback)
9. *People and Wildlife, Conflict or Co-existence?* Edited by Woodroofe *et al*. 0 521 82505 9 (hardcover), 0 521 53203 5 (paperback)
10. *Phylogeny and Conservation* Edited by Andrew Purvis, John L. Gittleman, Thomas Brooks 0 521 82502 4 (hardcover), 0 521 53200 0 (paperback)

Large Herbivore Ecology, Ecosystem Dynamics and Conservation

Edited by

KJELL DANELL

Swedish University of Agricultural Sciences, SE-90183 Umeå, Sweden.

PATRICK DUNCAN

Centre d'Études Biologiques de Chizé, Centre National de la Recherche Scientifique, 79 360 BEAUVOIR-sur-NIORT, France.

ROGER BERGSTRÖM

The Forestry Research Institute of Sweden, Uppsala Science Park, SE-73183 Uppsala, Sweden.

JOHN PASTOR

University of Minnesota, Duluth, MN 55811, USA.

CAMBRIDGE
UNIVERSITY PRESS

CAMBRIDGE UNIVERSITY PRESS
Cambridge, New York, Melbourne, Madrid, Cape Town, Singapore, São Paulo

Cambridge University Press
The Edinburgh Building, Cambridge CB2 2RU, UK

Published in the United States of America by Cambridge University Press, New York

www.cambridge.org
Information on this title: www.cambridge.org/9780521830052

First published 2006

Printed in the United Kingdom at the University Press, Cambridge

A catalogue record for this book is available from the British Library

ISBN-13 978-0-521-83005-2 hardback
ISBN-10 0-521-83005-2 hardback
ISBN-13 978-0-521-53687-5 paperback
ISBN-10 0-521-53687-1 paperback

Contents

Contributors

REIDAR ANDERSEN
Department of Biology, Norwegian University of Science and Technology, Høgskoleringen 5, N-7491 Trondheim, Norway.

ELISABETH BAKKER
Department of Plant–Animal Interactions Netherlands Institute of Ecology P.O. Box 1299 NL-3631 AC Maarssen, The Netherlands.

MARGARETA BERGMAN
Department of Animal Ecology, Swedish University of Agricultural Sciences, SE-90183 Umeå, Sweden.

ROGER BERGSTRÖM
The Forestry Research Institute of Sweden, Uppsala Science Park, SE-73183 Uppsala, Sweden.

RICHARD BODMER
Durrell Institute of Conservation and Ecology, University of Kent, Canterbury, Kent CT2 7NS, UK.

HARALD BUGMANN
Mountain Forest Ecology, Department of Environmental Sciences, ETH-Zentrum HG G 21.3, Rämistrasse 101, CH-8092 Zürich, Switzerland.

YOSEF COHEN
Department of Fisheries and Wildlife, University of Minnesota, St. Paul, MN 55105, USA.

MICHAEL B. COUGHENOUR
Natural Resource Ecology Laboratory, Colorado State University, Fort Collins, Colorado 80523-1499, USA.

KJELL DANELL
Department of Animal Ecology, Swedish University of Agricultural Sciences, SE-90183 Umeå, Sweden.

PATRICK DUNCAN
CNRS UPR 1934, Centre d'Études Biologiques de Chizé, 79 360 BEAUVOIR-sur-NIORT, France.

DOUGLAS A. FRANK
Biological Research Laboratories Syracuse University, Syracuse, NY 13244-1220, USA.

HERVÉ FRITZ
Centre d'Études Biologiques de Chizé, CNRS UPR 1934, F-79 360 Beauvoir-sur-Niort, France.

ROBIN GILL
Woodland Ecology Branch, Forest Research, Alice Holt Lodge, Wrecclesham, Surrey, GU10 4LH, UK.

IAIN J. GORDON
Macaulay Institute, Craigiebuckler, Aberdeen, AB15 8QH, UK. (Present address: Sustainable Ecosystems, CSIRO – Davies Laboratory, PMB PO Aitkenvale, Qld 4816, Australia.)

ALISON J. HESTER
Macaulay Institute, Craigiebuckler Aberdeen, AB15 8QH, UK

N. THOMPSON HOBBS
Natural Resource Ecology Laboratory, Colorado State University, Fort Collins, Colorado 80523-1499, USA.

GLENN IASON
Macaulay Institute, Craigiebuckler,
Aberdeen, AB15 8QH, UK.

ANDREW W. ILLIUS
Institute of Evolutionary Biology, School of
Biological Sciences, University of
Edinburgh, West Mains Road, Edinburgh
EH9 3JT, UK.

JOHN D.C. LINNELL
Norwegian Institute for Nature Research
(NINA), Tungasletta 2, N-7485 Trondheim,
Norway.

ANNE LOISON
Laboratory of Biometry and Biological
Evolution, CNRS-UMR 5558, Université
Claude Bernard Lyon 1, F-69622
Villeurbanne Cedex, France.

JON MOEN
Department of Ecology and Environmental
Sciences, Umeå University, SE-901 87
Umeå, Sweden.

HAN OLFF
Community and Conservation Ecology
Group, Centre for Ecological and
Evolutionary Studies, University of
Groningen, PO Box 14, NL-9750 AA
Haren, The Netherlands.

JOHN P. PASTOR
Department of Biology and Natural
Resources Research Institute, University of
Minnesota, Duluth, MN 55811, USA.

ERLING J. SOLBERG
Norwegian Institute for Nature Research
(NINA), Tungasletta 2, N-7485 Trondheim,
Norway.

OTSO SUOMINEN
Section of Ecology, Department of Biology,
University of Turku, FIN-20014 Turku,
Finland.

FRANS W.M. VERA
Staatsbosbeheer, PO Box 1300, NL-3970
BH Driebergen, The Netherlands.

DAVID WARD
School of Botany and Zoology, University
of KwaZulu-Natal, Scottsville 3209, South
Africa.

PETER WEISBERG
Department of Natural Resources and
Environmental Science, University of
Nevada, Reno, 1000 Valley Road / MS 186,
Reno, Nevada 89512-0013, USA.

Preface

Large herbivores are, and have for a long time been, among the major drivers for forming the shape and function of terrestrial ecosystems. These animals may modify primary production, nutrient cycles, soil properties, fire regimes as well as other biota. Some large herbivore species/populations are at the edge of extinction and great effort is being made to save them. Other species/populations are under discussion for reintroduction. Still other species occur in dense populations and cause conflicts with other land use interests. Overall, most large herbivores need some type of management and, according to our view, these operations should be scientifically based.

There is a great amount of scientific information on large herbivores in different regions of the world. We felt that there was an urgent need to bring this knowledge together and to make it available for a larger public outside the group of specialists. We also felt that synthesis of results from one region may be valuable for scientists working in other regions and with other species.

To initiate a first synthesis of the knowledge on large herbivores we held a workshop on 'The impact of large mammalian herbivores on biodiversity, ecosystem structure and function' 22–26 May 2002 at Kronlund outside Umeå in northern Sweden. The event brought together scientists from different disciplines and with experience of large herbivore research in different biomes. During the workshop the idea of a book was developed over time and some more specialists were invited to the synthesis.

We thank the financial support given by Swedish Environmental Protection Agency, The Swedish Research Council for Environment, Agricultural Sciences and Spatial Planning, Swedish Association for Hunting and Wildlife Management and the Faculty of Forest Sciences of the Swedish University of Agricultural Sciences. Special thanks are due to the representatives for the forest companies, the hunting organizations, and the

Saami people who gave valuable inputs and stimulated the discussions during the field trip of the workshop.

This book represents the culmination of the process initiated by the workshop. Edited volumes are by definition collaborative efforts. This book would not have been possible without the patience and strong commitment of all the contributors, including the numerous reviewers. We are deeply grateful for their efforts, collaboration and for allotting time and sharing insights and data. Special appreciation is due to Dr Tuulikki Rooke who provided excellent assistance during the last stage of the preparation of the book.

We are fully aware of the fact that this book gives only one perspective of large herbivores – the one seen by natural scientists. We hope that a similar effort will be made by scientists doing research on the human dimension of large herbivores. In concert, we hope these efforts will give valuable insights for managers and scientists, stimulate further studies and make further syntheses possible.

Introduction

PATRICK DUNCAN, KJELL DANELL,
ROGER BERGSTRÖM AND JOHN PASTOR

Biodiversity and productivity vary strongly among ecosystems: understanding the causes of these variations is a primary objective of ecology. To date a few overarching principles have been established. One is the species-area relationship: the species diversity of a system depends principally on its area, and some major mechanisms underlying this principle have been identified (Rosenzweig 1995). The structure and dynamics of plant communities also affect biodiversity profoundly. Edaphic conditions set the bounds for plant communities, and fire can be a key determinant of their structure and diversity. In addition, at least in some ecosystems, large herbivores are 'keystone' species, so the systems have very different structures according to whether large herbivores are present or absent. There is also some evidence that large herbivores affect plant productivity, from modelling (de Mazancourt et al. 1998) as well as empirical work (McNaughton 1985).

Understanding the role of large herbivores is therefore important for ecology, and also because the abundance of these animals can have profound effects on the conservation status of other species, through their impact on plant communities. However, the literature on these questions is rather difficult to access especially for people who are not academic ecologists. Reviewing the impact of large herbivores on ecosystems was identified as a priority in the Action Plan for the Large Herbivore Initiative for Europe and Central Asia (see http://www.largeherbivore.org). In some areas the ungulate populations are 'overabundant' and have serious negative impacts on forestry, agriculture and biodiversity. In other areas the

Large Herbivore Ecology, Ecosystem Dynamics and Conservation, ed. K. Danell, P. Duncan, R. Bergström & J. Pastor. Published by Cambridge University Press. © Cambridge University Press 2006.

ungulate populations are approaching extinction. There are thus many urgent management and conservation problems connected to large herbivores, and an accessible review of existing knowledge is urgently needed to underpin progress towards effective management.

In May 2002 Kjell Danell, Roger Bergström and John Pastor convened a workshop in Sweden to review 'The Impact of Large Mammalian Herbivores on Biodiversity, Ecosystem Structure and Function' and this book is the result of the work that started there. It focuses on wild large herbivores since information on domestic animals is voluminous and easier to access (though it could also benefit from being analysed to answer ecological questions!). Our main aim was to provide an up to date review of existing knowledge on the impact of large herbivores on species richness, ecosystem structure and function in the major habitats of the world. We also explore what is known about the consequences of global change on large herbivores populations, and their impact on ecosystems, and what needs to be done to improve our understanding of this crucial area.

The first chapter, **'Large herbivores across biomes' by H. Fritz and A. Loison**, presents the major communities of wild large herbivores in all the continents. For the purposes of this book, we define large herbivores as even-toed (Artiodactyla) and odd-toed ungulates (Perissodactyla) over 5 kg, and elephants (Proboscidea). The abundance of large herbivores, at least in Africa at a regional scale, are determined ultimately by the abundance of their resources. The general principles underlying the diversity of their communities in all the continents are reviewed, starting with what is known about their palaeohistory. The patterns of distribution of some of the key life history traits are also reviewed, body size, mating system, sexual dimorphism and litter weight. The different body sizes are distributed across habitats and feeding guilds in log normal (hump-backed) distributions, whose modes increase with openness of the habitats, and this is true for marsupials as well as eutherians. Dimorphism in body mass is closely related to polygyny in Artiodactyla, but not in the other groups, so other variables are clearly important here. Demographic strategies, which also vary considerably, nonetheless show some clear patterns: large herbivores share high and relatively constant adult survival, relatively early and variable age at maturity, and a relatively low and very variable juvenile survival. These patterns appear to hold true across phylogeny, biomes, habitat and feeding types.

The following chapters in the first part of the book deal with determinants of the dynamics of large herbivore populations and communities, notably the linkage between resource abundance and population dynamics, the capacity of large herbivores to cope with seasonality in resources and in climatic conditions, and the interplay between large herbivores and large predators.

In Chapter 2, 'Living in a seasonal environment' by J. Moen, R. Andersen and A.W. Illius, the focus is on a biome where seasonality is extreme, the Arctic. The effects of climatic variability on population sizes are analysed, and then the mechanisms are explored by evaluating the effects of environmental stochasticity on life history tactics of large herbivores (e.g. capital vs. income breeding), and the role of body size. Many models of global change predict an increase in the season of vegetative growth, which is already detectable, and the resulting increase in plant growth will generally be positive for large herbivores as both plant biomass and nutritional quality will increase. The decrease in snow cover (in some areas) will also be positive for large herbivores as they will have a longer period for body growth and an increased survival during the shorter winters. However, it is unclear what effect this will have on population dynamics: if climate change leads to increased animal growth and survival, the animal populations may enter winter at densities too high to be supported by winter resources. These climate changes may even result in lower accessibility of winter forage which could cause declines in calf body weight and survival during winter. Long-term monitoring is clearly essential, and coupled models of plant and animal dynamics like those of Illius and O'Connor (2000) could help to direct management of these systems, which are so sensitive to damage by overgrazing.

In Chapter 3, 'Linking functional responses and foraging behaviour to population dynamics' by A.W. Illius, an in depth review is given of what is known about a key interface – the interaction between large herbivores and their food resources. Our knowledge of the underlying principles is reviewed, distinguishing the way consumption rates respond to food abundance (i.e. the functional response) from the way the size of the consumer population responds to variations in food consumption (the numerical response). The work of Spalinger and Hobbs (1992) provides a systematic means of analysing functional responses and evaluating biologically meaningful parameters. This is used to review the state of the art in foraging behaviour, diet selection and food intake of wild and domestic herbivores. Andrew Illius concludes by stating 'there are a priori and empirical grounds for the propositions that optimal patch use is not an appropriate model of resource use by browsing mammalian herbivores, and that longer-term diet optimization, i.e. the trade-off between diet quality and daily intake rate, is a more likely explanation of their foraging behaviour'.

Approaches to describing how consumer populations change in response to the average per capita food intake are then reviewed, from the simplistic/abstract representations of ecological interactions, such as Lotka-Volterra coupled differential equations to the mechanistic approach of Illius and Gordon (1999). An alternative approach has been developed by Owen-Smith (2002) who describes consumer-resource systems in terms of biomass dynamics, rather than numbers of consumers, and uses aggregated efficiencies of assimilation, metabolism, repair and senescence to model aggregated population dynamics.

In Chapter 4, 'Impacts of large herbivores on plant community structure and dynamics' by A.J. Hester, M. Bergman, G.R. Iason and J. Moen, the focus is on the main direct impacts of herbivores on shrub and woodland systems to complement the later reviews, which cover more tree-dominated habitats. Their review covers the effects on individual plants (or ramets) and the range of responses of individual plants to herbivory, as a basis from which to explore the complexities of processes operating at the plant community level. Large herbivores make foraging decisions at a range of spatial (from bite to landscape) and temporal scales (from seconds to years), and plants also respond to herbivore impacts at a similar range of scale (plant part to community). This makes the identification of key processes affecting plant/herbivore interactions and the mechanisms driving plant community responses to herbivores quite a challenge. Some of the apparent controversies in the literature about herbivore influences on vegetation may be due to this difficulty.

Although most direct effects on plants, by grazing or browsing, are negative, indirect effects on seed dispersal, in the gut or on the body, are largely positive. Although some of the seeds do not survive herbivore digestive processes, others require passage through the gut of a herbivore for germination, or at least benefit from it. Further, the effects of large herbivores on seeding establishment are generally positive. Effects of large herbivore activities on plant growth and mortality can of course be strong; these are reviewed in relation to the type of tissue which is affected, the extent and frequency of off-take, and the herbivores involved.

Removal of plant parts above the ground inevitably affects belowground processes as well. Reallocation of resources, at least in grasses, usually leads to increased shoot growth (i.e. to restoration of root:shoot ratios after damage). Above-ground herbivory can also induce changes in mycorrhizal fungi, thereby affecting nutrient uptake and subsequent

growth and survival. Most studies show declines in mycorrhizal colonization as a result of herbivory, which can have powerful effects on the
dynamics of the plant communities.

Plant responses to herbivores are reviewed, including defences (physical and chemical) and tolerance. Plants can avoid large herbivores through
their spatial location, visibility (apparency), or by producing defence structures such as thorns, hairs or thick cuticles. They may also produce
'allelochemicals'; several hypotheses have been proposed to explain their
ecological and evolutionary occurrence: the merits of these hypotheses,
particularly the 'carbon-nutrient balance' hypothesis, are reviewed. The
conditions determining 'tolerance' and 'compensation' are reviewed: although plants are most commonly detrimentally affected by herbivory,
there is a long-running debate as there are examples of exact- or overcompensation in a considerable number of studies. Most of these, however,
were short-term responses and might not accurately reflect long-term
fitness – an important distinction.

There is a wealth of literature on the impact of large herbivores on
plant diversity (species, structure and genetic), but still much controversy. This is probably due to both the complexity of the subject and a
scarcity of long-term controlled studies where all main driving factors
are understood. Most studies indicate that herbivores are more likely to
increase the diversity and spatial heterogeneity of plant communities.
However, the authors of this chapter show that there are exceptions, and
that the conditions under which herbivores increase or decrease diversity and heterogeneity, and the mechanisms involved, are still not fully
understood.

Chapter 5, 'Long-term effects of herbivory on plant diversity and functional types in arid ecosystems' by D. Ward, addresses two contrasting yet
widely held beliefs about the dynamics of the vegetation in arid ecosystems: first, that abiotic factors have more impact than biotic factors
(principally because herbivores are limited at low densities by sparse
resources), so herbivory by mammals is relatively unimportant in ecosystem functioning and biodiversity maintenance, and secondly that heavy
grazing has caused land denudation and desertification in semi-arid
regions such as the Sahel of Africa. It is important here to distinguish
between short-term effects of herbivory (which lead to the removal of
phytomass) and long-term ones (which lead to changes in productivity
and the species composition of the plant communities). David Ward starts
by showing that the results of long-term studies of the effects of large
mammals on arid vegetation are not consistent. In some areas the impact

is strong, in others weak. Ward argues that the inconsistency in the results of the long-term studies may result from oscillations of vegetation and herbivore populations: migratory or nomadic movements of the animals could lead to contrasting pressure of herbivory at times of the year, such as the growing season, that are crucial for the dynamics of the plants.

Some of the most interesting effects of herbivory on plant diversity result from the effects of selective herbivory on the relationships among plant functional types, in particular herbaceous vs. woody plants. Ward focuses on the phenomenon of 'bush encroachment', as evidence is accumulating that suggests this trend is a general one in arid and semi-arid savannas throughout the world. He illustrates it from arid regions ranging from the Namib and Kalahari deserts, to the Mitchell grass plains of Australia via the southern Sahara, the Negev and central Asian deserts, and reviews the general explanations that have been proposed for bush encroachment. The first is Walter's two-layer hypothesis, based on tree-grass competition. Later models propose that trees and grasses coexist in a state between that of grassland and forest because the plant communities are 'pushed back' into the savanna state by frequent disturbances (human impact, fire, herbivory and drought). Ward then describes the results of experiments to test some of these models, and shows that the results open new perspectives for understanding the fundamental processes and for management of bush encroachment. Under the conventional two-layer competition hypothesis, grazing during years with less than average precipitation should be reduced to a minimum so as not to give the trees a competitive advantage. By contrast, the new results suggest that bush encroachment may not occur when water is limited and consequently such a management protocol would be futile.

Grazing responses in arid and semi-arid rangelands in winter rainfall regions differ from those in summer rainfall regions, and plant height may be a more important factor than palatability, life history or taxonomic affiliation in determining responses to herbivory. Ward argues that the 'classical' theory of grassland response to grazing which defines plants as increasers or decreasers has some value in explaining plant responses, but should be replaced by a theory which considers plant size and other relevant traits such as palatability and specific leaf area. More studies on more continents are also needed to tease apart the effects of evolutionary history of grazing and abiotic environmental factors on grazing responses and plant functional traits.

Chapter 6, '**The influence of large herbivores on tree recruitment and forest dynamics' by R. Gill**, shows that the effects of large herbivores on tree regeneration can be grouped broadly into two main types. Firstly, the effects of feeding on seeds, seedlings and bark, which are damaging, and delay forest succession or accelerate senescence. Secondly, the effects which promote regeneration and thus tend to advance forest succession. There appear to be at least four mechanisms involved in this latter group: regeneration may be promoted through seed dispersal, protection from thorny plants, reduced competition, or, lastly, by reduced fire frequency or fire temperatures as a result of reduced fuel. In general, the retarding effects of herbivory appear to be more prevalent in woodlands and forests, whereas facilitation is more likely to occur in open habitats. The fact that these two contrasting processes occur in different communities has led to the suggestion that large herbivores cause a cycle of succession, where the serial stages of open ground, young trees, maturing woodlands and senescent stands finally give way to open ground again. Large herbivores can therefore create more dynamic woodlands, where changes in tree cover occur continually, and where light-demanding species are favoured at the expense of shade-tolerant ones.

There is evidence for the simultaneous existence of all stages of this cycle, and there is no reason to suggest that the rates of regeneration and senescence will be balanced. Rates of tree regeneration and damage by large herbivores can be highly variable. Facilitation by thorny plants will depend on the suitability of the site for the nurse species. Each species of herbivore has a unique pattern of habitat and diet selection. As a result, the impact of large herbivores can lead to dominance of either grassland or of closed-canopy woodland. The effect of large herbivores on nutrient flows can bring about enduring changes in vegetation composition. Since the amount of food for herbivores can be sharply reduced by shade, animal populations will decline if trees grow dense enough to form closed-canopy woodland over an extensive areas, which then limits the extent to which herbivores can maintain openings. In the savanna regions of Africa, switching between woodland and grassland states can occur: as a result of a combination of grazing, elephants and fire, woodlands in the Serengeti-Mara region were opened up in the 1960s, but began to recover again in part of the region during the 1980s, when elephant numbers were severely reduced. These changes suggest that savanna ecosystems may be unstable, or have alternative stable states, and events affecting herbivore numbers or grazing pressure can prompt major changes in vegetation structure.

Evidence from exclosures suggests that the selective browsing by deer tends to reduce tree species diversity. Unfortunately there is insufficient information to generalize for other herbivores in forest habitats, although a study of the impact of elephants found that diversity of trees and shrubs were reduced, but diversity of plants near ground level was increased. A similar result was reported for moose browsing, where diversity of the smallest trees increased, but apparently not in older trees.

In Chapter 7, '**Large herbivores: missing partners of western European light-demanding tree and shrub species?' by F.W.M. Vera, E.S. Bakker and H. Olff**, the consequences of the presence of large herbivores for the vegetation and other biota are addressed. A major criterion for the selection of sites for the conservation of nature in western Europe has always been 'naturalness'. Curiously there has been little effort to analyse what the natural landscapes looked like. It has often been claimed that temperate Europe without human influence would have been almost entirely covered with a closed canopy broad-leaved forest, the 'classical' forest theory. However, these forests contained indigenous species of large herbivores (aurochs, tarpan, red deer, moose, roe deer and European bison). These animals were assumed not to have had a substantial influence on the forest, but to follow the development in the vegetation. Vera *et al.* reviews knowledge from a wide range of disciplines, including palaeontology, palynology, evolutionary ecology, and history, and presents a provocative point of view of the role of large herbivores in temperate forests. They suggest that large herbivores were in fact very important influences on natural temperate forests, and created a park-like landscape over much of temperate Europe with bulk grazers like cattle and horse playing key roles in the processes involved.

These 'wood pastures' have an extremely high diversity of plant and animal species, because of the structural diversity of the vegetation. The oak has a special place as a host for insects, since no other species of tree is associated with so many species of insects: more than 50% of all insect species found in Great Britain live in the 20 000 hectares of wood pasture in the New Forest alone, and this landscape is habitat for a great variety of bird species, especially songbirds. These observations are clearly highly relevant to current issues of nature management, at the reserve and the landscape scales.

In Chapter 8, '**Frugivory in large mammalian herbivores' by R. Bodmer and D. Ward**, the focus is changed to tropical and arid regions. On the basis of a survey of 178 large herbivores species in tropical regions, the occurrence of frugivory is described across the range of stomach complexity in large herbivores, from simple to advanced, and in animals with different adaptations to seed predation, including strengthened jaws, elaborate dentition and digestive systems. The occurrence of frugivory is compared between tropical forest and savannas, and across the range of body mass in large herbivores. Biomass density (kg km^{-2}) of large herbivores with different diets is compared across habitat types. The impact of frugivores on ecosystem dynamics is a consequence of both seed dispersal and seed predation: the importance of frugivory by mammals in the dynamics of ecosystems is difficult to assess because most of the studies lack detail, and very few measure the vital rates of the tree populations. These issues are illustrated by case studies in two extreme habitats, tropical rainforests and the Negev desert. Resource use by four species of Amazon ungulates in north-eastern Peru is compared using both stomach and faecal samples. The striking differences between the ungulate species are discussed in relation to the physical characteristics of the seeds and the adaptations of the large herbivores.

Work in the Negev on the ecologically important and complex interaction between Acacia trees, bruchid beetles and ungulates (which are both important seed predators) shows that, as expected, when ungulates are present, seed dispersal increases, thus reducing competition for the seedlings from the parent trees. However, contrary to the idea that large mammalian herbivores reduce the impact of seed predation by consuming seed pods before they can be infested, the results of this study indicate that ungulate activity does not reduce the impact of the bruchid beetles on seeds. Very few seeds eaten by bruchids germinate, and many eaten by ungulates do: interestingly the germination rate of Acacia seeds eaten by herbivores increases with the body size of the herbivores. The dispersal of Acacia seeds by large mammalian herbivores seems to have affected and, perhaps controls, the distribution of different ecotypes of Acacia trees on a large geographic scale in the Middle East. In conclusion, browsing by ungulates at high densities, reduced the growth rates of the young Acacia, but did not inhibit juvenile Acacia escaping above the browsing level. Negative effects of browsing on juvenile trees may not translate into changes in tree demography because of the enhancement of seed viability and germination by mammalian herbivores.

Chapter 9, '**Large herbivores as sources of disturbance in ecosystems**' **by N. Thompson Hobbs**, suggests that herbivores might be profitably viewed as agents of disturbance, or events which alter resource availability or substrates, thereby causing abrupt changes in states and rates of processes. Trampling is an unavoidable disturbance of large herbivores since a large body mass is supported on four hooves, creating a large force per unit area on ground vegetation and soil. Trampling area increases allometrically with body mass, but so does home range. Population density therefore decreases allometrically with body mass, effectively cancelling any relationship between body mass and the proportion of home range trampled, which is fairly uniform at approximately 7% of the home range trampled each year. But, notes Hobbs, if proportionally more time is spent in certain communities with a small area, then trampling is concentrated in those communities and can affect up to 50% of the area which is actually grazed. This explains the often highly trampled condition around water holes, for example. The effects of trampling are diverse. On the one hand, trampling compacts the soil and reduces water infiltration, but if the soil surface is covered with a biotic crust, as is often the case in arid environments, then trampling increases water infiltration by breaking the crust. Bare, trampled areas are available for colonization by seeds which require exposure to mineral soil, creating a matrix for high, small-scale plant species diversity. Trampling also fragments litter leading to faster decay. Finally, trampled areas are often sites of high colonization by nitrogen (N) fixing cyanobacteria.

Patches of faeces and urine can also be viewed as disturbances since they represent very abrupt changes in nutrient availability from the surrounding areas, a point which echoes that made by Frank in Chapter 11. Approximately 2% of an animal's home range is in urine patches at any one time, but if the animal urinates in certain types of sites more often than at random, then, like trampling, the proportion of actually grazed area affected by urination is much higher than expected at random. Hobbs presents equations demonstrating that faecal N deposition increases linearly with plant N concentration and body mass while urine N deposition increases quadratically with body mass and plant N. Therefore, very large herbivores which graze high N forage will return most of their N to the soil as urine, which is more readily available to plants than faecal material since the latter needs to be decomposed by soil microflora. This in turn results in higher plant N, higher productivity, and a higher probability that the herbivore will subsequently graze the urine patch and surrounding area.

Herbivores also modify the occurrence of other disturbances, most notably fire, by reducing standing fuels of dead straw, thereby reducing fire frequency. Herbivores also selectively forage in burned areas of grasslands because of the higher N availability in grass after a burn, and so herbivores can also increase the recurrence interval between fires on a site as well. However, browsers in forested areas tend to avoid plants which produce resinous tissues with high content of volatiles. Since these plant tissues are of high flammability, large herbivores increase the proportion of flammable species in forests and could possibly increase fire frequency.

In Chapter 10, **'The roles of large herbivores in ecosystem nutrient cycles' by J.P. Pastor, Y. Cohen and N. Thompson Hobbs**, the specific mechanisms by which herbivores affect the rate of nutrient cycling is discussed, using the Serengeti grasslands and the boreal forests as case studies where large herbivores have opposite effects. The herds of large herbivore grazers in the Serengeti increase rates of nitrogen cycling and productivity through deposition of faecal and urinary N. However, in boreal regions, ungulate browsers forage preferentially on tree species whose tissues are more digestible because they have low lignin and high N contents. Conversely, they often avoid conifers with tissues of high lignin and low N contents which decrease their digestibility. Over time, the browsed species are outcompeted by the unbrowsed species, whose litter comes to dominate inputs of N to the soil. The decay of these litters from unbrowsed species is slow because the same chemical properties which make them difficult to digest by the gut flora of the ruminant ungulates also slow decay by soil microflora. Therefore, in the long run selective browsing by ruminant ungulates in boreal regions decreases N cycling and productivity, exactly the opposite response to grazers in grasslands. Using equations presented by Hobbs in the previous chapter, Pastor *et al.* show that there is a critical plant N concentration, above which excretion is mainly as urea, which is readily available for plant uptake, and below which excretion is mainly as faecal material, which is less and less decomposable the lower the N concentration in the original forage. This critical N concentration is in the neighbourhood of 1.5% N, which is the lowest N concentration in the green graminoid forage consumed by grazers but the highest N concentration in twigs consumed by browsers. Pastor *et al.* suggest that positive feedbacks between the large herbivore, plant community and plant tissue chemistry, and soil nitrogen mineralization rates effectively cause divergence to either side of this critical level of plant N, leading to the difference between browsing- and grazing-dominated nutrient cycling regimes shown in the two case studies.

These positive feedbacks between herbivores, plant communities and soils have some interesting implications for the coevolution and conservation of herbivore-dominated ecosystems. Evolutionary stability is possible only when the herbivores increase nutrient cycling rates, as in the Serengeti. When the herbivore decreases nutrient cycling rates, as in boreal forests, the system is subject to invasion by another herbivore species which can reverse the process, and hence the system is not stable.

Conservation policies must also recognize the importance of these feed-backs which could move the system into unwanted states within a few decades or even years.

In Chapter 11, 'Large herbivores in heterogeneous grassland ecosystems' by D.A. Frank, it is discussed how ungulate decisions in grasslands relate to and change the spatial heterogeneity of food distribution over the seasonal home range, across portions of the landscape, and within a plant community. Ungulates in grasslands make a hierarchy of decisions, from where to move to seasonally across the home range, to which portions of a landscape to graze in within a season, and what plant or plant part to eat locally. All of these decisions are spatial because food is not distributed homogeneously. But the actions of the herbivores resulting from these decisions also affect the future spatial distribution of its food and therefore the future decisions the herbivore and its offspring must make.

Using the grasslands in Yellowstone National Park as an example, Frank shows that as much as 2 kg N per ha per year is moved by ungulates from their summer range at higher elevations to the winter range at lower elevations in carcasses, faeces and urine. This is substantial because it equals N inputs in precipitation; it also amounts to one-fifth to two-thirds of the N in above-ground green forage, a large proportion of annual plant uptake. Within the winter range, ungulates remain on a site in proportion to its productivity rather than its area. While feeding there, they defecate and urinate. Therefore, productive sites get fertilized proportionally more by the ungulates, further increasing their productivity and the contrast between their productivity and that of adjacent less productive sites. Even within a site, urine patches have obviously greener vegetation and are grazed at a higher rate than surrounding patches – up to 14% of the N consumed by an ungulate can come from urine patches. This sets up a positive feedback of nutrient transport to the winter range followed by selecting productive spots, fertilizing those spots, followed by enhanced feeding at those spots. Nitrogen is the nutrient which has the strongest limiting effect on grassland plant species and therefore is the nutrient with most influence on the outcome of competition. The enhanced N availability decreases competition between plant species, thereby promoting coexistence between plant species which can in turn supply a diverse diet. Therefore by concentrating nutrients in the most productive sites, ungulates in grasslands enhance spatial variability but also enhance productivity where they feed the most.

In Chapter 12 'Modelling of large herbivore-vegetation interactions in a landscape context' by P.J. Weisberg, M.B. Coughenour and H. Bugmann, the different modelling approaches for representing large herbivore-landscape interactions are reviewed. They characterize three general approaches: animal-focused, plant-focused, and integrated. The first two approaches are discussed briefly, and the remainder of the chapter focuses on integrated, spatially explicit models which become particularly valuable where research questions involve long time scales over which feedbacks between plant and animal components cannot reasonably be ignored.

Representing the critical, long-term interactions between large herbivores and vegetation requires that vegetation pattern and dynamics be linked to the landscape variability which actually influences large herbivore movement, foraging and distribution. A further problem is that linking large herbivore movements, habitat use, and ultimately population dynamics with landscape pattern requires a multi-scale approach. The authors propose that there is a fundamental mismatch (from the modelling perspective) between the scales at which herbivore and vegetation processes influence each other. Large herbivores influence vegetation proximately over very fine spatio-temporal scales, although ultimately their effects may become amplified over large areas and long time periods. Vegetation dynamics, however, directly influence large herbivores over a broad range of scales.

These issues are dealt with in the spatially explicit, process-oriented model of grassland, shrubland, savanna and forested ecosystems called SAVANNA. It is composed of a set of submodels which cover water balance, plant biomass production, plant population dynamics, litter decomposition and N cycling, ungulate herbivory, ungulate spatial distribution, ungulate energy balance and ungulate population dynamics. The model is described, and its strengths and weaknesses compared with the few other integrated models available.

Models which integrate large herbivore vegetation processes at landscape scales have yielded high rewards both for increasing our level of scientific understanding, and have potential for allowing managers to evaluate potential outcomes of their decisions. However, if they are to serve a useful function for management, i.e. decision support systems, the models need to be accessible and transparent, and developed in interaction with stakeholders and end-users. Only then are managers likely to use the models appropriately, since the analysis and use of simulation results require knowledge about the inner workings of a model. None of the models currently available are decision support systems. Scientists need to go to greater lengths to make their models accessible if they are to be useful for management decisions. Managers will need to become more willing to accept complexity and uncertainty, which is probably a good thing for nature!

In Chapter 13, 'Effects of large herbivores on other fauna' by O. Suominen and K. Danell, considerable evidence is provided that large mammalian herbivores cause declines in the abundance of other herbivores feeding upon the same types of plants. This is particularly true for small mammals whose densities can be reduced by an order of magnitude. Since these are important prey for a large number of vertebrate predators, some of which are endangered species, the effects of large herbivores on the predator communities are potentially more important, from a conservation point-of-view, than the impacts of large herbivores on small mammals themselves. The application of the 'intermediate disturbance' hypothesis (i.e. that moderate grazing intensity maximizes animal diversity) is reviewed, and shown to be true in some, but not all circumstances, since some studies have found a monotonic relationship (usually negative impact of grazing intensity on diversity) (e.g. small mammals, passerine birds, terrestrial gastropods, web spiders).

The 'evolutionary history' of the community and the differences in the impacts of native vs. introduced large herbivores are shown to be important, so the predominantly negative effects of introduced browsers on invertebrate abundance and plant diversity in New Zealand habitats could be partly explained by the absence of large mammalian herbivores until recently.

One area of research which has been inadequately addressed so far is that other biota may have threshold densities of large herbivores to which they respond, so the choice of study systems in the past may have skewed the picture we have of how large herbivores shape community structures. 'Overgrazing' by large herbivores has been seen as an environmental problem, mainly because of their powerful effects on plants, but also on animal communities. However, in many wetlands and grasslands, grazing by large herbivores is used as a management tool for the conservation of birds, butterflies and other invertebrates. The impacts of grazing at different spatial and temporal scales have also been little studied, since most studies have been short-term explorations at the local scale. There is clearly a need for much more research, theoretical as well as applied, on the roles of large herbivores as modifiers of assemblages of other animals.

In Chapter 14, 'The future role of large carnivores in terrestrial trophic interactions: the northern temperate view' by R. Andersen, J.D.C. Linnell

and E. J. Solberg, top-down and bottom-up views of population regulation in northern environments are reconciled, and the conditions under which herbivores can end up in a 'predator-pit' are explored. The authors show that the effect a large carnivore will have on a particular large herbivore population depends on (i) the presence of other predators, (ii) availability of alternative prey, (iii) the impact of food competition on the prey species, (iv) the degree of human harvest of both prey and predators, and (v) the mobility of the prey. The empirical evidence of the impact of predator control of northern boreal large herbivores leads to mixed conclusions, but it is widely recognized that most large carnivores are able to affect the abundance of their large herbivore prey strongly. The dichotomy of 'top-down' vs. 'bottom-up' regulation is too simplistic, and it is now widely accepted that it is the interaction of these processes that shapes the dynamics of herbivore populations.

A strong point of this chapter is that it shows that the subtle effects of a large carnivore on the behaviour of large herbivores can have strong effects on the use of resources, and on the population dynamics of the large herbivores. Because of fairly flat functional response curves (i.e. rapid increase up to a certain level) and strong human and intraspecific impact on large carnivore numerical responses, the impact of large carnivores will depend mainly on the large herbivore density. The authors conclude that the return of large carnivores to countries like Scotland/Germany (where roe deer, sika deer and red deer occur at very high densities) will do nothing to influence the dramatic impact of large herbivores on vegetation. Areas with mouflon and forest dwelling chamois could be an exception, where large carnivores like wolves and lynx could potentially exterminate mouflon and lead to marked changes in habitat use for chamois, from forest to mountain areas.

In multi-use landscapes it may be that large carnivores will have strong influences on large herbivore-habitat relationships locally, but weak effects regionally, because of the high densities (overabundance) of the large herbivores in these multi-use landscapes due to resource subsidies, management strategies of hunters etc. In contrast, in 'natural' systems or those with low productivity, large carnivores should limit ungulate population densities and therefore their impact on habitat. Humans now dominate both the top-down and bottom-up processes – often for the benefit of ungulates (at least in western Europe and North America). While fundamental research in 'pristine' areas is essential to allow basic ecological principles to be discovered, much more attention needs to be paid to multi-use landscapes, particularly long-term studies on trophic interactions and cascading effects in such systems. The authors conclude that 'There are today several studies in terrestrial ecosystems which indicate that the removal of large carnivores (and cessation of hunting by humans) have lead to dramatic increases in herbivore densities, which in turn have caused concern for long-term forest dynamics'.

The last two chapters of the book (Chapters 15 and 16) synthesizes the previous chapters. Chapter 15 describes the consequences for conservation of new insights in processes, and the very last chapter (16) highlights the general patterns which are emerging, generalizes our findings and identifies key areas for future research.

The previous chapters have shown how complex the large herbivore-vegetation interaction at the landscape scale can be, as it involves many different and interacting factors (e.g. plant competition, landscape pattern, climate, disturbance regimes and biogeochemical cycles). The earlier chapters demonstrate how difficult it is to find simple underlying principles. Simulation modelling has proved a useful tool for disentangling some of this complexity, and for integrating information across multiple scales. There are numerous modelling approaches, at varying levels of complexity which have been developed for different research objectives. Few models represent interactions between the two ecosystem components, animal and plant, in a balanced, integrated manner. Such integrated models include feedbacks and interactions between the components, typically including process-level representations for certain aspects of both plant and animal systems.

In Chapter 15, '**Restoring the functions of grazed ecosystems**' by **I.J. Gordon**, shows how the new understanding of the ecological roles of large herbivores can be used to restore and/or maintain the functioning of ecosystems and the goods and services they provide is discussed. The concept of ecosystem health is defined, and the ways in which ecosystems can become degraded (i.e. lose the ability to provide the goods and services to humans) are reviewed. Two examples of using scientific information to manage ecosystems are presented, first, the restoration of hydrological function in degraded semi-arid savanna systems, secondly, the restoration of woodland in degraded Scottish forest.

In the savanna systems the main issue is that heavy grazing causes a decline in the proportion of precipitation which infiltrates the soil, leading to reduced plant productivity and resilience to perturbations, especially droughts. Intermediate grazing pressure can solve the problems, through a number of ecological mechanisms involving interactions between hydrology, plants and microorganisms in the soil. Financial analyses show that the reduction in grazing pressure need not be linked to financial losses.

The Caledonian forests have been reduced to 1% of their historical area, so successful management of the remaining ones is crucial to preserve several species of plants and animals which depend on this ecosystem. The main issue is the lack of regeneration of the 'keystone species' the Scots pine. Also research on the domestic and wild herbivores shows that regeneration can increase when browsing is reduced to intermediate levels. The intermediate grazing hypothesis is based on a spatial framework. Iain Gordon argues that this hypothesis should also be considered on a temporal basis, and it could be worth testing the idea that grazing systems and their herbivore populations should be managed not for stability, often at levels well below carrying capacity (as has often been the case in the past), but for temporal as well as spatial variability. Introducing temporal variability is more complicated, but could have important benefits for biodiversity conservation.

It is clear that managers cannot succeed in changing grazing practices without the consent of the people affected by these restoration efforts since people will be affected by many of the changes (in water quality, the number of animals available to hunt etc.). Iain Gordon concludes that 'The future of many grazed ecosystems will depend upon scientists and practitioners forming a partnership in which scientists can investigate hypotheses at the landscape scale whilst managers can gain from the knowledge to provide guidance to management in the collaborative cycle for adaptive management.'

In Chapter 16, 'Themes and future directions in herbivore-ecosystem interactions and conservation' the editors identify four major themes or organizing principles which form a framework for understanding the richness of herbivore-ecosystem interactions described throughout this book. Two of these themes (body size and plant tissue chemistry) pertain to problems faced by large mammalian herbivores in securing enough resources to survive and reproduce in any ecosystem. The other two themes (the responses of individual plants to grazing or browsing and the alterations in plant and animal community composition) pertain to the effects of herbivores on ecosystems. Together, these themes could provide a framework for future directions in research in this area.

REFERENCES

de Mazancourt, C., Loreau, M. & Abbadie, L. (1998). Grazing optimization and nutrient cycling: when do herbivores enhance plant production? *Ecology*, **79**, 2242–52.

Illius, A.W. & Gordon, I.J. (1999). Scaling up from functional response to numerical response in vertebrate herbivores. In *Herbivores: Between Plants and Predators*, ed. H. Olff, V.K. Brown & R.H. Drent. Oxford: Blackwell Science, pp. 397–427.

Illius, A.W. & O'Connor, T.G. (2000). Resource heterogeneity and ungulate population dynamics. *Oikos*, **89**, 283–94.

McNaughton, S.J. (1985). Ecology of a grazing ecosystem: the Serengeti. *Ecological Monographs*, **55**, 259–94.

Owen-Smith, N. (2002). *Adaptive Herbivore Ecology*. Cambridge: Cambridge University Press.

Rosenzweig, M.L. (1995). *Species Diversity in Space and Time*. Cambridge: Cambridge University Press.

Spalinger, D.E. & Hobbs, N.T. (1992). Mechanisms of foraging in mammalian herbivores: new models of functional response. *American Naturalist*, **140**, 325–48.

1

Large herbivores across biomes

HERVÉ FRITZ AND ANNE LOISON

INTRODUCTION

The vertebrate herbivores cover a very wide range of body sizes from a few
tens of grams to more than a tonne. It is therefore necessary to define what
we consider as large herbivores: Bourlière (1975) described the bimodal
distribution of mammal body weights and defined large mammals as
being those with an adult body weight of more than 5 kg. A more recent
analysis on a restricted set of species from Africa and America (Lovegrove
& Haines 2004) also showed a bimodal distribution for herbivore body
weights, with a gap slightly before 10 kg, separating most micro-herbivores
(e.g. rodents, lagomorphs) from larger herbivores (mostly ungulates).
Recently, however, large herbivores are often defined as those with body
weight >2 kg (Ritchie & Olff 1999, Olff *et al.* 2002). We decided to keep
the 2 kg threshold, which restricts large herbivores to mostly ungulates
(*sensu lato*, i.e. Order Artiodactyla, Perissodactyla and including the Order
Proboscidea) and to most herbivorous marsupials (*sensu* Fisher *et al.*
2001), all belonging to the Order Diprotodonta, and mainly to the Family
Macropodidae. However we excluded from this synthesis the few large
rodent species (e.g. capybara *Hydrochaeris hydrochaeris*) and the very large
birds (e.g. ratites), which weigh over 2 kg. As it would take too long to show
the patterns exhibited by ungulates as well as those from marsupials,
we decided to comment on similarities and differences between these
phylums, but to limit our main descriptions to ungulates.

With this definition in mind, we will describe patterns of species
richness across a variety of biogeographical variables, such as continents,

Large Herbivore Ecology, Ecosystem Dynamics and Conservation, ed. K. Danell, P. Duncan, R.
Bergström & J. Pastor. Published by Cambridge University Press. © Cambridge University
Press 2006.

climate and habitat types. We will concentrate on ungulate community structure and diversity, rather than on the determinants of abundance. The ungulate communities of African savannas are the only ones on which extensive work has been done regarding their overall abundance. The results show that their abundance seems to be determined primarily by the quantity, and possibly the quality, of the primary production, as the overall biomass of African savanna ungulates is positively related to annual rainfall and soil nutrient quality (Coe *et al.* 1976, Bell 1982, Fritz & Duncan 1994). This is consistent with the pattern found across biomes that secondary production is positively related to primary production (McNaugthon *et al.* 1989). The determinants of the diversity of ungulates remain poorly understood, even in these well-studied and relatively intact communities. However, the interplay between the quantity and quality of primary production seems to drive the species richness of large herbivore communities, mainly through the trade-offs between digestive constraints and nutrient requirements, which are both primarily mediated by body size (Olff *et al.* 2002). The pattern described correctly fits the observed distribution, but the amount of unexplained variance calls for further investigations, including the implication of body size in interspecific competition and the role of other life history traits.

As diversity is the result of natural selection, which maximizes individual fitness through adjusting morphological, physiological, life history or behavioural traits to ecological conditions, we decided not to restrict ourselves to the description of taxonomic diversity, but also cover important traits. We have primarily used body size to describe diversity, as it is correlated with many morphological, physiological and life history attributes (e.g. Schmidt-Nielsen 1984, Gordon & Illius 1994). It also has the advantage of being available for a wide range of species, and has been the subject of analyses of basic spatio-temporal patterns (e.g. Rosenzweig 1995, Gaston & Blackburn 2000). Nonetheless, the debate on the mechanisms shaping the distribution of body sizes is still open (e.g. Kozlowski & Gawelczyk 2002). We used the recently published database on eutherian mammals (Ernest 2003) as the primary sources for this review (see Fisher *et al.* 2001 for a similar database on marsupials). In addition to body size, we have surveyed examples of the diversity of behavioural and life history traits in relation to ecological variables, in order to explore diversity with a broad life history strategy perspective. Our aim was to describe general patterns among ungulates and marsupials, and to discuss possible processes explaining these patterns at the scale of the continents, biomes and broad habitat types. Performing new comparative and multivariate analyses was, however, beyond the scope of this review. From the 1990s onward (e.g. Felsenstein 1985, Harvey & Pagel 1991, Garland *et al.* 1992), most comparative studies of life history traits accounted for phylogenetic inertia to avoid spurious relationships due to non-independence between data measured on closely related species (Stearns 1992). We nevertheless also refer to studies performed before phylogenetic inertia became the rule, as not all analyses have been updated.

Large herbivores also have the advantage, as most large body size vertebrates, of having a relatively well-known palaeoecological history. We have tried to incorporate in this synthesis the many useful insights this provides into the diversity of large herbivores today (e.g. Vrba 1992).

DEFINITIONS OF BIOGEOGRAPHICAL AND BEHAVIOURAL CATEGORIES

A habitat is a place that contains the resources necessary for maintaining all the stages of the life cycle of an organism or species. Using correspondence analysis, Greenacre and Vrba (1984) showed that the gross vegetational physiognomy (i.e. the wood-to-grass ratio) is a good proxy for the habitat specificities of antelopes (Vrba 1992). This specificity allows the species to be classified into broad categories that describe the patterns of herbivore distribution and diversity. However, the continuum in vegetation physiognomy requires some categorization. We chose to use an existing definition of broad habitat (Janis 1988, Loison *et al.* 1999, Pérez-Barbería *et al.* 2001), and to follow an existing classification of species-habitat relationship (Van Wieren 1996), which is consistent with another independent compilation (Pérez-Barbería *et al.* 2001a), but with more species. We also use information in Walker's encyclopedia of mammals (Nowack 1991), and an International Union for the Conservation of Nature (IUCN) specialist group database, Vrba and Schaller (2000) and Strahan (1983) to complete the information when necessary.

Closed-habitat dwellers are defined as those species that spend most of the year in dense habitats (e.g. forests, woodlands, bushlands, thickets). Open-habitat species are those that predominantly use grasslands, whilst mixed-habitat dwellers are those species that use savanna, forest ecotone or both closed and open habitats depending upon the season or the population within a species. However, these habitats do not translate directly into biomes, so we have associated each species with a climatic zone to give an idea of the corresponding biome: mountain, grassland, temperate woodland, temperate forest, desert, savanna, wooded savanna or rainforest.

Feeding style is defined by the predominant type of plant material (≥90%) in the year-round diet of the species (Janis 1988). Species whose diet is principally monocotyledons are classified as grazers; species with ≥90% dicotyledons (i.e. tree and shrub foliage, including herbaceous dicotyledons, or fruit eaters) in their diet as browsers. Mixed-feeders are those species with 10%–90% grass in their diet. For habitats we used an existing classification (Van Wieren 1996, Pérez-Barbería *et al.* 2001), which we completed from the same sources as for feeding style. We acknowledge the fact that more information and a finer dietary classification are available for African bovids (e.g. Gagnon & Chew 2000), but we kept very broad classes to allow the comparison between continents, climatic zones and biomes.

Average group size are not available for all species, as only African ruminants have been subject to extensive reviews of the relationship between group size, body size and some life history traits (e.g. Jarman 1974, Brashares *et al.* 2000). Recent meta-analyses on marsupial life history traits provided sources of typical group size for the large herbivorous species (e.g. Fisher & Owens 2000, Fisher *et al.* 2001, 2002). As this set of group size data does not cover all the species, we classified species into group size categories, which were more widely available: (1) Solitary or in pair-living, (2) Family unit (2–4 individuals), (3) Small groups (5–9 individuals), (4) Medium groups (10–25 individuals), and (5) Large groups (>25 individuals). Ungulates are present in all categories, whereas marsupials cover classes 1 to 4, and most are in 1 to 3.

TAXONOMIC DIVERSITY

The herbivore group is very diverse across biomes and continents, but it is unevenly spread, with most species in the tropics. The number of extant ungulate species included in the taxonomic classification of Family is also very unevenly distributed (Table 1.1). Most ungulates are found in Africa, twice as many as in Asia, followed by Europe, South America and North America. The ungulate hot-spot in Asia is in the tropical south-east, and most of the species live in forests and dry woodlands. Overall, the latitudinal distribution of large herbivore taxa conforms to the decreasing gradient of diversity from the tropics to the poles found in most organisms (Rosenzweig 1995). Europe and Asia have, as could be expected, many species in common especially in the cold and temperate climatic zone of the Eurasian land mass. Europe and North America, and to a lesser extent northern Asia, also share species, mostly those having a circumpolar

Table 1.1. A summary of the distribution of 227 large herbivore species within each main Family, and between the main continents. Ungulate distributions follow the standard classification (e.g. Ernest 2003), with the recent update of the Artiodactyls (Vrba & Schaller 2000)

Order	Suborder	Family	No. Species	Africa	Europe	Asia	North America	South America
Proboscidea	Euelephantoidea	Elephantidae	2	1		1		
Perissodactyla	Hippomorpha	Equidae	6	4	1	2£		
	Ceratomorpha	Tapiridae	4			1		3
		Rhinocerotidae	5	2		3		
Artiodactyla	Suina	Suidae	14	4	1	9£		
		Tayasuidae°	3					3
		Hippopotamidae	2	2				
	Tylopoda	Camelidae	6	1£		2£		2
	Ruminantia	Tragulidae	4					
		Moschidae	6		3£	4£		
		Giraffidae	2	2				
		Antilocapridae	1				1	
		Cervidae	42*		7£	22£	6£	10
		Bovidae	130*	74	21£	36£	6£	

Note: £ Some species may be present on two continents, e.g. the wild horses, Wild boar, dromedary, Roe deer, Moose, Red deer, Reindeer, Muskox. Species with subspecies that are sometimes considered as possible species, e.g. Bontebok and Blesbok are considered only once.
* Species with subspecies that are sometimes considered as possible species, e.g. Bontebok and Blesbok are considered only once.
° Tayasuidae are sometimes classified as Suidae.

distribution. Considerable movements occurred between the landmasses, especially between Eurasia and North America, and from Europe and Middle-East Asia to Africa, during the late Pliocene and Pleistocene time. In fact, most of the present day African Artiodactyls come from an influx of species from the Middle East (Colbert & Morales 1994). The difference in biodiversity between the Tropics and the temperate and cold zones could simply be due to the fact that the Tropics represent a much larger land area than any other climatic zone, as it is well known that diversity increases with area (Rosenzweig 1995). Diversity is also recognized to be increased by the productivity of ecosystems in conjunction with moderate levels of disturbance, which maintain the heterogeneity of habitats and presumably niches. In addition to the well-described latitudinal gradient in species diversity, there seems to be a longitudinal gradient in large herbivore species in the boreal zone, both in the Palearctic and Nearctic (Danell *et al.* 1996). Large herbivore diversity drops close to the Bering Strait and peaks in the interior of both landmasses, more weakly in the Palearctic. Interestingly, variables related to primary production (temperature, length of growing season) and habitat diversity (e.g. the number of tree species) influences species diversity in addition to the area of the boreal zone (Danell *et al.* 1996). This also suggests interplay between productivity, habitat diversity and herbivore diversity.

The classic humped-shaped relationship between primary production and species diversity has been found for East African ungulates (Western 1989) and more generally for East and Southern Africa (Fritz, unpublished 2003), with a recent study showing a log-normal shape (Ritchie & Olff 1999). This implies a maximum diversity at intermediate productivity, as is often found in studies of patterns in biodiversity (e.g. Rosenzweig 1995). As savannas are known to be subject to disturbances such as fire, it is possible that ungulate diversity is the result of the interaction between primary production and disturbance. However, Olff *et al.* (2002) demonstrated that the maximum diversity is found in sites with nutrient rich soils and intermediate productivity. Therefore there seems to be interplay between plant production and plant quality in limiting populations of ungulates of different sizes. These areas of high diversity in Africa correspond to open or wooded savannas in East and Southern Africa on volcanic soils (Olff *et al.* 2002). The prediction from their model seemed to fit reasonably well the predicted values from other hot-spots amongst the tropical climatic zone. However, there is a major difference between Africa and Asia for ungulates because it is in the tropical rainforests and woodlands that the highest diversity is found in Asia. This calls for an investigation of the role of human pressure on ungulate diversity, as it is in a remote rainforest that the last ungulate species was discovered, in this otherwise very densely populated continent. It is worth noting that the distribution of species between Families and Orders has changed considerably in historical times. These historical constraints on existing species and body size ranges calls for a short summary of the recent theory on large herbivore palaeohistory and palaeoecology, in order to set the scene for the description and understanding of modern day patterns.

PALAEONTOLOGY

The evolution of mammals is remarkably well documented, as they are large enough to have left many fossils (Vrba 1992). From the earliest ungulates, *Protogulatum* in the late Cretaceous, to present day ruminants the history of large mammalian herbivores is punctuated with regular radiations and extinctions (e.g. Eisenberg 1981, Vrba 1987). After the rise of ungulates in the Paleocene and Eocene (60–30 million years BP), the large herbivore taxa were dominated by the Proboscideans, with the Mastodonts thriving on most continents in the Pleistocene (1–0.01 million years BP). Most of these ancestors to the present day elephants had disappeared by the end of the Pleistocene, as well as many large herbivores, under what is often considered as human overkill (Martin & Klein 1984): North America lost 79 large mammal species including 44 herbivores, South America lost 68 including 25 herbivores, and Eurasia lost 11 mammal species, most of them in Europe. The Perissodactyls radiated in the Tertiary, when they became the dominant ungulates in the world, with horses predominating in the Oligocene (30–20 million years BP) and Miocene (20–5 million years BP), together with rhinos in the Miocene. The extant (or living) representatives of these ancient herbivores persist only in the Tropics, except for the horses and asses which occur in temperate and arctic biomes. The Perissodactyls gave way to the Artiodactyls as the dominant herbivores during the Pleistocene, although primitive Artiodactyls were present in the Eocene (e.g. Eisenberg 1981). The Pleistocene was also marked by massive extinctions in Australia (43 herbivore species). In the process, the community of large herbivorous marsupials lost its very large species (e.g. the very large kangaroos *Macropus ferragus*, *c.* 150 kg), including megaherbivores such as the *Diprodon optatum* or *Zygomaturus trilobus* (Murray 1984).

Recent analyses of the palaeohistory of ungulates suggest that the massive change in the trophic structure and species diversity of ungulate communities since the Miocene has been due to many factors (Janis *et al.* 2000, 2002, Cerling *et al.* 1997, 1998) in particular: the decline in atmospheric CO_2 that has slowly caused the reduction in abundance of C_3 plants in favour of C_4 plants that are less dependent on atmospheric CO_2; and an increase in temperature which has promoted arid climates over the globe, favouring more open habitats dominated by C_4 plants (Cerling *et al.* 1997, 1998). The main C_3/C_4 transition occurred sharply in the latest Miocene and early Pliocene (8–5 million years BP), and corresponded with a phase where open habitat ungulates (predominantly grazers) replaced those from more closed habitats (predominantly browsers). The observed changes in the structure and diversity of the ungulate community showed that grazers did not really replace browsers, but instead flourished after the rise of the mixed-feeders in the middle Miocene, when browsers were still numerous (Janis *et al.* 2000, 2002). The highest diversity of ungulates occurred in this period, all dietary types then decreased, in particular browsers, which were reduced by 80% in the Pleistocene. The fact that grazers and mixed-feeders became dominant is in agreement with the change in habitat structure. The change in the number of species strongly suggests that primary productivity of the planet also decreased severely in the last 14 million years BP or so (Janis *et al.* 2002), which is in agreement with the drop in atmospheric CO_2 from the middle Miocene with an accelerated decrease in the Pleistocene.

The gradual vegetation change, both in structure and in productivity, could be considered as an alternative non-exclusive hypothesis to the human overkill influence for the major Pleistocene extinctions in North America as well as in Europe (see Martin & Klein 1984). Recently Klein (2000) suggested that although humans have been eating ungulates for the last two million years, they might have had a dramatic impact only during the last glaciation (especially that of 11000 years ago) as many species or genera became extinct while they had survived previous glaciation/interglaciation events. Prior to 50000 years ago, and the advent of modern hunting techniques, human populations occurred at low densities, and their technologically primitive hunting methods were unlikely to have had a serious impact, so most extinctions before 50000 years ago were probably due to climatic/atmospheric changes. To conclude, if climate/vegetation changes may be considered as a likely explanation for changes in ungulate diversity and community structure from the Miocene to the early Pleistocene, most authors now concur that humans were the primary source of the rapid extinctions in the late Pleistocene, *c.* 10000 years BP (Smith *et al.* 2003). In Australia and New Guinea, the human overkill phenomenon seemed to have occurred earlier, *c.* 45 000 years BP (Smith *et al.* 2003, Johnson & Prideaux 2004). These very rapid changes in ungulate abundance and structure may also have had a more dramatic impact on the vegetation than the fairly gradual change started in the Miocene, which could question today the idea of what is considered as natural (Martin & Steadman 1999).

BODY SIZE, DIVERSITY AND DISTRIBUTION

Across the world, the distribution of ungulate body weight has a classic log-normal distribution (Fig. 1.1). The restricted range of body sizes in Australian marsupials does not allow for a comparison, but the level of diversity among marsupials is higher than the level of ungulate diversity in Europe, South and North America, where the range of their body size is comparable (Fig. 1.2). As expected from the taxonomic differences in diversity, Africa and Asia dominate the diversity of body sizes (Fig. 1.2), mostly because a large proportion occur in the tropical zone, which also contains a greater diversity of body sizes (Fig. 1.3).

There is much discussion about the reasons for the widespread, humped-shape distribution of body weights across taxa. The smaller number of large species is likely to be due to the fact that larger species face higher extinction rates and lower rates of evolutionary change (Fowler & MacMahon 1982, Vrba 1987). They also need more resources and more space, and hence live at lower densities than smaller species (Damuth 1981, Peters & Wassenberg 1983). The sharp decline in the number of small body sized species is less well understood. For ungulates there is a minimum size constraint for mammals which live exclusively on grass and browse (Van Soest 1994). Ungulates weighing less than 10 kg are forced to resort to frugivory or granivory, at least partly. However, the comparison between continents shows that it is not only the extreme range of sizes that make the difference in richness, but also a reduction in the number of medium sized species. This concurs with the information from palaeohistory, which suggests that medium sized herbivores, mostly browsers, disappeared in response to decreases in primary productivity in most ecosystems (see section above).

The nutritional explanation is the basis of a general conceptual model of large herbivore diversity (both in species number and body sizes), with primary production and soil fertility being the primary determinants of this diversity (Olff *et al.* 2002). The occurrence of larger herbivore species increases with plant moisture availability, almost independently of soil

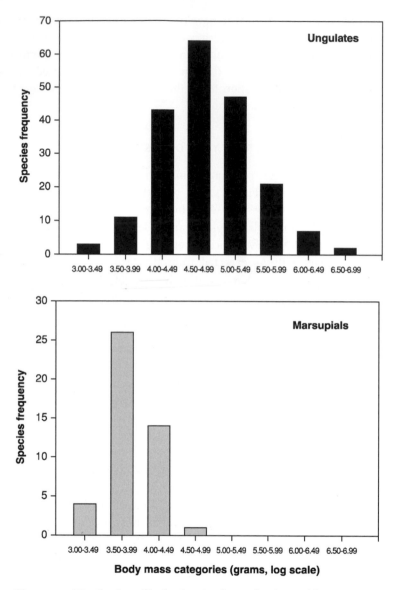

Figure 1.1. Distribution of body sizes in classes for the world ungulates and Australian herbivorous marsupials.

fertility, whereas small herbivores are mostly limited by soil fertility. Such patterns have been described in African savanna ungulate communities (Bell 1982, Fritz *et al.* 2002), for which the model was built originally, but the generality of this approach needs to be tested further. For instance, the

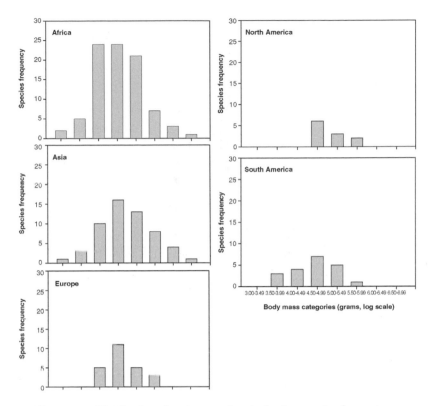

Figure 1.2. Distribution of native ungulate body sizes on the five main continents.

tropical rainforests with high moisture availability and, in general, low fertility are dominated by small species, when they should be dominated by megaherbivores (Fig. 1.4). The absence of these very large body sized herbivores may be due to extinctions, but the small number of medium sized ungulates is still puzzling. The relatively small number of species in the desert and mountain biomes, and their restricted body size range, is consistent with limitation by primary productivity, and with extra physiological constraints to cope with more extreme physical parameters. The savanna woodlands, and the temperate woodlands to a lesser extent, show a more uniform distribution of body masses than the more open or more forested biomes (Fig. 1.4). Interestingly, the distributions in body size show a tendency to be skewed to the right when compared in the broad habitat types (Fig. 1.5), with a wider range of species in less open habitat. The open habitat often comprised more seasonally stressed ecosystems,

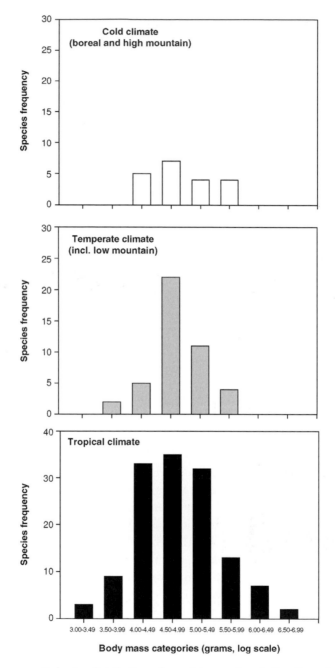

Figure 1.3. Body size distribution of ungulates per broad climatic region.

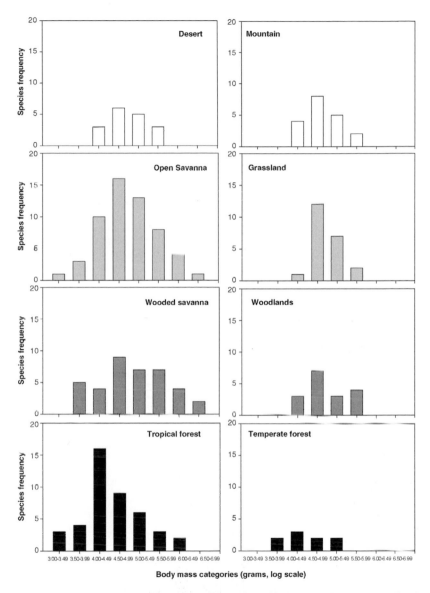

Figure 1.4. Body size distribution of ungulates in the main biomes (grassland and woodlands are the temperate equivalent of open savanna and wooded savanna in the Tropics).

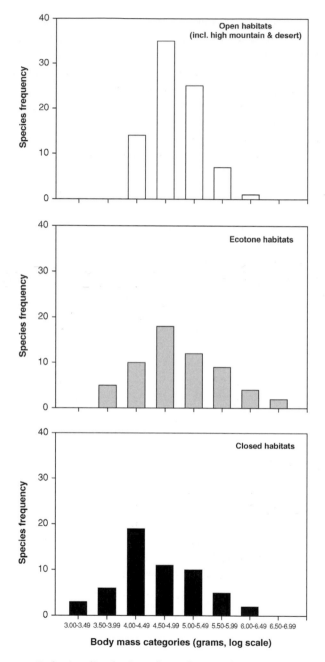

Figure 1.5. Body size distribution of ungulates in the main types of habitat.

which may result in greater constraints on the very large herbivores. Interestingly, the distribution of marsupials between the broad habitat types, does not match that of ungulates, as closed habitats have much greater diversity than open and ecotone habitats, but body size seems to increase slightly with habitat openness as in ungulates.

The different patterns between continents and biomes suggest that the feeding types of the herbivores may be important, as feeding types are likely not only to be correlated with habitat types, but also with the dynamics of their resources. For instance, browse resources are often less abundant and more heterogeneously distributed than grasses, and the relationship between the abundance of browse (shrubs or trees) and rainfall is not as simple as that for grasses, e.g. polynomial rather than linear (Lieth 1975, Deshmukh 1984, Le Houérou 1989). Consequently, the primary production structure and dynamics in different biomes and climatic zones is likely to affect feeding types differently.

GROUP SIZES AND FEEDING TYPES

The feeding types have different body weights, browsers being smaller than mixed-feeders, which are smaller than grazers, although there is considerable overlap in the range of body weights (Fig. 1.6). Interestingly, the largest ruminant is a browser. The distribution of body sizes within feeding types is slightly right-skewed, as in habitat types. This certainly reflects the link between habitat types and feeding types, but also suggests that the apparent log-normal distribution at the world level may in fact be the result of processes creating right-skewed distribution at the ecologically appropriate level of investigation. Although they have much in common, browsers and grazers may in fact differ sufficiently in the way they harvest food resources (e.g. review by Gordon 2003) to have different levels of constraints shaping their diversity.

Body size is perhaps more important in explaining differences in feeding types than morphological or physiological traits (Gordon & Illius 1994, Robbins et al. 1995, Pérez-Barbería & Gordon 1999). The ability to finely select plants and/or plant parts is associated with small muzzle size, which is strongly correlated to small body size. After controlling for phylogeny, only body size and two traits related to hypsodonty remained significant in the comparative analysis carried by Pérez-Barbería and Gordon (2001). Hypsodont (high-crowned) teeth in grazers are adapted to an abrasive diet, with high fibre, silicates and soil on the surface of leaves, i.e. plants growing in open areas. This suggests that the way food is

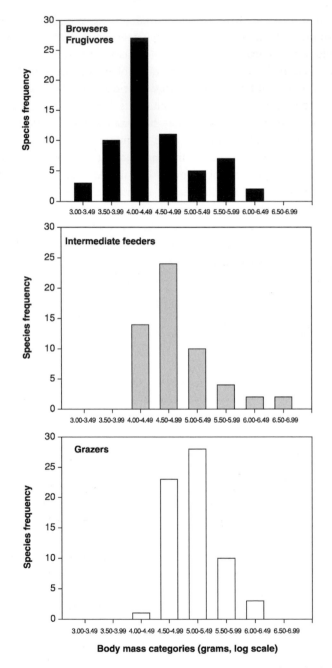

Figure 1.6. Body size distribution of ungulates in the main three feeding types.

processed in the mouth in relation to its structure (e.g. fibrousness) or composition (e.g. silicate) is more important in harvesting than mouth morphology. Low-crowned teeth are termed brachydont and correspond to a browse diet, medium-crowned teeth are termed mesodont and are those belonging to mixed-feeders (Janis *et al.* 2002). The hypsodonty index appears to be a good indicator of the broad feeding types, but also of the increase in abrasive particles in the diet within feeding types, i.e. a good indicator of the openness of the habitat: for instance the hypsodonty index increases from savanna to prairie in grazers, or from woodland to savanna for mixed-feeders (Janis *et al.* 2002). In a synthesis, Pérez-Barbería *et al.* (2001) proposed a scenario with a transition phase based on a diversification of mixed-feeder species both in closed and mixed habitat that lead to a multiplication of grazing species using mixed and open habitat. This is consistent with the reconstructed palaeohistory of dietary types (Janis *et al.* 2002) in which mesodonts (mostly mixed-feeders) flourished before hypsodont (grazers) started to diversify. It is also consistent with the relatively uniform distribution of body size in savanna woodlands and woodland, which are intermediate between forest and grassland dominated biomes, and hence have an intermediate structure (Fig. 1.4).

Since the seminal paper by Jarman (1974), it is known that ungulate feeding types, as well as other traits such as mating systems and predator avoidance, are associated with different group sizes. As group size is generally considered to be correlated with body size, this also reflects the correlation between feeding selectivity and body size, or between sexual dimorphism and body size (see sections below). Jarman's results and classification were revisited including a phylogenetic analysis, and although most of the relationships held qualitatively, there were large variations between Tribes (Brashares *et al.* 2000). Our descriptive approach to herbivore diversity exhibits some of these broad patterns. It appears that there are more solitary ungulate species at the small body size end of the spectrum, but the relationship is not striking (Fig. 1.7), and this pattern is not apparent in marsupials. The observed relationship between group size and habitat openness is more striking (Fig. 1.8), with species living in large groups being found primarily in open habitat. This is consistent with differences in anti-predator behaviour, the species in large groups in the open relying on vigilance and flight, whereas forest animals are hiders (Jarman 1974, Brashares *et al.* 2000). The cost of vigilance for the individual is a strong evolutionary force to promote aggregation (Giraldeau & Caraco 2000). The pattern does not appear as clearly in marsupials. The relationship between group size and feeding types is consistent with the

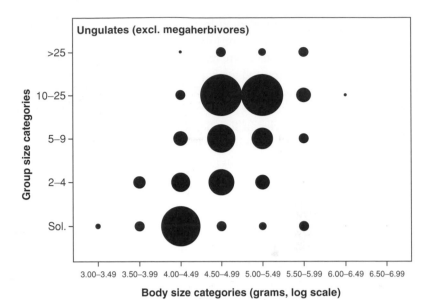

Figure 1.7. Density plot diagram of the relationship between the average group size per species and species body mass (the diameter of the circle is proportional to the number of species).

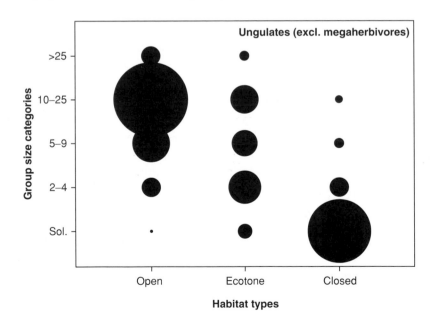

Figure 1.8. Density plot diagram of the relationship between the average group size of a species and its dominant habitat type (the diameter of the circle is proportional to the number of species).

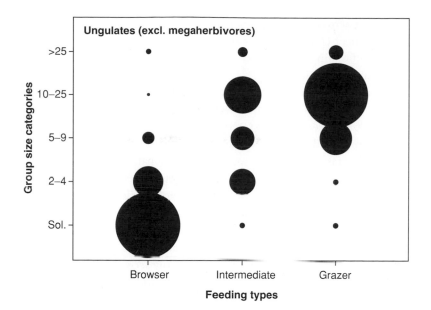

Figure 1.9. Density plot diagram of the relationship between the average group size of a species and its feeding type (the diameter of the circle is proportional to the number of species).

two previous patterns, grazers being in larger groups (Fig. 1.9). This was expected from the habitat relationship for the ungulates. But the distribution of resources could also be the main driver of aggregation rather than habitat structure: grass resources are abundant and mostly continuous in space; browse is more patchy and dispersed. This would be consistent with the idea that feeding type diversification, and not habitat change, is the primary driver of species diversity in ungulate communities (Pérez-Barbería *et al.* 2001).

THE DIVERSITY OF MATING SYSTEMS ACROSS CONTINENTS AND BIOMES

Most males of large herbivore species do not contribute to parental care, though in some of the smallest species of ungulates, males defend a common territory, which may contribute to female access to resources (Ralls 1977). Investment in reproduction by males is therefore generally restricted to mating. Mating systems vary from monogamy to polygyny; most monogamous species are territorial, while among polygynous species, diverse mating tactics (harem, tending, territory, leks) can be found, both across species (Jarman 1983, Clutton-Brock 1989, Lott 1991). The fallow deer (*Dama dama*) is an example of a species with intraspecific variability of mating tactics, since territorial behaviour can coexist with leks in the same population.

Monogamy and polygyny both occur in ungulates. Although the monogamy-polygyny gradient covaries with body weight (Loison *et al.* 1999), the relationship between mating systems and body weight is not very tight for species of intermediate size (Jarman 1983). There is indeed a great overlap between the ranges of body weight of monogamous and polygynous species. The smallest polygynous species weigh about 25–30 kg (female body weight in chamois, *Rupicapra rupicapra*), while the largest strictly monogamous species is the serow, *Capricornis sumatraensis*, weighing about 90 kg and the largest polygamous species can weigh more than 300 kg (female body weight in moose, *Alces alces*) (Loison *et al.* 1999).

Mating systems are not distributed randomly according to habitats and feeding types. They depend on female spatial and temporal distribution patterns, which are in turn determined by habitat and female social behaviour (Emlen & Oring 1977, Clutton-Brock & Harvey 1978, Clutton-Brock 1989). Among ungulates, polygynous mating systems are usually the rule in open habitat such as savanna, plains and mountain areas, where females tend to live in groups. Oligamy and monogamy appear to be restricted to closed habitat, where females live alone or in small family groups (see section above and Fig. 1.8 & Fig. 1.9). The covariation between habitat, female social grouping and male mating system has been extensively studied by Jarman (1974, 1983) and later by Clutton-Brock (1989). The latest review on ungulates, which adds historic and evolutionary perspectives to the evolution of this covariation (Pérez-Barbería *et al.* 2002), supports the view that the colonization of open habitat by an ancestral monogamous and forest-dwelling ungulate occurred before polygyny evolved (Jarman 1974). Covariation between habitat openness and mating systems, mediated through female social patterns appears to account for the distribution of mating systems found across continents and biomes in ungulates, but the loose relationship between body weight and mating system remains to be explained. For example, the small and polygynous chamois lives in open habitat while the large monogamous serow and moose live mainly in forests.

THE OCCURRENCE OF SEXUAL DIMORPHISM

Sexual dimorphism can be characterized by differences in size and body weight between the sexes, and by differences in the presence or size of secondary sexual characters (Jarman 1983, Caro *et al.* 2003). Large herbivores vary greatly along the gradient of size dimorphism, with at one end, females that are larger than males (e.g. forest duikers) and at the other, males that are more than twice the size of females (e.g. ibex, argali, markhor). Dimorphism is broadly correlated with body weight, whereby small species tend to show reverse size dimorphism (ungulates) or no dimorphism (marsupials), and large species with pronounced body weight dimorphism. The level of dimorphism among species of intermediate body weight is, however, quite variable among ungulates. The variance of male to female body weight ratio peaks for female body weights between 50 and 100 kg, but the greatest dimorphism is in species with female body weights greater than 100 kg. Dimorphism is even more variable and pronounced among marsupials (Jarman 1983).

Among ruminants, the relationship between dimorphism and body weight has been shown to be the by-product of the relationship between size and level of polygyny (Loison *et al.* 1999, Pérez-Barbería *et al.* 2002). For example, for similar body size, the dimorphic ibex is also highly polygynous, while the monomorphic serow is monogamous. Hence, for a given level of polygyny, there is no allometric increase of dimorphism with body weight (Loison *et al.* 1999). No additional influence of habitat type has been found either, once the level of polygyny is accounted for, possibly because the level of polygyny includes the influence of habitat (see previous section). The study of Loison *et al.* (1999), however, suggests that there may be an additional effect of feeding type on the level of dimorphism, even when the level of polygyny has been accounted for, with browsers being relatively less dimorphic in body weight than intermediate feeders or grazers. This strong relationship between level of polygyny and level of body weight dimorphism among ruminants does not hold true for non-ruminant ungulates, such as zebras and hippopotamus, which are relatively monomorphic despite a polygynous mating system and a large body size (Jarman 1983). This emphasizes that other constraints than the level of polygyny may act on either the male or the female body weight in these species (Clutton-Brock 1989, Martin *et al.* 1994, Loison *et al.* 1999). This aspect also needs further investigation, and extension to marsupials.

To sum up, the distribution of body weight dimorphism across biomes and continents in large herbivores is influenced by the level of polygyny of the species present in these biomes or continents, at least within the ruminants (Loison *et al.* 1999), and possibly, within the macropods (Fisher & Owens 2001).

VARIATIONS IN DEMOGRAPHIC STRATEGIES

Demographic strategies can be defined as the set of values of fitness components (e.g. adult or juvenile survival, age at first reproduction) and by their variability, exhibited by a species in a given environment. Large herbivores share some common patterns of covariation among life history traits (Eisenberg 1981, Gaillard *et al.* 2000, Fisher & Owens 2001) and belong to the long-lived and iteroparous mammals. Ungulates all give birth to precocious young, while in general herbivorous marsupials give birth to one embryo, whose development occurs in the pouch. Since body weight determines most physiological life history traits through negative allometric relationships in mammals (Peters 1983, Calder 1984), gestation length and birth weight are greatly dependent on female body weight among ungulates (Robbins & Robbins 1979). When compared to other mammal groups, ungulates are, however, characterized by a remarkably quick development and early age at maturity for their body size, in line with their precocious state at birth (Gaillard *et al.* 1997). Hence, ungulate species can be defined as 'fast' species within mammalian taxa, once the allometric component of their demographic strategy is accounted for. This common feature of all ungulates hold true across continents, biomes, habitats, and feeding categories and seems to be shared by marsupials (Gaillard *et al.* 2000, Fisher & Owens 2001).

Fitness components can be separated usefully into those related to reproduction and those related to survival. Contrary to gestation time or birth weight, adult survival hardly varies from species to species among ungulates and is remarkably high (>0.90) and constant over species despite variation in body size, biomes, habitat types and feeding regimes (Gaillard *et al.* 2000). Detailed long-term studies of roe deer, chamois, ibex, bighorn sheep, mountain goat and red deer survival living in temperate, mountainous, or forest habitat, illustrate that the adult survival and longevity varies little across species (females living to about 15–20 years). It may be more sensitive (although only to a small extent) to local conditions such as density, than to species-specific body weight (Loison *et al.* 1999, Loison *et al.* 2002, Toïgo & Gaillard 2003). The general pattern of a high and constant adult survival among large herbivores has been drawn from a small number of studies where reliable estimates of survival were obtained from long-term monitoring of marked individuals. More such studies are required on small and discreet species living in closed habitats, and more generally on species living in South America, Asia and Africa to test for the generality of this pattern across all taxonomic groups and habitat types.

Another general pattern among large ungulates is the relatively low and variable juvenile survival (Linnell *et al.* 1995, Gaillard *et al.* 2000), whether populations live under high or low predation pressure. Variations in weather from year to year generally have strong impact on the survival of juveniles, either indirectly by affecting the milk output of their mothers, or directly by causing deaths from starvation during droughts and long winters, or from freezing. The among-years variation in the level of juvenile survival leads to strong cohort effects (*sensu* Gaillard *et al.* 1998) in the dynamics of populations, whereby some cohorts can nearly disappear (e.g. up to 90% snow-related juvenile mortality reported for chamois kids, Crampe *et al.* 2002; in reindeer, Solberg *et al.* 2001; in roe deer, Gaillard *et al.* 1998) while other cohorts contribute to the future of adult populations to a greater extent (Coulson *et al.* 2004). Predation pressure is an additional cause of death that is biased towards juveniles in most ungulate species (Linnell *et al.* 1995). The main difference between continents, biomes or habitat types appears to be the timing of juvenile mortality, which may vary with environmental seasonality (Gaillard *et al.* 2000), and the diversity of the predator community encountered by the ungulate population (Sinclair *et al.* 2003). Predator pressure has probably also shaped the behaviour of offspring right after birth, which can be ranked along the hider-follower gradient both among ungulates and marsupials (Lent 1974, Fisher *et al.* 2002). Accordingly, species with following offspring preferentially inhabit open habitat, where a hiding strategy would not be efficient against predation, while species with hiding offspring are mainly found in closed habitat. Interestingly, the hider-follower gradient also correlates with patterns of maternal care. Species with hiding offspring appear to be closer to the fast extreme of the slow-fast continuum than species with following offspring (Fisher *et al.* 2002). This highlights an evolutionary pathway from ecological factors (habitat openness and predation risk) to life history strategies.

Reproductive performance can be further divided into four components: the age at maturity, the proportion of females that reproduce, the time interval between births, and the litter size. The first two components depend greatly on the density of the population, as they are among the first targets of the density-dependent response (Eberhardt 1985, Sæther 1997, Gaillard *et al.* 2000, Bonenfant *et al.* 2002). They are also dependent on the species' body size, but there is no evidence that these traits are specific to biomes, habitat or diet types. Litter size varies little among ungulates (between 1 and 3, Suidae excluded), with about 80% of cervids and bovids being monotocous on a regular basis. Some species can produce twins when environmental conditions are favourable (e.g. during colonization stages), but are not regular polytocous species (e.g. mountain goat). There are no clear patterns for the distribution of polytocous species among body weight, biomes, habitat and feeding regimes, and the patterns differ between bovids and cervids (see all polytocous cervids are forest-dwelling browsers, but most polytocous bovids are grazers on open or mixed habitat). Gaillard *et al.* (2000) reported an interesting trend for polytocous species to have a lower and more variable juvenile survival than mono-tocous species. The evolutionary, ecological and demographic correlates of litter size need to be investigated further, accounting for phylogenetic relationships between species (see Sæther & Gordon 1994). One trait that may be influenced by ecological factors is maternal expenditure, measured as the litter weight relative to the mother's weight. Because an allometric relationship is expected between these two variables, with a negative allo-metric coefficient of 0.75, Oftedal (1985) suggested measuring the relative prenatal maternal expenditure as the residual of the observed litter weight (log-transformed) to the expected litter weight. Preliminary investigation suggests that this relative litter weight may be correlated to biomes, habitat types or diet (Fig. 1.10) among bovids and cervids (Loison 1995, Gaillard *et al.*, unpublished), whereby grazers/open habitat dwellers appear to produce relatively heavier litters than browsers/forest habitat dwellers. Greater insights into the mechanisms behind such a relationship should be obtained by improved measuring of the environments faced by each species in terms of seasonality and predictability (Colwell 1974, Boyce 1979).

Large herbivores therefore share high and relatively constant adult survival, relatively early and variable age at maturity, and a relatively low and very variable juvenile survival. These patterns appear to hold true across phylogeny, biomes, habitat and feeding types. The subtle differ-ences suggested for the influence of ecological variables or taxonomy on these traits require more detailed studies.

CONCLUSIONS

In this chapter we explored the patterns of large herbivore diversity in different biomes, climates and habitats. We used the major taxonomic groups, and body size as a baseline descriptive variable for species attri-butes since body size is correlated with many morphological, physiological and life history traits. The distribution of body size follows a classic log-normal distribution, with a mode which increases with increasing habitat

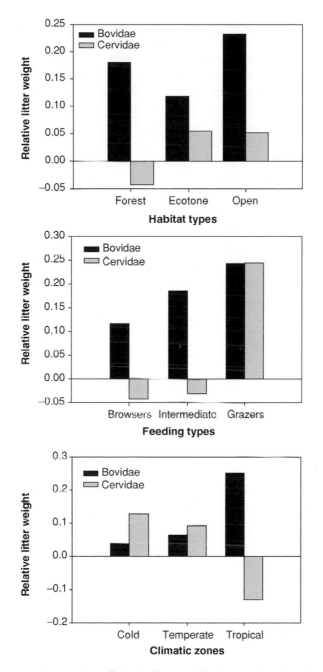

Figure 1.10. Comparison of relative litter weight between bovids and cervids, in the three main habitat types, feeding types and climatic zones.

openness, and a range which decreases with decreasing average temperature. Accordingly, the mode of distribution of body size in grazing species is
also greater than for browsers, both in marsupials and ungulates, with
group size being larger in open habitat and in grazers. Sexual dimorphism
increases with body size both for eutherians and marsupials, with a maximum variability in dimorphism at intermediate body size. Large herbivores
share high and relatively constant adult survival, relatively early and variable
age at maturity, and a relatively low and very variable juvenile survival. There
is some variability within the ungulates, and is greater in marsupials that
appear to be at the slow end of the slow-fast demographic continuum,
whereas the ungulate are at the fast end. These patterns appear to hold true
across phylogeny, biomes, habitat and feeding types. Palaeontology not only
provides some explanation for some of the missing species or species-types,
but also gives some insight into the drivers of the structure of ungulate
communities, among which vegetation change may have played a major
role prior to 50 000 years BP and human overkill around 10 000 years BP The
extinction of the megafaunal herbivores may have had cascading effects on
the dynamics and structure of unknown magnitude.

ACKNOWLEDGEMENTS

We thank Reidar Andersen, Kjell Danell and Bernt-Erik Sæther for helpful
comments on earlier drafts of this chapter, as well as Jean-Michel Gaillard
and Patrick Duncan for stimulating discussions.

REFERENCES

Bell, R.H.V. (1982). The effect of soil nutrient availability on the community
structure in African ecosystems. In *Ecology of Tropical Savannas*, ed.
B.J.Huntley & B.H. Walker, Berlin: Springer-Verlag, pp. 193–216.

Bonenfant, C., Gaillard, J.M., Loison, A. & Klein, F. (2002). Sex- and age-specific
effects of population density on life history traits of Red deer (*Cervus
elaphus*) in a temperate forest. *Ecography*, **25**, 446–58.

Bourlière, F. (1975). Mammals, small and large: the ecological implications of
body size. In *Small Mammals: Their Productivity and Population Dynamics*,
ed. F.B. Golley, K. Petrusewicz & L. Ryszkowski. Cambridge: Cambridge
University Press, pp. 1–8.

Boyce, M.S. (1979). Seasonality and patterns of natural selection for life histories.
American Naturalist, **114**, 569–83.

Brashares, J.S., Garland, T. & Arcese, P. (2000). Phylogenetic analysis of
coadaptation in behavior, diet and body size in the African antelope.
Behavioral Ecology, **11**, 452–63.

Calder, W.A. (1984). *Size, Function and Life History*. Cambridge, MA: Harvard University Press.

Caro, T.M., Graham, C.M., Stoner, C.J. & Flores, M.M. (2003). Correlates of horn and antler shape in bovids and cervids. *Behavioral Ecology and Sociobiology*, **55**, 32–41.

Cerling, T.E., Harris, J.M., MacFadden, B.J. *et al.* (1997). Global vegetation change through the Miocene/Pliocene boundary. *Nature*, **389**, 153–8.

Cerling, T.E., Ehleringer, J.R. & Harris, J.M. (1998). Carbon dioxide starvation, the development of C4 ecosystems, and mammalian evolution. *Philosophical Transactions of the Royal Society of London, Series B*, **353**, 159–71.

Clutton-Brock, T.H. (1989). Mammalian mating systems. *Proceedings of the Royal Society of London, Series B*, **236**, 339–72.

Clutton-Brock, T.H. & Harvey, P.H. (1978). Mammals, resources and reproductive strategies. *Nature*, **273**, 191–5.

Coe, M.J., Cumming, D.H.M. & Phillipson, J. (1976). Biomass and production of large African herbivores in relation to rainfall and primary production. *Oecologia*, **22**, 341–54.

Colbert, E.H. & Morales, M. (1994). *Evolution of the Vertebrates. a History of the Backboned Animals Through Time*. New York: Wiley-Liss, Inc.

Colwell, R.K. (1974). Predictability, constancy and contingency of periodic phenomena. *Ecology*, **55**, 1148–53.

Coulson, T., Guinness, F.E., Pemberton, J.M. & Clutton-Brock, T.H. (2004). The demographic consequences of releasing a population of red deer from culling. *Ecology*, **85**, 411–22.

Crampe, J.-P., Gaillard, J.-M. & Loison, A. (2002). L'enneigement hivernal: un facteur de variation du recrutement chez l'isard (*Rupicapra pyrenaica pyrenaica*). *Canadian Journal of Zoology*, **80**, 1306–12.

Damuth, J. (1981). Population density and body size in mammals. *Nature*, **290**, 699–700.

Danell, K., Lundberg, P. & Niemelä, P. (1996). Species richness in mammalian herbivores: patterns in the boreal zone. *Ecography*, **19**, 404–9.

Deshmukh, I.K. (1984). A common relationship between precipitation and grassland peak biomass for East and southern Africa. *African Journal of Ecology*, **22**, 181–6.

Eberhardt, L.L. (1985). Assessing the dynamics of wild populations. *Journal of Wildlife Management*, **49**, 997–1012.

Eisenberg, J.F. (1981). *The Mammalian Radiations: an Analysis of Trends in Evolution, Adaptation and Behavior*. Chicago: University of Chicago Press.

Emlen, S.T. & Oring, L.W. (1977). Ecology, sexual selection and the evolution of mammalian mating systems. *Science*, **197**, 215–23.

Ernest, M.S.K. (2003). Life history characteristics of placental non-volant mammals. *Ecology*, **84**, 3401.

Felsenstein, J. (1985). Phylogenies and the comparative method. *American Naturalist*, **125**, 1–15.

Fisher, D.O. & Owens, I.P.F. (2000). Female home range size and the evolution of social organisation in macropod marsupials. *Journal of Animal Ecology*, **69**, 1093–8.

Fisher, D.O., Owens, I.P.F. & Johnson, C.N. (2001). The ecological basis of life history variation in marsupials. *Ecology*, **82**, 3531–40.

Fisher, D.O., Blomberg, S.P. & Owens, I.P.F. (2002). Convergent maternal care strategies in ungulates and macropods. *Evolution*, **56**, 167–76.

Fowler, C.W. & MacMahon, J.A. (1982). Selective extinction and speciation: their influence on the structure and functioning of communities and ecosystems. *American Naturalist*, **119**, 480–98.

Fritz, H. & Duncan, P. (1994). On the carrying capacity for large ungulates of African savanna ecosystems. *Proceedings of the Royal Society of London, Series B*, **256**, 77–82.

Fritz, H., Duncan, P., Gordon, J. & Illius, A.W. (2002). Megaherbivores influence trophic guilds structure in African ungulate communities. *Oecologia*, **131**, 620–5.

Gaillard, J.M., Pontier, D., Allainé, A. *et al.* (1997). Variation in growth form and precocity at birth in eutherian mammals. *Proceedings of the Royal Society of London, Series B*, **264**, 859–68.

Gaillard, J.M., Festa-Bianchet, M. & Yoccoz, N.G. (1998). Population dynamics of large herbivores: variable recruitment with constant adult survival. *Trends in Ecology and Evolution*, **13**, 58–63.

Gaillard, J.M., Festa-Bianchet, M., Yoccoz, N.G., Loison, A. & Toïgo, C. (2000). Temporal variation in fitness components and population dynamics of large herbivores. *Annual Review of Ecology and Systematics*, **31**, 367–93.

Gagnon, M. & Chew, A.E. (2000). Dietary preferences in extant African bovidae. *Journal of Mammalogy*, **81**, 490–511.

Garland, T., Harvey, P.H. & Ives, A.R. (1992). Procedures for the analysis of comparative data using phylogenetically independent contrasts. *Systematics Biology*, **41**, 18–32.

Gaston, K.J. & Blackburn, T.M. (2000). *Pattern and Process in Macroecology*. Oxford: Blackwell Science.

Giraldeau, L.-A. & Caraco, T. (2000). *Social Foraging Theory*. Princeton: Princeton University Press.

Gordon, I.J. (2003). Browsing and grazing ruminants: are they different beasts? *Forest Ecology and Management*, **181**, 13–21.

Gordon, I.J. & Illius, A.W. (1994). The functional significance of the browser-grazer dichotomy in African ruminants. *Oecologia*, **98**, 167–75.

Greenacre, M.J. & Vrba, E.S. (1984). Graphical display and interpretation of antelope census data in African wildlife areas, using correspondence analysis. *Ecology*, **65**, 984–97.

Harvey, P.H. & Pagel, M.D. (1991). *The Comparative Method in Evolutionary Biology*. Oxford: Oxford University Press.

Janis, C.M. (1988). An estimation of tooth volume and hypsodonty indices in ungulate mammals, and the correlation of these factors with dietary preferences. In *Teeth Revisited*, ed. D.E. Russel, J.-P. Santoro & D. Sigoneau-Russel. Proceedings of the VIIth International Symposium on Dental Morphology. Paris: Musée d'Histoire Naturelle, pp. 367–87.

Janis, C., Damuth, J. & Theodor, J.M. (2000). Miocene ungulates and terrestrial primary productivity: where have all the browsers gone? *Proceeding of the National Academy of Science*, **97**, 7899–904.

Janis, C., Damuth, J. & Theodor, J.M. (2002). The origins and evolution of the North American grassland biome: the story from the hoofed mammals. *Palaeogeography, Palaeoclimatology, Palaeoecology*, **177**, 183–98.

Jarman, P.J. (1974). The social organisation of antelope in relation to their ecology. *Behaviour*, **48**, 215–65.

Jarman, P.J. (1983). Mating system and sexual dimorphism in large, terrestrial, mammalian herbivores. *Biological Reviews*, **58**, 485–520.

Johnson, C.N. & Prideaux, G.J. (2004). Extinctions of herbivorous mammals in the late Pleistocene of Australia in relation to their feeding ecology: no evidence for environment change as cause of extinction. *Austral Ecology*, **29**, 553–7.

Klein, R.G. (2000). Human evolution and large extinctions. In *Antelopes, Deer and Relatives*, ed. E.S. Vrba, & G.B. Schaller. London & New Haven: Yale University Press, pp. 128–42.

Kozlowski, J. & Gawelczyk, A.T. (2002). Why are species' body size distributions usually skewed to the right? *Functional Ecology*, **16**, 419–32.

Le Houérou, H.N. (1989). *The Grazing Land Ecosystems Of the African Sahel*. Berlin: Springer-Verlag.

Lent, P.C. (1974). Mother-infant relationships in ungulates. In *The Behaviour of Ungulates and its Relation to Management*, ed. V. Geist and F. Walther. IUCN Publications No. 24. Morges, Switzerland: International Union for Conservation and Natural Resources, pp. 14–55.

Lieth, H. (1975). Some prospects beyond production measurements. In *Primary Productivity of the Biosphere*, ed. H. Lieth & R.H. Whittaker. New York: Springer-Verlag, pp. 286–304.

Linnell, J.D.C., Aanes, R. & Andersen, R. (1995). Who killed Bambi? The role of predation in the neonatal mortality of temperate ungulates. *Wildlife Biology*, **1**, 209–23.

Loison, A., Gaillard, J.M., Pelabon, C. & Yoccoz, N.G. (1999). What factors shape sexual size dimorphism in ungulates? *Evolutionary Ecology Research*, **1**, 611–33.

Loison, A., Toigo, C., Appolinaire, J. & Michallet, J. (2002). Demographic processes in colonizing populations of isard (*Rupicapra pyrenaica*) and ibex (*Capra ibex*). *Journal of Zoology*, **256**, 199–205.

Lott, D.F. (1991). *Intraspecific Variation in the Social Systems of Wild Vertebrates*. Cambridge: Cambridge University Press.

Lovegrove, B.G. & Haines, L. (2004). The evolution of placental mammal body sizes: evolutionary history, form and function. *Oecologia*, **138**, 13–27.

Martin, P.S. & Klein, R.G. (eds.) (1984). *Quaternary Extinctions: a Prehistoric Revolution*. Tucson: University of Arizona Press.

Martin, P.S. & Steadman, D.W. (1999). Prehistoric extinctions on islands and continents. In *Extinctions in Near Time: Causes, Contexts and Consequences*, ed. R.D.E. MacPhee. New York: Kluwer Academic/Plenum Publishers, pp. 17–56.

Martin, R.D., Willner, L.A. & Dettling, A. (1994). The evolution of sexual dimorphism in primates. In *The Differences Between the Sexes*. ed. R.V. Short & E. Balaban. Cambridge: Cambridge University Press, pp. 159–200.

McNaughton, S.J., Oesterheld, D.A., Frank, D.A. & Williams, K.J. (1989). Ecosystem-level patterns of primary productivity and herbivory in terrestrial habitats. *Nature*, **341**, 142–4.

Nowak, R.M. (1991). *Walker's Mammals of the World*. Baltimore: Johns Hopkins University Press.

Oftedal, O.T. (1985). Pregnancy and lactation. In *Bioenergetics of Wild Herbivores.* ed. R.J. Hudson & R.E. White. Florida: CRD Press, Inc., pp. 215–38.

Olff, H., Ritchie, M.E. & Prins, H.H.T. (2002). Global environment controls of diversity in large herbivores. *Nature,* **415**, 901–4.

Pérez-Barbería, F.J. & Gordon, I.J. (1999). The functional relationship between feeding type and jaw and cranial morphology in ungulates. *Oecologia,* **118**, 157–65.

Pérez-Barbería, F.J. & Gordon, I.J. (2001). Relationships between oral morphology and feeding style in the Ungulata: a phylogenetically controlled evaluation. *Proceedings of the Royal Society of London, Series B,* **68**, 1021–30.

Pérez-Barbería, F.J., Gordon, I.J. & Nores, C. (2001). Evolutionary transitions among feeding styles and habitats in ungulates. *Evolutionary Ecology Research,* **3**, 221–30.

Pérez-Barbería, F.J., Gordon, I.J. & Pagel, M. (2002). The origins of sexual dimorphism in body size in ungulates. *Evolution,* **56**, 1276–85.

Peters, R.H. (1983). *The Ecological Implication of Body Size.* Cambridge: Cambridge University Press.

Peters, R.H. & Wassenberg, K. (1983). The effect of body size on animal abundance. *Oecologia,* **60**, 89–96.

Ralls, K. (1977). Sexual dimorphism in mammals: avian models and unanswered questions. *American Naturalist,* **111**, 917–38.

Ritchie, M.E. & Olff, H. (1999). Spatial scaling laws yield a synthetic theory of biodiversity. *Nature,* **400**, 557–60.

Robbins, C.T. & Robbins, B.L. (1979). Fetal and maternal growth patterns and maternal reproductive effort in ungulates and subungulates. *American Naturalist,* **114**, 101–16.

Robbins, C.T., Spalinger, D.E. & Van Hoven, W. (1995). Adaptation of ruminants to browse and grass diets: are anatomical-based browser-grazer interpretation valid? *Oecologia,* **103**, 208–13.

Rosenzweig, M.L. (1995). *Species Diversity in Space and Time.* Cambridge: Cambridge University Press.

Sæther, B.E. (1997). Environmental stochasticity and population dynamics of large herbivores: a search for mechanisms. *Trends in Ecology and Evolution,* **12**, 143–9.

Sæther, B.E. & Gordon, I.J. (1994). The adaptive significance of productive strategies in ungulates. *Proceedings of the Royal Society of London, Series B,* **256**, 263–8.

Schmidt-Nielsen, K. (1984). *Scaling: Why is Animal Size so Important?* Cambridge: Cambridge University Press.

Solberg, E.J., Jordhøy, P., Strand, O. *et al.* (2001). Effects of density-dependence and climate on the dynamics of a Svalbard reindeer population. *Ecography,* **24**, 441–51.

Sinclair, A.R.E., Mduma, S. & Brashares, J.S. (2003). Patterns of predation in a diverse predator-prey system. *Nature,* **425**, 288–90.

Smith, F.A., Lyons, S.K., Ernest, S.K.M. *et al.* (2003). Body mass of late quaternary mammals. *Ecology,* **84**, 3403.

Stearns, S.C. (1992). *The Evolution of Life Histories.* Oxford: Oxford University Press.

Strahan, R. (ed.) (1983). *The Australian Museum Complete Book of Australian Mammals*. North Ryde: Cornstalk Publishing, Collins Angus & Robertson Publishers.

Toïgo, C. & Gaillard, J.M. (2003). Causes of sex-biased adult survival in ungulates: sexual size dimorphism, mating tactic or environment harshness? *Oikos*, **101**, 376–84.

Van Soest, P.J. (1994). *Nutritional Ecology of the Ruminant*. Corvallis, Oregon: O & B Books.

Van Wieren, S.E. (1996). Digestive strategies in ruminants and nonruminants. Ph.D. thesis, Wageningen Agricultural University, Wageningen, The Netherlands.

Vrba, E.S. (1987). Ecology in relation to speciation rates: some case histories of Miocene-Recent mammal clades. *Evolutionary Ecology*, **1**, 283–300.

Vrba, E.S. (1992). Mammals as a key to evolutionary theory. *Journal of Mammalogy*, **73**, 1–28.

Vrba, E.S. & Schaller, G.B. (2000). *Antelopes, Deer and Relatives*. London & New Haven: Yale University Press.

Western, D. (1989). Conservation without parks: wildlife in rural landscape. In *Conservation for the 21st Century*, ed. D. Western & M. Pearl. Oxford: Oxford University Press, pp. 158–65.

2

Living in a seasonal environment

JON MOEN, REIDAR ANDERSEN AND ANDREW ILLIUS

INTRODUCTION

Accentuated seasons are a common phenomenon in large parts of the globe. This typically involves a pulse of plant growth during the favourable season, and an extended unfavourable season with no plant growth, which may be due to temperature variations in high latitudes or water limitations in arid environments. The consequences for large herbivores will be one season with abundant food resources and another season with very low food resources. This is especially pronounced in northern high latitudes where the favourable season can be as short as a month or less.

Polar areas receive less solar radiation than other parts of the globe on an annual basis, and this radiation is also to a large part lost to space due to reflection by clouds, snow and ice. This radiation imbalance gives low temperatures and low annual primary productivity. However, solar radiation levels vary greatly between seasons; in the summer the poles receive higher levels of radiation than any other place on Earth, whereas there may be a total lack of incoming solar radiation during winter. As plants experience 24 hours of daylight during summer, productivity on a daily basis may be very high in areas where the geology and topography are favourable for weathering and the transport of nutrients. Thus the pulsed plant growth may be of short duration but very strong.

The large annual variation in plant growth imposes constraints on herbivores as life history tactics must be adjusted to fit the seasonal pattern of the system. However, a seasonal environment imposes two types of environmental variation on the population dynamics of large herbivores. One type is the predictable within-year variation due to the seasons, but there will also be an unpredictable between-year variation caused by large-scale weather fluctuations. This between-year variation increases with increasing latitude (Ferguson & Messier 1996). In the northern hemisphere, climatic variability is mainly determined by large-scale alternations in atmospheric mass. The strongest regional expression of this is the so-called North Atlantic Oscillation (NAO), which affects the direction, magnitude and speed of westerly winds across the Atlantic Ocean (Rogers 1984, Hurrell *et al.* 2003). This large-scale climatic variation influences winter temperatures and precipitation patterns over both North America and northern Europe. The positive phase of the NAO is associated with relatively warm and moist air over much of northern Europe, while strong northerly winds will carry cold and dry air over Greenland and the Canadian Arctic (Hurrell *et al.* 2003). These variations especially in winter temperature and precipitation will have effects on the food supply of large herbivores (Post & Stenseth 1999). The NAO may explain >50% of inter-annual climatic variation, and it exhibits phases of increases and decreases that last for decades (Hurrell *et al.* 2003).

In this review, we will summarize findings showing that seasonality strongly influences life history tactics of large herbivores, and that the between-year variation has strong effects on population dynamics of the herbivores through effects on food availability during winter. Further, this dependence on winter forage will decouple population dynamics from summer grazing, giving only small impacts on food resources during summer. We will focus on the two most common large herbivores in the Arctic: muskox (*Ovibos moschatus* Zimmermann) and reindeer/caribou (*Rangifer tarandus* L.), but we will also give examples from other northern large herbivore populations. Finally, we will discuss possible effects of climate change on these plant-herbivore systems.

EFFECTS OF SEASONALITY ON LARGE HERBIVORE LIFE HISTORY TACTICS

Large herbivores adapt to seasonality in a variety of ways: for instance, breeding is timed so that calving is concentrated in the optimal period for offspring survival (e.g. Loudon & Brinklow 1992), growth is restricted to the period of summer food abundance, and herds may be highly migratory (Suttie & Webster 1995).

In both muskoxen and *Rangifer*, calves are born in spring around one month before fresh forage begins to be available. Females of both species use their body reserves to maintain growth of calves in the first postnatal period.

Growth rates in *Rangifer* are dependent on the condition of the summer ranges and on the availability of high quality forage and may thus vary between different herds in space and time (Reimers *et al.* 1983, Adamczewski *et al.* 1987, Finstad & Prichard 2000). Body growth is totally restricted to the summer months in both species, while life during the winter months is focused on survival (Reimers *et al.* 1983, Adamczewski *et al.* 1997).

Northern populations of large herbivores show different strategies of habitat use at different scales. At a larger scale, the animals may migrate between seasonally different areas, while on a smaller scale (within a season) animals choose how to utilize their ranges. Several *Rangifer* populations perform long seasonal migrations between distinct summer and winter ranges, whereas muskoxen are more sedentary. Muskoxen also have smaller home ranges within a season, while *Rangifer*, at least during the summer, tend to move over larger areas. This could be related to the larger body mass of muskox which enables them to exploit lower quality food, store more reserves and have a greater fasting endurance than *Rangifer* (Illius 1997). The Porcupine caribou herd in northern Alaska and Canada migrates in the order of 200–700 km between calving areas on the arctic coastal plain and winter areas in the mountainous interior (Fancy *et al.* 1994). Some reindeer populations in Sweden traditionally migrated between summer grounds on the Norwegian coast and winter grounds in the boreal forest in Sweden, a distance of some 400–500 km (Bernes 1996). However, conventions on grazing rights between the two countries have restricted these movements which, in some cases, have resulted in a change in the use of the landscape by the reindeer and detrimental effects on the vegetation (Moen & Danell 2003).

ENERGY USE IN ARCTIC/ALPINE LARGE HERBIVORES – CAPITAL VS. INCOME BREEDER STRATEGIES

Tactics of energy use varies among large herbivores. As in most other taxonomic groups, there is a continuum from capital breeders that use stored energy for reproduction, to income breeders that use energy acquired during the reproductive period (Jönsson 1997). These life history tactics involve different costs and benefits. A major disadvantage for a capital breeder is costs of storage (e.g. fat), while a major advantage is a spatial and temporal uncoupling between feeding and breeding. We argue that most of the large herbivores inhabiting arctic/alpine areas are closer to the capital breeder end of the continuum as they convert the strong seasonal pulse of plant growth into stored fat.

A capital breeder relies heavily on body reserves for raising their off-spring. The quality of the summer range is thus important as the females then build up their capital in terms of stored fat. Consequently, their body weight fluctuates widely, both seasonally and annually (Festa-Bianchet *et al.* 1996, 1998). This pattern is also evident in Arctic large herbivores: both muskox (Adamczewski *et al.* 1997) and *Rangifer* are able to deposit large fat stores, reaching more than 25% of ingesta-free body weight. Large seasonal variation in body weight is also reported for *Rangifer* (Finstad & Prichard 2000, Fig. 2.1).

In both muskox and *Rangifer*, timing of birth occurs slightly before spring flush (Reimers *et al.* 1983, Lent 1988, Flydal & Reimers 2002). For instance, populations of wild reindeer in Scandinavia give birth to calves in higher elevated alpine areas. They spend the first post-calving month in these areas before moving down to lower elevated summer grounds. Therefore, in this period the reindeer have only little access to edible forage, and the initial postnatal care depends to a large extent on the body reserves of the mother. Typical income breeders like roe deer, on the other hand, time the birth of young to the spring flush (Andersen *et al.* 2000). Only by having access to high quality forage after birth will such species be able to successfully raise the normally twin or triplet clutch, whereas

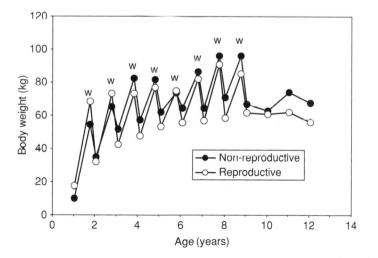

Figure 2.1. Seasonal body weight changes of female *Rangifer* in Alaska. W denotes winter weights (December–January). Data from Finstad and Prichard (2000), reproduced by permission of the Nordic Council for Reindeer Husbandry Research.

most capital breeders produce one offspring and use their fat deposits to meet the energy expenditure related to lactation.

The stability of large herbivore populations is closely linked to two factors: the specific growth rates close to the carrying capacity (set by winter resources in the case of Arctic large herbivores), and the environmental variance among years (Lande et al. 2003). As demonstrated by Clutton-Brock and Coulson (2002), it is clear that the timing of birth relative to the spring flush and energetic needs can exert very different effects on these matters. Contrasting Soay sheep (closer to the capital breeder end of the continuum) and red deer (closer to the income breeder end of the continuum) on the Hebridean Islands, they found interspecific variation in the effect of density-dependent factors. In Soay sheep, lambs are born in April, allowing ewes to regain body mass after June when lactation ceases, and enter the winter with a body mass similar to non-reproductive females. In fact, both in Soay sheep (Clutton-Brock & Coulson 2002) and big-horn sheep (a typical capital breeder; Festa-Bianchet 1998) it is found that females that have successfully reared lambs the previous season were more likely to give birth again than non-reproductive females, presumably reflecting phenotypic differences between individuals as body condition was similar. Consequently, density-dependent changes in fecundity had relatively little effect on population growth rates in these capital breeders, generating high rates of population increases during summer, leading eventually to over-compensatory mortality (Clutton-Brock et al. 1997). In fact, it was found that sheep populations close to winter carrying capacity can increase by over 50% the following summer (when resources are not limiting) and thus enter the following winter at levels that cannot be sustained by the winter food supplies (Clutton-Brock & Coulson 2002). In contrast, density-dependent factors depress growth rates in deer (income breeders) even at relatively low population densities, giving a greater annual stability in animal numbers (Fig. 2.2).

Both muskox and reindeer show many of the characteristics typical of capital breeders, such as large fat stores and seasonal variations in body weight (e.g. Adamczewski et al. 1987, 1997, White et al. 1989, Finstad & Prichard 2000). Further, it has been shown that calving is delayed if the female reindeer is in poor condition in the autumn (Flydal & Reimers 2002), and that both calving incidence and calf mass is affected by female reindeer mass (Rönnegård et al. 2002), indicating the importance of stored resources for breeding. However, contrary to Soay sheep, female *Rangifer* that have reared a calf weigh less in autumn than non-calving females (Kojola & Eloranta 1989, Chan-McLeod et al. 1999) showing that

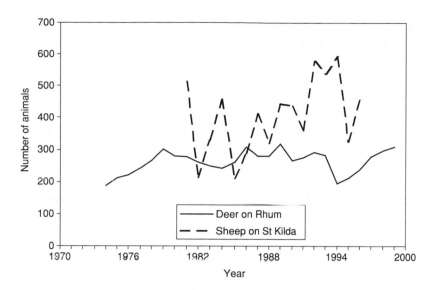

Figure 2.2. Population fluctuations for deer on Rhum and sheep on St Kilda, Hebridean Islands. Data from Clutton-Brock & Coulson (2002), reproduced by permission of the Royal Society and T. Clutton-Brock.

the females are not able to completely compensate for lost resources during the winter. It is also not clear if muskoxen and *Rangifer* have the capacity to maintain high population growth rates during the summer in situations where they are close to winter carrying capacity, and thus enter the next winter at population densities that cannot be sustained by the winter resources. However, before we can develop generalizations about the contrasting effects of capital and income breeders on their foraging resources, we need a more thorough understanding of the impact of differences in reproductive timing and population structure on demographic processes.

EFFECTS OF CLIMATIC VARIABILITY ON POPULATION DYNAMICS

The NAO causes variations in snow cover and winter temperatures, which in turn influences plant phenology and the nutritional value of plants for large herbivores (Mysterud *et al.* 2003). Body mass and fecundity of large herbivores thus varies with NAO, and these weather fluctuations operate mainly through cumulative effects on the condition of the mothers (Post & Stenseth 1999). Calves born after years of good or bad winter conditions may thus vary in condition, and this effect may persist into adulthood. This gives cohort effects on population dynamics (Albon *et al.* 1992), where the climatic conditions into which a cohort is born influences life-long differences in cohort reproduction and survival. The result of these effects is fluctuating numbers of animals as weak and strong cohorts are born.

Density-independent weather effects are very important for the food base of animal populations with low intrinsic rates of increase, and thus for population dynamics (Langvatn *et al.* 1996). Especially important for northern ungulates is ice-crust formations. These could be caused by sub-zero temperatures increasing to above 0°C and then falling to below zero again. Such periods, which could last from less than an hour to several hours, cause the upper layer of the snow to first melt and then freeze into an ice crust (Forchhammer & Boertmann 1993). Precipitation during periods with positive temperatures may also contribute to the ice-crust formation (Putkonen & Roe 2003). Animals cannot penetrate the hard layer of the ice crust, and these events will thus strongly influence forage availability. These density-independent decreases in forage availability may induce density-dependent decreases in fecundity, growth and/or survival as the animals are forced to forage on a reduced food resource. Density affects vital rates in a certain order: first juvenile survival is affected, then age at first reproduction, reproductive rates of adults, and finally adult survival. Juvenile survival also varies more than adult survival with environmental fluctuations (Gaillard *et al.* 1998). This is, for instance, the case in *Rangifer*, where density-dependent effects mainly operate through declines in fecundity (neonatal losses prior to, or at, calving rather than mortality of adult females; Skogland 1985).

Long delays (such as cohort effects) and overcompensation in the density-dependent feedback (as seen in Soay sheep), together with large-scale variations in climate (e.g. by variations in the NAO), can thus easily generate large fluctuations in population sizes of large herbivores. Because of this, a stable equilibrium between northern ungulates and their resource supply is unlikely, and large fluctuations in population size is a typical pattern (Sæther 1997).

Illius and O'Connor (2000) constructed a model to explore the effects of climatic variation on the dynamics of seasonal grazing systems (i.e. on both animal numbers and defoliation intensity). The model incorporated seasonal growth of the plants, body reserves of the animals, defoliation, and the functional and numerical responses of the animals. The model tested several predictions from Illius and O'Connor (1999): (1) animal numbers are regulated in a density-dependent manner by the limited forage available during the non-breeding season, (2) the animal population is uncoupled from resources in the favourable season, (3) the uncoupling of the animal population from vegetation in the favourable season could actually lead to an increased risk of heavy utilization, and (4) grazing systems prone to climatic variability may be more susceptible to extreme herbivore impacts because of intense localized defoliations. Their analyses showed that ungulate population size was regulated largely by non-breeding season resources, and that the population was largely, but not wholly, uncoupled from resources in the favourable season. The bottleneck in population dynamics of the animals is thus in the unfavourable season, while body and population growth is dependent on overabundant resources during the favourable season. Further, good resource situations during the unfavourable season supported many animals which could give rise to high defoliation intensities of resources in the favourable season, especially if the food resources during the favourable season are patchily distributed and if the animals tend to aggregate during feeding. This would be especially obvious in situations with supplemental feeding during the unfavourable season which will inflate the population densities entering the favourable season, and if the animals have the potential to affect the same food resource in both seasons. An example of the latter is seen in northern Finland where supplemental feeding in a stationary reindeer husbandry system has kept reindeer populations at high levels during winter. Summer grazing and trampling have then caused a nearly complete destruction of the natural winter forage (i.e. lichens; Väre et al. 1996).

Population dynamics of *Rangifer* and muskoxen: review of data

All or most *Rangifer* populations show considerable fluctuation in numbers. This is, for instance, seen in Peary caribou which show long periods of low numbers, followed by increases and sudden catastrophic die-offs (Fig 2.3; Conservation of Arctic Flora and Fauna (CAFF) 2001). Other examples are Svalbard reindeer which show large fluctuations between years (Fig. 2.4; CAFF 2001), and the caribou populations in Greenland (Meldgaard 1986). Population size of wild reindeer on Hardangervidda fluctuated five-fold during 1955–89 despite culling (Skogland 1990), and even semi-domesticated reindeer in Sweden show strong fluctuations during the entire last century (Moen & Danell 2003).

Many authors attribute these fluctuations to climatic variability, especially variations in winter precipitation which influences the availability of forage through deep snow and/or ice crust formations (e.g. Caughley & Gunn 1993, Heard & Ouellet 1994). This is, for instance, the case for

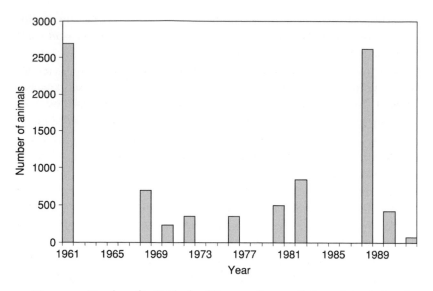

Figure 2.3. Number of individuals of Peary caribou on Bathurst Island, Canada. Data from CAFF (2001), obtained by permission from the CAFF International Secretariat, Akureyri, Iceland.

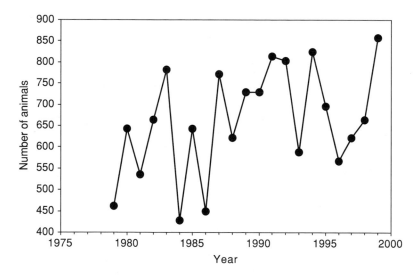

Figure 2.4. Number of individuals of Svalbard reindeer in Adventdalen, Spitsbergen. Data from CAFF (2001), obtained by permission from the CAFF International Secretariat, Akureyri, Iceland.

Svalbard reindeer (Aanes *et al.* 2000, CAFF 2001, Solberg *et al.* 2001), Scandinavian reindeer (Kumpula 2001), Peary caribou (Miller *et al.* 1975, CAFF 2001), and the George River caribou herd (Couturier *et al.* 1990).

Much less data exists for muskox populations, but the general pattern seems to be the same. Variations in winter precipitation have been suggested to cause strong variation in calf production and survival in northern Alaska (Reynolds 1998). Perhaps the best data comes from the northeast of Greenland (Fig. 2.5; Forchhammer & Boertmann 1993). It shows a generally favourable trend for muskox from the 1960s to the mid 1980s, but with considerable year-to-year variation around this trend, especially south of 75°. The northern areas have sparser vegetation, which is reflected in lower muskoxen densities, and more stable climate due to the existence of pack ice in the sea. In general, two different density-independent abiotic factors seem to be very important determinants of muskox population density and distribution: ice crust formations due to periods of above-freezing temperatures, and winter precipitation. Ice crust formations increase muskox mortality, especially in the southern part of the range, where foehn wind conditions create ablation periods. Winter precipitation,

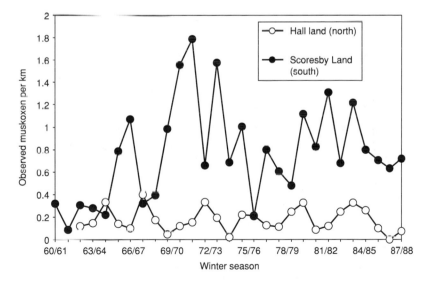

Figure 2.5. Number of observed muskox per travelled km in northeast Greenland. The northern observations are from Hall Land (approx. 80° N), and the southern observations are from Scoresby Land (approx. 73° N). Data from Forchhammer and Boertmann (1993), reproduced by permission of Blackwell Publishing.

on the other hand, seems to affect distribution patterns but not mortality, as heavy snowfall induces local migrations in muskoxen (Forchhammer & Boertmann 1993).

In the early 1960s, 27 muskoxen were moved from eastern Greenland to the Kangerlussuaq area in western Greenland. The original population increased and now occupy all the suitable habitats in the area (Linnell *et al.* 2000). Harvest of the population has been allowed through hunting quotas since 1988. Since the introduction the population has grown very quickly because of the availability of forage, which has led cows to give birth already from their second year. By 1990 the population had reached about 2500 animals (Fig. 2.6), and the population has continued to fluctuate around this value since then. It is tempting to conclude that the population has reached its carrying capacity (set by winter conditions), and that variation in weather conditions induce fluctuations around this long-term mean (Linnell *et al.* 2000). However, the relative importance of weather and culling for the population dynamics of the muskoxen should be evaluated.

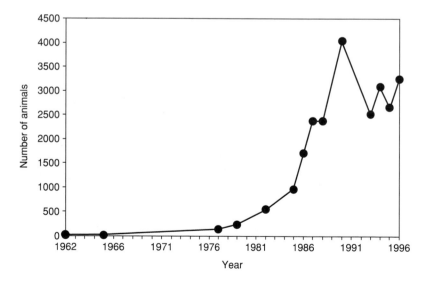

Figure 2.6. Population growth of an introduced muskox population in Kangerlussuaq, western Greenland. A total of 27 animals from northeast Greenland were released in 1962 and 1965. Data from Linnell *et al.* (2000), reproduced by permission of the Greenland Institute for Natural Resources and J. Linnell.

Large-scale climatic variability may synchronize population dynamics of ungulates over large areas (Stenseth *et al.* 2002). This is, for instance, seen in Svalbard reindeer, where two out of three populations showed synchronized dynamics (Aanes *et al.* 2003). Variations in local weather and animal densities between the populations may explain why only two of the three populations showed synchronized dynamics. Synchronization of dynamics of sheep populations on different islands in St. Kilda have also been demonstrated (Grenfell *et al.* 1998). Post & Forchhammer (2002) examined population dynamics of five muskox populations on the northeast coast of Greenland and six populations of caribou on the west coast of Greenland, together with data on climate variability measured by the NAO index. Their analyses showed that populations of both species are influenced by the effect of the NAO on local winter temperatures. They explained these effects as a result of ice-crust formation influencing juvenile mortality, together with spatial synchrony in plant phenology which may influence offspring production in the ungulates. In general, large-scale synchronization of population dynamics is likely to be mediated through climate effects on plant growth and thus on food resources for the ungulates (Aanes *et al.* 2003, Post 2003).

EFFECTS OF SEASONALITY ON IMPACT OF GRAZING

A decoupling of population dynamics and food resources as suggested by Illius and O'Connor (2000) may explain the apparently low effects on vegetation in summer grazing grounds reported from several northern large herbivore populations. In fact, in a description from the Russian Arctic, Chernov and Matveyeva (1997) write:

In spite of high numbers [of reindeer] in some tundra areas during summer and [their] comparatively large withdrawal of primary production from the ecosystems, this animal has no strong influence on vegetation. This is due to such special features in biology and behavior of the wild form of reindeer as seasonal migration. The influence of a reindeer herd is difficult to notice even immediately after grazing. Only wild reindeer can successfully utilize a wide range of low productive pastures without causing any real damage to the vegetation and without changing the natural succession.

The authors quantified this low impact on summer grazing grounds from the Taymyr Peninsula, Russia, to a removal of about 2% of the net annual primary production (NAP). This also seems to be true for wild reindeer on Hardangervidda, Norway (0.6% of NAP removed; Wielgolaski

1997) and of muskox from Devon Island, Canada (1%–2% of NAP removed; Bliss 1997). However, these numbers do not imply that large herbivores in Arctic and subarctic environments have no influence on vegetation in summer grazing grounds.

Animals do not use the landscape in a random fashion, and variations in habitat choice and food preferences will give uneven utilization of the vegetation both on landscape and local scales. Reindeer are highly dependent on high-quality forage during the summer to have as high a growth rate as possible (Aanes *et al.* 2002). To achieve this, they generally follow snow-melt patterns towards higher altitudes as the summer progresses to be able to forage on newly emerging shoots (Mårell 2001). In general they try to forage in spring conditions for as long as possible during the summer. This will result in patchy grazing effects on the landscape as the phenology of plants interacts with nutritional needs and behaviour of the herbivores. Muskox may preferentially use certain meadows within their home range and thus exert high grazing pressures on these localities. For instance, muskoxen on Ellesmere Island spent 83% of their total grazing time in meadows, even though the meadows only covered 31% of the study area (Raillard & Svoboda 2000). Grazing in these meadows resulted in an average of 48% of the available shoots being grazed. Similarly, muskoxen removed an estimated 15%–20% of NAP from select meadows during the summer on Devon Island (Bliss 1997).

Both *Rangifer* and muskoxen are able to strongly reduce preferred food plants during the summer. In an exclosure experiment in northern Norway, reindeer grazing during one season decreased the cover of 14% of the species present in the plots, all of them known to be preferred food plants (Bråthen & Oksanen 2001). A combination of grazing and trampling may severely depress the biomass of lichens in dry areas in Svalbard (van der Wal *et al.* 2001), Fennoscandia (Souminen & Olofsson 2000, Moen & Danell 2003), and North America (Klein 1987, Manseau *et al.* 1996). Reindeer grazing may also cause the establishment of grazing-tolerant graminoids and thus change plant community composition (Virtanen 1998, Bråthen & Oksanen 2001, Olofsson *et al.* 2001, 2004). Muskox grazing caused a reduction in plant size and in flowering for at least two years after grazing in *Oxytropis viscida* on Banks Island (Mulder & Harmsen 1995). Further, muskox grazing may change the competitive abilities of dominant graminoids, resulting in changes in relative abundances of species; *Carex stans* appeared to gain a competitive ability in grazed vegetation over *Carex membranacea* and *Eriophorum angustifolium* because of larger below-ground biomass, high phenotypic plasticity in rhizome lengths and more persistent rhizome connections than the other two species (Tolvanen & Henry 2000).

Many of the effects on vegetation of large herbivores in Arctic and subarctic areas (as in many other areas) seem to be related to changes in resource availability and the competitive abilities of plants (Mulder 1999). For instance, in cases where heavy reindeer grazing favours graminoid-dominated plant communities over moss- and shrub-rich communities, the produced litter is more easily decomposed which, together with increased soil temperatures in grazed areas, increases the rate of nutrient cycling as compared to ungrazed areas (Olofsson et al. 2001, 2004, Stark et al. 2002). Productivity may thus be increased in tundra sites where grazing pressure is high enough to cause a change in plant community structure. These sites may be where animals tend to aggregate, such as preferred feeding sites or where topography or man-made fences constrain movements.

Winter grazing effects should be much stronger than summer effects. However, less is known about winter grazing effects, but the few available studies do show grazing effects that are much stronger than the summer grazing effects described above. For example, winter grazing of semi-domesticated reindeer in Finland reduced total biomass to only 1%–20% of the biomass in lightly grazed areas (Helle & Aspi 1983). Muskox on Devon Island, Canada, removed 15% of the net annual production on the winter ranges, which is an order of magnitude larger than on the summer ranges (Bliss 1997). More studies on winter grazing effects are needed to enable a better understanding of the relationship between summer and winter ranges for large herbivores in Arctic and subarctic areas.

EFFECTS OF GLOBAL CLIMATE CHANGE ON LARGE HERBIVORE-PLANT INTERACTIONS

Northern areas are particularly vulnerable to projected climate changes, and, because of a variety of feedback mechanisms, are likely to respond more rapidly and severely than any other area on Earth (Anisimov et al. 2001). In general, predicted changes include warmer and wetter climate both in summer and winter. These trends began to be visible during the twentieth century. For instance, significant warming is indicated by reduced snow cover by about 10% since the early 1970s, and most Arctic regions have experienced increases in precipitation since at least the 1950s (Folland et al. 2001). Thawing of permafrost, and thus a thickening of the active layer, have also been reported (Anisimov et al. 2001). Other changes in terrestrial ecosystems during the last century include upward movements of the tree-limit (Kullman 2002), and significant range shifts of both plants and animals towards the poles or towards higher altitudes (Parmesan & Yohe 2003, Root et al. 2003).

Arctic plants will exhibit a wide range of physiological responses to climate change (e.g. Havström et al. 1993, Chapin et al. 1995, Callaghan et al. 1998). Growth may increase because of increased temperatures, and it is likely that graminoids, forbs and deciduous dwarf shrubs will respond more strongly than evergreen shrubs with changes in species composition as a result. Overall, the evidence indicates that responses will be on the level of individual species rather than groups of species or plant communities (Chapin et al. 1995, Callaghan et al. 1998). The Arctic tundra is thus likely to respond with important alterations to major vegetation types. For instance, a widespread increase in shrub abundance, covering more than 320 km², has been reported from Alaska (Sturm et al. 2001).

The increased plant growth will generally be positive for large herbivores as both plant biomass and nutritional quality will increase (Lenart et al. 2002). The longer vegetation period predicted by many models, which is evident in the already reported decrease in snow cover (Folland et al. 2001), will also be positive for large herbivores as they will have a longer period for growth and an increased survival during the short winter. However, it is unclear what effect this will have on population dynamics. If climate change results in increased animal growth and survival, the animal populations may enter winter at high densities that may not be supported by winter resources. The predicted warmer and wetter winter climate may further exacerbate the situation. Several authors suggest that these climate changes may result in lower accessibility of winter forage (Heggberget et al. 2002), followed by declines in calf body weights (Weladji & Holand 2003) and calf survival (Lee et al. 2000).

Other aspects of large herbivore-plant interactions will also change. For instance, increases in summer temperatures may increase insect-related stress on Rangifer with negative effects on body condition, caused by reduced grazing time and increased energy expenditure (Weladji et al. 2003). Changes in plant phenology and plant quality may influence habitat use and migration patterns (Mysterud et al. 2003). This may cause destruction of vegetation in sites where the animals may have to congregate, and exposure of soil that encourages the establishment of (southerly) weedy species under a warmer climate (Vilchek 1997). In general, the overall impact of climate change on large herbivores is controversial. One view is that there will be a decline in Rangifer and muskox, particularly if the climate becomes more variable and the probability of ice-crust formation increases (Gunn 1995, Gunn & Skogland 1997). An alternative view is that because caribou are generalist feeders and appear to be highly resilient they should be able to tolerate the predicted climate change (Callaghan *et al.* 1998). Only time will tell.

CONCLUSIONS

Seasonality will influence large herbivore life histories by forcing the animals to time breeding to the optimal period for offspring survival. Further, Arctic large herbivores are capital breeders that rely on stored resources for reproduction. This places a strong emphasis on the quality of the summer ranges to enable the animals to store fat. Weather fluctuations will cause variations in summer food quality which in turn will lead to the birth of strong or weak cohorts, resulting in large fluctuations in animal numbers due to cohort dynamics. This may be further accentuated through variations in snow cover and winter temperatures, especially in situations with ice-crust formations that decrease food availability. These density-independent weather effects may induce density-dependent effects on population dynamics. Cohort dynamics, together with climate variations, can easily generate large fluctuations in population sizes of large herbivores. This is also the general pattern for muskoxen and *Rangifer* populations. The dependence of winter conditions for survival effectively uncouples population dynamics and food resources which leads to a low utilization of summer food. However, both muskoxen and *Rangifer* have been shown to have strong effects on summer forage in preferred habitats.

ACKNOWLEDGEMENTS

We would like to thank R. Bergström, J. Olofsson and an anonymous reviewer for constructive comments. Jon Moen was supported by the Foundation for Strategic Environmental Research (MISTRA) through the Mountain Mistra Programme while writing the paper. Permission to use data for the figures in this chapter was given by the Royal Society, the Conservation of Arctic Flora and Fauna (CAFF) International Secretariat, Blackwell Publishing, the Nordic Council for Reindeer Husbandry Research and Greenland Institute for Natural Resources.

REFERENCES

Aanes, R., Sæther, B.-E. & Øritsland, N.A. (2000). Fluctuations of an introduced population of Svalbard reindeer: the effects of density dependence and climatic variation. *Ecography*, **23**, 437–43.

Aanes, R., Sæther, B.-E., Smith, F.M. *et al.* (2002). The Arctic Oscillation predicts effects of climate change in two trophic levels in a high-arctic ecosystem. *Ecological Letters*, **5**, 445–53.

Aanes, R., Sæther, B.-E., Solberg, E.J. *et al.* (2003). Synchrony in Svalbard reindeer population dynamics. *Canadian Journal of Zoology*, **81**, 103–10.

Adamczewski, J.Z., Gates, C.C., Hudson, R.J. & Price, M.A. (1987). Seasonal changes in body composition of mature female caribou and calves (*Rangifer tarandus groenlandicus*) on an arctic island with limited winter resources. *Canadian Journal of Zoology*, **65**, 1149–57.

Adamczewski, J.Z., Flood, P.F. & Gunn, A. (1997). Seasonal patterns in body composition and reproduction of female muskoxen (*Ovibos moschatus*). *Journal of Zoology*, **241**, 245–69.

Albon, S.D., Clutton-Brock, T.H. & Langvatn, R. (1992). Cohort variation in reproduction and survival: implications for population demography. New York: In *The Biology of Deer*, ed. R.D. Brown. Springer-Verlag, pp. 15–21.

Andersen, R., Gaillard, J.M., Linnell, J.D.C. & Duncan, P. (2000). Factors affecting maternal care in an income breeder, the European roe deer. *Journal of Animal Ecology*, **69**, 672–82.

Anisimov, O., Fitzharris, B., Hagen, J.O. *et al.* (2001). Polar regions (Arctic and Antarctic). In *Climate Change 2001: Impacts, Adaptation, and Vulnerability. Contribution of Working Group 2 to the Third Assessment Report of the Intergovernmental Panel on Climate Change*, ed. J.J. McCarthy, O.F. Canziani, N.A. Leary, D.J. Dokken & K.S.White. Cambridge: Cambridge University Press, pp. 801–41.

Bernes, C. (1996). *The Nordic Arctic Environment: Unspoilt, Exploited, Polluted?* Copenhagen: Nordic Council of Ministers.

Bliss, L.C. (1997). Arctic ecosystems of North America. In *Ecosystems of the World. 3. Polar and Alpine Tundras*, ed. F.E. Wielgolaski. Amsterdam: Elsevier, pp. 551–681.

Bråthen, K.A. & Oksanen, J. (2001). Reindeer reduce biomass of preferred plant species. *Journal of Vegetation Science*, **12**, 473–80.

Callaghan, T.V., Körner, C., Lee, S.E. & Cornelison, J.H.C. (1998). Part 1: scenarios for ecosystem responses to global change. In *Global Change in Europe's Cold Regions*, ed. O.W. Heal, T.V. Callaghan, J.H.C. Cornelison, C. Körner & S.E. Lee. European Commission Ecosystems Research Report, 27, L-2985, Luxembourg, pp. 11–63.

Caughley, G. & Gunn, A. (1993). Dynamics of large herbivores in deserts: kangaroos and caribou. *Oikos*, **67**, 47–55.

Chapin, F.S., III, Shaver, G.S., Giblin, A.E., Nadelhoffer, K.G. & Laundre, J.A. (1995). Response of arctic tundra to experimental and observed changes in climate. *Ecology*, **66**, 564–76.

Chan-McLeod, A.C.A., White, R.G. & Russell, D.E. (1999). Comparative body composition strategies of breeding and nonbreeding female caribou. *Canadian Journal of Zoology*, **77**, 1901–7.

Chernov, Y.I. & Matveyeva, N.V. (1997). Arctic ecosystems in Russia. In *Ecosystems of the World. 3. Polar and Alpine Tundras*. ed. F.E. Wielgolaski. Amsterdam: Elsevier, pp. 361–507.

Clutton-Brock, T.H. & Coulson, T. (2002). Comparative ungulate dynamics: the devil is in the detail. *Philosophical Transactions of the Royal Society of London Series B*, **357**, 1285–98.

Clutton-Brock, T.H., Illius, A., Wilson, K. et al. (1997). Stability and instability in ungulate populations: an empirical analysis. *American Naturalist*, **149**, 195–219.

Conservation of Arctic Flora and Fauna (CAFF) (2001). *Arctic Flora and Fauna: Status and Conservation*. Helsinki: Edita.

Couturier, S., Brunelle, J., Vandal, D. & St-Martin, G. (1990). Changes in the population dynamics of the George River caribou herd, 1976–1987. *Arctic*, **43**, 9–20.

Fancy, S.G., Whitten, K.R. & Russell, D.E. (1994). Demography of the Porcupine caribou herd, 1983–1992. *Canadian Journal of Zoology*, **72**, 840–6.

Ferguson, S.H. & Messier, F. (1996). Ecological implication of a latitudinal gradient in inter-annual climatic variability: a test using fractal and chaos theories. *Ecography*, **19**, 382–92.

Festa-Bianchet, M.(1998). Condition-dependent reproductive success in bighorn ewes. *Ecology Letters*, **1**, 91–4.

Festa-Bianchet, M., Jorgenson, J.T., King, W.J., Smith, K.G. & Wishart, W.D. (1996). The development of sexual dimorphism: seasonal and lifetime mass changes of bighorn sheep. *Canadian Journal of Zoology*, **74**, 330–42.

Festa-Bianchet, M., Gaillard, J.M. & Jorgenson, J.T. (1998). Mass- and density-dependent reproductive success and reproductive costs in a capital breeder. *American Naturalist*, **152**, 367–79.

Finstad, G.L. & Prichard, A.K. (2000). Growth and body weight of free-range reindeer in western Alaska. *Rangifer*, **20**, 221–7.

Flydal, K. & Reimers, E. (2002). Relationship between calving time and physical condition in three wild reindeer *Rangifer tarandus* populations in southern Norway. *Wildlife Biology*, **8**, 145–51.

Folland, C.K., Karl, T.R., Christy, J.R. et al. (2001). Observed climate variability and change. In *Climate Change 2001: The Scientific Basis. Contribution of Working Group 1 to the Third Assessment Report of the Intergovernmental Panel on Climate Change*. ed. J.Y. Houghton, Y. Ding, D.J. Griggs, M. Noguer, P.J. van der Linden, X. Dai, K. Maskell & C.A. Johnson. Cambridge: Cambridge University Press, pp. 99–181.

Forchhammer, M. & Boertmann, D. (1993). The muskoxen *Ovibos moschatus* in north and northeast Greenland: population trends and the influence of abiotic parameters on population dynamics. *Ecography*, **16**, 299–308.

Gaillard, J.-M., Festa-Blanchet, M. & Yoccoz, N.G. (1998). Population dynamics of large herbivores: variable recruitment with constant adult survival. *Trends in Ecology and Evolution*, **13**, 58–63.

Grenfell, B.T., Wilson, K., Finkenstädt, B.F. et al. (1998). Noise and determinism in synchronized sheep dynamics. *Nature*, **394**, 674–77.

Gunn, A. (1995). Responses of Arctic ungulates to climate change. In *Human Ecology and Climate Change*, ed. D.L. Peterson & D.R. Johnson. Washington: Taylor & Francis, pp. 89–104.

Gunn, A. & Skogland, T. (1997). Responses of caribou and reindeer to global warming. *Ecological Studies*, **124**, 189–200.

Havström, M., Callaghan, T.V. & Jonasson, S. (1993). Differential growth responses of *Cassiope tetragona*, an arctic dwarf-shrub, to environmental perturbations among three contrasting high- and subarctic sites. *Oikos*, **66**, 389–402.

Heard, D.C. & Ouellet, J.-P. (1994). Dynamics of an introduced caribou population. *Arctic*, **47**, 88–95.

Heggberget, T.M., Gaare, E. & Ball, J.P. (2002). Reindeer (*Rangifer tarandus*) and climate change: importance of winter forage. *Rangifer*, **22**, 13–32.

Helle, T. & Aspi, J. (1983). Effects of winter grazing by reindeer on vegetation. *Oikos*, **40**, 337–43.

Hurrell, J.W., Kushnir, Y., Ottersen, G. & Visbeck, M. (2003). An overview of the North Atlantic Oscillation. In *The North Atlantic Oscillation. Climate Significance and Environmental Impact*, ed. J.W. Hurrell, Y. Kushnir, G. Ottersen & M. Visbeck. American Geophysical Union, Washington, pp. 1–35.

Illius, A.W. (1997). Physiological adaptation in savanna ungulates. *Proceedings of the Nutrition Society*, **56**, 1041–8.

Illius, A.W. & O'Connor, T.G. (1999). On the relevance of nonequilibrium concepts to arid and semiarid grazing systems. *Ecological Applications*, **9**, 798–813.

Illius, A.W. & O'Connor, T.G. (2000). Resource heterogeneity and ungulate population dynamics. *Oikos*, **89**, 283–94.

Jönsson, K.I. (1997). Capital and income breeding as alternative tactics of resource use in reproduction. *Oikos*, **78**, 57–66.

Klein, D.R. (1987). Vegetation recovery patterns following overgrazing by reindeer on St. Matthew Island. *Journal of Range Management*, **40**, 336–8.

Kojola, I. & Eloranta, E. (1989). Influences of maternal body weight, age and parity on sex ratio in semidomesticated reindeer (*Rangifer t. tarandus*). *Evolution*, **43**, 1331–6.

Kullman, L. (2002). Recent reversal of Neoglacial climate cooling trend in the Swedish Scandes as evidenced by mountain birch tree-limit rise. *Global Planetary Change*, **36**, 77–8.

Kumpula, J. (2001). Productivity of the Semidomesticated Reindeer (*Rangifer t. tarandus L.*) stock and carrying capacity of pastures in Finland during 1960–1990's. Ph.D. thesis, University of Oulu, Oulu, Finland.

Lande, R., Engen, S. & Sæther, B.-E. (2003). *Stochastic Population Dynamics in Ecology and Conservation*. Oxford; Oxford University Press.

Langvatn, R., Albon, S.D., Burkey, T. & Clutton-Brock, T.H. (1996). Climate, plant phenology and variation in age of first reproduction in a temperate herbivore. *Journal of Animal Ecology*, **65**, 653–70.

Lee, S.E., Press, M.C., Lee, J.A., Ingold, T. & Kurttila, T. (2000). Regional effects of climate change on reindeer: a case study of the Muotkatunturi region in Finnish Lapland. *Polar Research*, **19**, 99–105.

Lenart, E.A., Bowyer, R.T., Ver Hoef, J. & Ruess, R.W. (2002). Climate change and caribou: effects of summer weather on forage. *Canadian Journal of Zoology*, **80**, 664–78.

Lent, P.C. (1988). *Ovibos moschatus. Mammalian Species*, **302**, 1–9.

Linnell, J.D.C., Cuyler, C., Loison, A. *et al.* (2000). *The Scientific Basis for Managing the Sustainable Harvest of Caribou and Muskoxen in Greenland for the 21st Century: an Evaluation and Agenda*. Technical Report no. 34, 2000. Greenland Institute of Natural Resources, Nuuk.

Loudon, A.S.I. & Brinklow, B.R. (1992). Reproduction in deer: adaptations for life in seasonal environments. In *The Biology of Deer*, ed. R.D. Brown. New York; Springer-Verlag, pp. 261–78.

Manseau, M., Huot, J. & Crête, M. (1996). Effects of summer grazing by caribou on composition and productivity of vegetation: community and landscape level. *Journal of Ecology*, **84**, 503–13.

Mårell, A. (2001). Summer Feeding Behaviour of Reindeer and its Relation to the Food Resource. Licentiate thesis, Swedish University of Agricultural Sciences.

Meldgaard, M. (1986). *The Greenland Caribou: Zoogeography, Taxonomy, and Population Dynamics*. Meddelelser om Grønland; Bioscience.

Miller, F. L., Russell, R. H. & Gunn, A. (1975). The recent decline of Peary caribou on western Queen Elizabeth Islands of Arctic Canada. *Polarforschung*, **45**, 17–21.

Moen, J. & Danell, Ö. (2003). Reindeer in the Swedish mountains: an assessment of grazing impacts. *Ambio*, **32**, 397–402.

Mulder, C. P. H. (1999). Vertebrate herbivores and plants in the Arctic and subarctic: effects on individuals, populations, communities and ecosystems. *Perspectives in Plant Ecology, Evolution and Systematics*, **2**, 29–55.

Mulder, C. P. H. & Harmsen, R. (1995). The effect of muskox herbivory on growth and reproduction in an Arctic legume. *Arctic and Alpine Research*, **27**, 44–53.

Mysterud, A., Stenseth, N.C., Yoccoz, N., Ottersen, G. & Langvatn, R. (2003). The response of terrestrial ecosystems to climate variability associated with the North Atlantic Oscillation. In *The North Atlantic Oscillation. Climate Significance and Environmental Impact*, ed. J.W. Hurrell, Y. Kushnir, G. Ottersen & M. Visbeck. Washington; American Geophysical Union, pp. 235–262.

Olofsson, J., Kitti, H., Rautiainen, P., Stark, S. & Oksanen, L. (2001). Effects of summer grazing by reindeer on composition of vegetation, productivity and nitrogen cycling. *Ecography*, **24**, 13–24.

Olofsson, J., Stark, S. & Oksanen, L. (2004). Reindeer influence on ecosystem processes in the tundra. *Oikos*, **105**, 386–6.

Parmesan, C. & Yohe, G. (2003). A globally coherent fingerprint of climate change impacts across natural systems. *Nature*, **421**, 37–42.

Post, E. (2003). Large-scale climate synchronizes the timing of flowering by multiple species. *Ecology*, **84**, 277–81.

Post, E. & Forchhammer, M.C. (2002). Synchronization of animal population dynamics by large-scale climate. *Nature*, **420**, 168–71.

Post, E. & Stenseth, N.C. (1999). Climatic variability, plant phenology, and northern ungulates. *Ecology*, **80**, 1322–39

Putkonen, J. & Roe, G. (2003). Rain-on-snow events impact soil temperatures and affect ungulate survival. *Geophysical Research Letters*, **30**, 37.

Raillard, M. & Svoboda, J. (2000). High grazing impact, selectivity, and local density of muskoxen in Central Ellesmere Island, Canadian High Arctic. *Arctic, Antarctic and Alpine Research*, **32**, 278–85.

Reimers, E., Klein, D.R. & Sørumgård, R. (1983). Calving time, growth rate, and body size of Norwegian reindeer on different ranges. *Arctic and Alpine Research*, **15**, 107–18.

Reynolds, P.E. (1998). Dynamics and range expansion of a reestablished muskox population. *Journal of Wildlife Management*, **62**, 734–44.

Rogers, J.C. (1984). The association between the North Atlantic Oscillation and the Southern Oscillation in the northern hemisphere. *Monthly Weather Review*, **112**, 1999–2005.

Rönnegård, L., Forslund, P. & Danell, Ö. (2002). Lifetime patterns in adult female mass, reproduction, and offspring mass in semidomestic reindeer (*Rangifer tarandus tarandus*). *Canadian Journal of Zoology*, **80**, 2047–55.

Root, T., Price, J.T., Hall, K.R. *et al.* (2003). Fingerprints of global warming on wild animals and plants. *Nature*, **421**, 57–60.

Sæther, B.-E. (1997). Environmental stochasticity and population dynamics of large herbivores: a search for mechanisms. *Trends in Ecology and Evolution*, **12**, 143–9.

Skogland, T. (1985). The effects of density-dependent resource limitations on the demography of wild reindeer. *Journal of Animal Ecology*, **54**, 359–74.

Skogland, T. (1990). Density dependence in a fluctuating wild reindeer herd; maternal vs. offspring effects. *Oecologia*, **84**, 442–50.

Solberg, E., Jordhøy, J.P., Strand, O. *et al.* (2001). Effects of density-dependence and climate on the dynamics of a Svalbard reindeer population. *Ecography*, **24**, 441–51.

Stark, S., Strömmer, R. & Tuomi, J. (2002). Reindeer grazing and soil microbial processes in two suboceanic and two subcontinental tundra heaths. *Oikos*, **97**, 69–78.

Stenseth, N.C., Mysterud, A., Ottersen, G. *et al.* (2002). Ecological effects of climate fluctuations. *Science*, **297**, 1292–96.

Sturm, M., Racine, C. & Tape, K. (2001). Increasing shrub abundance in the Arctic. *Nature*, **411**, 546–7.

Suominen, O. & Olofsson, J. (2000). Impacts of semi-domesticated reindeer on structure of tundra and forest communities in Fennoscandia: a review. *Annales Zoologica Fennica*, **37**, 233–49.

Suttie, J.M. & Webster, J.R. (1995). Extreme seasonal growth in Arctic deer: comparisons and control mechanisms. *American Zoologist*, **35**, 215–21.

Tolvanen, A. & Henry, G.H.R. (2000). Population structure of three dominant sedges under muskox herbivory in the high arctic. *Arctic, Antarctic and Alpine Research*, **32**, 449–55.

van der Wal, R., Brooker, R., Cooper, E. & Langvatn, R. (2001). Differential effects of reindeer on high Arctic lichens. *Journal of Vegetation Science*, **12**, 705–10.

Väre, H., Ohtonen, R. & Mikkola, K. (1996). The effect and extent of heavy grazing by reindeer in oligotrophic pine heaths in northeastern Fennoscandia. *Ecography*, **19**, 245–53.

Vilchek, G.E. (1997). Arctic ecosystem stability and disturbance. In *Disturbance and Recovery in Arctic Lands*, ed. R.M.M. Crawford. NATO-ASI series, no. 2, Environment. Dordrecht: Kluwer, pp. 179–89.

Virtanen, R. (1998). Impact of grazing and neighbour removal on a heath plant community transplanted onto a snowbed site, NW Finnish Lapland. *Oikos*, **81**, 359–67.

Weladji, R.B. & Holand, Ø. (2003). Global climate change and reindeer: effects of winter weather on the autumn weight and growth of calves. *Oecologia*, **136**, 317–23.

Weladji, R.B., Holand, Ø. & Almøy, T. (2003). Use of climatic data to assess the effect of insect harrassment on the autumn weight of reindeer (*Rangifer tarandus*) calves. *Journal of Zoology, London*, **260**, 79–85.

White, R.G., Holleman, D.F. & Tiplady, B.A. (1989). Seasonal body weight, body condition, and lactational trends in muskoxen. *Canadian Journal of Zoology*, **67**, 1125–33.

Wielgolaski, F.E. (1997). Fennoscandian tundra. In *Ecosystems of the World. 3. Polar and Alpine Tundras*, F.E. Wielgolaski. Amsterdam: Elsevier, pp. 27–83.

3

Linking functional responses and foraging behaviour to population dynamics

ANDREW W. ILLIUS

INTRODUCTION

This chapter reviews the connection between large herbivores and their food sources, and asks how the population dynamics of large herbivores are related to their foraging behaviour, diet selection and food intake. Large herbivores are a well-studied group because they include cattle and sheep, which have been the subjects of a huge amount of agricultural research. Accordingly, much is known, or can be deduced, about their response to resources.

It is useful to distinguish the way consumption rate responds to food abundance (i.e. the functional response) from the way the size of the consumer population responds to food consumption (the numerical response). The first two sections in the chapter review the mechanistic approach to describing the functional response, and its implications, and the next section discusses the modelling of the numerical response. The final two sections consider the relationship between large herbivore population dynamics and the selection and consumption of resources.

RECENT MODELS OF FUNCTIONAL RESPONSE

The functional response describes how a consumer's rate of food intake varies with the abundance of food. It is, therefore, a crucial link in consumer-resource dynamics, as well as being fundamental to classical foraging models that predict the diet or patch residence time that would

Large Herbivore Ecology, Ecosystem Dynamics and Conservation, ed. K. Danell, P. Duncan, R. Bergström & J. Pastor. Published by Cambridge University Press. © Cambridge University Press 2006.

maximize intake rate. Hobbs *et al.* (2003) discuss and distinguish mechanistic models of functional response and more empirical approaches. The former are intended to increase understanding of the foraging process. An example of the latter, which Hobbs *et al.* (2003) term the biomass model, seeks to explain variation in intake in terms of available biomass (e.g. Fryxell *et al.* 1988) and is applicable to the study of higher-level phenomena such as population and community processes.

Conventionally, the activities of searching for and handling prey are assumed to be mutually exclusive components of foraging, with the consequence that both prey abundance and the time required to handle prey affect intake rate. Spalinger and Hobbs (1992) recognized that, in mammalian herbivores, handling can overlap to some degree with searching, because herbivores can use the time spent chewing (i.e. handling) previous bites to search for the next bite. If food is scarce, intake rate will be limited by the time taken to search for the next bite. Conversely, if food is abundant, intake rate may be limited by the time taken to chew and swallow ingested forage. So, the abundance and size of food items determines the mathematical form of functional response that applies.

In developing this mechanistic framework, Spalinger and Hobbs (1992) derived equations for the functional response under conditions where intake rate is limited by one of three processes: rate of encounter with cryptic food items encountered at random (Process 1); rate of encounter with apparent items that the animal can move directly between (Process 2); and rate at which food can be chewed and swallowed (Process 3). Adapting their derivation slightly, we can describe the time between successive bites as consisting of the time devoted exclusively to cropping each bite (h, s) and either the time between encounters (Process 1 or 2) or the time required to handle ingested forage (Process 3). Given an animal with maximum foraging velocity V_{max} (m s^{-1}), maximum eating rate R_{max} (mg s^{-1}), with a search path of width W (m), foraging on plants offering bites at density D (m^{-2}), and a size of bite S (mg), then the time between bites T (s) is:

$$\text{Process 1}: \quad T_1 = h + \frac{1}{V_{max}WD}$$

$$\text{Process 2}: \quad T_2 = h + \frac{1}{V_{max}a\sqrt{D}} \tag{3.1}$$

$$\text{Process 3}: \quad T_3 = h + \frac{S}{R_{max}}$$

The rate of biting B (s^{-1}) $= 1/T$ can then be written as:

$$\text{Process 1:} \quad B_1 = \frac{V_{max} WD}{(1 + hV_{max} WD)}$$

$$\text{Process 2:} \quad B_2 = \frac{V_{max} a\sqrt{D}}{(1 + hV_{max} a\sqrt{D})} \tag{3.2}$$

$$\text{Process 3:} \quad B_3 = \frac{R_{max}}{(S + R_{max} h)}$$

Intake rate is simply the product of B and S. The first two equations describe rate of biting as being limited by encounter rate, and distinguish cases where potential bites can only be detected at close range, and are therefore encountered at random, from those where bites can be detected at a distance. Process 1 applies where the average distance between bites is greater than the detection distance, i.e. where $1/a \sqrt{D} > W$, otherwise the forager can move directly from bite to bite (Process 2). The parameter a is a unitless constant related to the spatial arrangement of bites, with $a = 2$ when the pattern is random and $a = 1$ when the pattern is uniform (see Hobbs et al. 2003). Equation (3.3) describes the case where encounters with large S are sufficiently frequent to cause bite rate to be limited by chewing rate. The actual rate of biting will be governed by whichever is the rate-limiting Process, i.e. the lowest for any combination of variables, so:

$$\begin{aligned} & B = min(B_1, B_3) \quad 1/a\sqrt{D} > W \\ or, \quad & B = min(B_2, B_3) \quad 1/a\sqrt{D} \le W \end{aligned} \tag{3.3}$$

The combined response of biting rate is illustrated in Fig. 3.1. It shows how Process 1 or 2 applies when food is scarce and bites are small, and Process 3 applies when food is sufficiently abundant. The cut-off point separating encounter-limited and handling-limited foraging is visible as a discontinuity, or boundary. The boundary conditions can be defined in terms of D and S (Spalinger & Hobbs 1992, Illius et al. 2002). These are illustrated in Fig. 3.2, and can also be seen as the projection of the discontinuity in Fig. 3.1 onto the S–D plane.

We can observe how a herbivore's intake rate changes as food becomes less abundant in each of two distinct ways. First, imagine a browser successively removing discrete food items, such as leaves, from a branch. That will reduce bite density D but leave bite mass S unaffected. In contrast, grazing involves progressive removal of biomass from the surface of a sward, but without completely removing plants. As defoliation proceeds and residual biomass declines, S will be reduced, but D will be unaffected. This contrast between browsing and grazing was first made

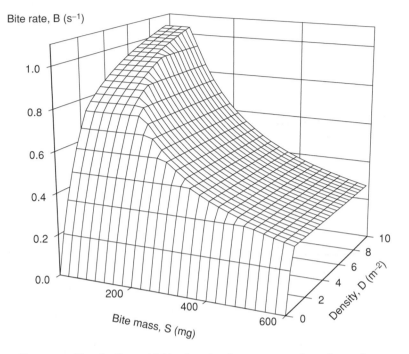

Figure 3.1. The Spalinger-Hobbs functional response surface, drawn from equation (3.3). Bite rate increases with density if bite size is sufficiently small, and decreases with bite size at high density. Reproduced from Illius *et al.* (2002), by permission of Blackwell Publishing.

by Jarman (1974), in the context of inter- and intraspecific competition. Figure 3.3 illustrates the difference between these modes of resource depletion. Note the quite different shapes of these composite functional responses, with browsers' intake rates showing no diminution until depletion is virtually complete. In order to show the full range of constraints on intake, the longer term of daily intake has been estimated, assuming that animals will either forage for 10 hours per day or until their digestive capacity has been reached. Further details of the relationships between short term and daily intake are discussed by Illius and Gordon (1999a,b).

The work of Spalinger and Hobbs (1992) provides a systematic means of analysing the functional response and evaluating biologically meaningful parameters. For example, Gross *et al.* (1993) applied the Process 3 model to analysis of the functional response by mammalian herbivores feeding on artificial patches of lucerne (or alfalfa, *Medicago sativa*). Hobbs *et al.* (2003) have recently shown how the discontinuity between encounter- and

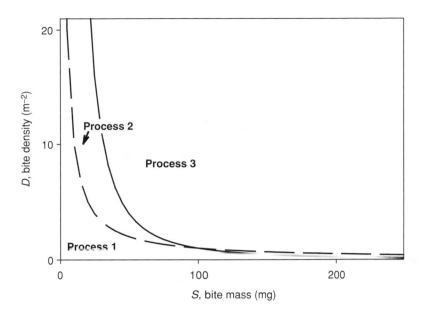

Figure 3.2. Boundary conditions distinguishing three mechanisms of functional response as functions of bite density and bite mass (Spalinger & Hobbs 1992). The dashed line separates Process 1 and 2, and is $D^* = \frac{R_{max}}{SV_{max}W}$; the solid line separates Process 2 and 3, and is $D^* = \left[\frac{R_{max}}{SV_{max}}\right]^2$, with $R_{max} = 100$ mg.s^{-2}, $V_{max} = 1$ m^{-2}, $W = 1$ m. See text for definition of parameters. Reproduced from Illius *et al.* (2002), by permission of Blackwell Publishing.

handling-limited foraging processes applies in heterogeneous environments. They found that the threshold plant spacing between these processes scales allometrically with animal body size as $M^{-0.06}$, which shows that animals of quite divergent body size react remarkably similarly to heterogeneity in plant distribution. Illius *et al.* (2002) examined the functional responses of roe deer using 11 commonly browsed plant species, finding that both h and R_{max} differed widely between plant species. The effect of spinescence on these parameters was also investigated by comparing responses to branches with the thorns removed or left intact. The results suggested that animal size and thorn spacing interact in a way that may allow small-bodied animals to evade or mitigate the negative effects of thorns on intake rate (see also Cooper & Owen-Smith 1986). Thus, *Prunus* has few, widely spaced thorns that the small-mouthed roe deer were apparently able to avoid while foraging, and hence there was no significant effect of the presence of thorns on either parameter of the

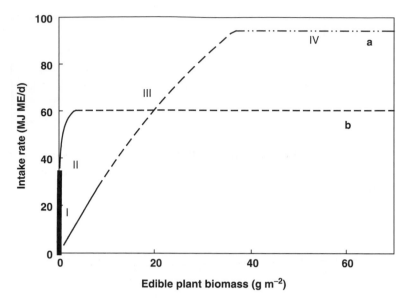

Figure 3.3. Functional responses (daily energy intake rate) during two contrasting modes of depletion. (a) Sward depletion reduces bite mass S, but bite density D remains constant (100 m^{-2}). (b) Removal of successive items reduces bite density, but S remains constant (200 mg). Roman numerals indicate the applicable Spalinger-Hobbs Process: I (thick line), II (thin solid), III (dashed). IV (dash-dot) indicates daily intake being limited by digestive constraints on daily intake, predicted to apply in case **a**. Calculated for an animal of mass 500 kg foraging for 10 h on food with digestibility 0.6.

functional response. In contrast, the effect of thorns in *Crataegus* was to increase the time taken to prehend bites (h), implying that evasion of the thorns had a time cost. Thorns in this species are more densely packed than in *Prunus*, and very sharp. Lastly, in *Rubus*, there are many thorns on the midrib of the leaves and the deer were obliged to eat considerable amounts of them. The thorns appear to be painful to chew, which may have slowed the chewing process, resulting in lower R_{max}.

Because the parameters are associated with mechanisms, such as movement velocity and chewing rate, they can readily be evaluated as allometric functions of body mass. Shipley *et al.* (1994) showed that R_{max} scaled as the 0.71 power of body mass (i.e. close to the 0.75 scaling of energy requirements with mass), and a number of other scaling rules and assumptions can be applied to evaluate the other parameters of the functional responses (Illius & FitzGibbon 1994, Illius & Gordon 1999b). In this way, bite rate and intake rate can be estimated for given S and D in mammalian herbivores of a given body mass. An example of this is shown in Fig. 3.2, where the boundaries between Processes for a small-bodied animal like a roe deer are drawn. We can deduce from this that there are good a priori grounds for thinking that exploitation of patches (e.g. branches with leaves) by small browsing herbivores is governed by either Process 2 or 3: food items are apparent rather than cryptic and may be encountered at a sufficiently high rate and mass for oral processing rate to be the most likely constraint on intake rate. This was tested by Illius *et al.* (2002), who applied an optimization procedure to discriminate between encounter- and handling-limited processes in roe deer, and confirmed that the functional response applicable to patch browsing is governed by the rate of oral processing and not by the rate of encounter.

These new models of functional response can also be used to predict diet choice in foraging herbivores. For example, Shipley *et al.* (1999) made predictions of the optimal twig diameters that browsing roe deer, red deer and moose should select. Larger bite mass can be obtained by biting off longer sections of twigs than just the tips, and that means biting at a larger diameter. Increased bite mass means increased short-term dry matter intake rate. But thicker twigs are more woody and less digestible (i.e. energy intake rate does not increase linearly with dry matter intake rate), and digestive constraints will limit daily intake to a lower dry mass than could be eaten from smaller and more digestible twigs. Accordingly, the model to examine this trade-off assumed that short-term intake rate is governed by oral processing rate (Process 3), and that daily intake rate is constrained by digestive capacity (Process 4). It predicted that larger-bodied animals should browse twigs at a greater diameter than small bodied animals, because of the interplay of these constraints and the way they scale allometrically between species. An experimental test (Shipley *et al.* 1999) provided strong supporting evidence: observed bite diameters were extremely close to those predicted and were larger in the larger-bodied species.

IMPLICATIONS OF NEW MODELS OF FUNCTIONAL RESPONSES FOR FORAGING AND DIET OPTIMIZATION

Conflicts between the way animals spend their time (e.g. between handling the item at hand or searching for a better one, and between foraging and vigilance) lie at the heart of many classical foraging problems. Accordingly, the potential overlap of handling with searching has a number of implications for foraging behaviour and diet optimization in large herbivores.

1. *Diet choice.* The conventional model of optimal prey choice (e.g. Stephens & Krebs 1986) illustrates the principle of lost opportunity. The forager can maximize its intake rate whilst foraging by adding food types to the diet in order of their profitability. As more food types are accepted on encounter, less time is spent between encounters and more time is spent handling. The diet should broaden until the profitability of the next-ranked food type is lower than the average intake rate of the diet. Then, spending time handling inferior food types would cost the opportunity of encountering better food types. Note that the intake rate of this diet is both encounter- and handling-limited, because these are mutually exclusive activities for the conventional forager. In herbivores, relaxation of this constraint means that different prey models apply according to whether the intake rate of the diet is encounter-limited or handling-limited (Farnsworth & Illius 1998, Fortin 2001). Herbivores may save time by searching while chewing, and so their rate-maximizing diets are broader if food is scarce, because less opportunity is lost in accepting the last item in the diet than a conventional forager would lose by accepting that item. This might go some way towards explaining a classical observation of herbivore diets: that they contain a mixture of items (Westoby 1978). A further feature of herbivores is that their intake rates are higher than conventional foragers faced with the same array of food items (see Fig. 3.4a). As more and more food types are added to the herbivore's diet, encounters become sufficiently frequent for the diet to become handling-limited, in which case no lower-ranked prey should be taken. Indeed, the optimal diet may sometimes include just enough of a food item to make the diet handling-limited (and no more), and so only that much of it should be eaten (Fig. 3.4b). In other words, it should not always be consumed on encounter, and the 'zero-one' rule of the classical model does not apply in this particular case.

2. *Patch exploitation.* Foragers removing prey successively from a patch cause a decline in encounter rate, and this reduces intake rate (termed patch depression). This is the conventional explanation of diminishing returns to patch residence, and assumes mutually exclusive searching and handling, uniform prey size, and non-systematic

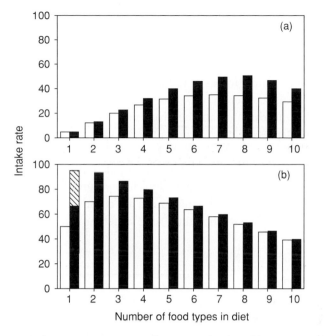

Figure 3.4. Changes in average intake rate as diet breadth is increased in the conventional prey model (open bars) and in models applicable to mammalian herbivores (closed bars). In both cases, food types are included in the diet in rank order of profitability. (a) When food is scarce, the conventional forager maximizes its long-term average intake rate by including the top seven types in its diet, and the herbivore the top eight. (b) When food is more abundant, intake rates increase in both foragers, and diets narrow. The conventional forager should now include the top three food types. The herbivore maximizes its long-term intake rate by taking the highest ranked type, and by taking only enough of the second-ranked type (shown contributing to its intake rate by the hatched bar) to make the diet handling-limited.

searching. Ungulates which browse on woody plants can be thought of as exploiting patches of food items (usually bunches of leaves or twigs) which are concentrated in space. Because foraging is likely to be handling-limited, rather than encounter-limited (see Fig. 3.2), the explanation of patch depression by lengthening encounter intervals would not apply until the patch were severely depleted. In general, provided that the parameters and independent variables in the relevant functional response remain constant, the gain curve will be linear. Browsers may also systematically search branches for prey items, which would also have the effect of avoiding patch depression. Systematic search is described by Process 2, where animals move directly between apparent food items, rather than encountering them at random and with decreasing frequency as depletion proceeds. The overlap of handling and searching that underlies the Process 3 functional response offers an alternative mechanism whereby the same effect can be achieved: no time is wasted in searching and herbivores should therefore experience less patch depression than a conventional forager, given equivalent patch characteristics. Figure 3.5 shows that a herbivore would not experience patch depression until a patch of uniformly sized prey had become almost totally depleted. A greater degree of patch depression would be experienced by a conventional forager with mutually exclusive handling and searching. In either case, there

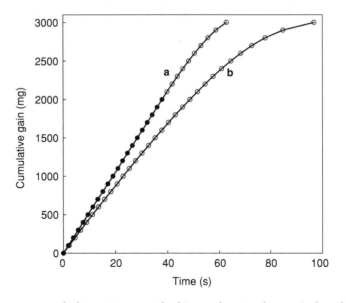

Figure 3.5. Patch depression. (a) A herbivore whose intake rate is described by the Spalinger-Hobbs equations (see text for details). The example shows the progressive depletion of a patch of 30 items each of 100 mg distributed over 10 m². (b) A conventional predator that searches randomly, that cannot simultaneously handle and search for prey, and whose functional response is represented by a Holling-type function: $I = \frac{aD}{1+aDT_h}$, where I is intake rate, $a = 1$ is search efficiency and $T_h = \left(h + \frac{S}{R_{\max}} \right)$ is handling time. Open symbols denote the part of the gain curve where intake rate is limited by encounter rate. Parameter values as in Fig. 3.2.

would be no patch depression if searching was systematic and encounter rate thus remained constant.

Support for the proposed near-linearity of the gain curve was provided by the roe deer data analysed by Illius *et al.* (2002), who showed that gain curves were virtually linear for each plant species studied, with the exception of *Prunus*. Roe deer were selective during patch exploitation, selecting the larger items to eat first. Only in *Prunus* was the decline in bite mass during patch exploitation sufficient to produce patch depression. In grazing ungulates, bite mass decreases as animals bite deeper into grass swards and to a sufficient extent to cause patch depression (Laca *et al.* 1994, Ginnett *et al.* 1999).

What are the implications of linear gain functions for our understanding of herbivore foraging? Rather obvious features of patch use by browsers in the studies of Åström *et al.* (1990), and Shipley and Spalinger (1995) are the wider range of patch exploitation times and lower patch depletion observed than would be predicted from nearly linear gain functions. The fact that patch-use by browsers is hard to predict with any accuracy is in contrast to the success in predicting diet optimization at the bite scale (e.g. Vivås & Sæther 1987, Vivås *et al.* 1991, Shipley *et al.* 1999). Shipley *et al.* (1999) successfully predicted browse selection from consider-ations of diet quality, and it has been noted that browsers respond to both food quality and availability by eating a higher quality diet and taking less from each plant at high food densities (Vivås & Sæther 1987, Andersen & Sæther 1992, Shipley & Spalinger 1995). This suggests that diet optimization under digestive constraints may be the fundamental process in browser foraging, as it appears to be in other mammalian herbivores (Belovsky 1978, Lundberg & Åström 1990, Fryxell 1991, Doucet & Fryxell 1993, Wilmshurst *et al.* 1999). As Fortin *et al.* (2002) make clear, the important question is one of time scale. Foraging behaviour that would maximize energy intake rate over the short-term cycle of patch residence and inter-patch travel (typically minutes) would not necessarily maximize energy intake rate over the longer time scale at which digestive constraints operate (typically hours to days). The model of Shipley *et al.* (1999) can be used to show that the patch residence time that maximizes daily energy intake under digestive constraints is generally shorter than the residence time that maximizes energy intake rate under ingestive constraints, especially in small-bodied animals and when diet quality declines with increasing intensity of patch utilization.

Therefore, short-term optimization based on MVT (Marginal Value Theorem) may well be subordinated to long-term optimization of diet quality, regardless of the fact that successive removal of food items in order of diet quality is a patch depletion process. In summary, there are a priori and empirical grounds for the propositions that optimal patch use is not an appropriate model of resource use by browsing mammalian herbivores, and that longer-term diet optimization, i.e. the trade-off between diet quality and daily intake rate, is a more likely explanation of their foraging behaviour.

3. *Costs of vigilance*. When scanning for predators is incompatible with foraging, then reduced intake rate will be a cost of vigilance. Illius and FitzGibbon (1994) showed that ungulates can be vigilant without incurring this cost, if plant density and biomass is high enough to allow Process 3 foraging to occur. Then, anti-predator vigilance can take place at no cost to rate of intake during the time spent chewing after detection of the next bite. Recent empirical evidence provides some support for this (Fortin *et al.* 2004).

DESCRIBING THE NUMERICAL RESPONSE

Approaches to describing how the consumer population changes in response to its average per capita food intake can vary from the simplistic or abstract to the complicated and fully detailed. Simplified representations of ecological interactions, such as Lotka-Voltera coupled differential equations, are tractable and allow the effects of each parameter to be examined analytically. They are also appropriate in the absence of sufficient knowledge of underlying mechanisms to build more detailed and, hence, more realistic models. A compromise approach developed by Owen-Smith (2002a,b) describes consumer-resource systems in terms of biomass dynamics, rather than numbers of consumers, and uses aggregated efficiencies of assimilation, metabolism, repair and senescence to model aggregated population dynamics.

Considerable progress has been made in the last few decades towards a mechanistic understanding of the relations between vertebrate herbivores and their food supply (see Illius & Gordon 1999b for review and details). Mechanistic approaches, addressing the physiological processes which relate food intake to its consequences for population dynamics, are now set to augment the classical theoretical descriptions of predator-prey dynamics. Instead of treating population dynamics explicitly, as for example in setting a parameter governing density dependence, mechanistic modelling attempts to build an accurate description of the underlying processes. For example, the savanna dynamics model of Illius et al. (1998, 1999b) takes daily rainfall data and calculates daily growth of trees and grass, and the allocation of growth to plant parts, the selection and intake of these by animals, the animals' consequent energy and protein balances, body growth, reproduction and mortality. It therefore simulates animal population dynamics mechanistically, by coupling nutritional influences on vital rates (reproduction and mortality) to vegetation biomass dynamics, allowing the underlying mechanisms to dictate the performance of the system over the chosen time scale. The model quite accurately predicts the observed relationship between rainfall and herbivore abundance. Illius and Gordon (1999b) also give an example of mechanistic modelling of a temperate grazing system, and show that mechanistic modelling can be used to explain the physiological basis of over-compensatory population dynamics.

The ability of a model to give good predictions of component processes is clearly a prerequisite of scaling up from the functional to numerical response in mechanistic terms. It is an important principle that modelling of the component processes is kept separate from study of how these components affect the behaviour of the system as a whole. It is legitimate and desirable to model those components as accurately as possible, in their own right. Provided that only the performance of individual components, and not the whole system's response, are modified by the modeller to accord with expectation, the investigation of the system's behaviour is a true test of the underlying assumptions. Such an approach can then be used to investigate hypotheses about the way that physiological properties and activities of animals and plants determine system dynamics.

One of the prices of the mechanistic approach is the greater complexity of the description, and it is only viable if the greater amount of detail is all sufficiently robust to realize the goal of an accurate description of the system. Arguably, the substantial literature on the physiology of domestic and wild ruminants allows a robust mathematical description, and the many parameters can be defined with sufficient confidence. This has allowed fairly detailed descriptions of how foraging behaviour and energy balance can be used to predict population dynamics in large herbivores (e.g. Moen et al. 1998, Weisberg et al. 2002), both for theoretical and management purposes.

DIET SELECTION, RESOURCE HETEROGENEITY AND LARGE HERBIVORE POPULATION DYNAMICS

Resource heterogeneity and the way animals select their diets, especially at times of scarcity, can have important consequences for their population dynamics. Large herbivores usually are subject to considerable seasonal, climatic and spatial variation in resources, especially in arid and semi-arid tropical environments, where such variation is extreme. Alternating wet and dry seasons impose a cycle of plant growth and phenology that results in a cycle of food abundance and quality. Resource limitation occurs during the dry season, when low food quality causes animals to lose weight; their survival then depends on the adequacy of body fat reserves carried over from the growing season (Sinclair 1975, Fryxell 1987). Annual rainfall in semi-arid environments typically has a coefficient of variation greater than 25%, with the result that droughts are common causes of herbivore mortality (Ellis & Swift 1988, Owen-Smith 1990). In general, large herbivore populations are regulated mainly through density-dependent mortality outside the breeding season, with environmental stochasticity often combining with density-dependence through a common effect on resource supply (Caughley & Gunn 1993, Sæther 1997). An important qualification to this generality is that heterogeneity in vital rates across the sexes and age-classes means that they respond differentially to environmental conditions, with younger animals typically being sensitive to temporal variations in resource supply in a way that adults are not (Clutton-Brock et al. 1997, Gaillard et al. 1998). Nevertheless, variation in the quantity and quality of the food supply has a fundamental effect on herbivore population dynamics.

Spatial variation in semi-arid grazing systems arises from variation in soil characteristics and topography, causing variation in nutrient content and hydrology. Therefore, low-lying areas that receive run-off from up-slope have longer growing seasons and may have plant communities, including woody browse, that differ from those on the more arid land further up the catena. Access to drinking water is an additional spatial variable. As the dry season progresses, surface water sources become depleted and dry up, forcing herbivores to range over areas that are accessible from permanent sources of drinking water, and to abandon outlying areas that are beyond herbivores' foraging radius, regardless of the abundance of food there. This spatial separation of the area over which herbivores can range during the dry season and the outlying areas accessible only during the wet season is reinforced by the distinctions between the botanical and phenological characteristics of the forage in the two areas.

The potentially important role played by spatial and temporal hetero-geneity in the dynamics of semi-arid grazing systems was recognized by Scoones (1995), who studied seasonal diet shifts in livestock under com-munal grazing management in southern Zimbabwe. He argued that livestock were dependent on 'key resource' areas during the dry season. Generalizing this, Illius and O'Connor (2000) defined 'key resource' in relation to the key factor (*sensu* Varley & Gradwell 1960): given that the key factor determining animal population size is survival over the season of plant dormancy, key resources are those eaten then. In other words, we can posit that key resources limit population size via the key factor. Reduction in these resources would cause the population to decline. In most large herbivore populations, survival over the season of plant dormancy (winter, or dry season) is the key factor, and so key resources are those resources used then. In roe deer, on the other hand, fawn survival during the summer appears to be the critical phase (Gaillard *et al.* 1993, 1998), and so resources used during lactation would be expected to be the key resources.

We can observe the importance of resource heterogeneity even in highly variable arid and semi-arid environments. In these, it has been argued that plant production is largely determined by rainfall and is unaffected by animal population density, because intermittent die-offs during extended droughts keeps densities below equilibrium (Ellis & Swift 1988). In contrast to the earlier view that plants and animals exist in some sort of equilibrium, and are regulated by density-dependent processes, it is now argued that populations subject to sufficient environmental variability are governed by fundamentally different, 'non-equilibrial' processes in which plant and animal dynamics are largely independent of one another (Behnke & Scoones 1993, Scoones 1994). Yet Ellis and Swift (1988), referring to earlier work of Hobbs and Swift (1985), identify the small subset of resources that are of high quality, and that herbivore populations are, hypothetically, limited by. Hobbs and Swift (1985) presented a method of determining the quantity of resources that, selected from a range varying in nutrient concentration, would supply a diet of a specified quality. The selection of scarce, high quality resources balance, and hence make possible the consumption of, lower quality and more abundant resources. Their results 'demonstrate clearly the density-dependent nature of animal forage interactions' and 'even when the total amount of available forage is not limiting, increases in animal density may compel deterioration of the nutritional status of individuals'.

The implication of some subset of resources having a key role in herbivore population dynamics is, of course, that the remaining resources have a lesser or unimportant role. Thus, we can now begin to distinguish resources in terms of whether consumer population dynamics are coupled to them or not. Illius and O'Connor (1999) analysed the 'non-equilibrium' view of animal population dynamics and concluded that, despite the apparent lack of equilibrium, animal numbers are regulated in a density-dependent manner by the limited forage available in key resource areas, especially during droughts. They argued that, spatially and temporally, the whole system is heterogeneous in the strength of the forces tending to equilibrium, these diminishing with the distance from watering and key resource areas. This model asserts that strong equilibrial forces exist over a limited part of the system, with the animal population being virtually uncoupled from resources elsewhere in the system, except in drought years. Non-equilibrium conditions merely pertain in patches of the wet-season range to which the consumer population is not coupled – as doubtless occurs in virtually all consumer-resource systems considered at a scale sufficient to encompass spatial and temporal heterogeneity.

These ideas were tested by Illius and O'Connor (2000), who described a simple rainfall-plant-animal model that allowed long-term mean animal abundance to be predicted from two distinct resource types, and under chosen conditions of annual variability in primary production. Intake was modelled using a simple empirical model of functional response, with upper limits imposed by digestive and metabolic constraints. The resource types were, for convenience, specified as areas of rangeland available to the animal population during the wet and dry seasons, and the exclusivity of use of the two types in each season could be set by the user. The animal component was described by two state variables, animal numbers and mean body fat reserves, for each of four age classes: juveniles, yearlings, two-year-olds and adults. Note that some of the sources of demographic variation in vital rates are incorporated in the model. Detail was restricted to the level that would capture the main features of the system, namely, starvation-induced mortality, carry-over of body reserves between seasons and resource types, and state- (i.e. fat-) dependent reproduction.

When there is some degree of separation in seasonal use of resources (i.e. wet-season range, WSR, and dry-season range, DSR), Illius and O'Connor (2000) found that long-term mean animal abundance was largely determined by the quantity of resources available during the dry season, when the key factor of mortality operates, and scarcely at all by resources available in the wet season (see Fig. 3.6). Increasing degrees of variability in primary production on areas used by animals for surviving the dry season increased the annual variation in livestock numbers and reduced the mean (Fig. 3.7). Nevertheless, the animal population is in long-term equilibrium with dry-season resources, because as the abundance of key resources is increased, so animal numbers increase. The fact that the size of the available wet-season range had very little effect on year-round carrying capacity is perhaps surprising, given that the model allowed fat reserves built up during the growing season to be carried over to the dry season. The explanation is that fat reserves cannot be deposited without limit, and so provided that summer resources are sufficient to allow animals to establish maximum fatness, additional resources are useless from the viewpoint of winter survival.

Environmental variability disturbs the equilibrium that could be reached between consumers and resources under stable conditions. This

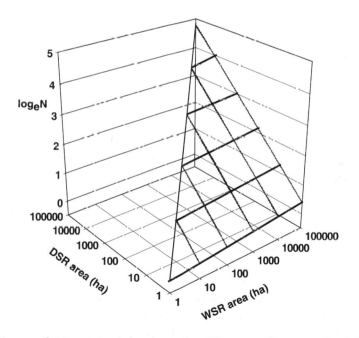

Figure 3.6. Mean animal abundance ($\log_e(N)$), mean of 100-year simulations) in response to increasing availability of dry-season range (DSR) and of wet-season range (WSR). Animal numbers are rather insensitive to WSR area, but respond sharply to availability of dry-season resources.

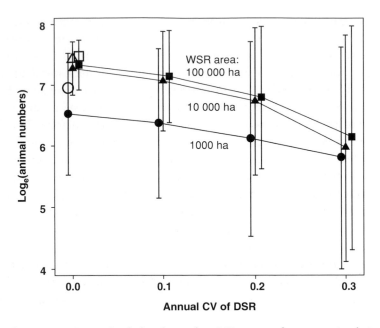

Figure 3.7. Mean animal abundance ($\log_e(N)$), mean of 100-year simulations) in response to increasing variability of primary production in the dry season range (DSR) and with wet season range (WSR) area of 1000 ha (●), 10000 ha (▲), or 100000 ha (■). DSR range area was 1000 ha, and WSR inter-annual cv of primary production was 0.3 throughout. The error bars show the inter-annual SD of $\log_e(N)$. Open symbols show $\log_e(N)$ predicted by the model when it was run without climatic variation.

condition of disequilibrium arising from climatic variation is different from non-equilibrium, which is the absence of coupling between the animal population's dynamics and the subset of resources not associated with key factors. Wet season rangeland can therefore be classed as a non-equilibrium resource, because the animal population's dynamics are not coupled to it. Superabundance of non-key resources is likely to be observed during the growing season, because the animal population is typically limited by scarcer, high quality resources during the dormant season. Note also that the key and non-equilibrium resources need not be widely separated in space. Given a distribution of food quality, as described by Hobbs and Swift (1985), a consumer population will tend towards equilibrium with the quantity of resources above the minimum quality threshold, and will not be in equilibrium with the remaining (= non-equilibrium) resources below the threshold. Diet selection from heterogeneous resources will naturally cause the animal population's dynamics to depend differentially on different resources. But this is not primarily the consequence of climatic variability, and nor can we characterize entire grazing systems in highly variable climates as 'non-equilibrial', as was asserted by Ellis and Swift (1988).

A corollary of this analysis is that the extent to which the non-equilibrium part of consumer-resource systems is prone to impact will depend on the relative abundance of the two resource types. Because animal numbers are regulated by key resources and are not coupled to nonequilibrium resources, high ratios of key-to-nonequilibrium resources could support animal populations which are sufficient to result in quite high defoliation intensities of the non-equilibrium resources. An extreme case of this effect would occur if animals were maintained on supplementary food over the dry season. Then, their numbers would tend to become completely uncoupled from wet season or summer resources, and defoliation intensity there would be purely a function of the numbers maintained. In principle, the same would apply to summer range in the case of migration away from there during the winter.

We may also correct, in passing, the conclusion of Hairston *et al.* (1960) that herbivores are seldom food-limited but are instead predator-limited, because green plants are normally abundant whilst herbivores are normally scarce. If herbivores are limited by scarce key resources, the remaining vegetation may very well be abundant. So the abundance of resources cannot be read as a sign that herbivores are not resource-limited, and accordingly must be predator-limited.

STABILIZING AND DESTABILIZING INFLUENCES ON LARGE HERBIVORE POPULATION DYNAMICS

Large herbivores' functional response shows, especially for browsers, little diminution in intake rate until depletion is almost complete (see Fig. 3.3). Owen-Smith (2002a) reached the same conclusion from a functional response derived on a similar though less mechanistic basis than that of Spalinger and Hobbs (1992), including digestive constraints as an upper limit on daily food intake. The steeply saturating form of the functional response should have, from a classical perspective, a destabilizing effect on consumer-resource dynamics in constantly productive and uniform environments (Caughley 1976, Crawley 1983). In effect, the animal population can grow rapidly without diminishing intake until resources virtually disappear, and then over-compensatory mortality causes a population crash. However, rather few cases of population instability in herbivores have been documented (see Clutton-Brock *et al.* 1997), which raises the question of what intrinsic or extrinsic factors counter-act the apparent tendency to instability inherent in the functional response.

One possibility is that linear functional response is only observed over short time scales and homogeneous vegetation conditions, and that the necessity to move about and select diets over a longer time scale and in complex environments produces an aggregate functional response that is less steeply saturating. This possibility is supported by the results of Owen-Smith (2002a,b), who addressed the question using a metaphysiological modelling approach, which is similar to that used by Illius and O'Connor (2000), but simpler and less mechanistic. Owen-Smith (2002a,b) was able to show that, in seasonally varying environments, stabilization can result when resources are heterogeneous in quality and herbivores are able to select diets adaptively over the course of the year. Three main resource types can be identified, in order of quality: prime, reserve and buffer. The animal population uses these in order of profitability, depletion of the better types, mainly during the growing season, leading to use of the poorer types, especially in the dormant season. When prime resources are of high enough quality to allow rapid population growth, the population may overshoot and crash due to starvation in the dormant season. The effect is more pronounced if reserve and buffer vegetation is also of fairly high quality: body condition remains high over the dormant season, leading to maximum reproductive output in the following season, and eventual over-compensation. When reserve and buffer vegetation are of poorer quality, animals do not starve but lose more condition over the dormant season, limiting future reproductive investment and population growth, and reducing the tendency of the population to overshoot its equilibrium. But with even poorer reserve and buffer vegetation, the population begins to starve as soon as it is large enough to exhaust the prime vegetation, causing a crash. The population rebuilds from a low level using only the prime resources until it reaches the point when the cycle is repeated. The effect is illustrated in Fig. 3.8, using the model of Illius and O'Connor (2002). Population variability of *c.* 30% indicates gross cyclicity in these simulations, and occurs when both prime and reserve resources are of high quality, or when both reserve and buffer vegetation are of low quality. Note that these simulations were carried out assuming that dead vegetation had a digestibility 0.9 of live vegetation, with senescence of live vegetation and decomposition of dead vegetation being modelled as described by Illius and O'Connor (2000). In other words,

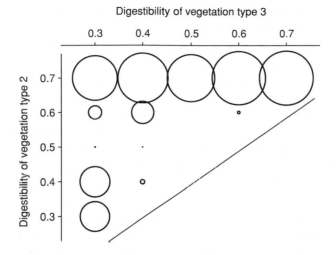

Figure 3.8. Effect on modelled animal population variability when three vegetation types are available, using the model of Illius & O'Connor (2000) without climatic variation. Variability was assessed as the inter-annual coefficient of variation $(SD(\log_e N))/\log_e N$ over the last 100 years of 125-year simulations) and is shown by the diameter of circles, with the top right circle indicating a cv of 30%. The digestibility of vegetation type 1 was 0.7 throughout. Combinations of vegetation types 2 and 3 without symbols showed no appreciable variation. Digestibility of live vegetation is plotted; dead vegetation was assumed to be 0.9 of live digestibility.

forage quality within a vegetation type would decline during the season over only a narrow range. If, instead, we assume that dead vegetation has only half the digestibility of live, which is perhaps more realistic, the modelled dynamics are stable for all combinations of prime, reserve and buffer quality. Conversely, introducing a prime vegetation digestibility of 0.8 increases instability. This emphasizes that the effect is driven by the presence of sufficiently high quality vegetation to allow animals to survive and carry adequate body reserves through the dormant season and hence to reproduce at a maximum rate regardless of density.

In investigating the reasons for erratic population dynamics in a feral population of Soay sheep, Clutton-Brock *et al.* (1997) related over-compensation to intrinsic physiological attributes of the sheep. They concluded that over-compensatory mortality could arise because the period of reproductive investment (late pregnancy and lactation) of Soay sheep is sufficiently brief, in accordance with their small body size, to allow them to regain body condition before the next breeding season, resulting in high subsequent fecundity regardless of density (Clutton-Brock *et al.* 1997, Illius & Gordon 1999b, Fig. 3.5). Is Owen-Smith's (2002a,b) demonstration of the role of resource heterogeneity an alternative explanation? The resources available to the Soay sheep on Hirta are quite varied in quality, ranging from *Holcus* and *Agrostis-Fescue* to low-productivity *Molinia* and *Calluna* heath. We can identify *Calluna* as a low-quality buffer, while the vegetation types predominately used during the growing season are all fairly high quality. Digestibility of vegetation in the summer is in the 0.6–0.7 range, and in winter in the 0.3–0.6 range, even excluding *Calluna*, which forms up to 30% of faecal fragments in winter (Milner & Gwynne 1974). It would seem that these are conditions that might promote stability, based on Owen-Smith's (2002b) work and the example above. However, the population is not stable, and the rather detailed model of Soay sheep dynamics of Illius and Gordon (1999b) is not sensitive to alterations in the range of vegetation quality in a way that stabilizes the dynamics of the population (A. W. Illius, unpublished data 1998).

The common ground between these approaches to population instability is the seasonal cycle of energy balance, with its implications for mortality and fecundity. The steeply saturating functional response of large herbivores is an inherent source of population instability, as are physiological factors that allow animals to regain body reserves after reproduction during the growing season at higher population densities than winter forage conditions can support. Extrinsic factors such as resource heterogeneity, duration of the dormant season and the rate of decline in vegetation quality evidently have the potential to alter the seasonal cycle of energy intake in such a way that starvation-induced mortality may be attenuated, thereby having a stabilizing effect.

CONCLUSIONS

The Spalinger-Hobbs functional response provides a sound mechanistic basis for analysing herbivore-resource relations, at least at the fine scale and over short time-periods. It has provided fertile ground for the investigation of a number of classical problems in foraging behaviour, such as prey choice, patch use and the cost of vigilance. Allied to careful experimentation, it is now providing insights into the next challenge: the way herbivores integrate small-scale responses in heterogeneous environments and at scales above the feeding station (Hobbs *et al.* 2003). Much has been learnt about how species differences in body size affect these foraging processes, but little is yet known about individual differences within species, nor about how differences across the sexes and age-classes translate into demographic variation in vital rates.

Linking the behaviour of individuals with the consequences for populations remains an important challenge in ecological research. Progress with large herbivores has perhaps exceeded that in other animals, simply because they are a well-studied group. Modelling that is to some degree mechanistic has been an important feature of this progress. It must now address a major challenge: the interaction of spatial and temporal heterogeneity in resources with herbivore foraging responses and population dynamics. Spatially explicit representations of foraging behaviour are an active topic of research, but most have not moved much beyond the approach of cellular automata, and have unknown predictive ability. Investigations of herbivore populations' responses to resource heterogeneity will be important for testing the proposition that a limited subset of the vegetation is relevant, in trophic terms. Future studies should aim to identify and quantify key resources, and test the significance of their role in supporting herbivore populations and modifying plant community composition.

ACKNOWLEDGEMENTS

To Tom Hobbs, John Pastor, Patrick Duncan and Jean-Michel Gaillard, for helpful comments on the manuscript.

REFERENCES

Andersen, R. & Sæther, B.E. (1992). Functional-response during winter of a herbivore, the moose, in relation to age and size. *Ecology*, **73**, 542–50.

Åström, M., Lundberg, P. & Danell, K. (1990). Partial prey consumption by browsers: trees as patches. *Journal of Animal Ecology*, **57**, 287–300.

Behnke, R.H. & Scoones, I. (1993). Rethinking range ecology: implications for rangeland management in Africa. In *Range Ecology at Disequilibrium*, ed. R.H., Behnke, I. Scoones & C. Kerven. London: Overseas Development Institute, pp. 1–30.

Belovsky, G.E. (1978). Diet optimization in a generalist herbivore: the moose. *Theoretical Population Biology*, **14**, 105–34.

Caughley, G. (1976). Plant-herbivore systems. In *Theoretical Ecology: Principles and Applications*, ed. R.M. May. Oxford: Blackwell Scientific Publications, pp. 94–113.

Caughley, G. & Gunn, A. (1993). Dynamics of large herbivores in deserts: kangaroos and caribou. *Oikos*, **67**, 47–55.

Cooper, S. & Owen-Smith, N. (1986). Effects of plant spinescence on large mammalian herbivores. *Oecologia*, **68**, 446–55.

Clutton-Brock, T.H., Illius, A.W., Wilson, K. *et al.* (1997). Stability and instability in ungulate populations: an empirical analysis. *American Naturalist,* **149,** 195–219.

Crawley, M.J. (1983). *Herbivory: The Dynamics of Animal-Plant Interactions.* Oxford: Blackwell Scientific Publications.

Doucet, C.M. & Fryxell, J.M. (1993). The effect of nutritional quality on forage preference by beavers. *Oikos,* **67,** 201–8.

Ellis, J.E. & Swift, D.M. (1988). Stability of African pastoral ecosystems: alternate paradigms and implications for development. *Journal of Range Management,* **41,** 450–9.

Farnsworth, K. & Illius, A.W. (1998). Optimal diet choice for large herbivores: an extended contingency model. *Functional Ecology,* **12,** 74–81.

Fortin, D. (2001). An adjustment of the extended contingency model of Farnsworth and Illius (1998). *Functional Ecology,* **15,** 138–9.

Fortin, D., Fryxell, J.M. & Pilote, R. (2002). The temporal scale of foraging decisions in bison. *Ecology,* **83,** 970–82.

Fortin, D., Boyce, M.S., Merrill, E.H. & Fryxell, J.M. (2004). Foraging costs of vigilance in large mammalian herbivores. *Oikos,* **107,** 172–80.

Fryxell, J.M. (1987). Food limitation and demography of a migratory antelope, the white-eared kob. *Oecologia,* **72,** 83–91.

Fryxell, J.M. (1991). Forage quality and aggregation by large herbivores. *American Naturalist,* **138,** 478–98.

Fryxell, J.M., Greever, J. & Sinclair, A.R.E. (1988). Why are migratory ungulates so abundant? *American Naturalist,* **131,** 781–98.

Gaillard, J.M., Delorme, D., Boutin, J.M. *et al.* (1993). Roe deer survival patterns: a comparative analysis of contrasting populations. *Journal of Animal Ecology,* **62,** 778–91.

Gaillard, J.M., Liberg, O., Andersen, R., Hewison, A.J.M. & Cederlund, G. (1998). Population dynamics of roe deer. In *The European Roe Deer: the Biology of Success,* ed. R. Andersen, P. Duncan & J.D.C. Linnell. Oslo: Scandinavian University Press, pp. 309–35.

Gaillard, J.M., Festa-Bianchet, M. & Yoccoz, N.G. (1998). Population dynamics of large herbivores: variable recruitment with constant adult survival. *Trends in Ecology & Evolution,* **13,** 58–63.

Ginnet, T.F., Dankosky, J.A., Deo, G. & Demment, M.W. (1999). Patch depression in grazers: the roles of biomass distribution and residual stems. *Functional Ecology,* **13,** 37–44.

Gross, J.E., Shipley, L.A., Hobbs, N.T., Spalinger, D.E. & Wunder, B.A. (1993). Funtional response of herbivores in food concentrated patches: test of a mechanistic model. *Ecology,* **74,** 778–91.

Hairston, N.G., Smith, F.E. & Slobodkin, L.B. (1960). Community structure, population control, and competition. *American Naturalist,* **44,** 421–5.

Hobbs, N.T. & Swift, D. (1985). Estimates of habitat carrying capacity incorporating explicit nutritional constraints. *Journal of Wildlife Management,* **49,** 814–22.

Hobbs, N.T., Gross, J.E., Shipley, L.A., Spalinger, D.E. & Wunder, B.A. (2003). Herbivore functional response in heterogeneous environments: a contest among models. *Ecology,* **84,** 666–81.

Illius A.W. & FitzGibbon, C. (1994). Costs of vigilance in foraging ungulates. *Animal Behaviour*, **47**, 481–4.

Illius, A.W. & Gordon, I.J. (1999a). Physiological ecology of mammalian herbivory. In *Vth International Symposium on the Nutrition of Herbivores*, ed. H.-J.G. Jung & G.C. Fahey, Jr. Savoy, IL: American Society of Animal Science, pp. 71–96.

Illius, A.W. & Gordon, I.J. (1999b). Scaling up from functional response to numerical response in vertebrate herbivores. In *Herbivores: Between Plants and Predators*, ed. H. Olff, V.K. Brown & R.H. Drent. Oxford: Blackwell Science, pp. 397–427.

Illius, A.W. & O'Connor, T.G. (1999). On the relevance of nonequilibrium concepts to semi-arid grazing systems. *Ecological Applications*, **9**, 798–813.

Illius, A.W. & O'Connor, T.G. (2000). Resource heterogeneity and ungulate population dynamics. *Oikos*, **89**, 283–94.

Illius, A.W., Derry, J.F. & Gordon, I.J. (1998). Evaluation of strategies for tracking climatic variation in semi-arid grazing systems. *Special Issue on Drought, Agricultural Systems*, **57**, 381–98.

Illius, A.W., Duncan, P., Richard, C. & Mesochina, P. (2002). Mechanisms of functional response and resource exploitation in browsing roe deer. *Journal of Animal Ecology*, **71**, 723–34.

Jarman P.J. (1974). The social organization of antelope in relation to their ecology. *Behaviour*, **48**, 215–66.

Laca, E., Distel, R.A., Griggs, T.C. & Demment, M.W. (1994). Effects of canopy structure on patch depression by grazers. *Ecology*, **75**, 706–16.

Lundberg, P. & Åström, M. (1990). Low nutritive quality as a defense against optimally foraging herbivores. *American Naturalist*, **135**, 547–62.

Milner, C. & Gwynne, D. (1974). The Soay sheep and their food supply. In *Island Survivors*, ed. P.A. Jewell, C. Milner & J. Morton Boyd. London: Athlone Press, pp. 160–94.

Moen, R., Cohen, Y. & Pastor, J. (1998). Linking moose population and plant growth models with a moose energetics model. *Ecosystems*, **1**, 52–63.

Owen-Smith, N. (1990). Demography of a large herbivore, the greater kudu, *Tragelaphus strepsiceros*, in relation to rainfall. *Journal of Animal Ecology*, **59**, 893–913.

Owen-Smith, N. (2002a). A metaphysiological modelling approach to stability in herbivore-vegetation systems. *Ecological Modelling*, **149**, 153–78.

Owen-Smith, N. (2002b). *Adaptive Herbivore Ecology*. Cambridge: Cambridge University Press.

Sæther, B.-E. (1997). Environmental stochasticity and population dynamics of large herbivores: a search for mechanisms. *Trends in Ecology and Evolution*, **12**, 143–9.

Scoones, I. (1994). New directions in pastoral development in Africa. In *Living with Uncertainty*, ed. I. Scoones. London: Intermediate Technology Publications, pp. 1–36.

Scoones, I. (1995). Exploiting heterogeneity: habitat use by cattle in dryland Zimbabwe. *Journal of Arid Environments*, **29**, 221–37.

Sinclair, A.R.E. (1975). The resource limitation of trophic levels in tropical grassland ecosystems. *Journal of Animal Ecology*, **44**, 497–520.

Spalinger, D.E. & Hobbs, N.T. (1992). Mechanisms of foraging in mammalian herbivores: new models of functional response. *American Naturalist*, **140**, 325–48.

Shipley, L.A. & Spalinger, D.E. (1995). Influence of size and density of browse patches on intake rates and foraging decisions of young moose and white-tailed deer. *Oecologia*, **104**, 112–21.

Shipley, L.A., Gross, J.E., Spalinger, D.E., Hobbs, N.T. & Wunder, B.A. (1994). Scaling of functional response in mammalian herbivores. *American Naturalist*, **143**, 1055–82.

Shipley, L.A., Illius, A.W., Danell, K., Hobbs, N.T. & Spalinger, D.E. (1999). Predicting bite size selection of mammalian herbivores: a test of a general model of diet optimization. *Oikos*, **84**, 55–68.

Stephens D.W. & Krebs J.R. (1986). *Foraging theory*. Princeton, New Jersey: Princeton University Press.

Varley, G.C. & Gradwell, G.R. (1960). Key factors in population studies. *Journal of Animal Ecology*, **29**, 399–401.

Vivås, H.J. & Sæther, B.E. (1987). Interactions between a generalist herbivore, the moose *Alces alces*, and its food resources: an experimental study of winter foraging behaviour in relation to browse availability. *Journal of Animal Ecology*, **56**, 509–20.

Vivås, H.J., Sæther, B.E. & Andersen, R. (1991). Optimal twig-size selection of a generalist herbivore, the moose *Alces alces*: implications for plant-herbivore interactions. *Journal of Animal Ecology*, **60**, 395–408.

Weisberg, P.J., Hobbs, N.T., Ellis, J.E. & Coughenour, M.B. (2002). An ecosystem approach to population management of ungulates. *Journal of Environmental Management*, **65**, 181–97.

Westoby, M. (1978). What are the biological bases of varied diets? *American Naturalist*, **112**, 627–31.

Wilmshurst, J.E., Fryxell, J.M. & Colucci, P.E. (1999). What constrains daily intake in Thomson's gazelles? *Ecology*, **80**, 2338–47.

4

Impacts of large herbivores on plant community structure and dynamics

ALISON J. HESTER, MARGARETA BERGMAN,
GLENN R. IASON AND JON MOEN

INTRODUCTION

How do large herbivores affect plant community structure and dynamics? Here we review the main direct impacts of herbivores on plant communities. We briefly review effects on individual plants (or ramets) and the range of responses of individual plants to herbivory, as a basis from which to explore the complexities of processes operating at the plant community level. Large herbivores make foraging decisions at a range of spatial (from bite to landscape) and temporal (from seconds to years) scales, and plants also respond to herbivore impacts at a similar ranges of scales (plant part to community) (Bailey *et al.* 1996, Hodgson & Illius 1996, Crawley 1997). This provides a challenge for the identification of key processes affecting plant-herbivore interactions and the mechanisms driving plant community responses to herbivore damage under different conditions. Scale issues (both temporal and spatial) are paramount to the study of herbivore impacts on plant community dynamics (Crawley 1997, Olff & Ritchie 1998), and scale is implicitly or explicitly brought into many of the sections in this review. Scale issues can also underlie apparent controversies in the literature about herbivore influences on vegetation, and an awareness of their implications is fundamental.

The impacts of large herbivores on vegetation have been particularly widely studied in relation to range management and pasture plants, primarily grasses (Rosenthal & Kotanen 1994, Hodgson & Illius 1996,

Large Herbivore Ecology, Ecosystem Dynamics and Conservation, ed. K. Danell, P. Duncan, R. Bergström & J. Pastor. Published by Cambridge University Press. © Cambridge University Press 2006.

Crawley 1997, Olff & Ritchie 1998). In this chapter, we focus on shrub and woodland systems where possible to complement earlier reviews.

HOW DO LARGE HERBIVORES DIRECTLY AFFECT INDIVIDUAL PLANTS?

Grazing and trampling are probably the most important direct impacts of herbivores and they affect all key stages of plant development, through germination, establishment, growth and seed production. Grazing is always accompanied by trampling at the scale of the herbivore or larger, although at smaller scales individual plants could be only grazed, only trampled or both. However, trampling can (and frequently does) occur in the absence of grazing, particularly in areas used primarily for resting or for travelling (Milne *et al.* 1998, Hester & Baillie 1998, Oom & Hester 1999, Oom 2002). Grazing impacts form the main focus of this review, primarily because they have been most studied. But direct, non-grazing impacts are also referred to where important and where relevant information exists. Indirect impacts are covered in Chapter 9.

Grazing removes plant tissue (which involves loss of photosynthetic material, nutrients and carbon), and/or meristems, and/or flowers and seeds. Grazing by large herbivores rarely causes plant death directly, except for very small/young, poorly established plants (Crawley 1983), although there are exceptions, particularly in relation to woody species or extremely large herbivores whose activities can often uproot whole plants, such as elephants (Laws *et al.* 1975, Grant *et al.* 1978, Pamo & Chamba 2001, Tafangenyasha 2001, see also Chapter 9).

Trampling by large herbivores involves plant tissue damage or breakage, often resulting in the death of that shoot or that part of the shoot above the point of damage (Crawley 1997). Unlike grazing, which is usually of leaves or upper portions of shoots, trampling can affect any part of a plant (if shorter than the herbivore), but is normally more frequent close to its base (especially for large, upright plants). Hence the greater likelihood of consequential plant death, particularly for chamaephytes, with their perennating buds above the ground surface. Trampling can also have indirect effects on plants and plant communities, such as soil compaction (see Chapter 9).

Bark stripping and fraying also impact directly on plants, especially woody species; severe damage of this sort often kills the plant (Gill 1992a, Reimoser *et al.* 1999, see also Chapter 6). Discharges from animals, i.e. saliva, urination and defecation, are also important. During feeding, animals deposit saliva onto the plant, which has variously been shown to result in growth promotion (McNaughton 1979a), amplified branching responses (Bergman 2002, Rooke 2003), reduced growth (Capinera & Roltsch 1980, Detling *et al.* 1981) or no effects (Reardon *et al.* 1974). Urine and faecal deposition directly onto plants can cause physical damage or local toxic effects (Harper 1977, Haynes & Williams 1993), but the main effects are probably indirect through nutrient recycling and/or dispersal of seed (Welch 1986, Pakeman *et al.* 1998, Mitlacher *et al.* 2002, see also Chapter 9). Other direct effects include digging and scraping activities, which can damage or uproot plants, although the main effects of such processes are indirect, through soil disturbance and provision of new germination niches (see Chapter 9).

Herbivore activities can have very different effects at each stage of plant development; positive effects at one stage can be detrimental or even fatal at another, as outlined below.

Seedling establishment

Many species of plant require gaps for germination (Miles 1973, Grubb 1976, Thompson *et al.* 1977, Miles & Kinnaird 1979) and these can be created by large herbivore trampling, although this is mostly anecdotal and has been rarely measured (Miles & Kinnaird 1979, Hester *et al.* 2000b). New seedlings (<1 year) are extremely vulnerable to a wide range of abiotic and biotic factors; under most conditions only a small proportion survive these early stages (Miles & Kinnaird 1979, Pigott 1985, Crawley 1997). Although abiotic factors are probably the major causes of mortality at this stage, and small herbivore impacts the next most important, trampling by large herbivores can also kill small seedlings (Milchunas *et al.* 1992). Overall, the balance of large herbivore impacts on seed germination and establishment at the population level appears to be mainly positive, with greater seedling establishment overall in grazed than ungrazed areas (Miles & Kinnaird 1979, Bullock *et al.* 1994a,b, Hester *et al.* 1996, Crawley 1997).

Plant growth

Type of tissue damage

Growth of established plants can be dramatically affected by large herbivore activities, depending on the type of tissue which is damaged or removed and the location of that tissue on the plant (Richards 1993). For example, losses of meristematic tissue have been shown to have proportionally greater effects than losses of non-meristematic tissue (Richards 1993). Removal of, or damage to, apical meristems results in loss of apical dominance, with increased branching and/or leaf production and increased production of lateral or basal buds (Danell & Huss-Danell 1985, Bergström & Danell 1987, Raven et al. 1992, Richards 1993, Reinhardt & Kuhlemeier 2002, Hester et al. 2004). Removal of leaves results in loss of photosynthetic material and, particularly in the case of evergreen species in winter, may also cause the loss of significant amounts of nitrogen (N) or carbohydrate reserves, which may also significantly inhibit new growth (Crawley 1983, Rosenthal & Kotanen 1994, Honkanen et al. 1999, Millard et al. 2001). Regrowth after pruning or browsing reduces the overall physiological age of the plant (Kozlowski 1971), with increased proportions of new shoots often containing higher tissue N and different chemical composition as compared to older shoots (Bryant et al. 1991b, Richards 1993). Such effects have important implications both for the plant and the likelihood of subsequent herbivory.

Severity and timing of tissue damage

In general terms, the more severe the tissue damage or removal, the more severe the impact, but the limits of plant tolerance depend on a variety of factors including the availability of nutrients. Plants may show a range of linear responses to increased severity of damage (Strauss & Agrawal 1999), or various types of curvilinear response (Fig. 4.1); thus the same level of herbivore damage could have a range of different effects (varying between physiological stage as well as species). In general, management to keep damage below 'acceptable' levels (e.g. Palmer 1997, Oom 2002) will be more critical for species exhibiting curvilinear responses.

In relation to timing, in general terms, the earlier in the growing season the damage is sustained, the less severe the effect on the plant, as it has a longer time to recover before the end of the growing season (Fig. 4.2, Gill 1992a,b, Honkanen et al. 1999, Bullock et al. 2001, Millard et al. 2001, Hester et al. 2004). Furthermore, the impacts of damage during dormancy depend more on sites of winter storage of nutrients, which differ between different species (Millard et al. 2001). Thus the interaction between severity and timing is important in determining plant responses, but this has only been studied a little in relation to herbivore management. As well as the importance of understanding changes in herbivore diet selection through the year, the timing of domestic herbivore grazing/browsing can also be manipulated through management to avoid or reduce pressure on specific plant communities at certain times of year. There is a strong need for the development and testing of hypotheses such as those shown in Fig. 4.2.

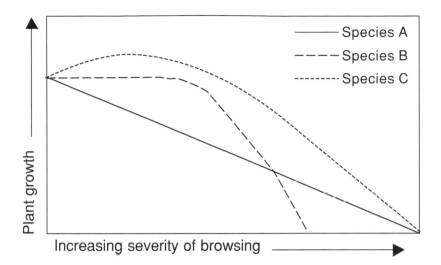

Figure 4.1. Examples of hypothetical relationships between woody plant growth (fitness) and herbivore browsing severity. Plant growth (or fitness) and severity of browsing are represented on arbitrary scales. Species A shows a linear response to browsing. Species B shows a clear threshold below which the effects of browsing on plant growth dramatically increase. Species C shows initial over-compensation where plant growth as a result of light browsing is enhanced (see section, Implications for plant community structure and diversity) after which additional browsing leads to ever increasing detrimental effects on plant growth.

Finer-scale temporal responses have also been measured: for example, experiments removing buds from birch (*Betula pendula*) just before or after budburst showed how responses could vary even between days at that key time of year (Senn & Haukioja 1994). Both age and location of leaves removed has been shown to affect plant response, for example, removal of older or shaded leaves will have less effect on photosynthesis than removal of younger leaves or leaves in full light (Richards 1993, Lindroth *et al.* 2002).

Defoliation interval

The effects of defoliation interval have also been shown to be important in determining plant response; most work has been on grasses (Crawley 1983, 1997, Chapman & Lemaire 1993, Richards 1993, Hodgson & Illius 1996, Lemaire & Chapman 1996). For example, continuous grazing of grass swards tends to reduce overall photosynthetic capacity as well as N,

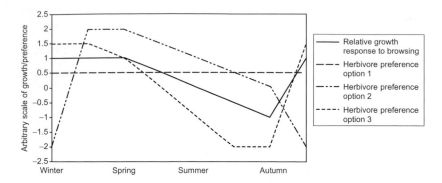

Figure 4.2. Hypothesized relationships between responses of a tree sapling to browsing and herbivore selection through the year. The diagram shows: (a) the hypothesized growth response of a tree sapling to a given level of browsing at different times of the year (solid line), with compensatory growth following damage during dormancy or spring, but increasingly detrimental effects as the growing season proceeds (based on evidence from Miller, Kinnaird & Cummins 1982, Gill 1992b, Senn & Haukioja 1994, Hester *et al.* 1996, Honkanen *et al.* 1999; Hester *et al.* 2005; Hester *et al.* 2004) and (b) three possible seasonal patterns of herbivore browsing selection for that species (broken lines). Option 1: no change in selection through the year. Thus plant response patterns are neither enhanced nor offset. Option 2: sapling is avoided in the winter, highly preferred in the spring, then preference declines through the growing season in line with plant growth response, thus offsetting changes in plant response. Option 3: highest preference through the winter, offsetting the reduced effect of browsing at that time of year. Preferences during the growing season reduce faster than the rate of reduction in growth, resulting in a net positive effect on sapling growth.

as the youngest leaves have the highest capacity and these are the parts grazed most frequently (Lemaire & Chapman 1996). Conversely, the negative effects of self-shading and senescence on growth are reduced. So called cyclic grazing, or 'feeding loops', where herbivores return to previously browsed or grazed plants or patches has been shown for a variety of vertebrates: wildebeest (McNaughton 1979b), geese (Drent & van der Wal 1999) and moose (Danell *et al.* 1985, Löyttyniemi 1985, Bergqvist *et al.* 2003). This may represent herbivore manipulation of their food plants, making them more attractive for subsequent herbivory (see Chapters 3, 6 and 10).

Flowering and seed production
Removal of flowering stems prevents flowering and seed production, thus favouring species that reproduce vegetatively over those that do not, and

favouring perennials over annuals. Removal of other parts of the plant can also lead to reduced flowering or size/number of seeds as a result of reduced resources available (Crawley 1997). According to Bullock (1996), the effects of grazing on the net reproductive rate of populations are therefore generally negative, although this will presumably only be a problem for species that are seed-limited. For example, grazing of flowering stems of *Calluna vulgaris* by sheep in a Scottish site reduced seed production to virtually zero, but this species has persistent, long-lived seeds and so many years of heavy grazing had little measurable effect on soil seed stores, unlike species such as *Deschampsia flexuosa* with short-lived seeds and little soil storage (Hester et al. 1991a). In summary, although most direct effects (grazing/browsing) are negative, indirect effects of seed dispersal (on the body or in the gut) are largely positive (see Chapter 8). If seeds are eaten, although some seeds do not survive herbivore digestive processes, others require, or at least benefit from, passage through the gut for germination (Welch 1985, Pakeman et al. 1998, Pakeman et al. 2002).

Below-ground processes

Removal of above-ground plant parts inevitably affects below-ground processes as well, but below-ground responses to large herbivore activities have been much less studied (Holland & Detling 1990, Huntly 1991, Richards 1993). Plants reallocate assimilates to new growth regions in response to defoliation; in some situations reallocation takes place between above-ground parts, but preferential allocation to shoot growth for restoration of root : shoot ratios after damage has been widely recorded (Crawley 1983, Richards 1993, Crawley 1997, Ruess et al. 1998). Most grassland-related studies, and a few from other systems, have measured significant below-ground plant responses to the effects of herbivory, particularly when severe, for example, reduced root biomass, N fixation, root respiration and/or nutrient absorbtion (e.g. Crawley 1983, Richards 1993, Vare et al. 1996, Ruess et al. 1998, Hester et al. 2004). In contrast, a study of Serengeti grasslands by McNaughton et al. (1998) found no effects, even of intense grazing, on root biomass or productivity. However, some studies have shown that above-ground herbivory can induce changes in mycorrhizal fungi, thereby affecting nutrient uptake and subsequent growth and survival in the affected plants, with most studies suggesting a decline in mycorrhizal colonization as a result of herbivory (see review by Gehring & Whitham 1994). Rossow et al. (1997) showed that winter browsing by moose (*Alces alces*) and snowshoe hare (*Lepus timidus*) decreased the percentage ectomycorrhizal infection in willow (*Salix* spp.) and balsam poplar (*Populus balsamifera*) fine root tips, thereby potentially reducing their competitive ability with the mycorrhizal tree species alder (*Alnus tenuifolia*), rarely browsed by snowshoe hare and moose. The conclusion of their study was that a reduction in competitive ability in the two salicaceous species may contribute to the shift in community composition in taiga forests where, as a result of mammal browsing, palatable deciduous species are replaced by less palatable ones.

HOW DO PLANTS AVOID OR RESPOND TO LARGE HERBIVORE IMPACTS?

Plants may avoid, resist and/or tolerate large herbivore impacts – but definitions and uses of these terms are not always consistent (e.g. Fritz & Simms 1992, Rosenthal & Kotanen 1994, Crawley 1997, Strauss & Agrawal 1999). We primarily follow Rosenthal and Kotanen (1994) in our ordering of this section and Fig. 4.3. Rosenthal and Kotanen (1994) use the term resistance to encompass both avoidance (escape and defence, both physical and chemical) and tolerance strategies. Resistance to herbivory in most forms is costly to the plant and most current theories of inducible plant defences consider cost: benefit trade-offs with allocation to plant growth and/or reproduction (Rosenthal & Kotanen 1994, Strauss & Agrawal 1999, Strauss *et al.* 2002, Ward & Young 2002).

Physical avoidance

Plants may physically avoid large herbivores through location, visibility (apparency), or by producing defence structures such as thorns, hairs or thick cuticles. Avoidance through location includes: (a) growing in places inaccessible to large herbivores; or (b) growing in proximity to neighbouring plants whose presence may reduce the likelihood of herbivore browsing. Tall growing plants may also minimize susceptibility to large mammal herbivory by growing out of reach as rapidly as possible. Avoidance of herbivory through low apparency, or 'susceptibility to discovery' (Feeny 1976), is determined not only by a plant's own characteristics, but by environmental influences. These include its microenvironment, which affect phenotype and visibility, and by the characteristics of the whole plant community, such as species of neighbouring plants or density of the plant's own species (e.g. Spalinger & Hobbs 1992, Diaz *et al.* 2001). Avoidance of mammalian herbivory through production of structures such as thorns is particularly prevalent in semi-arid shrubland systems and

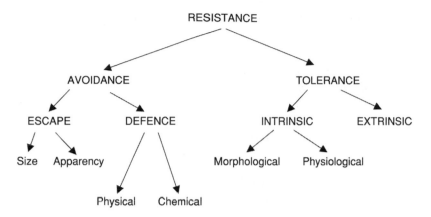

Figure 4.3. Plant resistance to herbivores – conceptual strategies (derived from Rosenthal & Kotanen 1994, Strauss & Agrawal 1999; Kotanen & Rosenthal 2000), as described in the text.

many studies have shown strong evidence that such defences are inducible or facultative (Milewski *et al.* 1991, Myers & Bazeley 1991, Young & Okello 1998, Karban *et al.* 1999, Ward & Young 2002). The two-way interactions between herbivory and plant physiological stage are crucially important in such interactions (Moorby & Waring 1963, Kozlowski 1971, Fox & Bryant 1984, Danell & Huss-Danell 1985, Bryant 2003).

Chemical avoidance
Avoidance of herbivory by constitutive chemical defence
There is little doubt that plant secondary metabolites (PSMs) are active against vertebrate and insect herbivores and constitute a form of defence against them (Rosenthal & Janzen 1979, Palo & Robbins 1991). Constitutive defences are hypothesized to be an evolutionary response to intensive herbivory which reduces the likelihood of attack. This can be due to a direct behavioural inhibition, such as altered taste and smell. But to be retained in evolutionary time, defences would also have to reduce the quality of the plant material to a herbivore, for example, by being toxic, having lower digestibility or reducing the rate of foraging (Foley *et al.* 1999).

Since the identification of the allelochemical role of PSMs (Fraenkl 1959), several key hypotheses have been proposed to explain their ecological and evolutionary occurrence (Table 4.1). The utility and merits of these hypotheses, particularly the applicability of the carbon-nutrient balance hypothesis (Bryant *et al.* 1983, 1991c) have recently come under scrutiny (Hamilton *et al.* 2001, Koricheva 2002, Lerdau & Coley 2002,

Table 4.1. *Overview of hypotheses on the role of plant secondary metabolites (PSMs) as defences against herbivores*

Hypothesis	Main characteristics	References
Optimal defence hypothesis	Evolutionary; trade-offs with other traits	Feeney 1976, Rhoades & Cates 1976, Rhoades 1979
Carbon-nutrient hypothesis	Phenotypic; allocations of resources to PSMs in relation to resource availability	Bryant *et al.* 1983
Growth-rate hypothesis	Evolutionary; defence allocations as functions of growth rates and resource availability	Coley, Bryant & Chapin 1985
Growth-differentiation balance hypothesis	Evolutionary, phenotypic; PSM production in relation to the balance between new tissue growth and differentiation	Herms & Mattson 1992

Nitao *et al.* 2002, Stamp 2003). The hypotheses have different strengths, are not mutually exclusive and none has been comprehensively falsified (Koricheva 2002, Stamp 2003). All four hypotheses have, as their basis, the concept that allocation to defence has costs. This is central to ecological and evolutionary thinking, but is very difficult to rigorously quantify, owing to the range of forms that such costs might take. Costs to the plants of maintaining a defence in the absence of herbivores can be described as allocation costs, as resource-based trade-offs or as ecological costs, where lowered fitness of a plant results from interactions with other species (Strauss *et al.* 2002). Costs should ultimately be expressed in terms of plant fitness, but are usually expressed in the form of some component or subset of it (Cipollini *et al.* 2003). Consequently, the absence of costs cannot be definitively demonstrated. Similarly, the costs of production of a particular PSM can theoretically be at the expense of allocating substrate or other resources necessary for synthesis or storage, to other processes. Without quantification of the full suite of primary and secondary metabolites of the plant, such costs cannot be quantified.

Much work on the evolution of chemical defences derives from studies of insects, which can be highly specific in their interactions with plants, mediated by phytochemicals (Feeney 1991). It is generally assumed that vertebrates are more generalist foragers than invertebrates (Crawley 1983). In the few studies of vertebrates that have been performed, some specific compounds have been shown to be particularly active repellents (Pass *et al.* 1998), or particularly active toxins (Foley *et al.* 1999).

During the development of plant defence hypotheses, it has been stated that PSMs are the primary determinant of palatability of plants to herbivores (Bryant *et al.* 1991c, Stamp 2003). Whilst this may be true in certain cases (see below), several lines of evidence question this assertion of omnipotence of PSMs as determinants of diet choices and diet quality. Production by mammals of salivary tannin binding proteins, which reduce the inhibition of protein digestion by condensed tannins, (Austin *et al.* 1989, Mole *et al.* 1990, Juntheikki 1996) are among a large number of counter-adaptations to PSMs which reduce the costs of ingestion (Foley *et al.* 1999). The negative effects of plant toxins on herbivores may be ameliorated by ingestion of food with higher nutrient content (Bidlack *et al.* 1986), which clearly leads to the expectation that food selection by vertebrates is likely to be due to a combination of PSMs, fibre and nutrient content (Hjältén & Palo 1992, McArthur *et al.* 1993, Foley *et al.* 1999).

Responding to herbivory by induced chemical defence

Induced chemical defences represent phenotypic plasticity, which is thought to be adaptive to reduce the detrimental effects to plants by only incurring the costs of defence when it is required, rather than continuously, as is the case with constitutive defences (Cipollini *et al.* 2003). Induced chemical responses can be either within the damaged tissue or can affect adjacent tissue (Edwards *et al.* 1991). It can be short-term, occurring in hours or days (Raupp & Sadof 1991, Schittko & Baldwin 2003), or can occur over longer time scales (Bryant *et al.* 1991a, Zangerl 2003). The vast majority of work on induced chemical defences of woody plants has been conducted on responses to insect herbivores. However, the mechanisms of browsing by mammals often involve removal of whole leaves which, if applied rapidly, in some plant species, causes no chemical induction (Cipollini & Sipe 2001). Defoliation by a mammalian browser may also occur rapidly at any given point in a tree. By contrast, defoliation by insects, for example, of birch (*Betula* spp.) by the autumnal moth (*Epirrita autumnata*), or heather (*Calluna vulgaris*) by the heather beetle (*Lochmaea suturalis*) (Bokdam 2001), can occur gradually on individual leaves or shoots unless the insect population is moderate or high, in which case defoliation may be locally similar or even greater in extent to damage inflicted by browsing mammals. Tissue damage by any cause can also open a plant to invasion by pathogens; induced defences are not only effective against the initiating herbivore, but can be anti-pathogenic

(Karban & Baldwin 1997) and can also attract enemies of insect herbivores (Dicke *et al.* 2003).

Tolerance

Plant 'tolerance' is the term most widely used to describe a composite of a plant's responses to herbivore damage at any or all stages of development (Rosenthal & Kotanen 1994, Briske 1996, Strauss & Agrawal 1999, Kotanen & Rosenthal 2000). Our working definition of tolerance is 'the capacity of a plant to maintain its fitness through growth and reproduction after sustaining herbivore damage' (Rosenthal & Kotanen 1994). The evolutionary and ecological significance of plant tolerance can be examined by two main groups of mechanisms: intrinsic and extrinsic factors, i.e. those determined genetically or developmentally, and those determined by external factors such as environmental resources available for growth (Rosenthal & Kotanen 1994). In general, tolerance to vertebrate herbivores should require broad responses promoting growth and resource acquisition, to cope with impacts which are often sporadic and non-specific. Tolerance is predicted to vary between plant life forms, plant species and individuals of the same species (van der Meijden *et al.* 1988, Rosenthal & Kotanen 1994, Haukioja & Koricheva 2000), as well as plant age or developmental stage. In general, younger plants are less tolerant than older plants, although they may be more defended (Bryant *et al.* 1985, Chapin *et al.* 1985, Huntly 1991).

Intrinsic morphological features promoting plant tolerance of herbivory by large herbivores include protected and/or numerous meristems, wide distribution of leaves and buds, branching or tillering responses, stolons or rhizomes, and seed numbers, viability, longevity and size. The presence of active meristems after damage is clearly a crucial trait conferring tolerance (Richards 1993). Dicotyledons and grasses in particular have been shown to respond to herbivory in different ways due the positions of their meristems (e.g. Rosenthal & Kotanen 1994, Crawley 1997, Strauss & Agrawal 1999). Woody plants and forbs have their apical meristems at the tip of their branches, vulnerable to large herbivore browsing (unless out of reach), whereas most or all meristems on grasses are basal (much less likely to be grazed), until flowering, after which expansion of internodes occurs.

Two important intrinsic physiological features promoting plant tolerance of herbivory by large herbivores are growth rate and growth plasticity (Bradshaw 1965). In general terms, slower growing plants should be less tolerant of large herbivore damage because it takes longer for them to replace plant parts lost through herbivory, particularly in low-resource environments where opportunities for new uptake are limited (Coley et al. 1985, Rosenthal & Kotanen 1994). Growth plasticity relates to the capacity of a plant to release previously dormant buds, modify nutrient uptake and allocation, and increase photosynthetic activity, carbon fixation and/or growth rate; all key determinants of plant tolerance to herbivore damage. Storage of reserves in tissue that is unlikely to be grazed or browsed can also increase plant tolerance to herbivore damage (e.g. Richards 1993, Millard et al. 2001), and shallow rooting has also been proposed to increase tolerance by allowing faster uptake of nutrients close to the soil surface (Jefferies et al. 1994). The relative importance of stored resources (carbohydrates and nutrients) versus new uptake for regrowth following herbivore damage has been shown to vary for different plant species (Chapin et al. 1990, Richards 1993, Rosenthal & Kotanen 1994, Millard et al. 2001).

Tolerance is by implication normally linked to the effects of herbivore grazing; but features promoting tolerance to grazing may not protect the plant against other herbivore impacts such as trampling or bark stripping. Storage of nutrients in woody tissue, for example, may confer an advantage in relation to grazing (as the youngest shoots tend to be those grazed), but storage in roots would be required to safeguard against trampling. Thus it is important to consider plant 'tolerance' in relation to all herbivore impacts, not just grazing, as non-grazing impacts may be the main drivers of change in some systems (e.g. Hester & Baillie 1998, Oom 2002). Extrinsic factors affecting plant tolerance are normally those which may allow increased plant growth, nutrient uptake and/or light acquisition following grazing or trampling damage. Soil nutrient status is thus a key factor; it seems logical that plants growing on higher nutrient soils should be more tolerant of large herbivore damage, through greater productivity and a greater opportunity for increased nutrient uptake after tissue damage (Coley et al. 1985, Richards 1993, Crawley 1997, Bergman et al. 2001). This is not always supported by experimental results (e.g. Meyer & Root 1993, Hawkes & Sullivan 2001) perhaps as a result of higher ecological costs in high nutrient conditions. Furthermore, the interactions between soil nutrient status and plant productivity can also affect the *probability* of herbivore damage and the amount eaten. The plant vigour hypothesis (Price 1991) states that more productive plants should be more attractive to herbivores. If this is the case, then slow growing plants should be less susceptible to herbivore damage (Coley et al. 1985), in which case the consequences of any tissue removal would be more serious. Hence the widely stated hypothesis that fast growing plants should 'require' less chemical defence than slow growing plants (Coley *et al.* 1985, Bryant *et al.* 1991b). The plant stress hypothesis states, conversely, that stressed plants may actually be more attractive to herbivores as they tend to have higher tissue N and/or lower concentrations of defensive chemicals (White 1993). The generality of all these hypotheses has been questioned, particularly in relation to large herbivores, as so much 'evidence' comes from insect studies alone (e.g. Briske 1996, Crawley 1997).

Compensation

Plant compensation involves a positive response of a plant to injury to reduce the impacts of damage on their growth and reproduction, for example through faster relative growth rates and/or increased seed production, requiring alterations in resource allocation and patterns of growth (McNaughton 1983, Belsky 1986, Richards 1993). 'Compensation' and 'tolerance' are closely linked; the intrinsic and extrinsic factors discussed under 'tolerance' above will all affect the ability of a plant to compensate for tissue removed (e.g. McNaughton 1983, Briske 1996).

Do plants 'over-compensate' for tissue loss/damage, and if so, under what conditions? This controversial topic also fuels the questions of whether herbivory might even be 'good' for some plants under certain conditions and whether or not it has actually evolved as a response to herbivory in some species subjected to long histories of grazing (McNaughton 1983, Belsky 1986, Crawley 1997, Belsky *et al.* 1993, Bergelson *et al.* 1996, Agrawal 2000, Hawkes & Sullivan 2001). 'Over-compensation' is generally defined as increased plant (Darwinian) fitness as a result of herbivory, as indexed by various (not always consistent) measures of plant growth and reproduction (McNaughton 1983, Crawley 1997, Strauss & Agrawal 1999).

One main area of controversy appears to relate to whether or not records of 'over-compensation' are simply: (a) a result of short-term or poorly designed experiments; and/or (b) due to indirect benefits of release from some other constraint being greater than any direct negative effect of tissue removal *per se*. Other constraints 'released after grazing' could include competition from neighbours (e.g. if they were also grazed), light or nutrient limitations. For example, despite the losses of photosynthetic material, carbohydrates and nutrients incurred by grazing, many grass species actually increase their rates of tillering following grazing due to stimulation of tiller production by increased intensity and red:far-red ratio of the light reaching the basal meristems (Langer 1956, Deregibus *et al.*

1985, Richards 1993). Furthermore, a strategy of rapid regrowth after tissue damage could alternatively be an adaptation to factors such as fire, frost, drought or wind, rather than herbivory *per se* (McNaughton 1983, Belsky *et al.* 1993, Crawley 1997). A meta-analysis of data sets on dicot herbs, woody plants and monocot herbs showed that, although plants were most commonly *detrimentally* affected by herbivory, there were examples of exact- or over-compensation in 26%–44% of records analysed, particularly under high resource conditions for monocots and low resource conditions for dicot herbs (Hawkes & Sullivan 2001). The authors did acknowledge, however, that these were short-term responses and might not accurately reflect long term fitness – an important distinction.

The over-compensation controversy is well exemplified by the long-running debate concerning *Ipomopsis aggregata*, which gives a good demonstration of the main issues (e.g. Paige & Whitham 1987, Bergelson & Crawley 1992a,b, Paige 1992, 1994, 1999, Bergelson *et al.* 1996, Juenger & Bergelson 1997, 2000, Paige *et al.* 2001).

IMPLICATIONS FOR PLANT COMMUNITY STRUCTURE AND DIVERSITY

Plants normally grow with other plants, be that in single species groups (populations) or multispecies assemblages (communities). The impacts of large herbivores discussed above in the context of individual plants all apply, but with the added complication of neighbours. Plant populations and communities contain mixtures of life stages, and in the latter case species, which compete for resources but exhibit a range of different traits, leading both to differential herbivore damage and differential responses to that damage. As so many features of herbivore impact are similar in both populations and communities (Crawley 1997), for the purpose of brevity and simplicity we focus on plant communities in this review. Not surprisingly, it is notoriously difficult to isolate the main drivers of plant community dynamics, although many researchers have attempted to find unifying hypotheses (Huntly 1991, Bullock 1996, Crawley 1997, Olff & Ritchie 1998, Ritchie & Olff 1999). Moreover, scales of plant response may not relate directly to the scale of herbivore selection, and this underlies many of the points outlined in the following sections. A change from one plant community to another may be the result of processes occurring at much smaller scales, such as one or more individual species, or plant part. For example, removal of flowering stems of a key species by grazing could easily result in the loss of that species (particularly if both adult plants and seeds are not long-lived), with cascading effects on the composition of the whole community (Dormann & Bakker 1999).

Inter- and intraspecific competitive interactions

Interactions between large herbivore impacts and plant competition are the key to understanding large herbivore effects on plant communities. Plant competition, as per Begon *et al.* (1990), is an interaction between individual plants with a shared requirement for a resource in limited supply, which results in reduced growth, reproduction and/or survival of one or all of the individual plants involved. Herbivores can affect competition by reducing or increasing the competitive abilities of individual plants for light, nutrients and/or water. For example, grazing a tall plant will reduce the competitive advantage of that individual in relation to light, but might also increase the amount of light available to other surrounding plants which are not grazed or are grazed less. However, if grazing on the surrounding plants (even if less severe) has a stronger negative effect on water or nutrient uptake, then this might negate the advantage inferred by the increase in availability of light. Thus, the degree of impact of herbivores on competition depends very much on how they affect plant uptake of the most limiting resource(s), as well as the physical form of the plant itself (Grime 1979, Tilman 1988, Gough & Grace 1998, Louda *et al.* 1990, Huntly 1991, Bullock 1996, Crawley 1997). Competitive interactions between neighbouring plants may be increased, decreased or altered by herbivore activities. Situations where one plant may benefit (through reduced grazing) from association with another are commonly termed *associational resistance* or *avoidance* (e.g. reviews by Huntly 1991, Olff *et al.* 1999). Hjältén *et al.* (1993), for example, found avoidance of preferred species by association with less palatable species, using mountain hares, voles and deciduous tree species. If a plant is more detrimentally affected by herbivores through its association with another (which might benefit from the association), then the effect is commonly termed *associational susceptibility* or *apparent competition* (Holt 1977, Strauss 1991, Holt & Lawton 1994). Prieur-Richard *et al.* (2002), for example, found increased herbivory on two *Conyza* species when growing within grass-dominated vegetation, as compared to communities dominated by Asteraceae or Fabaceae. Similarly, the dwarf shrub, *Calluna vulgaris*, was found to be much more heavily grazed when growing adjacent to grass (Hester & Baillie 1998, Palmer *et al.* 2003). Several such examples have also been found between different temperate grass species in grazed swards (e.g. Bullock 1996). McNaughton (1978) found reduced grazing by buffalo

and wildebeest on the grass *Themeda triandra* in plots with higher proportions of less palatable plant species. This was not so for the more selective
Thompson's gazelles and zebra, illustrating (as per Hjältén *et al.* 1993) that
the expression of associational resistance or susceptibility depends on the
types of herbivore present.

Few studies have attempted to compare the relative importance of
apparent versus 'actual' competition in driving plant community dynamics under grazing, particularly in relation to large herbivores (Grace &
Tilman 1990, Huntly 1991, Crawley 1997, Bonsall & Hassell 1997,
Milchunas & Noy-Meir 2002). Hambäck and Ekerholm (1997) tested
this for voles but found only weak evidence that they might mediate
apparent competition between different plants. Animals do not forage
randomly, but select their food plants to a greater or lesser degree using
olfactory and/or visual cues (Bailey *et al.* 1996, Bergman *et al.*, in press).
However, these cues will also be affected by plant growth pattern, chemical
composition and plant spacing, as well as their position relative to other
plants in the plant community. Hambäck and Beckerman (2003), for
example, hypothesized that herbivore species which recognize their hosts
by general plant characteristics such as height and colour are more confounded by plant neighbours than herbivore species which recognize their
host plants by specific characteristics, such as the distinct odour of a plant
species.

There is evidence for a range of trade-offs between traits which increase
plant competitive abilities under ungrazed conditions and their ability to
avoid or tolerate grazing (e.g. Grime 1979, Tilman 1988, Huntly 1991,
Rosenthal & Kotanen 1994, Briske 1996, Augustine & McNaughton
1998). Large herbivore grazing is more likely to reduce or alter competitive
interactions between species than to increase their magnitude (Bullock
1996, Olofsson *et al.* 2002). However, the effects of such a reduction on
plant community dynamics depend very much on the relationships between competitive ability and tolerance or resistance to herbivory. For
example, if resistance to (or defence against) herbivores is negatively
correlated with competitive ability, then the relative benefits to the plant
of any one strategy will change as herbivore activities shift the balance of
effects between different plant strategies. At some mid-point this would
thus be hypothesized to increase diversity, as found by many studies.
However, if competitive ability and tolerance are positively related then
the presence of herbivores could reduce diversity through their greater
detrimental effects on those species already competitively inferior, as
demonstrated by Welch (1986).

Trade-offs between competitive ability and other strategies, such as colonization, can also be variously affected by the presence of herbivores. For example, the net result of a negative correlation between colonization ability and competitive ability (*sensu* Tilman 1994) would depend on the action of the herbivore: creation of gaps by herbivore activities could favour colonizer species in a sward, offsetting the disadvantage of reduced competitive abilities. In the absence of gaps, the relative advantage of competitors over colonizers would depend on the effect of the herbivores on plant competition. Although relatively little conclusive field data exists (most on insects), this is a dynamic field of theoretical research (Crawley 1983, Pacala & Crawley 1992, Kotanen & Rosenthal 2000, Crawley 1997, Chase *et al.* 2000).

Diversity

Across the globe, many changes in plant species diversity have been attributed to grazing, either directly or indirectly (e.g. Briske 1996, Bullock 1996, Crawley 1997, Austrheim & Eriksson 2001, Hart 2001). There is a wealth of literature on the subject, but still much controversy about the likely effects of herbivores on plant species diversity under different conditions (Grime 1973, Jefferies *et al.* 1994, Milchunas *et al.* 1998, Olff & Ritchie 1998, Ritchie & Olff 1999, Stohlgren, *et al.* 1999, Brockway *et al.* 2002). This is probably due to both the complexity of the subject and a scarcity of long-term controlled studies where all main driving factors are understood. Other complications include the fact that diversity is measured in many different ways and abiotic conditions as well as herbivore influences are not always taken into account. Furthermore, assessment of the influence of herbivores on diversity also depends very much on the spatial scale at which it is measured (Crawley 1997, Ritchie & Olff 1999).

Colonization and extinction

In basic terms, plant species richness results from the balance between local colonization and extinction rates of species (Crawley 1997, Olff & Ritchie 1998), thus any impacts that herbivores have on these processes will have effects on diversity. Seed dispersal on fur or in dung, for example, can significantly increase plant diversity, particularly where gaps in established vegetation occur (created by herbivores or other causes) (Miles & Kinnaird 1979, Pakeman *et al.* 1998, Mitlacher *et al.* 2002). Bullock *et al.* (2001) found that timing of grazing was also important in defining herbivore effects on colonizer species, finding a positive relationship between colonizer species and heavy grazing only during the summer over a 12-year mesophytic grassland study. Recruitment is the most difficult stage for many plant species and some species readily capitalize on windows of opportunity for germination and establishment. They may be through herbivore activities or other factors such as favourable climatic conditions, producing a cohort of seedlings, some of which survive until the next combination of favourable conditions (this is termed the storage effect) (Chesson & Huntly 1989). Herbivores can also increase or decrease extinction rates of different species, depending on both species tolerance and the relative effects on competition with surrounding vegetation.

Plant species coexistence and diversity

If herbivores tend to reduce or alter competitive interactions between plants, then their presence is likely to allow greater coexistence between species and thus increase diversity (e.g. Bakker 1989, Bullock et al. 1994a, Olff & Ritchie 1998, Austrheim & Eriksson 2001, Hart 2001, Virtanen et al. 2002). However, in situations where grazing acts to increase the dominance of an already dominant species (Crawley 1988), or under prolonged heavy grazing, species diversity has been shown to decline, as only the most grazing-resistant species can survive (Welch 1986, Olff & Ritchie 1998, Austrheim & Eriksson 2001, Hart 2001). This concords with the classic Intermediate Disturbance Model (Grime 1973) which predicts that herbaceous species richness is highest at intermediate levels of biomass (e.g. under intermediate grazing levels), recently also tested for arid-zone grazing lands by Oba et al. (2001). Bullock et al. (2001) found differential effects of grazing on mesotrophic grassland diversity according to season, with increased species richness under spring and winter grazing but decreased richness under heavy summer grazing. They used this data to test three hypotheses relating to plant species traits and plant community responses to large herbivore grazing: (1) that preferentially grazed species will decline under heavier grazing and less preferred species will increase; (2) that species more able to colonize gaps will increase under heavier grazing; and (3) that species with greater competitive abilities will increase under reduced grazing. Results confirmed hypothesis 2 under summer grazing, but showed the opposite to hypothesis 1 under spring and winter grazing. One possible explanation for the latter result is that plant selection and regrowth ability (tolerance) might be positively related. This requires further research.

Gradients of herbivory have been variously used to explain or predict different plant community responses to herbivores, with both herbivore selection and plant responses varying with increasing herbivore densities (e.g. Huntly 1991, Crawley 1997). Olff and Ritchie (1998) proposed, primarily based on grassland studies, a series of relationships between herbivore abundance, body size and their effects on plant diversity. They proposed that as well as factors promoting colonization and extinction, herbivore body size could explain the direction, magnitude and scale of herbivore effects on plant species diversity, in conjunction with resource availability for plant growth. In brief, small non-digging herbivores would be expected to have weak or negative effects on diversity unless at high densities; digging herbivores or herbivores of intermediate size, however, would be expected to increase diversity under certain conditions (see below). Large herbivores would be expected to more consistently increase diversity due to the fact that they can use abundant (dominant), low quality food, create spatial heterogeneity through their grazing, urination and defecation, and generally transport seeds over longer distances.

Factors affecting herbivore species selection

Crawley (1997) suggested that the most likely mechanism affecting species diversity would be a correlation between palatability and competitive ability of different plant species, with a positive correlation leading to increased species richness and a negative correlation the opposite. One of the reasons for the great variety of measured effects of herbivores on diversity is that herbivore selection (and therefore 'palatability' of a plant in its broadest sense) is not consistent, either in space or time (Fig. 4.2; see also Chapters 6 & 10). Furthermore, if preferred species decline and become less available, even highly selective herbivores may shift to more abundant species; similarly if the spatial distribution of preferred species makes some or all individuals less accessible to herbivores, then the same may occur. Herbivores (although mostly insect studies) have variously been shown to respond to differences in plant species composition, frequency and density (Crawley 1983, Huntly 1991, Crawley 1997).

Some herbivores have also been shown to alter their diet as a response to the presence of other herbivores, making it difficult to predict whether the addition of herbivores to a system will have additive or compensatory effects on plant diversity (Ritchie & Olff 1999). Most plant communities are grazed by a range of herbivores and, although many studies have involved multiple herbivore assemblages, few have specifically tested how different herbivores interact and how this affects their impact on the vegetation (Ritchie & Olff 1999). Cid et al. (1991) reported additive effects of bison and prairie dog as a result of similar vegetation responses (e.g. species diversity and community structure) after removal of one or both herbivores from the system. Hester *et al.* (1999) also found additive effects of sheep and red deer on grass:shrub mosaics, as the herbivores showed no significant diet shifts in the presence or absence of the other herbivore species. However, early results from a long-term experiment set up by Fahnestock and Detling (2002) to examine the interactive effects of prairie dog colonies and bison, found strong and persistent effects of prairie dogs on plant diversity but no significant additional effects of bison exclusion or inclusion, indicating compensatory effects. Ritchie and Olff (1999) proposed a range of conditions under which herbivore effects might be expected to be additive or compensatory. For example, if herbivores consume the same plant species then they may have additive effects on a community; alternatively they may have compensatory or opposing effects if they consume different species. They provided a range of examples primarily for grassland systems, proposing the importance of herbivore body size as well as resource competition between plants in determining the impacts on plant community dynamics.

Abiotic factors and diversity

Abiotic factors clearly affect plant diversity. This has been widely shown in both natural situations and controlled experiments where, for example, light and nutrient levels have been manipulated (Crawley 1983, 1997, Gough & Grace 1998). The interactions between abiotic factors and herbivore impacts on plant diversity are not straightforward and have been much debated (reviews by Gough & Grace 1998, Olff & Ritchie 1998). Olff and Ritchie (1998) reviewed grassland literature on herbivore influences across environmental gradients, and Proulx and Mazumder (1998) analysed data from many types of ecosystems on the effect of herbivory on species richness. Both studies concluded that herbivores tend to reduce diversity or have no effect on poor soils but increase diversity on richer soils, which concords with more recent studies (Virtanen *et al.* 2002). Olff and Ritchie (1998) further developed this concept to distinguish between the four main combinations of soil fertility and moisture and herbivore body size. They proposed few or negative effects of herbivores on plant diversity on dry, poor soils, assuming that such habitats would only support few, small, specialist herbivores which could increase local extinctions of palatable species but would have little effect on colonization or coexistence. On dry, fertile soils herbivores were predicted to have weak negative effects on diversity, through greater tolerance of many plant species to herbivory due to high nutrient availability. Impacts on plant diversity on wet, infertile soils were predicted to be positive, through the

preponderance of large, non-selective herbivores, shifting plant competition from light- to nutrient-limitation. Finally, herbivore impacts on
wet, fertile soils were predicted to vary most, as they would support
multiple assemblages of large and small herbivores with different selection and impacts on colonization, coexistence and extinction. Proulx and
Mazumder (1998) proposed that the decline in species richness with
grazing in nutrient-poor sites is due to a limitation in available resources
which prevents regrowth. The increase in nutrient-rich areas could be due to
abundant resources allowing ungrazed (or unpalatable) species to respond
quickly to herbivory. Ritchie and Olff (1999) more recently proposed that
simple constraints on how organisms acquire resources in space can explain many species-diversity patterns found, although they do acknowledge
the importance of other factors in influencing diversity patterns as well.
Although the models of Olff and Ritche (1998), Proulx and Mazumder
(1998), and Ritchie and Olff (1999) are compelling in their simplicity, they
still encompass a large range of possible impacts of herbivores on diversity,
and as such do not greatly simplify the task of predicting herbivore impacts
in different systems. However, they do provide an ordered framework
within which to test various hypotheses.

Grazing refuges

Another important factor affecting herbivore influences on plant diversity is
the presence of grazing refuges. Milchunas and Noy-Meir (2002) reviewed
different types of grazing refuges and their impacts on plant diversity. From
their interpretation of various studies, they concluded that associational
avoidance of grazing was uncommon for terrestrial mammalian herbivores,
whilst indirect avoidance was probably common but little documented.
However, most important for plant diversity was what they termed 'geo-
logic' refuges (rock outcrops, cliffs, etc.) They found that 86% of small
refuge studies reported positive effects of their presence on plant diversity,
with the effects of such protection being greatest in communities with long
evolutionary histories of grazing. Such effects will clearly vary according to
the herbivore species present; for example, few areas remain effective
refuges in areas where goats are present as compared to less agile species.

Genetic diversity

Understanding the effects of herbivores on genetic diversity is hampered
by a lack of studies in areas where long-term grazing regimes are well
understood (Ledig 1992, Crawley 1997, Meikle *et al.* 1999, Simon *et al.*
2001, Cadenasso *et al.* 2002). There is some evidence for the evolution of

certain genotypes under long-term grazing, indicating selection for features such as more prostrate growth form under long-grazed conditions (e.g. Jaindl *et al.* 1994, Hartvigsen & McNaughton 1995, Strauss & Agrawal 1999), although such responses may sometimes be phenotypic rather than genotypic (Thomas *et al.* 2000). Sward studies of *Trifolium repens* (Lemaire & Chapman 1996) showed how genetic types with larger leaves did better under intermittent defoliation, whereas genotypes with smaller leaves did better under severe defoliation. Charles (1961) also found differential survival of cultivars of three grass species under different grazing regimes. The complexity of genotype-environment interactions in growth and insect herbivore resistance has probably played an important part in the evolution of current plant traits (Tikkanen *et al.* 2003), for example, the magnitude of change in primary and secondary metabolites is dependent on nutrient availability as well as on genotype (Lindroth *et al.* 2002). However, it is more difficult to make such links with traits conferring resistance to large herbivores rather than to insect herbivores.

Structural diversity

Grazing by large herbivores generally reduces plant size and height, leading to overall reductions in mean plant size and fewer or no large individuals within a plant community. If herbivores preferentially graze smaller plants they may simply increase plant size variation. In plant populations, plant size is one of the major determinants of the outcome of competition between individuals – the greater the size difference, the greater the competitive advantage of the larger plant (symmetric to asymmetric competition) (Hutchings 1997). Therefore, if herbivores reduce variation in plant size, this should result in reduced plant mortality due to competition, and vice versa. A whole range of structural responses to grazing have been recorded in the field; in most cases heavy grazing has indeed reduced structural diversity (e.g. Smit *et al.* 2001), but a variety of outcomes have been recorded under moderate or no grazing (Hutchings 1997, Crawley 1997). Husheer *et al.* (2003) illustrated how herbivore selectivity can alter the structural composition of different components of a plant community, with suppression of regeneration of palatable, fast growing species leading to overall reductions in new recruits and consequent reductions in structural variation. Olff *et al.* (1999) showed how large herbivores can induce and maintain structural diversity in other situations, through their selective foraging driving the alternation of plant facilitation (through associational resistance) and competition, leading to cyclic patch dynamics (see Chapter 7).

Spatial heterogeneity

It is important to stress that heterogeneity and diversity are clearly closely inter-linked, and so much of the discussion under 'Diversity' above is also relevant here.

Heterogeneity in resource distribution and herbivore distribution

Resource distribution is not uniform in space or time and this is one of the main factors affecting the spatial distribution of plants. Spatial heterogeneity in resource distribution allows species coexistence; if herbivores alter resource distribution then they inevitably affect the spatial distribution of plants as well. Herbivores themselves are also affected by heterogeneity in resource distribution (see Chapters 9 and 10). There is widespread support for the hypothesis that the distribution patterns of large herbivores are actually primarily determined by abiotic factors, such as terrain and distance to water, and these act as constraints within which mechanisms involving biotic factors (i.e. amount and quality of forage) operate (e.g. Bailey et al. 1996, Tainton et al. 1996). Water, for example, is a particularly strong cause of spatial heterogeneity in herbivore locations in arid or semi-arid systems. Topography acts to determine shelter or resting areas, particularly in more extreme climates (Staines 1977, Senft et al. 1987, Bailey et al. 1996, Pickup et al. 1998, Hobbs 1999, Wilmshurst et al. 1999). The relative importance of abiotic factors is likely to decrease in more moderate environments, for example, strong effects of plant distribution on herbivore location have been demonstrated in temperate or boreal regions (e.g. Heikkilä & Mikkonen 1992, Hester et al. 1999, Oom et al. 2002, see also Chapters 9 and 10). Other factors affecting herbivore distribution include avoidance of predators and avoidance of areas recently grazed, urinated or defecated on (see Chapter 9). It is clear from earlier discussions that heterogeneity of herbivore activities can clearly promote heterogeneity in vegetation at all plant life stages, from seed transport and germination through to extinction. Several authors have considered the implications of multiple interactions between heterogeneity in abiotic factors, herbivore distribution and their effects on vegetation, but relatively little data exists, particularly for large herbivores (Huntly 1991, Hobbs 1996, Hester et al. 2000a, Adler et al. 2001, Augustine & Frank 2001).

Scale dependence

Spatial heterogeneity in both vegetation and herbivores is strongly scale-dependent (Bakker et al. 1984, Olff et al. 1999, Wallis de Vries et al. 1999,

Rietkerk *et al.* 2000, Adler *et al.* 2001, Augustine & Frank 2001). At small scales under heavy grazing, for example, factors affecting seed germination could be most influential in driving local species composition (probably increasing local diversity), whereas at the landscape scale increasing dominance of grazing-tolerant species might act to reduce diversity. Herbivore body size is also hypothesized to interact with the scale of diversity (Holling 1992, Olff & Ritchie 1998), with larger herbivores generally having larger scale effects. A study of vegetation changes in New Mexico following removal of 'keystone' herbivores also illustrates the scale issue well, with many multi-directional vegetation changes at the site level but no major changes at the landscape level over a 20-year period (Ryerson & Parmenter 2001). Similarly, multi-scale sampling of long-term grazing exclosure sites across several USA states (Stohlgren *et al.* 1999) revealed many local differences but no clear effects of herbivores on plant species diversity at landscape scales. Others have argued that at large (landscape) scales the impacts of herbivores on vegetation are inversely proportional to variation in climatic variables. For example, it has been hypothesized that herbivores tend to have stronger effects in humid systems than in arid or semi-arid areas, where interactions between herbivores and their food sources are argued to be weaker due to the importance of abiotic factors (Ellis & Swift 1988, Tainton *et al.* 1996). However, there have been strong arguments presented against this idea (e.g. Olff & Ritchie 1998, Illius & O'Connor 1999).

At several scales, abiotic factors are likely to impact upon how plants ultimately will respond to herbivory, therefore spatial variability in such factors will also affect spatial heterogeneity of the vegetation. Augustine and Frank (2001) examined the spatial heterogeneity of soil N in a grazed grassland system, testing for differences in spatial patterns at a range of scales and finding evidence for herbivore influences on N at all scales measured. They challenged the widely stated hypothesis that increased heterogeneity in grazed vegetation relates strongly to deposition of dung and urine (see Chapter 9). They hypothesized instead that grazers promote fine-scale heterogeneity by increasing the spatial variability in plant litter inputs and/or diversifying the effects of plants on soils.

Grazing vs. non-grazing impacts on heterogeneity

Heterogeneity in herbivore distributions does not necessarily match the heterogeneity of their activities, for example they generally show different locational preferences for grazing and resting. As discussed before, non-grazing activities have also been shown to promote heterogeneity in vegetation composition. Trampling, for example, promotes strong spatial heterogeneity in plant species structure and composition with the formation of distinct communities along paths, containing a different mixture of species from the vegetation surrounding the paths (MacLennan 1979, Crawley 1997, Milne *et al.* 1998, Hester & Baillie 1998, Oom & Hester 1999); the same can also occur in preferred resting areas (Oom 2002). The relative importance of grazing and non-grazing impacts on heterogeneity will depend very much on the tolerance of the plant species present to those impacts. For example, trampling impacts within *Calluna vulgaris* dominated heath, an internationally important vegetation type in northern Europe (Gimingham 1972, Thompson *et al.* 1995), can locally change the composition of this community from woody-shrub-dominated to grass-dominated within less than one growing season, which is probably faster than the effects of grazing (Hester & Baillie 1998, Hester *et al.* 1999, Fig. 4.4). This hypothesis is further supported by recent air photo analysis demonstrating that the main areas of vegetation change over three years of sheep grazing at a range of densities were associated with resting areas and paths, rather than those areas consistently most heavily grazed (Oom 2002). If trampling rather than grazing is indeed the main driver of change, it raises a question as to the validity of the primary focus of management on the proportion of grazed shoots that *Calluna vulgaris* can tolerate, with little or no consideration of trampling impacts (Grant *et al.* 1982, Palmer 1997). This question is probably relevant to many other habitats, especially those containing woody shrubs or other highly trampling-sensitive species.

What further complicates matters is the fact that large herbivores are mobile, with movement patterns that may vary dramatically depending on time of year. Persson *et al.* (2000) reviewed literature on moose from Fennoscandia, North America and the former Soviet Union to estimate average daily food intake, area moved, and dung and urine deposition. Their study showed that area trampled, food intake and urine deposition were about twice as high during the summer as compared with winter. Further, when they took into account that Sweden currently has a population of about 350 000 moose, they calculated an annual trampled area of 3255 km^2, an annual amount of dung deposition of about 3×10^8 kg (containing 5.6×10^6 kg N), and an annual amount of urine deposition of 1.3×10^6 m^3. Clearly, the moose population in Sweden has a strong potential for non-browsing as well as browsing impacts on vegetation dynamics and other processes!

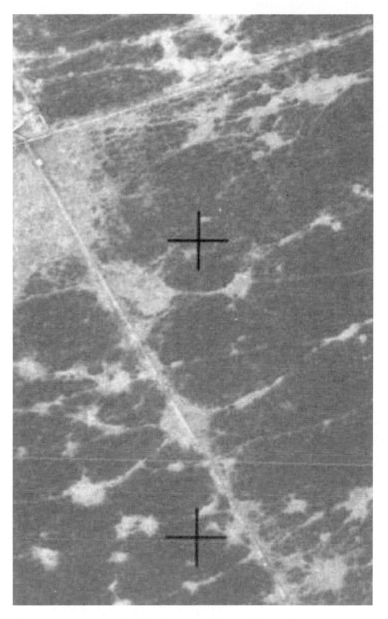

Figure 4.4. Photograph of sheep-grazed plots within *Calluna vulgaris*-dominated vegetation, illustrating local effects of trampling changing heather to grass-dominance within 1 to 3 years.

Do herbivores always increase heterogeneity?

Most studies indicate that herbivores are more likely to increase spatial heterogeneity, but, as ever, there are exceptions and, as with diversity, the reasons for herbivores increasing or decreasing heterogeneity under different conditions are still not fully understood (Adler *et al.* 2001). Adler *et al.* (2000) reviewed a range of studies to try to develop some predictive understanding of the conditions under which herbivores have been shown to increase heterogeneity. They found no consistent links with ecosystem type, productivity, or grazer selectivity but they did find interactions between the spatial pattern of the vegetation and the spatial pattern of grazing at a given scale of observation. They hypothesized that if, for example, at a given scale, vegetation heterogeneity was greater than grazing heterogeneity, then the vegetation heterogeneity would decrease under grazing (termed 'homogeneous grazing'), and vice versa ('patch grazing'). Several examples of patch grazing were found in the literature and many showed increases in heterogeneity of vegetation where appropriate measurements had been made. Examples of homogeneous grazing were found to occur most commonly at smaller scales, as one would expect, but their effects on heterogeneity were variable. 'Selective grazing' (*sensu* Senft *et al.* 1987) was also distinguished where both herbivores and vegetation responded to the same spatial patterning agent, for example, topography. In this type of scenario, herbivore influences on vegetation heterogeneity would depend on whether they increased or decreased the abundance of the selected vegetation. Their ideas present a useful synthesis of some possible predictors of herbivore impacts on spatial heterogeneity of vegetation, and an interesting model developed from these ideas, but testing of their ideas suffered from a lack of appropriate data, as few studies have measured spatial heterogeneity in a consistent manner, if at all. The advent of increasingly sophisticated spatial analysis tools has already facilitated wider analysis of the drivers of spatial heterogeneity in both plant and herbivore distributions at different scales (e.g. Olff & Ritchie 1999, Adler *et al.* 2000, Olff *et al.* 2002). This new body of hypotheses now needs to be accompanied with a drive for new field data collection and analysis.

Temporal dynamics

Many of the factors discussed earlier that vary in space also vary in time, and so much of the discussion above also applies to a consideration of herbivore influences on temporal plant community dynamics. The time scale of herbivore impacts on vegetation dynamics also varies depending

on the plant unit under consideration. For example, trees have two organ-
izational levels, modules and genets, and ungulate activities affect both
levels but at different time scales. Responses at the module level (i.e. as
defined as annual shoots and leaves of woody species) are generally more
dynamic and more short-term, whereas responses at the genet (zygote)
level tend to have longer-term effects, such as rates of birth, death, immigration or emigration (Danell *et al.* 2003). As with spatial considerations,
scale issues are paramount at all levels – a 'stable' grazed system in the
time scale of a five-year research programme, for example, may be highly
unstable if studied over longer time scales. Similarly, a directional change
over a short time scale may simply be a fluctuation over a longer time
(Miles 1979, 1985). In general terms, temporal factors affecting grazing
impacts range from seasonal changes in both species selection by herbivores and the responses of plants to herbivore damage (e.g. Hester *et al.*
1996, Smith *et al.* 2000, Bullock *et al.* 2001). This occurs through between-year variation in either or both of the above (e.g. Chesson & Huntly
1989), up to medium- to long-term changes in, for example, herbivore
densities, community structure and composition (e.g. Huntly 1991, Dlott
& Turkington 2000, Bullock *et al.* 2001).

Apart from assemblages of annuals, the structure and spatial arrangement of many populations and communities of plants is generally more a
reflection of many years of past events than present conditions (Archer
1996, see also Chapter 7). Thus the current effects of herbivores are
intricately inter-linked with the past as well as the present, although the
long-term past is rarely a direct component of study! This makes it a
difficult challenge to fully understand the impacts of herbivores on the
longer-term dynamics of any systems. Forests are one of the most obvious
examples of this problem – what we see now may be the result of hundreds
of years of particular combinations of biotic and abiotic conditions (Kirby
2003, see also Chapter 7). Archer (1996) offers a useful résumé of many
techniques available to assess historical changes in vegetation for the
purposes of reconstructing site or vegetation histories.

Herbivore effects on longer-term directional, i.e. successional, processes depend on the stage of growth that they affect most and its importance in the succession (e.g. Gray *et al.* 1986). For example, creation of
gaps by trampling can allow the entry of new individuals by facilitating
germination. If the species colonizing gaps are early successional species,
then gap creation by herbivores could slow down, arrest or reverse a
succession, whereas if the gap colonizers are later successional species
then succession could be accelerated. Crawley (1997) argued that, in

general, herbivores will slow down primary successions or seed-limited successions, whereas they are likely to speed up secondary successions limited by inhibition. Briske (1996) discussed the influence of generalist herbivores versus specialist herbivores on succession, demonstrating how studies have shown different herbivores variously to prefer early-, mid- or late-successional species, depending on conditions. Ritchie & Olff (1999) confirmed that herbivores could variously accelerate, arrest or retard succession depending on their effects on limiting factors at different successional stages. Olff *et al.* (1999) also presented evidence for large herbivores changing directional successions to 'shifting mosaics' by their differential impacts on different growth stages of key species. For example, with positive facilitation interactions at one growth stage but competitive displacement at another (see Chapter 7). To give some examples, suppression of later-stage competitive dominants by grazing may slow down, arrest or reverse a succession (Miles 1988, Jefferies *et al.* 1994, Briske 1996). However, if early-successional species are more selected or more vulnerable to grazing and/or browsing than later-successional ones, then herbivore browsing can speed up successional processes (e.g. Hester *et al.* 1991b, Pastor & Naiman 1992). Drent and van der Wal (1999) found that hares tended to slow down saltmarsh succession (as they grazed the late-successional dominants during winter) whereas geese had few effects (preferring early-successional species). Pastor and Naiman (1992) modelled the effects on succession in boreal forests caused by different foraging strategies by two different herbivores, i.e. moose and beaver. They focused on two key plant species, aspen being the early-successional, easily decomposable, more palatable species, which is fed on by both moose and beaver, and spruce as the late-successional, slowly decomposable species, rejected as food by both animal species. Moose browsing on aspen occurs early in the succession, accelerating succession towards spruce, whereas beaver fell aspen later, during 'mid-succession', resulting in 'arresting' of the succession for longer at the aspen stage. They suggested that the same traits determining digestibility of plants also determine litter decomposition in the ground as well as in the herbivores, which were hypothesized to have further effects on directions of succession (see Chapter 10).

Reversal of some successional changes is often not simply a matter of reversal of the conditions under which that particular vegetation state was formed (Miles 1985, 1988, Archer 1996). Several studies have reported very few changes in plant community composition following grazing removal from heavily grazed systems, even over long time scales, for example, unproductive communities dominated by species such as *Calluna vulgaris*,

Nardus stricta or *Molinia caerulea* (Welch 1986, Hill *et al.* 1992, Virtanen *et al.* 2002). Many examples of herbivore-driven vegetation changes which are difficult to reverse involve the loss of species (plants and propagule stores) from a system (e.g. loss of forest trees) (Pastor & Naiman 1992, Hester *et al.* 2000a), and/or the loss of essential conditions for germination (e.g. loss of shrubs and development of dense, grazed swards which are very difficult to re-invade) (Hester & Baillie 1998, Palmer *et al.* 2003).

CONCLUSIONS

This chapter has outlined some of the main herbivore impacts on plant community structure and dynamics, through a consideration of individual plants up to the community level. Although many questions still remain over the precise impacts of herbivores on individual plants, it is much easier to demonstrate how herbivores affect individual plants, particularly under highly controlled conditions, than to demonstrate how they affect the dynamics of plant communities. In our view the main questions requiring further work on individual plants relate to thresholds of herbivore damage to different plant parts, under a range of abiotic conditions. Many more studies have been carried out on invertebrate herbivory than large mammalian herbivory and this imbalance has clearly affected the degree of understanding of large herbivore impacts. At the plant community level there is also a relative lack of good, controlled experimental data on large herbivore impacts on plant community processes. However, in recent years there has been active development of new and stimulating hypotheses seeking to find unifying concepts to explain the complexity of large herbivore interactions with vegetation dynamics at a range of spatial and temporal scales. An increasing number of these contemporary ideas are aiming to find unifying theories across whole ecosystems rather than separating the effects of herbivory for different ecosystems. The obvious advantage with this approach is that it makes the theoretical framework less complex, thereby enabling a broader view of processes occurring not only on different scales, but also across different environments. However, ecosystem properties vary to such an extent that it is still difficult to make generalizations about the impact of herbivores even within small limited areas, let alone on an ecosystem scale. Care has to be taken when dynamics occurring on smaller scales are multiplied up to predict large-scale processes. The ever increasing availability of better computational analysis tools should facilitate the continued development of new, unifying ideas, but there also needs to be a concerted approach to targeted data collection to provide sound information on which to test and refine these ideas. Long-term data is, as ever, particularly scarce. In relation to future management of grazing systems, the challenge also remains in defining what types of community structure and diversity we are aiming for, at all scales. Here, grazing history is also a fundamental guiding tool when setting future management goals and conservation priorities.

ACKNOWLEDGEMENTS

Thanks to the Scottish Executive Environment and Rural Affairs Department for funding the work of Alison J. Hester and Glenn R. Iason, and to the Carl Tryggers Foundation for their Postdoctoral Scholarship funding for Margareta Bergman. We are grateful to Colin Birch and an anonymous referee for their helpful comments on the manuscript.

REFERENCES

Adler, P.B., Raff, D.A. & Lauenroth, W.K. (2001). The effect of grazing on the spatial heterogeneity of vegetation. *Oecologia*, **128**, 465–79.

Agrawal, A.A. (2000). Overcompensation of plants in response to herbivory and the by-product benefits of mutualism. *Trends in Plant Science*, **5**, 309–13.

Archer, S. (1996). Assessing and interpreting grass-woody plant dynamics. In *The Ecology and Management of Grazing Systems*, ed. J. Hodgson & A.W. Illius. Wallingford: CAB International, pp. 101–36.

Augustine, D.J. & Frank, D.A. (2001). Effects of migratory grazers on spatial heterogeneity of soil nitrogen properties in a grassland ecosystem. *Ecology*, **82**, 3149–62.

Augustine, D.J. & McNaughton, S.J. (1998). Ungulate effects on the functional species composition of plant communities: herbivore selectivity and plant tolerance. *Journal of Wildlife Management*, **62**, 1165–83.

Austin, P.J., Suchar, L.A., Robbins, C.T. & Hagerman A.E. (1989). Tannin-binding proteins in saliva of deer and their absence in saliva of sheep and cattle. *Journal of Chemical Ecology*, **15**, 1335–47.

Austrheim, G. & Eriksson, O. (2001). Plant species diversity and grazing in the Scandinavian mountains – patterns and processes at different spatial scales. *Ecography*, **24**, 683–95.

Bailey, D.W., Gross, J.E., Laca, E.A. *et al.* (1996). Mechanisms that result in large herbivore grazing distribution patterns. *Journal of Range Management*, **49**, 386–400.

Bakker, J.P. (1989). *Nature Management by Grazing and Cutting*. Dordrecht: Kluwer Academic Publishers.

Bakker, J.P., de Leeuw, J. & van Wieren, S.E. (1984). Micro-patterns in grassland vegetation created and sustained by sheep grazing. *Vegetatio*, **55**, 153–61.

Begon, M., Harper, J.L. & Townsend, C.R. (1990). *Ecology: Individuals, Populations and Communities,* 2nd edn. Oxford: Blackwell Scientific Publications.

Belsky, A.J. (1986). Does herbivory benefit plants? A review of the evidence. *American Naturalist*, **127**, 870–92.

Belsky, A.J., Carson, W.P., Jensen, C.L. & Fox, G.A. (1993). Overcompensation by plants: herbivore optimisation or red herring? *Evolutionary Ecology*, **7**, 109–21.

Bergelson, J. & Crawley, M.J. (1992a). The effects of grazers on the performance of individuals and populations of scarlet gilia, *Ipomopsis aggregata*. *Oecologia*, **90**, 435–44.

Bergelson, J. & Crawley, M.J. (1992b). Herbivory and *Ipomopsis aggregata*: the disadvantages of being eaten. *American Naturalist*, **139**, 870–82.

Bergelson, J., Juenger, T. & Crawley, M.J. (1996). Regrowth following herbivory in *Ipomopsis aggregata*: compensation but not overcompensation. *American Naturalist*, **148**, 744–55.

Bergman, M. (2002). Can saliva from moose, *Alces alces*, affect growth responses in the sallow, *Salix caprea*? *Oikos*, **96**, 164–8.

Bergman, M., Edenius, L. & Danell, K. (2001). The effect of browsing on *Sorbus aucuparia* in high- and low-resource environments. In *Ungulate Effects on Their Food Plants: Responses Depending on Scale*. M. Bergman Ph.D Thesis, Department of Animal Ecology, Swedish University of Agricultural Sciences, Umea.

Bergman, M., Iason, G.R. & Hester, A.J. (2005). Feeding patterns by roe deer and rabbits on pine, willow and birch in relation to spatial arrangement. *Oikos*, **109**, 513–20.

Bergqvist, G., Bergström, R. & Edenius, L. (2003). Effects of moose (*Alces alces*) rebrowsing on damage development in young stands of Scots pine (*Pinus sylvestris*). *Forest Ecology and Management*, **176**, 397–403.

Bergström, R. & Danell, K. (1987). Effects of simulated browsing by moose on morphology and biomass of two birch species. *Journal of Ecology*, **75**, 533–44

Bidlack, W.R., Brown, R.C. & Mohan, C. (1986). Nutritional parameters that alter hepatic drug metabolism, conjugation and toxicitiy. *Federation Proceedings*, **45**, 142–8.

Bokdam, J. (2001). Effects of browsing and grazing on cyclic succession in nutrient-limited ecosystems. *Journal of Vegetation Science*, **12**, 875–86.

Bonsall, M.B. & Hassell, M.P. (1997). Apparent competition structures ecological assemblages. *Nature*, **388**, 371–3.

Bradshaw, A.D. (1965). Evolutionary significance of phenotypic plasticity in plants. *Advances in Genetics*, **13**, 115–55.

Briske, D.D. (1996). Strategies of plant survival in grazed systems: a functional interpretation. In *The Ecology and Management of Grazing Systems*, ed. J. Hodgson & A.W. Illius. Wallingford: CAB International, pp. 37–68.

Brockway, D.G., Gatewood, R.G. & Paris, R.B. (2002). Restoring grassland savannas from degraded pinyon-juniper woodlands: effects of mechanical overstory reduction and slash treatment alternatives. *Journal of Environmental Management*, **64**, 179–97.

Bryant, J.P. (2003). Winter browsing on Alaska feltleaf willow twigs improves leaf nutritional value for snowshoe hares in summer. *Oikos*, **102**, 25–32.

Bryant, J.P., Chapin, F.S., III. & Klein, D.R. (1983). Carbon/nutrient balance of boreal plants in relation to vertebrate herbivory. *Oikos*, **40**, 357–68.

Bryant, J.P., Clausen, T. & Kuropat, P. (1985). Interactions of snowshoe hare and feltleaf willow in Alaska. *Ecology*, **66**, 1564–73.

Bryant, J.P., Danell, K., Provenza, F.D. *et al.* (1991a). Effects of mammal browsing on the chemistry of deciduous woody plants. In *Phytochemical Induction by Herbivores*, ed. D. Tallamy & M.J. Raupp. New York: Wiley, pp. 135–54.

Bryant, J.P., Provenza, F.D., Pastor, J. *et al.* (1991b). Interactions between woody plants and browsing animals mediated by secondary metabolites. *Annual Review of Ecology and Systematics*, **22**, 431–46.

Bryant, J.P., Reichardt, P.B., Clausen., T.P., Provenza F.D. & Kuropat, P.J. (1991c). Woody plant-mammal interactions. In *Herbivores: Their Interactions with Secondary Plant Metabolites. Vol II. Ecological and Evolutionary Processes*, ed. G.A. Rosenthal & M.R. Berenbaum. San Diego, California: Academic Press, pp. 344–71.

Bullock, J.M. (1996). Plant competition and population dynamics. In *The Ecology and Management of Grazing Systems*, ed. J. Hodgson & A.W. Illius Wallingford: CAB International, pp. 69–100.

Bullock, J.M., Clear Hill, B. & Silvertown, J. (1994a). Demography of *Cirsium vulgare* in a grazing experiment. *Journal of Ecology*, **82**, 101–11.

Bullock, J.M., Clear Hill, B., Dale, M.P. & Silvertown, J. (1994b). An experimental study of vegetation change due to grazing in a species-poor grassland and the role of the seed bank. *Journal of Applied Ecology*, **31**, 737–47.

Bullock, J.M., Franklin, J., Stevenson, M.J. *et al.* (2001). A plant trait analysis of responses to grazing in a long-term experiment. *Journal of Applied Ecology*, **38**, 253–67.

Cadenasso, M.L., Pickett, S.T.A. & Morin, P.J. (2002). Experimental test of the role of mammalian herbivores on old field succession: community structure and seedling survival. *Journal of the Torrey Botanical Society*, **129**, 228–37.

Capinera, J.L. & Roltsch, W.J. (1980). Response of wheat seedlings to actual and simulated migratory grasshopper defoliation. *Journal of Economic Entomology*, **73**, 258–61.

Chapin, F.S., Bryant, J.P. & Fox, J.F. (1985). Lack of induced chemical defence in juvenile Alaskan woody plants in response to simulated browsing. *Oecologia*, **67**, 457–9.

Chapin, F.S. Schultze, E.D. & Mooney, H.A. (1990). The ecology and economics of storage in plants. *Annual Review of Ecology and Systematics*, **21**, 423–47.

Chapman, D.F. & Lemaire, G. (1993). Morphogenetic and structural determinants of plant regrowth after defoliation. In *Grasslands for our World*, ed. M.J.Baker. Proceedings of the XVII International Grassland Congress. Wellington: SIR publishing, pp. 95–104.

Charles, W.N. (1961). Differential survival of cultivars of *Lolium, Dactylis* and *Phleum. Journal of the British Grassland Society*, **16**, 69–75.

Chase, J.M., Leibold, M.A. & Simms, E. (2000). Plant tolerance and resistance in food webs: community-level predictions and evolutionary implications. *Evolutionary Ecology*, **14**, 289–14.

Chesson, P. & Huntly, N. (1989). Short-term instabilities and long-term community dynamics. *Trends in Ecology and Evolution*, **4**, 293–8.

Cid, M.S., Detling, J.K., Whicker, A.D. & Brizuela, M.A. (1991). Vegetational responses of a mixed-grass prairie site following exclusion of prairie dogs and bison. *Journal of Range Management*, **44**, 100–5.

Cipollini, D. & Sipe M. (2001). Jasmonic acid treatment and mammalian herbivory differentially affect chemical defence expression and growth of *Brassica kaber. Chemoecology*, **11**, 137–43.

Cipollini, D., Purringnton, C.B. & Bergelson, J. (2003). Costs of induced responses in plants. *Basic and Applied Ecology*, **4**, 79–89.

Coley, P.D., Bryant, J.P. & Chapin, F.S. (1985). Resource availability and plant antiherbivore defense. *Science*, **230**, 895–9.

Crawley, M.J. (1983). *Herbivory. The Dynamics of Animal-Plant Interactions*. Studies in Ecology Volume 10. Oxford: Blackwell Scientific Publications.

Crawley, M.J. (1988). Herbivores and plant population dynamics. In *Plant Population Ecology*, ed. A.J. Davy, M.J. Hutchings & A.R. Watkinson. Oxford: Blackwell Scientific Publications, pp. 367–92.

Crawley, M.J. (ed.) (1997). *Plant Ecology*, 2nd edition. Oxford: Blackwell Science.

Danell, K. & Huss-Danell, K. (1985). Feeding by insects and hares on birches earlier affected by moose browsing. *Oikos*, **44**, 75–81.

Danell, K., Huss-Danell, K. & Bergström, R. (1985). Interactions between browsing moose and two species of birch in Sweden. *Ecology*, **66**, 1867–78.

Danell, K., Bergström, R., Edenius, L. & Ericsson, G. (2003). Ungulates as drivers of tree population dynamics at module and genet levels. *Forest Ecology and Management*, **181**, 67–76.

Deregibus, V.A., Sanches, R.A., Casal, J.J. & Trlica, M.J. (1985). Tillering responses to enrichment of red light beneath the canopy in a humid natural grassland. *Journal of Applied Ecology*, **22**, 199–206.

Detling, J.K., Ross, C.W., Walmsley, M.H. *et al.* (1981). Examination of North American bison saliva for potential growth regulators. *Journal of Chemical Ecology*, **7**, 239–46.

Diaz, S., Noy-Meir, I. & Cabido, M. (2001). Can grazing response of herbaceous plants be predicted from simple vegetative traits? *Journal of Applied Ecology*, **38**, 497–508.

Dicke, M., van Poecke, M.P. & de Boer, J. (2003). Inducible indirect defense of plants: from mechanisms to ecological functions. *Basic and Applied Ecology*, **4**, 27–42.

Dlott, F. & Turkington, R. (2000). Regulation of boreal forest understory vegetation: the roles of resources and herbivores. *Plant Ecology*, **154**, 239–51.

Dormann, C.F. & Bakker, J.P. (1999). The impact of herbivory and competition on flowering and survival during saltmarsh succession. *Plant Biology*, **2**, 68–76.

Drent, R.H. & van der Wal, R. (1999). Cyclic grazing in vertebrates and the manipulation of the food resource. In *Herbivores: Between Plants and Predators*, ed. H. Olff, V.K. Brown, R.H. Drent. Oxford: Blackwell Science, pp. 271–99.

Edwards, P.J., Wratten, S.D. & Gibberd, R.M. (1991). The impact of inducible phytochemicals on food selection by insect herbivores and its consequences for the distribution of grazing damage. In *Phytochemical Induction by Herbivores*, ed. D. Tallamy & M.J. Raupp. New York: Wiley, pp. 205–22.

Ellis, J.E. & Swift, D.M. (1988). Stability of African pastoral systems: alternate paradigms and implications for development. *Journal of Range Management*, **41**, 450–9.

Fahnestock, J.T. & Detling, J.K. (2002). Bison-prairie dog-plant interactions in a North American mixed-grass prairie. *Oecologia*, **132**, 86–95.

Feeney, P. (1976). Plant apparency and chemical defence. *Recent Advances in Phytochemistry*, **10**, 1–40.

Feeney, P. (1991). The evolution of chemical ecology: contributions from the study of herbivorous insects. In *Herbivores: Their Interactions with Secondary Plant Metabolites. Vol II. Ecological and Evolutionary Processes*, ed. G.A. Rosenthal & M.R. Berenbaum. San Diego, California: Academic Press, pp. 1–44.

Foley, W.J., Iason, G.R. & MacArthur, C. (1999). Role of plant secondary metabolites in the nutritional ecology of mammalian herbivores. How far have we come in 25 years? In *Nutritional Ecology of Herbivores*, ed. H.J.G. Jung & G.C. Fahey. Savoy, IL: American Society of Animal Science, pp. 130–209.

Fox, J.F. & Bryant, J.P. (1984). Instability of the snowshoe hare and woody plant interaction. *Oecologia*, **64**, 128–35.

Fraenkel, G.S. (1959). The raison d'etre of secondary plant substances. *Science*, **129**, 1466–70.

Fritz, R.S. & Simms, E.L. (eds.) (1992). *Plant Resistance to Herbivores and Pathogens: Ecology, Evolution and Genetics*. Chicago: University of Chicago Press.

Gehring, C.A. & Whitham, T.G. (1994). Interactions between aboveground herbivores and the mycorrhizal mutualists of plants. *Trends in Ecology and Evolution*, **9**, 251–5.

Gill, R.M.A. (1992a). A review of damage by mammals in north temperate forests. 1. Deer. *Forestry*, **65**, 145–69.

Gill, R.M.A. (1992b). A review of damage by mammals in north temperate forests. 3. Impact on trees and forests. *Forestry*, **65**, 363–88.

Gimingham, C.H. (1972). *Ecology of Heathlands*. London: Chapman & Hall.

Gough, L. & Grace, J.B. (1998). Herbivore effects on plant species density at varying productivity levels. *Ecology*, **79**, 1586–94.

Grace, J.B. & Tilman, D. (eds.) (1990). *Perspectives on Plant Competition*. San Diego: Academic Press.

Grant, S.A., Barthram, G.T., Lamb, W.I.C. & Milne, J.A. (1978). Effects of season and level of grazing on the utilization of heather by sheep. 1. Responses of the sward. *Journal of British Grassland Society*, **33**, 289–300.

Grant, S.A., Milne, J.A., Barthram, G.T. & Souter, W.G. (1982). Efects of season and level of grazing on the utilization of heather by sheep. III. Longer-term responses and sward recovery. *Grass and Forage Science*, **37**, 311–20.

Gray, A.J., Crawley, M.J. & Edwards, P.J. (eds.) (1986). *Colonisation, Succession and Stability*. Oxford: Blackwell Scientific Publications.

Grime, J.P. (1973). Competitive exclusion in herbaceous vegetation. *Nature*, **242**, 344–7.

Grime, J.P. (1979). *Plant Strategies and Vegetation Processes*. Chichester: John Wiley & Sons.

Grubb, P.J. (1976). The maintenance of species richness in plant communities: the importance of the regeneration niche. *Biological Reviews*, **52**, 107–45.

Hambäck, P.A. & Beckerman, A.P. (2003). Herbivory and plant resource competition: a review of two interacting interactions. *Oikos*, **101**, 26–37.

Hambäck, P.A. & Ekerholm, P. (1997). Mechanisms of apparent competition in seasonal environments: an example with vole herbivory. *Oikos*, **80**, 276–88.

Hamilton, J.G., Zangerl, A.R., DeLucia, E.H. & Berenbaum, M.R. (2001). The carbon-nutrient balance hypothesis: its rise and fall. *Ecology Letters*, **4**, 86–95.

Harper, J.L. (1977). *Population Biology of Plants*. London: Academic Press.

Hart, R.H. (2001). Plant biodiversity on shortgrass steppe after 55 years of zero, light, moderate or heavy cattle grazing. *Plant Ecology*, **155**, 111–18.

Hartvigsen, G. & McNaughton, S.J. (1995). Trade-off between height and relative growth rate in a dominant grass from the Serengeti ecosystem. *Oecologia*, **102**, 273–6.

Haukioja, E. & Koricheva, J. (2000). Tolerance to herbivory in woody vs. herbaceous plants. *Evolutionary Ecology*, **14**, 551–62.

Hawkes, C.V. & Sullivan, J.J. (2001). The impact of herbivory on plants in different resource conditions. A meta-analysis. *Ecology*, **82**, 2045–58.

Haynes, R.J. & Williams, P.H. (1993). Nutrient cycling and soil fertility in the grazed pasture ecosystem. *Advances in Agronomy*, **49**, 119–99.

Heikkilä, R. & Mikkonen, T. (1992). Effects of density of young scots pine (*Pinus sylvestris*) stand on moose (*Alces alces*) browsing. *Acta Forestalia Fennica*, **231**, 3–14.

Herms, D.A. & Mattson, W.J. (1992). The dilemma of plants: to grow or defend. *Quarterly Review of Biology*, **67**, 283–335.

Hester, A.J. & Baillie, G.J. (1998). Spatial and temporal patterns of heather use by sheep and red deer within natural heather/grass mosaics. *Journal of Applied Ecology*, **35**, 772–84.

Hester, A.J., Gimingham, C.H. & Miles, J. (1991a). Succession from heather moorland to birch woodland. III. Seed availability, germination and early growth. *Journal of Ecology*, **79**, 329–44.

Hester, A.J., Miles, J. & Gimingham, C.H. (1991b). Succession from heather moorland to birch woodland. I. Experimental alteration of specific environmental conditions in the field. *Journal of Ecology*, **79**, 303–15.

Hester, A.J., Mitchell, F.J.G. & Kirby, K.J. (1996). Effects of season and intensity of sheep grazing on tree regeneration in a British upland woodland. *Forest Ecology and Management*, **88**, 99–106.

Hester, A.J., Gordon, I.J., Baillie, G.J. & Tappin, E. (1999). Foraging behaviour of sheep and red deer within natural heather/grass mosaics. *Journal of Applied Ecology*, **36**, 133–46.

Hester, A.J., Edenius, L., Buttenshøn, R.M. & Kuiters, A.T. (2000a). Interactions between forests and herbivores: the role of controlled grazing experiments. *Forestry*, **73**, 381–91.

Hester, A.J., Stewart, F.E., Racey, P.A. & Swaine, M.D. (2000b). Can gap creation by red deer enhance the establishment of birch (*Betula pubescens*)? *Scottish Forestry*, **54**, 143–51.

Hester, A.J., Millard, P., Baillie, G.J. & Wendler, R. (2004). How does timing of browsing affect above- and below-ground growth of *Betula pendula*, *Pinus sylvestris* and *Sorbus aucuparia*? *Oikos*, **105**, 536–50.

Hester, A. J., Lempa, K. & Neuvonen, S. *et al.* (2005). Birch sapling responses to severity and timing of domestic herbivore browsing – implications for management. In *Plant Ecology, Herbivory and Human Impacts in Nordic Mountain Birch Forests*, ed. F. E. Wielgolaski. Berlin: Springer-Verlag, pp. 139–55.

Hill, M. O., Evans, D. F. & Bell, S. A. (1992). Long term effects of excluding sheep from hill pastures in north Wales. *Journal of Ecology*, **80**, 1–13.

Hjältén, J. & Palo, R. T. (1992). Selection of deciduous trees by free-ranging voles and hares in relation to plant chemistry. *Oikos*, **63**, 477–84.

Hjältén J., Danell, K. & Lundberg, P. (1993). Herbivore avoidance by association – vole and hare utilization of woody-plants. *Oikos*, **68**, 125–31.

Hobbs, N. T. (1996). Modification of ecosystems by ungulates. *Journal of Wildlife Management*, **60**, 695–713.

Hobbs, N. T. (1999). Responses of larger herbivores to spatial heterogeneity in ecosystems. In *Nutritional Ecology of Herbivores*, ed. H. G. Jung & G. C. Fahey. Proceedings of the Vth International Symposium on the Nutrition of Herbivores. Savory, Illinois: American Society of Animal Science, pp. 97–129.

Hodgson, J. & Illius, A. W. (eds). (1996). *The Ecology and Management of Grazing Systems*. Wallingford: CAB International.

Holland, E. A. & Detling, J. K. (1990). Plant response to herbivory and below-ground nitrogen cycling. *Ecology*, **71**, 1040–9.

Holling, C. S. (1992). Cross-scale morphology, geometry and dynamics of ecosystems. *Ecological Monographs*, **62**, 447–502.

Holt, R. D. (1977). Predation, apparent competition, and the structure of prey communities. *Theoretical Population Biology*, **12**, 197–229.

Holt, R. D. & Lawton, J. H. (1994). The ecological consequences of shared natural enemies. *Annual Review of Ecology and Systematics*, **25**, 495–520.

Honkanen, T., Haukioja, E. & Kitunen, V. (1999). Responses of *Pinus sylvestris* branches to simulated herbivory are modified by tree sink/source dynamics and by external resources. *Functional Ecology*, **13**, 126–40.

Huntly, N. J. (1991). Herbivores and the dynamics of communities and ecosystems. *Annual Review of Ecology and Systematics*, **22**, 477–503.

Husheer, S. W., Coomes, D. A. & Robertson, A. W. (2003). Long-term influences of introduced deer on the composition and structure of New Zealand *Nothofagus* forests. *Forest Ecology and Management*, **181**, 99–117.

Hutchings, M. J. (1997). The structure of plant populations. In *Plant Ecology*, 2nd edn, ed. M. J. Crawley. Oxford: Blackwell Science, pp. 325–58.

Iason G. R & Van Wieren S. E. (1999). Digestive and ingestive adaptations of mammalian herbivores to low quality forage. In *Herbivores: Between Plants and Predators*, ed. H. Olff, V. K. Brown & R. H. Drent. 38th Symposium of the British Ecological Society. Oxford: Blackwell Scientific Publications, pp. 337–69.

Illius, A. W. & O'Connor, T. G. (1999). On the relevance of nonequilibrium concepts to arid and semi-arid grazing systems. *Ecological Applications*, **9**, 798–813.

Jaindl, R. G., Doescher, P., Miller, R. F. & Eddleman, L. E. (1994). Persistence of idaho fescue on degraded rangelands – adaptation to defoliation or tolerance. *Journal of Range Management*, **47**, 54–9.

Jefferies, R.L., Klein, D.R. & Shaver, G.R. (1994). Vertebrate herbivores and northern plant communities – reciprocal influences and response. *Oikos*, **71**, 193–206.

Juenger, T. & Bergelson, J. (1997). Pollen and resource limitation of compensation to herbivory in scarlet gilia, *Ipomopsis aggregata*. *Ecology*, **78**, 1684–95.

Juenger, T. & Bergelson, J. (2000). The evolution of compensation to herbivory in scarlet gilia, *Ipomopsis aggregata*: herbivore-imposed natural selection and the quantitative genetics of tolerance. *Evolution*, **54**, 764–77.

Juntheikki, M.R. (1996). Comparison of tannin-binding proteins in saliva of Scandinavian and North American moose (*Alces alces*). *Biochemical Systematics and Ecology*, **24**, 595–601.

Karban, R. & Baldwin I.T. (1997). *Induced Responses to Herbivory*. Chicago: University of Chicago Press.

Karban, R., Agrawal, A.A., Thaler, J.S & Adler, L.S. (1999). Induced plant responses and information content about risk of herbivory. *Trends in Ecology and Evolution*, **14**, 443–7.

Kirby, K.J. (2003). What might a British forest-landscape driven by large herbivores look like? *English Nature Research Reports*, **530**, 1–51.

Koricheva, J. (2002). The carbon-nutrient balance hypothesis is dead; long live the carbon-nutrient balance hypothesis? *Oikos*, **98**, 537–9.

Koricheva, J., Larsson, S., Haukioja, E. & Keinanen, M. (1998). Regulation of woody plant secondary metabolism by resource availability: hypothesis testing by means of meta-analysis. *Oikos*, **83**, 212–26.

Kotanen, P.M. & Rosenthal, J.P. (2000). Tolerating herbivory: does the plant care if the herbivore has a backbone? *Evolutionary Ecology*, **14**, 537 49.

Kozlowski, T.T. (1971). *Growth and Development of Trees*, vol. 1. New York: Academic Press.

Langer, R.H.M. (1956). Growth and nutrition of timothy (*Phleum pratense*). I. The life-history of individual tillers. *Annals of Applied Biology*, **44**, 166–87.

Laws, R.M., Parker, I.S.C. & Johnstone, R.C.B. (1975). *Elephants and their Habitat*. Oxford: Clarendon Press.

Ledig, F.T. (1992). Human impacts on genetic diversity in forest ecosystems. *Oikos*, **63**, 87–108.

Lemaire, G. & Chapman, D. (1996). Tissue flows in grazed plant communities. In *The Ecology and Management of Grazing Systems*, ed. J. Hodgson & A.W. Illius. Wallingford: CAB International, pp. 3–36.

Lerdau, M. & Coley P.D. (2002). Benefits of the carbon-nutrient balance hypothesis. *Oikos*, **98**, 534–6.

Lindroth, R.L., Osier, T.L., Barnhill, H.R.H. & Wood, S.A. (2002). Effects of genotype and nutrient availability on phytochemistry of trembling aspen (*Populus tremuloides* Michx.) during leaf senescence. *Biochemical Systematics and Ecology*, **30**, 297–307.

Louda, S.M., Keeler, K.H. & Holt, R.D. (1990). Herbivore influences on plant performance and competitive interactions. In *Perspectives on Plant Competition*, ed. J.B. Grace & D. Tilman. New York: Academic Press, pp. 413–44.

Löyttyniemi, K. (1985). On repeated browsing of Scots pine saplings by moose (*Alces alces*). *Silva Fennica*, **19**, 387–91.

McArthur C., Robbins, C.T., Hagerman, A.E. & Hanley, T.A. (1993). Diet selection by a ruminant generalist browser in relation to plant chemistry. *Canadian Journal of Zoology*, **71**, 2236–43.

MacLennan, A.S. (1979). Soil Erosion in Strathconon, Central Ross, with Special Reference to the Effects of Animal Grazing and Trampling. Ph.D. thesis, University of Aberdeen, UK.

McNaughton, S.J. (1978). Serengeti ungulates; feeding selectivity influences the effectiveness of plant defense guilds. *Science*, **199**, 806–7.

McNaughton, S.J. (1979a). Grazing as an optimization process: grass-ungulate relationships in the Serengeti. *American Naturalist*, **113**, 691–703.

McNaughton, S.J. (1979b). Grassland-herbivore dynamics. In *Serengeti: Dynamics of an Ecosystem*, ed. A.R.E. Sinclair & M. Northon-Griffiths. Chicago: Chicago University Press. pp. 46–81.

McNaughton, S.J. (1983). Compensatory growth as a response to herbivory. *Oikos*, **40**, 329–36.

McNaughton, S.J. Banyikwa, F.F. & McNaughton, M.M. (1998). Root biomass and productivity in a grazing ecosystem: the Serengeti. *Ecology*, **79**, 587–92.

Meikle, A., Paterson, S., Finch, R.P., Marshall, G. & Waterhouse, A. (1999). Genetic characterisation of heather (*Calluna vulgaris* (L.) Hull) subject to different management regimes across Great Britain. *Molecular Ecology*, **8**, 2037–47.

Messina, F.J., Durham, S.L., Richards, J.H. & McArthur, E.D. (2002). Trade-offs between plant growth and defense? A comparison of sagebrush populations. *Oecologia* **131**, 43–51.

Meyer, G.A. & Root, R.B. (1993). Effects of herbivorous insects and soil fertility on reproduction of goldenrod. *Ecology*, **74**, 1117–28.

Milchunas, D.G. & Noy-Meir, I. (2002). Grazing refuges, external avoidance of herbivory and plant diversity. *Oikos*, **99**, 113–30.

Milchunas, D.G., Lauenroth, W.K. & Chapman, P.L. (1992). Plant competition, abiotic, and long term and short term effects of large herbivores on demography of opportunistic species in a semi-arid grassland. *Oecologia*, **92**, 520–31.

Milchunas, D.G., Lauenroth, W.K. & Burke, I.C. (1998). Livestock grazing: animal and plant biodiversity of shortgrass steppe and the relationship to ecosystem function. *Oikos*, **83**, 65–74.

Milewski, A.V., Young, T.P. & Madden, D. (1991). Thorns as induced defences: experimental evidence. *Oecologia*, **86**, 70–5.

Miles, J. (1973). Natural recolonisation of experimentally bared soil in Callunetum in north-east Scotland. *Journal of Ecology*, **61**, 399–412.

Miles, J. (1979). *Vegetation Dynamics*. London: Chapman & Hall.

Miles, J. (1985). The pedogenic effects of different species and vegetation types and the implications of succession. *Journal of Soil Science*, **36**, 571–84.

Miles, J. (1988). Vegetation and soil change in the uplands. In *Ecological Change in the Uplands*, ed. M.B. Usher & D.B.A. Thompson. Oxford: Blackwell Scientific Publications, pp. 57–70.

Miles, J. & Kinnaird, J.W. (1979). The establishment and regeneration of birch, juniper and Scots pine in the Scottish Highlands. *Scottish Forestry*, **33**, 102–19.

Millard, P., Hester, A.J., Wendler, R. & Baillie, G. (2001). Remobilization of nitrogen and the recovery of *Betula pendula, Pinus sylvestris*, and *Sorbus aucuparia* saplings after simulated browsing damage. *Functional Ecology*, **15**, 535–43.

Miller, G.R., Kinnaird, J.W. & Cummins, R.P. (1982). Liability of saplings to browsing on a red deer range in the Scottish Highlands. *Journal of Applied Ecology*, **19**, 941–51.

Milne, J.A., Birch, C.P.D., Hester, A.J., Armstrong, H. & Robertson, A. (1998). The impact of vertebrate herbivores on the natural heritage of the Scottish uplands – a review. *Scottish Natural Heritage Reviews*, (SNH, Edinburgh) **95**, 1–127.

Mitlacher, K., Poschlod, P., Rosen, E. & Bakker, J.P. (2002). Restoration of wooded meadows – a comparative analysis along a chronosequence on Oland (Sweden). *Applied Vegetation Science*, **5**, 63–73.

Mole, S., Butler, L.G. & Iason, G.R. (1990). Defense against dietary tannin in herbivores: a survey for proline rich salivary proteins in mammals. *Biochemical Systematics and Ecology*, **18**, 287–93.

Moorby J. & Waring, P.F. (1963). Aging in woody plants. *Annals of Botany*, **27**, 291–309.

Myers, J.H. & Bazeley, D. (1991). Thorns, spines, prickles and hairs: are they stimulated by herbivory and do they deter herbivores? In *Phytochemical Induction by Herbivores*, ed. D.J. Tallamy & M.J. Raupp. New York: Academic Press, pp. 326–43.

Nitao, J.K., Zangerl, A.R., Berenbaum, M.R., Hamilton, J.G. & DeLucia, E.H. (2002). CNB: requiescat in pace? *Oikos*, **98**, 540–546.

Oba, G., Vetaas, O.R. & Stenseth, N.C. (2001). Relationships between biomass and plant species richness in arid zone grazing lands. *Journal of Applied Ecology*, **38**, 836–45.

Olff, H. & Ritchie, M.E. (1998). Effects of herbivores on grassland plant diversity. *Trends in Ecology and Evolution*, **13**, 261–5.

Olff, H., Vera, F.W.M., Bokdam, J. et al. (1999). Shifting mosaics in grazed woodlands driven by the alternation of plant facilitation and competition. *Plant Biology*, **1**, 127–37.

Olff, H., Ritchie, M.E. & Prinz, H.H.T. (2002). Global environmental controls of diversity in large herbivores. *Nature*, **415**, 901–4.

Olofsson, J., Moen, J. & Oksanen, L. (2002). Effects of herbivory on competition intensity in two arctic-alpine tundra communities with different productivity. *Oikos*, **96**, 265–72.

Oom, S. (2002). Spatial Pattern and Process in Fragmenting Heather Moorland. Ph.D. thesis, University of Aberdeen, UK.

Oom, S. & Hester, A.J. (1999). Heather utilization along paths by red deer and sheep in a natural heather/grass mosaic. *Botanical Journal of Scotland*, **51**, 23–38.

Oom, S.P., Hester, A.J., Elston, D.A. & Legg, C.J. (2002). Spatial interaction models: from human geography to plant-herbivore interactions. *Oikos*, **98**, 65–74.

Pacala, S.W. & Crawley, M.J. (1992). Herbivores and plant diversity. *American Naturalist*, **140**, 243–60.

Paige, K. N. (1992). The effects of fire on scarlet gilia: an alternative selection pressure to herbivory? *Oecologia*, **92**, 229–35.

Paige, K. N. (1994). Herbivory and *Ipomopsis aggregata*: differences in response, differences in experimental protocol: a reply to Bergelson and Crawley. *American Naturalist*, **143**, 739–49.

Paige, K. N. (1999). Regrowth following ungulate herbivory in *Ipomopsis aggregata*: geographic evidence for overcompensation. *Oecologia*, **118**, 316–23.

Paige, K. N. & Whitham, T. G. (1987). Overcompensation in response to mammalian herbivory: the advantage of being eaten. *American Naturalist*, **129**, 407–16.

Paige, K. N., Williams, B. & Hickox, T. (2001). Overcompensation through the paternal component of fitness in *Ipomopsis arizonica*. *Oecologia*, **128**, 72–6.

Pakeman, R. J., Attwood, J. P. & Engelen, J. (1998). Sources of plants colonising experimentally disturbed patches in an acidic grassland, in eastern England. *Journal of Ecology*, **86**, 1032–41.

Pakeman, J. P., Digneffe, G. & Small, J. L. (2002). Ecological correlates of endozoochory by herbivores. *Functional Ecology*, **16**, 296–304.

Palmer, S. C. F. (1997). Prediction of the shoot production of heather under grazing in the uplands of Great Britain. *Grass and Forage Science*, **52**, 408–24.

Palmer, S. C. F., Hester, A. J., Elston, D., Gordon, I. J. & Hartley, S. E. (2003). The perils of having tasty neighbours. *Ecology*, **84**, 2877–90.

Palo, R. T. & Robbins, C. T. (eds.) (1991). *Plant Defenses Against Mammalian Herbivory*. Boca Raton: CRC Press, Inc.

Pass D. M., Foley W. J. & Bowden B. (1998). Vertebrate herbivory on *Eucalyptus* – Identification of specific feeding deterrents for common ringtail possums (*Pseudocheirus peregrinus*) by bioassay-guided fractionation of *Eucalyptus ovata* foliage. *Journal of Chemical Ecology*, **24**, 1513–27.

Pastor, J. & Naiman, R. J. (1992). Selective foraging and ecosystem processes in boreal forests. *American Naturalist*, **139**, 690–705.

Pamo, E. T. & Chamba, M. N. (2001). Elephants and vegetation change in the Sahelo-Soudanian region of Cameroon. *Journal of Arid Environments*, **48**, 243–53.

Persson, I.-L. Danell, K. & Bergström, R. (2000). Disturbance by large herbivores in boreal forests with special reference to moose. *Annales Zoologici Fennici*, **37**, 251–63.

Pickup, G., Bastin, G. N. & Chewings, V. H. (1998). Identifying trends in land degradation in non-equilibrium rangelands. *Journal of Applied Ecology*, **35**, 365–77.

Pigott, C. D. (1985). Selective damage to tree-seedlings by bank voles (*Clethrionomys glareolus*). *Oecologia*, **67**, 367–71.

Price, P. W. (1991). The plant vigour hypothesis and herbivore attack. *Oikos*, **62**, 244–51.

Prieur-Richard, A. H., Lavorel, S., Linhart, Y. B. & Dos Santos, A. (2002). Plant diversity, herbivory and resistance of a plant community to invasion in Mediterranean annual communities. *Oecologia*, **130**, 96–104.

Proulx, M. & Mazumder, A. (1998). Reversal of grazing impact on plant species richness in nutrient-poor vs. nutrient-rich ecosystems. *Ecology*, **79**, 2581–92.

Raupp, M.J. & Sadof, C.S. (1991). Responses of leaf beetles to injury-related changes in their salicaceous hosts. In *Phytochemical Induction by Herbivores*, ed. D. Tallamy & M.J.Raupp. New York: Wiley, pp. 183–204.

Raven, P.H., Evert, R.F. & Eichhorn, S.E. (1992). *Biology of Plants*. New York: Worth Publishers.

Reardon, P.O., Leinweber, C.L. & Merrill, L.B. (1974). Response of Sideoats grama to animal saliva and thiamine and bovine saliva. *Journal of Range Management*, **27**, 400–1.

Reimoser, F., Armstrong, H. & Suchant, R. (1999). Measuring forest damage of ungulates: what should be considered. *Forest Ecology and Management*, **120**, 47–58.

Reinhardt, D. & Kuhlemeier, C. (2002). Plant arctitecture. *EMBO Reports*, **3**, 846–51.

Rhoades, D.F. (1979). The evolution of plant chemical defense against herbivores. In *Herbivores: Their Interaction with Secondary Plant Metabolites*, ed. G.A. Rosenthal & D.H. Janzen. New York: Academic Press, pp. 1–55.

Rhoades, D.F. & Cates, R.G. (1976). Towards a general theory of plant antiherbivore chemistry. *Recent Advances in Phytochemistry*, **10**, 168–213.

Richards, J.H. (1993). Physiology of plants recovering from defoliation. In *Grasslands for our World*, ed. M.J. Baker. Proceedings of the XVII International Grassland Congress. Wellington: SIR Publishing, pp. 85–94.

Rietkerk, M., Ketner, P., Burger, J., Hoorens, B. & Olff, H. (2000). Multiscale soil and vegetation patchiness along a gradient of herbivore impact in a semi-arid grazing system in West Africa. *Plant Ecology*, **148**, 207–24.

Ritchie, M.E. & Olff, H. (1999). Spatial scaling laws yield a synthetic theory of biodiversity. *Nature*, **400**, 557–60.

Rooke, T. (2003). Growth responses of a woody species to clipping and goat saliva. *African Journal of Ecology*, **41**, 324–8.

Rosenthal, G.A. & Janzen, D.H. (1979). *Herbivores: Their Interaction with Plant Secondary Metabolites*. New York: Academic Press.

Rosenthal, J.P. & Kotanen, P.M. (1994). Terrestrial plant tolerance to herbivory. *Trends in Ecology and Evolution*, **9**, 145–8.

Rossow, L.J., Bryant, J.P. & Kielland, K. (1997). Effects of above-ground browsing by mammals on mycorrhizal infection in an early successional taiga ecosystem. *Oecologia*, **110**, 94–8.

Ruess, R.W., Hendrick, R.L. & Bryant, J.P. (1998). Regulation of fine root dynamics by mammalian browsers in early successional Alaskan taiga forests. *Ecology*, **79**, 2706–20.

Ryerson, D.E. & Parmenter, R.R. (2001). Vegetation change following removal of keystone herbivores from desert grasslands in New Mexico. *Journal of Vegetation Science*, **12**, 167–80.

Schittko, U. & Baldwin, I.T. (2003). Constraints to herbivore-induced systemic responses: bi-directional signalling along orthostichies in *Nicotiana attenuata*. *Journal of Chemical Ecology*, **29**, 763–70.

Senft, R.L., Cougenhour, M.B., Bailey, D.W. *et al.* (1987). Large herbivore foraging and ecological heirarchies. *Bioscience*, **37**, 789–99.

Senn, J. & Haukioja, E. (1994). Reactions of the mountain birch to bud removal: effects of severity and timing, and implications for herbivores. *Functional Ecology*, **8**, 494–501.

Simon, J., Bosch, M., Molero, J. & Blanche, C. (2001). Conservation biology of the Pyrenean larkspur (*Delphinium montanum*): a case of conflict of plant versus animal conservation? *Biological Conservation*, **98**, 305–14.

Smit, R., Bokdam, J., den Ouden, J. *et al.* (2001). Effects of introduction and exclusion of large herbivores on small rodent communities. *Plant Ecology*, **155**, 119–27.

Smith, R.S., Shiel, R.S., Millward, D. & Corkhill, P. (2000). The interactive effects of management on the productivity and plant community structure of an upland meadow: an 8 year field trial. *Journal of Applied Ecology*, **37**, 1029–43.

Spalinger, D.E. & Hobbs, N.T. (1992). Mechanisms of foraging in mammalian herbivores: new models of functional response. *American Naturalist*, **140**, 325–48.

Staines, B.W. (1977). Factors affecting the seasonal distribution of red deer (*Cervus elaphus*) at Glen Dye, north-east Scotland. *Annals of Applied Biology*, **87**, 495–512.

Stamp, N. (2003). Out of the quagmire of plant defense hypotheses. *Quarterly Review of Biology*, **78**, 23–55.

Stohlgren, T.J., Schell, L.D. & van den Heuvel, B. (1999). How grazing and soil quality affect native and exotic plant diversity in rocky mountain grasslands. *Ecological Applications*, **9**, 45–64.

Strauss, S.Y. (1991). Indirect effects in community ecology: their definition, study and importance. *Trends in Ecology and Evolution*, **6**, 206–10.

Strauss, S.Y. & Agrawal, A.A. (1999). The ecology and evolution of plant tolerance to herbivory. *Trends in Ecology and Evolution*, **14**, 179–85.

Strauss, S.Y., Rudgers, J.A., Lau, J.A. & Irwin, R.E. (2002). Direct and ecological costs of resistance to herbivory. *Trends in Ecology and Evolution*, **17**, 278–81.

Tafangenyasha, C. (2001). Decline of the mountain acacia, *Brachystegia glaucescens* in Gonarezhou National Park, southeast Zimbabwe. *Journal of Environmental Management*, **63**, 37–50.

Tainton, N.M., Morris, C.D. & Hardy, M.B. (1996). Complexity and stability in grazing systems. In *The Ecology and Management of Grazing Systems*, ed. J. Hodgson & A.W. Illius. Wallingford: CAB International, pp. 275–300.

Thomas, M.A., Carrera, A.D. & Poverene, M. (2000). Is there any genetic differentiation among populations of *Piptochaetium napostaense* (Speg.) Hack (Poaceae) with different grazing histories? *Plant Ecology*, **147**, 227–35.

Thompson, D.B.A., Hester, A.J. & Usher, M.B. (eds.) (1995). *Heaths and Moorland: Cultural Landscapes*. Edinburgh: HMSO.

Thompson, K., Grime, J.P. & Mason, G. (1977). Seed germination in response to diurnal fluctuations in temperature. *Nature*, **267**, 147–9.

Tikkanen, O.-P., Rousi, M., Ylioja, T. & Roininen, H. (2003). No negative correlation between growth and resistance to multiple herbivory in a deciduous tree, *Betula pendula*. *Forest Ecology and Management*, **177**, 587–92.

Tilman, D. (1988). *Plant Strategies and the Dynamics and Structure of Plant Communities*. Princeton: Princeton University Press.

Tilman, D. (1994). Competition and biodiversity in spatially structured habitats. *Ecology*, **75**, 2–16.

van der Meijden, E., Wijn, M. & Verkaar, H.J. (1988). Defence and regrowth, alternative plant strategies in the struggle against herbivores. *Oikos*, **51**, 355–63.

Vare, H., Ohtonen, R. & Mikkola, K. (1996). The effect and extent of heavy grazing by reindeer on young sitka spruce trees in western Scotland. 1. Damage rates and the influence of habitat factors. *Forestry*, **64**, 61–82.

Virtanen, R., Edwards, G.R. & Crawley, M.J. (2002). Red deer management and vegetation on the Isle of Rum. *Journal of Applied Ecology*, **39**, 572–83.

Wallis de Vries, M.F., Laca, E.A. & Diemont, M.W. (1999). The importance of scale of patchiness for selectivity in grazing herbivores. *Oecologia*, **121**, 355–63.

Ward, D. & Young, T.P. (2002). Effects of large mammalian herbivores and ant symbionts on condensed tannins of *Acacia drepanolobium* in Kenya. *Journal of Chemical Ecology*, **28**, 913–29.

Welch, D. (1985). Studies in the grazing of heather moorland in north-east Scotland. IV. Seed dispersal and plant establishment in dung. *Journal of Applied Ecology*, **22**, 461–72.

Welch, D. (1986). Studies in the grazing of heather moorland in north-east Scotland. V. Trends in *Nardus stricta* and other unpalatable graminoids. *Journal of Applied Ecology*, **23**, 1047–58.

White, T.C.R. (1993). *The Inadequate Environment. Nitrogen and the Abundance of Animals*. Berlin: Springer-Verlag.

Wilmshurst, J.F., Fryxell, J.M., Farm, B.P., Sinclair, A.R.E. & Henschel, C.P. (1999). Spatial distribution of Serengeti wildebeest in relation to resources. *Canadian Journal of Zoology*, **77**, 1223–32.

Young, T.P. & Okello, B.D. (1998). Relaxation of an induced defence after exclusion of herbivores: spines on *Acacia drepanolobium*. *Oecologia*, **111**, 508–13.

Zangerl, A. (2003). Evolution of induced plant responses to herbivores. *Basic and Applied Ecology*, **4**, 91–103.

Long-term effects of herbivory on plant diversity and functional types in arid ecosystems

DAVID WARD

INTRODUCTION

There is a widely held belief that abiotic factors outweigh biotic factors in arid ecosystems, and that herbivory by mammals is relatively unimportant in ecosystem functioning and biodiversity maintenance (reviewed by Noy-Meir 1973). The over-riding importance of abiotic factors in arid regions is ascribed to the high temporal and spatial variation in rainfall. Indeed, changes in plant species composition in arid and semi-arid regions of Africa and Asia as a consequence of grazing are positively correlated with mean annual rainfall (Milchunas & Lauenroth 1993, Ward 2004). There is a strong negative correlation between the coefficient of variation in mean annual rainfall among years and median annual rainfall of arid regions (Ward 2001, 2004). Similarly, spatial variation in rainfall is high and is not correlated with distance among stations (Ward 2001, Ward *et al.* 2000, 2004). This high variability in rainfall results in high spatio-temporal variability in plant abundance and availability to herbivores. For example, Ward *et al.* (2000) showed that, in the Negev desert of Israel, only 1% of plant species were present in their permanent plots in all years and approximately half the plant species were found once only in ten years. Spatial variation in forage availability is also enormous (see e.g. Fig. 5.1) and most plants may be restricted to ephemeral water courses (so-called *contracted vegetation*) (Whittaker 1975) in some arid regions. Furthermore, geological substrates vary considerably among arid regions, particularly in their nutrient status and distribution, as well as in their

Large Herbivore Ecology, Ecosystem Dynamics and Conservation, ed. K. Danell, P. Duncan, R. Bergström & J. Pastor. Published by Cambridge University Press. © Cambridge University Press 2006.

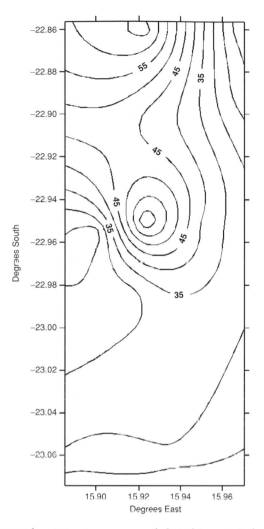

Figure 5.1. Spatial variation in recommended stocking rate in large stock units (~450 kg cow) per hectare over 32 000 ha in an arid region (mean annual rainfall = 80–120 mm) of Namibia in 1997–98. Grass biomass was calculated monthly at 14 stations situated approximately evenly over the ranching area. Recommended stocking rate was then calculated by dividing grass biomass by the mean amount of grass consumed by a 450 kg cow (3% of body mass per day) per annum (from Ward *et al.* 2003).

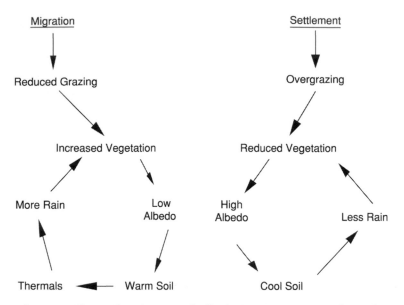

Figure 5.2. Plant-soil-environment feedbacks in migratory (nomadic) and settlement-based African grazing systems. From Sinclair and Fryxell (1985).

water retention capacities. This leads to considerable differences in plant composition and nutritional quality among habitats (Stafford Smith & Morton 1990, Ward & Olsvig-Whittaker 1993, Ward *et al.* 1993, Ward 2004). The high spatio-temporal variability in the availability of plants to herbivores necessarily limits the numbers of herbivores that can be sustained in arid ecosystems, which is considered to limit their impacts on plant resources.

The above-mentioned claims contrast strongly with claims that heavy grazing has caused land denudation and desertification of the Sahel of Africa and in other regions. This land denudation has been claimed to have resulted in a negative feedback loop via decreased soil nutrient status and increased soil albedo (caused by lower vegetation cover), thereby causing increased evaporation and decreased precipitation, which in turn reduces the stocking capacity, further exacerbating the negative effects of grazing (Sinclair & Fryxell 1985, Schlesinger *et al.* 1990, Fig. 5.2). These studies, which are based on changes in vegetation recorded by satellite photographs of large geographic regions, have been criticized because they focus heavily on biomass removal (as indicated by changes in Normalized Difference Vegetation Indices (NDVI)) rather than on changes in diversity, species composition and nutritional quality of vegetation. Changes in vegetation density may be confounded with the effects of natural climatic variation (or even man-induced global climatic change) on vegetation density. Pickup and Chewings (1994) stress that remote-sensing studies need to focus on vegetation recovery by the end of the wet season because dry season estimates may indicate short-term and trivial effects of consumption but may say little or nothing about whether long-term vegetation change and/or degradation is occurring. Additionally, Saltz *et al.* (1999) have demonstrated that the reliability of NDVI is low in arid systems where reflectance from the large bare soil surfaces creates considerable vegetation density artifacts (dependent on soil type).

LONG-TERM STUDIES OF EFFECTS OF LARGE MAMMALS ON ARID VEGETATION

What do field-based studies of the effects of herbivory by large mammals tell us about the effects of large mammals on vegetation of arid zones? Several modelling studies have shown that vegetation change as a result of herbivory may be a slow process in arid ecosystems because of the high inter-annual variation in precipitation and, consequently, variation in plant presence and abundance (Wiegand & Milton 1996, Weber *et al.* 2003). Hence, longer-term studies need to be considered when assessing the impact of herbivory in arid-zone vegetation. Although the list below is not intended to be exhaustive, such studies show inconsistent patterns in vegetation response to mammalian herbivory:

(1) Goldberg and Turner (1986) analysed vegetation changes in nine permanent 100 m^2 plots first established in 1906 near Tucson, Arizona (mean annual rainfall = 250mm). These plots were fenced to exclude large herbivores in 1906 and were examined periodically until 1978. There were no consistent, directional changes in vegetation composition between 1906 and 1978, despite large fluctuations in absolute cover and density of the species. For most species, and in most plots, the changes in absolute cover and density appear to have been a response to sequences of either exceptionally wet years or exceptionally dry years. Only two species, *Krameria grayi* and *Janusia gracilis*, appeared to increase more or less continuously over the study period – the former species is reported to be very palatable to livestock. A study comparing vegetation inside and outside of the above-mentioned fenced areas

following 50 years of protection showed that total plant density was significantly higher within the fenced areas. However, there were no strong differences in the composition of the vegetation (Blydenstein *et al.* 1957).

(2) Ward *et al.* (1998a, 2000) and Saltz *et al.* (1999) examined the effects of reintroduced (in 1983) Asiatic wild asses, *Equus hemionus onager*, in 11 pairs of permanent plots in the central Negev desert of Israel (mean annual rainfall = 56 mm) from 1992–97. There has been considerable concern that the reintroduction of such a large equid (~200 kg) can cause habitat degradation through heavy grazing because:

    (i) large, hindgut fermenters are dependent on processing large quantities of low quality forage. Their ability to survive on low quality forage indicates that poor habitat conditions caused by environmental fluctuations and their heavy grazing would have little impact on their survival;

    (ii) an ungulate of this size is expected to show density-dependent responses only when the population approaches *K* (= high inflection point in the logistic curve) (Fowler 1988).

    (iii) the long gestation period creates the potential for a delayed response to environmental conditions, which will produce cycling dynamics (Saltz 2001).

Hence, the asses could potentially degrade the habitat before they suffer the consequences in terms of reduced fitness (Saltz 2001). We found that fenced plots (wild asses excluded) had significantly higher plant cover than unfenced plots when differences in rainfall among plots were accounted for, although there were no significant differences in plant species richness, diversity or dominance between fenced and unfenced plots. Three plant species showed significant increases in percentage cover in the fenced plots, and one species significantly increased in cover in the unfenced plots. Eight plant species invaded the fenced plots, three species invaded the unfenced plots and one species disappeared from the unfenced plots during the study. Unfenced plots showed a directional change away from their original species composition (although richness and diversity remained the same) while vegetation in fenced plots did not change over the period (Ward *et al.* 2000). These results indicate that herbivory by asses is causing a change in the relative abundance of certain species (unfenced plots) and that competitive effects in the protected plots have not occurred or are not strong enough to cause a change in species composition when plants are protected from grazing. However, I note that species composition changes were generally underwhelming (Ward *et al.* 2000, Ward 2001).

(3) Ward and Saltz (1994), Ward *et al.* (1997, 2000), Saltz and Ward (1999), Ruiz *et al.* (2002a, b) studied the interactions between the dorcas gazelle, *Gazella dorcas*, and the desert lily, *Pancratium sickenbergeri*, in sand dunes in the central Negev desert from 1990 to 2002. Gazelles dig in the sand to remove all or part of the bulbs of the lilies during the dry summer months, while in the winter months they consume the leaves (leaves are not present on the sand surface during the summer) and in October–December they consume virtually all flowers when available – flowers have a 1:30000 chance of surviving (Saltz & Ward 2000). We found that the gazelles entirely consume about 5% of the plants per annum, but may eat part of 50%–60% of plants each year. Lily populations enclosed in 1994 now have about twice as many plants as populations outside the enclosures (478 ± 159 vs. 255 ± 52 plants per 225 m^2 plot), indicating a significant negative impact of herbivory. Due to the almost complete removal of all flowers by the gazelles (and absence of vegetative reproduction in this species), the lily populations in the dunes can only be maintained by seed dispersal from source populations outside the dunes where gazelles are rare or absent (due to low lily densities in the compact loess substrate).

We found that there is strong selection on lilies to minimize the effects of gazelle herbivory: lilies that have their bulbs partially consumed in one year are less likely to produce flowers and produce fewer, smaller leaves in the following season. Ward and Saltz (1994) found that the gazelles select lilies according to their size in a manner consistent with an optimal foraging model. We found that the lilies grow their bulbs down deeper into the sand (pulling them down with contractile roots) to minimize the effects of herbivory in populations where gazelles are common but have bulbs under the surface in populations where gazelles are absent (Ward *et al.* 1997). Lilies protect their leaves with calcium oxalate crystals (called 'raphides') – gazelles eat only the unprotected tips. Lily populations where gazelles are common have more crystals in their leaves than where gazelles are absent (Ward *et al.* 1997). This was the first study to demonstrate that calcium oxalate is produced in leaves to protect them against herbivory – raphides in geophytes had previously been assumed to have developed as a consequence of excessive calcium uptake from the soil. The close coevolution of the gazelle (optimal foraging behaviour, avoidance of chemically defended parts of leaves) and the lily (evolution of deeper bulbs and chemical investment in leaves) indicates that strong biotic interactions between herbivore and plant can and do develop in arid regions in spite of the great impact of abiotic factors on plant populations.

(4) Ward *et al.* (1998b) compared the diversity of plants in a communal ranch at Otjimbingwe in Namibia (mean annual rainfall = 165 mm) that had been heavily grazed for at least 150 years with that of several surrounding commercial cattle and sheep ranches where mean stocking density was about ten times lower. No significant difference in diversity, plant species richness or soil quality was found. However, within the 117 000 ha communal ranch, vegetation around water points that had been in use for 150 years was more degraded than vegetation near water points that had only been in use for about ten years. This indicates that herbivores can have strong negative impacts on vegetation of deserts but that such impacts may take a very long time to manifest themselves.

(5) In a large-scale study in Namibia at 31 sites along a rainfall gradient from 100 to 450 mm per annum, there was no correlation between the residuals of grass production (regressed against mean annual rainfall) and stocking density either in the current season or when averaged over the past 11 years (Ward & Ngairorue 2000). However, when we compared data along the same gradient between 1939 and 1997, grass production in 1997 was approximately 50% lower than in the earlier period (Ward & Ngairorue 2000). This is yet another example of the longer-term impact of herbivory in such systems.

(6) It has been reported in many arid ecosystems that annual species replace perennials following heavy grazing, owing to their ability to invade open spaces quickly and utilize soil resources (e.g. Kelly & Walker 1977, Cheal 1993, Freeman & Emlen 1995). Perennials are always present and thus are permanently available to browsers. The transient nature of the annual lifestyle means that herbivores are less likely to encounter them and, thus, they increase in abundance while perennials decrease with grazing. However, in a

study of permanent plots from 1989 to 1996 in Namaqualand, South Africa (mean annual rainfall = 76 mm), Milton and Dean (2000) found that reduction of perennial grasses by cattle grazing favoured annual plants in wet years only. Dry conditions prohibited the establishment of annual plants regardless of whether perennial grasses were present or not. This pattern has also been reported by Van Rooyen *et al.* (1991) and Jeltsch *et al.* (1997) in the Kalahari desert, South Africa. Similarly, in a long-term study in a Chihuahuan desert site in southeastern Arizona, North America, Kelt and Valone (1995) found that the removal of herbivores (cattle) had little impact on the abundance and diversity of annual plants. Historical effects of grazing may cloud our ability to detect differences in the effects of herbivory on perennial and annual plants. For example, Jauffret and Lavorel (2003) were unable to detect decreases in perennial grasses in heavily grazed regions of arid Tunisian steppe vegetation and ascribed this to the near or complete elimination of these species over thousands of years of heavy grazing. This heavy grazing has left Tunisian ecosystems with a homogenized flora consisting only of species that are highly tolerant of herbivory and other forms of disturbance. In such instances, we might not expect to see changes in dominance of different life history forms with changes in grazing pressure.

OSCILLATIONS OF VEGETATION AND HERBIVORE POPULATIONS

Researchers have become increasingly aware in recent years that arid grazing ecosystems are non-equilibrial, event-driven systems (see e.g. Westoby 1980, O'Connor 1985, Milchunas *et al.* 1988, 1989, Venter *et al.* 1989, Hoffman & Cowling 1990). Ellis and Swift (1988) contend that rainfall in arid regions is the major driving variable and has the ability to 'recharge' a system that suffers heavy grazing pressure. This can lead to oscillations of herbivore and plant populations, as envisaged for the arid Turkana region of Kenya by Ellis and Swift (1988) (Fig. 5.3). Indeed, it has been claimed that where pastoralists are able to maintain their activities on a large spatial scale by migrating to areas where key rich resources can be exploited, allowing previously used resources time to recover, negative density-dependent effects of grazing on plant biodiversity do not develop (Sinclair & Fryxell 1985, Ellis & Swift 1988, Behnke & Abel 1996). Illius

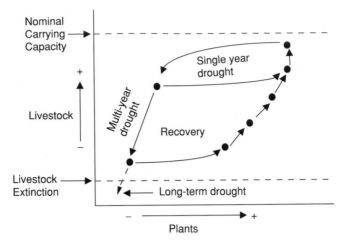

Figure 5.3. Oscillations in herbivore numbers and vegetation in the Turkana region of Kenya (from Ellis & Swift 1988).

and O'Connor (2000) disagree and have suggested that herbivore populations use key preferred habitats or resources for much of the year and only move out of those habitats when resources are limiting. Consequently, one might not find any significant effects of mammalian herbivory in arid ecosystems at large, yet negative density-dependent effects of heavy grazing are likely to be found in these key habitats. Spatially explicit modelling by Weber *et al.* (2003), based on field data from a Kalahari desert grazing system, indicates that the existence of long-term negative effects of herbivory depends closely on whether herbivores cause reductions in plant productivity (rather than short-term reductions in phytomass) and local mortality of plant species during periods of reduced plant availability (see also O'Connor 1991). Such mortality may result in a change in plant species composition and, if the newly dominant species are less palatable to herbivores, will ultimately lead to rangeland degradation. Thus, Ellis and Swift's (1988) model may be a suitable one for arid vegetation only if grazing does not differentially affect species and thereby alter species composition through changes in competitive interactions.

EFFECTS OF HERBIVORY ON RELATIONSHIPS AMONG PLANT FUNCTIONAL TYPES

Some of the most interesting effects of herbivory on plant diversity are through the effects of selective herbivory on the relationships among plant functional types. Here, I illustrate this phenomenon from three semi-arid ecosystems:

(1) Bush encroachment

One of the most interesting, and enigmatic, of purported effects of herbivory by large mammals is in the initiation of bush encroachment (also known as shrub encroachment). In the past 50 years, evidence has accumulated suggesting that arid and semi-arid savannas throughout the world are being altered by bush encroachment (e.g. Hennessey *et al.* 1983, Idso 1992, reviewed by Archer *et al.* 1995, Scholes & Archer 1997). Bush encroachment is the suppression of palatable grasses and herbs by encroaching woody species often unpalatable to domestic livestock (Lamprey 1983, Scholes & Walker 1993).

Factors causing bush encroachment are poorly understood. The first attempt at a general explanation for bush encroachment was Walter's (1939) two-layer hypothesis for tree-grass coexistence (Walter 1954, Noy-Meir 1982). Walter (1939, 1971) explained the coexistence of these two different life forms in terms of root separation; he assumed water to be the major limiting factor for both grassy and woody plants and hypothesized that grasses use only topsoil moisture, while woody plants mostly use subsoil moisture. Under this assumption, removal of grasses, e.g. by heavy grazing, allows more water to percolate into the sub-soil, where it is available for woody plant growth. This allows for mass recruitment of trees, leading to bush encroachment. Note that, in arid and semi-arid ecosystems, cohorts of similarly aged trees have been widely reported, indicating repeated phases of mass recruitment (Reid & Ellis 1995, Wiegand *et al.* 1999, 2005). Hence, it is the initiation of bush encroachment that is considered the crucial stage in arid savannas and not the control of adult tree densities as may be the case in mesic regions (*sensu* Higgins *et al.* 2000).

Although the two-layer theory is still widely accepted (Skarpe 1990a), field data and theoretical models have produced conflicting evidence. Several field studies have shown the increase of shrub or tree abundance under heavy grazing (van Vegten 1983, Skarpe 1990a,b, Perkins & Thomas 1993). However, recruitment in honey mesquite, *Prosopis glandulosa*, a bush-encroaching tree in North America, is unrelated to herbaceous biomass or density, indicating that release from competition with grasses is not required for mass tree recruitment to occur (Brown & Archer 1989, 1999). Similarly, while some models have shown that the two-layer hypothesis may indeed lead to tree-grass coexistence (Walker *et al.* 1981,

Walker & Noy-Meir 1982), a spatially explicit simulation model by Jeltsch *et al.* (1996) showed that rooting niche separation might not be sufficient to warrant coexistence under a range of climatic situations.

Field studies investigating root distribution and water uptake also produced mixed results. In the different studies, great differences were observed in the degree of niche separation, depending on abiotic factors and the species involved (Hesla *et al.* 1985, Knoop & Walker 1985, Weltzin & McPherson 1997; see also Scholes & Archer 1997 and Higgins *et al.* 2000 for further references). Clearly, rooting niche separation cannot be an explanation for the *initiation* of bush encroachment because young trees use the same subsurface soil layer as grasses in the sensitive early stages of growth. Heavy grazing is not a sufficient cause of bush encroachment. For example, the naturalist, Charles John Andersson (1856), reported heavy bush encroachment in areas of Namibia that were, according to his and other independent historical records, not heavily grazed. Thus, rooting niche separation cannot be a general mechanism explaining tree-grass coexistence, and heavy grazing is unlikely to be the most important factor causing bush encroachment. Furthermore, heavy grazing in combination with rooting niche separation is not a prerequisite for bush encroachment because bush encroachment sometimes occurs on soils too shallow to allow for root separation (Wiegand *et al.* 2005). To date, mitigation protocols based on the two-layer theory, e.g. reducing livestock densities in years with below-average rainfall, have failed to reduce bush encroachment, indicating that the causes of the problem are poorly understood (Teague & Smit 1992, Smit *et al.* 1996).

As a consequence of the inadequacy of previous explanations for the occurrence of bush encroachment, several new hypotheses have been put forward to explain tree-grass coexistence. Disturbances have been mooted as major determinants of savanna structure, with savannas being portrayed as inherently unstable ecosystems that oscillate in an intermediate state between those of stable grasslands and forests because they are pushed back into the savanna state by frequent disturbances such as human impact (Scholes & Archer 1997, Jeltsch *et al.* 1998, Jeltsch *et al.* 2000), fire (Higgins *et al.* 2000), herbivory or drought (Scholes & Walker 1993), and spatial heterogeneities in water, nutrient and seed distribution (Jeltsch *et al.* 1996). These disturbance-based hypotheses all suggest that bush encroachment occurs when disturbances shift savannas from the open grassland towards the forest end of the environmental spectrum. All of these hypotheses may be valid for specific situations but may lack generality. None of these purported mechanisms of bush encroachment has been convincingly demonstrated under field conditions.

In an attempt to tease apart the various purported factors causing bush encroachment, we have been running multi-factorial field and pot experiments in a semi-arid savanna north of Kimberley (Northern Cape, South Africa) (see e.g. Kraaij & Ward 2005 in press) using encroaching *Acacia mellifera*. In the pot experiment (large (100 litre) garbage bins were used), we planted grasses growing naturally in our study area and allowed them to reach maturity and cover the surface of the bins entirely. Then we added 100 *Acacia mellifera* seeds per bin. In a replicated, balanced, completely crossed experimental design, we used the following experimental factors: rainfall frequency (water supplied to saturation once every 3 days and once very 10 days), clipping (clipped all grass to the surface once every 3 weeks, and unclipped) and nutrients (nitrogen added [equivalent of $30\,\mathrm{g\,m^{-2}}$] and control) (see Kraaij & Ward 2005, in press, for more details). Rainfall frequency was the most important factor affecting germination and survival of *Acacia* seedlings (Fig. 5.4). There was also a significant difference between nitrogen addition and control treatments (Fig. 5.4); nitrogen addition increased grass growth, suppressing tree germination and survival. In the field experiment, in 48 5 m × 5 m plots, with a completely crossed randomized block design with the same factors and the addition of fire, we found that rainfall addition increased *Acacia* germination and survival (Fig. 5.5a), while nitrogen addition decreased *Acacia* germination and survival (Fig. 5.5b). Fire and grazing (and seed addition in the second year of the experiment) did not affect tree seedling germination and survival. I stress that, in both the pot and field experiments, it was the high rainfall frequency rather than the rainfall amount that resulted in germination and survival of *Acacia* trees. Doubling the annual mean rainfall (800 mm as opposed to 400 mm) did not lead to bush encroachment in the field when added twice per month over the growing season, while applying the same amount every two days for a month led to significant germination.

I believe that these results will dramatically alter the way we approach the problem of bush encroachment, i.e. as a problem initiated by unique rainfall conditions that may or may not be exacerbated by certain types of grazing or fire conditions (Ward 2002). We can model the management implications of rainfall effects on the initiation of bush encroachment as follows. Without grazing, both grass and tree biomass increase linearly with increasing rainfall. In an open savanna, grass biomass always exceeds tree biomass (Fig. 5.6a). When heavy grazing occurs, grass biomass per

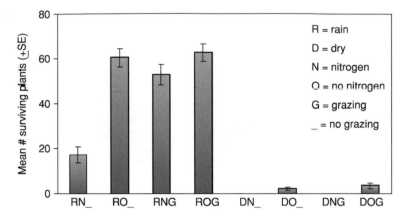

Figure 5.4. Effects of watering, grazing, fire and nutrient addition on *Acacia mellifera* recruitment and survival in a pot experiment (from Kraaij & Ward 2005). Note that all treatment combinations with the high water level (water added to saturation every 3 days) resulted in higher *Acacia* seedling germination and survival, regardless of the combination. Furthermore, addition of nitrogen resulted in lower *Acacia* seedling germination and survival due to increased competition with grasses.

unit rainfall is reduced, reducing competition with trees (Fig. 5.6b). This releases water and nutrient resources for trees to germinate en masse. Because there is a greater probability that trees will recruit when rainfall is higher, the difference between tree and grass biomass increases with increasing rainfall. The management consequence thereof in areas prone to bush encroachment is that farmers should limit stock in *wet* years and not in dry years (because trees cannot germinate) as is usually the case.

Thus, the mitigation protocol for bush encroachment under this hypothesis differs considerably from those under the two-layer competition hypothesis. Under the conventional two-layer competition hypothesis, grazing during years with less than average precipitation should be reduced to a minimum so as not to give the trees a competitive advantage. By contrast, our results from the multi-factorial experiments mentioned above, demonstrate that bush encroachment does not occur when water is limited and consequently such a management protocol would be futile. Thus, if tree-grass competition occurs, grazing should be reduced in years with greater than average rainfall, especially in open grazing lands (Fig. 5.6b).

(2) Size matters in rangelands with winter rainfall

Arid regions that experience summer rainfall are usually grass-dominated (e.g. Namib and Kalahari deserts, southern Sahara, Mitchell grass plains

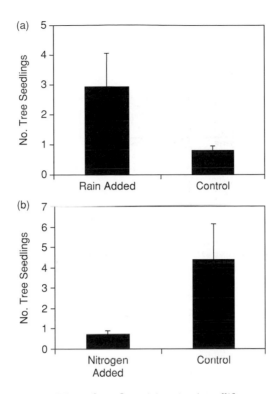

Figure 5.5. Mean | SE number of surviving *Acacia mellifera* tree seedlings with: (a) irrigation used to double annual rainfall, and (b) when nitrogen is added to the soil. Note that increasing water availability allows the trees to germinate and survive effectively. Increasing soil nitrogen makes the grasses more competitive against the trees, and reduces tree germination and survival.

of Australia), while deserts with winter rainfall (e.g. Negev and central Asian deserts) are usually dominated by asteraceous and other dicotyledonous annual plants (Louw & Seely 1990). The above-mentioned bush encroachment scenario does not occur in these winter rainfall deserts, although a spiny perennial shrub species, *Sarcopoterium spinosum*, can become dominant in some areas under heavy grazing. This species acts as a nurse plant to annual plants, protecting them from herbivory and locally increasing diversity. However, more conventionally (in the Middle East at least), the most important changes in vegetation in response to herbivory occur in the relative abundance of tall and short annual and perennial plants (Noy-Meir *et al.* 1989).

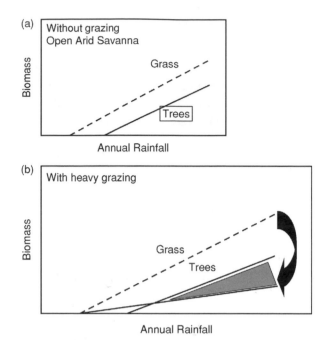

Figure 5.6. Schematic diagram of the relationships between tree and grass biomass and rainfall in arid regions. (a) Relationships between plant biomass and rainfall in the absence of herbivory. (b) Effects of heavy grazing on grass biomass. Note that tree biomass only exceeds that of grass biomass at a higher rainfall because trees require more rain to germinate and survive than grasses.

Noy-Meir *et al.* (1989) tested some of the hypotheses generated by the 'classical' theory of grassland response to grazing (Clements 1928, Smith 1940, Dyksterhuis 1949) using experimental paddocks in semi-arid range-lands in the upper Galilee and Golan Heights of Israel that have had known and controlled cattle grazing treatments from 1960 until 1982–83. The 'classical' theory postulates that the main effect of grazers is through differential removal of plant parts among plant species. This shifts the balance of relative species abundances established in the ungrazed ('climax') state, mainly by competition for water, light and nutrients, to a new stable balance which depends on differential defoliation and regrowth. Noy-Meir *et al.* (1989) used fenceline contrasts of paddocks ranging from protected (grazing intensity = 0) through lightly and moderately grazed (intensity = 1–3) to heavily grazed (intensity = 4–5) to test the following specific hypotheses that form part of this 'classical' theory:

(1) the relative abundance of some plants in a community decreases consistently in response to increased grazing intensity ('decreasers'), while that of others increases consistently ('increasers'), while some species only appear above a certain threshold of grazing intensity ('invaders');

(2) decreasers are plants with attributes that favour them in competition for space and other resources but disadvantage them under differential defoliation. Such attributes include erect tall shoots with elevated renewal buds, long growing season, perennial life cycles, and readily palatable and available to grazers (especially grasses and legumes). Increasers (and invaders) are plants with at least some of the converse attributes: low or prostrate shoots with renewal buds close to or below ground, short growing season, annual or short perennial life cycle and lower palatability to grazers due to chemical or morphological 'defensive' characters (especially forbs (non-legume dicots)).

They found that plant responses to different levels of grazing intensity were more diverse than could be expressed in a simple increaser-decreaser continuum as mooted by the 'classical' theory. Consistent grazing increasers were the largest group, followed by consistently neutral species. Species that were consistent in their responses to grazing (increasers, decreasers or neutral) accounted for 56% of the 73 common species. Weakly consistent species (i.e. tended to either increase or decrease in most comparisons) constituted another 11% of species. Many species in this region did not respond consistently to grazing intensity (33% of 73 common species); that is, they sometimes increased with increasing grazing intensity and, in other comparisons, they decreased with increased grazing. Some species preferred intermediate grazing intensities. These species were typically more abundant in the grazed area when the fence separated a completely protected enclosure (grazing intensity 0) from a lightly or moderately grazed paddock (grazing intensity 2 or 3). When the fence separated a lightly grazed from a heavily grazed paddock (intensity 4–5), these species were usually more abundant on the more protected side of the fence. This unimodal pattern of responses is consistent with the hypothesis that these species are most favoured by grazing at light-moderate intensity, and are depressed by complete protection and heavy

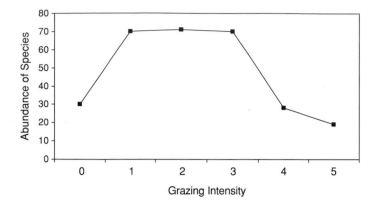

Figure 5.7. Hypothetical unimodal response of abundance of a plant species to grazing intensity in a Middle Eastern rangeland. Grazing intensity 0 = protected from herbivory, 1–3 = light to moderate herbivory, and 4–5 = heavy grazing. The plant species will appear as a grazing increaser when comparing areas with grazing intensities 0/1, 0/2 or 0/3, as neutral at 1/2, 1/3 or 1/4, or as a protection increaser (= 'decreaser' or 'invader' in conventional rangeland management terminology) at 1/4, 2/4, 3/4, 1/5, 2/5 or 3/5 (from Noy-Meir *et al.* 1989).

grazing (Fig. 5.7). Noy-Meir *et al.* (1989) suggested that the classical theory needs to incorporate an additional response type to accommodate these plants and termed them 'increaser-decreasers' or 'moderate grazing increasers'.

Noy-Meir *et al.* (1989) found that there were only marginally more perennial species among the protection increasers and that grazing response was only weakly associated with taxonomic affiliation. Palatability was not a major factor determining plant selection by herbivores (*contra* the observations of Jauffret & Lavorel 2003 in arid Tunisian rangelands); spiny plants were not more frequent among grazing increasers. In fact, there was a trend, albeit not significant, in the opposite direction (Noy-Meir *et al.* 1989). Indeed, other studies have shown that spiny species such as *Echinops polyceras* and *Acacia raddiana* are favoured food plants of wild asses and camels, respectively (Ward & Rohner 1997, Ward *et al.* 1998a). However, a very strong and significant association was found between grazing response and growth form. Tall plants that are erect from the seedling stage and grow tall at maturity (>50 cm) were mostly protection increasers and made up the majority of this response type (Fig. 5.8). Only one tall plant, *Asphodelus aestivus*, was a grazing increaser and it is totally

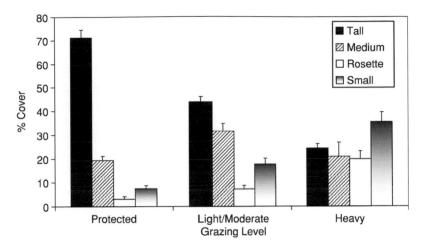

Figure 5.8. Responses (% cover + SE) of plant growth forms to different intensities of grazing. Data are summarized from Noy-Meir *et al.* (1989).

unpalatable to cattle while green, apparently due to its chemical constitution. Small plants, including prostrate plants and erect plants that remain small (<20 cm) at maturity were mostly grazing increasers (Fig. 5.8) and accounted for more than half the species in this response type. 'Rosette' plants, with prostrate basal leaves in the seedling stage and erect inflorescences at maturity, were mostly either grazing increasers or had an intermediate response. Medium height plants, with erect seedlings but medium final height (20–50 cm), were most frequent in the intermediate response group but were also common in the other two groups. The rosette and medium plants accounted for most of the species with an apparently unimodal response.

Thus, the responses of many species appear to be consistent with a modified version of the 'classical' theory of grazing response, with its basic mechanism being a balance between competition and differential defoliation. Cattle in these rangelands mainly graze from above, and their bite sizes and intake rates decline sharply as plant height decreases below 5 cm. Thus, in general, differential defoliation is not highly species-selective and is a *vertical gradient* that is the converse of that induced by competition for light. This gradient is probably strongest in the early part of the growing season, when the sward is short, leading to a competitive advantage for prostrate and rosette plants over plants with erect seedlings under heavy grazing.

In long-protected enclosures, most of the area is covered by tall plants that are capable of forming a dense sward of leaves soon after the first rain and elevate this sward rapidly. In the dry season, they leave a large amount of dead material in the absence of grazing. This material forms a mulch mat after the first rains of the following season through which they are able to regenerate, either by sprouting or germination. Once established, these species are able to persist in the absence of disturbance, and are able to impede the germination, establishment and reproduction of plants that do not have these characteristics. Noy-Meir et al. (1989) hypothesize that, as grazing increases from protection to light to moderate grazing, the sward of the dominants is increasingly fragmented by disturbed patches (caused by trampling and vegetation removal), creating a *horizontal gradient* in grazing intensity. A patchy and diverse grassland is formed that includes species with a wide range of competitive abilities and grazing resistance. Some of them may form locally dominant patches; which species do so at any site may be largely a matter of chance and is thus not consistent between sites with similar grazing intensity. Although many species can germinate and establish, those with tall-growing seedlings are reduced and eliminated while rosette, prostrate and small plants prevail. Although not specifically covered by Noy-Meir et al. (1989), geophytes, such as *Urginea maritima*, are also widespread and abundant in the Middle East, particularly where there is heavy grazing and trampling (see e.g. Hadar et al. 1999). Like prostrate and rosette plants, they are close to or under the ground and unavailable to grazers for much of the year. When they produce leaves in the winter months, they are largely untouched by grazers because of the defensive chemicals in the leaves (Ward et al. 1997). Furthermore, the short reproductive period enables early flowering, seed setting and dispersal despite heavy grazing (Hadar et al. 1999).

In more arid rangelands, evidence supports the vertical but not the horizontal grazing gradient. For example, in the wild ass study mentioned above, the change in vegetation composition in unfenced but not in fenced plots is consistent with Noy-Meir et al. (1989) vertical gradient but there is no evidence (yet) that interspecific interactions are occurring or have occurred in protected plots so that competitively dominant tall plants exclude the short species. The absence of a horizontal gradient is likely due to rainfall and edaphic limitations on total plant cover in the arid region. These limitations reduce the ability of tall plants to exclude short plants by overgrowing them and, especially, retard the formation of a mulch mat that is impenetrable to the short plants. The horizontal gradient is likely to develop once mean annual rainfall exceeds 200 mm or in regions with lower mean rainfall where run-on precipitation from other habitats (e.g. in ephemeral rivers (wadis)) increases net annual precipitation.

The Noy-Meir et al. (1989) model of vegetation response to grazing in semi-arid rangelands is more deterministic than the state-and-transition models outlined by Westoby (1980) and others (e.g. Westoby et al. 1989, Milton & Hoffman 1994, Milton et al. 1994), although Noy-Meir et al. (1989) recognize that there are many species' responses to grazing (33% of species showed inconsistent responses) that are unexplained by their model. The Noy-Meir et al. (1989) model is mechanistic while state-and-transition models are phenomenological in that they describe vegetation community composition as either being the same over a long period (= 'state') or changing to another state (= 'transition'). State-and-transition models were developed because the 'classical' theory of vegetation response was deemed too deterministic (and simplistic) in arid regions where large changes and fluctuations in vegetation state are related to environmental (mostly rainfall) fluctuations and not to density-dependent interactions among species mediated by selective herbivory. States and transitions are ascribed only in retrospect and causes are assigned by way of correlation. Consequently, state-and-transition models have little predictive value. Clearly, correlations generated from state-and-transition models may be used in hypothesis development for subsequent generations of mechanistic models.

I believe that we must pursue the mechanistic approach mooted by Noy-Meir et al. (1989) if we are to understand and manage semi-arid and arid rangelands appropriately. Indeed, Noy-Meir and others (Diaz et al. 2001) have attempted to extend this approach by relating plant traits to grazing responses in a comparison of sub-humid grasslands in Argentina and Israel. They found that plant species that decrease in abundance under increased grazing pressure are characterized (in decreasing order of importance) by tall height, perenniality, large leaves and low specific leaf area (SLA) (Diaz et al. 2001, see also Vesk et al. 2004). Height decreases under increased grazing pressure because tall species receive most grazing pressure, perennials decrease because they are more available to herbivores, leaf size decreases because larger leaves provide larger bites for grazers, and high SLA species (which have thin, soft leaves) may be favoured by selective grazers (Vesk et al. 2004). Westoby (1999) pointed out that, under intense, non-selective grazing, all species are grazed and high SLA species may have an advantage because they have faster regrowth, which is due to quicker leaf turnover and a greater rate of regrowth per unit of carbon invested in leaf tissue (see also Vesk *et al.* 2004).

While the results of Noy-Meir *et al.* (1989) generally do not indicate that plant palatability plays a large role in grazing responses, I believe that this is somewhat overstated. Ward *et al.* (2000) and Jauffret and Lavorel (2003), among others, have shown that palatability may play an important role in determining the effects of mammalian herbivory on arid ecosystems. Indeed, the dominance of geophytes in the Noy-Meir *et al.* (1989) study, may be ascribed at least in part to their unpalatability (see also Ward *et al.* 1997 and Ward 2004). Jauffret and Lavorel (2003) consider the fact that long-spined species such as *Astragalus armatus* and toxic, highly fibrous species such as *Thymelaea hirsuta* are dominant in arid Tunisian rangelands, a consequence of the long grazing history. Similarly, unpalatable shrubs such as *Hammada scoparia*, *Thymelaea hirsuta* and *Anabasis articulata* are often dominant in heavily grazed arid regions of the Middle East (Ward *et al.* 2000, Ward 2004).

(3) Is Australia a special case? – a meta-analysis

Vesk *et al.* (2004) performed a meta-analysis of 11 lists of grazing responses from five published Australian semi-arid and arid shrubland and woodland studies in an attempt to assess the generality of the results of the Diaz *et al.* (2001) study mentioned above. They found that the traits shown to predict grazing responses in the Argentinean and Israeli studies did not adequately explain responses in Australian semi-arid and arid rangelands. They found no effects of plant height or leaf size on grazing. Annuals were no less likely than perennials to decrease with increased grazing pressure. Analyses of traits within growth forms provided little evidence for relationships between traits and responses other than that annual grasses, which have a high SLA, tend to be increasers. Vesk *et al.* (2004) believe that because the Australian rangelands have lower productivity, less continuous sward, higher growth form diversity and more bare ground than ecosystems in the Diaz *et al.* (2001) study, grazers can move through vegetation and taller species do not necessarily receive more grazing pressure because grazers can access short species from the side rather than by grazing the sward down to them. In contrast with Vesk *et al.*'s (2004) general conclusions, an earlier study of two arid Australian shrublands (which was included in the meta-analysis of Vesk *et al.* 2004) found associations between increased grazing pressure and small plant size, small leaves, high fecundity and plasticity of growth form (Landsberg et al. 1999). However, many attributes of plants recorded in the Landsberg et al. (1999) study varied independently of each other and grazing-related attributes were only convincingly demonstrated in grasses. Landsberg et al. (1999) suggested that 'large erect tussocks branching above-ground' and 'small, sprawling basal tussocks' may potentially be recognized as functional grass types that are reliable indicators of light and heavy grazing, respectively. However, these authors noted the general absence of clear patterns and pointed to the complexity of grazing effects (such as strength of selection, degree of defoliation and variance in recruitment opportunities) and lack of evolutionary history of grazing by large mammalian herbivores in Australia as reasons for weak selective pressure for grazing-related traits (Landsberg et al. 1999, see also Milchunas & Lauenroth 1993 for a general discussion of the role of evolutionary history of grazing in grazing responses). Vesk et al. (2004) recognized that they could not discount evolutionary history of grazing or the 'Australia is a special case argument' for the differences between their results and those of Diaz et al. (2001). Milchunas and Lauenroth (1993) showed convincingly that evolutionary history of grazing had an effect on grazing responses inside and outside herbivore exclosures in North America. Interestingly, re-examination of the same data for Africa and Asia (Ward 2004) shows no such effect for Africa and Asia, and indicates that grazing responses are positively correlated with mean annual rainfall in those studies. Relationships between grazing intensity and plant functional traits were not examined by Milchunas and Lauenroth (1993). Clearly, further controlled studies and meta-analyses on other continents differing in evolutionary grazing history are needed.

CONCLUSIONS

The effects of mammalian herbivores on the vegetation of arid and semi-arid regions vary considerably and may be negative, positive or non-existent. Short-term studies may be unable to reveal significant effects of herbivory because the rate of vegetation change in arid regions is slow and high spatio-temporal variation in vegetation presence and abundance limits the effects of herbivory. We need to focus on the effects of large mammalian herbivores on differential mortality and rate of recovery of different plant species from herbivory and not allow ourselves to be unduly influenced by the effects of biomass removal.

One of the most interesting vegetation changes occurring in arid rangelands is bush or shrub encroachment. We have been lulled into the perception that we understand this problem. We do not. We need more models and more experiments to fully understand this phenomenon.

Grazing responses in arid and semi-arid rangelands in winter rainfall regions differ from those in summer rainfall regions. Rangelands in winter rainfall regions have vertical and horizontal gradients of grazing effects (semi-arid regions) or vertical gradients only (arid regions). Plant height may be a more important factor than palatability, life history or taxonomic affiliation in determining responses to herbivory. The 'classical' theory of grassland response to grazing which defines plants as increasers or decreasers has some value in explaining plant responses but is unduly simplistic. It should be replaced by a theory that considers: plant size and other relevant traits such as palatability and specific leaf area; includes unimodal responses to grazing; and incorporates grazing height ('vertical gradient') and degree of disturbance of the sward by trampling and vegetation removal ('horizontal gradient'). More studies on more continents are also needed to tease apart the effects of evolutionary history of grazing and abiotic environmental factors on grazing responses and plant functional traits.

ACKNOWLEDGEMENTS

I thank Kjell Danell and the organizing committee for the opportunity to participate in the workshop. Partial financial support for the research reported on here was obtained from the National Research Foundation of South Africa, the Volkswagen Foundation, Israel National Science Foundation and the United States Agency for International Development.

REFERENCES

Andersson, C.J. (1856). *Lake Ngami; or Explorations and Discoveries, During Four Years' Wanderings in the Wilds of South Western Africa.* London: Hurst and Blackett.

Archer, S. (1996). Assessing and interpreting grass-woody plant dynamics. In *The Ecology and Management of Grazing Systems,* ed. J. Hodgson & A.W. Illius. Wallingford: CAB International, pp. 101–34.

Archer, S., Schimel, D.S. & Holland, E.A. (1995). Mechanisms of shrubland expansion – land-use, climate or CO_2. *Climatic Change,* **29**, 91–9.

Behnke, R. & Abel, N. (1996). Revisited: the overstocking controversy in semiarid Africa. *World Animal Review,* **87**, 4–27.

Blydenstein, J., Hungerford, C.R., Day, G. I. & Humphrey, R. (1957). Effect of domestic livestock exclusion on vegetation in the Sonoran Desert. *Ecology*, **38**, 522–6.

Brown, J.R. & Archer, S. (1989). Woody plant invasion of grasslands: establishment of honey mesquite (*Prosopis glandulosa* var. *glandulosa*) on sites differing in herbaceous biomass and grazing history. *Oecologia*, **80**, 19–26.

Brown, J.R. & Archer, S. (1999). Shrub invasion of grassland: recruitment is continuous and not regulated by herbaceous biomass or density. *Ecology*, **80**, 2385–96.

Cheal, D.C. (1993). Effects of stock grazing on the plants of semi-arid woodlands and grasslands. *Proceedings of the Royal Society of Victoria*, **105**, 57–65.

Clements, F.E. (1928). *Plant Succession and Indicators*. New York: Hafner.

Diaz, S., Noy-Meir, I. & Cabido, M. (2001). Can grazing response of herbaceous plants be predicted from simple vegetative traits? *Journal of Applied Ecology*, **38**, 497–508.

Dyksterhuis, E.J. (1949). Condition and management of range land based on quantitative ecology. *Journal of Range Management*, **2**, 104–5.

Ellis, J.E. & Swift, D.M. (1988). Stability of African pastoral ecosystems: alternate paradigms and implications for development. *Journal of Range Management*, **41**, 450–9.

Fowler, C.W. (1988). Population dynamics as related to rate of increase per generation. *Evolutionary Ecology*, **2**, 197–204.

Freeman, D.C. & Emlen, J.M. (1995). Assessment of interspecific interactions in plant communities: an illustration of the cold desert saltbush grasslands of North America. *Journal of Arid Environments*, **31**, 179–98.

Goldberg, D. & Turner, R.M. (1986). Vegetation change and plant demography in permanent plots in the Sonoran desert. *Ecology*, **67**, 695–712.

Hadar, L., Noy-Meir, I. & Perevolotsky, A. (1999). The effect of shrub clearing and grazing on the composition of a Mediterranean plant community: functional groups versus species. *Journal of Vegetation Science*, **10**, 673–82.

Hennessey, J T, Gibbens, R.P., Tromble, J.M. & Cardenas, M. (1983). Vegetation changes from 1935 to 1980 in mesquite dunelands and former grasslands of southern New Mexico. *Journal of Range Management*, **36**, 370–4.

Hesla, B.I., Tieszen, L.L. & Boutton, T.W. (1985). Seasonal water relations of savanna shrubs and grasses in Kenya. *Journal of Arid Environments*, **8**, 15–31.

Higgins, S.I., Bond, W.J. & Trollope, S.W. (2000). Fire, resprouting and variability: a recipe for grass-tree coexistence in savannna. *Journal of Ecology*, **88**, 213–29.

Hoffman, M.T. & Cowling, R.M. (1990). Vegetation change in the semi-arid Karoo over the last 200 years: an expanding Karoo–fact or fiction? *South African Journal of Science*, **86**, 286–94.

Idso, S.B. (1992). Shrubland expansion in the American Southwest. *Climate Change*, **22**, 85–6.

Illius, A.W. & O'Connor, T.G. (2000). Resource heterogeneity and ungulate population dynamics. *Oikos*, **89**, 283–94.

Jauffret, S. & Lavorel, S. (2003). Are plant functional types relevant to describe degradation in arid, southern Tunisian steppes? *Journal of Vegetation Science*, **14**, 399–408.

Jeltsch, F., Milton, S.J., Dean, W.R.J. & Van Rooyen, N. (1996). Tree spacing and coexistence in semiarid savannas. *Journal of Ecology*, **84**, 583–95.

Jeltsch, F., Milton, S.J., Dean, W.R.J. & Van Rooyen, N. (1997). Simulated pattern formation around artificial waterholes in the semi-arid Kalahari. *Journal of Vegetation Science*, **8**, 177–81.

Jeltsch, F., Weber, G., Dean, W.R.J. & Milton, S.J. (1998). Disturbances in savanna ecosystems: modelling the impact of a key determinant. In *Ecosystems and Sustainable Development*, ed. J.L. Usó, C.A. Brebbia & H. Power. Southampton: Computational Mechanics Publications, pp. 233–42.

Jeltsch, F., Weber, G.E. & Grimm, V. (2000). Ecological buffering mechanisms in the savannas: a unifying theory of long-term tree-grass coexistence. *Plant Ecology*, **150**, 161–71.

Kelly, R.D. & Walker, B.H. (1977). The effects of different forms of land use on the ecology of a semi-arid region in south-eastern Rhodesia. *Journal of Ecology*, **62**, 553–74.

Kelt, D.A. & Valone, T.J. (1995). Effects of grazing on the abundance and diversity of annual plants in Chihuahuan desert scrub habitat. *Oecologia*, **103**, 191–5.

Knoop, W.T. & Walker, B.H. (1985). Interactions of woody and herbaceous vegetation in a southern African savanna. *Journal of Ecology*, **73**, 235–53.

Kraaij, T. & Ward, D. (2005). Effects of rain, nitrogen, fire and grazing on tree recruitment and early survival in bush-encroached savanna. *Plant Ecology*, in press.

Lamprey, H.F. (1983). Pastoralism yesterday and today: the overgrazing problem. In *Tropical Savannas: Ecosystems of the World*, ed. F. Bouliere. Amsterdam: Elsevier, pp. 643–66.

Landsberg, J., Lavorel, S. & Stol, J. (1999). Grazing response groups among understorey plants in arid rangelands. *Journal of Vegetation Science*, **10**, 683–96.

Louw, G.N. & Seely, M.K. (1990). *Ecology of Desert Organisms*. London: Longmans.

Milchunas, D.G., Sala, O.E. & Lauenroth, W.K. (1988). A generalized model of the effects of grazing by large herbivores on grassland community structure. *American Naturalist*, **132**, 87–106.

Milchunas, D.G., Lauenroth, W.K., Chapman, P.L. & Kazempour, K. (1989). Effects of grazing, topography, and precipitation on the structure of a semi-arid grassland. *Vegetatio*, **80**, 11–23.

Milchunas, D.G. & Lauenroth, W.K. (1993). Quantitative effects of grazing on vegetation and soils over a global range of environments. *Ecological Monographs*, **63**, 327–66.

Milton, S.J. & Dean, W.R.J. (2000). Disturbance, drought and dynamics of desert dune grassland, South Africa. *Plant Ecology*, **150**, 37–51.

Milton, S.J. & Hoffman, M.T. (1994) The application of state-and-transition models to rangeland research and management in arid succulent and semi-arid grassy Karoo, South Africa. *African Journal of Range and Forage Science*, **11**, 18–26.

Milton, S.J., Dean, W.R.J., du Plessis, M.A. & Siegfried, W.R. (1994). A conceptual model of arid rangeland degradation. *Bioscience*, **44**, 70–6.

Noy-Meir, I. (1973). Desert ecosystems: environment and producers. *Annual Review of Ecology and Systematics*, **4**, 25–51.

Noy-Meir, I. (1982). Stability of plant-herbivore models and possible applications to savanna. In *Ecology of Tropical Savannas*, ed. B.J. Huntley & B.H. Walker. Ecological Studies. Berlin: Springer Verlag, pp. 591–609.

Noy-Meir, I., Gutman, M. & Kaplan, Y. (1989). Responses of Mediterranean grassland plants to grazing and protection. *Journal of Ecology*, **77**, 290–310.

O'Connor, T.G. (1985). *A Synthesis of Field Experiments Concerning the Grass Layer in the Savanna Regions of Southern Africa*. South African National Scientific Programmes Report 114. CSIR, Pretoria.

O'Connor, T.G. (1991). Local extinction in perennial grasslands: a life-history approach. *American Naturalist*, **137**, 753–73.

Perkins, J.S. & Thomas, D.S.G. (1993). Spreading deserts or spatially confined environmental impacts? Land degradation and cattle ranching in the Kalahari desert of Botswana. *Land Degradation and Rehabilitation*, **4**, 179–94.

Pickup, G. & Chewings, V.H. (1994). A grazing gradient approach to land degradation assessment in arid areas from remotely-sensed data. *International Journal of Remote Sensing*, **15**, 597–617.

Reid, R.S. & Ellis, J.E. (1995). Impacts of pastoralists on woodlands in south Turkana, Kenya: livestock-mediated tree recruitment. *Ecological Applications*, **5**, 978–92.

Ruiz, N., Ward, D. & Saltz, D. (2002a). Crystals of calcium oxalate in leaves: constitutive or induced defence? *Functional Ecology*, **16**, 99–105.

Ruiz, N., Ward, D. & Saltz, D. (2002b). Responses of *Pancratium sickenbergeri* to simulated bulb herbivory: combining defense and tolerance strategies. *Journal of Ecology*, **90**, 472–9.

Saltz, D. (2001). Ungulates of Makhtesh Ramon: dynamics, behaviour, and their conservation implications. In *The Makhteshim Country: a Laboratory of Nature*, ed. B. Krasnov & E. Mazor. Sofia, Bulgaria: Pensoft, pp. 273–87.

Saltz, D. & Ward, D. (2000). Responding to a three-pronged attack: desert lilies subject to herbivory by dorcas gazelles. *Plant Ecology*, **148**, 127–38.

Saltz, D., Schmidt, H., Rowen, M. *et al.* (1999). Assessing grazing impacts by remote sensing in hyper-arid environments. *Journal of Range Management*, **52**, 500–7.

Schlesinger, W., Reynolds, J.F., Cunningham, G.L. *et al.* (1990). Biological feedbacks in global desertification. *Science*, **247**, 1043–8.

Scholes, R.J. & Archer, S.R. (1997). Tree-grass interactions in savannas. *Annual Review of Ecology and Systematics*, **28**, 545–70.

Scholes, R.J. & Walker, B.H. (1993). *An African Savanna: Synthesis of the Nylsvley Study*. Cambridge: Cambridge University Press.

Sinclair, A.R.E. & Fryxell, J.M. (1985). The Sahel of Africa: ecology of a disaster. *Canadian Journal of Zoology*, **63**, 987–94.

Skarpe, C. (1990a). Shrub layer dynamics under different herbivore densities in an arid savanna, Botswana. *Journal of Applied Ecology*, **27**, 873–85.

Skarpe, C. (1990b). Structure of the woody vegetation in disturbed and undisturbed arid savanna. *Vegetatio*, **87**, 11–18.

Smit, G.N., Rethman, N.F.G. & Moore, A. (1996). Review article: vegetative growth, reproduction, browse production and response to tree clearing of woody plants in African savanna. *African Journal of Range and Forage Science*, **13**, 78–88.

Smith, C.C. (1940). The effect of overgrazing and erosion upon the biota of the mixed-grass prairie of Oklahoma. *Ecology*, **21**, 381–97.

Stafford Smith, D.M. & Morton, S.R. (1990). A framework for the ecology of arid Australia. *Journal of Arid Environments*, **18**, 255–78.

Teague, W.R. & Smit, G.N. (1992). Relations between woody and herbaceaous components and the effects of bush-clearing in southern African savannas. *Journal of the Grassland Society of South Africa*, **9**, 60–71.

Van Rooyen, N., Bredenkamp, G.J. & Theron, G.K. (1991). Kalahari vegetation: veld condition trends and ecological status of species. *Koedoe*, **34**, 61–72.

van Vegten, J.A. (1983). Thornbush invasion in eastern Botswana. *Vegetatio*, **56**, 3–7.

Venter, J., Liggitt, B., Tainton, N.M. & Clarke, G.P.M. (1989). The influence of different land use practices on soil erosion, herbage production, and grass species richness and diversity. *Journal of the Grassland Society of Southern Africa*, **6**, 89–98.

Vesk, P.A., Leishman, M.R. & Westoby, M. (2004). Simple traits do not predict grazing response in Australian shrublands and woodlands. *Journal of Applied Ecology*, **41**, 22–31.

Walker, B.H. & Noy-Meir, I. (1982). Aspects of the stability and resilience of savanna ecosystems. In *Ecology of Tropical Savannas*, ed. B.J. Huntley & B.H. Walker. Berlin: Springer Verlag, pp. 556–90.

Walker, B.H., Ludwig, D., Holling, C.S. & Peterman, R.M. (1981). Stability of semi-arid savanna grazing systems. *Journal of Ecology*, **69**, 473–98.

Walter, H. (1939). Grassland, Savanne und Busch der ariden Teile Afrikas in ihrer oekologischen Bedingheit. *Jaarboek wissenschaftelike Botaniek*, **87**, 750–860.

Walter, H. (1954). Die Verbuschung, eine Erscheinung der subtropischen Savannengebiete, und ihre ökologischen Ursachen. *Vegetatio*, **5/6**, 6–10.

Walter, H. (1971). *Ecology of Tropical and Subtropical Vegetation*. Edinburgh: Oliver & Boyd.

Ward, D. (2001). Plant species diversity and population dynamics in Makhtesh Ramon. In *The Makhteshim Country: a Laboratory of Nature*, ed. B. Krasnov & E. Mazor. Sofia, Bulgaria: Pensoft, pp. 171–86.

Ward, D. (2002). Do we understand the causes of bush encroachment? In *Multiple Use Management of Natural Forests and Woodlands: Policy Refinements and Scientific Progress*, ed. A.W. Seydack, T. Vorster, W.J. Vermeulen & I.J. Van Der Merwe. Pretoria: DWAF, pp. 189–201.

Ward, D. (2004). The effects of grazing on plant biodiversity in arid ecosystems. In *Biodiversity in Drylands: Towards a Unified Framework*, ed. M. Shachak, S.T. A. Pickett, J.R. Gosz & A. Perevolotsky. Oxford: Oxford University Press, pp. 233–49.

Ward, D. & Ngairorue, B.T. (2000). Are Namibia's grasslands desertifying? *Journal of Range Management*, **53**, 138–44.

Ward, D. & Olsvig-Whittaker, L. (1993). Plant species diversity at the junction of two desert biogeographic zones. *Biodiversity Letters*, **1**, 172–85.

Ward, D. & Rohner, C. (1997). Anthropogenic causes of high mortality and low recruitment in three *Acacia* tree taxa in the Negev desert, Israel. *Biodiversity and Conservation*, **6**, 877–93.

Ward, D. & Saltz, D. (1994). Foraging at different spatial scales: dorcas gazelles foraging for lilies in the Negev desert. *Ecology*, **75**, 48–58.

Ward, D., Olsvig-Whittaker, L. & Lawes, M.J. (1993). Vegetation-environment relationships in a Negev desert erosion cirque. *Journal of Vegetation Science*, **4**, 83–94.

Ward, D., Spiegel, M. & Saltz, D. (1997). Gazelle herbivory and interpopulation differences in calcium oxalate content of leaves of a desert lily. *Journal of Chemical Ecology*, **23**, 333–46.

Ward, D., Saltz, D., Rowen, M. & Schmidt, I. (1998a). Effects of grazing by re-introduced *Equus hemionus* on the vegetation in a Negev desert erosion cirque. *Journal of Vegetation Science*, **10**, 579–86.

Ward, D., Ngairorue, B.T., Kathena, J., Samuels, R. & Ofran, Y. (1998b). Land degradation is not a necessary outcome of communal pastoralism in arid Namibia. *Journal of Arid Environments*, **40**, 357–71.

Ward, D., Saltz, D. & Olsvig-Whittaker, L. (2000). Distinguishing signal from noise: long-term studies of vegetation in Makhtesh Ramon erosion cirque, Negev desert, Israel. *Plant Ecology*, **150**, 27–36.

Ward, D., Saltz, D. & Ngairorue, B.T. (2004). Spatio-temporal rainfall variation and stock management in arid Namibia. *Journal of Range Management*, **57**, 130–40.

Weber, G.E., Moloney, K. & Jeltsch, F. (2003). Simulated long-term vegetation response to alternative stocking strategies in savanna rangelands. *Plant Ecology*, **150**, 77–96.

Weltzin, J.F. & McPherson, G.R. (1997). Spatial and temporal soil moisture partitioning by trees and grasses in a temperate savanna, Arizona, USA. *Oecologia*, **112**, 156–64.

Westoby, M. (1980). Elements of a theory of vegetation dynamics in arid rangelands. *Israel Journal of Botany*, **28**, 169–94.

Westoby, M. (1999). The LHS strategy scheme in relation to grazing and fire. In *Sixth International Rangeland Congress Vol. 2*, ed. D. Eldridge & D. Freudenberger. Townsville, Australia: International Rangeland Congress, pp. 893–6.

Westoby, M., Walker, B. & Noy-Meir, I. (1989). Opportunistic management for rangelands not at equilibrium. *Journal of Range Management*, **42**, 266–74.

Whittaker, R.H. (1975). *Communities and Ecosystems*. New York: MacMillan.

Wiegand, T. & Milton, S.J. (1996) Vegetation change in semiarid communities: simulating probabilities and time scales. *Vegetatio*, **125**, 169–83.

Wiegand, K., Jeltsch, F. & Ward, D. (1999). Analysis of the population dynamics of *Acacia* trees in the Negev desert, Israel with a spatially explicit computer simulation model. *Ecological Modeling*, **117**, 203–24.

Wiegand, K., Ward, D. & Saltz, D. (2005). Multi-scale patterns encroachment in an arid savanna with a shallow soil layer. *Journal of Vegetation Science*, **16**, 311–20.

6

The influence of large herbivores on tree recruitment and forest dynamics

ROBIN GILL

INTRODUCTION

In recent years, concern for the damage caused by herbivores, or the absence of young trees in forests appears to have been growing. Many of these problems can be linked to changes in ungulate populations. Deer have been increasing intermittently in the temperate region for 100–200 years, and some problems with forest regeneration can be linked directly to these increases.

The fossil record shows that very large herbivores, related to those present in Africa and Asia today, were prevalent throughout the temperate region. Herbivores, including ancestral forms of the tapirs, horses and rhinos, and later many proboscidians (elephants and mammoths) and artiodactyls (cattle, deer, hippos and giraffe), have been present almost continuously since the Eocene, with browsing species particularly linked with forested environments (Yalden 1999, Agusti & Anton 2002). The last of the large herbivores disappeared only around 11 000 years ago. In the last few hundred years there have been further losses: the distribution of bison, *Bison bonasus* and *B. bison*, has shrunk dramatically in both Europe and North America, and Aurochsen, *Bos primigenius* (wild cattle), have gone extinct.

The disappearance of large wild herbivores from temperate regions at the end of the last ice age was followed sometime later by the arrival of domestic livestock. Grazing by early pasturalists in forests presumably dates from the time when livestock husbandry first spread from the Middle East to

Large Herbivore Ecology, Ecosystem Dynamics and Conservation, ed. K. Danell, P. Duncan, R. Bergström & J. Pastor. Published by Cambridge University Press. © Cambridge University Press 2006.

western Europe between 10 000 and 5000 years ago (Clutton-Brock 1989). Livestock grazing in forests also spread to the Americas in the last 500 years following settlement by Europeans. Although livestock are now excluded from woodlands in most areas, grazing appears to have been widespread, since both historical and pollen evidence indicates that areas now covered with closed-canopy woodland were once subject to grazing (Williams 1989, Segerström *et al.* 1996, Mitchell & Cole 1998, Vera 2000). Although there are important differences in the species and grazing pressures involved, livestock therefore replaced wild herbivores that preceded them. Historically, the word 'forest' in Europe referred to places containing trees and herbivores, and in places may have resembled parkland or savanna more than closed-canopy woodland. As tree cover shrank and livestock numbers increased with settlement, systems of managing both animals and tree regeneration together, such as pollarding, compartmentalizing and encouraging protection with thorns, were developed (Flower 1980, Rackham 1998, Vera 2000). The management of forests and grazing in this way became uneconomic in Europe by the start of the industrial period, and now only relict areas of ancient grazed woodland remain (Rackham 1998). However, it is clear that large mammalian herbivores, either wild or domestic, have been present in most forested environments for the greater part of the last 50 million years and the current regime, where one or two species of deer may be the only herbivores, is relatively atypical.

Ecologists have become increasing interested in the effect these large herbivores must have had on the vegetation. What was the structure of temperate forests like during periods when large herbivores were present? If problems of regeneration exist today, then how could temperate forests have persisted with the existence of larger species in the past? How can forested landscapes, or the herbivores in them, be managed to ensure adequate regeneration or to minimize unwanted consequences of selective foraging? Changes in forest structure and composition come about as a result of changes in the abundance and composition of seedlings and young trees, the age class that is of course most vulnerable to damage by herbivores. In this chapter, the various effects that herbivores have on the process of tree regeneration are explored to assess the implications they have for forest structure and composition.

LARGE HERBIVORE DIETS

Large herbivores have a variety of feeding behaviours which directly affect trees. The most prevalent is browsing on leaves and young shoots.

Table 6.1. *Composition (%) of the diet of large herbivores that use woodland habitats*

Species	Grass	Forb + Fruit	Tree/shrub
Giraffe *Giraffa camelopardalis*	1	1	98
Moose *Alces alces*	2	8	90
Roe deer *Capreolus capreolus*	7	15	78
Japanese serow *Capricornis crispus*	–	25	75
White-tailed deer *Odocoileus virginianus*	10	30	60
Mule/Black-tailed deer *Odocoileus hemionus*	13	28	59
Goat	29	12	59
Sika deer *Cervus nippon*	34	7	59
Kudu *Tragelaphus strepsciceros*	18	21	51
Elephant *Loxodonta africana*	46	10	44
Fallow deer *Dama dama*	42	15	43
Red deer *Cervus elaphus*	40	21	39
European bison *Bison bonasus*	61	6	33
Sheep	50	30	20
Horse *Equus caballus*	69	15	16
Elk/Wapiti *Cervus elaphus*	69	14	17
Cattle	72	15	13
Wild boar *Sus scrofa*	36	62	2

Source: Van Dyne *et al.* 1980.

However, they can also damage young trees by bark stripping, breaking or trampling, or by using their antlers, horns or tusks (Laws *et al.* 1975, Gill 1992a, Heraldová *et al.* 2003). Elephants will go as far as pushing trees over and eating the roots. Some tree species have edible seeds and these may be consumed in large quantities. This may either deplete seedling abundance or promote seed dispersal, if the seeds can survive passage through the digestive tract.

The diets of large herbivores can be distinguished broadly by the degree to which they contain browse, grasses or fruit (Table 6.1). The herbivores that are most committed to woodland in terms of habitat use and diet are true browsers, for example, the giraffe, serow, moose, roe, white-tailed deer and spiral-horned antelopes (Tragelaphini). These species include the greatest number and widest range of woodland plants in their diet. The majority of medium sized herbivores are grazers or mixed feeders. Many of these species concentrate much of their feeding outside woodlands, or, if in woodland, use openings or savanna habitats which provide mixed feeding. Nonetheless, by feeding on seedling trees and shrubs opportunistically they can have a significant effect on regeneration. Some of the smaller antelopes, Cephalophini and Neotragini (duikers and dwarf antelope), may also have an important influence on regeneration by foraging on fallen fruit and browsing, however, the effects they have on vegetation appear not to have been investigated directly. Most Suidae (pigs) influence regeneration through seed consumption and digging, which may bury seeds as well as uproot seedlings and other plants. However, they rarely browse.

The amount eaten by large herbivores is dependent on body size. Average daily food intake rate tends to increase with body weight, but very large herbivores eat relatively less for their body weight (Owen-Smith 1988). Larger herbivores are also able to bite through twigs of a greater diameter and since gut retention time also increases with weight, they can consume material of lower digestibility, and a greater proportion of the vegetation biomass is therefore food (Shipley et al. 1999, Wilson & Kerley 2003). When browsing shoots, larger herbivores can take more than the current annual growth. Moose, for example, bite twigs approximately 1 mm thicker on average than current annual growth, whereas roe deer take twigs approximately 0.5 mm less (Jia et al. 1995, Shipley et al. 1999). Such a difference may be significant in affecting subsequent growth and survival of young trees and shrubs. The height at which animals feed affects forest structure by depleting vegetation within a particular height zone. Small deer (e.g. muntjac, *Muntiacus reevesi*) feed mainly within 50 cm of ground level, and may maintain a relatively open ground layer (Fuller 2001). Larger deer (e.g. white-tailed deer) will feed up to 1.5 m in height. The largest herbivores (elephants and giraffes), focus most of their browsing above 2 m in height (Pellew 1983), with the result that small trees and other low vegetation may receive more light and hence some benefit (Laws et al. 1975, Lenzi-Grillini et al. 1996).

PLANT DEFENCES

Large herbivores exhibit important differences in species selection, and this is particularly clear in their ability to tolerate some of the defensive mechanisms of plants. Cattle, for example, feed with a tongue sweep and usually avoid thorny species (Buttenschøn & Buttenschøn 1985). However, browsing herbivores are able to feed on many thorny plants, although thorns can slow down the rate of feeding and reduce bite size on shoots (Cooper & Owen-Smith 1986, Gowda 1996, Wilson & Kerley 2003). In experiments to measure foraging efficiency on winter shoots, Illius et al. (2002) found that removing thorns reduced the time taken for roe deer to feed on *Rubus fruticosus*, but not *Prunus spinosa* or *Crataegus monogyna*, which have more widely spaced thorns. Differences in the effectiveness of straight and hooked thorns, as well as differences in the ability of herbivore species to cope with them, were also found by Cooper and Owen-Smith (1986).

Diet choice in large herbivores is known to be influenced by concentrations of secondary compounds, although their role in different species is still not well known. The concentration of monoterpenes has been found to affect the rate of browsing by red deer amongst clones of Sitka spruce (Duncan et al. 2001). Recent studies on the diet of roe deer and mule deer, however, indicate that their diets include many plants with a high tannin or terpene content, and that they may be able to reduce the effect of some secondary compounds by the precipitating action of salivary proteins (McArthur et al. 1993, Tixier et al. 1997). There are marked differences in palatability of conifers (both amongst tree species and between herbivores for some species) and some (e.g. *Taxus baccata*) are known to be toxic to cattle and horses but readily eaten by deer (Cooper & Johnson 1984, James et al. 1989).

Introductions of ungulates into areas with no recent history of large herbivores reveal evidence that natural selection has favoured trees with higher concentrations of secondary compounds. Black-tailed deer were introduced into the Queen Charlotte Islands in 1901 and after increasing rapidly, now severely limit regeneration of western red cedar, *Thuja plicata*. However, regeneration of this species is normally successful on suitable sites on the adjacent mainland (Klinka 1999). Comparisons of browsing damage to nursery grown seedlings indicate that seedlings of island origin are browsed more than those of mainland origin and have a lower monoterpene concentration (Vourc'h et al. 2001), suggesting that the absence of herbivory in the post-glacial period has favoured selection for reduced browse resistance.

Many studies have reported changes in palatability or nutritional quality following browsing or other forms of damage. Some thorny species (e.g. bramble, *Rubus fruticosus*, and holly, *Ilex aquifolium*) have been found to grow shoots with more thorns after being browsed (Bazely et al. 1991, Obeso 1997), indicating an ability to increase defence against further browsing. In contrast, there are species which become more palatable after browsing, as a result of mobilization of nutrients and changes in shoot morphology or possibly plant architecture (Danell et al. 2003). In many species, trees that have been damaged once have been found to be more likely to be damaged again (Löyttyniemi 1985, Welch et al. 1991, Bergström et al. 2000, Skarpe et al. 2000, Bergqvist et al. 2003).

EFFECTS OF BROWSERS ON TREE GROWTH AND SURVIVAL

Browsing on leaves and shoots

Feeding by large herbivores is often focused on the upper shoots of young trees and shrubs, parts of the plant usually containing the most actively growing foliage and highest nitrogen concentrations. The loss of these tissues is more serious than damage to leaves or shoots lower down (Furuno & Yamazaki 1973, Bassman & Dickman 1985, Ericsson *et al.* 1985, Harper 1989). Browsing on trees reduces height growth rates, and subsequent growth is dependent on the severity of damage or the number of times a plant is browsed (Eiberle 1975, Bergström & Danell 1987, Crawley 1989, Cooke & Lakhani 1996). Repeated browsing may keep trees within reach of browsing ungulates for years. Enclosures used in Europe to monitor the effects of deer browsing have indicated that beech, *Fagus sylvatica*, growth may be delayed by 3–4 years and silver fir, *Abies alba*, by 9–13 years (Roth 1996). Growth of oak, *Quercus robor*, has been found to be held in check for 25 years or more by browsing (Shaw 1974).

Although browsing almost invariably reduces height growth, growth of individual shoots may be enhanced. The length and diameter of shoots, leaf size and frequency of buds or branching have all been reported to increase following browsing in several tree species (Bergström & Danell 1987, Wilson 1993, Danell *et al.* 1994, Bergström *et al.* 2000). In some cases, these effects are dependent on the season of damage, and the severity or frequency. In birch, *Betula* sp., shoot size increases after winter damage but decreases after summer damage (Danell *et al.* 1994), and in Scots pine, shoot length increases more after moderate than severe damage (Edenius 1993). The retarding effect of browsing on height growth, coupled with positive responses in side shoot growth, mean that resources for browsers can be temporarily increased as a result of browsing.

Besides affecting growth, browsing can also decrease the chance of survival, with the probability of death increasing with the severity or repetition of damage (Eiberle 1975, Eiberle & Nigg 1987, Tsiouvaras 1988). Younger or smaller trees are generally more susceptible than larger or older trees (Krefting & Stoeckeler 1953). In particular, very small seedlings are likely to be most vulnerable to damage if the cotyledons are lost before the first leaf forms. As young trees grow and the shoots become thicker and more lignified, digestibility declines and only the distal parts are likely to be browsed. As a result, browsing is more likely to affect only the growth rate or growth form, rather than survival (Bergerud & Manuel 1968, Dimock 1970, Lewis 1980). Since young trees can withstand some browsing pressure, much of the mortality that occurs appears to be due to a reduced ability to compete with other plants, rather than the damage itself.

Many tree species are able to reproduce asexually from buds near the base of the main stem or on roots. In some species dormant buds are only activated following damage to the main stem, for example, by fire, cutting or breakage. Because the tree is drawing on reserves in the stem or roots, the growth of such coppice shoots (if unbrowsed) are much more rapid than that of seedlings and they may escape damage by growing out of reach of herbivores in only one or two seasons. However, because the shoots are located near the stem, herbivores can discover all the recruits quickly and they may then be killed by repeated browsing.

Bark stripping

Large herbivores have been widely reported to strip or gnaw bark whilst feeding, and in some cases the activity is considered serious enough to threaten the survival of certain tree species or stands (Parks *et al.* 1998, Vera 2000, Yokoyama *et al.* 2001). The herbivores most commonly reported to strip bark are the large browsers or intermediate feeders (elephant, European bison, moose, and red, sika and sambar deer, *Cervus unicolor*). Bark stripping is occasionally inflicted by fallow and white-tailed deer as well as sheep, goats, cattle and horses (Kinnaird *et al.* 1979, Michael 1987). Smaller ungulates do not appear to strip bark.

Most reports of bark stripping suggest that bark is only eaten in small quantities, and a certain level of stripping appears to be normal. Extensive surveys of damage have yielded rates of damage of 1% per year (Welch *et al.* 1987) and 0.7%–3.4% per year (Gill *et al.* 2000) by red deer to conifers, and <5% per year by moose on Scots pine (Faber & Edenius 1998). However, severe outbreaks of bark stripping are also quite commonly reported, resulting in high levels of damage occurring in a short time (Faber 1996). Many of these include situations where relatively high numbers of animals are confined in a limited area, for example, when enclosed by fencing (Anderson *et al.* 1985) or when using woodland following heavy snow fall (Ueda *et al.* 2002). In one example, when fence removal enabled red deer to gain access to a conifer woodland, as many as 31.6% of the trees were damaged in one year (Scott 1998). European bison have been reported to strip as many as 481 trees each in 4 months (Borowski & Kossak 1972). Following such a period of severe damage, the majority of trees of a species in a stand may get damaged (Santiapillai *et al.* 1981, Parks *et al.* 1998, Akashi and Nakashizuka 1999, Scharf & Hirth 2000, Yokoyama *et al.* 2001).

Bark stripping appears to occur mostly in the winter in temperate regions and during the dry season in the Tropics (Laws *et al.* 1975, Welch *et al.* 1987, Gill 1992a, Khan *et al.* 1994, Ueda *et al.* 2002), however, there is considerable variation in this pattern and it may occur at any time of year (e.g. Faber 1996). Large herbivores are very selective when stripping bark, focusing on particular species and age classes (Borowski & Kossak 1972, Laws *et al.* 1975, Gill 1992a, Khan *et al.* 1994). Most bark stripping by ungulates occurs on sapling or pole-sized trees, usually less than 40 years old (in temperate regions). The age or size classes of trees vulnerable to stripping tends to reflect morphological development, with damage starting when the main stem becomes rigid and accessible, and ending when the bark becomes rough and thick. *Pinus sylvestris*, *P. contorta* and *Larix decidua*, for example, are vulnerable for younger age classes than *Picea sitchensis* and *P. abies* (Gill 1992a, Gill *et al.* 2000). Some investigations have also shown that in even-aged stands, deer tend to select above-average size trees in the early part of the vulnerable age range and, conversely, they select below-average sized trees during the later stages of the vulnerable period (Welch *et al.* 1987). Both the adhesion of the bark and digestibility (*in vitro*) have been found to decline with increasing thickness (McIntyre 1975, Wästerlund 1985) suggesting that the decline in rate of stripping with increasing age is due to reduced digestibility not ease of removal from the tree (Gill 1992a). The observation that larger herbivores (which have longer gut retention time and increased digestive efficiency) are more prone to bark stripping is consistent with the conclusion that digestibility imposes some limit to bark stripping activity. However, there does not appear to be a unifying explanation for the variability in levels of bark stripping damage, nor the sudden outbreaks.

If bark is removed from the entire circumference, phloem translocation is interrupted and death is normally inevitable. Most stripping by ungulates, however, removes bark from only a proportion of the stem circumference and trees usually survive and continue to grow. When bark is removed, xylem cells near the wound surface close, and water translocation is restricted to the parts of the stem away from the wound surface. Resin and antifungal compounds are released near the wound, however, a proportion of wounds become infected with microorganisms leading to decay, the extent of which is usually proportional to wound size (Pawsey & Gladman 1965, Isomaki & Kallio 1974, Gregory 1986, Vasiliauskas

1998). Many wounds, however, will subsequently be re-covered as bark grows from the wound edges, and this is likely to restrict further decay (Girompaire & Ballon 1992, Han *et al.* 2000).

Bark loss can affect tree survival although it is questionable whether or not there is any significant effect on growth. Several studies have concluded that growth loss does not occur even if bark loss extends to 90% of the circumference (Pels Rijcken 1965, Luitjes 1971, Welch & Scott 1998). The exceptions are investigations of damage caused by small mammals or invertebrates, which affect other parts of the stem and may be more extensive than ungulate damage (Storm & Halvorson 1967, Cerezke 1974). Since ungulates sometimes select suppressed trees when stripping, subsequent growth loss may be due more to competition than wounding (Akashi & Nakashizuka 1999). Similarly, mortality after partial girdling appears unusual and confined to trees with about two-thirds or more of the circumference stripped (Luitjes 1971, Miquelle & Van Ballenberghe 1989, Scharf & Hirth 2000). Trees can be physically weakened by severe bark damage and some species (e.g. *Pinus sylvestris* and *P. contorta*) may be killed by a break at the wound in a subsequent storm (Scott 1998). Norway spruce, *Picea abies*, has been found to be more prone to snow damage after fungal infection develops from a bark wound (Fruhman & Roeder 1981).

In the Tropics, bark stripping is widely reported to make trees more vulnerable to fire (Laws *et al.* 1975, Hiscocks 1999). Browsing by elephants can also reduce canopy density leading to more vegetation growth near ground level, which in turn increases fuel for dry season fires. Thus trees that survive damage directly may ultimately be killed by fire, and elephants may indirectly alter tree species composition, favouring fire-resistant trees (Laws *et al.* 1975, Jachmann & Croes 1991). Laws *et al.* (1975) reported as much as 95% mortality in *Terminalia glaucescens* due to the combined effects of bark stripping and fire.

Many studies indicate a positive association between the proportion of trees damaged and the number that are either severely stripped or completely girdled (e.g. Kinnaird *et al.* 1979). Mortality is therefore likely to be proportionately greater where damage is most severe. In some examples of severe bark stripping, mortality rates of 18% (with many more senescent) have been recorded in a stand of *Taxus brevifolia* (Parks *et al.* 1998) and 24%–43% in *Abies homolepis* in Japan, although a proportion of these were suppressed (Yokoyama *et al.* 2001). Elephants have been recorded to ring-bark as much as 58% of a sample of *Acacia tortilis* trees in less than 10 years (Mwalyosi 1990). However, it is unusual for ungulates to completely ring-bark trees, and where damage does occur, it is usually focused on younger trees and particular species. Therefore, unless elephants are present, bark stripping is unlikely to be the cause of significant mortality amongst mature trees, although if severe, it may reduce thickets or pole-stage stands.

EFFECTS OF BROWSERS ON TREE REGENERATION

Consumption of seeds

The larger seeds and seed pods of some tree species (e.g. *Quercus* sp. and *Castanea*) are readily consumed by some herbivore species. Seed production in *Quercus* is highly variable and appears to be synchronized on climatic cues. Correlation in masting has been recorded at distances of up to 800 km (Koenig & Knops 2002). The quantities of seed produced are extremely variable, but can be enough to yield up to 250 000 seedlings ha^{-1}. The variation in acorn yield is sufficient to influence the fecundity and density of wild boar populations (Groot Bruinderink & Hazebroek 1995) and growth of white-tailed deer fawns (Feldhamer 2002). Direct comparisons of relative losses due to consumption of oak mast versus consumption of seedlings by ungulates appear not to have been carried out. The fact that performance of herbivore populations is linked to acorn availability and that the abundance of small oak seedlings are often found to be depleted more than other tree species (e.g. Healy 1997), suggests that much of the loss of oak seedlings is due to consumption of acorns in addition to seedlings.

Large herbivores are capable of dispersing seeds on their coats or by passage through the intestine after they are ingested. While there are several examples of this occurring in tropical and sub-tropical environments (Cochrane 2003, see also Chapter 5), reviews of seed dispersal amongst temperate tree species have revealed few examples (Gill & Beardall 2001). Instead, birds and small mammals are likely to be the most important dispersal agents for species with larger seeds. Small mammals may be effective at dispersing seeds into small canopy gaps close to the parent tree, but dispersal over longer distances is most likely to be done by birds, which can transport acorns greater distances and bury them in open ground (Bossema 1979, Darley-Hill & Johnson 1981).

Seedling abundance

The combined effects of growth loss and an increased rate of mortality can have a substantial effect on the density of young trees. The general tendency is to reduce the density, and this effect is most apparent where ungulate densities are greatest (Table 6.2, Watson 1983, Risenhoover & Maass 1986, McInnes et al. 1992, Beaumont et al. 1995, Healy 1997). There are, however, large differences between sites and vegetation types. In some cases, regeneration is almost entirely eliminated (Table 6.2, Watson 1983, Putman et al. 1989) whereas in others seedling densities may still exceed 10^5 per hectare, even under relatively high ungulate densities (e.g. Tilghman 1989).

Besides the density of ungulates, there are a number of other factors which affect seedling density. Most tree species regenerate more readily in canopy openings or clearings, and many studies indicate that seedling densities are substantially lower under un-thinned or closed-canopy stands than under openings or thinned stands, and that a lower proportion survive browsing (Table 6.2). The effects of browsing can therefore be compounded by competition or shading from other trees or vegetation.

By reducing seedling density and growth rates, ungulates have the effect of accelerating the process of thinning in forest stands. This can have a marked effect on the age and size structure of woodlands, reducing or eliminating cohorts of young trees for many years. The density of shrubs and small trees are reduced, creating a more open under-storey. As browsing pressure increases, or if regeneration continues to fail, the density of more mature trees will also be reduced, and savanna or parkland conditions may then develop (Stromayer & Warren 1997, Rooney 2001). The more open under-storey created by browsing may favour plant establishment at ground level (Kirby 2001), and in some cases tree seedlings may germinate in even greater numbers as a result (Tilghman 1989, Table 6.2). This effect is, however, likely to be short-lived, if the seedlings are killed by browsing or shade from trees that have already grown beyond browsing reach.

The supply of seeds or initial density of seedlings have been found to have an influence on the effect of regeneration for some tree species. Investigations of moose browsing in relation to stand density have revealed that although the number of browsed saplings increase approximately in proportion to stem density, the bite diameter, bite weight and number of bites per sapling all decline with increasing stem density, resulting in relatively less damage when tree density is high (Heikkila & Mikkonen 1992). Barandun (1983) reported that regeneration of Norway spruce, Picea abies, in the presence of red and roe deer was possible in small groups of 7000–8000 stems ha^{-1}, because only trees on the edges of the groups were damaged.

Table 6.2. *Changes in tree seedling densities under browsing pressure. The effects of increasing ungulate density (if reported) have been indicated by listing results in classes I–IV*

Age (yrs)	Stand Type	Size Class	Protected	Browsed Ungulate — Density Class I	II	III	IV	Ungulate Species, Location and Density
6	Unthinned	Total	8 708	8 063	3 166			White-tailed deer, USA Density I: 4.5; II: 13.5 Km^{-2} (Healy 1997)
		>90 cm ht	1 354	2 042	729			
	Thinned	Total	26 417	35 500	9 417			
		>90 cm ht	7 938	17 504	1 792			
14		<10 cm dbh	6 440	20				Fallow deer, UK Density 100 Km^{-2} (Putman et al. 1989)
11			3 323	2 539				Red deer, roe deer, Poland (Mean of 7 sites) (Dzieciolowski 1980)
6	Heathland	Total	5 686	3 800				Red deer, roe deer, wild boar, Germany (Luthardt & Beyer 1998)
		>130 cm ht	601	266				
6			627	488				Red deer, roe deer, Netherlands (Van Hees et al. 1996)
	Clearing		13 045	10 989				
	Unthinned		4 215	1 162				
2	Closed canopy	Total	31 960	15 333				Red deer, UK Density: 7.0 Km^{-2} (Langbein 1997)
		>35 cm ht	520	0				
	Open canopy	Total	43 019	32 466				
		>35 cm ht	1 100	1 022				

Table 6.2. *(cont.)*

| Age (yrs) | Stand Type | Size Class | Density of Tree Seedlings, ha^{-1} | | | | | | Ungulate Species, Location and Density |
| | | | Protected | Ungulate Browsed Density | | | | | |
				I	II	III	IV		
5	Thinned	Total	207 200	219 500	226 600	296 400	241 700		White-tailed deer, USA Density I: 3.7; II: 7.7; III: 14.8; IV: 26.8 Km^{-2} (Tilghman 1989)
		>100 cm ht	7 200	8 400	6 400	3 000	3 200		
	Unthinned	Total	180 900	130 200	157 600	109 800	83 800		
		>100 cm ht	900	700	500	700	0		
	Clearing	Total	139 900	122 900	115 400	130 300	177 600		
		>150 cm ht	32 900	33 100	30 100	168 00	9 700		
10	Heathland	Total	627	468					Red deer, roe deer, wild boar, Netherlands Density: 13.6 Km^{-2} (Kuiters & Slim 2002)
	Pine forest		1 855	1 089					
	Oak forest		1 990	570					
	Beech forest		4 295	0					

INDIRECT EFFECTS OF LARGE HERBIVORES

The success of tree regeneration can be strongly influenced by either competitive or facultative interactions with neighbouring plants. There is now increasing evidence that browsing and grazing herbivores can affect regeneration *indirectly* by altering the relative strength of these effects.

Grasses compete with tree seedlings, by reducing sites for germination as well as limiting growth and survival rates of established seedlings (Davies 1987). By virtue of having low meristems, grasses are well-adapted to withstand repeated defoliation by herbivores, and seeds of some species are also dispersed through the gut (Malo & Suarez 1995). In woodland environments, grasses are not grazed short, and they usually increase in cover as result of deer browsing pressure (Putman *et al.* 1989, Kirby 2001). In the eastern USA, browsing by white-tailed deer results in increased and persistent cover of grasses and unpalatable ferns, which restricts regeneration of many broad-leaved tree species (Horsley & Marquis 1983). Once established, grasses or other plants can persist, preventing tree establishment even if the deer population subsequently declines (Stromayer & Warren 1997, Rooney 2001). Such non-reversible effects may have long-lasting implications for the effects of deer on vegetation.

In spite of the competition, tree seedlings can establish themselves successfully in grasslands and there are a number of mechanisms which enable this to happen. Grazing reduces shading and hoof pressure can break roots or rhizomes creating niches suitable for trees to germinate in. Once germinated, the seedlings themselves are often browsed but may succeed in growing if subsequent damage is not too severe. Pigott (1983), for example, reported that seedlings of birch *Betula* spp. would germinate in grass shortly after fencing out sheep, but as soon as the grasses became too tall and dense, germination of birch was prevented. On the other hand, seedlings of oak were able to germinate successfully inside the fence in spite of competition from grasses. In another example, Vinther (1983) found that regeneration of alder, *Alnus glutinosa*, into a meadow was possible only at moderate densities of cattle. Seedlings could not germinate if grazing pressure was too low, but were damaged too frequently if it was too high. Seedlings of many tree species (e.g. *Pinus elliotti, P. ponderosa, P. palustris*) are relatively unpalatable to cattle and grazing has sometimes been deliberately employed to reduce competition and improve seedling growth and survival (Adams 1975, Doescher *et al.* 1987, Ratliff & Denton 1995). Livestock grazing has been found to cause the expansion of scrub from grassland in tropical or arid regions (Madany & West 1983, Westoby *et al.* 1989). Several factors contribute to shrub establishment, including seed dispersal (endozoochory) and reduced fire frequency caused by reduction in biomass following grazing (Roques *et al.* 2001). These factors are discussed in more detail in Chapter 5.

Established shrubs, particularly those of thorny or unpalatable species can protect seedlings from grazing damage. The survival of oak seedlings, *Quercus* sp., in areas grazed by cattle or horses can increase under the protection of bushes of *Prunus spinosa, Juniperus communis, Buxus sempervirens* and *Rubus fruticosus* (Watt 1919, Buttenschøn & Buttenschøn 1985, Rousset & Lepart 1999, Bakker 2003, Kuiters & Slim 2003). Similarly, the survival of beech, *Fagus sylvatica*, yew, *Taxus baccata*, and oak can be facilitated by protection from holly, *Ilex aquifolium* (Morgan 1991, Garcia & Obeso 2003). In the latter case, the authors noted that yew was better protected if the holly had itself been browsed and developed a more spreading growth form. Since deer and other browsing herbivores are able to eat thorny plants, this form of protection may be less effective against them than grazers. Buttenschøn and Buttenschøn (1985), for example, noted that oak did not regenerate in the *absence* of cattle or in the *presence* of sheep. Many authors report that deer browsing acts to *retard* woodland succession on open ground or near woodland edges (Okuda & Nakane 1990, Cooke 1994, Lawson *et al.* 1999), which suggests that if any facilitation is operating, sufficient browsing on trees is occurring to overwhelm it. However, Hamard and Ballon (1998) found that woody plants (only some of which were thorny species) grown close to young *Q. rubra* seedlings offered sufficient protection from roe deer, *Capreolus capreolus*, to improve growth and survival. In Scotland, young conifer trees can escape damage until they grow above surrounding heather, *Calluna vulgaris*, plants (Welch *et al.* 1991). Neighbouring plants may therefore be capable of offering protection by reducing detection rates or access, not solely by reducing biting rates. In temperate regions, the majority of thorny plants are light-demanding species, and thus are most likely to offer protection to other light-demanding tree species colonizing open ground or large canopy gaps. Oak is a widespread species in northwest Europe but failure of regeneration has been noticed for some time (Watt 1919). It is particularly palatable to deer and sheep, intolerant of shade and may be restricted by competition from under-storey species such as *Rubus* sp. (Pigott 1983, Rozas 2003). As a result, it was unclear how it became so prevalent in the pollen and historical records, but recent reviews (Vera 2000) have suggested that protection from thorny plants was the main vehicle for regeneration, and that the reduction of extensive stock grazing in wood-lands and wood-pastures is largely responsible for the recent failure of regeneration.

The influence of large herbivores on soil nutrient availability has important implications for tree regeneration. Large herbivores may either increase or decrease nutrient flows, depending on the environment and herbivore density (Pastor *et al.* 1992, see also Chapter 10). This will affect growth of the tree both directly and indirectly, either by changing the balance of competition or the growth of facilitating species. In forests, browsing by moose and deer has been linked to declining nutrient avail-ability and regeneration of some tree species (Pastor *et al.* 1998, Ritchie *et al.* 1998). Many of the thorny species that function as nurse plants grow best on high nutrient status sites, and may therefore benefit from high grazing pressures. The changes in soil nutrient status may also contribute to changes in plant and tree species composition.

CHANGES IN TREE SPECIES COMPOSITION

Large herbivores need to feed selectively and the effects of this selection are very evident on forest vegetation. Some tree species are browsed more heavily than others, as well as differing in their ability to recover from damage (Eiberle 1975, Gill 1992b, Miller *et al.* 1998). The result is that recruits of the more palatable or sensitive species are depleted. Less palatable trees, or other plants, may increase at their expense. In the northeast USA, Tilghman (1989), for example, found that tree species richness declined with increasing deer density (particularly at higher densities) but one unpalatable species, black cherry, *Prunus serotina*, in-creased. Some authors have commented that deer appear to change their diet as the most palatable species decline (Beals *et al.* 1960, Stewart & Burrows 1989).

Since deer populations have increased in many temperate regions, recruitment failure of sensitive species is being increasingly reported. In the Great Lake states, recruitment of hemlock, *Tsuga canadensis*, Canadian yew, *Taxus canadensis*, and white cedar, *Thuja occidentalis*, are being de-pleted by white-tailed deer (Anderson & Loucks 1979, Frelich & Lorimer 1985, Alverson *et al.* 1988). These species are browsed heavily in the winter, and losses have been particularly evident in winter-yarding areas. However, extensive surveys have indicated that the problem is region-wide, not merely local (Rooney 2001). Further, comparisons of contemporary forest composition with pre-settlement times in Michigan have revealed a decline in *Tsuga canadensis* (Van Deleen *et al.* 1996). Besides affecting growth, browsing on Canada yew also reduces flowering and pollination success (Allison 1990a,b). On Anticosti Island, Quebec, Balsam fir, *Abies balsamea*, has been declining, following the introduction of white-tailed deer during the last century (Potvin *et al.* 2003). In the western USA, aspen, *Populus tremuloides*, has been declining under the effects of ungulate browsing. Selective exclosure experiments have revealed that most damage is being done by elk, *Cervus elaphus*, but the combination of mule deer, elk and cattle reduce abundance even more (Kay & Bartos 2000, Kay 2001). Decreases in the abundance of riparian willows, *Salix* spp. in Colorado are also thought to be due to browsing by elk (Zeigenfuss *et al.* 2002). Another sensitive species is the European silver fir, *Abies alba*, which fails to regenerate adequately due to browsing by roe deer, red deer and chamois, *Rupicapra rupicapra* (Zeltner 1979, Konig & Baumann 1990). Eiberle (1975) noted that silver fir was both very palatable and slow to recover from the effects of browsing.

In view of the fact that the majority of tree species are palatable, the tendency is for deer to decrease tree species diversity (Table 6.3, Fig. 6.1a,b). In this analysis, the influence of deer to tree species richness and diversity was examined both by comparing fenced and unfenced plots, as well as by including deer density as a variable in a general linear model. The results show that deer reduce both richness and diversity, and that there tends to be a greater loss at higher densities. Although there was insufficient data for shrubs to be analysed in the same way, the results reported by several authors (Kraus 1987, Gerber & Schmidt 1996, Martin & Daufresne 1999) indicate that shrub diversity also declines at high deer densities.

Where tree seedlings receive protection from other shrubs or thorny plants it is possible that browsing or grazing will promote or maintain diversity, rather than decrease it. Provided the dominant plants are not unpalatable, grazing usually acts to reduce competition and this promotes diversity (Olff & Ritchie 1998, see also Chapter 4). The reason why seedling diversity is often reduced in woodlands is, not only because many tree species' seedlings are relatively palatable, but because they are subject to competition from trees in the over-storey, which are unaffected by browsing. As yet there appears to be little direct evidence that grazing and browsing in openings, particularly where protection from other plants occurs, actually results in increased tree species diversity, but there are at least theoretical reasons why it may occur. It is therefore possible that feeding by herbivores acts to increase tree seedling diversity in openings but decreases it in a more shaded under-storey.

Table 6.3. *Results of the general linear models to assess the effect of deer browsing on tree species richness (N) and diversity (H)*

Model	F	d.f.	r^2	Name	F	d.f.	P
				Explanatory Variable			
1 $N = 9.64 + L - 1.645d$	10.39	12,68	0.65	L	10.39	11	0.0001
				d	10.36	1	0.002
2 $H = 2.07 + L - 0.352d$	5.43	9,44	0.53	L	5.1	8	0.0002
				d	8.06	1	0.0068
3 $N_d = 2.2092 + 0.796N_o$ $+ L - 0.165D$	10.6	6,15	0.81	N_o	47.9	1	0.0001
				L	1.9	4	0.1(ns)
				D	4.9	1	0.02
4 $H_d = 1.1372 + 0.708H_o$ $+ L - 0.0826D$	64.8	4,4	0.98	H_o	62.2	1	0.002
				L	70.9	2	0.001
				D	55.2	1	0.002

Diversity H' was calculated using the Shannon index, $H' = -E\ pi\ \ln\ pi$, where pi is the proportional abundance of species i, $pi = ni/N$ (Magurran 1988). In models 1 and 2, richness and diversity were compared between paired fenced ($d = 0$) and unfenced controls ($d = 1$) after accounting for between site variation (L). Models 3 and 4 test the effect of deer density (D deer km^{-2}) on richness (N_d) and diversity (H_d) after accounting for the effect of location (L). These models were based on a smaller sample where deer density had been recorded, and used the values of richness and diversity recorded in exclosures (N_o, H_o) as a covariate. Analyses were based on data for young trees only (<11 years old), obtained from 13 studies carried out in temperate woodland sites in both Europe and North America: Dzieciolowski (1980); Kraus (1987); Tilghman (1989); Putman et al. (1989); Jones et al. (1993); Gerber & Schmidt (1996); Van Hees et al. (1996); Ammer (1996); Healy (1997); Scrinzi et al. (1997); Langbein (1997); Luthardt & Bayer (1998). Shrub species were excluded from these analyses because the majority of authors did not report them. Reproduced from Gill and Beardall (2001), by permission of Oxford University Press.

It is evident that deer do not always have the same effect on vegetation composition. Distinctions can be made between tree species that are almost always depleted by browsing and those that decrease in some sites but increase in others (Table 6.4). In European conditions, oak, willow and hornbeam have been reported to decline in all cases, implying that reduction of at least these three species is inevitable. In contrast, species such as beech and birch can occasionally increase. There are likely to be a variety of reasons why browsing may not create a consistent change in species composition. The rate of browsing on any species of medium or low preference is likely to vary in relation to the abundance of more preferred species. Browsing by roe deer on yew (*Taxus baccata*) has been found to increase where a more palatable shrub, bilberry, *Vaccinium myrtillus*, is

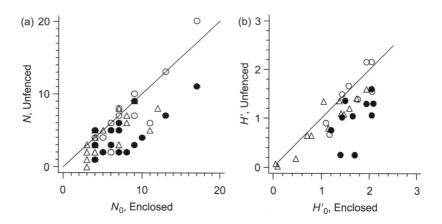

Figure 6.1. The effect of deer browsing pressure on tree species richness and diversity, assessed by comparison between fenced enclosures and unfenced controls. (a) The numbers of tree species. (b) Tree species diversity. Data points have been represented by open circles where deer density was below the median for a particular study or site and solid circles where it is above. Triangles represent sites where density was not recorded. The straight line marks the line of equal diversity. Data obtained from the same sources as used in Table 6.3. Reproduced from Gill and Beardall (2001), by permission of Oxford University Press.

present, or when it is covered with snow (Mysterud & Ostbye 1995). Similarly, browsing on beech, *Fagus sylvatica*, and Norway spruce, *Picea abies*, was found to be reduced where silver fir, *Abies alba*, was more abundant (Eiberle & Bucher 1989). Selection can also depend on the relative abundance of each species. Silver birch, *Betula pendula*, appears to be preferentially selected by moose when it occurs in low proportions to downy birch, *B. pubescens*, but not when it is above 60% (Danell & Ericson 1986). In contrast ash, *Fraxinus exelsior*, has been found to be browsed more than willow, *Salix* sp., by red deer, irrespective of their relative densities (Chevallier-Redor *et al.* 2001).

TEMPORAL AND SPATIAL VARIATIONS IN HERBIVORE DENSITIES

There are many examples showing how seedling survival and growth rates of seedlings or coppice shoots are increasingly limited at higher herbivore densities (Table 6.2, Tilghman 1989, Hester *et al.* 1996). Natural fluctuations in herbivore populations will therefore be followed by changes in tree seedling recruitment rate and forest vegetation structure. The New

Table 6.4. *The effect of exclusion from deer on the relative abundance of some woody plant species*

	Proportion of cases %		
	Abundance *decreasing* under browsing pressure	Abundance *increasing* under browsing pressure	Sample size (*n*)
Trees			
Oak *Quercus* sp.	100		24
Willow *Salix* sp.	100		10
Hornbeam *Carpinus betula*	100		8
Rowan *Sorbus aucuparia*	91		11
Ash *Fraxinus excelsior*	83		6
Aspen *Populus tremula*	83	17	6
Birch *Betula* sp.	70	30	10
Scots Pine *Pinus sylvestris*	60	30	10
Field maple *Acer campestre*	60	40	5
Beech *Fagus sylvatica*	54	38	13
Shrubs and climbers			
Bramble *Rubus fruticosus*	92	8	12
Ivy *Hedera helix*	83	17	6
Hawthorn *Crataegus monogyna*	80	20	5
Honeysuckle *Lonicera periclymenum*	50	50	4

Data have been summarized from ten European studies: Dzieciolowski (1980); Kraus (1987); Putman *et al.* (1989); Gerber and Schmidt (1996); Van Hees (1996); Ammer (1996); Scrinzi *et al.* (1997); Langbein (1997); Luthardt & Bayer (1998); Author's unpublished data. The sample sizes indicate the total number of sites where more than 5 individuals of the species were recorded. The sum of the two percentages is <100 where no change in abundance were recorded at one or more of the sites.

Forest is one of the few remaining areas in Europe where grazing in woodlands has been carried out for several centuries and analysis of the stand age structure has revealed distinct pulses of regeneration, coinciding with periods when historical records show that herbivore numbers were low (Peterken & Tubbs 1965). More dramatic changes in woodland cover have occurred in East Africa following the decimation of herbivore populations (both wild and domestic) by rinderpest epidemics in the late nineteenth century. The age of existing mature woodlands can be traced to the periods following this epidemic (Prins & Van Der Jeugd 1993). Extensive areas of the Serengeti-Mara ecosystem developed into woodland during the early part of the twentieth century, only to revert back to grassland again when ungulate and elephant populations recovered (Dublin 1995).

Short-term fluctuations in herbivore numbers are likely to be key events in the maintenance of woodlands. Trees have a long life span (in comparison to most herbivores) and many species exhibit a high inter-annual variation in seed output creating frequent opportunities for repro-duction. Further, many tree species can re-sprout quickly from coppice shoots after damage to the main stem. These strategies provide short time windows for regeneration, if sufficient growth can be achieved in time. Several mechanisms have been identified indicating that herbivores can promote tree regeneration (endozoochory, protection from thorny plants, by reducing competition from grasses). These effects mainly operate on open ground, and will mitigate the destructive effects of browsing in denser woodlands to some extent. As yet, there appears to be little direct evidence that rates of tree regeneration are *positively* related to herbivore densities, although it is plausible that it may occur.

Although it is clear that variation in herbivore density through time is often associated with varying rates of tree regeneration, there are enor-mous differences between areas, with regeneration succeeding in some areas but not in others. In Scotland, various studies have concluded that regeneration of Scots pine is only possible where densities of red deer are between 4–8 km^{-2} (a biomass of 3–7 kg ha^{-1}) or less (Beaumont *et al.* 1995, Scott *et al.* 2000). In contrast, Mwalyosi (1990) concluded that regeneration of *Acacia tortilis* in Manyara, Tanzania, was still successful where the biomass of herbivores was in the region of 120–150 kg ha^{-1}. There are of course many differences between areas that can contribute to such differences in rates of regeneration. One reason is that very large herbivores feed at a greater height in the canopy, thus reducing competi-tion with smaller ungulates. However, very large herbivores will also increase light penetration to the ground layer, which will stimulate tree regeneration as well as the productivity of browse for small-medium sized ungulates. Although elephants can feed on seedling trees (Dublin 1995, Barnes 2001), several studies have concluded that loss of regeneration or suppression of seedling growth can be attributed more to browsing by smaller ungulates, such as impala, *Aepyceros melampus,* or kudu, than very large herbivores (Mwalyosi 1990, Prins & Van Der Jeugd 1993, Barnes 2001).

Herbivores select habitats within their home range and damage to young trees may therefore be most severe where animals concentrate feeding effort. The effects of elk, *Cervus elaphus*, and deer, for example, can be greatest where animals congregate in winter. By modelling habitat suitability, aspen productivity and off-take, Weisberg and Coughenour

(2003) were able to show that regeneration of aspen would vary throughout the area, being increasingly restricted to sites used least in winter as elk population density increased. In an investigation of herbivore impacts in Australia, sheep were found to cause more damage in drought years than kangaroos, *Macropus rufus*, because they were not able to extend their foraging to better sites as conditions deteriorated (Tiver & Andrew 1997). Concentrations of herbivores will also act to redistribute nutrients and seeds, and create greater disturbance (Pastor *et al.* 1998). Recruitment and early growth of *Acacia tortilis* in Kenya was found to be enhanced near corrals, where livestock concentrations are greatest, because of elevated soil nutrient levels and improved moisture retention (Reid & Ellis 1995). There is a need for more information on the various relationships between herbivore impact and dispersal movements. It is likely that damage will be more severe if herbivores become confined or restricted in fragmented landscapes (e.g. Dublin 1995). To address problems of this kind, dispersal corridors have been proposed to link protected areas isolated by urban or intensive agricultural land in northwestern Europe (Groot Bruinderink *et al.* 2002).

CONCLUSIONS

There is clearly abundant evidence that herbivores have a major effect on trees, by causing damage and affecting survival rates. However, there is a shortage of direct evidence of the long-term consequences of these effects on vegetation structure. This is particularly the case in the temperate regions, where there has been such a loss of large herbivores in the historic and pre-historic time periods. The effects of large herbivores on tree regeneration can be grouped broadly into two main types: firstly, the effects of feeding on seeds, seedlings and bark, which are damaging and delay forest succession or accelerate senescence; and secondly, the effects which promote regeneration and thus tend to advance forest succession. There appear to be at least four mechanisms involved in this latter group: regeneration may be promoted through seed dispersal; protection from thorny plants; reduced competition; or lastly, by reduced fire frequency or fire temperatures as a result of reduced fuel biomass. In general, the retarding effects of herbivory appear to be more prevalent in woodlands or existing areas of tree cover, whereas facilitation is more likely to occur in grasslands or other open ground used by grazing animals. The fact that these two contrasting processes occur in different communities has led to the suggestion that large herbivores cause a cycle of succession (Vera 2000, Kirby 2003), including several stages of open ground, tree colonization, maturing woodlands and senescent stands which finally give way to open ground again. Large herbivores will therefore create a more dynamic woodland, one where changes in tree cover may be continually occurring and one where light-demanding tree species are likely to be favoured at the expense of shade-tolerant species.

Although there is evidence to support the existence of all stages of this cycle, there are also processes involved which are progressive and include positive feed-backs. Apart from the presence of the herbivores themselves, there is also little reason to suggest that the rates of regeneration and senescence will be balanced. Rates of both tree regeneration and damage by large herbivores can be highly variable, and facilitation by thorny plants will depend on the suitability of the site for the nurse species. Further, each species or guild of herbivores will have a unique pattern of habitat and diet selection. As a result, successional changes could lead to dominance of either open ground grassland or closed-canopy woodland. The effect of herbivores on nutrient flows, for example, may bring about enduring changes in vegetation composition. Since the amount of food for herbivores can be sharply reduced by shade, populations will decline if trees grow dense enough to form closed-canopy woodland over an extensive area (Gill *et al.* 1996). This may then limit the extent to which herbivores can maintain openings. In Africa, switching between woodland and grassland states appears to occur in savanna regions. As a result of a combination of grazing, elephants and fire, woodlands in the Serengeti-Mara region were transformed into grassland in the 1960s, but began to recover again in part of the region during the 1980s, when elephant numbers were severely reduced (Dublin *et al.* 1990, Dublin 1995). These changes suggest that savanna ecosystems may be unstable, or have alternate stable states, and events affecting herbivore numbers or grazing pressure could prompt major changes in vegetation structure.

Evidence from exclosures suggests that the selective browsing by deer tends to reduce tree species diversity. Unfortunately, there is insufficient information to generalize for other herbivores in forest habitats. However, a study of the impact of elephants found that diversity of trees and shrubs was reduced, but diversity of plants near ground level was increased (Lenzi-Grillini *et al.* 1996). A similar result was reported for moose browsing, where diversity of the smallest trees (<1 m) increased, but apparently not for trees above this height class (Risenhoover & Maass 1986). These results indicate that diversity will be promoted only if it is maintained by the time the smallest class attain maturity. It should not be assumed that the effects on stand diversity will be reflected in reduced diversity at the landscape scale: in fact the reverse is likely to be the case. Because herbivores vary foraging effort amongst habitats, the impact they have on vegetation and nutrient flows will be uneven, and this will promote spatial diversity. Herbivores also promote structural variation in woodland and help to maintain openings. In grassland, herbivores have long been known to enhance plant diversity (Olff & Ritchie 1998). Lastly, the protection provided by thorny plants would be expected to increase diversity by permitting the growth of other trees and shrubs. There are therefore cogent reasons for encouraging free-ranging herbivores to meet woodland conservation objectives. However, it needs to be recognized that these cannot easily be met simply by protecting woodland areas alone with a resident deer population. Instead, greater diversity is likely to be achieved by linking open ground and woodland, restoring large grazing animals and allowing natural successional pathways to develop.

ACKNOWLEDGEMENTS

I would like to thank the Swedish University of Agricultural Sciences for financial support for a workshop in Umeå which provided many opportunities for helpful discussions with colleagues. I would also like to thank Helen Armstrong, Frans Vera and an anonymous referee for comments on an earlier draft of this manuscript.

REFERENCES

Adams, S. N. (1975). Sheep and cattle grazing in forests: a review. *Journal of Applied Ecology*, **12**, 143–52.

Agusti, J. & Anton, M. (2002). *Mammoths, Sabertooths and Hominids: 65 Million Years of Mammalian Evolution in Europe*. New York: Columbia University Press.

Akashi, N. & Nakashizuka, T. (1999). Effects of bark stripping by sika deer (*Cervus nippon*) on population dynamics of a mixed forest in Japan. *Forest Ecology and Management*, **113**, 75–82.

Allison, T. (1990a). The influence of deer browsing on the reproductive biology of Canada yew (*Taxus canadensis* Marsh). 1. Direct effect on pollen, ovule, and seed production. *Oecologia*, **83**, 523–9.

Allison, T. (1990b). The influence of deer browsing on the reproductive biology of Canada yew (*Taxus canadensis* Marsh). 2. Pollen limitation: an indirect effect. *Oecologia*, **83**, 530–4.

Alverson, W. S., Waller, D. M. & Solheim, S. L. (1988). Forests too deer: edge effects in northern Wisconsin. *Conservation Biology*, **2**, 348–58.

Ammer, C. (1996). Impact of ungulates on structure and dynamics of natural regeneration of mixed mountain forests in the Bavarian Alps. *Forest Ecology and Management*, **88**, 43–53.

Anderson, G. W., Hawke, M. & Moore, R. W. (1985). Pine needle consumption and bark stripping by sheep grazing annual pastures in young stands of widely spaced *Pinus radiata and P. pinaster*. *Agroforestry Systems*, **3**, 37–45.

Anderson, R. C. & Loucks, O. L. (1979). White-tail deer (*Odocoileus virginianus*) influence on structure and composition of *Tsuga canadensis* forests. *Journal of Applied Ecology*, **16**, 855–61.

Bakker, E. S. (2003). *Herbivores as Mediators of their Environment: the Impact of Large and Small Species on Vegetation Dynamics*. Ph.D. thesis, Wageningen University, Netherlands.

Barandun, J. (1983). Afforestation at high altitudes. *Schweizerische Zeitschrift für Forstwesen*, **134**, 431–41.

Barnes, M. E. (2001). Effects of large herbivores and fire on the regeneration of *Acacia erioloba* woodlands in Chobe National Park, Botswana. *African Journal of Ecology*, **39**, 340–50.

Bassman, J. H. & Dickmann, D. I. (1985). Effects of defoliation in the developing leaf zone on young *Populus × euamericana* plants. 2. Distribution of 14-C photosynthesate after defoliation. *Forest Science*, **31**, 358–66.

Bazely, D. R., Myers, J. H. & Dasilva, K. B. (1991). The response of numbers of bramble prickles to herbivory and depressed resource availability. *Oikos*, **61**, 327–36.

Beals, E. W., Cottam, G. W. & Vogal, R. J. (1960). Influence of deer on vegetation of the apostle islands, Wisconsin. *Journal of Wildlife Management*, **24**, 68–79.

Beaumont, D., Dugan, D. & Evans, G. (1995). Deer management and tree regeneration in the RSPB Reserve at Abernethy. *Scottish Forestry*, **49**, 155–61.

Bergerud, A. T. & Manuel, F. (1968). Moose damage to balsam fir–white birch forests in central Newfoundland. *Journal of Wildlife Management*, **32**, 729–46.

Bergqvist, G., Bergström, R. & Edenius, L. (2003). Effects of moose (*Alces alces*) rebrowsing on damage development in young stands of Scots pine (*Pinus sylvestris*). *Forest Ecology and Management*, **176**, 397–403.

Bergström, R. & Danell, K. (1987). Effects of simulated winter browsing by moose on morphology and biomass of two birch species. *Journal of Ecology*, **75**, 533–44.

Bergström, R., Skarpe, C. & Danell, K. (2000). Plant responses and herbivory following simulated browsing and stem cutting of *Combretum apiculatum*. *Journal of Vegetation Science*, **11**, 409–14.

Borowski, S. & Kossak, S. (1972). The natural food preferences of the European bison in the season of snow cover. *Acta Theriologica*, **17**, 151–69.

Bossema I. (1979). Jays and oaks: an eco-ethological study of a symbiosis. *Behaviour*, **70**, 1–117.

Buttenschøn, J. & Buttenschøn R. M. (1985). Grazing experiments with cattle and sheep on nutrient poor, acidic grassland and heath. IV. Establishment of woody species. *Natura Jutlandica*, **21**, 47–140.

Cerezke, H. F. (1974). Effects of partial girdling on growth in Lodgepole pine with application to damage by the weevil *Hylobius warreni* wood. *Canadian Journal of Forest Research*, **4**, 312–20.

Chevallier-Redor, N., Verheyden-Tixier, H. & Verdier, M. (2001). Foraging behaviour of red deer *Cervus elaphus* as a function of the relative availability of two tree species. *Animal Research*, **50**, 57–65.

Clutton-Brock, J. (1989). Five thousand years of livestock in Britain. *Biological Journal of the Linnean Society*, **38**, 31–7.

Cochrane, E. P. (2003). The need to be eaten: *Balanites wilsoniana* with and without elephant seed-dispersal. *Journal of Tropical Ecology*, **19**, 579–89.

Cooke, A. S. (1994). *Long-term Scrub Succession Deflected by Fallow Deer at Castor Hanglands NNR*. ITE Annual Report 1993/4.

Cooke, A. S. & Lakhani, K. H. (1996). Damage to coppice regrowth by muntjac deer *Muntiacus reevesi* and protection with electric fencing. *Biological Conservation*, **75**, 231–8.

Cooper, M. R. & Johnson, A. W. (1984). *Poisonous Plants in Britain and their Effects on Animals and Man*. HMSO, Reference Book 161. London: Ministry of Agriculture, Fisheries and Food.

Cooper, S. M. & Owen-Smith, N. (1986). The effects of plant spinescence on large mammalian herbivores. *Oecologia*, **68**, 446–55.

Crawley, M. J. (1989). The relative importance of vertebrate and invertebrate herbivores in plant population dynamics. In *Insect-Plant Interactions*, ed. E. A. Bernays. Boca Raton, Florida: CRC Press, pp. 45–71.

Danell, K. & Ericson, L. (1986). Foraging by moose on two species of birch when these occur in different proportions. *Holarctic Ecology*, **9**, 79–84.

Danell, K., Bergström, R. & Edenius, L. (1994). Effects of large mammalian browsers on architecture, biomass, and nutrients of woody plants. *Journal of Mammalogy*, **75**, 833–44.

Danell, K., Bergström, R., Edenius, L. & Ericsson, G. (2003). Ungulates as drivers of tree population dynamics at module and genet levels. *Forest Ecology and Management*, **181**, 67–76.

Darley-Hill, S. & Johnson, W. C. (1981). Acorn dispersal by the Blue jay (*Cyanocitta cristata*). *Oecologia*, **50**, 231–2.

Davies, R. J. (1987). *Trees and Weeds*. Forestry Commission Handbook 7. London: HMSO.

Dimock, E. J. (1970). Ten year height growth of Douglas fir damaged by hare and deer. *Journal of Forestry*, **68**, 285–8.

Doescher, P. S., Teasch, S. D. & Alejandro Castro, M. (1987). Livestock grazing: a silvicultural tool for plantation establishment. *Journal of Forestry*, **40**, 29–37.

Dublin, H. (1995). Vegetation dynamics in the Serengeti-Mara ecosystem: the role of elephants, fire and other factors. In *Serengeti II, Dynamics, Management and Conservation of an Ecosystem*, ed. A. R. E. Sinclair & P. Arcese. Chicago: University of Chicago Press, pp. 71–90.

Dublin, H., Sinclair, A. R. E. & McGlade, J. (1990). Elephants and fire as causes of multiple stable states in the Serengeti-Mara woodlands. *Journal of Animal Ecology*, **59**, 1147–64.

Duncan, A. J., Hartley, S. E. & Thurlow, M. (2001). Clonal variation in mono-terpene concentrations in Sitka spruce (*Picea sitchensis*) saplings and its effect on their susceptibility to browsing damage by deer (*Cervus elaphus*). *Forest Ecology and Management*, **148**, 259–69.

Dzięciołowski, R. (1980). Impact of deer browsing upon forest regeneration and undergrowth. *Ekologia Polska*, **28**, 583–99.

Edenius, L. (1993). Browsing by moose on Scots pine in relation to plant resource availability. *Ecology*, **74**, 2261–9.

Eiberle, K. (1975). Result of simulation of game damage through shoot cutting. *Schweizerische Zeitschrift für Forstwesen*, **126**, 821–38.

Eiberle, K. & Bucher, H. (1989). Interdependence between browsing of different tree species in a selection forest region. *Zeitschrift für Jagdwissenschaft*, **35**, 235–44.

Eiberle, K. & Nigg, H. (1987). Basis for assessing game browsing in montane forests. *Schweizerische Zeitschrift für Forstwesen*, **138**, 747–85.

Ericsson, A., Hellquist, C. & Långström, B. (1985). Effects on growth of simulated and induced shoot pruning by *Tomicus piniperda* as related to carbohydrate and nitrogen dynamics in Scots pine. *Journal of Applied Ecology*, **22**, 105–24.

Faber, W. E. (1996). Bark stripping by moose on young *Pinus sylvestris* in south-central Sweden. *Scandinavian Journal of Forest Research*, **11**, 300–6.

Faber, W. E. & Edenius, L. (1998). Bark stripping by moose in commercial forests of Fennoscandia – a review. *Alces*, **34**, 1–8.

Feldhamer, G. (2002). Acorns and white-tailed deer: interrelationships in forest ecosystems. In: *Oak Forest Ecosystems*, ed. W. J. McShea, & W. M. Healy. Baltimore: Johns Hopkins University Press, pp. 215–223.

Flower, N. (1980). The management history and structure of unenclosed woods in the New Forest, Hampshire. *Journal of Biogeography*, **7**, 311–28.

Frelich, L. E. & Lorimer, C. G. (1985). Current and predicted long-term effects of deer browsing in hemlock forests in Michigan, USA. *Biological Conservation*, **34**, 99–120.

Fruhmann, M. & Roeder, A. (1981). Increased risk of snow breakage in Norway spruce stands caused by red deer bark-stripping damage. *Allgemeine Forstzeitschrift*, **21**, 528–9.

Fuller, R. J. (2001). Responses of woodland birds to increasing numbers of deer: a review of evidence and mechanisms. *Forestry*, **74**, 289–98.

Furuno, T. & Yamazaki, T. (1973). Effects of artificial deprivation of shoots on stem upon the growth of some pine species. *Bulletins of the Kyoto University Forests*, **45**, 9–26.

Garcia, D. & Obeso, J. R. (2003). Facilitation by herbivore-mediated nurse plants in a threatened tree, *Taxus baccata*: local effects and landscape level consistency. *Ecography*, **26**, 739–50.

Gerber, R. & Schmidt, W. (1996). Influence of roe deer in the vegetation of oak-hornbeam forests in southern Steigerwald. *Verhandlungen der Gesellschaft für Oekologie*, **26**, 345–53.

Gill, R. M. A. (1992a). A review of damage by mammals in north temperate forests. 1. Deer. *Forestry*, **65**, 145–69.

Gill, R. M. A. (1992b). A review of damage by mammals in north temperate forests. 3. Impact on trees and forests. *Forestry*, **65**, 363–88.

Gill, R. M. A. & Beardall, V. (2001). The impact of deer on woodlands: the effects of browsing and seed dispersal on vegetation structure and composition. *Forestry*, **74**, 209–18.

Gill, R. M. A., Johnson, A. L., Francis, A., Hiscocks, K. & Peace, A. J. (1996). Changes in roe deer (*Capreolus capreolus* L.) population density in response to forest habitat succession. *Forest Ecology and Management*, **88**, 31–41.

Gill, R. M. A., Webber, J. & Peace, A. (2000). *The Economic Implications of Deer Damage: a Review of Current Evidence*. Inverness: Deer Commission for Scotland.

Girompaire, L. & Ballon, P. (1992). Consequences of bark stripping by red deer in the Alsatian Vosges massif. *Revue Forestière Française*, **44**, 501–11.

Gowda, J. H. (1996). Spines of *Acacia tortilis*: what do they defend and how? *Oikos*, **77**, 279–84.

Gregory, S. C. (1986). The development of stain in wounded Sitka spruce stems. *Forestry*, **59**, 199–208.

Groot Bruinderink, G. W. T. A. & Hazebroek, E. (1995). Modelling carrying capacity for wild boar *Sus scrofa scrofa* in a forest/heathland ecosystem. *Wildlife Biology*, **1**, 81–7.

Groot Bruinderink, G. W. T. A., Lammertsma, D. R. & Hengeveld, R. (2002). Make way for the European ecological network. *Vakblad Natuurbeheer*, **41**, 51–3.

Han, H. S., Kellogg, L. D., Filip, G. M. & Brown, T. D. (2000). Scar closure and future timber value losses from thinning damage in western Oregon. *Forest Products Journal*, **50**, 36–42.

Hamard, J. P. & Ballon, P. (1998). Browsing on red oak (*Quercus rubra* L.) by roe deer (*Capreolus capreolus* L.) and accompanying vegetation. *Gibier Faune Sauvage*, **15**, 231–45. (in French)

Harper, J. L. (1989). The value of a leaf. *Oecologia*, **80**, 53–8.

Healy, W. M. (1997). Influence of deer on the structure and composition of oak forests in Central Massachusetts. In *The Science of Overabundance: Deer Ecology and Population Management*, ed. W. J. McShea, H. B. Underwood & J. H. Rappole. Washington: Smithsonian Institution Press, pp. 249–66.

Heikkila, & Mikkonen (1992). Effects of density of young Scots pine (*Pinus sylvestris*) stands on moose (*Alces alces*) browsing. *Acta Forestalia Fennica*, **231**, 4–14.

Heraldová, M., Homolka, M. & Kamler, J. (2003). Breakage of rowan caused by red deer – an important factor for *Sorbeto-Piceetum* stand regeneration? *Forest Ecology and Management*, **181**, 131–8.

Hester, A., Mitchell, F. J. G. & Kirby, K. (1996). Effects of season and intensity of sheep grazing on tree regeneration in a British upland woodland. *Forest Ecology and Management*, **88**, 99–106.

Hiscocks, K. (1999). The impact of an increasing elephant population on the woody vegetation in southern Sabi Sand Wildtuin, South Africa. *Koedoe*, **42**, 47–55.

Horsley, S. B. & Marquis, D. A. (1983). Interference by weeds and deer with Allegheny hardwood reproduction. *Canadian Journal of Forest Research*, **13**, 61–9.

Illius, A. W., Duncan, P. & Richard, C. (2002). Mechanisms of functional response and resource exploitation in browsing roe deer. *Journal of Animal Ecology*, **71**, 723–34.

Isomaki, A. & Kallio, T. (1974). Consequences of injury caused by timber harvesting machines on the growth and decay of spruce (*Picea abies* (L.) Karst.). *Acta Forestalia Fennica*, **136**, 1–25.

Jachmann, H. & Croes, T. (1991). Effects of browsing by elephants on the *Combretum terminalia* Woodland at the Nazinga Game Ranch, Burkina-Faso, West Africa. *Biological Conservation*, **57**, 13–24.

James, L. F., Short, R. E. & Panter, K. E. (1989). Pine needle abortion in cattle: a review and report of 1973–1984 research. *Cornell Veterinarian*, **79**, 39–52.

Jia, J., Niemelä, P. & Danell, K. (1995). Moose *Alces alces* bite diameter selection in relation to twig quality on four phenotypes of Scots pine *Pinus sylvestris*. *Wildlife Biology*, **1**, 47–55.

Jones, S. B., de Calesta, D. & Chunko, S. E. (1993). White-tails are changing our woodlands. *American Forests*, **Nov/Dec**, 20–54.

Kay, C. E. (2001). Long-term aspen exclosures in the Yellowstone ecosystem. In *Sustaining Aspen in Western Landscapes: Symposium Proceedings*. Grand Junction, Colorado, 13–15 June **2000**, pp. 225–40.

Kay, C. E. & Bartos, D. L. (2000). Ungulate herbivory on Utah aspen: assessment of long-term exclosures. *Journal of Range Management*, **53**, 145–53.

Khan, J. A., Rodgers, W. A., Johnsingh, A. J. T. & Mathur, P. K. (1994). Tree and shrub mortality and debarking by sambar *Cervus unicolor* (Kerr) in Gir after a drought in Gujarat, India. *Biological Conservation*, **68**, 149–54.

Kinnaird, J. W., Welch, D. & Cummins, C. (1979). Selective stripping of rowan (*Sorbus aucuparia* L.) bark by cattle in North-east Scotland. *Transactions of the Botanical Society of Edinburgh*, **43**, 115–25.

Kirby, K. J. (2001). The impact of deer on the ground flora of British woodland. *Forestry*, **74**, 219–30.

Kirby, K. J. (2003). *What Might a British Forest-Landscape Driven by Large Herbivores Look Like?* Peterborough: English Nature Research Reports.

Klinka, K. (1999). Update on silvics of Western red cedar and yellow cedar. In *The Cedar Symposium, 28–30 May 1996*, ed. G. Wiggins. Queen Charlotte Islands/Haida Gwaii: Ministry of Forests, BC.

Koenig, W. B. & Knops, J. M. H. (2002). The behavioural ecology of masting in oaks. In *Oak Forest Ecosystems*, ed. W. J. McShea & W. M. Healy. Baltimore: Johns Hopkins University Press, pp. 129–48.

Konig, E. & Baumann, B. (1990). The influence of roe deer browse on the natural regeneration in mixed-conifer stands. *Allgemeine Forst Und Jagdzeitung*, **161**, 170–6.

Kraus, P. (1987). The use of vegetation by red deer as an indicator of their population density. *Zeitschrift für Jagdwissenschaft*, **33**, 42–59.

Krefting, L. W. & Stoekeler, J. H. (1953). Effect of simulated snowshoe hare and deer damage on planted conifers in the Lake States. *Journal of Wildlife Management*, **17**, 487–94.

Kuiters, A. T. & Slim, P. A. (2002). Regeneration of mixed deciduous forest in a Dutch forest-heathland, following a reduction of ungulate densities. *Biological Conservation*, **105**, 65–74.

Kuiters, A. T. & Slim, P. A. (2003). Tree colonisation of abandoned arable land after 27 years of horse grazing: the role of bramble as a facilitator of oak wood regeneration. *Forest Ecology and Management*, **181**, 239–51.

Langbein, J. (1997). *The Ranging Behaviour, Habitat Use and Impact of Deer in Oak Woods and Heather Moors of Exmoor and the Quantock Hills*. Fordingbridge, UK: The Deer Society.

Laws, R. M., Parker, I. S. C. & Johnstone, R. C. B. (1975). *Elephants and Their Habitats*. Oxford: Clarendon Press.

Lawson, D., Inouye, R., Huntly, N. & Carson, W. P. (1999). Patterns of woody plant abundance, recruitment, mortality and growth in a 65 year chronosequence of old-fields. *Plant Ecology*, **145**, 267–79.

Lenzi-Grillini, C. R., Viskanic, P. & Mapesa, M. (1996). Effects of 20 years of grazing exclusion in an area of the Queen Elizabeth National Park, Uganda. *African Journal of Ecology*, **34**, 333–41.

Lewis, C. (1980). Simulated cattle injury to planted slash pine: defoliation. *Journal of Range Management*, **33**, 337–40.

Löyttyniemi, K. (1985). On repeated browsing of Scots pine saplings by moose (*Alces alces*). *Silva Fennica*, **19**, 387–91.

Luitjes, J. (1971). The effect of barking by red deer on height growth and mortality of Corsican pine. *Nederlands Bosbouw Tijdschrift*, **43**, 112–18.

Luthardt, M. & Beyer, G. (1998). The effect of game animals on forest vegetation. *Wald Und Wild*, **17**, 890–4.

Madany, M. H. & West, N. E. (1983). Livestock grazing-fire regime interactions within montane forests of Zion National Park, Utah. *Ecology*, **64**, 661–7.

Magurran, A. E. (1988). *Ecological Diversity and its Measurement*. London: Croom Helm.

Malo, J. E. & Suarez, F. (1995). Herbivorous mammals as seed dispersers in a Mediterranean *Dehesa*. *Oecologia*, **104**, 246–55.

Martin, J. L. & Daufresne, T. (1999). Introduced species and their impacts on the forest ecosystem of Haida Gwaii. In *The Cedar Symposium*, ed. G. Wiggins, 28–30 May 1996. Queen Charlotte Islands/Haida Gwaii: Ministry of Forests, British Columbia.

McArthur, C., Robbins, C. T. & Hagerman, A. E. (1993). Diet selection by a generalist browser in relation to plant chemistry. *Canadian Journal of Zoology*, **71**, 2236–43.

McInnes, P. F. Naiman, R. J., Pastor, J. & Cohen Y. (1992). Effects of moose browsing on vegetation and litter of the boreal forest, Isle Royale, Michigan, USA. *Ecology*, **73**, 2059–75.

McIntyre, E. B. (1975). Bark stripping by ungulates. Ph.D. thesis, University of Edinburgh.

Michael, E. D. (1987). Bark Stripping by white-tailed deer in West Virginia. *Northern Journal of Applied Forestry*, **4**, 96–7.

Miller, G. R., Cummins, R. P. & Hester, A. J. (1998). Red deer and woodland regeneration in the Cairngorms. *Scottish Forestry*, **52**, 14–20.

Miquelle, D. G. & Van Ballenberghe, V. (1989). Impact of bark stripping by moose on aspen-spruce communities. *Journal of Wildlife Management*, **53**, 577–86.

Mitchell, F. J. G. & Cole, E. (1998). Reconstruction of long-term successional dynamics of temperate woodland in Białowieża Forest, Poland. *Journal of Ecology*, **86**, 1042–59.

Morgan, R. K. (1991). The role of a protective understorey in the regeneration system of a heavily browsed woodland. *Vegetatio*, **92**, 119–32.

Mwalyosi, R. B. B. (1990). The dynamic ecology of *Acacia tortilis* woodland in Lake Manyara National Park, Tanzania. *African Journal of Ecology*, **28**, 189–99.

Mysterud, A. & Ostbye, E. (1995). Bed-site selection by European roe deer (*Capreolus capreolus*) in southern Norway during winter. *Canadian Journal of Zoology*, **73**, 924–32.

Obeso, J. R. (1997). The induction of spinescence in European holly leaves by browsing ungulates. *Plant Ecology*, **129**, 149–56.

Okuda, T. & Nakane, K. (1990). Effects of deer browsing on the early stage of pyrogenic succession on Miyajima Island, Southwestern Japan. *Ecological Research*, **5**, 353–66.

Olff, H. & Ritchie, M. E. (1998). Effects of herbivores on grassland plant diversity. *Trends in Ecology and Evolution*, **13**, 261–65.

Owen-Smith, R. N. (1988). *Megaherbivores*. Cambridge: Cambridge University Press.

Parks, C. G., Bednar, L. & Tiedemann, A. R. (1998). Browsing ungulates – an important consideration in dieback and mortality of Pacific yew (*Taxus brevifolia*) in a Northeastern Oregon stand. *Northwest Science*, **72**, 190–7.

Pastor, J. & Naiman, R. J. (1992). Selective foraging and ecosystem processes in boreal forests. *American Naturalist*, **139**, 690–705.

Pastor, J., Dewey, B., Moen, R. *et al.* (1998). Spatial patterns in the moose-forest-soil ecosystem on Isle Royale, Michigan, USA. *Ecological Applications*, **8**, 411–24.

Pawsey, R. G. & Gladman, R. J. (1965). Decay in standing conifers developing from extraction damage. *Forest Record*, Forestry Commission.

Pellew, R. (1983). The impacts of elephant, giraffe and fire upon the *Acacia tortilis* woodlands of the Serengeti. *African Journal of Ecology*, **21**, 41–74.

Peterken, G. F. & Tubbs, C. R. (1965). Woodland regeneration in the New Forest, Hampshire, since 1650. *Journal of Applied Ecology*, **2**, 159–70.

Pigott, C. D. (1983). Regeneration of oak-birch woodland following exclusion of sheep. *Journal of Ecology*, **71**, 629–46.

Potvin, F., Beaupre, P. & Laprise, G. (2003). The eradication of balsam fir stands by white-tailed deer on Anticosti Island, Quebec: a 150-year process. *Ecoscience*, **10**, 487–95.

Prins, H. H. T. & Van Der Jeugd, H. P. (1993). Herbivore population crashes and woodland structure in East Africa. *Journal of Ecology*, **81**, 305–14.

Putman, R. J., Edwards, P. J., Mann, J. C. E., How, R. C. & Hill, S. D. (1989). Vegetational and faunal change in an area of heavily grazed woodland following relief of grazing. *Biological Conservation*, **47**, 13–32.

Pels Rijcken, H. (1965). Bark-stripping damage to Scots pine by red deer. *Nederlandse Bosbouw Tijdschrift*, **37**, 353–65.

Rackham, O. (1998). Savanna in Europe. In *The Ecological History of European Forests*, ed. K. J. Kirby & C. Watkins. New York: CAB International, pp. 1–24.

Ratliff R. D. & Denton R. G. (1995). Grazing on regeneration sites encourages pine seedling growth. *USDA Forest Service Research Paper PSW-RP-223*.

Reid, R. S. & Ellis, J. E. (1995). Impacts of pastoralists on woodlands in South Turkana, Kenya: livestock-mediated tree recruitment. *Ecological Applications*, **5**, 978–92.

Risenhoover, K. L. & Maass, S. A. (1986). The influence of moose on the composition and structure of Isle Royale forests. *Canadian Journal of Forest Research*, **17**, 357–64.

Ritchie, M. E., Tilman, D. & Knops, J. M. H. (1998). Herbivore effects on plant and nitrogen dynamics in oak savanna. *Ecology*, **79**, 165–77.

Rooney, T. (2001). Deer impacts on forest ecosystems: a North American perspective. *Forestry*, **74**, 2001–8.

Roques, K. G., O'Connor, T. G. & Watkinson, A. R. (2001). Dynamics of shrub encroachment in an African savanna: relative influences of fire, herbivory, rainfall and density dependence. *Journal of Applied Ecology*, **38**, 268–80.

Roth, R. (1996). The effect of deer on naturally regenerating forest. *Zeitschrift für Jagdwissenschaft*, **42**, 143–56.

Rousset, O. & Lepart, J. (1999). Shrub facilitation of *Quercus humilis* regeneration in succession on calcareous grasslands. *Journal of Vegetation Science*, **10**, 493–502.

Rozas, V. (2003). Regeneration patterns, dendroecology, and forest-use history in an old-growth beech-oak lowland forest in Northern Spain. *Forest Ecology and Management*, **182**, 175–94.

Santiapillai, C., Chambers, M. R. & Balasubramaniam, S. (1981). A preliminary study of bark damage by cervids in the Ruhuna National Park, Sri Lanka. *Spixiana*, **4**, 247–54.

Scharf, C. M. & Hirth, D. H. (2000). Impact of moose bark stripping on mountain ash in Vermont. *Alces*, **36**, 41–52.

Scott, D. (1998). Impact of red deer on a Scots pine plantation after removal of deer fencing. *Scottish Forestry*, **52**, 8–13.

Scott, D., Welch, D. & Thurlow, M. (2000). Regeneration of *Pinus sylvestris* in a natural pinewood in NE Scotland following reduction in grazing by *Cervus elaphus*. *Forest Ecology and Management*, **130**, 199–211.

Scrinzi, G., Floris, A. & Pignatti, G. (1997). Impacts of large wild ungulates on the vegetation and its regeneration in Trentino's mountain forests: biodiversity and bioindicators. *ISAFA Comunicazioni Di Ricerca* 97.

Segerström, U., Hörnberg, G. & Bradshaw, R. (1996). The 9000 year history of vegetation development and disturbance patterns of a swamp-forest in Dalarna, northern Sweden. *The Holocene*, **6**, 37–48.

Shaw, M. W. (1974). The reproductive characteristics of oak. In *The British Oak: its History and Natural History*, ed. M. G. Morris & F. H. Perring. Conference Report 14. Classey. Farringdon, Berks: The Botanical Society of the British Isles.

Shipley, L. A., Illius, A. W. & Danell, K. (1999). Predicting bite size selection of mammalian herbivores: a test of a general model of diet optimization. *Oikos*, **84**, 55–68.

Skarpe, C., Bergström, R., Bråten, A. L. & Danell, K. (2000). Browsing in a heterogenous savanna. *Ecography*, **23**, 632–40.

Stewart, G. H. & Burrows, L. E. (1989). The impact of white-tailed deer *Odocoileus virginianus* on regeneration in the coastal forests of Stewart-Island, New-Zealand. *Biological Conservation*, **49**, 275–93.

Storm, G. & Halvorson, C. (1967). Effect of injury by porcupines on radial growth of Ponderosa pine. *Journal of Forestry*, **65**, 740–3.

Stromayer, K. A. K. & Warren, R. J. (1997). Are overabundant deer herds in the eastern United States creating alternate stable states in forest plant communities? *Wildlife Society Bulletin*, **25**, 227–34.

Tilghman, N. G. (1989). Impacts of white-tailed deer on forest regeneration in northwestern Pennsylvania. *Journal of Wildlife Management*, **53**, 524–32.

Tiver, F. & Andrew, M. H. (1997). Relative effects of herbivory by sheep, rabbits, goats and kangaroos on recruitment and regeneration of shrubs and trees in eastern South Australia. *Journal of Applied Ecology*, **34**, 903–14.

Tixier, H., Duncan, P. & Scchovic, J. (1997). Food selection by European roe deer (*Capreolus capreolus*): effects of plant chemistry, and consequences for the nutritional value of the diets. *Journal of Zoology*, **242**, 229–45.

Tsiouvaras, C. N. (1988). Long-term effects on production and vigor of kermes oak (*Quercus coccifera*). *Forest Ecology and Management*, **24**, 159–66.

Ueda, H., Takatsuki, S. & Takahashi, Y. (2002). Bark stripping of hinoki cypress by sika deer in relation to snow cover and food availability on Mt. Takahara, central Japan. *Ecological Research*, **17**, 545–51.

Van Deleen, T. R., Pregitzer, K. S. & Haufler, J. B. (1996). A comparison of presettlement and present-day forests in two northern Michigan deer yards. *The American Midland Naturalist*, **135**, 181–94.

Van Dyne, G. M., Brockington, N. R. & Szocs, Z. (1980). Large herbivore subsystem. In *Grasslands, Systems Analysis and Man*, ed. A. I. Breymer & G. M. Van Dyne. Cambridge: Cambridge University Press, pp. 269–538.

Van Hees, A. F. M., Kuiters, A. T. & Slim, A. (1996). Growth and development of silver birch, pedunculate oak and beech as affected by deer browsing. *Forest Ecology and Management*, **88**, 55–63.

Vasiliauskas, R. (1998). Patterns of wounding and decay in stems of *Quercus robur* due to bark peeling. *Scandinavian Journal of Forest Research*, **13**, 437–41.

Vera, F. W. M. (2000). *Grazing Ecology and Forest History*. Oxford: CABI.

Vourc'h, G., Martin, J. L. & Duncan, P. (2001). Defensive adaptations of Thuya plicata to ungulate browsing: a comparative study between mainland and island populations. *Oecologia*, **126**, 84–93.

Vinther, E. (1983). Invasion of *Alnus glutinosa* (L.) Gaerth in a former grazed meadow in relation to different grazing intensities. *Biological Conservation*, **25**, 75–89.

Wästerlund, I. (1985). *The Strength of Bark on Scots pine and Norway spruce trees,* Garpenberg: Swedish University of Agricultural Sciences.

Watson, A. (1983). Eighteenth century deer numbers and pine regeneration near Braemar, Scotland. *Biological Conservation*, **25**, 289–305.

Watt, A. S. (1919). On the causes of failure of regeneration in British oakwoods. *Journal of Ecology*, **7** 173–203.

Weisberg, P. J. & Coughenour, M. B. (2003). Model-based assessment of aspen responses to elk herbivory in Rocky Mountain National Park, USA. *Environmental Management*, **32**, 152–69.

Welch, D. & Scott, D. (1998). Bark-stripping damage by red deer in a Sitka spruce forest in western Scotland. IV. Survival and performance of wounded trees. *Forestry*, **71**, 225–35.

Welch D., Staines, B. W. & Scott, D. (1987). Bark stripping damage by red deer in a Sitka spruce forest in western Scotland. I: Incidence. *Forestry*, **60**, 249–62.

Welch D., Staines, B. W., Scott, D., French, D. D. & Catt, D. C. (1991). Leader browsing by red and roe deer on young Sitka spruce trees in western Scotland. 1. Damage rates and incidence. *Forestry*, **64**, 61–82.

Westoby, M., Walker, B. & Noy-Meir, E. (1989). Opportunistic management for rangelands not at equilibrium. *Journal of Range Management*, **42**, 266–74.

Williams, M. (1989). *Americans and Their Forests*. Cambridge: Cambridge University Press.

Wilson, B. F. (1993). Compensatory shoot growth in young black birch and red maple trees. *Canadian Journal of Forest Research*, **23**, 302–6.

Wilson, S. L. & Kerley, G. I. H. (2003). Bite diameter selection by thicket browsers: the effects of body size and plant morphology on forage intake and quality. *Forest Ecology and Management*, **181**, 51–66.

Yalden, D. (1999). *The History of British Mammals*. London: T. & A. D. Poyser Ltd.

Yokoyama, S., Maeji, I. & Ueda, T. (2001). Impact of bark stripping by sika deer *Cervus nippon*, on subalpine coniferous forests in central Japan. *Forest Ecology and Management*, **140**, 93–9.

Zeigenfuss, L. C. Singer, F. J., Williams, S. A. & Johnson, T. L. (2002). Influences of herbivory and water on willow in elk winter range. *Journal of Wildife Management*, **66**, 788–95.

Zeltner, J. (1979). Impoverishment of tree species mixtures as a result of roe deer populations. *Schweizerische Zeitschrift für Forstwesen*, **130**, 81–4.

7

Large herbivores: missing partners of western European light-demanding tree and shrub species?

FRANS W. M. VERA, ELISABETH S. BAKKER AND
HAN OLFF

INTRODUCTION

The landscape of the temperate zone of western Europe has a long history of human occupation and impact. As the development of agriculture and the growth of the human population coincided with climate change since the last ice age, it is difficult to picture the landscape without human intervention. Based on palaeoecological data and reference sites, several authors state that temperate Europe without human influence would have been covered with a closed-canopy broad-leaved forest in places where trees can grow (Ellenberg 1988, Peterken 1996). This perception is hereafter called 'the classical forest theory'. This forest type is thought to have regenerated by means of small or large gaps, or large windblown areas, where young trees could grow up. Indigenous species of large herbivores that lived within the range of this forest ecosystem are considered forest dwellers. In temperate Europe this applies to the Holocene aurochs (*Bos primigenius*), tarpan (*Equus przewalski gmelini*), red deer (*Cervus elaphus*), moose (*Alces alces*), roe deer (*Capreolus capreolus*) and European bison (*Bison bonasus*). The animals would not have had a substantial influence on the forest, but have followed the development in the vegetation (Tansley 1935, Iversen 1960, Whittaker 1977). The role of large herbivores in the broad-leaved forests is often discussed because the animals can prevent the regeneration of trees in the forest (see Chapter 6 in this book). When large herbivores, such as deer,

Large Herbivore Ecology, Ecosystem Dynamics and Conservation, ed. K. Danell, P. Duncan, R. Bergström & J. Pastor. Published by Cambridge University Press. © Cambridge University Press 2006.

cattle and horses, are excluded from forests, this usually stimulates recruitment (Peterken & Tubbs 1965, Putman *et al.* 1989, Mountford *et al.* 1999). This has been used as an argument especially to exclude large ungulates like cattle and horses, because they are considered as an 'unnatural' component of forest ecosystems. Recent ecological and historical research on the role of these large herbivores in temperate wood-pastures (Vera 1997, 2000, Olff *et al.* 1999, Bakker *et al.* 2004), however, sheds doubt on the picture of the primaeval vegetation being a forest as well as on the view that large herbivores are not very important in temperate vegetation in its natural state. Wood-pasture ecosystems are found in places with a very long history of what is commonly considered as extensive livestock grazing. These are park-like landscapes grazed and browsed by livestock, like cattle and horses. They consist of a mosaic of grassland and thorny scrub thickets, with or without trees and forests (groves). Thorny shrubs mark the transition of the grassland to the forest, and form a so-called mantle and fringe vegetation (Watt 1924, Ellenberg 1988). Some authors consider wood-pastures as high forest, degraded by livestock because the animals prevented the regeneration of trees in the forest. As a consequence the forest became more and more open and transformed through so-called retrogressive succession into the park-like landscape that is characteristic of the wood-pasture (Moss 1913, Tansley 1953, Ellenberg 1988).

In this paper, we will discuss oak (pedunculate and sessile oak) and hazel in wood-pastures and forest reserves as a case study for trees with properties that may reflect adaptations to now-extinct large grazers, aurochs and tarpan. This discussion is important because it may yield that cattle and horses are to be key species in the ecology of temperate natural vegetation, in acting as ecological proxies for their extinct ancestors.

THE DISAPPEARANCE OF LIGHT-DEMANDING TREE AND SHRUB SPECIES

In central and western Europe many wood-pastures have been declared as forest reserves during the nineteenth and twentieth century. Cattle and horses were subsequently removed, because they were considered as alien species, introduced by man. Indigenous species like red deer, if present, were reduced to such low densities that they did not prevent the regeneration of trees in the forest. This caused wood-pastures to develop spontaneously into a closed-canopy high forest. These forests are then considered to be modern analogues of the primaeval vegetation (Falinski 1986, Peterken 1996).

In these forest reserves light-demanding woody species like pedunculate oak (*Quercus robur*), sessile oak (*Q. petraea*) and the shrub hazel
(*Corylus avellana*) disappear. They are outcompeted by shade-tolerant
species like beech (*Fagus sylvatica*), elm (*Ulmus glabra* and *U.
laevis*), hornbeam (*Carpinus betulus*), lime (*Tilia cordata* and *T. platyphyllos*), field
maple (*Acer campestre*), sycamore (*A. pseudoplatanus*) and ash (*Fraxinus
excelsior*) (Emborg et al. 1996, Vera 2000). Pollen analysis of both regional
and local pollen grains, however, shows that both oak and hazel were very
well represented in the primaeval vegetation in central and western Europe
in the Atlantic period (8000–5000 BP). This is the period before the
introduction of livestock when the primaeval forest is thought to have
been optimally developed. In this period, the percentage of oak and hazel
together in pollen diagrams varies between 20%–50% up to 60%–75% of
the total pollen sum (Huntley & Birks 1983). This also shows that both taxa
were present for thousands of years in the presence of shade-tolerant
species. This raises the question whether the natural vegetation of temperate Europe was indeed a closed-canopy forest as is stated by the classical
forest theory. Because the disappearance of these light-demanding taxa
correlates with the removal and subsequent absence of the grazing large
ungulates, cattle and horses, the question is raised whether these
large herbivores may have maintained ecological conditions that are no
longer present in the current forest reserves. Cattle and horses were in
fact present in the primaeval vegetation by means of their wild progeni-
tors, aurochs and tarpan (Söffner 1982, von Koeningswald 1983, Guintard
& Tardy 1994), from which they are shaped in a process of domestication
(Felius 1995). Aurochs and tarpan went extinct in 1627 and 1887, respectively (Szafer 1968, Pruski 1963, Vereshchagin & Baryshnikov 1989). It is
generally difficult to reconstruct ecological properties of species and
ecosystems that do not exist anymore. However, the ecological properties
of still existing tree and shrub species like oak and hazel can also tell us a
lot about the prevailing ecological conditions in the past (Janzen & Martin
1982, Barlow 2000, Bakker et al. 2004).

OAK AND HAZEL IN FOREST RESERVES

As mentioned above, in the lowlands of Europe, wood-pastures became
forest reserves over the last two centuries. This happened, for example, in
the reserves: La Tillaie and Le Gros-Fouteau in the Forêt de Fontainebleau
in France; the Hassbruch and the Neuenburger Urwald in Germany; the
Dalby Söderskog in Sweden; the National Park Bialowieza in the Forest of

Bialowieza in Poland; and the Suserup Skov in Denmark (Emborg *et al.* 1996, Vera 2000). In these reserves, light-demanding oak, whether pedunculate oak or sessile oak, and hazel disappear and are replaced by shade-tolerant tree species like lime, beech, ash, elm, sycamore and hornbeam (Vera 2000). This also happened in parts of forests in the still existing wood-pasture of the New Forest, England, where cattle and horses were excluded by fences (Mountford *et al.* 1999, Mountford & Peterken 2003). Despite the presence of many seedlings on the forests floor, no new generations enter the older diameter classes, while the oldest classes that date from the time that cattle and horses grazed the area disappear because of mortality. Oak does not regenerate successfully in small or large gaps. Only shade-tolerant species grow, inhibiting the oak seedlings (Vera 2000). Oak also fails to regenerate in large wind blown areas. These areas might act as a window of opportunity for the light demanding oak. However, shade-tolerant species having established a seedling bank under the closed-canopy, are released after a storm removed the canopy (Peltier *et al.* 1997, Houtzagers *et al.* 2000). The failure to regenerate results in a 'clock shaped' diameter distribution pattern of oak trees in these forest reserves (Fig. 7.1). This is a pattern that is typical for a population on the road to extinction (Christensen 1977). On the other hand, shade-tolerant species show a diameter distribution of an inverse J-curve. This means that many specimens of the younger age classes are present whereas the numbers decrease towards the older ages. This is considered as a sign of a successfully regenerating population (Malmer *et al.* 1978, Lemée 1978, 1987, Emborg *et al.* 1996, Fig. 7.1).

Long-term spontaneous vegetation development in forest reserves also showed a strong decline in the cover of hazel (Malmer *et al.* 1978, Hytteborn 1986). This species disappears when it becomes overtopped by a closed canopy (Malmer *et al.* 1978, Hytteborn 1986, Peterken & Jones 1987).

COMPETITION FOR LIGHT IN A CLOSED-CANOPY FOREST

Oak seedlings seem to be shade-tolerant because they grow well under low amounts of daylight in the first years of their lives (Jarvis 1964, Shaw 1974). However, the mechanism behind this phenomenon is not shade-tolerance, but rather a re-allocation of nutrients from the acorn into the taproot (Jarvis 1964, Brookes *et al.* 1980, Ziegehagen & Kausch 1995). Immediately after germination, seedlings of oak form an extremely extensive root system with a long taproot unparalleled by any other tree

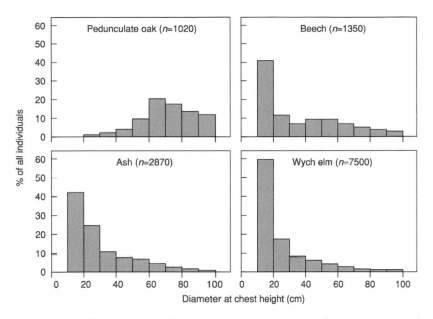

Figure 7.1. The percentage distribution per tree species in diameter categories per species of pedunculate oak, beech, ash and wych elm in Dalby Söderskog, Sweden. Only trees with a trunk diameter of >10 cm at chest height are included (redrawn from Malmer *et al.* 1978, from Vera 2000).

species in Europe (Jarvis 1964, Newbold & Goldsmith 1981, Van Hees 1997). If low amounts of daylight persist, the seedlings survive for some years on the nutrients in their taproots, but eventually die. Consequently, oak seedlings disappear from a forest within 3–5 years after germination (Watt 1919, Lemée 1987, 1992). Under similar amounts of reduced daylight, seedlings of shade-tolerant species like beech, lime, sycamore, field maple, wych elm (*Ulmus glabra*), European white elm (*U. laevis*), common elm (*U. minor/carpinifolia*) and ash persist for several to many years longer than oak (Vera 2000). Seedlings of beech, lime and hornbeam also show a morphological adaptation to conditions of low amounts of daylight. They have reduced height growth and form side branches. This gives them a wide shape (Pockberger 1963, Belostokov 1980, Suner & Röhrig 1980, Dupré *et al.* 1986, Pigott 1988), a greater leaf surface for catching the sparse daylight, and, therefore, a competitive advantage over oak seedlings.

The above mentioned characteristics give the shade-tolerant species the capability to establish a seedling bank under a closed canopy. This pool of seedlings is released as soon as a gap in the canopy or a large windblown area is formed (Mayer & Tichy 1979, Raben 1980, Wolf 1982, 1988). The height growth of the shade-tolerant seedlings is fast, giving light-demanding young oaks virtually no chance (Eichhorn 1927, Bezacinsky 1971, Peltier *et al.* 1997). Sometimes, oaks do grow up in large gaps and remain ahead of beech in height growth for several years and up to a few decades (Von Lüpke 1982). None the less, eventually young oak becomes overgrown and out-competed by beech or other shade-tolerant species like lime, hornbeam, sycamore and elm (Bonnemann 1956a,b, Von Lüpke & Hauskeller-Bullerjahn 1999). Seedlings of oak can only grow up successfully in the presence of seedlings of shade-tolerant species if the latter are constantly trimmed, as is done in forestry practice with natural regeneration of oak (Vanselow 1926, Krahl-Urban 1959, Von Lüpke & Hauskeller-Bullerjahn 1999). Even mature oak are out-competed by shade-tolerant species if the soil properties allow these species to grow higher than mature oak (Bonnemann 1956a,b, Malmer *et al.* 1978, Ponge & Jean-Baptiste 1997).

Like oak, hazel re-allocates nutrients from the hazelnut into the tap-root in the first growing season (Sanderson 1958). A reduction of daylight results in a clearly reduced development of the seedling. Under a closed canopy, hazel seedlings survive for not much longer than one year (Sanderson 1958, Vera 2000).

Altogether, these data show that in a closed-canopy forest, where regeneration of trees takes place in small or large gaps, or in large wind-blown areas, oak and hazel cannot persist in the presence of shade-tolerant tree species (Vera 2000).

REGENERATION OF OAK AND HAZEL IN WOOD-PASTURES

Contrary to the situation in closed-canopy forest, oak and hazel do regenerate very well in the presence of shade-tolerant tree species in wood-pastures that are grazed by large true grazers like cattle and horses (Watt 1919, Burrichter *et al.* 1980, Rackham 2003). They do so with densities of cattle, horses and deer as high as 110–130 and up to 187 kg ha^{-1} (Flower 1977, Putman 1986, Rackham 2003). Among these observations were densities of red deer of 30 animals per 100 ha (20 kg ha^{-1}) (Hart 1966, Vera 2000). These densities are far higher than 0.5 to 3 deer 100 ha^{-1} (0.4–3.2 kg ha^{-1}) that is usual for forests, as defined from the classical forest theory of a closed-canopy forest as climax vegetation (Wolfe & Von Berg 1988, Remmert 1991).

In wood-pastures, the seedlings of oak and hazel, as well as other tree and shrub species, establish in open grassland. In these grazed systems, such palatable seedlings can only survive there if they are close to or in the direct vicinity of shrub or herb species that have defences against large ungulates (Rousset & Lepart 1999, Vera 1997, 2000, Olff *et al.* 1999). Plant species with physical defences against herbivores are, for instance, blackthorn, hawthorn, juniper and brambles (*Rubus* spp.) that are 'armed by spines or thorns', while bracken (*Pteridium aquilinum*) and heather (*Calluna vulgaris*) are defended by chemical substances (Iason & Alison 1993, Mountford & Peterken 2003, Bakker *et al.* 2004). These species act as nurse species for palatable tree and shrub species. This defence of palatable species through spatial association is called associational resistance (Olff *et al.* 1999, Callaway *et al.* 2000, Milchunas & Noy-Meir 2002). In a recent study (Bakker *et al.* 2004), experimental evidence was found indicating that oaks do indeed need spiny shrubs (blackthorn) for their recruitment in grazed systems (Fig. 7.2). One-year-old seedlings of *Quercus robur* were planted in open grassland, between young spiny shrubs, in old

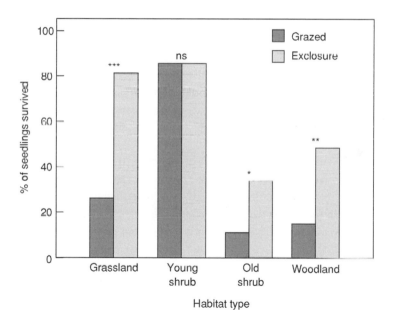

Figure 7.2. Effect of grazing on the survival of transplanted oak seedlings in different vegetation structure types in the Junner Koeland reserve, The Netherlands. Different symbols indicate statistically different percentages of seedlings at the levels ns: $p > 0.05$; *: $p < 0.05$; **: $p < 0.01$; ***: $p < 0.001$. From Bakker *et al.* (2004).

spiny shrub thickets and between large established oaks. In each vegetation structure, oaks were planted inside and outside exclosures, to separate low resource availability (light, nutrients) from herbivory as mortality causes. It was found that amongst young shrubs, the survival of the oaks was very high. In open grassland, recruitment failed because all oaks were grazed heavily. In the old thickets and under the established trees, establishment failed probably due to a combination of low light levels and grazing. The young shrub thickets provided protection while not being tall enough to out shade the seedlings. When the oaks then grow up, they out shade the plants that facilitated their survival (Watt 1934, Bakker et al. 2004, Fig. 7.3). Spiny species, however, are not absolutely defended against the large herbivores. Seedlings and new root suckers of blackthorn and seedlings of hawthorn, as well as young twigs of blackthorn and hawthorn are not spiny (Heukels & Van der Meijden 1983). The spines only harden at the end of the growing season. Therefore, young seedlings and the annual shoots of mature shrubs can be consumed by large herbivores (Buttenschøn & Buttenschøn 1978, Bokdam 1987). The browsing of annual shoots induces a dense canopy that is almost impenetrable to the snouts of large herbivores. This enhances the protection of the undefended palatable tree and shrub species that grow in spatial association with the spiny species (Bakker et al. 2004). Unarmed seedlings, however, can rapidly disappear during their first growing season (Buttenschøn & Buttenschøn 1985, Mountford & Peterken 2003). On the other hand, both seedlings and mature shrubs can expand rapidly in open grassland when grazing pressure is reduced for a number of growing seasons, or if it suddenly stops altogether (Tansley 1922, Watt 1934, Smith 1980, Buttenschøn & Buttenschøn 1985).

Light-demanding shrub and tree species other than hazel and oak, that disappear in wood-pastures that have become forest reserves (Vera 2000), regenerate in wood-pastures through spatial association with spiny or thorny shrub species as well. Such shrub species are guelder rose (*Viburpulus*), wayfaring tree (*V. lantana*), dogwood (*Cornus sanguinea*), bird cherry (*Prunus padus*), spindle tree (*Euonymus europaeus*), elder (*Sambucus nigra*) and privet (*Ligustrum vulgare*). The tree species are wild cherry (*Prunus avium*), wild apple (*Malus sylvestris*), wild pear (*Pyrus communis*), rowan (*Sorbus aucuparia*), wild service tree (*S. torminalis*), whitebeam (*S. aria*) and true service tree (*S. domestica*) (Vera 2000). Several of them are nowadays endangered species (Dagenbach 1981, Rackham 2003). Besides hazel, all these shrub and tree species bear fruits eaten by birds (Passeriformes), which defecate the seeds below thorny shrubs (Namvar & Spethmann

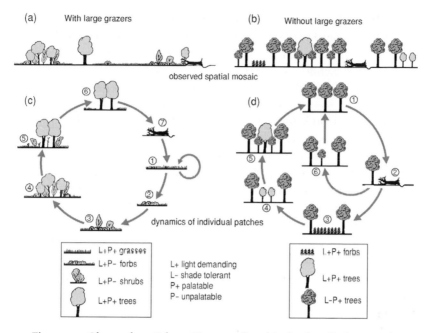

Figure 7.3. Observed spatial mosaic as mediated by local cyclical succession of plant functional types in temperate woodlands (a) with and (b) without free-ranging large grazers, such as cattle and horses. Protection of palatable (P+) plant species by defended, spiny (P−) plant species is an important mechanism causing the dynamics of local cyclical succession in the presence of large grazers. This dynamics is therefore very different with (c) versus without (d) large herbivores. The differences are also caused by the interaction of palatability with light demand of the different woody species. Light-demanding trees and shrubs (L+) co-occur with grasses in the presence of large grazers, while shade-tolerant trees (L−) dominate in the absence of large grazers. From Olff *et al.* (1999).

1985, Snow & Snow 1988). Shade-tolerant tree species also regenerate in wood-pasture in spatial association with thorny and spiny species (Tansley 1953, Hart 1966, Rackham 2003). A remarkable phenomenon is that compared to shade-tolerant tree species, oak (pedunculate and sessile oak) is very common in wood-pastures (Watt 1919, Pott & Hüppe 1991, Rackham 2003). This is caused by the activity of the jay (*Garrulus glandarius*).

THE JAY AND THE OAK

The jay (*Garrulus glandarius*) collects acorns and buries them from a few metres to up to several kilometres from the site of collection (Schuster

1950, Chettleburgh 1952, Bossema 1979). Schuster (1950) concluded that in 4 weeks, approximately 65 birds dispersed at least 500 000 acorns throughout the area. The jay performs a clear preference for open terrain (Kollmann & Schill 1996, Hauskeller-Bullerjahn et al. 2000, Stähr & Peters 2000) where they select short grass or the outer edge of hedges, the fringes of thorny scrub of blackthorn and the base of the stem of a thorny shrub like hawthorn or juniper (Bossema 1979, Vullmer & Hanstein 1995, Rousset & Lepard 1999). Shade-tolerant tree species lack a vector that plants their seeds in the direct vicinity of a nurse species. Compared to shade-tolerant tree species it seems that the jay gives oak an advantage in its establishment in wood-pastures. Mice also distribute acorns, but they do so over distances less than tens of metres (Jensen & Nielsen 1986, Rousset & Lepart 1999). Although mice hoard beechnuts as well, the infrequent appearance of beech seedlings and the frequent establishment of oak seedlings in grassland and thorny scrub near beech woods, shows that oak seems to have an advantage over beech (Tansley 1922, Watt 1925).

Hazelnuts have a vector as well, namely the Nuthatch (Sitta europaea). This bird species plants hazelnuts (Sanderson 1958, F.W.M. Vera, personal observation 1995). The presence of hazel seedlings is limited to areas with open daylight like the thorny shrub species blackthorn and hawthorn, which are transitional area from forest to grassland, as well as open grasslands close to this transition. Because of this, hazel becomes part of mantle and fringe vegetation. It seems, however, that hazel is also able to persist in the presence of large ungulates without a nurse species (Bär 1914, Jahn 1991, Coppins et al. 2002).

THE FORMATION OF A PARK-LIKE LANDSCAPE

Blackthorn spreads clonally into open grassland and tree seedlings establish in the fringes of the advancing blackthorn. In this way, trees advance into the grassland at the same pace as the spreading fringes of the thorny scrub (Watt 1924, Pott & Hüppe 1991). Only rabbits can inhibit the clonal expansion of blackthorn (Bakker et al. 2004). Because blackthorn spreads from a nucleus in every direction, a characteristic convex shaped group of trees, called a grove can establish within the scrub (Vera 2000, Bakker et al. 2004). An expanding spiny mantle and fringe vegetation consisting of blackthorn and the associated seedlings, saplings and young trees that grow up in association with blackthorn surrounds the grove (Pott & Hüppe 1991, Vera 2000, Bakker et al. 2004). Inside the scrub itself the establishment of light-demanding as well as shade-tolerant trees is impossible because of the very low density of daylight (Dierschke 1974, Tubbs 1988), which may reach less than 2% of total daylight (Dierschke 1974). Light-demanding thorny nurse shrubs disappear from the grove because they are killed by shade cast by the crowns of trees they nursed that also shape the grove (Watt 1924, 1934, Ekstam & Sjögren 1973, Coops 1988). Regeneration of trees inside the grove is also limited due to grazing and trampling by large ungulates present in the wood-pastures (Mountford et al. 1999, Mountford & Peterken 2003, Bakker et al. 2004). Because the animals prevent the regeneration of trees within the grove, they prevent shade-tolerant species from growing up under oak and ousting it, as happens in forest reserves (Mountford & Peterken 2003). Because of the lack of regeneration within the grove, oak remains in the presence of shade-tolerant tree species and is part of the canopy of the grove. If a gap in the canopy of the grove is formed, the establishment of young trees is still prevented by the large herbivores. Fungi may facilitate the process of opening up the canopy and demise of the trees (Green 1992, Dobson & Crawley 1994) as well drought and storms (Mountford & Peterken 2003). Grasses, whose seeds often are brought in by large ungulates by means of their dung and fur, establish themselves and lawns are formed (Bokdam 2003, Mountford & Peterken 2003). As more trees die, the grove becomes more and more open, from the centre where the oldest trees stand, onwards. In this way the grove changes gradually (degrades in the classical forest theory) from the centre into grassland (Goriup et al. 1991, Peterken 1996, Mountford et al. 1999, Mountford & Peterken 2003). This process is known as retrogressive succession in the 'classical forest theory' and has resulted in the large ungulates gaining the reputation of potential destroyers of the forest (Tansley 1911, Moss 1913, Ellenberg 1988). Light-demanding shrub species do not establish because there is still too much shade or the local grazing pressure is so high that the young seedlings of spiny species whose thorns are not yet hardened disappear (Mountford & Peterken 2003, Bakker et al. 2004). Tree species will not be able to establish, because they are not protected by thorny species. Only in the newly developed open grassland in the end, light-demanding thorny shrubs become established and again they protect young trees against the large herbivores. In this way a new grove can emerge from the grassland (Vera 1997, 2000, Olff et al. 1999).

It is not yet known what role ungulates like European bison, moose, red deer and horses may play in this process. Because they strip bark from trees and shrubs (Borowski & Kossak 1972, Falinski 1986), they may speed up the opening up of the grove.

The above-described process shows that large herbivores like cattle and horses facilitate the establishment of trees in open grassland and prevent the regeneration in closed-canopy forest. In fact they induce a non-linear succession, namely: grassland → thorny shrubs → grove → grassland → thorny shrub → grove, etc. This theory is called *the cyclic turnover of vegetation* (Vera 2000). The resulting spatial shifting mosaic is very different from the mosaic in an ungrazed forest (Vera 1997, 2000, Olff *et al.* 1999, Fig. 7.3). Variations on this basal process are possible. The pattern of tree establishment may depend on the shrub species that nurse the tree and on the soil type. Blackthorn may lead to characteristic convex shaped groves, because the shrub reproduces vegetatively from a nucleus. Hawthorn on the other hand does not exhibit clonal vegetative reproduction and may nurse a solitary tree that will develop into an open grown tree. This will result in a more savanna-like landscape. On more basic as well as more acidic soils bramble will nurse trees and on acidic soils holly (*Ilex aquifolium*), juniper or even old shrubs of heather will do so (Olff *et al.* 1999, Vera 2000, Bakker *et al.* 2004). Holly and juniper can also form low lying branches in between which the jay can plant several acorns. This results in small groups of oak in open vegetation. Bramble can nurse a similar or somewhat bigger group because of its ability to spread by runners. The shrub eventually becomes ousted by the shade cast by the open grown wide crowned trees.

The landscape may be more open in cases of very fertile soil because of the high densities of large ungulates that can occur on these soils. Seedlings of spiny species may have problems becoming established because their spines are formed at the end of the growing season and they may be grazed before that time. The Oostvaardersplassen in the Netherlands may be an illustration of this type of landscape. Without supplementary feeding the population densities of wild cattle, red deer and horses reach *c.* 1 animal 4 ha^{-1}, 1 animal 2 ha^{-1} and 1 animal 4 ha^{-1}, respectively, and hundreds of hectares of grassland remain open.

PROCESSES IN THE WOOD-PASTURE AS MODERN ANALOGUES OF FORMER RELATIONS?

If we compare forest reserves with wood-pastures, the forest reserves differ from the latter by the removal or absence of true grazers among the large herbivores. This results in the absence of light-demanding shrub and tree species. Although man introduced cattle and horses, he in fact replaced their two wild ancestral species, aurochs and tarpan, from which cattle and horses are derived by domestication. As far as their feeding strategies are concerned (Fig. 7.4), there is no difference between these domestic ungulates in the wood-pastures and their wild forms (Hofmann 1973, 1976, 1985, Van de Veen & Van Wieren 1980). Therefore, the processes that cattle and horses initiate in the wood-pasture can be considered as modern analogues of the former relationship between the vegetation and large ungulates. In conclusion, the wood-pasture is the closest modern analogue of the primaeval natural vegetation in areas where large ungulates like aurochs and tarpan lived.

A question that remains to be answered is whether the densities of livestock in wood-pastures mimic those of their wild ancestors, or rather, were densities of wild ungulates in primaeval vegetation as high as the densities of livestock in wood-pastures? There will not have been one overall density. Like in wood-pastures, there will have been differences because of the difference in accessibility and productivity because of soil fertility. However, the fossil records cannot answer the question about density because, first, the chance of fossilization depends on special conditions and is generally very small and, second, the chance of finding fossilized bones is very small (Davis 1987). What remains is indirect proof, like, for instance, the high proportion of pollen of oak and hazel in the pollen spectra, together with pollen of shade-tolerant tree species in periods when or areas where agriculture was absent (Vera 2000).

OTHER LINES OF EVIDENCE

There are other lines of evidence that support the theory that the uncultivated wilderness was a park-like landscape instead of a closed-canopy forest (Vera 2000). Lines of evidence are charters from the sixth century AD onwards, which regulated the use of the wilderness. These regulations concerned the fattening of pigs and the protection of so-called fruitful (light-demanding) trees such as oak, wild cherry, wild pear and crab apple that produced food (the mast) for pigs. The grazing of cattle and horses was regulated from the thirteenth century onwards in order to protect the re-sprouting stools of 'hazel and thorn', which were cut for firewood. The regulations ordered to spare the young trees that grew in between the thorny shrubs, like they do in the wood-pasture. Oak was particularly mentioned, because of its importance for the fattening of pigs and shipbuilding (Vera 2000). The places where this happened were indicated in

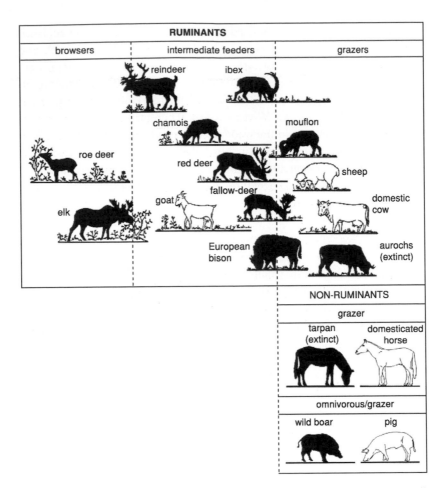

Figure 7.4. The different species of large herbivores indigenous in Europe, as well as the omnivorous wild boar, classified according to their feeding strategy. The domesticated species are shown in white. The indigenous species of the lowlands of central and western Europe include aurochs, tarpan, European bison, red deer, elk, roe deer and wild boar (redrawn from Hofmann 1973, 1976, 1985, Van de Veen & Van Wieren 1980, from Vera, 2000).

charters with the terms 'silva', 'forest', 'forêt', 'Forst', 'Wald', 'woud', 'bos', 'Busch' and 'wood' in Latin, French, German, Saxon and Dutch. They did not mean forest or woodland in the modern sense of these words, but referred to places where there were trees with 'wood' as material as well as grassland and even treeless raised bogs (Vera 2000).

Other lines of evidence are pollen diagrams from areas from before the introduction of agriculture in the Holocene. The proportion of arboreal pollen (trees, including oak, and shrubs, including hazel) and non-arboreal pollen (grasses and forbs) from that period varies mostly between 90% and 95% arboreal pollen. The dominance of arboreal pollen is in the 'classical forest theory' interpreted as proof of the presence of a closed-canopy forest. However, pollen analyses of modern landscape show that such pollen diagrams can also be interpreted as park-like landscapes. For instance, an area with 30% open terrain with grasses and grains showed a percentage of non-arboreal pollen of 4.5% and 2.0%, respectively (Gaillard *et al.* 1998, Sugita *et al.* 1999). A closed zone of trees situated along the bank of a sampled lake (0.2 ha) surrounded by a landscape that consisted of more than 50% open cultivated land and of 30% semi-open land (20% to 50% tree coverage) in a radius up to 1000 m, showed a pollen image of 90% tree pollen (arboreal pollen) (Broström *et al.* 1998). All these data show that there is no linearity between the openness of a landscape and the percentage of non-arboreal pollen (Sugita *et al.* 1997, 1999, Gaillard *et al.* 1998). Besides these data, the high proportion of pollen of oak and hazel together varies from 20%–50% up to 60%–75% of the total pollen sum (Huntley & Birks 1983). This is also an important indication towards the park-like landscape (Vera 2000).

PRESERVING BIODIVERSITY

Because of the high variety of types of vegetation, wood-pastures have an extremely high diversity of plant and animal species (Harding & Rose 1986, Tubbs 1988, Rackham 2003). Bulk grazers like cattle and horses are key elements in the processes that are responsible for this high diversity (Vera 2000). The oak itself has a special place as a host for insects. There is no other species of tree in Europe associated with so many species of insects (Darlington 1974, Morris 1974). More than 50% of all the species of insects found in the whole of Great Britain live in the wood-pasture of the New Forest alone (20 000 hectares) (Tubbs 1988, Alexander 1998). Of all the European species of butterflies, 80% live in a habitat combining grasslands, scrub and groves with mantle vegetation (Bink 1992). Furthermore, there is an enormous variety of species of birds, especially songbirds (Smith 1980, Hondong *et al.* 1993, Cramp 1988, 1992).

SUMMING UP THE VIEWPOINTS

The disappearance of oak and hazel and other light-demanding species in the forest reserves shows that oak and hazel reflect past environmental adaptations that no longer exist in these reserves. In forest reserves these species as well as other light-demanding species are ecological anachronisms. The presence and the successful regeneration in wood-pastures of light-demanding tree and shrub species shows that the environmental conditions these species require are still there. The large ungulates, cattle and horses, play a key role in the processes of creating these environmental conditions. Being modern analogues of aurochs and tarpan, cattle and horses highlight that in wood-pastures light-demanding oak and hazel and other light-demanding tree and shrub species, reflect adaptations of the now-extinct grazers aurochs and tarpan.

In wood-pastures the natural interplay of herbivores and plant defences is still at work. The evolution of spiny and thorny shrub species that protect palatable tree and shrub species through associational resistance may have been enforced by large herbivores (Milewski et al. 1991). The presence of these taxa as well as large ungulates goes back through the Pleistocene to as far as the Tertiary (Tallis 1991, Agusti & Anton 2002). They lived together for millions of years. It is striking that the current ecological distribution of woody species with thorns and spines in the Netherlands coincides with the preferred distribution of large herbivores in grazed landscapes, namely on dry, fertile soils.

In conclusion, the wood-pasture can be considered as the closest modern analogue of the primaeval natural vegetation in situations where large ungulates lived (Vera 1997, 2000). Contrary to the classic forest theory, the wood-pasture system can explain the presence of light-demanding as well as shade-tolerant species in the primaeval vegetation, together with the presence of large grazing ungulates. Our study provides an interesting case showing that current ecological traits of species can tell us something about their ecological context in the past – which can have important lessons for current conservation strategies.

THE THEORY IN A BROADER PERSPECTIVE

This is not the only theory about a key role for large herbivores with regard to the structure and species composition of the natural vegetation. It is suggested that in Beringia, the Pleistocene megafauna played a key role in maintaining grass-dominated steppe conditions, and that the disappearance of these animals at the end of the Pleistocene, probably because of the hunting pressure by anatomically modern people, caused a shift of grass-dominated steppe to moss dominated tundra, irrespective of climatic change (Zimov et al. 1995).

The theory of wood-pasture as the nearest modern analogue of prim-aeval vegetation has been commented on and criticized by several authors (Svenning 2002, Bradshaw *et al.* 2003, Rackham 2003, Whitehouse & Smith 2004). In a review of palaeoecological data Svenning (2002) states that a closed forest would predominate in so-called normal upland situations, but includes localized longer-lasting openings. Open vegetation would have been frequent on floodplains, infertile soils, chalklands and in continental and sub-Mediterranean areas. Large herbivores and fire would have been potential key factors in creating open vegetation in northwestern Europe.

Svenning (2002) states that the low percentage of non-arboreal pollen can indeed be interpreted as proof for the presence of a closed canopy forest, because among fossil beetles there is a similar low percentage of species connected with vegetation openness. He then concludes that, therefore, oak and hazel can persist in a closed-canopy deciduous species-rich forest. Data from the large island Zealand in Denmark would support his conclusion. Aurochs and moose would have become extinct there 7000–8000 years BP, because no fossils are found afterwards (Aaris-Sørensen 1980). Oak and hazel remained there during the mid-Holocene (6200–5200 BP) with shade-tolerant species like lime, ash and sycamore. Therefore oak and hazel occurred in a species-rich forest with shade-tolerant species even in the absence of large grazers.

This interpretation disregards the facts revealed by the developments in forest reserves. One of them is on the island Zealand itself. It is called Suserup Skov and is a former wood-pasture (Fritzbørger & Emborg 1996). It was protected in 1854. There are oaks of 250 to 500 years old and many have wide crowns and short boles, showing they grew up in open conditions. Nowadays it is a closed-canopy forest where oak and hazel are replaced by shade-tolerant species like lime, ash, sycamore, beech and hornbeam (Emborg *et al.* 1996), of which the first three taxa were present during the mid-Holocene together with oak and hazel (Hannon *et al.* 2000). Concerning the absence of grazers on the island of Zealand, it should be stressed that one of the basic rules in palaeoecology is that absence of proof is no proof of absence (Davis 1987).

The data concerning beetles used by Svenning (2002) are according to Whitehouse & Smith (2004) less convincing. The percentages of open-area taxa, routinely presented by palaeoentomologists, reflect abundance within the sample and do not indicate *direct proportions of associated habitat* (italics by Whitehouse & Smith 2004). Although she states that using fossil beetles to examine openness has potential, it is presently not possible to estimate percentages of landscape openness/closedness from beetle records. The interpretations have been largely intuitive (Dinnin & Sadler 1999, Whitehouse & Smith 2004).

Svenning (2002) as well as Whitehouse and Smith (2004) refer to fire as an important disturbance agency. Especially in the eastern United States, fire received much attention in relation to the failure of oak to regenerate in closed-canopy forests (Abrams 1992, 2003, Frelich & Reich 2002). Here there are about 30 species of oak (Abrams 1996), almost all of which are light-demanding (Smith 1993, Dey 2002). As in Europe light-demanding oak species do not regenerate successfully in forest reserves, either in small or large gaps. They are replaced by shade-tolerant species like American beech (*Fagus grandifolia*), sugar maple (*Acer saccharum*), silver maple (*A. saccharinum*), red maple (*A. rubrum*), basswood (*Tilia americana*), white ash (*Fraxinus americana*) and American elm (*Ulmus americana*). Also the light-demanding fast-growing yellow poplar (*Liriodendron tulipifera*) that can, like oak, be long lived, can suppress oak (Peterken 1996, Brose *et al.* 1999, McCarthy *et al.* 2001). Even in large wind blown areas created by catastrophic storms, only shade-tolerant species are released (Spurr 1956, Hibbs 1983, Peterson & Picket 1995). Such events actually speed up the replacement of oak (Nowacki & Abrams 1992). Oak only regenerates in circumstances where the shade-tolerant species cannot thrive like xeric conditions (McCune & Cottam 1985, Orwig & Abrams 1994, Frelich & Reich 2002). According to pollen diagrams, oak, however, survived next to shade-tolerant taxa such as *Tilia, Acer, Fagus, Ulmus* and *Fraxinus*. The percentage of pollen from oak forms a much larger portion of the pollen diagrams than in Europe, namely from 40% to up to 70% (Watts 1979, Delcourt & Delcourt 1991, Clark 1997).

According to Abrams (1992, 2002, 2003), the successional replacement of oak by shade-tolerant species is caused by the suppression of wildfires, that started around the 1930s. He formulated the so-called fire and oak hypothesis (Abrams 2002). According to this hypothesis, fire eliminated the regeneration of shade-tolerant species. Fire also created open landscape that would be necessary for the light-demanding oak to survive. He refers to historical descriptions of the east of the United States, indicating the presence of open, park-like landscapes with open forests and areas where forests alternated regularly with grasslands (Cronon 1983, Whitney & Davis 1986, Covington & Moore 1994). The burning by Native Americans would have created this open park-like landscape. Therefore, fire could explain why oak continued to exist in the presence of shade-tolerant species like maple, lime, beech and ash for thousands of years (Abrams & Seischab 1997).

There is doubt about the evidence for large-scale burning of forests by Native Americans (Day 1953, Russell 1983). Russell (1983) states that the openness of the landscape in itself is used as the evidence of large-scale burning. Because there were open forests everywhere, there must have been burning everywhere, because otherwise the phenomenon cannot be explained. Several authors (Whitney & Davis 1986, Huddle & Pallardy 1996, Arthur *et al.* 1998) also pointed out that fire is not as selective with respect to oak as is assumed. Therefore, it is not clear at all whether oak species, for instance white oak (*Quercus alba*), do benefit from fire. This species is the most widely distributed light-demanding oak species in the eastern United States and a common species before European colonization in so-called pre-settlement forests. White oaks, 300–500 years old, became established in a period without clear traces of fire. Even during a recent historic fire regime no successful regeneration took place (McCarthy *et al.* 2001).

Abrams (2002, 2003) considered the presence of charcoal to be an indication of the role of fire in prehistoric times. However, from analyses of pollen and charcoal in sediments, it appears that fire cannot have played the role in forests in the eastern United States that has been ascribed to it (Clark 1997, Clark & Royall 1995, Clark *et al.* 1996). In most of the east of the United States, oak appears to have maintained itself in the company of shade-tolerant genera in more moist regions on soils with good moisture levels for thousands of years without clear palaeoevidence of fire. Therefore, other factors must have allowed the subsistence of oak in the long-term in the absence of fire (Clark 1997). It cannot have been catastrophic storms, because as mentioned earlier, only shade-tolerant species will be released. Therefore, as Frelich and Reich (2002) stated, in the absence of fire the mechanism for the establishment of oaks within the mesic forests dominated by shade-tolerant species remains a mystery.

However, the development of closed-canopy forests in the east of the United States did not only take place in the absence of fire. As in Europe, large grazing ungulates were absent as well. However, in the eastern United States prior to the early nineteenth century, the large grazer bison (*Bison bison*) was present (Vera 2000). At the time of colonization by the Europeans large numbers were there (Smith 1962, McHugh 1972, Joke & Sawtelle 1985, cited in Crow *et al.* 1994). They left traces in the landscape, as is shown by the first railroads that were constructed through the Appalachians from the east in a westerly direction that were laid on bison trails (Smith 1962, McHugh 1972). For example, around 1770 more than 10 000 bison were present in North Pennsylvania. The bison disappeared soon after colonization of the east of the United States. In North

Pennsylvania none were left 70 years later in 1840 (McHugh 1972, Day 1989). In 1825, the bison was extinct in West Virginia (Day 1989).

Being a specialized grazer, the influence of the bison in the eastern United States could have been analogous to specialized grazers like cattle and horses in Europe. Trees would have regenerated in open grassland with thorny bushes as nurse species, while groves would have changed into grassland. There are more than 30 species of hawthorn in the eastern United States, most of which are thorny (Britton & Brown 1947). This process could explain the permanent presence of open, park-like land-scapes known from the historical descriptions, without the presence of fire. In the eastern United States oak does regenerate in thorny bushes in grassland grazed by cattle (Scot 1915, Marks 1942). It is striking that in Ohio where there was heavy grazing by cattle until 1940, white oak was present in all year classes (Whitney & Somerlot 1985). Concerning the role of fire in the regeneration of oak, it should be kept in mind that fire has been proposed as a disturbance agency within the framework of the natural vegetation being a closed-canopy forest. This framework implied that large grazers would not have had a substantial influence on the forest and followed the development in the vegetation. Our study of oak in the eastern United States indicates that the answer to the question posed by Abrams and Seischab (1997): 'What disturbance factor other than fire could historically have prevented these species from replacing oak?', may be large grazers like bison. Burning by Native Americans would then have made the landscape more open than it already was.

ACKNOWLEDGEMENTS

We thank D. Wisser for drawing the figures.

REFERENCES

Aaris-Sørensen, K. (1980). Depauperation of the mammalian fauna of the island of Zealand during the Atlantic period. *Videnskabelige Meddelelser fra Dansk Naturhistorisk Forening*, **142**, 131–8.

Abrams, M.D. (1992). Fire and the development of oak forests. *BioScience*, **42**, 346–53.

Abrams, M.D. (1996). Distribution, historical development and ecophysiological attributes of oak species in the eastern United States. *Annales des Sciences Forestières*, **53**, 487–512.

Abrams, M.D. (2002). The postglacial history of oak forests in eastern North America. In *Oak Forests Ecosystems: Ecology and Management for Wildlife*, ed. W.J. McShea & W.M. Healy. Baltimore and London: The Johns Hopkins University Press, pp. 34–45.

Abrams, M.D. (2003). Where has all the white oak gone? *BioScience*, **53**, 927–39.
Abrams, M.D. & Seischab, F.K. (1997). Does the absence of sediment charcoal provide substantial evidence against the fire and oak hypothesis? *Journal of Ecology*, **85**, 373–5.
Agusti, J. & Anton, M. (2002). *Mammoths, Sabertooth's, and Hominids*. New York: Columbia University Press.
Alexander, K.N.A. (1998). The links between forest history and biodiversity: the invertebrate fauna of ancient pasture-woodlands in Britain and its conservation. In *The Ecological History of European Forests*, ed. K.J. Kirby & C. Watkins. Wallingford: CAB International, pp. 73–80.
Arthur, M.A., Paratley, R.D. & Blankenship, B.A. (1998). Single and repeated fires affect survival and regeneration of woody and herbaceous species in an oak-pine forest. *Journal of the Torrey Botanical Society*, **125**, 225–36.
Bakker, E.S., Olff, H., Vandenberghe, C., De Maeyer, K., Smit, R., Gleichman, J.M. and Vera, F.W.M. (2004). Ecological anachronisms in the recruitment of temperate light-demanding tree species in wooded pastures. *Journal of Applied Ecology*, **41**, 571–82.
Bär, J. (1914). Die flora des Val Onsernone. *Mitteilungen aus dem botanischen Museum der Universität Zürich*, **59**, 223–563.
Barlow, C. (2000). *The Ghosts of Evolution: Nonsensical Fruit, Missing Partners, and Other Ecological Anachronisms*. New York: Basic Books.
Bradshaw, R.H.W., Hannon, G.E. & Lister, A.M. (2003). A long-term perspective on ungulate-vegetation interactions. *Forest Ecology and Mangement*, **181**, 267–80.
Belostokov, G.P. (1980). Morphogenesis of *Tilia cordata* Mill.; bush-shaped regrowth. *Lesoved*, **6**, 53–9.
Bezacinský, H. (1971). Das Hainbuchenproblem in der Slowakei. *Acta Facultatis Forestalis*, **8**, 7–36.
Bink, F.A. (1992). *Ecologische Atlas van de Dagvlinders van Noordwest-Europa*. Haarlem: Instituut voor Bos- en Natuuronderzoek en Unie van Provinciale Landschappen, Schuyt & Co.
Bokdam, J. (1987). Foerageergedrag van jongvee in het Junner Koeland in relatie tot het voedselaanbod. In *Begrazing in de natuur*, ed. S. de Bie, W. Joenje & S.E. van Wieren. Wageningen: Pudoc, pp. 165–86.
Bokdam, J. (2003). *Nature Conservation and Grazing Management. Free-Ranging Cattle as Driving Force for Cyclic Vegetation Succession*. Ph.D. thesis, Wageningen University, Wageningen.
Bonnemann, A. (1956a). Eichen-Buchen mischbestände. *Allgemeine Forst- und Jagdzeitung*, **127**, 33–42.
Bonnemann, A. (1956b). Eichen-Buchen mischbestände. *Allgemeine Forst- und Jagdzeitung*, **127**, 118–26.
Borowski, S. & Kossak, S. (1972). The natural food preferences of the European bison in seasons free of snow cover. *Acta Theriologica*, **17**, 151–69.
Bossema, J. (1979). Jays and Oaks: An Eco-Ethological Study of a Symbiosis. Ph.D. thesis, Rijksuniversiteit Groningen, Groningen. (Also published in *Behaviour*, **70**, 1–117.)
Britton, N.L. & Brown, H.A. (1947). *An Illustrated Flora of the Northern United States, Canada and the British Posessions*, Volume II. New York: New York Botanical Garden.

Brookes, P.C., Wigston, D.L. & Bourne, W.F. (1980). The dependence of *Quercus robur* and *Q. petraea* seedlings on cotyledon potassium, magnesium, calcium and phosphorus during the first year of growth. *Forestry*, **53**, 167–77.

Brose, P.H., Van Lear, D.H. & Keyser, P.D. (1999). A shelterwood-burn technique for regenerating productive upland oak sites in the Piedmont region. *Southern Journal of Applied Forestry*, **23**, 158–63.

Broström, A., Gaillard, M.-J., Ihnse, M. & Odgaard, B. (1998). Pollen-landscape relationships in modern analogues of ancient cultural landscapes in southern Sweden – a first step towards quantification of vegetation openness in the past. *Vegetation History and Archaeobotany*, **7**, 189–201.

Burrichter, E., Pott, R., Raus, T. & Wittig, R. (1980). Die Hudelandschaft 'Borkener Paradies' im Emstal bei Meppen. *Abhandlungen aus den Landesmuseum für Naturkunde zu Münster in Westfalen*. Münster 42. Jahrgang 4.

Buttenschøn, J. & Buttenschøn, R.M. (1978). The effect of browsing by cattle and sheep on trees and bushes. *Natura Jutlandica*, **20**, 79–94.

Buttenschøn, J. & Buttenschøn, R.M. (1985). Grazing experiments with cattle and sheep on nutrient poor, acidic grassland and heath. IV. Establishment of woody species. *Natura Jutlandica*, **21**, 47–140.

Callaway, R.M., Kikvidze, Z. & Kikodze, D. (2000). Facilitation by unpalatable weeds may conserve plant diversity in overgrazed meadows in the Caucasus Mountains. *Oikos*, **89**, 275–82.

Chettleburgh, M.R. (1952). Observations on the collection and burial of acorns by jays in Hinault Forest. *British Birds*, **45**, 359–64. Also further note (1955); **48**, 183–4.

Christensen, N.L. (1977). Changes in structure, pattern, and diversity associated with climax forest maturation in Piedmont, North Carolina. *American Midland Naturalist*, **97**, 176–88.

Clark, J.S. (1997). Facing short-term extrapolation with long-term evidence: Holocene fire in the north-eastern US forests. *Journal of Ecology*, **85**, 377–80.

Clark, J.S. & Royall, P.D. (1995). Transformation of a northern hardwood forest by aboriginal (Iroquois) fire: charcoal evidence from Crawford Lake, Ontario, Canada. *The Holocene*, **5**, 1–9.

Clark, J.S. Royall, P.D. & Chumbley, C. (1996). The role of fire during climate change in an eastern deciduous forest at Devil's Bathtub, New York. *Ecology*, **77**, 2148–66.

Coops, H. (1988). Occurrence of blackthorn (*Prunus spinosa* L.) in the area of Mols Bjerge and the effect of cattle- and sheep-grazing on its growth. *Nature Jutlandica*, **9**, 169–76.

Coppins, A., Coppins, B. & Quelch, P. (2002). Atlantic hazelwoods. Some observations on the ecology of this neglected habitat from a lichenological perspective. *British Wildlife*, **14**, 17–26.

Covington, W.W. & Moore, M.M. (1994). Southwestern Ponderosa forest structure. Changes since Euro-American settlement. *Journal of Forestry*, **92**, 39–47.

Cramp, S. (ed.) (1988). *Handbook of the Birds of Europe, the Middle East, and North Africa. The Birds of the Western Palaearctic, Vol. V. Tyrant Flycatchers to Thrushes*. Oxford: Oxford University Press.

Cramp, S. (ed.) (1992). *Handbook of the Birds of Europe, the Middle East, and North Africa. The Birds of the Western Palaearctic, Vol. VI. Warblers*. Oxford: Oxford University Press.

Cronon, W. (1983). *Changes in the Land: Indians, Colonists, and the Ecology of New England*. New York: Hill and Wang.

Crow, T.R., Johnson, W.C. & Atkinson, C.S. (1994). Fire and recruitment of *Quercus* in a postagricultural field. *American Midland Naturalist*, **131**, 84–97.

Dagenbach, H. (1981). Der Speierling, ein seltener Baum in unseren Wäldern und Obstgärten. *Allgemeine Forstzeitschrift*, **36**, 214–17.

Darlington, A. (1974). The galls on oak. In *The British Oak: Its History and Natural History*, ed. M.G. Morris & F.H. Perring. Berkshire: The Botanical Society of the British Isles, E.W. Classey, pp. 298–311.

Davis, S.J. M. (1987). *The Archeology of Animals*. London: B.T. Batsford.

Day, D. (1989). *Vanished Species*. New York: Gallery Books.

Day, G.M. (1953). The Indian as an ecological factor in the northeastern forest. *Ecology*, **34**, 329–46.

Delcourt, H.R. & Delcourt, P.A. (1991). *Quaternary Ecology: A Paleoecological Perspective*. London: Chapman and Hall.

Dey, D. (2002). Fire history and postsettlement disturbance. In *Oak Forests Ecosystems: Ecology and Management for Wildlife*, ed. W.J. McShea & W.M. Healy. Baltimore and London: The Johns Hopkins University Press, pp. 60–79.

Dierschke, H. (1974). Saumgesellschaften im Vegetations- und Standortsgefälle an Waldrändern. *Scripta Geobotanica*, **6**, 3–246.

Dinnin, M.H. & Sadler, J.P. (1999). 10 000 years of change: the Holocene entomofauna of the British Isles. *Quaternary Proceedings*, **7**, 545–62.

Dobson, A. & Crawley, M. (1994). Pathogens and the structure of plant communities. *Trends in Ecology and Evolution*, **9**, 303–98.

Dupré, S., Thiébaut, S. & Teissier du Cros, E. (1986). Morphologie et architecture des jeunes hêtres (*Fagus sylvatica* L.). Influence du milieu, variabilité génétique. *Annales des Sciences Forestières*, **43**, 85–102.

Eichhorn (1927). Waldbauliche Erfahrungen in den Hardtwaldungen des unteren Rheintales. *Allgemeine Forst- und Jagdzeitung*, **103**, 169–85.

Ekstam, U. & Sjögren, E. (1973). Studies on past and present changes in deciduous forest vegetation on Öland. *Zoon* (Uppsala) Suppl., **1**, 123–35.

Ellenberg, H. (1988). *Vegetation Ecology of Central Europe*. 4th edn. Cambridge: Cambridge University Press.

Emborg, J., Christensen, M. & Heilmann-Clausen, J. (1996). The structure of Suserup Skov. A near-natural temperate deciduous forest in Denmark. *Forest and Landscape Research*, **1**, 311–33.

Falinski, J.B. (1986). *Vegetation Dynamics in Temperate Lowland Primaeval Forests*. Ecological studies in Bialowieza forest, Geobotany 8. Dordrecht: Dr. W. Junk Publishers.

Felius, M. (1995). *Cattle Breeds. An Encyclopedia*. Doetinchem: Misset.

Flower, N. (1977). An historical and ecological study of inclosed and uninclosed woods in the New Forest, Hampshire. M.Sc. thesis, King's College, University of London.

Frelich, L.E. & Reich, P.B (2002). Dynamics of old-growth oak forests in eastern United States. In *Oak Forests Ecosystems: Ecology and Management for Wildlife*, W.J. McShea & W.M. Healy. Baltimore and London: The Johns Hopkins University Press, pp. 113–26.

Fritzbøger, B. & Emborg, J. (1996). Landscape history of the deciduous forest Suserup Skov, Denmark, before 1925. *Forest and Landscape Research*, 1, 291–309.

Gaillard, M.-J., Birks, H.J. B., Ihse, M. & Runberg, S. (1998). Pollen/landscape calibration based on modern pollen assemblages from surface-sediments samples and landscape mapping – a pilot study in south Sweden. In *Quantification of Land Surfaces Cleared of Forest During the Holocene-Modern Pollen/Vegetation/Landscape Relationships as an Aid to the Interpretation of Pollen Data.* Paläoklimaforschung/Palaeoclimate Research 7, 31–52.

Green, T. (1992). The forgotten army. *British Wildlife*, 4, 85–6.

Goriup, P.D., Batten, L.A. & Norton, J.A. (eds.) (1991). The conservation of lowland dry grassland birds in Europe. *Proceedings of an International Seminar held at the University of Reading, 20–22 March 1991.* Peterborough: Joint Nature Committee.

Guintard, G. & Tardy, F. (1994). Les bovins de l'Île Amsterdam. Un example d'isolement génétique. In *Aurochs. Le retour. Aurochs, vaches et autres bovins de la préhistoire à nos jours* ed. L. Bailly & A.-S. Cohën. Lons-le-Saunier Centre Jurassien du Patrimoine, pp. 203–9.

Hannon, G.E., Bradshaw, R. & Emborg, J. (2000). 6000 years of forest dynamics in Suserup Skov, a semi-natural Danish woodland. *Global Ecology and Biogeography*, 9, 101–14.

Harding, P.T. & Rose, F. (1986). *Pasture-Woodlands in Lowland Britain. A Review of their Importance for Wildlife Conservation.* Huntingdon: Natural Environment Research Council, Institute of Terrestrial Ecology.

Hart, G.E. (1966). *Royal Forests. A History of Dean's Woods as Producers of Timber.* London: Clarendon Press.

Hauskeller-Bullerjahn, K., von Lüpke, B., Hauskeller, H.-M. & Dong, P.H. (2000). Versuch zur natürlichen Verjüngung der Traubeneiche im Pfälzerwald. *AFZ/DerWald*, 10, 514–17.

Hibbs, D.E. (1983). Forty years of forest succession in central New England. *Ecology*, 64, 1394–401.

Heukels, H. & Van der Meijden, R. (1983). *Flora van Nederland.* Groningen: Wolters-Noordhoff.

Hofmann, R.R. (1973). *The Ruminant Stomach: Stomach Structure and Feeding Habits of East African Game Ruminants.* Nairobi, Kenya: East African Literature Bureau.

Hofmann, R.R. (1976). Zur adaptiven Differenzierung der Wiederkäuer: Untersuchungsergebnisse auf der Basis der Vergleichenden funktionellen Anatomie des Verdauungstrakts. *Praktische Tierärtzt*, 57, 351–58.

Hofmann, R.R. (1985). Digestive physiology of the deer. Their morphophysiological specialisation and adaptation. *The Royal Society of New Zealand Bulletin*, 22, 393–407.

Hondong, H., Langner, S. & Coch, T. (1993). *Untersuchungen zum Naturschutz an Waldrändern.* Bristol-Schriftenreihe, Band 2, Bristol-Stiftung, Ruth und Herbert UHL - Forschungsstelle für Natur- und Umweltschutz.

Houtzagers, M., Neutel, W., Rosseel, A. & Swart, B. (2000). Fontainebleau (re)visited. Effect van storm in bosreservaat in Fontainebleau. *Nederlands Bosbouw Tijdschrift*, 72, 228–33.

Huddle, J.A. & Pallardy, S.G. (1996). Effects of long-term annual and periodic burning on tree survival and growth in a Missouri Ozark oak-hickory forest. *Forest Ecology and Management*, **82**, 1–9.

Huntley, B. & Birks, H.J.B. (1983). *An Atlas of Past and Present Pollen Maps of Europe: 0–13 000 Years Ago*. Cambridge: Cambridge University Press,

Hytteborn, H. (1986). Methods of forest dynamics research. In *Forest Dynamics Research in Western and Central Europe*. ed. I. Fanta. Wageningen: Pudoc, pp. 17–31.

Iason, G.R. & Alison, H. (1993). The response of heather (*Calluna vulgaris*) to shade and nutrients – predictions of the carbon-nutrient balance hypothesis. *Journal of Ecology*, **81**, 75–80.

Iversen, J. (1960). Problems of the early post-glacial forest development in Denmark. *Danmarks Geologiske Undersøgelse*, IV. Raekke Bd. 4, 3 (Geological Survey of Denmark. IV Series, 4, 3).

Jahn, G. (1991). Temperate deciduous forests of Europe. In *Temperate Deciduous Forests*, ed. R. Röhrig & B. Ulrich. Ecosystems of the World, 7. Amsterdam: Elsevier, pp. 377–503.

Janzen, D.H. & Martin, P.S. (1982). Neotropical anachronisms: the fruits the gomphoteres ate. *Science*, **215**, 19–27.

Jarvis, P.G. (1964). The adaptability to light intensity of seedlings of *Quercus petraea* (Matt.) Liebl. *Journal of Ecology*, **52**, 545–71.

Jensen, T.S. & Nielsen, O.F. (1986). Rodents as seed dispersers in a heath–oak wood succession. *Oecologia*, **70**, 214–21.

Kollmann, J. & Schill, H.-P. (1996). Spatial patterns of dispersal, seed predation and germination during colonization of abandoned grassland by *Quercus petraea* and *Corylus avellana*. *Vegetatio*, **125**, 193–205.

Krahl-Urban, J. (1959). *Die Eichen. Forstliche Monographie der Traubeneiche und der Stieleiche*. Berlin: Paul Parey.

Lemée, G. (1978). La hêtraie naturalle de Fontainbleau. In *Problèmes d'ecologie: structure et fonctionnement des écosystèmes terrestres*, ed. M. Lamotte & F. Boreslière. Paris: Masson, pp. 75–128.

Lemée, G. (1987). Les populations de chênes (*Quercus petraea* Liebl.) des réserves biologiques de La Tillaie et du Gros Fouteau en forêt de Fontainebleau: structure, démographie et évolution. *Revue d'Ecologie*, **42**, 329–55.

Lemée, G., Faille, A., Pontailler, J.Y. & Roger, J.M. (1992). Hurricanes and regeneration in a natural beech forest. In *Responses of Forest Ecosystems to Environmental Changes*, ed. A. Teller, P. Malthy & J.N.R. Jeffers. London & New York: Elsevier Applied Science, pp. 987–8.

Malmer, N. Lindgren, K. & Persson, S. (1978). Vegetational succession in a south-Swedish deciduous wood. *Vegetatio*, **36**, 17–29.

Marks, J.B. (1942). Land use and plant succession in Coon Valley, Wisconsin. *Ecological Monographs*, **12**, 113–33.

Mayer, H. & Tichy, K. (1979). Das Eichen-Naturschutzgebiet Johannser Kogel im Lainzer Tiergarten, Wienerwald. *Centralblatt für das Gesamte Forstwesen*, **4**, 193–226.

McCarthy, B.C., Small, J.C. & Rubino, D.L. (2001). Composition, structure and dynamics of Dysart Woods, an old-growth mixed mesophytic forest of southeastern Ohio. *Forest Ecology and Management*, **140**, 193–213.

McCune, B. & Cottam, G. (1985). The successional status of a southern Wisconsin oak wood. *Ecology*, **66**, 1270–78.

McHugh, T. (1972). *The Time of the Buffalo*. Lincoln: University of Nebraska Press.

Milchunas, D.G. & Noy-Meir, I. (2002). Grazing refuges, external avoidance of herbivory and plant diversity. *Oikos*, **99**, 113–30.

Milewski, A.V., Young, T.P. & Madden, D. (1991). Thorns as induced defences: experimental evidence. *Oecologia*, **86**, 70–5.

Morris, M.G. (1974). Oak as a habitat for insect life. In *The British Oak: Its History and Natural History*, ed. M.G. Morris & F.H. Perring. Berkshire: The Botanical Society of the British Isles, E.W. Classey, pp. 274–97.

Moss, C.E. (1913). *Vegetation of the Peak District*. Cambridge: Cambridge University Press.

Mountford, E.P. & Peterken, G. (2003). Long-term change and implications for the management of wood-pastures: experience over 40 years from Denny Wood, New Forest. *Forestry*, **76**, 19–43.

Mountford, E.P., Peterken, G.F., Edwards, P.J. & Manners, J.G. (1999). Long-term change in growth, mortality and regeneration of trees in Denny Wood, an old-growth wood-pasture in the New Forest (UK). *Perspectives in Plant Ecology, Evolution and Systematics*, **2**, 223–72.

Namvar, K. & Spethmann, W. (1985). Waldbaumarten aus der Gattung *Ulmus* (Ulme, Rüster). *Allgemeine Forstzeitschrift*, **40**, 1220–5.

Newbold, A.J. & Goldsmith, F.B. with an addendum on birch by Harding, J.S. (1981). *The Regeneration of Oak and Beech: A Literature Review*. Discussion Papers in Conservation. No. 33. London University College: London.

Nowacki, G.J. & Abrams, M.D. (1992). Community, edaphic, and historical analysis of mixed oak forests of the Ridge and Valley Province in central Pennsylvania. *Canadian Journal of Forest Research*, **22**, 790–800.

Olff, H., Vera, F.W.M., Bokdam, J., Bakker, E.S., Gleichman, J.M., De Maeyer, K. & Smit, K. (1999). Shifting mosaics in grazed woodlands driven by the alternation of plant facilitation and competition. *Plant Biology*, **1**, 127–37.

Orwig, D.A. & Abrams, M.D. (1994). Land-use history (1720–1992), composition, and dynamics of oak-pine forests within the Piedmont and Coastal Plain of northern Virginia. *Canadian Journal of Forest Research*, **24**, 1216–25.

Peltier, A., Toezet, M.-C., Armengaud, C. & Ponge, J.-F. (1997). Establishment of *Fagus sylvatica* and *Fraxinus excelsior* in an old-growth beech forest. *Journal of Vegetation Science*, **8**, 13–20.

Peterken, G.F. (1996). *Natural Woodland. Ecology and Conservation in Northern Temperate Regions*. Cambridge: Cambridge University Press.

Peterken, G.F. & Jones, E.W. (1987). Forty years of change in Lady Park Wood: the old growth stands. *Journal of Ecology*, **75**, 477–512.

Peterken, G.F. & Tubbs, C.R. (1965). Woodland regeneration in the New Forest, Hampshire, since 1650. *Journal of Applied Ecology*, **2**, 159–70.

Peterson, C.J. & Picket, S.T.A. (1995). Forest reorganization: a case study in an old-growth forest catastrophic blowdown. *Ecology*, **76**, 763–74.

Pigott, C.D. (1988). The ecology and silviculture of limes (*Tilia* spp.). In *O.F.I. Occasional Papers, No 37. National Hardwoods Programme. Report of the Eighth Meeting and Second Meeting of the un-even Aged Silviculture Group 7 January 1988*, ed. P.S. Savill. Oxford: Oxford Forestry Institute, University of Oxford, pp. 27–32.

Pockberger, J. (1963). Die Linden. Ein Beitrag zur Bereicherung des Mitteleuropäischen Waldbildes. *Centralblatt für das Gesamte Forstwesen*, **80**, 99–123.

Ponge, J.-F. & Ferdy, J.-B. (1997). Growth of *Fagus sylvatica* saplings in an old growth forest as affected by soil and light conditions. *Journal of Vegetation Science*, **8**, 789–96.

Pott, R. & Hüppe, J. (1991). *Die Hudenlandschaften Nordwestdeutschlands.* Westfälisches Museum für Naturkunde, Landschafsverband Westfalen-Lippe. Veröffentlichung der Arbeitsgemeinschaft für Biol.-ökol. Landesforschung, ABÖL, nr. 89, Münster.

Pruski, W. (1963). Ein Regenerationsversuch des Tarpans in Polen. *Zeitschrift für Tierzüchtung und Züchtungsbiologie*, **79**, 1–30.

Putman, R.J. (1986). *Grazing in Temperate Ecosystems: Large Herbivores and the Ecology of the New Forest.* London: Croom Helm.

Putman, R.J., Edwards, P.J., Mann, J.C. E., How, R.C. & Hill, S.D. (1989). Vegetational and faunal changes in an area of heavily grazed woodland following relief of grazing. *Biological Conservation*, **47**, 13–22.

Raben, G.(1980). Geschichtliche Betrachtung der Waldwirtschaftung im Naturwaldreservat Priorteich und deren Einfluss auf den heutigen Bestand. Diplomarbeit. Göttingen: Institut für Waldbau der Universität Göttingen.

Rackham, O. (2003). *Ancient Woodland: Its History, Vegetation and Uses in England*, New Edition. Kirkcudbrightshire: Castlepoint Press.

Remmert, H. (1991). The mosaic-cycle concept of ecosystems. An overview. In *The Mosaic-Cycle Concept of Ecosystems*, ed., H. Remmert. Berlin: Springer, pp. 11–21.

Rousset, O. & Lepart, J. (1999). Shrub facilitation of *Quercus humilis* regeneration in succession on calcareous grasslands. *Journal of Vegetation Science*, **10**, 493–502.

Russell, F.W. B. (1983). Indian-set fires in the forests of the northeastern United States. *Ecology*, **64**, 78–88.

Sanderson, J.I. (1958). The autecology of Corylus avellana (L.). in the neighbourhood of Sheffield with special reference to its regeneration. Ph.D. thesis, The University of Sheffield, Sheffield.

Schuster, L. (1950). Über den Sammeltrieb des Eichelhähers (*Garrulus glandarius*). *Vogelwelt*, **71**, 9–17.

Scot, F.I. (1915). A study of pasture trees and shrubbery. *Bulletin of the Torrey Botanical Club*, **42**, 451–61.

Shaw, M.W. (1974). The reproductive characteristics of oak. In *The British Oak: Its History and Natural History*, ed. M.G. Morris & F.H. Perring. Berkshire: The Botanical Society of the British Isles, F.W. Classey Ltd., pp. 162–81.

Smith, C. (1993). Regeneration of oaks in the Central Appalachians. In *Oak Regeneration: Serious Problems, Practical Recommendations. Symposium Proceedings, Knoxville, Tennessee, 8–10 September 1992*, ed. D.L. Loftis & C.E. McGee. Ashville: Southeastern Forest Experiment Sation, pp. 211–21.

Smith, C.J. (1980). *Ecology of the English Chalk.* London: Academic Press.

Smith, D.M. (1962). The forest of the United States. In *Regional Silviculture of the United States*, ed. J.W. Barrett. New York: The Ronald Press Componay, pp. 3–29.

Snow, B. & Snow, D. (1988). *Birds and Berries. A Study of an Ecological Interaction.* Calton: T. and A.D. Poyser.

Söffner, W. (1982). *Über die Grosssäugerfauna Mitteleuropas im Postglazial. Ein Beitrag zur Kenntnis der Beziehungen zwischen Wild und Vegetation. Zulassungsarbeit.* Institut für Botanik der Universität Hohenheim.

Spurr, H. S. (1956). Natural restocking of forests following the 1938 hurricane in central New England. *Ecology*, **33**, 426–7.

Stähr, F. & Peters, T. (2000). Hähersaat – Qualität und Vitalität natürlicher Eichenverjüngung im nordostdeutschen Tiefland. *AFZ/Der Wald*, **32**, 1231–5.

Sugita, S. MacDonald, G. & Larsen, C. P. S. (1997). Reconstruction of fire disturbance and forest succession from fossil pollen in lake sediments: potential and limitations. In *Sediment Records of Biomass Burning and Global Change*, ed. J. S. Clark, H. Cashier, J. G. Goldmmer & B. J. Stocks. Berlin: Springer, pp. 387–412.

Sugita, S., Gaillard, M.-J. & Broström, A. (1999). Landscape openness and pollen records: a simulation approach. *The Holocene*, **9**, 409–21.

Suner, A. & Röhrig, E. (1980). Die Entwicklung der Buchennaturverjüngung in Abhängigkeit von der Auflichtung des Altbestandes. *Forstarchiv*, **51**, 145–9.

Svenning, J.-S. (2002). A review of natural vegetation openness in north-western Europe. *Biological Conservation*, **104**, 133–48.

Szafer, W. (1968). The ure-ox, extinct in Europe since the seventeenth century: an early attempt at conservation that failed. *Biological Conservation*, **1**, 45–7.

Tallis, J. H. (1991). *Plant Community History: Long-term Changes in Plant Distribution and Diversity*. London: Chapman and Hall.

Tansley, A. G. (ed.) (1911). *Types of British Vegetation*. Cambridge: Cambridge University Press.

Tansley, A. G. (1922). Studies on the vegetation of the English chalk. II. Early stages of redevelopment of woody vegetation on chalk grassland. *Journal of Ecology*, **10**, 168–77.

Tansley, A. G. (1935). The use and abuse of vegetational concepts and terms. *Ecology*, **16**, 284–307.

Tansley, A. G. (1953). *The British Islands and their Vegetation*, Vol. 1, 2nd, 3rd edn. Cambridge: Cambridge University Press.

Tubbs, C. R. (1988). *The New Forest, A Natural History*. London: The New Naturalist, Collins.

van Hees, A. F. M. (1997). Growth and morphology of pedunculate oak (*Quercus robur* L) and beech (*Fagus sylvatica* L) seedlings in relation to shading and drought. *Annales des Sciences Forestières*, **54**, 9–18.

Van de Veen, H. E. & Van Wieren, S. E. (1980). *Van Grote Grazers, Kieskeurige Fijnproevers en Opportunistische Gelegenheidsvreters; over het Gebruik van Grote Herbivoren bij de Ontwikkeling en Duurzame Instandhouding van Natuurwaarden*. Rapport 80/11, Instituut voor Milieuvraagstukken, Amsterdam.

Vanselow, K. (1926). *Die Waldbautechnik im Spessart*. Eine historisch-kritische Untersuchung ihrer Epochen. Berlin: Verlag von Julius Springer.

Vera, F. W. M. (1997). Metaforen voor de wildernis. Eik, hazelaar, rund en paard. Ph.D. thesis, Wageningen University, Wageningen.

Vera, F. W. M. (2000). *Grazing Ecology and Forest History*. Wallingford, UK: CAB International.

Vereshchagin, N. K. & Baryshnikov, G. F. (1989). Quaternary mammalian extinctions in northern Eurasia. In *Quaternary Extinctions: A Prehistoric Revolution*, ed. P. S. Martin & R. G. Klein. Tucson: The University of Arizona Press, pp. 483–516.

von Koenigswald, W. (1983). Die Säugetierfauna des süddeutschen Pleistozäns. In *Urgeschichte in Baden-Württemberg*, ed. H. J. Müller-Beck. Stuttgart: Konrad Theiss Verlag, pp. 167–216.

von Lüpke, B.V. (1982). Versuche zur Einbringung von Lärche und Eiche in Buchenbestände. *Schriften aus der Forstlichen Fakultät der Universität Göttingen und der Niedersächsischen Forstlichen Versuchsanstalt 74*.

von Lüpke, B.V. & Hauskeller-Bullerjahn, K. (1999). Kahlschlagfreire Waldbau: wird die Eiche an den Rand gedrängt? *Forst und Holz*, **18**, 563–8.

Vullmer, H. & Hanstein, U. (1995). Der Beitrag des Eichelhähers zur Eichenverjüngung in einem Naturnah Bewirtschafteten Wald in der Lünerburger Heide. *Forst und Holz*, **50**, 643–6.

Watt, A.S. (1919). On the causes of failure of natural regeneration in British oakwoods. *Journal of Ecology*, **7**, 173–203.

Watt, A.S. (1924). On the ecology of British beech woods with special reference to their regeneration. Part II. The development and structure of beech communities on the Sussex downs. *Journal of Ecology*, **12**, 145–204.

Watt, A.S. (1925). On the ecology of British beech woods with special reference to their regeneration. Part II, sections II & III. The Development and structure of beech communities. *Journal of Ecology*, **13**, 27–73.

Watt, A.S. (1934) The vegetation of the Chiltern Hills with special reference to the beechwoods and their seral relationship. Part II. *Journal of Ecology*, **22**, 445–507.

Watts, W.A. (1979). Late Quaternary vegetation of central Appalachia and the New Jersey coastal plain. *Ecological Monographs*, **49**, 427–69.

Whitehouse, N.J. & Smith, D.N. (2004). 'Islands' in Holocene forests: implications for forest openness, landscape clearance and 'culture-steppe' species. *Environmental Archaeology*, **9**, 203–12.

Whitney, G.C. & Davis, W.C. (1986). From primitive woods to cultivated woodlots: Thoreau and the forest history Concord, Massachusetts. *Journal of Forest History*, **30**, 70–81.

Whitney, G.G. & Somerlot, W.J. (1985). A case study of woodland continuity and change in the American midwest. *Biological Conservation*, **31**, 265–87.

Whittaker, R.H. (1977). Animal effects on plant species diversity. In *Vegetation und Fauna*. Berichte der Internationalen Symposium der Internationalen Vereinigung für Vegetationskunde, ed. R. Tüxen. Vaduz: Cramer, pp. 409–25.

Wolf, G. (1982). Beobachtungen zur Entwicklung von Baumsämlingen im Eichen-Hainbuchen und Eichen-Buchenwald. In *Struktur und Dynamik von Wäldern*. ed. H. Dierschke. Berichte der Internationale Symposium der Internationale Verein für Vegetationskunde. Valduz: J. Cramer, pp. 475–94.

Wolf, G. (1988). Dauerflächen-Beobachtungen in Naturwaldzellen der Niederrheinischen Bucht. Veränderungen in der Feldschicht. *Natur und Landschaft*, **63**, 167–72.

Wolfe, M.L. & Von Berg, F.C. (1988). Deer and forestry in Germany. Half a Century after Aldo Leopold. *Journal of Forestry*, **86**, 25–31.

Ziegenhagen, B. & Kausch, W. (1995). Productivity of young shaded oaks (*Quercus robur* L.) as corresponding to shoot morphology and leaf anatomy. *Forest Ecology and Management*, **72**, 97–108.

Zimov, S.A., Chuprynin, V.I., Oreshko, A.P. Chapin, F.S., III, Reynolds, J.F., & Chapin, M.C. (1995). Steppe-tundra transition: a herbivore-driven biome shift at the end of the Pleistocene. *American Naturalist*, **146**, 765–94.

8

Frugivory in large mammalian herbivores

RICHARD BODMER AND DAVID WARD

INTRODUCTION

Body size and complexity of digestive systems are key factors in the herbivore ecology of mammals (Langer 1987), and much attention has been devoted to herbivory in browsing and grazing forms and how this relates to conservation (Sinclair & Arcese 1995, Owen-Smith 2002). However, frugivory, or fruit feeding, is equally important in the ecology of mammalian herbivores and the conservation of biodiversity (Bodmer 1990, Andresen 2000, Levey *et al.* 2002). This chapter looks at frugivory in large mammalian herbivores. It focuses on the tropical regions, but we must stress that frugivory is equally important in temperate habitats. The chapter examines: (1) the relationships between frugivores and the evolution of browsing and grazing herbivory; (2) the ecology of frugivory in relation to seed dispersal and seed predation; and (3) two case studies of frugivory, one in the Negev desert and the other in Amazonia. The case studies show the importance of frugivory in the ecology of large herbivores, and the links between frugivory and conservation.

Successful biological conservation requires an understanding of the ecology of species and their interactions with human resource use (Freese 1997). Frugivory in large herbivores exemplifies these relations and the need for studying ecological interactions to understand the application of successful conservation (Levey *et al.* 2002). For example, the bush meat crisis in tropical forests is currently one of the most important conservation issues that must be addressed (Robinson & Bennett 2000). The majority of bush meat species are frugivores and their conservation

Large Herbivore Ecology, Ecosystem Dynamics and Conservation, ed. K. Danell, P. Duncan, R. Bergström & J. Pastor. Published by Cambridge University Press. © Cambridge University Press 2006.

requires a deeper understanding of the ecology of frugivory and how this relates to sustainable use (Bodmer *et al.* 1999). To solve the bush meat crises we must understand the underlying ecology of the species; why are they frugivorous, how do their frugivore diets relate to habitat structure, and how can human resource use of plants and bush meat enhance sustainability and conservation.

FRUGIVORES AND THE EVOLUTION OF HERBIVORY IN MAMMALS

It is generally accepted that mammalian herbivores originated from frugivores (Collinson & Hooker 1987, Bodmer 1989), and the transition from simple monogastric mammals to the complex stomachs of browsing and grazing mammals were initially developed via frugivory (Janis 1976, Bodmer 1989). Fruit resources have both pulp and seed components which provide sufficient variation in structure and difficulty of digestion for the evolution of complex digestive systems. Frugivorous mammals and angiosperm plants have coevolved and this relationship is symbiotic in many cases with frugivory being one of the most important dispersal mechanisms of angiosperm plants (Wing & Tiffney 1987). This coevolution was most common in closed-canopy plant communities, such as forests. Today, seed dispersal by mammals continues to be the major mechanism of plant regeneration in tropical forests (Andresen 2000).

The evolution of herbivory in mammals initially began with ancestral forms that used their simple primitive stomachs to consume the readily digestible pulp of fleshy fruits. As frugivores became more advanced those that overcame seed defences by evolving more complex digestive systems or specialized dental adaptations had a competitive advantage, because they could exploit nutrient-rich seed embryos. Consequently, when drier habitats expanded mammals which developed more complex guts through frugivory could switch to browse or grass, because they could digest higher fibre diets.

The earliest mammals were small insectivores that appeared during the Late Triassic and Early Jurassic (Carroll 1988). One major difference between these early mammals and their reptilian predecessors was an increased metabolic rate that supported an endothermic physiology. This higher metabolic rate required more efficient processing of food and constrained ancestral mammals to more nutritious diets (Crompton *et al.* 1978). Mammalian herbivores initially radiated in the Late Paleocene to Middle Eocene when climates were hot and humid, and habitats were dominated by tropical forests (Wolfe 1985, Parrish 1987). Mammalian herbivores of these periods had dental structures that suggest they were predominantly frugivorous (Collinson & Hooker 1987) and the little evidence available from palaeontological finds suggests that the diets of Eocene herbivores were dominated by fruits (Wing & Tiffney 1987). Indeed, the Late Paleocene coincided with the widespread occurrence of large angiosperm fruits (Wing & Tiffney 1987). During the Late Eocene and Early Oligocene when the climate of the Earth began to cool, and open woodlands replaced tropical forests in northern and southern latitudes, larger bodied mammalian herbivores appeared which consumed more fibrous diets (Langer 1987, Janis 1989).

FRUGIVORY AND LARGE HERBIVORES OF THE TROPICS

Contemporary mammalian herbivores in tropical forests and tropical savanna/grasslands demonstrate how the structural components of fruits provide the conditions necessary for the initial evolution of complex digestive systems in mammalian herbivores. Comparisons of mammalian herbivores in tropical zones show the relationships between habitat, digestive morphology and feeding strategies. Here we use comparisons on the generic level, because of relatively consistent feeding strategies within genera and the problem that many individual species evolved as a result of geographic isolation, independent of feeding ecology.

Diets of mammalian herbivore genera can be categorized along a frugivore/browser/grazer continuum which is based on nutritional differences between fruits, browse and grass (Hofmann 1989, Bodmer 1990). This classification includes frugivores, intermediate frugivore/browsers, browsers, intermediate browser/grazers and grazers.

Mammals can exploit fruit resources if they have simple or more complex digestive systems (Chivers & Hladik 1980, Fleming 1988, Bodmer 1989). However, browsing and grazing herbivory requires complex digestive tracts (Van Soest 1982, Demment & Van Soest 1985). If genera of mammalian herbivores are categorized along a continuum representing complexity of digestive tracts from simple, to intermediate through advanced systems we can see the relationship between gut complexity and diet (Langer 1984). Mammals with simple digestive systems include frugivorous bats, because of their primitive morphology (Fleming 1988, Stevens 1988). Those categorized with digestive systems having intermediate complexity include rodents and primates (Chivers & Hladik

1980, Stevens 1988). Those categorized with advanced digestive systems include non-ruminant ungulates and ruminant Artiodactyla (Van Soest 1982).

Information on 178 genera of mammalian herbivores from tropical regions of the world (58 genera from the Neotropics, 40 genera from tropical Asia and 80 genera from tropical Africa) show that ones with simple digestive systems have a greater proportion of frugivorous genera than those with intermediate and advanced digestive tracts, and herbivores with simple digestive systems do not have browsing or grazing forms (Fig. 8.1a). Likewise, mammalian herbivores with intermediate complexity of digestive systems have a greater proportion of frugivorous genera than those with advanced digestive tracts, the latter having greater proportions of browsing and grazing forms. There are greater numbers of herbivores with the intermediate category, because of the large diversity of rodents many of whom have an intermediate complexity in their digestive systems. Indeed, this relationship between complexity of digestive systems and frugivory is upheld when habitat types are separated into tropical forests and tropical savanna/grasslands (Fig. 8.1b). Mammalian herbivores with simple digestive systems are frugivorous even when they live in tropical savanna/grasslands and those with intermediate complexity of digestive systems have many frugivorous forms in these more open habitats.

Mammals can digest the readily available pulp of fruits or the more protected and nutrient rich seeds. However, seed predation requires either specific dental or digestive adaptations to overcome seed defences (Hulme 2002). Mammalian genera that have simple digestive systems and little or no dental adaptations for cracking hard structures, such as bats, only consume fruit pulp (Fleming 1991). In contrast, primates and rodents which have intermediate digestive systems and advanced dental adaptations for cracking or gnawing hard structures exploit seeds by opening protective structures with their teeth (Ayres 1989, Kinzey & Norconk 1990). On the other hand, ruminant Artiodactyla which have advanced digestive tracts use their reticulo-rumen to break down seed defences (Bodmer 1989, Taylor 1990), and non-ruminant ungulates use a mixture of digestive and dental adaptations for seed predation (Janzen 1981, Kiltie 1982).

Fruits appear to play an important role in the evolution of herbivory in different lineages of mammals. For example, mammals that have dental adaptations as their major mechanism for seed predation, such as primates and rodents, do not have many browsing or grazing forms from a

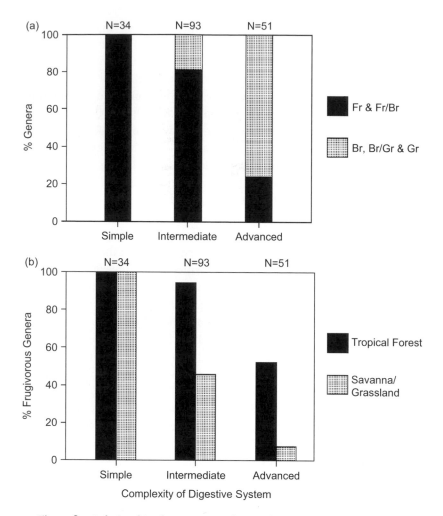

Figure 8.1. Relationships between complexity of digestive systems in mammals and diet. (a) Complexity of digestive system in relation to frugivores (Fr) and frugivore/browsers (Fr/Br) versus browsers (Br), browser/grazers (Br/Gr) and grazers (Gr). (b) Relationship between frugivorous genera (Fr and Fr/Br) and type of habitat (tropical forest versus savanna/grasslands). Data are from a literature survey of 178 mammalian genera of tropical regions.

literature survey of 178 tropical mammalian genera, because they often lack digestive systems necessary for exploiting high fibre forages (Fig. 8.2a). In contrast, mammals that use complex digestive systems for seed predation, such as ungulates, have many browsing and grazing

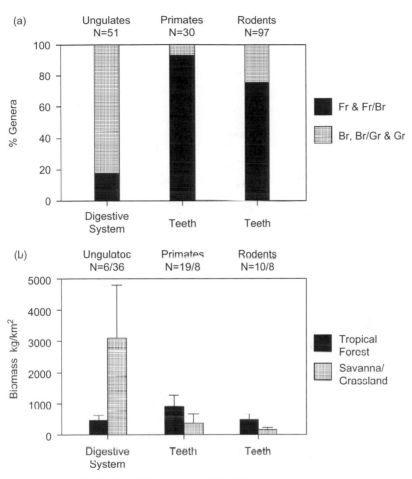

Figure 8.2. (a) Relationships between predominant mechanisms of seed predation of mammals and diet. Data are from a literature survey of 178 mammalian genera of tropical regions. (b) Relationship between predominant mechanisms of seed predation of mammals and crude biomass (kg/km²) in tropical forest and tropical savanna/grassland habitats. Bars represent standard error of mean of biomass for study sites. Data are from a literature survey and the N represents number of tropical sites.

genera. The differences in the feeding strategies and complexity of digestive systems between tropical forests and tropical savanna/grasslands are also reflected in the differences in mammalian biomass. In tropical forests the biomass of rodent, primate and ungulate communities is similar (Kruskal-Wallis statistic = 1.16, p = 0.56) (Fig. 8.2b). However, in tropical savanna/grasslands mammalian herbivores are dominated by the ungulate community and the majority of these genera are browsers, browser/grazers and grazers that can exploit the abundant higher fibre forages (Kruskal-Wallis statistic = 18, p = 0.02). Many rodents and primates that occur in savanna/grasslands remain as frugivores and frugivore/browsers despite the scarcity of fruit resources in these habitats, presumably because they do not have digestive adaptations to exploit higher fibre forages.

In addition, mammalian herbivores with small body sizes feed on higher quality fruit and fruit/browse diets, while larger bodied ones feed on browse and grass diets (Langer 1986). This is based on the relationship between metabolic rate, body size and food quality (Demment & Van Soest 1985). Smaller mammals require relatively greater quantities of nutrients than larger mammals, because they have relatively greater metabolic rates for their body size (Clutton-Brock & Harvey 1983). However, smaller mammals ingest less food than larger ones in absolute terms and usually consume the scarcer high quality foods, such as fruits, while large-bodied mammals consume the more plentiful lower quality foods, such as browse and grasses (Foose 1982, Demment & Van Soest 1985). Indeed, body weights from a literature survey of 178 genera of non-flying tropical mammals fit well with predicted relationships of feeding categories. Frugivores and frugivore/browsers are smaller than browsers, browser/grazers and grazers using all taxa (Kruskal-Wallis statistic = 66.5, d.f. = 4, p < 0.0001) (Fig. 8.3). This relationship is upheld when controlling for generic effects of taxa for ungulates (Kruskal-Wallis statistic = 12.0, d.f. = 4, p = 0.017) rodents (Kruskal-Wallis statistic = 11.7, d.f. = 4, p = 0.019) and primates (Kruskal-Wallis statistic = 10.9, d.f. = 2, p = 0.004).

Relationships between habitats and feeding strategies of mammalian herbivores in tropical regions are based on the linkages between food availability and habitat. Fruits are most abundant in tropical forests (Terborgh 1986), whereas browse is most plentiful in woodlands/savannas, and grass in open grasslands. The relatively closed-canopy of tropical forests means that there is little primary production occurring at the ground and shrub layers. The available biomass of browse is limited and fruit production, usually produced in the canopy layer, is the most abundant food available for large terrestrial herbivores. In contrast, the savannas and grasslands have the majority of primary production occurring at the field and shrub layers. There are fewer tree species and

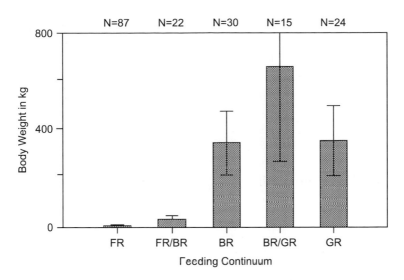

Figure 8.3. Relationship between the body weight of tropical herbivores and feeding strategy. FR = frugivore, FR/BR = frugivore/browser, BR = browser, BR/GR = browser/grazer and GR = grazer. Data are from a literature survey of 178 mammalian genera of tropical regions.

generally less fruit production. Thus, there is a shift in feeding strategies (frugivores to browsers to grazers) when moving from tropical forests to mixed habitats to open grasslands.

The relationship between diet and habitat is reflected in differences in herbivory. Of the frugivore genera surveyed from the literature, 84% were found in tropical forests and 16% in savanna/grasslands. Among the frugivore-browsers, 71% were found in tropical forests and 29% in savanna/grasslands. Browsers were more evenly distributed among the habitats with 39% found in tropical forests and 51% in savanna/grasslands. Browser/grazers and grazers were most abundant in savanna/grassland habitats with the former having 94% of genera occurring in these drier habitats and the latter 96%.

Crude biomass of mammalian herbivores, or the kilograms of mammals per kilometre squared, also shows a clear relationship between habitat and herbivory. Crude biomass of frugivores and frugivore/browsers in tropical forests is greater than crude biomass of browsers, browser/grazers and grazers (Mann-Whitney U statistic = 35, $p = 0.046$). Likewise, crude biomass of browsers and grazers in tropical savanna/grasslands is greater than frugivores and frugivore/browsers (Mann-Whitney U statistic = 5, $p = 0.022$) (Fig. 8.4).

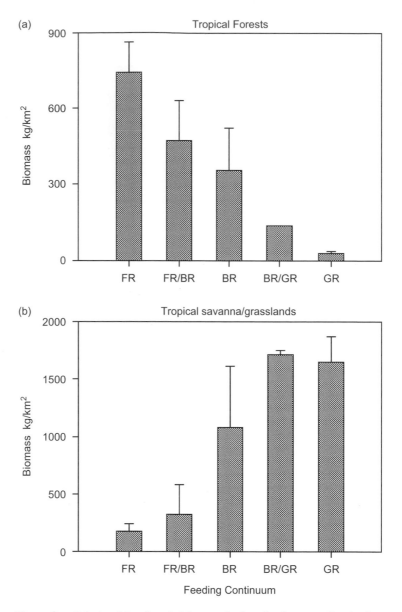

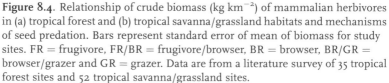

Figure 8.4. Relationship of crude biomass (kg km^{-2}) of mammalian herbivores in (a) tropical forest and (b) tropical savanna/grassland habitats and mechanisms of seed predation. Bars represent standard error of mean of biomass for study sites. FR = frugivore, FR/BR = frugivore/browser, BR = browser, BR/GR = browser/grazer and GR = grazer. Data are from a literature survey of 35 tropical forest sites and 52 tropical savanna/grassland sites.

SEED DISPERSAL AND SEED PREDATION

The role of large herbivores in ecosystem dynamics is exemplified by frugivory. Seed dispersal by mammalian frugivores is a major mechanism determining plant species composition and forest structure in many terrestrial habitats (Fleming & Sosa 1994, Tabarelli & Peres 2002). Whilst studies on primates, rodents and bats have given considerable attention to seed dispersal, only recently have studies on ungulates begun to realize the importance of frugivory and seed dispersal (Bodmer 1991, Fragoso *et al.* 2003).

Plants produce fruits and seeds to disperse their offspring into favourable environments or 'safe sites' that permit sprouting and growth (Fleming & Sosa 1994, Fragoso *et al.* 2003). Seeds are dispersed by physical mechanisms (i.e. wind and water) or animal vectors (i.e. fish, birds and mammals). Seeds dispersed by animal vectors often produce attractants that are used by animals, in order to achieve dispersal via vertebrate guts, spitting or scatterhoarding (Smythe *et al.* 1982, Forget 1991). Plants that produce animal attractants aim only to have the pulp consumed and seeds left intact (Hulme 2002). Seeds are rich in energy and nutrient content to facilitate germination and early development of seed embryos, and most fruits protect themselves against seed predators (Murray 1984). Thus, plants have evolved mechanisms of seed protection, including physical mechanisms such as hardness or spines, chemicals involving toxic compounds and saturation strategies via mast fruiting.

Fruit production in tropical forests is concentrated in the canopy strata. Arboreal vertebrates such as primates, bats, arboreal rodents and birds have first choice of fruit crops, and can reject rotten, parasitized or abnormal fruits (Andresen 2000). Because arboreal frugivores have much greater choice in fruit parts and have relatively small body sizes, they usually consume the nutritious pulps and reject hard or toxic seeds (Estrada & Coates-Estrada 1986). In absolute terms these small bodied mammals require small quantities of high quality food which can be obtained from nutrients provided in the fruit pulp, and they have not evolved mechanisms to overcome protective strategies of seeds (Levey *et al.* 2002).

Terrestrial species, such as ungulates and large rodents, are more restricted in their choice of fruit and generally have larger body sizes. These two factors have led many terrestrial species to evolve mechanisms for seed predation (Kiltie 1982, Bodmer 1990). Only the residual fruit production is available to terrestrial mammals. That is, those fruits not consumed by arboreal frugivores. These fruits often consist only of seed parts, rotten pulp and parasitized or other abnormal fruits. The terrestrial ungulates usually have large body sizes and require larger quantities of food than arboreal species. Seed predation appears to be a better strategy for these ungulates than consuming the toxic and sparsely distributed browse.

Seeds become most important to vertebrate seed predators during periods of resource scarcity or 'bottlenecks' (when fruit production is lowest). During these bottlenecks frugivores must subsist on a small variety of often highly protected seeds or 'keystone' resources (Terborgh 1986). Animals, such as capuchin monkeys, often switch from seed dispersers to seed predators during these periods (Kinzey 1974, Terborgh 1983). Other species, such as agouti and acouchi, resort to exploiting caches that have been scatterhoarded during times of fruit abundance (Smythe 1970, Smythe *et al.* 1982, Hallwachs 1986). During exceptionally harsh dry seasons, such as that on Barro Colorado Island in 1970, fruit production decreased to an extent that famine and massive die-offs occurred, even among seed predators (Foster 1982).

CASE STUDIES ON FRUGIVORY AND SEED DISPERSAL FROM EXTREME HABITATS

Frugivory and seed dispersal by ungulates are widespread and occur in a wide range of diverse habitats. Here, we illustrate the importance of frugivory in mammals from case studies in two extreme habitats, deserts and tropical rainforests.

(1) Large mammalian herbivores as *Acacia* seed dispersers in the Negev desert

Acacia savannas in Africa and the Middle East support large numbers of large mammalian herbivores and frugivores. There has been a considerable amount of coevolution between *Acacia* trees and these mammals (see e.g. Coe & Coe 1987, Scholes & Walker 1993). For example, *Acacia* trees produce condensed tannins to retard digestion, and increase thorn length and reduce leaf size in the presence of herbivores (Rohner & Ward 1997, Ward & Young 2002). *Acacia* trees produce seed pods with high protein concentration (about 35%) to attract mammals, thereby facilitating dispersal. The hard seed coats are scarified by the mammalian digestive process, thereby increasing germination (Halevy 1974, Or & Ward 2003). Furthermore, because the mammalian herbivores frequently eat the seed pods while they are still on the trees, it has been claimed that they may significantly reduce the effects of seed predators (mostly bruchid beetles: family Bruchidae) by consuming the seed pods before the bruchids can infest them (Halevy 1974, Coe & Coe 1987, Miller 1994). In addition to the positive effects that the mammalian herbivores may have on the trees, they may have significant negative effects, especially by restricting the growth and survival of young trees (Dublin *et al.* 1990, Mwalyosi 1990, Rohner & Ward 1999).

On account of the evolutionary interactions between the trees and mammalian herbivores, we might expect that changes in the population dynamics of either group might have adverse effects on the other. In arid savannas in the Middle East, there is high mortality of *Acacia* trees in some areas (up to 60% of trees in some areas are dead) (Ward & Rohner 1997). Some of the major human disturbances involve lowering of ground-water levels through extraction for agricultural purposes and road construction which alters natural patterns of run-off (Ward & Rohner 1997). Additionally, several ungulate species have been extirpated since the 1800s, while increasing human populations and concomitant changes in livestock populations have led to heavy grazing in some areas that may have negative effects on the tree populations.

A decline in *Acacia* tree populations may have serious negative consequences for biodiversity because of their role as keystone species (Munzbergova & Ward 2002). The disappearance of *Acacia* trees from Negev desert ecosystems may lead to the loss of up to five other species of perennial plants that grow beneath the canopy of these trees and which are dependent on the trees owing to their properties of nitrogen fixation (which improves soil quality), shade and reduced evaporation from the soil (Ward & Rohner 1997, Munzbergova & Ward 2002). Additionally, the Bedouin people of the Middle East depend on *Acacia* trees as fodder for livestock and as a source of fuel wood. The identity of the species that suffer as a result of *Acacia* mortality varies somewhat between sites, although the shrubs *Ochradenus baccatus*, *Zilla spinosa* and *Fagonia arabica* are most commonly associated with *Acacia* tree canopies (55%–60% of sites). *Ochradenus baccatus* and *Zilla spinosa* form important nesting sites for birds owing to their tangled and thorny canopies, and tenebrionid beetles (one of the most important groups of desert detritivores) form a conspicuous part of the under-shrub fauna. Consequently, the loss of these shrub species may have considerable trickle-down effects in the ecosystem.

Rohner and Ward (1999) investigated the effects of large mammalian herbivores on recruitment in *Acacia raddiana* and *A. tortilis* trees in the hyper-arid Negev desert of Israel (mean annual rainfall = 25–100 mm). Wiegand *et al.* (1999) showed in spatially explicit models of two *Acacia raddiana* populations that recruitment was the limiting stage in the population dynamics of these trees. Rohner and Ward (1999) tested the following predictions related to the purported effects of large mammalian herbivores on these trees:

(1) An absence of ungulates will lead to a decrease in seed dispersal in *Acacia* trees.

(2) Seeds not ingested by ungulates will suffer high damage from insect seed predators.

(3) Consumption of seeds by ungulates will cause a reduction in seed predator populations, which in turn will lead to reduced seed damage.

(4) Ingestion of seeds by ungulates will result in ungulate species-specific increases in germination owing to differences in the degree of scarification of the hard seed coat.

(5) Survival rates of seedlings will be lower when mammalian herbivores are present.

(6) High densities of large mammalian herbivores will prevent escape of juvenile trees above browsing height and subsequent recruitment into mature size classes.

Rohner and Ward (1999) found that many seeds accumulated under trees in areas where large herbivores were excluded, but ungulates quickly removed the seeds and they did not accumulate on the ground (Fig. 8.5). The main mode of foraging of ungulates in the vicinity of *Acacia* trees was clearly seed pod consumption (Rohner & Ward 1999). Ungulates were more likely to defecate away from trees rather than under them, which increases dispersal and reduces competition with parent trees.

Seeds that were not ingested by ungulates suffered very high levels of bruchid infestation (97% in *Acacia raddiana* and 96% in *A. tortilis*). Thus, virtually all seeds not ingested by mammalian herbivores were infested by bruchid beetles. However, there was no evidence that seed infestation by bruchid beetles was reduced by large mammal consumption of pods (Rohner & Ward 1999); bruchid beetles infest the seed pods while the seeds are still on the trees and the pods are still green. This contradicts the claim of Halevy (1974) and Coe and Coe (1987) that large mammalian herbivores reduce the impact of seed predation by consuming seed pods before they can be infested. These results also indicate that ungulate activity does not reduce activity or population sizes of the bruchid beetles.

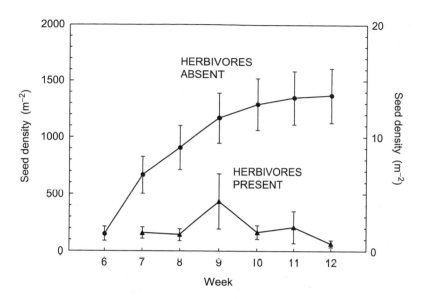

Figure 8.5. Accumulation of seed pods under *Acacia tortilis* trees (mean + SE seed density) over a season and the effects of large mammalian herbivores on seed removal. Note the different scales on the y1 and y2 axes; axis y1 pertains to seed density with herbivores absent and axis y2 to seed density under trees where herbivores are present (from Rohner & Ward 1999).

Germination trials showed that germination percentages were significantly higher when seeds were consumed by dorcas gazelles, *Gazella dorcas* (30% vs. 13.5% for unconsumed seeds), and Arabian oryx, *Oryx beisa* (51% for *Acacia raddiana* and 34% for *Acacia tortilis*). Contrastingly, seeds predated by bruchid beetles had a very low (but non-zero) percentage germination (2.1% for *A. raddiana* and 3.7% for *A. tortilis*). These results are consistent with the generally accepted conclusion that bruchids damage the cotyledons and radicle of seeds and thereby reduce seed viability (Miller & Coe 1993). Rohner and Ward (1999) found, in a review of the literature, that there is a strong positive correlation between percentage germination in *Acacia* seeds and the size of the herbivore that ingests the seeds (Fig. 8.6). This correlation is likely due to the allometric scaling of digestion time (passage rate) to herbivore body mass (Robbins 1983), which results in greater removal of the seed coat. This result indicates that the species composition of the ungulate community may have important consequences for the recruitment of *Acacia* populations. The role of camels, as the largest herbivores in these ecosystems, needs to be re-evaluated. Camels, which are entirely domesticated and owned

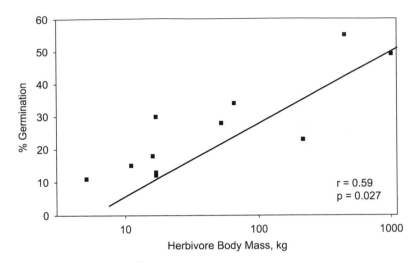

Figure 8.6. Correlation between percentage germination of *Acacia* seeds and the body mass of the mammalian herbivore that ingested and defecated the seeds (from Rohner & Ward 1999).

by Bedouin people, could be used as a management tool to aid recruitment if they could be introduced to areas to increase seed germination after winter rain and then removed so that they do not retard tree growth and seedling survival by browsing.

Large herbivores had a pronounced effect on the size distribution of juvenile trees; the cumulative effect of heavy browsing over many years was apparent in the reduced height of juvenile trees (for their stem diameters) relative to the heights of trees where browsers were absent. Waves of recruitment (as indicated by the presence of distinct cohorts) contrasted with an increasing under-representation of taller trees under high browsing pressure. However, high densities of ungulates did not inhibit the escape of juvenile *Acacia* trees above browsing level and therefore limit recruitment in *Acacia* trees. Negative effects of browsing on juvenile trees may not translate into changes in tree demography because of the enhancement of seed viability and germination by mammalian herbivores. That is, if more seeds germinate in the presence of these herbivores, the higher density of juvenile trees may compensate for a smaller proportion of individuals escaping browsing height (see also Coughenour & Detling 1986).

Seed dispersal by large mammalian herbivores also significantly affects and, indeed, controls the biogeography of *Acacia* trees in the Middle East

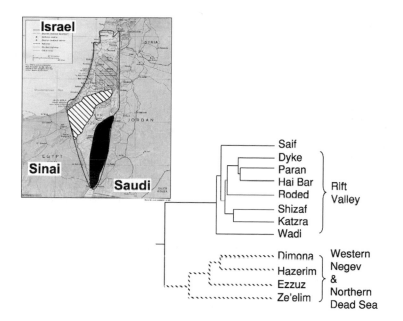

Figure 8.7. Cluster analysis of the population genetics of *Acacia raddiana* in Israel using RAPD analysis (from Shrestha *et al.* 2002). Dashed lines (and dashed region – inset) indicate the western Negev and northern Dead Sea populations and the solid black lines (and black region in the inset) indicate the Syrian-African Rift valley populations.

on a large geographic scale. Shrestha *et al.* (2002), using Randomly Amplified Polymorphic DNA (RAPD) analyses, showed that there are two main genetic groups of *Acacia raddiana* trees in the Negev desert, one in the western Negev, extending to the northern shores of the Dead Sea and the other along the Syrian-African Rift valley from the Red Sea to the southern end of the Dead Sea (Fig. 8.7). As these trees have large, heavy seeds, they must have been dispersed from Africa (where the main populations of this species are found) by mammalian herbivores across the flat expanses of the western Negev desert to the northern Dead Sea. Independently, seeds must have been carried from south to north in the Syrian-African Rift valley from the Sinai (Egypt) and/or Saudi Arabia and up the ephemeral rivers ('wadis' in Arabic) entering the valley by large mammals as water-borne transport of seeds in the west-east running wadis cannot account for the upward movement of seeds in the wadis nor the north-south directionality in *Acacia raddiana* genetics.

(2) Frugivory in Amazonian ungulates: a case study from the Peruvian Amazon

Tropical forest ungulates have efficient mechanisms for seed predation to exploit the entire fruit resource including both the pulp and the seed (Bodmer 1989). Tropical forests have the majority of plant production in the canopy well out of reach of terrestrial ungulates. Shade-tolerant plants of the forest floor are low in nutrients and high in fibre and chemical protectants, and have little value as food for most terrestrial ungulates (Leigh 1999). This has resulted in many tropical forest ungulates, especially the smaller species, relying on fruits, having advanced mechanisms for seed predation in order to use the entire fruit resource including pulp and seed (Kiltie 1981a).

Amazonian ungulates show how the ecology of fruit feeding and seed predation is influenced by body size, gut morphology and methods of ingestion. Species include red brocket deer (*Mazama americana*), grey brocket deer (*Mazama gouazoubira*), collared peccary (*Tayassu tajacu*), white-lipped peccary (*Tayassu pecari*) and lowland tapir (*Tapirus terrestris*). The two brocket deer species are ruminants, with the red brocket deer weighing an average of 32 kg and the grey brocket deer 15 kg. The peccaries are non-ruminant artiodactyls with a limited amount of pre-gastric fermentation in their sacculated stomachs. The collared peccary weighs an average of 25 kg and the white-lipped peccary 32 kg. The lowland tapir is the largest species weighing on average 200 kg and, like other perissodactyls, has post-gastric fermentation.

Many plants in Amazonia use fruits as a means of dispersal and most of the fruits are animal dispersed (Peres & van Roosmalen 2002). These fruits have a palatable and nutritional attractant that the animal consumes, usually in the form of fruit pulp. Indeed, in the Peruvian Amazon animal dispersed fruits make up 80% of the dry weight of fruit production. These fruits included drupes, berries and pods. Hard nuts, which are adapted for scatterhoarding, make up 18% and physical dispersed seeds from winged or exploding fruits make up 2%.

Whilst the pulp of fruits is palatable and readily digestible by most vertebrate digestive systems, the seeds have considerable amounts of nutrients. But plants do not want animals destroying the seeds and protect them through structural and chemical defences. For example, in the animal dispersed fruits of the Peruvian Amazon the majority of dry weight is in the seed portion of the fruit. Seeds make up an average of 71% of the fruit production, whereas, pulp makes up around 29% of the fruit production (Table 8.1). Palm fruits are an important component of the fruit

Table 8.1. *Average pulp and seed dry weights of palm fruits frequently consumed by Amazonian ungulates in north-eastern Peru*

Species	Dry Weight (g)	
	Pulp	Seed
Euterpe sp. (N = 21)	0.2	0.9
Iriartea sp. (N = 25)	0.5	2.3
Jessenia sp. (N = 12)	1.8	4.1
Mauritia flexuosa (N = 10)	7.6	12.2

Pulp and seed weights were taken from whole fruits collected in fruit traps. Fruits were collected weekly from 100 fruit traps of 1 m² placed along transects in the forest for 12 months.

production in Amazonian forests and make up 53% of the dry weight of fruits.

The peccaries and brocket deer consume large proportions of their diet in the form of fruit and they can be considered as frugivores. For example, the diet of the red brocket deer in the Peruvian Amazon consists of 81% fruit, grey brocket deer 87%, collared peccary 59% and white-lipped peccary 66%. The lowland tapir also consumes large quantities of fruit making up 34% of its diet, but in smaller proportions than the deer and peccaries.

The deer and collared peccaries are specialized seed predators. They digest seeds of virtually every fruit they consume (Bodmer 1991). The most common food items consumed by brocket deer in the Peruvian Amazon are seeds of *Euterpe* sp. and *Iriartea* sp. These palm seeds occur in 80% of grey brocket deer samples and 59% of red brocket deer samples (Table 8.2). *Euterpe* sp. and *Iriartea* sp. use hardness to protect their seeds from seed predators and require 162 and 288 kg, respectively, to crack (Table 8.3). The seeds are an important source of nutrients for the deer and have a much greater dry weight of nutrients in their seeds than in their pulp. Deer are able to eat these seeds by overcoming the protective strategy of hardness by using their rumens as a mechanism of seed predation. Deer swallow palm seeds of *Iriartea* sp. and *Euterpe* sp. whole, thus enabling these palms to be digested and softened by rumen microbes. These palm seeds appear to be digested at the same rate as non-palm seeds since there is no difference between the occurrence of whole and digested palm and non-palm seeds in rumen samples. Rumination, or the process of regurgitation and re-chewing, allows the deer to re-chew the seeds once the microbes have softened and partly digested them.

Table 8.2. *Percent occurrence of fruit types from combined stomach and faecal samples of Amazon ungulates from north-eastern Peru*

Food type	Red brocket N = 91	Grey brocket N = 26	Collared peccary N = 121	White-lipped peccary N = 46	Lowland tapir N = 44
Palm foods (Palmae)					
Astrocaryum sp.	3	o	45	48	5
Bactris sp.	9	o	o	o	o
Euterpe sp.	44	48	8	16	o
Iriartea sp.	34	36	28	75	o
Jessenia sp.	1	o	46	59	24
Mauritia flexuosa	9	8	12	45	76
Scheelea sp.	o	o	o	o	13
Palmae leaf and flower	o	o	11	5	16
Non-palm fruits					
Araceae	1	o	o	o	8
Anacardiaceae – Spondias sp.	11	12	14	11	3
Annonaceae	31	32	19	18	3
Apocinaceae	5	8	2	o	o
Bombaceae	11	12	4	2	o
Boraginaceae – Cordia sp.-type 1	8	8	12	2	3
Boraginaceae – Cordia sp.-type 2	11	16	4	o	o
Chrysobalanaceae	24	7	o	o	8
Convolvulaceae – Maripa sp.	21	28	5	2	o
Flacourtiaceae – Carpotroche sp.	1	8	o	o	o
Guttiferae – Rheedia sp.	25	20	1	o	o
Hippocrateaceae	6	o	1	o	o
Lecythidaceae – Eschweilera sp.	10	4	o	o	o
Leguminosae – Inga sp.	20	28	17	9	3
Leguminosae – Swartzia sp.	17	20	2	o	o
Leguminosae – U. I. type	13	o	37	18	8
Linaceae	21	20	5	2	o
Loganiaceae	21	16	2	o	3
Lorantaceae	9	8	9	7	o
Menispermaceae	6	o	40	50	8
Moraceae – Brosimum sp.	17	32	9	18	3
Moraceae – Pourouma sp.	5	12	o	o	o
Myrististicaceae – Virola sp.	5	20	4	2	o
Rubiaceae	3	8	8	o	5
Sapindaceae – Paullinia sp.	6	o	8	7	o
Sapotaceae	33	36	47	52	11

Only food types with a percent occurrence of 5% or greater for at least one ungulate species are listed.

Table 8.3. *Load required to reach breaking point and strength of various palm seeds eaten by Amazon ungulates*

Palm species	Load to break (kg) (Mean ± SD)	Strength ($N\ mm^{-2}$) (Mean ± SD)
Mauritia flexuosa	408 ± 59 (3)	4.5 ± 0.4 (3)
Iriartea sp.	288 ± 55 (9)	13.8 ± 2.6 (9)
Euterpe sp.	162 ± 54 (10)	14.4 ± 6.6 (10)
Astrocaryum sp.	140 ± 30 (34)*	1.7 ± 0.3 (4)
Jessenia sp.	100 ± 40 (20)*	——

Load and strength were measured with an Instron 1122 to determine load at breaking point (p). Strength was calculated by (p)/volume where volume was estimated by (length*breadth*height)2/3. (Reproduced from Bodmer 1989, by permission of Cambridge University Press.)
* Data from Kiltie (1981b).

Both peccary species also consume large quantities of palm fruits, with hard palm seeds occurring in 91% of white-lipped peccary samples and in 43% of collared peccary samples. The most common food item of white-lipped peccary is the palm seeds of *Iriartea* sp. which occur in 75% of stomach samples. Peccaries are able to overcome the protective strategies of seeds by cracking seeds using their strong adductive jaw muscles, thick skull bones, strong resilient teeth and interlocking canines. The strong adductive jaw muscles are attached to a large sagital crest and large lower jaw bone allowing the peccary to exert massive pressure on the seeds. The thick bones of the skull can withstand the pressure required to crack palm nuts. Premolar and molar teeth of peccaries are extremely strong and difficult to dislocate from the jaw. Interlocking canines are an adaptation to prevent the jaw from dislocating during the excretion of massive pressure (Kiltie 1981b).

Peccaries commonly eat *Astrocaryum* sp. fruits that are not consumed by brocket deer. These palms are coconut-type nuts with lignified shells and highly nutritious endocarps. Peccaries are able to crack the lignified shell and consume the endocarp. However, deer are unable to consume *Astrocaryum* sp. fruits because their rumen microbes cannot digest the lignified covering. The nutritious pulp of *Mauritia flexuosa* palm fruits is also consumed by deer and peccaries. However, the very hard seeds of this palm are only swallowed by brocket deer and appear to be digested in a similar way as *Iriartea* sp. and *Euterpe* sp.

The peccaries have a sacculated fore-stomach that has microbial fermentation, similar to the deer rumen. Microbial fermentation in the stomach of peccaries occurs in three blind sacs, whilst gastric digestion occurs in the central main sac (Langer 1974, Sowls 1984). These blind sacs are efficient at fermenting low fibre plant products, but not plant material with high concentrations of cell wall (Sowls 1997). The blind sacs probably help soften and digest the hard palm seeds once they are cracked into small pieces by peccaries. However, since peccaries do not ruminate they must crack the seeds into small pieces before ingesting them into the blind sacs.

The peccary and the deer are good examples of how small bodied tropical ungulates cope with the forest environment. The peccaries and deer meet their nutritional requirements by eating the fruits on the forest floor. This fruit production is made up in large part of seeds, especially those with effective seed protection strategies. Seed predation is costly to plants because it reduces the proportion of seeds that can successfully reproduce. Plants have evolved a variety of seed protection mechanisms to deter seed predators, the most common being hardness and toxicity (Janzen 1981). Likewise, seed predators have evolved strategies to overcome seed protection because of the scarcity of nutrient-rich foods on the forest floor. This has resulted in an evolutionary arms race between seed and predator. The Amazon palm and ungulate communities appear to be entwined in an arms race between seed hardness and ingestive/digestive mechanisms. Many palms are sufficiently hard to deter arboreal predators, but not hard enough to deter terrestrial ungulates. Only the very hard *Mauritia flexuosa* seeds appear able to deter both arboreal and terrestrial seed predators.

The diet of lowland tapir differs from peccary and deer. The food habits of the lowland tapir resemble those of other large non-ruminant herbivores, because of the greater quantities of low quality browse that tapirs consume. Large non-ruminant herbivores are efficient at digesting low quality forage per unit time, because their large digestive systems allow both long retention time and uninterrupted throughput (Demment & Van Soest 1985, Parra 1978). Large ungulates use the strategy of consuming large quantities of the more abundant low quality forage rather than consuming lesser quantities of the scarcer high quality forage (Bell 1971, Foose 1982). The use of abundant forages has the important advantage of reducing search effort. It appears likely that large non-ruminant ungulates would not meet their nutritional demands if they concentrated on searching for scarce high quality forages (Demment & Van Soest 1985).

However, lowland tapirs differ from other large non-ruminant herbivores in that they do consume relatively large quantities of fruit.

The *Mauritia flexuosa* drupe is the most common fruit eaten by the lowland tapir, and it occurs in 76% of the lowland tapir samples (Table 8.2). The next most common fruit eaten by the tapir is the *Jessenia* sp. drupe that occurs in 24% of the samples. The only other fruits occurring in greater than 10% of the tapir samples are *Scheelea* sp. (13%) and Sapotaceae (11%).

The lowland tapir prefers the *M. flexuosa* drupe more than any other fruit type and considerably more than any other ungulate species. *M. flexuosa* drupes occur in larger patches than any other palm fruit of the Peruvian Amazon and has an order of magnitude greater in the degree of patchiness (Kiltie & Terborgh 1983). *M. flexuosa* palms grow in swampy habitats often in virtually monotypic stands. These fruits are a relatively constant source of food and are present throughout most of the year (78%) in fruit traps. *M. flexuosa* palm swamps occupy approximately 2.35% of the forests in the Peruvian Amazon (Bodmer *et al.* 1999).

M. flexuosa fruits are oval drupes of approximately 2–3 cm long by 1–2 cm wide. Pulp makes up 38% of the entire fruit and the seeds are very strong and require a load of 408 kg to reach their breaking point (Table 8.3). The pulp is nutritionally rich and consists of 53% fat, 43% carbohydrate and 4% protein (Lopes *et al.* 1980). The tapirs appear only to digest the pulp portion of the drupes, and either spit out the seeds or ingest them whole and pass them through their digestive systems. During feeding trials with captive adult tapir the pulp was stripped off the fruit and the seeds always spat out. Intact seeds of *M. flexuosa* are found regularly in defecation samples of wild tapir.

Theories on optimal foraging would predict that large-bodied, non-ruminant herbivores should only resort to frugivory if the nutritional gains outweigh the searching costs (Stephens & Krebs 1986). The lowland tapir is an example of how a large-bodied, tropical forest ungulate is able to maintain a higher rate of frugivory than would be predicted from foraging models by exploiting a nutritionally rich fruit source that occurs in large patches.

IMPLICATIONS FOR CONSERVATION

Currently, the greatest threat to Amazonian ungulates is unregulated bush meat hunting (Peres 2000). Ungulates make up the majority of animals used for bush meat, both in terms of individuals hunted and in terms of biomass hunted (Bodmer & Pezo 2001). Managing bush meat hunting at sustainable levels is a priority for conservation in the Peruvian Amazon.

Table 8.4. *Palm trees commonly used by people living in the north-eastern Peruvian Amazon*

Common name	Species	Part used	Method of harvesting
Aguaje	*Mauritia flexuosa*	fruit	climbing/felling
Aguajillo	*Mauritiella peruviana*	fruit	climbing/felling
Chambira	*Astrocaryum* spp.	fruit	picking
		fronds	felling
Huasai	*Euterpe precatoria*	apex	felling
		wood	felling
		fruit	climbing/felling
Irapay	*Lepidocaryum tessmannii*	leaf	selective leaf removal
Pijuayo	*Bactris gasipaes*	fruit	climbing/felling
Pona	*Iriartea* sp.	wood	felling
Sinamillo	*Oenocarpus mapora*	fruit	climbing/felling
Ungurahui	*Jessenia bataua*	fruit	climbing/felling
		wood	felling
Yarina	*Phytelephas macrocarpa*	leaf	felling
		fruit	picking

From Bodmer *et al.* (1997).

But, managing hunting levels is only part of the problem. Managing wildlife habitat is equally important, and this is directly linked to frugivory.

As described above, Amazonian ungulates rely extensively on palm fruits in their diets. People living in the Peruvian Amazon also use palms for food, fibres and building material. Indeed, the palm resources used by people overlap directly with the palm fruits eaten by ungulates (Bodmer *et al.* 1999). For example, all of the top food items in Amazonian ungulate diets are also used by people. The *M. flexuosa* are eaten and fruits sold in city markets, *Iriartea* are used for palm hearts and building material, *Euterpe* fruits are used for drink as are *Jessenia* fruits, *Astrocaryum* fruits are eaten and their leaves used for fibres, just to give a few examples (Table 8.4).

Palm fruits are determining, in large part, the carrying capacity of Amazonian ungulates. The level of sustainable bush meat hunting will be determined by the species carrying capacity. If the carrying capacity is larger, then the level of sustainable hunting is greater. In turn, if the carrying capacity is reduced then the level of sustainable hunting will be less (Caughley & Sinclair 1994).

In the Peruvian Amazon, people are reducing the carrying capacity of Amazonian ungulates by felling palm trees. Most of the palm resources used by people require destruction of adult trees. For example, palm hearts are collected from *Iriartea* trees by felling adults. Fruits of *M. flexuosa* are collected by felling adult trees, since they are usually too tall to climb. Building material from *Euterpe* and *Iriartea* are gathered by cutting down adult trees. And the list goes on as seen in Table 8.4.

People who live in the Peruvian Amazon will only be able to use both palm resources and ungulate bush meat if the use of both resources is managed more sustainably (Bodmer *et al.* 1999). Deforestation in this region is less of an issue than the unsustainable use of palm trees and other non-timber forest resources. The people are destroying the plant resources, and this is directly impacting animal populations.

CONCLUSIONS

In the Amazon there are clearly relationships between frugivores and biodiversity conservation that require conservation actions (Moegenburg 2002). When people no longer gain sufficient economic benefits from intact forests they will be more inclined to deforestation and conversion of forests to cattle ranching, thus almost completely destroying the biodiversity. If solutions can be found that incorporate the relationships between frugivores, bush meat hunting and non-timber forest exploitation, then people will continue to gain economic benefits from intact forests. This will provide an economic argument for maintaining intact forests and avert major deforestation of the Amazon.

We note that the conservation implications for maintaining the ungulate-*Acacia* systems in the hyper-arid Negev desert are as clear and important as those in the Amazon. The ungulate frugivores are responsible for the most important stage in the population dynamics of these trees, namely recruitment. Seed germination is substantially enhanced by the ungulates and they are responsible for the removal of virtually all seeds and dispersing them over wide areas. At a local scale, dispersal by ungulates ensures that seeds do not compete with adult trees because the seeds are defecated in open areas between trees. Furthermore, ungulates are responsible for the transport of seeds up wadi systems (where the best environmental conditions for seed germination and survival are) (Ward & Rohner 1997). On a larger, biogeographic scale, dispersal of seeds by large mammals is responsible for the two separate genetic groups of *Acacia raddiana* trees in Israel. Thus, in spite of the fact that large mammals are also herbivores on these plants, their positive role outweighs the negative effect of biomass removal. It is, therefore, imperative that ungulate densities be maintained in the Middle East, particularly because the *Acacia* trees are keystone species upon which many other plant species depend. The evidence for allometric scaling of germination to herbivore body size provides a particularly interesting view on the relative importance of these animals for the *Acacia* trees and indicates that the largest herbivore in these systems, the camel, although now domesticated, has a key role to play in the maintenance of these *Acacia*-dominated ecosystems.

ACKNOWLEDGEMENTS

Drs George Rabb, Tim Clutton-Brock and Nigel Leader-Williams provided important contributions to the analysis on frugivory in herbivores. The Chicago Zoological Society and the Wildlife Conservation Society are thanked for sponsoring the work conducted in the Amazon. David Ward thanks Iris Musli and Sonia Rosin for technical assistance and the Israel Science Foundation and Keren Keyemet L'Israel for financial support.

REFERENCES

Andresen, E. (2000). Ecological roles of mammals: the case of seed dispersal. In *Priorities for the Conservation of Mammalian Diversity: Has the Panda had its Day?*, ed. A. Entwistle & N. Dunstone. Cambridge: Cambridge University Press, pp. 11–25.

Ayres, J.M. (1989). Comparative feeding ecology of the uakari and bearded saki, Cacajao and Chiropotes. *Journal of Human Evolution*, **18**, 697–716.

Bell, R.H.V. (1971). A grazing ecosystem in the Serengeti. *Scientific American*, **255**, 86–93.

Bodmer, R.E. (1989). Frugivory in Amazonian Artiodactyla: evidence for the evolution of the ruminant stomach. *Journal of Zoology*, **219**, 457–67.

Bodmer, R.E. (1990). Ungulate frugivores and the browser-grazer continuum. *Oikos*, **57**, 319–25.

Bodmer, R.E. (1991). Strategies of seed dispersal and seed predation in Amazonian ungulates. *Biotropica*, **23**, 255–61.

Bodmer, R.E. & Pezo Lozano, E. (2001). Rural development and sustainable wildlife use in the tropics. *Conservation Biology*, **15**, 1163–70.

Bodmer, R.E., Penn, J.W., Puertas, P.E., Moya I.L. & Fang, T.G. (1997). Linking conservation and local people through sustainable use of natural resources: community-based management in the Peruvian Amazon. In *Harvesting Wild Species*, ed. C. Freese. Baltimore, MD: Johns Hopkins University Press, pp. 315–58.

Bodmer, R.E., Allen, C.M., Penn, J.W., Aquino, R. & Reyes, C. (1999). Evaluating the sustainable use of wildlife in the Pacaya-Samiria National Reserve, Peru. *America Verdi*, **4a**, 1–36.

Carroll, R.L. (1988). *Vertebrate Paleontology and Evolution*. New York: W.H. Freeman & Co.

Caughley, G. & Sinclair, A.R.E. (1994). *Wildlife Ecology and Management*. Oxford: Blackwell Scientific Publications.

Chivers, D.J. & Hladik, C.M. (1980). Morphology of the gastrointestinal tract in primates: comparisons with other mammals in relation to diet. *Journal of Morphology*, **166**, 337–86.

Clutton-Brock, T.H. & Harvey, P.H. (1983). The functional significance of variation in body size among mammals. *Special Publication of the American Society of Mammalogy*, **7**, 632–63.

Coe, M. & Coe, C. (1987). Large herbivores, *Acacia* trees and bruchid beetles. *South African Journal of Science*, **83**, 624–35.

Collinson, M.E. & Hooker, J.J. (1987). Vegetational and mammalian faunal changes in the Early Tertiary of southern England. In *The Origins of Angiosperms and their Biological Consequences*, ed. E.M. Friis, W.G. Chalconer & P.R. Crane. Cambridge: Cambridge University Press, pp. 359–04.

Coughenour, M.B. & Detling, J.K. (1986). *Acacia tortilis* seed germination responses to water potential and nutrients. *African Journal of Ecology*, **24**, 203–5.

Crompton, A.W., Taylor, C.R. & Jagger, J.A. (1978). Evolution of homeothermy in mammals. *Nature*, **272**, 333–6.

Demment, M.W. & Van Soest, P.J. (1985). A nutritional explanation for body-size patterns of ruminant and nonruminant herbivores. *American Naturalist*, **125**, 641–72.

Dublin, H.T., Sinclair, A.R.E. & McGlade, J. (1990). Elephants and fire and causes of multiple stable states in the Serengeti-Mara woodlands. *Journal of Animal Ecology*, **59**, 1147–64.

Estrada, A. & Coates-Estrada, R. (1986). Frugivory in howling monkeys (*Alouatta palliata*) at Los Tuxtlas, Mexico: dispersal and fate of seeds. In *Frugivores and Seed Dispersal*, ed. A. Estrada & T.H. Fleming. Lancaster: Dr. W. Junk Pub., pp. 93–104.

Fleming, T.H. (1988). *The Short-tailed Fruit Bat: A Study in Plant-Animal Interactions*. Chicago: The University of Chicago Press.

Fleming, T.H. (1991). The relationship between body size, diet, and habitat use in frugivorous bats, genus *Carollia* (Phyllostomidae). *Journal of Mammalogy*, **72**, 493–501.

Fleming, T.H. & Sosa, V.J. (1994). Effects of nectarivotous and frugivorous mammals on reproductive success of plants. *Journal of Mammalogy*, **75**, 845–51.

Foose, T.J. (1982). Trophic strategies of ruminant versus nonruminant ungulates. *Unpublished Ph.D. thesis, University of Chicago*.

Forget, P. (1991). Scatterhoarding of *Astrocaryum paramaca* by *Proechimys* in French Guiana: comparison with *Myoprocta exilis*. *Tropical Ecology*, **32**, 155–7.

Foster, R.B. (1982). Famine on Barro Colorado Island. In *The Ecology of a Tropical Forest: Seasonal Rhythms and Long-term Change*, ed. E.G. Leigh, A.S. Rand & D.M. Windsor. Washington, DC: Smithsonian Institution Press, pp. 201–12.

Fragoso, J.M.V., Silvius, K.M. & Correa, J.A. (2003). Long-distance seed dispersal by tapirs increases seed survival and aggregates tropical trees. *Ecology*, **84**, 1998–2006.

Freese, C. (1997). *Harvesting Wild Species*. Baltimore: Johns Hopkins University Press.

Halevy, G. (1974). Effects of gazelles and seed beetles (Bruchidae) on germination and establishment of *Acacia* species. *Israel Journal of Botany*, **23**, 120–6.

Hallwachs, W. (1986). Agoutis (*Dasyprocta punctata*), the inheritos of guapinol (*Hymenaea courbaril*: Leguminosae). In *Frugivores and Seed Dispersal*, ed. A. Estrada & T.H. Fleming. Lancaster: Dr W. Junk Publisher, pp. 285–304.

Hofmann, R.R. (1989). Evolutionary steps of ecophysiological adaptation and diversification of ruminants: a comparative view of their digestive system. *Oecologia*, **78**, 443–57.

Hulme, P.E. (2002). Seed eaters: seed dispersal, destruction and demography. In *Frugivory and Seed Dispersal: Ecological, Evolutionary and Conservation Issues*, D. Levey, M. Galetti & W. Silva. Oxford: CAB International Publishing, pp. 257–73.

Janis, C.M. (1976). The evolutionary strategy of the Equidae and the origins of rumen and cecal digestion. *Evolution*, **30**, 757–74.

Janis, C.M. (1989). A climatic explanation for patterns of evolutionary diversity in ungulate mammals. *Palaeontology*, **32**, 463–81.

Janzen, D.H. (1981). Digestive seed predation by a Costa Rican Baird's tapir. *Biotropica*, **13** (Supplement), 59–63.

Kiltie, R.A. (1981a). Stomach contents of rain forest peccaries (*Tayassu tajacu* and *T. pecari*). *Biotropica*, **13**, 234–6.

Kiltie, R.A. (1981b). The significance of interlocking canines in rain forest peccaries (Tayassuidae). *Journal of Mammalogy*, **62**, 459–69.

Kiltie, R.A. (1982). Bite force as a basis for niche differentiation between rain forest peccaries (*Tayassu tajacu* and *T. pecari*). *Biotropica*, **14**, 188–95.

Kiltie, R.A. & Terborgh, J. (1983). Observations on the behavior of rain forest peccaries in Peru: why do white-lipped peccaries form herds? *Zeitschrift für Tierpsychologia*, **62**, 241–55.

Kinzey, W.G. (1974). Ceboid models for the evolution of hominoid dentition. *Journal of Human Evolution*, **3**, 193–203.

Kinzey, W.G. & Norconk, M.A. (1990). Hardness as a basis of fruit choice in two sympatric primates. *Journal of Physical Anthropology*, **18**, 5–15.

Langer, P. (1974). Stomach evolution in the Artiodactyla. *Mammalia*, **38**, 295–314.

Langer, P. (1984). Anatomical and nutritional adaptations in wild herbivores. In *Herbivore Nutrition in the Subtropics and Tropics*, F.M.C. Gilchrist & R.I. Mackie. Craighall: Science Press, R.S.A., pp. 185–203.

Langer, P. (1986). Large mammalian herbivores in tropical forests with either hindgut- or forestomach-fermentation. *Zeitschrift für Säugetierkunde*, **51**, 173–87.

Langer, P. (1987). Evolutionary patterns of Perissodactyla and Artiodactyla (Mammalia) with different types of digestion. *Zeitschrift für Zoologische Systematik und Evolutionsforschung*, **25**, 212–36.

Leigh, E.J., Jr. (1999). *Tropical Forest Ecology: A View from Barro Colorado Island*. Oxford: Oxford University Press.

Levey, D., Galetti, M. & Silva, W. (2002). *Frugivory and Seed Dispersal: Ecological, Evolutionary and Conservation Issues*. Oxford: CAB International Publishing.

Lopes A.J.P., Albuquerque M.H., Silva R.Y. & Shrimpton, R. (1980). Aspectos nutritivos de alguns frutos da Amazônia. *Acta Amazonica*, **10**, 755–8.

Miller, M.F. (1994). Large African herbivores, bruchid beetles and their interactions with *Acacia* seeds. *Oecologia*, **97**, 265–70.

Miller, M.F. & Coe, M. (1993). Is it advantageous for *Acacia* seeds to be eaten by ungulates? *Oikos*, **66**, 364–8.

Moegenburg, S.M. (2002). Harvest and management of forest fruits by humans: implications for fruit-frugivore interactions. In *Frugivory and Seed Dispersal: Ecological, Evolutionary and Conservation Issues*, ed. D. Levey, M. Galetti & W. Silva. Oxford: CAB International Publishing, pp. 479–94.

Munzbergova, Z. & Ward, D. (2002). *Acacia* trees as keystone species in Negev desert ecosystems. *Journal of Vegetation Science*, **13**, 227–36.

Murray, M.G. (1984). The 24 species of grazing antelope. In *The Encyclopedia of Mammals*: 2, ed. D.W. Macdonald. London: George Allen and Unwin, pp. 570–1.

Mwalyosi, R.B.B. (1990). The dynamic ecology of *Acacia tortilis* woodlands in Lake Manyara National Park, Tanzania. *African Journal of Ecology*, **33**, 64–70.

Or, K. & Ward, D. (2003). Three-way interactions between *Acacia*, large mammalian herbivores and bruchid beetles – a review. *African Journal of Ecology*, **41**, 257–65.

Owen-Smith, R.N. (2002). *Adaptive Herbivore Ecology*. Cambridge: Cambridge University Press.

Parra, R (1978). Comparison of foregut and hindgut fermentation in herbivores. In *The Ecology of Arboreal Folivores*, ed. G.G. Montgomery. Washington, DC: Smithsonian Institution Press, pp. 205–29.

Parrish, J.T. (1987). Global palaeogeography and palaeoclimate of the Late Cretaceous and Early Tertiary. In *The Origins of Angiosperms and their Biological Consequences*, ed. E.M. Friis, W.G. Chaloner & P.R. Crane. Cambridge: Cambridge University Press, pp. 51–73.

Peres, C.A. (2000). Evaluating the impact and sustainability of subsistence hunting at multiple Amazonian forest sites. In *Hunting for Sustainability in Tropical Forests*, ed. J.G. Robinson & E.L. Bennett. New York: Columbia University Press, pp. 31–56.

Peres, C.A. & van Roosmalen, M.G.M. (2002). Patterns of primate frugivory in Amazonia and the Guianan shield: implications to the demography of large-seeded plants in overhunted forests. In *Frugivory and Seed Dispersal: Ecological, Evolutionary and Conservation Issues*, ed. D. Levey, M. Galetti & W. Silva. Oxford: CAB International Publishing, pp. 407–21.

Robinson, J.G. & Bennett, E.L. (2000). *Hunting for Sustainability in Tropical Forests*. New York: Columbia University Press.

Rohner, C. & Ward, D. (1997). Chemical and mechanical defense against herbivory in two sympatric species of desert *Acacia*. *Journal of Vegetation Science*, **8**, 717–26.

Rohner, C. & Ward, D. (1999). Large mammalian herbivores and the conservation of arid *Acacia* stands in the Middle East. *Conservation Biology*, **13**, 1162–71.

Scholes, R.J. & Walker, B.H. (1993). *An African Savanna: Synthesis of the Nylsvley Study*. Cambridge: Cambridge University Press.

Shrestha, M.K., Golan-Goldhirsh, A. & Ward, D. (2002). Population genetic structure in isolated populations of *Acacia raddiana* investigated by random amplified polymorphic DNA (RAPD) markers. *Biological Conservation*, **108**, 119–27.

Sinclair, A.R.E. & Arcese, P. (1995). *Serengeti II: Dynamics, Management, and Conservation of an Ecosystem*. Chicago: The University of Chicago Press.

Smythe, N. (1970). Relationships between fruiting seasons and seed dispersal methods in a neotropical forest. *American Naturalist*, **104**, 25–35.

Smythe, N., Glanz, W.E. & Leigh, E.G. (1982). Population regulation in some terrestrial frugivores. In *The Ecology of a Tropical Forest: Seasonal Rhythms and Long-term Changes*, ed. E.G. Leigh, A.S. Rand & D.M. Windsor. Washington, DC: Smithsonian Institution Press, pp. 227–38.

Sowls, L.K. (1984). *The Peccaries*. Tucson, Arizona: The University of Arizona Press.

Sowls, L.K. (1997). *Javelinas and other Peccaries: Their Biology, Management, and Use*. College Station, Texas: Texas A & M University Press.

Stephens, D.W. & Krebs, J.R. (1986). *Foraging Theory*. Princeton, New Jersey: Princeton University Press.

Stevens, C.V. (1988). *Comparative Physiology of the Vertebrate Digestive System*. Cambridge: Cambridge University Press.

Tabarelli, M. & Peres, C.A. (2002). Abiotic and vertebrate seed dispersal in the Brazilian Atlantic forest: implications for forest regeneration. *Biological Conservation*, **106**, 165–76.

Taylor, M.A. (1990). Two dietary developments. *Nature*, **346**, 14–15.

Terborgh, J. (1983). *Five New World Primates: A Study in Comparative Ecology*. Princeton, New Jersey: Princeton University Press.

Terborgh, J. (1986). Community aspects of frugivory in tropical forests. In *Frugivores and Seed Dispersal*, ed. A. Estrada & T.H. Fleming. Dordrecht: Dr. W. Junk Pub., pp. 371–84.

Van Soest, P.J. (1982). *Nutritional Ecology of the Ruminant*. Corvallis, Oregon: O & B Books Inc.

Ward, D. & Rohner, C. (1997). Anthropogenic causes of high mortality and low recruitment in three *Acacia* tree taxa in the Negev desert, Israel. *Biodiversity and Conservation*, **6**, 877–93.

Ward, D. & Young, T.P. (2002). Effects of large mammalian herbivores and ant symbionts on condensed tannins of *Acacia drepanolobium* in Kenya. *Journal of Chemical Ecology*, **28**, 913–29.

Wing, S.L. & Tiffney, B.H. (1987). Interactions of angiosperms and herbivorous tetrapods through time. In *The Origins of Angiosperms and their Biological Consequences*, ed. E.M. Friis, W.G. Chaloner & P.R. Crane. Cambridge: Cambridge University Press, pp. 203–24.

Wiegand, K., Jeltsch, F. & Ward, D. (1999). Analysis of the population dynamics of *Acacia* trees in the Negev desert, Israel with a spatially explicit computer simulation model. *Ecological Modeling*, **117**, 203–24.

Wolfe, J.A. (1985). Distribution of major vegetational types during the Tertiary. *Geophysical Monograph*, **32**, 357–75.

9

Large herbivores as sources of disturbance in ecosystems

N. THOMPSON HOBBS

INTRODUCTION

Understanding the causes and consequences of spatial heterogeneity in ecosystems has emerged as a fundamental challenge for contemporary ecologists worldwide (Levin 1992, Pickett & Cadenasso 1995, Pascual & Levin 1999, Allen & Holling 2002, Ettema & Wardle 2002, Perry 2002, Hobbs 2003). Abiotic sources of heterogeneity, variation in soils for example, are described relatively easily. A much more difficult task is to understand how spatial heterogeneity arises from biotic interactions (Augustine & Frank 2001, Steinauer & Collins 2001). These biotic sources of spatial variation can give rise to complex feedbacks in ecosystems; feedbacks that shape the operation of ecological processes across scales and levels of organization (e.g. Holling 1992, Pickett et al. 1992, Tilman 1994, Pastor et al. 1997, 1998, Polis et al. 1997, Van Buskirk & Ostfeld 1998, Keeling 1999, Illius & O'Connor 2000, Augustine & Frank 2001, Steinauer & Collins 2001, van de Koppel et al. 2002).

Much effort has been invested in identifying biotic sources of spatial variation in grassland, steppe and forested ecosystems, particularly in describing the reciprocal role played by large herbivores in responding to landscape heterogeneity and in creating it (Jefferies et al. 1994, Laca & Ortega 1995, Scoones 1995, Hobbs 1996, 1999, Pastor et al. 1997, 1998, 1999, Fuhlendorf & Smeins 1999, Adler et al. 2001, Augustine & Frank 2001, Steinauer & Collins, 2001). Herbivores respond to spatial

Large Herbivore Ecology, Ecosystem Dynamics and Conservation, ed. K. Danell, P. Duncan, R. Bergström & J. Pastor. Published by Cambridge University Press. © Cambridge University Press 2006.

heterogeneity in plants across a range of scales by selecting locations for feeding and resting (Senft *et al.* 1987, McNaughton 1989, Coughenour 1991, Laca & Ortega 1995, Bailey *et al.* 1996, Wallis De Vries *et al.* 1999, Johnson *et al.* 2001). This selectivity amplifies abiotic heterogeneity by creating patchy patterns of forage consumption (Hobbs *et al.* 1991, Hester & Baillie 1998), physical disturbance (Polley 1984, Coppedge & Shaw 2000, Posse *et al.* 2000), and deposition of faeces and urine (Day & Detling 1990, Steinauer & Collins 1995, 2001). These herbivore-induced patterns modulate nutrient cycles (Hobbs *et al.* 1991, Frank & Groffman 1998, Augustine & Frank 2001, Zacheis *et al.* 2002), influence plant productivity (Bergström 1992, Jaramillo & Detling 1992a, Semmartin & Oesterheld 2001), modify disturbance regimes (Madany & West 1983, Zimmerman & Neuenschwander 1984, Frost & Robertson 1987, Hobbs *et al.* 1991) and alter plant community structure (Dublin *et al.* 1990, Glenn *et al.* 1992, Jefferies *et al.* 1994, Steinauer & Collins 1995, 2001, Hartnett *et al.* 1996). It follows that understanding the dynamics of ecosystems throughout the world requires understanding the role of large herbivores in creating spatial heterogeneity across a range of scales.

My purpose is to describe how large herbivores disturb ecosystems, and in so doing, how they influence biological diversity and spatial heterogeneity. I will begin this chapter by defining disturbance. Next, I will review the role of large herbivores as agents of disturbance, treating direct physical effects of trampling and wallows, additions of dung and urine, and indirect effects on large-scale disturbance regimes, particularly fire. I will conclude by discussing the interacting and amplifying effects of large herbivores as sources of biotic disturbance in ecosystems.

WHAT IS DISTURBANCE?

This chapter will use the definition of disturbance offered by Krebs (2001), 'A disturbance is any discrete event that disrupts community structure and changes available resources, substrate availability, or the physical environment.' Despite its apparent simplicity, the concept of disturbance can be confusing because it is possible to measure disturbance directly as a physical change in variables, such as biomass or canopy cover. Alternatively, disturbance can be assessed indirectly through changes in populations, communities or ecosystems relative to their 'normal' state (see review of White & Jentsch 2001). Direct measurements of disturbance are tidy to quantify, but fail to assess the ecological dynamics that make disturbance worthy of study in the first place. Indirect measurements are vague because of their dependence on defining 'normal' but are, nonetheless, explicitly relevant to understanding the dynamics of interest.

The tension between cause and effect in definitions of disturbance has motivated some authors to treat the concept narrowly to mean events that create space by killing, displacement or damage (Sousa 1984, Begon *et al.* 1996, Persson *et al.* 2000). Some workers have gone so far as to restrict the definition to include events that reset succession to its earliest stage (Turner *et al.* 1993). However, these narrow definitions only apply to systems where competition for space mediated by the availability of light or substrate determines the structure of the community. It ignores communities where changes in the availability of nutrients facilitate invasion. For example, one of the original non-equilibrium explanations for the effects of disturbance on community diversity was offered by Hutchinson (1961), who proposed that the remarkable diversity of planktonic communities might be due to short-term heterogeneity in nutrient supply rates, such that no single species could assume competitive dominance. Thus, in these systems, important disturbances included short-term mixing events that redistributed nutrients in such a way as to favour competitively inferior species.

A broad definition of disturbance is required for terrestrial systems as well. Changes in community structure occur abruptly when invasion and colonization by non-resident species are permitted by disturbance. Contemporary theory on invasibility predicts that fluctuation in resource availability is the key factor controlling invasibility (Davis *et al.* 2000, Davis & Pelsor 2001). Thus, events like urine deposition may not cause mortality or damage, or create space for colonization. Instead, these events are disturbances because they create opportunity for invasion by dramatically changing nutrient availability, altering competitive relationships among plants and propagating additional disturbance from patch grazing (Steinauer & Collins 1995, 2001).

A broad definition of disturbance to include all changes in resources that promote colonization and invasion will provide a framework for the review that follows. In each section I will assess the direct, measurable magnitude of disturbance by large herbivores and then will discuss consequences of these disturbances for plant communities, paying particular attention to the role of disturbance by herbivores as a source of spatial heterogeneity.

PHYSICAL DISTURBANCE: TRAMPLING

Magnitude of trampling effects

One of the most frequent interactions between large herbivores and the habitats they use occurs at the junction between the animal and the ground. Hooves come in contact with vegetation and soil thousands of times daily, and it follows that trampling would seem to be an important source of disturbance by virtue of its frequency alone. Although trampling is often cited in textbooks as one of the principal impacts of large herbivores on soils and vegetation (Stoddart *et al.* 1975, Steinauer & Collins 1995), until recently (Cumming & Cumming 2003) there had been no attempt to develop general estimates of the area of landscape affected by trampling. So, the first question I address is this: how much area of a given landscape is likely to be impacted by trampling? How does the importance of this impact vary with scale of habitat use?

Cumming and Cumming (2003) assembled data on morphometric traits of 44 species of African large herbivores and used these data to calculate the area trampled by single species populations and multi-species communities. Their results show that most species have a relatively small impact on the landscape – most of the species they studied trampled less than 10% of the area used by the population per year (Fig. 9.1). However, the effects of the community taken together were quite large, and tended to be dominated by a particularly abundant species (i.e. impala) or species of particularly large mass (i.e. elephant, buffalo, Fig. 9.1).

It is possible to estimate the daily trampling rate during foraging (A, area/time) by individual herbivores based on published scaling relationships. Simple algebra shows that $A = 2\sigma Tp\theta$, where σ is the stride frequency (time^{-1}), T is the foraging time per day (time/time), p is the proportion of the foraging time spent moving, and θ is the hoof area. Using $1.54 M^{-.24}$ for the scaling of stride frequency (s^{-1}, Shipley *et al.* 1996), $0.242 M^{0.12}$ for the scaling of foraging time (day, OwenSmith 1988), and $0.942 M^{0.99}$ for the scaling of hoof area (cm^2, Cumming & Cumming 2003), I calculated the area trampled per individual herbivore per day (Fig. 9.1). Converting units and multiplying the trampling rate by the scaling of population density, $0.995 M^{-0.75}$ (ha^{-1}, Damuth 1981) allows calculation of the percentage of the area used by an individual that is trampled per year, P (Fig. 9.2). This calculation estimates P as roughly 15%–25% of an individual's home range. However, these effects can be much greater when summed over a community of herbivores (Fig. 9.1).

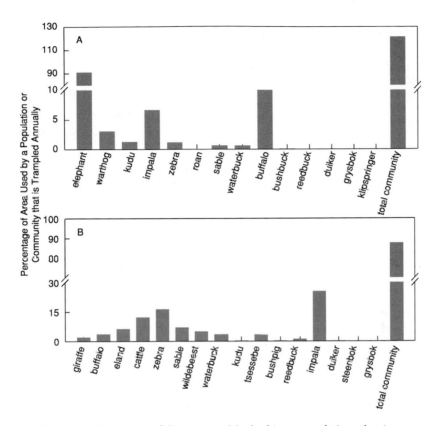

Figure 9.1. Percentage of the area used by herbivore populations that is trampled annually in two multispecies assemblages in South Africa (A – Sengwa Wildlife Research Area, B – Imire Game Park). Data recalculated from Cumming and Cumming (2003).

The theoretical predictions (Fig. 9.2) diverge from observations (Fig. 9.1) because observed population densities are different from the theoretical scaling. It is notable that my calculation indicates body mass has a relatively small influence on area trampled unlike the conclusion of Cumming and Cumming (2003). This is important because if the scaling exponent of trampling effects approaches 0 (Fig. 9.2), then the composition of the herbivore community is largely irrelevant to the estimation of trampling effects (contra Cumming & Cumming 2003).

Because animals concentrate their foraging activity on favoured areas of landscape, trampling effects will be amplified at local scales. For example, if only 20% of the total habitat is used for foraging, then this

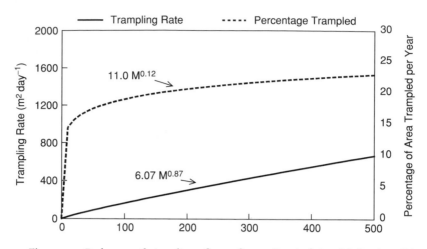

Figure 9.2. Body mass (kg) scaling of rate of trampling (m² day⁻¹, left axis, solid line) and the percentage of area used by an individual that is trampled annually (right axis, dashed line).

means that roughly 100% of the foraging area will be trampled by a population. Such concentrating effects are particularly acute around water points and along trails in arid and semi-arid ecosystems (Andrew 1988, Jeltsch *et al.* 1997, Thrash 1998, James *et al.* 1999, Larson 2003), and along trails used for movement among habitats (Ganskopp *et al.* 2000, Larson 2003). Although the magnitude of trampling losses relative to consumption has not been widely studied, Laycock & Harniss (1974) estimated that the amount of forage damaged by trampling was roughly equivalent to the amount consumed by livestock on grass-forb rangelands.

Effects on hydrology

Trampling can create spatial heterogeneity by cutting and compressing vegetation, and by changing properties of soils. Direct effects of trampling on plants are covered in Chapter 4. Here, I will review effects on soils. Soil properties are altered when trampling fractures biotic crusts (cyanobacteria, fungi, lichens), creates mineral crusts and increases bulk density of subsurface layers by compacting pore spaces. Probably the best studied outcomes of trampling are effects on hydrologic properties of soils. In arid and semi-arid systems, trampling can have opposing effects on infiltration of soil water (Fig. 9.3). Infiltration is retarded by effects of trampling that reduce pore space in the soil, cause formation of mineral crust or 'caps' on the soil surface, and reduce the sinuosity of microchannels at the

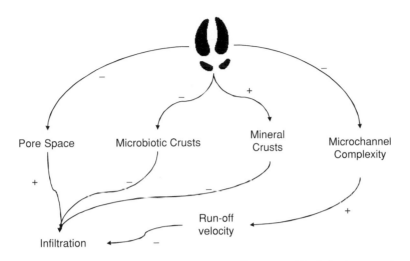

Figure 9.3. Conceptual model of trampling effects on soil hydrologic properties. Minus signs indicate reducing effects; plus signs indicate increasing effects.

soil surface, thereby accelerating run-off. In contrast, hooves can break microbiotic crusts leading to enhanced infiltration.

For example, Hiernaux *et al.* (1999) studied effects of sheep grazing on spatial patterns of sandy soils of Sahel rangelands. Soil and hydrologic properties were compared among ungrazed, moderately grazed and heavily grazed pastures. Trampling reduced the total area of biotic crusts on the soil surface and fractured the remaining crust. These effects increased infiltration rates relative to the control (Fig. 9.4). Heavily grazed pastures also experienced reduced biotic crusts, but caused a marked increase in the surface area of mineral crusts, which made the soil surface less permeable. As a result, the net effect of heavy grazing was a reduction in infiltration (Fig. 9.4). Thus, the magnitude of the effect of trampling on infiltration depended strongly on herbivore density.

In arid systems, the direct effects of trampling on soil properties interact with indirect effects on soil biota to reduce infiltration (Holt *et al.* 1996). Termites and soil arthropods increase porosity by creating macro pores. Heavy grazing causes elevated soil temperature due to loss of vegetative cover and reduces the amount of litter available to soil invertebrates like termites. These combined effects cause declines in soil fauna. Thus, deterioration in soil hydraulic properties in heavily grazed areas appears to result partly from direct effects of trampling on soil properties, and partly from indirect effects mediated through loss of activity by soil invertebrates.

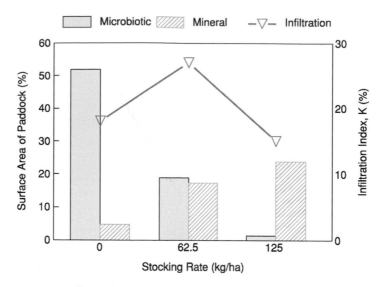

Figure 9.4. Effects of livestock stocking on area of pasture with mineral and microbiotic crusts (cyanobacteria, fungi, lichens) and infiltration rate in sandy soils of Sahelian rangelands. Figure drawn from data in Hiernaux *et al.* (1999).

Interactions also arise in more mesic systems where the magnitude of the effects of trampling depend on soil moisture (Taboada & Lavado 1993). Soils with low to medium moisture content are simply compressed as the hoof collapses larger pores by disruption of aggregates. However, when soils are wet, plastic flow occurs around the hoof, leaving deep prints that disturb the sward, opening up space for colonization.

Effects of trampling on infiltration also result from changes in patterns of run-off. Trampling can reduce stem densities and diminish sinuosity of microchannels that carry run-off, thereby accelerating velocity of overland flow (Flenniken *et al.* 2001). Effects of trampling on the velocity of flow are additive to effects of grazing (Flenniken *et al.* 2001).

Effects on plant community composition

Although it is clear that trampling can create bare areas of soil that provide opportunities for colonization, changes in plant communities in response to trampling by large herbivores are not extensively documented. There are strong associations between soil disturbance resulting from trampling and species richness in grazing lawns (Posse *et al.* 2000). Physical disturbance by ungulates is believed to inhibit invasion of grasslands by woody deciduous plant communities (Campbell *et al.* 1994). Changes in species plant cover around watering points and along trails are well documented, and many of these changes are attributed to effects of trampling (Andrew 1988, Jeltsch et al. 1997, Thrash 1998, James et al. 1999, Larson 2003). Moreover, although effects of trampling by herbivores on plant community composition are difficult to disentangle from effects of consumption, trampling by people has been extensively studied (Parikesit et al. 1995, deGouvenain 1996, Kobayashi et al. 1997, Posse et al. 2000, Kitazawa & Ohsawa 2002) and does not suffer from these confounding effects. In these studies, trampling created spatial heterogeneity in soil conditions, which tended to elevate plant diversity among patches.

Effects on nutrient dynamics

Trampling can exert direct and indirect effects on nitrogen cycling, effects that have been extensively studied in Alaskan salt marshes grazed by snow geese (Zacheis et al. 2001, 2002). Litter accumulation was reduced in areas grazed by geese compared with ungrazed areas (Zacheis et al. 2001). Trampling of the previous year's litter accelerated incorporation of litter into soils, which in turn accelerated nitrogen mineralization. In addition, trampling created areas of bare soil, which elevated rates of nitrogen fixation by cyanobacteria. Nitrogen dynamics were most responsive to effects of trampling on litter; trampling effects on nitrogen fixation were of secondary importance, and faecal additions had little effect relative to those of trampling (Zacheis et al. 2002).

Effects on herbivore patch use

As described above, trampling by herbivores creates heterogeneity in soils and vegetation on the landscape. How do herbivores respond to trampled areas? Dry matter intake rate can be greater in mature, high biomass patches that are lodged (Dougherty & Cornelius 1999), presumably because animals are able to obtain large bites from recumbent plants. However, cattle prefer to graze patches that are unlodged, suggesting a negative feedback between effects of trampling on sward structure and future regrazing (Dougherty & Cornelius 1999). However, if trampled patches also offer immature, rapidly growing plants, they may be used in preference to the untrampled matrix (Posse et al. 2000).

It is plausible that the nature of the feedback between trampled areas and regrazing depends on time scale and other effects of grazing. It is likely that other features of grazed patches, such as maintenance of immature, high-quality forage (McNaughton 1984, Jefferies et al. 1994, Wilmshurst et al. 2000), can cause animals to congregate in these areas

(Fryxell 1991), and thus, concentrates trampling. This congregation is likely to be a result rather than a cause of patch selection by herbivores.

PHYSICAL DISTURBANCE: WALLOWS

Many species of large herbivores create patches of bare soil by deliberately pawing the soil surface and rolling in pawed areas, thereby creating 'wallows'. The purpose of wallowing has been variously ascribed to insect protection, thermoregulation and attraction of mates. Buffalo wallows in the North American tallgrass prairie have been particularly well studied. Once a wallow is established, it is revisited frequently, which hardens the soil and creates depressions where water accumulates (Collins & Uno 1983), creating small, ephemeral ponds. There are dramatic changes in soil physical properties, soil nutrients and composition of vegetation along the prairie-wallow gradients for both active and inactive wallows (Collins & Uno 1983, Polley 1984). Vegetation patterns are directly correlated with moisture gradient and soil texture; ruderal species compose almost 60% of vegetation sampled within wallows. Trampling in wallows leads to dominance by sedges which form dense rhizomatous mats well adapted to trampling and seasonal fluctuations in standing water (Polley 1984). Effects of wallows on vegetation can persist for more than 100 years (Collins & Uno 1983). Although wallows may affect only a small area of landscape, they can exert strong effects on plant diversity (Knapp et al. 1999).

Effects of wallows on spatial heterogeneity of landscape are not random, but rather are entrained by larger-scale patterns. The distribution of wallows differs from the distribution of habitat use by ungulates (Coppedge & Shaw 2000). Bison preferentially formed wallows on relatively level portions of tallgrass prairie landscape that burned in the spring and autumn while they avoided summer burns, unburned areas, and steep slopes. Thus, areas disturbed by fire were more likely to be disturbed by wallows.

ADDITIONS OF DUNG, URINE AND CARCASSES

Magnitude of effects

Heterogeneity in resources is believed to be a primary mechanism promoting coexistence of competing species in plant communities (Chesson 2000). Addition of nutrients in dung, urine and carcasses can be considered disturbances because they create heterogeneity in resource availability, and in so doing, create opportunities for shifts in competitive dominance among species with different resource use efficiencies.

Hobbs (1996) provided simple equations for estimating the rate of the addition of nitrogen to ecosystems by large herbivores as a function of herbivore body mass and dietary nitrogen content. However, these equations assumed that dry matter intake was a constant proportion of body mass and did not respond to differences in forage quality; an assumption that limits the value of the approach. Here, I improve the equations of Hobbs (1996) by developing a model including effects of forage quality on dry matter intake in calculations of nitrogen excretion.

Nitrogen is excreted by large herbivores in urine and faeces. This excreted nitrogen has two origins: plant and animal. Thus, four sources of excretion must be accounted for: plant faecal nitrogen, plant urinary nitrogen, endogenous faecal nitrogen, and endogenous urinary nitrogen. Three of these quantities depend on daily dry matter intake which responds dynamically to forage quality. To represent this response, I begin by modifying the equation of Illius and O'Connor (2000) to predict dry matter intake (I, g day^{-1}) as a function of herbivore body mass (M, kg) and dietary digestibility (d, proportion):

$$I = 90\, d^{1.1} M^{0.81} \tag{9.1}$$

Using data from Baker and Hobbs (1982) and Hobbs et al. (1979), I developed a relationship between dry matter digestibility and plant nitrogen content (N, g/g dry matter), $d = 0.362 + 0.144\ N$, which I substitute this for d in Equation 9.1, obtaining:

$$I = 0.90(0.362 + 0.144\ N)^{1.1} M^{0.81}. \tag{9.2}$$

This expression is needed to estimate three pathways of nitrogen loss from the animal. First, nitrogen of plant origin in the faeces (F_p, g/day) can be calculated as a function of I, the true indigestibility of plant nitrogen, estimated as .05, and plant nitrogen (Robbins 1983, Hobbs 1996):

$$F_p = 0.05\ IN. \tag{9.3}$$

Similarly, we can now calculate plant urinary nitrogen (U_p, g/day) based on I, the biological value of plant nitrogen, and true nitrogen digestibility (Robbins 1983, Hobbs 1996),

$$U_p = 0.208 \ IN + 0.11 \ N^2. \tag{9.4}$$

Endogenous faecal nitrogen (F_e) can be estimated as a constant fraction of I (Robbins 1983),

$$F_e = 0.00421 \ I \tag{9.5}$$

and endogenous urinary nitrogen (U_e, g/day) can be estimated as a function of body mass (Robbins 1983),

$$U_e = 0.1 \ M^{0.75}. \tag{9.6}$$

Summing equations representing urinary and faecal nitrogen excretion ($F_P + U_p + F_e + U_e$) and substituting Equation 9.1 for I in the sum, provides an equation for total nitrogen added to the environment per individual as a function of body mass and plant nitrogen content.

The magnitude of nitrogen excreted by large herbivores increases with animal body mass and plant nitrogen content (Fig. 9.5). Large bodied species can excrete as much as 300 g nitrogen per individual per day when

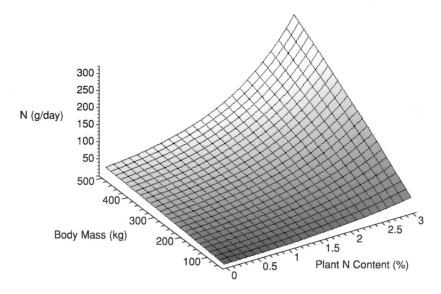

Figure 9.5. Total additions of nitrogen to ecosystems by large herbivores as a function of body mass and dietary nitrogen content.

consuming high nitrogen plants. Including effects of plant nitrogen content on dry matter intake rate, as has been done here, results in estimates of nitrogen excretion that are higher than previous estimates (Hobbs 1996) for high nitrogen diets and lower than previous estimates for low nitrogen diets.

How significant are additions of nitrogen in urine and faeces? It is possible to estimate roughly the area of habitat affected by urination using the scaling relationship for population density and by assuming that large herbivores urinate about ten times per day (Belovsky & Jordan 1981, Sawyer et al. 1993, Gassett et al. 1998, Aland et al. 2002), and that each urination affects a patch about 1/2 m in area (Afzal & Adams 1992, Williams & Haynes 1994). It follows from these assumptions that approximately 2% of the habitat used by large herbivores is affected by urination, an approximation that closely agrees with field measurements for wild herbivores (Day & Detling 1990, Augustine & Frank 2001), but that is approximately ten times lower than estimates for domestic herbivores confined to pastures (Afzal & Adams 1992, Williams & Haynes 1997).

To estimate the magnitude of total nitrogen additions per unit area of habitat, I scaled estimates of additions per individual by the reciprocal of population density (Damuth 1981). Estimates scaled this way reveal that additions of nitrogen per unit area of landscape are largely independent of herbivore body mass, but increase dramatically with increasing nitrogen content of consumed plants (Fig. 9.6). On high nitrogen diets, nitrogen excretion approaches 1 kg ha^{-1} year^{-1}. Thus, averaged over the total area of

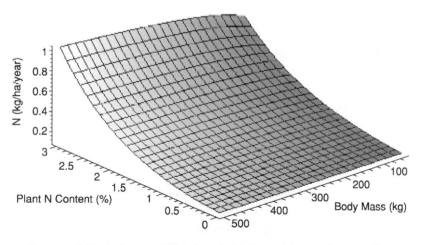

Figure 9.6. Total nitrogen additions to habitats used by populations of large herbivores as a function of dietary nitrogen content and herbivore body mass.

habitat used by an ungulate, nitrogen additions are quite small, less than 1% of what would be expected from net mineralization (Olff *et al.* 1994, Gill *et al.* 1995, Reich *et al.* 2001, Collins & Allinson 2002) and less than half of what would be expected from even lower levels of atmospheric deposition (Swank 1984, Boring *et al.* 1988). However, Frank *et al.* (1994) measured nitrogen additions to temperate grasslands by elk and bison, and found that nitrogen additions by these migratory ungulates could be far higher, averaging 27% of net mineralized nitrogen. This difference illustrates that inputs may be small when averaged over the home range of an individual, but can be substantial whenever animals are concentrated spatially by migrating to habitats of a restricted area, or by choosing sites for feeding and resting within those habitats. It also illustrates that multispecies communities will have larger impacts than single populations.

Effects on plant communities and herbivore foraging

Effects of additions of nitrogen on nutrient cycles will be considered in Chapter 10. Here, I concentrate on reviewing the effects on plant communities and herbivore foraging behaviour. Nitrogen additions can dramatically change availability of nitrogen to plants at local scales, and this change promotes shifts in plant community composition by altering competitive interactions. Urine deposition forms distinct patches in grasslands (Steinauer & Collins 2001) because urine is a concentrated solution deposited on a small area, and as such, urine patches are likely to contain nitrogen in excess of plant demand (de Mazancourt *et al.* 1999). Biomass is higher and nitrogen is more concentrated in these patches than in the surrounding landscape (Day & Detling 1990). Above-ground biomass of grasses can increase by a factor of four one year after urine deposition and nitrogen yield can increase by six-fold (Jaramillo & Detling 1992a).

Unlike other small-scale disturbances in grasslands (like wallows and trampling) that disrupt vegetation, and in so doing, favour colonization by early successional species, urine additions change competitive relationships in intact vegetation (Steinauer & Collins 1995), often favouring late-successional species. Thus, changes in plant community structure are driven primarily by increases in abundance of species that are strong competitors for nitrogen, which tend to characterize mature grasslands (Steinauer & Collins 1995). As a result, urine patches can elevate or reduce plant diversity in grasslands, and the direction of these effects depends on other sources of disturbance (Steinauer & Collins 1995, 2001). Urine additions to burned grasslands tend to reduce alpha and beta diversity, while the opposite responses are seen in unburned landscapes (Steinauer

& Collins 1995). This is likely to be the case because nitrogen additions favour late-successional species which are less dominant in recently burned areas. Similarly, the magnitude of the effect of additions of synthetic urine on species richness, evenness, and overall community composition depends on the effects of grazing (Steinauer & Collins 2001). Urine deposition is a small-scale, patch-forming event that increases the likelihood that a patch and its surroundings will be grazed, thereby amplifying the effects of the original disturbance (Jaramillo & Detling 1992b, Steinauer & Collins 2001). These feedbacks between urine deposition and future grazing can be very strong; although only 2% of the landscape may be affected by urine, and as much as 7% of biomass consumed by ungulates and 14% of nitrogen they consume can come from urine patches (Day & Detling 1990).

Carcasses of large herbivores add pulses of nutrients to landscapes in excess of all other natural sources (Knapp *et al.* 1999). In the tallgrass prairie, bison carcasses create zones of high soil fertility 5 m in diameter (Knapp *et al.* 1999, Towne 2000). Soil cores extracted from the centre of carcass sites had inorganic nitrogen concentrations two to three times higher than surrounding prairie (Towne 2000). These sites are frequently invaded by early-successional species. Five years after death, ungulate carcass sites in tallgrass prairie remained in disturbed patches containing vegetation markedly different in composition and height from surrounding, undisturbed vegetation (Towne 2000). By providing conditions favouring species not normally found in undisturbed prairie, carcasses increased community diversity and enhanced landscape heterogeneity.

Additions of dung, urine and carcasses affect composition of the soil biota (Sagara 1995). These additions stimulate production of a particular group of fungi. Both field observations and simulation experiments show that, when animal waste products are deposited in forests of ectomycorrhizal trees, ectomycorrhizal fungi will fruit during the late phase in the succession (Sagara 1995). Thus, pulsed additions of animal wastes and dead bodies above-ground can drive marked shifts in fungal dynamics below-ground.

INTERACTIONS OF LARGE HERBIVORES WITH OTHER SOURCES OF DISTURBANCE

Effect of grazing on fire regimes in grasslands and savannas

One of the most important ways that herbivores disturb ecosystems is by modifying the effect of other agents of disturbance, notably fire (Fig. 9.7). Herbivores shape the frequency, intensity and spatial distribution of fire in

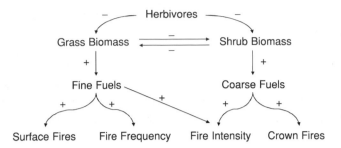

Figure 9.7. Herbivores can exert direct and indirect effects on fire regimes. Grazing directly reduces the amount of fine, herbaceous fuels, thereby reducing the frequency of surface fires. Browsing reduces the amount of coarse fuels, thereby reducing fire intensity. However, herbivores can indirectly affect fire regimes by altering the competitive balance between woody and herbaceous species.

grasslands by influencing fuel supplies (Bachelet *et al.* 2000). There is a strong, positive correlation between grass biomass and frequency of fire (Bond *et al.* 2001), and a strong negative correlation between grass biomass and intensity of grazing by ungulates. These relationships explain why the total area burned in East African grasslands is strongly related to ungulate population size (McNaughton 1992). In the Serengeti, there appears to be a threshold population size of approximately 600 000 wildebeest that causes qualitative changes in fire regimes; when populations exceed this threshold, only 20% of the region burns. At populations less than this threshold, most of the region burns.

Reduction in fire frequency and intensity resulting from grazing are attributable to 'fire breaks' created by grazed patches (McNaughton 1992). Patch grazing by large herbivores creates heterogeneity in fire behaviour; grazed patches burn less intensely than ungrazed ones, or may not burn at all (Hobbs *et al.* 1991). In annually burned tallgrass prairie, these feedbacks create a mosaic of unburned, grazed patches and burned, ungrazed ones (Knapp *et al.* 1999). Thus, in grasslands, herbivores create discontinuities in fuels and these gaps constrain fire spread (Fig. 9.7).

Because ungulates prefer to forage on burned areas in grasslands (Vinton *et al.* 1993, Biondini *et al.* 1999), it is plausible that this grazing causes the reductions in fuels, preventing intense burning in the same place year after year. Moreover, fire prevents recurrent, patch grazing (Hobbs *et al.* 1991). On unburned landscapes, grazed patches are likely to be regrazed the following year. Burning interrupts this feedback by reducing the differences in residual biomass between grazed and ungrazed patches (Hobbs *et al.* 1991).

Interactions between large herbivores and fire regimes have important implications for plant community structure. In the tallgrass prairie, grazing amplifies the enhancing effects of fire on species diversity (Hartnett *et al.* 1996), and these effects may be particularly large for annual species (Collins 1987). Species diversity in African grasslands is promoted by the creation of grazing lawns allowing establishment of *Acacia nilcotica*, which can tolerate browsing, but not fire. Fire favours establishment of *A. karroo* in ungrazed areas that have high fuel loads and burn frequently (Bond *et al.* 2001). In savannas, browsers assure that tree canopies are exposed to fire by maintaining them within 'ground fire' zones. Tree canopies cannot escape fire by growing upward because ungulate browsing maintains them at a low stature (Frost & Robertson 1987, Bergström 1992, McNaughton 1992). Thus, browsing, interacting with fire, maintains grassland conditions. In the absence of such browsing, tree canopies reach heights allowing them to escape the effects of surface fires and out compete grasses (Dublin *et al.* 1990, Skarpe 1992) causing a conversion from grassland to forest. Thus, although disturbance by fire may cause conversion of forests to grasslands, browsing by ungulates maintains the grassland state (Dublin *et al.* 1990) by altering the way future fires affect trees.

Effects of large herbivores on fire regimes in forests and shrublands

Grazing by large herbivores reduces the frequency and intensity of fires in grasslands by creating horizontal discontinuities in fuels. Reductions in fine herbaceous fuels in forests and shrublands act in a similar way to reduce the probability of ignition events, and hence, to dampen the frequency of fire. However, indirect, successional effects of large herbivores on community composition of woody plant communities can make them more prone to intense fires. These effects include increases in the vertical continuity of fuels and increases in the dominance of plants containing volatile compounds in leaves and stems.

Grazing by large herbivores affects the competitive balance between herbaceous plants and shrubs (Fig. 9.7). Heavy grazing can allow unpalatable shrubs to invade otherwise open, park-like forests. This invasion of shrubs creates a new layer of fuel, intermediate in height, between the herbaceous layer and the tree canopy (Madany & West 1983, Zimmerman & Neuenschwander 1984). In so doing, invading shrubs allow ground fires to reach the canopy of trees in a process called 'laddering', which promotes the frequency of crown fires, even if the frequency of surface

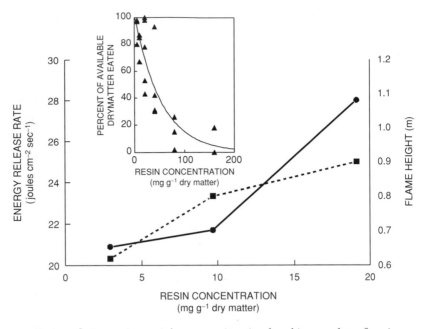

Figure 9.8. Increasing resin concentrations in plant biomass deter foraging by herbivores and increase the intensity of fire. Main figure: energy release (dashed line, squares) and flame height (solid line, circles) as a function of resin concentration in woody fuels. Drawn from data in Rundel (1981). Inset: proportion of available browse consumed by snowshoe hares as a function of browse resin concentration. Drawn from data in Bryant (1981).

fires is reduced (Madany & West 1983, Zimmerman & Neuenschwander 1984). These effects of grazers in forests resemble the effects of browsers in grasslands. In both cases, large herbivores make crown fires more likely.

Large herbivores can also make plant communities more flammable by selecting plants containing low levels of volatile compounds. Many of the compounds that deter browsing (e.g. resins, volatile oils) are also highly flammable (Fig. 9.8). Consequently, if herbivores avoid plants containing these compounds, they may favour dominance by flammable plant species by providing a competitive advantage to unbrowsed, defended plants over browsed, undefended ones. A notable example of this shift can be seen in chaparral where browsing by large and small mammals allows a flammable species, chamise, to out compete a less flammable one, ceanothus. In the absence of browsing, dominance of the two species is reversed (Mills 1983) (Fig. 9.9). Thus, herbivores create conditions in plant communities that fundamentally alter the fire regime.

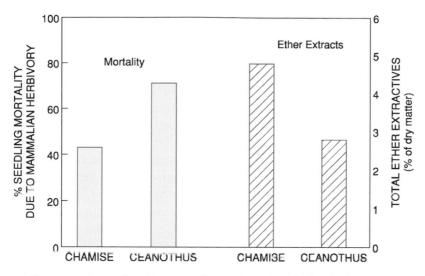

Figure 9.9. Rates of seedling mortality resulting from feeding by deer and small mammalian herbivores (light bars, left axis) in chaparral shrubs and total ether extractives in those shrubs (hatch bars, right axis). Drawn from data in Mills (1983).

CONCLUSIONS

One of the most prominent features of the ecology of large herbivores is selectivity. Animals discriminate among areas of landscapes for feeding and resting, and this discrimination creates non-random patterns of landscape use at several scales of time and space. When animals use areas of the landscape selectively, the disturbances associated with their choices may increase the likelihood of future use, creating a positive feedback. Alternatively, disturbance by herbivores may diminish the likelihood of future use, creating a negative feedback.

Many of the disturbances discussed above involve positive feedbacks; that is, the occurrence of a disturbance increases the likelihood that the disturbed area will be used by herbivores again in the future, and hence, increases the probability of future disturbance nearby. There are many examples of these feedbacks: trampled areas are more likely to be used for travelling and creating trails; urine patches may be used in preference to urine-free areas; and wallows are revisited rather than created anew. These positive feedbacks create patchiness in disturbances because one disturbance increases the likelihood of another nearby. Disturbed patches tend to contrast with the surrounding landscape, and this contrast increases the heterogeneity of landscapes.

Scale dependence occurs in ecological phenomena whenever spatial patterns are patchy (Schneider 1998). It follows that the clustering of disturbances resulting from positive feedbacks between current and future disturbances creates strong scale-dependence in disturbance effects. This means that the magnitude of the effect of disturbance depends on the scale over which it is measured. For example, the total area disturbed by herbivores (above) is relatively small at the scale of the landscape. However, this disturbance can have tremendous impacts at local scales. So, considering the area over which we 'average' is critical to assessing the importance of the effects of herbivore disturbance. Many of the initial effects of disturbance are most recognizable at scales of 1–20 m (Jefferies et al. 1994), but as discussed below, these initial events can propagate disturbances at larger scales.

Positive feedbacks concentrate the effects of disturbance in space, while negative feedbacks tend to expand the area affected by disturbance. For example, in domestic grazing systems where animals are stocked at high densities, animals may avoid trampled areas of pastures, seeking portions of the pasture that are lightly used. Negative feedbacks, like this one, tend to increase the uniformity of landscape use by large herbivores, thereby reducing landscape heterogeneity.

There appear to be non-linear effects of population density on the nature of the disturbance feedback. The best example of this dependence is seen in the effects of urine and faecal deposition on herbivore selectivity. When animals graze landscapes at low or moderate densities, there is strong evidence for a positive feedback between urine deposition and future use of urine patches. However, the opposite is seen when stocking densities are high – herbivores avoid 'fouled areas' where urine and faeces accumulate. These non-linearities could create powerful switches in relationships between herbivore density and landscape heterogeneity – low population densities may enhance landscape heterogeneity while high densities reduce it.

All of the disturbances discussed above are discrete, perturbing events that occur at relatively fine scales. However, these localized perturbations can propagate disturbances affecting much larger areas. For example, urine patches are localized disturbances affecting less than 5% of the landscape. However, large herbivores are attracted to these areas, and this attraction creates grazed patches that occupy a much larger footprint than the original disturbance, of the order of 20% of the landscape (Steinauer

& Collins 2001). Direct effects of urine patches on plant community composition may be relatively small, but larger effects result indirectly as herbivores select areas adjacent to urine patches for feeding (Steinauer & Collins 2001), creating additional positive feedbacks as grazing promotes regrazing (Hobbs et al. 1991). Thus, urine patches can propagate patch grazing at specific locations on the landscape, and patch grazing perpetuates itself by the creation of additional urine patches and by maintaining plants in an immature state. Patch grazing, in turn, can affect the frequency and intensity of fires by creating breaks in otherwise homogeneous fuels (Hobbs et al. 1991). This effect on the fire regime can be seen across entire landscapes. This example illustrates how feedbacks from initial, small-scale disturbances create multiplying effects that expand the scale of influence of disturbance from metres to kilometres.

In addition to effects on landscape heterogeneity, disturbance by large herbivores influences biological diversity directly by the effects of trampling, wallowing, urination and defecation, and indirectly by influencing the other sources of disturbance. By creating local conditions that contrast with the surrounding landscape, disturbance by ungulates has the potential to increase beta diversity (e.g. Collins & Uno 1983, Polley 1984, Steinauer & Collins 1995). Increases in the availability of substrate and/ or nutrients within patches can promote colonization that enhances alpha diversity (Posse et al. 2000, Steinauer & Collins 2001). However, the effects of local disturbance may depend on the larger context. For example, Steinauer and Collins (2001) found that the effect of simulated additions of nutrients in urine on species diversity depended on the effect of grazing. On grazed landscapes, additions of urine enhanced species diversity by creating a positive feedback with grazing. In the absence of this feedback, no effects of urine additions were detected.

In conclusion, disturbances by large herbivores shape spatial heterogeneity and biological diversity of ecosystems. Feedbacks created by selectivity cause the magnitude and direction of these effects to depend on the scale at which they are measured. These feedbacks can propagate other sources of disturbance, thereby magnifying the spatial extent and the importance of the original event.

ACKNOWLEDGEMENTS

This work was supported by grants (DEB 9981368, DEB 0119618) from the United States National Science Foundation to Colorado State University.

REFERENCES

Adler, P.B., Raff, D.A. & Lauenroth, W.K. (2001). The effect of grazing on the spatial heterogeneity of vegetation. *Oecologia*, **128**, 465–79.

Afzal, M. & Adams, W.A. (1992). Heterogeneity of soil mineral nitrogen in pasture grazed by cattle. *Soil Science Society of America Journal*, **56**, 1160–6.

Aland, A., Lidfors, L. & Ekesbo, I. (2002). Diurnal distribution of dairy cow defecation and urination. *Applied Animal Behaviour Science*, **78**, 43–54.

Allen, C.R. & Holling, C.S. (2002). Cross-scale structure and scale breaks in ecosystems and other complex systems. *Ecosystems*, **5**, 315–18.

Andrew, M.H. (1988). Grazing impacts in relation to livestock watering points. *Trends in Ecology and Evolution*, **3**, 336–9.

Augustine, D.J. & Frank, D.A. (2001). Effects of migratory grazers on spatial heterogeneity of soil nitrogen properties in a grassland ecosystem. *Ecology*, **82**, 3149–62.

Bachelet, D., Lenihan, J.M., Daly, C. & Neilson, R.P. (2000). Interactions between fire, grazing and climate change at Wind Cave National Park, SD. *Ecological Modelling*, **134**, 229–44.

Bailey, D.W., Gross, J.E., Laca, E.A. *et al.* (1996). Mechanisms that result in large herbivore grazing distribution patterns. *Journal of Range Management*, **49**, 386–400.

Baker, D.L. & Hobbs, N.T. (1982). Composition and quality of elk summer diets in Colorado. *Journal of Wildlife Management*, **46**, 694–703.

Begon, M., Harper, J.L. & Townsend, C.R. (1996). *Ecology: Individuals, Populations, and Communities*. Oxford: Blackwell Science.

Belovsky, G.E. & Jordan, P.A. (1981). Sodium dynamics and adaptations of a moose population. *Journal of Mammalogy*, **62**, 613–21.

Bergström, R. (1992). Browse characteristics and impact of browsing on trees and shrubs in African savannas. *Journal of Vegetation Science*, **3**, 315–24.

Biondini, M.E., Steuter, A.A. & Hamilton, R.G. (1999). Bison use of fire-managed remnant prairies. *Journal of Range Management*, **52**, 454–61.

Bond, W.J., Smythe, K.A. & Balfour, D.A. (2001). *Acacia* species turnover in space and time in an African savanna. *Journal of Biogeography*, **28**, 117–28.

Boring, L.R., Swank, W.T., Waide, J.B. & Henderson, G.S. (1988). Sources, fates, and impacts of nitrogen inputs to terrestrial ecosystems. Review and synthesis. *Biogeochemistry*, **6**, 119–59.

Bryant, J.P. (1981). Phytochemical deference of snowshoe hare browsing by adventitious shoots of four Alaskan trees. *Science* **23**, 889–90.

Campbell, C., Campbell, I.D., Blyth, C.B. & McAndrews, J.H. (1994). Bison extirpation may have caused aspen expansion in western Canada. *Ecography*, **17**, 360–2.

Chesson, P. (2000). Mechanisms of maintenance of species diversity. *Annual Review of Ecology and Systematics*, **31**, 343–66.

Collins, A. & Allinson, D.W. (2002). Nitrogen mineralization in soil from perennial grassland measured through long-term laboratory incubations. *Journal of Agricultural Science*, **138**, 301–10.

Collins, S.L. (1987). Interaction of disturbances in tallgrass prairie – a field experiment. *Ecology*, **68**, 1243–50.

Collins, S.L. & Uno, G.E. (1983). The effect of early spring burning on vegetation in Buffalo wallows. *Bulletin of the Torrey Botanical Club*, **110**, 474–81.

Coppedge, B.R. & Shaw, J.H. (2000). American bison (*Bison bison*) wallowing behavior and wallow formation on tallgrass prairie. *Acta Theriologica*, **45**, 103–10.

Coughenour, M.B. (1991). Spatial components of plant-herbivore interactions in pastoral, ranching, and native ungulate ecosystems. *Journal of Range Management*, **44**, 530–42.

Cumming, D.H.M. & Cumming, G.S. (2003). Ungulate community structure and ecological processes: body size, hoof area and trampling in African savannas. *Oecologia*, **134**, 560–8.

Damuth, J. (1981). Population-density and body size in mammals. *Nature*, **290**, 699–700.

Davis, M.A. & Pelsor, M. (2001). Experimental support for a resource-based mechanistic model of invasibility. *Ecology Letters*, **4**, 421–8.

Davis, M.A., Grime, J.P. & Thompson, K. (2000). Fluctuating resources in plant communities: a general theory of invasibility. *Journal of Ecology*, **88**, 528–34.

Day, T.A. & Detling, J.K. (1990). Grassland patch dynamics and herbivore grazing preference following urine deposition. *Ecology*, **71**, 180–8.

de Mazancourt, C., Loreau, M. & Abbadie, L. (1999). Grazing optimization and nutrient cycling: potential impact of large herbivores in a savanna system. *Ecological Applications*, **9**, 784–97.

deGouvenain, R.C. (1996). Indirect impacts of soil trampling on tree growth and plant succession in the North Cascade Mountains of Washington. *Biological Conservation*, **75**, 279–87.

Dougherty, C.T. & Cornelius, P.L. (1999). Intake of cattle offered normal and lodged tall fescue swards. *Journal of Range Management*, **52**, 508–14.

Dublin, H.T., Sinclair, A.R.E. & McGlade, J. (1990). Elephants and fire as causes of multiple stable states in the Serengeti-Mar woodlands. *Journal of Animal Ecology*, **59**, 1147–64.

Ettema, C.H. & Wardle, D.A. (2002). Spatial soil ecology. *Trends in Ecology and Evolution*, **17**, 177–83.

Flenniken, M., McEldowney, R.R., Leininger, W.C., Frasier, G.W. & Trlica, M.J. (2001). Hydrologic responses of a montane riparian ecosystem following cattle use. *Journal of Range Management*, **54**, 567–74.

Frank, D.A. & Groffman, P.M. (1998). Ungulate vs. landscape control of soil C and N processes in grasslands of Yellowstone National Park. *Ecology*, **79**, 2229 41.

Frank, D.A., Inouye, R.S., Huntly, N., Minshall, G.W. & Anderson, J.E. (1994). The biogeochemistry of a north-temperate grassland with native ungulates: nitrogen dynamics in Yellowstone National Park. *Biogeochemistry*, **26**, 163–88.

Frost, P.H.G. & Robertson, F. (1987). The ecological effects of fire in savannas. In *Determinants of Tropical Savannas*, ed. B.H. Walker. Paris: International Union of Biological Sciences, pp. 93–140.

Fryxell, J. M. (1991). Forage quality and aggregation by large herbivores. *American Naturalist*, **138**, 478–98.

Fuhlendorf, S. D. & Smeins, F. E. (1999). Scaling effects of grazing in a semi-arid grassland. *Journal of Vegetation Science*, **10**, 731–8.

Ganskopp, D., Cruz, R. & Johnson, D. E. (2000). Least-effort pathways?: a GIS analysis of livestock trails in rugged terrain. *Applied Animal Behaviour Science*, **68**, 179–90.

Gassett, J. W., Osborn, D. A., Rickard, J. K., Marchinton, R. L. & Miller, K. V. (1998). Stimuli-related variation in urination frequency of female white-tailed deer during the estrous cycle. *Applied Animal Behaviour Science*, **56**, 71–5.

Gill, K., Jarvis, S. C. & Hatch, D. J. (1995). Mineralization of nitrogen in long-term pasture soils. Effects of management. *Plant and Soil*, **172**, 153–62.

Glenn, S. M., Collins, S. L. & Gibson, D. J. (1992). Disturbance in tallgrass prairie: local and regional effects on community heterogeneity. *Landscape Ecology*, **7**, 243–51.

Hartnett, D. C., Hickman, K. R. & Walter, L. E. (1996). Effects of bison grazing, fire, and topography on floristic diversity in tallgrass prairie. *Journal of Range Management*, **49**, 413–20.

Hester, A. J. & Baillie, G. J. (1998). Spatial and temporal patterns of heather use by sheep and red deer within natural heather/grass mosaics. *Journal of Applied Ecology*, **35**, 772–84.

Hiernaux, P., Bielders, C. L., Valentin, C., Bationo, A. & Fernandez-Rivera, S. (1999). Effects of livestock grazing on physical and chemical properties of sandy soils in Sahelian rangelands. *Journal of Arid Environments*, **41**, 231–45.

Hobbs, N. T. (1996). Modification of ecosystems by ungulates. *Journal of Wildlife Management*, **60**, 695–713.

Hobbs, N. T. (1999). Responses of large herbivores to spatial heterogeneity in ecosystems. In *Nutritional Ecology of Herbivores: Proceedings of the Vth International Symposium on the Nutrition of Herbivores*, ed. H. G. Jung & G. C. Fahey. Savory, IL: American Society of Animal Science, pp. 97–129.

Hobbs, N. T. (2003). Challenges and opportunities for integrating ecological knowledge across scales. *Forest Ecology and Management*, **181**, 222–38.

Hobbs, N. T., Baker, D. L., Ellis, J. E. & Swift, D. M. (1979). Composition and quality of elk diets during summer and winter: a preliminary analysis, In *North American Elk: Ecology, Behavior, and Management*, ed. M. S. Boyce & L. D. Hayden-Wing. Laramie, Wyoming: University of Wyoming, pp. 47–54.

Hobbs, N. T., Schimel, D. S., Owensby, C. E. & Ojima, D. J. (1991). Fire and grazing in the tallgrass prairie: contingent effects on nitrogen budgets. *Ecology*, **72**, 1374–82.

Holling, C. S. (1992). Cross-scale morphology geometry and dynamics of ecosystems. *Ecological Monographs*, **62**, 447–502.

Holt, J. A., Bristow, K. L. & McIvor, J. G. (1996). The effects of grazing pressure on soil animals and hydraulic properties of two soils in semi-arid tropical Queensland. *Australian Journal of Soil Research*, **34**, 69–79.

Hutchinson, G. E. (1961). The paradox of the plankton. *American Naturalist*, **95**, 137–45.

Illius, A.W. & O'Connor, T.G. (2000). Resource heterogeneity and ungulate population dynamics. *Oikos,* **89,** 283–94.

James, C.D., Landsberg, J. & Morton, S.R. (1999). Provision of watering points in the Australian arid zone: a review of effects on biota. *Journal of Arid Environments,* **41,** 87–121.

Jaramillo, V.J. & Detling, J.K. (1992a). Small-scale heterogeneity in a semi-arid North American grassland. 1. Tillering, N-uptake and retranslocation in simulated urine patches. *Journal of Applied Ecology,* **29,** 1–8.

Jaramillo, V.J. & Detling, J.K. (1992b). Small-scale heterogeneity in a semi-arid North American grassland. 2. Cattle grazing of simulated urine patches. *Journal of Applied Ecology,* **29,** 9–13.

Jefferies, R.L., Klein, D.R. & Shaver, G.R. (1994). Vertebrate herbivores and northern plant communities: reciprocal influences and responses. *Oikos,* **71,** 193–206.

Jeltsch, F., Milton, S.J., Dean, W.R.J. & vanRooyen, N. (1997). Simulated pattern formation around artificial waterholes in the semi-arid Kalahari. *Journal of Vegetation Science,* **8,** 177–88.

Johnson, C.J., Parker, K.L. & Heard, D.C. (2001). Foraging across a variable landscape: behavioral decisions made by woodland caribou at multiple spatial scales. *Oecologia,* **127,** 590–602.

Keeling, M.J. (1999). The effects of local spatial structure on epidemiological invasions. *Proceedings of the Royal Society of London, Series B – Biological Sciences,* **266,** 859–67.

Kitazawa, T. & Ohsawa, M. (2002). Patterns of species diversity in rural herbaceous communities under different management regimes, Chiba, central Japan. *Biological Conservation,* **104,** 239–49.

Knapp, A.K., Blair, J.M., Briggs, J.M. et al. (1999). The keystone role of bison in North American tallgrass prairie. Bison increase habitat heterogeneity and alter a broad array of plant, community, and ecosystem processes. *Bioscience,* **49,** 39–50.

Kobayashi, T., Hori, Y. & Nomoto, N. (1997). Effects of trampling and vegetation removal on species diversity and micro-environment under different shade conditions. *Journal of Vegetation Science,* **8,** 873–80.

Krebs, C.J. (2001). *Ecology: The Experimental Analysis of Distribution and Abundance.* New York: Benjamin Cummings.

Laca, E. & Ortega, I.M. (1995). Integrating foraging mechanisms across spatial and temporal scales. In *Rangelands in a Sustainable Biosphere,* ed. N.E. West. Denver, CO: Society for Range Management, pp. 129–32.

Larson, D.L. (2003). Native weeds and exotic plants: relationships to disturbance in mixed-grass prairie. *Plant Ecology,* **169,** 317–33.

Laycock, W.A. & Harniss, R.O. (1974). Trampling damage on native forb grass ranges grazed by sheep and cattle. *Grassland Utilization. Proceedings of the 12th International Grassland Congress.* Moscow, USSR, pp. 349–54.

Levin, S.A. (1992). The problem of pattern and scale in ecology. *Ecology,* **73,** 1943–67.

Madany, M.H. & West, N.E. (1983). Livestock grazing-fire regime interactions within montane forests of Zion National Park, Utah. *Ecology,* **64,** 661–7.

McNaughton, S.J. (1984). Grazing lawns: animals in herds, plant form, and coevolution. *American Naturalist*, **124**, 863–6.

McNaughton, S.J. (1989). Interactions of plants of the field layer with large herbivores. *Symposium of the Zoological Society of London*, **61**, 15–29.

McNaughton, S.J. (1992). The propagation of disturbance in savannas through food webs. *Journal of Vegetation Science*, **3**, 301–14.

Mills, J.N. (1983). Herbivory and seedling establishment in post-fire southern California chaparral. *Oecologia*, **60**, 267–70.

Olff, H., Berendse, F. & Devisser, W. (1994). Changes in nitrogen mineralization, tissue nutrient concentrations and biomass compartmentation after cessation of fertilizer application to mown grassland. *Journal of Ecology*, **82**, 611–20.

Owen-Smith, N. (1988). *Megaherbivores: The Influence of Very Large Herbivores on Ecology*. Cambridge, UK: Cambridge University Press.

Parikesit, P., Larson, D.W. & Matthessears, U. (1995). Impacts of trails on cliff-edge forest structure. *Canadian Journal of Botany – Revue Canadienne De Botanique*, **73**, 943–53.

Pascual, M. & Levin, S.A. (1999). From individuals to population densities: searching for the intermediate scale of nontrivial determinism. *Ecology*, **80**, 2225–36.

Pastor, J., Moen, R. & Cohen, Y. (1997). Spatial heterogeneities, carrying capacity, and feedbacks in animal-landscape interactions. *Journal of Mammalogy*, **78**, 1040–52.

Pastor, J., Dewey, B., Moen, R. *et al.* (1998). Spatial patterns in the moose-forest-soil ecosystem on Isle Royale, Michigan, USA. *Ecological Applications*, **8**, 411–24.

Pastor, J., Cohen, Y. & Moen, R. (1999). Generation of spatial patterns in boreal forest landscapes. *Ecosystems*, **2**, 439–50.

Perry, G.L.W. (2002). Landscapes, space and equilibrium: shifting viewpoints. *Progress in Physical Geography*, **26**, 339–59.

Persson, I.L., Danell, K. & Bergström, R. (2000). Disturbance by large herbivores in boreal forests with special reference to moose. *Annales Zoologici Fennici*, **37**, 251–63.

Pickett, S.T.A. & Cadenasso, M.L. (1995). Landscape ecology: spatial heterogeneity in ecological systems. *Science*, **269**, 331–4.

Pickett, S.T.A., Parker, V.T. & Fiedler, P.L. (1992). The new paradigm in ecology: implications for conservation biology above the species level, In *Conservation Biology: The Theory and Practice of Nature Conservation, Preservation, and Management*, ed. P.L. Fiedler & S.K. Jain. New York: Chapman and Hall, pp. 65–88.

Polis, G.A., Anderson, W.B. & Holt, R.D. (1997). Toward an integration of landscape and food web ecology: the dynamics of spatially subsidized food webs. *Annual Review of Ecology and Systematics*, **28**, 289–316.

Polley, H.W. (1984). Relationships of vegetation and environment in Buffalo Wallows. *American Midland Naturalist*, **112**, 178–86.

Posse, G., Anchorena, J. & Collantes, M.B. (2000). Spatial micro-patterns in the steppe of Tierra del Fuego induced by sheep grazing. *Journal of Vegetation Science*, **11**, 43–50.

Reich, P.B., Peterson, D.W., Wedin, D.A. & Wrage, K. (2001). Fire and vegetation effects on productivity and nitrogen cycling across a forest-grassland continuum. *Ecology*, **82**, 1703–19.

Robbins, C.T. (1983). *Wildlife Feeding and Nutrition*. New York: Academic Press.

Rundel, P.W. (1981). Structural and chemical components of flammability. In *Fire Regimes and Ecosystem Properties*, ed. H.A. Mooney, T.A. Bonnicksen, N.L. Christensen, J.E. Lotan & W.A. Reiners USDA. Forest Service General Technical Report WO-26, pp. 183–207.

Sagara, N. (1995). Association of ectomycorrhizal fungi with decomposed animal wastes in forest habitats – a cleaning symbiosis. *Canadian Journal of Botany – Revue Canadienne De Botanique*, **73**, S1423–33.

Sawyer, T.G., Miller, K.V. & Marchinton, R.L. (1993). Patterns of urination and rub-urination in female white-tailed deer. *Journal of Mammalogy*, **74**, 477–9.

Schneider, D.C. (1998). Applied scaling theory. In *Ecological Scale: Theory and Applications*, ed. D.L. Peterson & V.T. Parker. New York: Columbia University Press, pp. 253–69.

Scoones, I. (1995). Exploiting heterogeneity: habitat use by cattle in dryland Zimbabwe. *Journal of Arid Environments*, **29**, 221–37.

Semmartin, M. & Oesterheld, M. (2001). Effects of grazing pattern and nitrogen availability on primary productivity. *Oecologia*, **126**, 225–30.

Senft, R.L., Coughenour, M.B., Bailey, D.W. *et al.* (1987). Large herbivore foraging and ecological hierarchies. *Bioscience*, **37**, 789–99.

Shipley, L.A., Spalinger, D.E., Gross, J.E., Hobbs, N.T. & Wunder, B.A. (1996). The dynamics and scaling of foraging velocity and encounter rate in mammalian herbivores. *Functional Ecology*, **10**, 234–44.

Skarpe, C. (1992). Dynamics of savanna ecosystems. *Journal of Vegetation Science*, **3**, 293–300.

Sousa, W.P. (1984). The role of disturbance in natural communities. *Annual Review of Ecological Systems*, **15**, 353–91.

Steinauer, E.M. & Collins, S.L. (1995). Effects of urine deposition on small-scale patch structure in prairie vegetation. *Ecology*, **76**, 1195–205.

Steinauer, E.M. & Collins, S.L. (2001). Feedback loops in ecological hierarchies following urine deposition in tallgrass prairie. *Ecology*, **82**, 1319–29.

Stoddart, L.A., Smith, A.D. & Box, T.W. (1975). *Range Management*. New York: McGraw-Hill.

Swank, W.T. (1984). Atmospheric contributions to forest nutrient cycling. *Water Resources Bulletin*, **20**, 313–21.

Taboada, M.A. & Lavado, R.S. (1993). Influence of cattle trampling on soil porosity under alternate dry and ponded conditions. *Soil Use and Management*, **9**, 139–43.

Thrash, I. (1998). Impact of water provision on herbaceous vegetation in Kruger National Park, South Africa. *Journal of Arid Environments*, **38**, 437–50.

Tilman, D. (1994). Competition and biodiversity in spatially structured habitats. *Ecology*, **75**, 2–16.

Towne, E.G. (2000). Prairie vegetation and soil nutrient responses to ungulate carcasses. *Oecologia*, **122**, 232–9.

Turner, G., Romme, W., Gardner, R., O'Neill, R. & Kratz, T. (1993). A revised concept of landscape equilibrium: disturbance and stability on scaled landscapes. *Landscape Ecology*, **8**, 213–27.

Van Buskirk, J. & Ostfeld, R.S. (1998). Habitat heterogeneity, dispersal, and local risk of exposure to Lyme disease. *Ecological Applications*, **8**, 365–78.

van de Koppel, J., Rietkerk, M., van Langevelde, F. *et al.* (2002). Spatial heterogeneity and irreversible vegetation change in semiarid grazing systems. *American Naturalist*, **159**, 209–18.

Vinton, M.A., Hartnett, D.C., Finck, E.J. & Briggs, J.M. (1993). Interactive effects of fire, bison grazing and plant community composition in the tall grass prairie. *American Midland Naturalist*, **129**, 10–18.

Wallis De Vries, M.F., Laca, E.A. & Demment, M.W. (1999). The importance of scale of patchiness for selectivity in grazing herbivores. *Oecologia*, **121**, 355–63.

White, P.S. & Jentsch, A. (2001). The search for generality in studies of disturbance and ecosystem dynamics. *Progress in Botany*, **62**, 399–449.

Williams, P.H. & Haynes, R.J. (1994). Comparison of initial wetting pattern, nutrient concentrations in soil solution and the fate of N-15-labeled urine in sheep and cattle urine patch areas of pasture soil. *Plant and Soil*, **162**, 49–59.

Williams, P.H. & Haynes, R.J. (1997). Recovery of N derived from 15N-labelled grass/clover residues recently immobilised urine 15N or native soil organic N by a wheat crop following cultivation of a pasture soil. *Agriculture Ecosystems and Environment*, **63**, 67–72.

Wilmshurst, J.F., Fryxell, J.M. & Bergman, C.M. (2000). The allometry of patch selection in ruminants. *Proceedings of the Royal Society of London, Series B – Biological Sciences*, **267**, 345–9.

Zacheis, A., Hupp, J.W. & Ruess, R.W. (2001). Effects of migratory geese on plant communities of an Alaskan salt marsh. *Journal of Ecology*, **89**, 57–71.

Zacheis, A., Ruess, R.W. & Hupp, J.W. (2002). Nitrogen dynamics in an Alaskan salt marsh following spring use by geese. *Oecologia*, **130**, 600–8.

Zimmerman, G.T. & Neuenschwander, L.F. (1984). Livestock grazing influences on community structure, fire intensity, and fire frequency within the Douglas-Fir Ninebark habitat type. *Journal of Range Management*, **37**, 104–10.

The roles of large herbivores in ecosystem nutrient cycles

JOHN PASTOR, YOSEF COHEN AND
N. THOMPSON HOBBS

INTRODUCTION

The question of how herbivores control various ecosystem processes has had a long history in modern ecology. In a now much-cited paper, Hairston *et al.* (1960) proposed that in the absence of predators, herbivore populations increase to the limit set by their food supply and thus control net or actual productivity and energy flow. With the addition of predators, herbivore populations become controlled from above; plant productivity is then released from direct control by herbivores and instead is limited by abiotic processes such as climate. These ideas have been developed further by Oksanen and colleagues (Oksanen *et al.* 1981, Oksanen 1983, 1988). In order to simplify the concepts and models, these studies have ignored the way that the cycling of nutrients between decomposers and higher trophic levels limits net primary productivity in most ecosystems, and the many mechanisms by which herbivores alter nutrient flows through decomposers and soils.

Early recognition of the roles of herbivores in regulating nutrient cycles focused on phytophagous insects (Mattson & Addy 1975) or phytoplanktivorous zooplankton (Kitchell *et al.* 1979). Perhaps this was because of their ubiquity, rapid population growth rates, high turnover rates and because (at least in the case of zooplankton) they consume most of the primary production (Macfadyen 1964). With the exception of large herds in grasslands (Sinclair & Norton-Griffiths 1979) and microtine populations in tundra (Schultz 1964), the possibility that mammals could also regulate

Large Herbivore Ecology, Ecosystem Dynamics and Conservation, ed. K. Danell, P. Duncan, R. Bergström & J. Pastor. Published by Cambridge University Press. © Cambridge University Press 2006.

Table 10.1. *Direct and indirect mechanisms by which large mammalian herbivores affect nutrient cycling and productivity in ecosystems*

Direct Effects	Indirect Effects (Consequences)
Consume parts of plants	Cause reallocation of carbon and nutrients within the plant; possibly stimulate production of carbon or nitrogen based secondary compounds
Consume leaves or twigs and excrete urine and faeces	Shift arrays of litter to urine and faeces with faster turnover rates than plant parts
Eat species with high N, low lignin, and low secondary compound concentrations	Shift species composition to those species that produce slowly decomposing litter of slow turnover rate
Kill plants	Reduce plant biomass, increase litter inputs to soil, including woody litter with slow turnover rates

nutrient cycles was generally ignored for quite some time. This was because they typically comprise a negligible proportion of the nutrient content and biomass of an ecosystem, and consume a relatively small proportion of its productivity (Wiener 1975). Yet recent theoretical (DeAngelis 1992, Holland *et al.* 1992, Loreau 1995, de Mazancourt *et al.* 1998, Pastor & Cohen 1997, Cohen *et al.* 2000) and empirical (Schimel *et al.* 1986, Hobbs *et al.* 1991, Pastor *et al.* 1993, McNaughton *et al.* 1997, Ritchie *et al.* 1998) studies show that large mammalian herbivores can alter rates of nutrient cycling far out of proportion to their nutrient contents or even consumption rates. This suggests that the effects of large mammalian herbivores on nutrient cycles and productivity are magnified through positive and negative feedbacks with other trophic levels, including decomposers (McNaughton & Georgiadis 1986, Bryant *et al.* 1991, Huntly 1991, Jefferies *et al.* 1994, Hobbs 1996, Pastor *et al.* 1997, Adler *et al.* 2001, Wardle & Bardgett 2004).

Large mammalian herbivores directly affect nutrient cycles through a number of mechanisms that have a variety of indirect effects or consequences (Table 10.1). First, there are response mechanisms internal to the plants. Plants that are browsed or grazed often reallocate carbon and nutrient resources in response to the intensity of grazing/browsing and the particular tissue consumed, processes that are treated in more detail elsewhere in this volume (see Chapter 4). The intensity of browsing or grazing may also depend on carbon or nitrogen based secondary compounds, and consumption may (or may not) stimulate the subsequent production of such compounds. This phenomenon is beyond the scope of this paper, but the interested reader is referred to Bryant and Kuropat (1980), Coley *et al.* (1985), Bryant *et al.* (1991, 1992), and Stamp (2003) for an introduction to this literature.

Large mammalian herbivores enhance local soil nutrient availability when they gather food over a wide area and concentrate it in small spots in dung, urine and carcasses. These concentrated nutrient spots may persist for several years or more and are reflected in higher nutrient concentrations in surrounding vegetation (Ruess & McNaughton 1987, Ruess & Seagle 1994, Danell *et al.* 2002). On the other hand, mammalian herbivores forage selectively on the most nutritious plant parts and plant species. This exerts a long-term and widespread selection pressure on the plant community and alters the arrays of plant litter returned to the soil. As a result, plant litter quantity and quality is usually reduced. Soil nitrogen mineralization rate, or the rate by which microbes convert organic nitrogen in plant residues and humus to inorganic forms available for plant uptake, then eventually declines (Pastor & Naiman 1992). Consequently, large mammalian herbivores can either accelerate (e.g. Hobbs *et al.* 1991, Frank & Evans 1997, McNaughton *et al.* 1997) or retard (e.g. Pastor *et al.* 1993, Pastor & Cohen 1997, Ritchie *et al.* 1998) rates of nutrient cycling, depending on the relative balance of these processes.

It is important to recognize at the outset that any combination or all of these mechanisms operate simultaneously in all ecosystems but at different spatial scales and at different rates. It follows that conclusions about the roles of herbivores depend on the scale of observation: experimental results obtained at fine scales (e.g. a urine spot) may differ in fundamental ways from those obtained at coarse scales (e.g. the landscape) and over short compared with long time scales (Sirotnak & Huntly 2000). Furthermore, the greater mobility of herbivores compared with the rate of spread of populations of their forage species can generate spatial patterns of productivity and nutrient cycling rates across landscapes (Ruess & Seagle 1994, Pastor *et al.* 1998, 1999a, Adler *et al.* 2001, see also Chapter 11). Therefore, herbivores not only respond to the spatial scales of variation in nutrient availability and productivity, they can sometimes be the dominant factor causing them. Understanding the interactions between herbivores and the nutrient cycles and net primary productivity of ecosystems requires simultaneous consideration of all these processes at the multiple scales over which they occur.

One of the essential features of the interaction between large herbivores and plants is that the chemistry of large mammalian herbivores is very different from that of their food. Nutrient concentrations of mammalian biomass are higher than that of their forage. For example, the whole body nitrogen content of large mammalian herbivores is typically between 2.5 % and 3%, depending on fat content (Robbins 1983), but in the forage only newly expanded green leaves of deciduous, herbaceous or graminoid plants have concentrations this high, and only then when soil nitrogen availability does not limit plant growth (Larcher 1995). When soil nitrogen availability is limiting, which is usually the case, nitrogen concentrations in green leaves and in evergreen needles can fall as low as 1%–2% and in woody shoots nitrogen concentrations can be as low as 0.5% (Larcher 1995). Consequently, because the stoichiometries of herbivores and their forage differ widely, one gram of forage cannot simply be converted into one gram of herbivore biomass. These differences between the chemistries of the forage that herbivores consume compared with that of their own flesh necessitate a variety of behavioural and digestive adaptations, such as selective foraging and rumen vs. hindgut fermentative digestive systems (White 1993). Although these adaptations allow the herbivore to convert forage into flesh, they also result in a variety of long-term consequences for ecosystem nutrient cycles. These ecosystem-level effects are related to the differences in turnover rates and chemistries of plant species or plant parts that the herbivore selects compared with those that are avoided, and to the much faster turnover rates of hindgut fermenters compared with ruminants. These differences in organism chemistry conspire to produce non-linear dynamics of nutrient cycling and require careful theoretical and empirical analysis.

Forage in turn contains high proportions of high molecular weight/low nutrient carbohydrates such as secondary compounds, cellulose and lignin. These compounds are unpalatable and difficult for the herbivore to digest (Bryant et al. 1991, 1992), and decrease decay rates of litter (Melillo et al. 1983, Flanagan & Van Cleve 1983). Also, because they are energetically costly to produce, they decrease the relative growth rates of plants (Coley et al. 1985, Bryant et al. 1989). The correlations amongst these plant traits that simultaneously control palatability, digestibility, decomposition and relative growth (Grime et al. 1996) underlie many of the indirect consequences of herbivore foraging behaviour listed in Table 10.1.

We will explore the relationship between herbivores and the production and chemistry of their forage by reviewing three particularly well-studied, contrasting case studies: the grazing ecosystem of the Serengeti; the moose-boreal forest browsing system; and the mixed grazing-browsing system of reindeer in the tundra. We focus on these three case studies because plant productivity, nutrient cycles and herbivore impacts are especially well documented with regard to them and because they represent differing responses of ecosystem processes to herbivores. We will then explore some of the underlying reasons why large mammals affect nutrient cycles in such contrasting ways in these ecosystems. We will conclude with some speculations about the implications of the phenomena for evolution and conservation.

THE SERENGETI: INCREASED NUTRIENT CYCLING IN A GRAZING ECOSYSTEM

The Serengeti includes a vast landscape defined by the migration patterns of large mammalian herbivores who move seasonally along gradients of green vegetation. Interactions between large herbivores and plants in this ecosystem offer the canonical example of how grazers increase rates of nutrient cycling in grasslands (Sinclair & Norton-Griffiths 1979, McNaughton et al. 1997). The landscape is divided into three parts: the southernmost Serengeti Plains of low rainfall supporting short grass species; the western Serengeti of intermediate rainfall and grasses of moderate height; and the northern Serengeti of taller grass species and higher rainfall. There are at least six large herbivore species resident in the Serengeti, of which the zebra (*Equus burchelli*), wildebeest (*Connochaetes taurinus*) and Thomson's gazelle (*Gazella thomsonii*) are the major ones. These and other species migrate between the three subregions of the Serengeti following seasonal rainfall. Within each subregion (but especially in the southern Plains), successional waves of these herbivores graze different plant species in turn, but in aggregate the herbivore trophic level consumes almost all net primary production in the proportions that it is distributed amongst the different plant species (McNaughton 1985).

The zebra, wildebeest and gazelle present interesting contrasts in digestive physiology and foraging strategies (Bell 1971) that underlie interactions with plants and define their aggregate effects on nutrient cycles (McNaughton 1985, McNaughton et al. 1997). The problem presented to all herbivores is that the plant cell wall, consisting mainly of cellulose shielded by lignin, protects the more nutritious cytoplasm where the protein resides. Ruminants such as wildebeest and gazelle, solve this problem by fermenting the cellulose and lignin in the rumen followed by repeated regurgitation and mastication in the mouth. These chemical and mechanical processes degrade the structure of the cell wall and increase the specific gravity of ingested particles. When sufficient break-down has occurred, the plant material sinks in the rumen and is passed into the stomach where the protein contents are subsequently extracted with a high degree of efficiency. Ruminants thus maximize the efficiency of protein absorption by first breaking down the cell walls that shield them, but at the expense of a slow turnover rate of the food, the necessity to stop eating until the rumen can be emptied and high maintenance require-ments of the rumen. The rate of passage of the food with its residual nutrients through the gut and back to the soil is limited by the rate of cell wall breakdown in the rumen, and higher cell wall contents lead to slower passage. What is passed to the soil as faecal material is often of lower nutrient concentration than the forage, the proteins being very effectively assimilated in the stomach. High cell wall contents in the food prevent the ruminant from assimilating enough protein for maintenance of the rumen, and so the ruminant must forage selectively on plant species or plant parts that have thin cell walls and high nutrient contents, such as leaves or small diameter shoots or twigs.

In contrast to ruminants, hindgut fermenters, such as the zebra, ferment cellulose and lignin in the colon and large intestine after extrac-tion of protein in the stomach. The hindgut fermenter does not have the advantage of the ruminant in preprocessing the cell wall to enhance efficient extraction of proteins. Hindgut fermenters are less efficient in assimilating protein than ruminants. But, unlike the ruminants they pass food rapidly through the gut and, consequently, their total daily intake is not nearly so constrained as the intake of ruminants. Thus, even though the hindgut fermenter is only two-thirds as efficient as a ruminant in assimilating protein, it can process twice as much food per unit time because it does not have to wait for a rumen to be emptied (Bell 1971). Therefore, hindgut fermenters assimilate protein at four-thirds the rate of ruminants but also pass relatively less digested food through their gut to the soil (Bell 1971).

In the Serengeti grasslands, the quality of food presented to these herbivores varies vertically down through the plant canopy. Zebras, which form the first wave of the three herbivores, eat mainly the abundant graminoid stems that are highest in the canopy and have the high cell wall constituents. Because zebras have a hindgut digestive system, much of the protein in this material passes through relatively undigested at a rapid rate. But this grazing on upper layers by zebra opens up the leafy layer lower on the grass stem to the ruminant wildebeest, who arrive after the zebra have moved to new, ungrazed patches of plants. The leafy material consumed by wildebeest has relatively less cell wall contents than the stem-dominated fraction consumed by zebra and hence is more easily broken down in the rumen, thereby exposing the proteins relatively quickly. This sequential foraging by zebras and then wildebeest exposes the lowermost layer of the plant canopy, consisting mainly of nutritious dicotyledons and emerging grass tillers, to the gazelles that follow in the grazing sequence.

The different foraging strategies of zebra, wildebeest and gazelle are also partly determined by body size. Average body mass of zebra is 360 kg while that of wildebeest is approximately 180 kg and that of the diminutive gazelle only about 20 kg (Kingdon 1982). Relative metabolic rate (metabolic rate per unit body mass) declines with increasing mass because of the proportionally greater amount of skeletal tissue of low metabolic rate in larger animals (Sterner & Elser 2002). Therefore, the relative metabolic rate of zebra is lowest. This low metabolic rate allows it to eat the less nutritious graminoid stems, thereby opening the canopy and allowing access to the more nutritious green material required by the smaller wildebeest and gazelle with higher relative metabolic rates.

Thus, each successive wave of herbivores exposes food for the next, whose digestive system and body size is suited for processing the plants that remain. Although the zebra, wildebeest and gazelle select the most apparent plant species or plant parts exposed by the previous wave of herbivores, the herbivore assemblage as a whole consumes almost all above-ground production and thus forages on each type of food in proportion to its abundance. Selective foraging by individual herbivore species thus disappears at the aggregate trophic level and so overall there is no selective foraging pressure on the plant community. These waves of successive herbivores feeding lower in the exposed canopy result in the formation of a relatively uniform 'grazing lawn' (McNaughton 1984).

Early in the growing season on the Serengeti Plains, the nitrogen concentration of the young shoots that these species consume is relatively high – generally over 3%, but it declines as the growing season advances because of increased grazing pressure and increased drought (Georgiadis et al. 1989). Because of this seasonal decline in nutritional quality of their forage, the animals migrate west and north to areas of higher rainfall in search of taller grass with higher nitrogen concentrations. With the renewal of the rainy season in the south, the grass there recovers from previous grazing and the animals migrate from the north back to the southern Plains.

The search for and consumption of high nitrogen forage results in manuring of the soils through excretion from the herbivores. With diets as high in nitrogen as 3%, the animal must convert ammonium formed during metabolism of the protein to urea and excrete it in urine before it becomes toxic (Robbins *et al.* 1974, Mould & Robbins 1981, Robbins 1983, Hobbs 1996). Nitrogen in excreted urine is readily available to plants (Doak 1952, Floate 1970, Ruess & McNaughton 1987, Seagle *et al.* 1992). The dung derived from this green plant material also has a relatively high concentration of nitrogen, sometimes even higher than the dead plant litter – approximately 1.6% compared with 1.2% for leaf and stem litter (Ruess & McNaughton 1987). The slightly higher nitrogen concentration of dung compared with plant litter reflects the high metabolism of simple carbohydrates by the microbial community of the ruminant digestive system, which concentrates the remaining nitrogen. Moreover, the plant particles contained in dung are orders of magnitude smaller than those in plant litter. This small particle size facilitates microbial attack and mineralization in the soil. Soils amended with this dung have higher nitrogen mineralization rates than soils amended with litter alone (Ruess & McNaughton 1987).

The high nitrogen availability in soils in turn supports the continuous production of high protein forage. In fact, the high supply of forage where the animals are grazing depends in part on rapid compensatory regrowth of the above-ground plant parts (McNaughton 1983, 1984, 1985). The physiology of compensatory regrowth of browsed or grazed plants and reallocation of carbon and nutrients amongst plant parts is treated in more detail elsewhere in this volume (see Chapter 4). But it is pertinent to point out that compensatory regrowth is only possible if nutrients are available from the soil to support it (Georgiadis *et al.* 1989). Therefore, the stimulation of nitrogen availability by grazers in the Serengeti may be a necessary condition for compensatory regrowth of forage and stability of the system (McNaughton *et al.* 1997). The evolutionary implications are interesting and will be treated below.

The only way that grazing can permanently increase rates of nitrogen cycling is if it increases plant growth rates by subsidizing them with increased nitrogen availability in the soil, either by increasing transfers from plant material to urine and faeces (McNaughton *et al.* 1997) or by importing nitrogen from outside the ecosystem (de Mazancourt *et al.* 1998). Not only must the herbivore increase soil nitrogen turnover rate, but nitrogen must also be retained in the system and not exported in herbivore biomass or leached from the soil (Pastor & Cohen 1997, de Mazancourt *et al.* 1998). Although there are other losses of nitrogen from this system via fire and inputs via nitrogen fixation, at present how herbivores affect these inputs and outputs is unknown. The ability of the herbivore trophic level in the Serengeti to increase nitrogen cycling across all ecosystems is predicated on the assumption that transfers of nitrogen between southern, northern, and western portions of their range are in steady state. But if they are not, then there must be a non-linearity or threshold beyond which too much removal of nitrogen from an area will slow nitrogen cycling rates (de Mazancourt *et al.* 1998).

Lest we give the impression that the Serengeti grasslands form the norm for East Africa, we wish to call attention to a paper by Bell (1982), in which he makes the suggestion that the positive effects of grazers on productivity and nitrogen cycling in the Serengeti, and similar systems of East Africa, may be facilitated by the underlying rich sub-soils from volcanic ash. In other parts of East Africa, where the sub-soils are highly weathered, nutrient-poor and have low ion exchange capacity to retain mineral (plant-available) forms of nutrients, grasslands are temporarily created when elephants (*Eluphus africanus*) remove trees by browsing or simply pushing them over (Laws *et al.* 1975, Bell 1982). But the poor quality and unproductive grasslands on these highly weathered soils cannot support a high herbivore biomass which can then further enhance nitrogen cycling as in the Serengeti, and so the system eventually reverts to woodland, which is then reoccupied by elephants and the cycle repeats itself.

THE MOOSE IN THE BOREAL FOREST: DECREASED NUTRIENT CYCLING IN A BROWSING SYSTEM

Large mammalian herbivores in boreal regions are all ruminants belonging to the order Artiodactyla, of which the signature species is the circumpolar moose (*Alces alces*). Hindgut fermenters consist mainly of small mammal lagomorphs such as snowshoe hare (*Lepus americanus*) and mountain hare (*Lepus timidus*), and rodents such as beaver (*Castor canadensis*) as well as a variety of voles and mice. This system contrasts greatly with the grazing system of the Serengeti. First, all large and most small mammalian herbivores are browsers rather than grazers. Second, both the quality and productivity of forage is much lower than in grasslands, especially during the long winter months when the preferred forage for all mammalian herbivores consists of twigs of deciduous species, although a few conifers such as balsam fir (*Abies balsamea*) in North America and Scots pine (*Pinus sylvestris*) in Scandinavia and Siberia are also browsed. Spruce (*Picea* spp.) is almost never browsed to any great extent by these mammals. None of these herbivores can survive for extended periods on exclusive diets of slowly growing evergreens, with poorly digestible leaves and shoots of low nutrient, high cell wall and toxic secondary compound contents (Bryant & Kuropat 1980). Consequently, there is a strong selective pressure on deciduous species by the entire mammalian herbivore community. This selective foraging is especially striking in the foraging strategy of moose (Pastor & Danell 2003). Moose browse the deciduous species, especially of the genera *Salix* and *Populus*, far out of proportion to their abundance, but browse conifers in proportions lower or equal to their abundance (Bryant & Chapin 1986, Shipley *et al.* 1998), except when rare (Brandner *et al.* 1990).

Although in the summer the diet of moose consists of relatively nutritious and digestible leaves, the low digestibility of winter browse presents severe problems for the moose's energy balance. Moose maximize energy intake per unit time by browsing larger shoots, especially of deciduous species (Belovsky 1978, Bryant & Kuropat 1980, Spalinger & Hobbs 1992, Shipley *et al.* 1998). As bite size increases, so does energy intake rate, but digestibility decreases because larger shoots contain higher proportions of lignified woody material (Vivås & Saether 1987). Moose therefore optimize selection of shoot diameter to maximize energy intake rate within the constraints of decreasing digestibility; the optimal shoot diameter selected across a wide range of species appears to be between 3–5 mm, depending on the plant species (Shipley *et al.* 1998), or approximately 3.5 g per bite (Risenhoover 1987, Gross *et al.* 1993, Pastor *et al.* 1999b, and others reviewed in Renecker & Schwartz 1998). These bites are concentrated on apical meristems of the few preferred plant species. Moose usually take only 20% of bites available at any given spot, or 1–2 bites per individual plants (Shipley *et al.* 1998), except when a food species is rare, whereupon it is heavily and repeatedly browsed (Brandner *et al.* 1990). But by concentrating their impact on the growing tips of a few plant species, moose have a great ability to affect growth of plants, competitive abilities between browsed and adjacent unbrowsed plants, plant succession and ecosystem properties.

The browsed plants, especially those of preferred birch, aspen and willow, respond with compensatory regrowth of twigs, an increasingly branched morphology and changes in tissue chemistry. Moderate browsing increases long shoot dry mass, leaf dry mass, leaf number, leaf area, and chlorophyll and nitrogen content of leaves on *Betula pendula* and *B. pubescens* compared with slightly browsed trees (Danell *et al.* 1985, Bergström & Danell 1987). Some short shoots on moderately browsed birch develop into more nutritious long shoots (Danell *et al.* 1985). The frequency of branched shoots, and hence shoot density, also increases (Bergström & Danell 1987). Senn and Haukioja (1994) show that these growth responses primarily result from removal of the apical buds with subsequent reduction in hormonal suppression of buds lower on the stem. Regrown shoots of browsed birch have higher leaf and stem chemical quality and density than unbrowsed shoots, and there is a greater proportion of shoots, within reach of the moose (Bergström 1984, Danell & Huss-Danell 1985, Danell *et al.* 1985, 2003). Therefore, previously browsed birch have a higher probability of being browsed again than unbrowsed or slightly browsed birch. Thus, the compensatory growth response of birch to browsing establishes a positive feedback loop between birch and moose that results in even greater consumption in subsequent years.

Although the total dry matter production of an individual plant is often not decreased outright by browsing (Danell *et al.* 1985, Bergström & Danell 1987, Hjältén *et al.* 1993), height growth of browsed seedlings and suckers is often curtailed in favour of increased production of new side shoots or new ramets. Defoliation of *B. pubescens* by leaf-stripping during the summer also decreases height growth by almost 50% (Bergström & Danell 1987, Hjältén *et al.* 1993), presumably because of decreased shoot growth due to reductions in photosynthate. Height growth of *P. sylvestris* was also similarly decreased when 100% of current shoots were clipped (Edenius *et al.* 1995).

In boreal forests, the suppression of height growth by increased browsing intensity increases mortality of individual plants (Danell *et al.* 2003). In boreal forests, the more preferred and shade-intolerant deciduous plant species have higher rates of mortality compared with the less preferred conifers (Krefting 1974, Risenhoover & Maass 1987, Heinen & Sharik 1990, McInnes *et al.* 1992, Edenius *et al.* 1995, Danell *et al.* 2003). This suggests that browsed individuals die because light limitations increase when they are overtopped by adjacent unbrowsed individuals (Pastor *et al.* 1993). However, this association between browsing and shade intolerance may not hold outside the boreal forest – species of maple (*Acer*) and oak (*Quercus*) which are shade tolerant seem able to tolerate browsing quite well even in the under-storey (see Chapter 6).

Nonetheless, the combination of browsing intolerance and shade intolerance amongst preferred boreal species causes rapid changes in boreal regions in response to mammalian browsing pressure. Numerous studies comparing plant community composition inside and outside exclosures have shown that the abundances of preferred, shade-intolerant deciduous species decline as they are replaced by unpreferred species, especially *Picea* (Krefting 1974, Snyder & Janke 1976, Risenhoover & Maass 1987, McInnes *et al.* 1992, Thompson *et al.* 1992). In North America, increased moose population density consistently shifts an aspen-birch-spruce-fir community to a more open and unbrowsed spruce (*Picea glauca, P. mariana*) community with an under-storey of heavily browsed preferred species (see previous references). In many areas, unbrowsed spruce is often the only species able to grow above browse height (Bryant & Chapin 1986, McInnes *et al.* 1992, Thompson & Curran 1993).

Browsing also generally decreases plant sexual reproduction. The number of female catkins (and hence seed production) is reduced in *B. pendula* and *B. pubescens* with higher browsing intensity, although mean viable seed mass increased slightly, suggesting partial compensation in potential seed germination success to the reduction of seed number (Bergström & Danell 1987). Beaked hazelnut (*Corylus cornuta*), an important winter forage species for moose in North America, usually does not set seed when browsed (Trottier 1981). Browsing also decreases cone production in *P. sylvestris*, especially with severe browsing on productive sites (Edenius *et al.* 1995).

These long-term successional shifts in plant community composition towards unpreferred species greatly depress rates of ecosystem properties such as net primary productivity (McInnes *et al.* 1992) and nitrogen cycling (Pastor *et al.* 1993). The decline in productivity occurs for two reasons. First, unpreferred species grow more slowly than preferred species (Danell *et al.* 1985, Bryant & Chapin 1986, McInnes *et al.* 1992, Pastor & Naiman 1992). Second, unpreferred species have litter that is difficult to decompose because of low nitrogen and high lignin contents, the same reason why moose, with microbially mediated ruminant digestion, avoid them (Bryant & Chapin 1986, Pastor & Naiman 1992). The same chemical properties of tissues that cause moose to forage selectively also depress soil nitrogen mineralization by as much as 50% (Pastor *et al.* 1993, 1998, Pastor & Cohen 1997). Thus, foraging decisions made by moose at the individual plant level are reflected at the ecosystem level because the same plant chemical properties affect both digestive rate and nutrient cycling.

The decrease in nitrogen cycling because of the browsing-induced shift towards unpreferred species with poorer quality litter may be partly offset by occasional increased nitrogen concentrations in green leaves (Danell & Huss-Danell 1985) and litter (Kielland & Bryant 1998), and faster decay rates of litter (Irons *et al.* 1991) from browsed individuals compared to unbrowsed individuals in the same species. It is currently not known to what extent browsing changes litter quality of browsing other species. But in the long run, this does not appear to completely offset the larger differences between unpreferred and preferred species in litter decay rates, so long-term browsing-induced shifts in species composition probably eventually outweigh this compensatory adjustment of litter quality within a browsed species.

This long-term decrease in the rate of nitrogen cycling coincident upon species replacement is not offset by deposition and decay of faecal material. First, the amount of nitrogen deposited by moose (or most other mammalian herbivores in boreal forests) is small compared to the deposition of plant litter (Pastor *et al.* 1996). Second, faecal pellets egested after digestion of twigs are extremely low in nitrogen – being mainly sawdust in which almost all nitrogen has been extracted by the efficient ruminant digestive system – and in fact mineralize what nitrogen remains more slowly than soil from locations whose vegetation has not been altered by moose (Pastor *et al.* 1993). Thus, if anything, deposition of dung produced from woody forage by browsers may even exacerbate the decrease in nitrogen availability caused by successional replacement of forage species of highly digestible and decomposable tissues with unpreferred species.

Such effects on ecosystem properties are widely distributed across the landscape in characteristic patterns: patches of high browse availability are heavily browsed, allowing unbrowsed conifers to invade and create coincident patches of low nitrogen availability (Pastor *et al.* 1998). Moose must therefore contend not only with changes at individual plant levels, but also the effect of these plant responses on the distribution of food across the landscape and the cycling of limiting nutrients to support that food. Theoretically, some foraging strategies may produce a landscape in which the spatial distribution of food leads to a negative energy or nutrient balance imposed on the animal as it searches for food, leading to local extinction (Moen *et al.* 1998).

REINDEER IN TUNDRA: MIXED EFFECTS ON NUTRIENT CYCLING

Recent research appears to show that reindeer (*Rangifer tarandus*) in tundra systems of Fennoscandinavia may have mixed effects on nutrient cycling. Reindeer sometimes increase rates of nitrogen cycling and productivity (Olofsson *et al.* 2001, Olofsson & Oksanen 2002) and sometimes decrease it (Grellmann 2002, Stark & Grellmann 2002, Stark *et al.* 2003). The tundra ecosystem is composed of graminoids whose litter decays rapidly, ericaceous shrubs whose litter decomposes more slowly, and lichens and mosses whose litter decomposes most slowly (Hobbie 1996, Olofsson & Oksanen 2002). Lichens comprise the major food of reindeer, especially in winter (Väre *et al.* 1996). Because reindeer eat nutrient-poor lichens, they may form an exception to the hypothesis of Pastor and Naiman (1992) and Grime *et al.* (1996) that food preference by boreal herbivores is correlated with decay rates of the plant litter (Stark *et al.* 2000). Therefore, reindeer may increase nitrogen mineralization rates in soil by consuming recalcitrant materials and shifting litter quality to dominance by more nutrient-rich and easily decomposable litter (Stark *et al.* 2000), which appears unusual amongst mammalian herbivores. Trampling of shrubs and mosses on the summer range by reindeer may also increase dominance of graminoids with high quality litter, thereby also enhancing nitrogen mineralization and nitrogen cycling (Bråthens & Oksanen 2001, Olofsson & Oksanen 2002, see also Chapter 9 for discussion of the effects of trampling by large herbivores on ecosystems).

In contrast to their stimulation of nitrogen mineralization on their summer range, reindeer decrease rates of nutrient cycling and productivity on their winter range, partly because the nitrogen deposited in urea and faeces on the winter range may simply be leached from the system during spring snowmelt and thus exported from the ecosystem before plant uptake begins (Grellmann 2002, Stark & Grellmann 2002). In addition, by removing lichens, which comprise the bulk of their winter diet, reindeer expose soil biota to drier microclimates which may inhibit decay during the ensuing summer (Stark *et al.* 2000). Reindeer may also export nitrogen during migration through their wintering grounds on the way to their summer ranges (Stark & Grellmann 2002). Thus, reindeer may represent an intermediate case between a purely grazing, migratory system (as in the Serengeti) and a purely non-migratory, browsing system (as in the moose example).

WHEN IS NUTRIENT CYCLING AND PRODUCTIVITY ENHANCED AND WHEN IS IT DECREASED?

The Serengeti and the boreal forest represent two poles of how large mammalian herbivores affect nutrient cycles. The first is a grazing system where a wide diversity of hindgut fermenters and ruminants consume almost all above-ground vegetation and, by converting it into faeces and urine, increase nitrogen availability and hence productivity. The second is a browsing system where a few large herbivores (mainly ruminants) select-ively forage on the growing tips of a few preferred deciduous plant species whose tissues are lowest in lignin. This accelerates replacement by un-browsed conifers with low litter quality, which in turn depresses soil nitrogen availability and hence productivity. Other systems seem to fit the Serengeti grazing example, e.g. bison on Yellowstone grasslands (Coughenour 1991, Frank & Evans 1997, see also Chapter 11), bison and cattle on the Great Plains (Hobbs et al. 1991, Holland et al. 1992, Shariff et al. 1994, Biondini et al. 1998), or lemmings in the tundra (Schultz 1964, McKendrick et al. 1980). Alternatively, other systems fit the boreal forest browsing example, e.g. deer in temperate forests (Ritchie et al. 1998) or ungulate browsers in South African brushland (du Toit 1991). Elk (Cervus elaphus) appear to increase nitrogen cycling and productivity when they graze in grasslands (Frank & Evans 1997, Singer & Schoenecker 2003), but decrease it when they browse in forests (Singer & Schoenecker 2003), an example to which we shall return shortly.

Mixed effects in the same ecosystem are also possible, as in the case of reindeer in tundra reviewed above. In addition, Sirotnak and Huntly (2000) found that voles grazing in Yellowstone National Park grasslands increased nitrogen mineralization in the short term by depositing faeces and urine. However, in the long term nitrogen mineralization declined as selective grazing by voles on the more palatable plant species altered species composition to decreased dominance by nitrogen fixing legumes, and dominance by unpalatable and slowly decomposing plants. The recal-citrant soil organic pool increased as a result of these long-term effects. This study is interesting for showing both stimulation and depression of nitrogen cycling by a herbivore but at different time scales.

Ritchie et al. (1998) term these two scenarios of herbivore-ecosystem interactions the *nutrient accelerating* and *nutrient decelerating* scenarios, respectively. It is an interesting question, and one worthy of further research, as to how such a dichotomy between grazing (accelerating) and browsing (decelerating) systems arises in the first place. One might simply accept grazing and browsing systems as fundamentally two distinct modes of the roles of large mammalian herbivores in controlling ecosystem properties, but this seems unsatisfactory to us. De Mazancourt et al. (1998) suggest that herbivores increase or decrease rates of nutrient cycling depending on the quantity of nutrients they import to or export from a system. This is an interesting hypothesis, worthy and conducive of further experimentation. Essentially, they suggest that herbivores determine boundary conditions of nutrient fluxes through ecosystems. This can certainly affect equilibrium nutrient cycling rates, but it is unclear without further experimental studies how this affects trajectories far from equilibrium. Certainly the effect of altering inputs and outputs to and from the ecosystem depends to some extent on the magnitudes of these fluxes relative to the magnitudes of internal cycles, and the strengths of sinks for nutrients within the ecosystem. Singer and Schoenecker (2003) suggest that perhaps the effects of herbivores are mediated partly through their biomass densities and therefore through bulk consumption rates, and that greater herbivore biomass potentially leads to decreases in nutrient cycling rates, especially if the nutrients which are incorporated into herbivore biomass are exported via migration. This is plausible if for no other reason than that, to a first approximation, consumption is proportional to biomass density. We have already noted above that differences in body size, which contribute to biomass density, must be taken into account when making cross-system comparisons. But not all data support this conclusion – ungulate grazing increases nitrogen mineralization rates in both Yellowstone and Serengeti grasslands despite a two-fold difference in herbivore biomass densities (Frank et al. 2000). Clearly, additional factors must also play a role in determining whether herbivores increase or decrease nutrient cycling rates and productivity.

We wish instead to suggest an additional and plausible set of positive feedbacks between herbivores, plant tissue chemistry and soil properties to account for the dichotomous responses of ecosystems to herbivore consumption. This set of feedbacks may force systems into either mode. The basis for this set of feedbacks is the observation by Hobbs (1996) that nitrogen excreted in faeces increases linearly with respect to forage nitrogen concentration, while nitrogen excreted in urine increases quadratically over a wide range of body sizes (Fig. 10.1; original equations for these surfaces are given as Eq. (7) and (8) in the appendix to Hobbs (1996); see Chapter 9 for further elaboration of these equations). Setting Eqs. (7) and (8) from Hobbs (1996) equal to each other yields a critical plant nitrogen concentration in the relatively narrow range of 1.3%–1.7% over a wide range of herbivore body masses (this is easily seen in Fig. 10.1 where the two planes cross). Therefore, there is a critical nitrogen concentration in the forage above which mammalian herbivores excrete nitrogen primarily as urea in order to remove excess nitrogen from their system; this urea is readily available to plants. When consuming forage below this value,

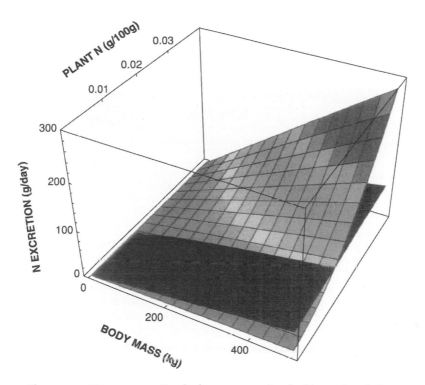

Figure 10.1. Nitrogen excretion by large mammalian herbivores in relation to body mass and plant nitrogen concentration (original equations in the appendix of Hobbs 1996; also see text and Chapter 9 for elaboration). The surface of faecal excretion is in black and that of urinary excretion is grey-tone. Note that the two surfaces cross with a very narrow range of plant nitrogen concentration around 1.5% for a wide range of body sizes.

mammalian herbivores must retain as much nitrogen as possible (through ruminant digestion and slower turnover rates) and the nitrogen is excreted primarily in faecal material which may mineralize the nitrogen even more slowly than soil humus (Pastor *et al.* 1993). Further elaborations and refinements to these equations (see Chapter 9) may result in slightly different critical values, but these elaborations do not alter the qualitative importance of these conclusions. So long as faecal nitrogen excretion increases linearly and urinary nitrogen excretion increases quadratically with plant nitrogen concentration, there will almost certainly be some critical value of plant nitrogen concentration above which excretion is primarily in urea and below which excretion is primarily in faeces.

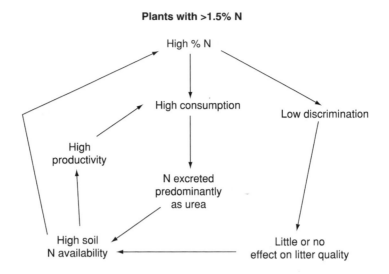

Figure 10.2. Positive feedbacks between plants, herbivores and soil nitrogen availability that increase rates of nitrogen cycling when plant nitrogen concentrations exceed 1.5% (the critical value where the surfaces in Fig. 10.1 cross). These may be characteristic of grazing systems.

We do not believe it is a coincidence that this critical nitrogen concentration is in the vicinity of the highest nitrogen concentration in twigs consumed by browsers (Shipley *et al.* 1998), and near the lowest nitrogen concentration in green graminoid forage consumed by grazers (Georgiadis *et al.* 1989). Interactions between plant tissue chemistry, the processing and mode of excretion of nitrogen by the herbivore, and soil microbial activity establishes positive feedbacks to either side of this critical nitrogen concentration that would tend to move the ecosystem away from it (Figs. 10.2 and 10.3). This critical plant nitrogen concentration ranges from 1.3%–1.7%, and the mean (1.5%) would thus be an unstable bifurcation point demarcating green forage above it from structural woody tissues below it. While others have also recognized the role of forage chemical quality (especially the difference between green tissues and structural woody tissues) in determining herbivore productivity (Caughley 1976, Bell 1982), the positive feedbacks that result from exploiting these two different types of plant tissues in Figs. 10.2 and 10.3 were not completely recognized in these earlier papers.

When the forage contains greater than this concentration of nitrogen, excretion as metabolic waste in urea promotes higher microbial activity

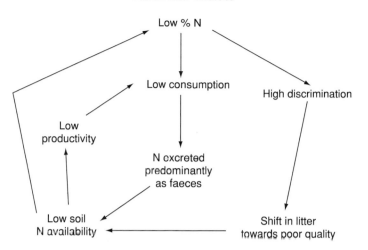

Figure 10.3. Positive feedbacks between plants, herbivores and soil nitrogen availability that decrease rates of nitrogen cycling when plant nitrogen concentrations are below 1.5% (the critical value where the surfaces in Fig. 10.1 cross). These may be characteristic of browsing systems.

in soils, greater forage production with higher nitrogen concentration, and greater herbivore biomass (Fig. 10.2, Ruess & McNaughton 1987, Georgiadis *et al.* 1989, McNaughton *et al.* 1997). The high production of generally high quality forage allows the formations of large herds of various herbivores behaviourally specialized to forage on different plant species to avoid competition (McNaughton 1985). Consequently almost all of the above-ground net primary production can be consumed and selection pressure towards ungrazed species is low. This low selection pressure is also made possible by the large-scale migrations, which reduce the possibility of overgrazing (McNaughton *et al.* 1997). The implications of this for evolution and conservation will be discussed below.

When the nitrogen concentration of forage is less than this critical value (as in browsing systems), nitrogen excretion mainly as residual (and undigestible) compounds in faeces rather than as metabolic waste in urea conserves body nitrogen. In addition, the faeces themselves may be low in nitrogen and mineralize it very slowly. Moreover, with forage this poor in protein, the herbivore must forage very selectively on plant parts and species of the highest nitrogen concentrations, thus giving a competitive advantage to less preferred plant species with lower nitrogen concentration, lower digestibility and slower decay rate. These feedbacks decrease in microbial activity and nitrogen availability, reduce forage production, decrease nitrogen concentration in forage, reduce herbivore biomass, and exert an even greater pressure towards selective foraging and conservation of nitrogen by the digestive system of the herbivore. Thus, positive feedbacks in browsing systems move the system away from the critical nitrogen concentration but in the opposite direction of grazing systems. Browsing and grazing systems may be two different stable states of terrestrial ecosystems that support herbivores separated by a bifurcation at a critical level of approximately 1.5% plant nitrogen concentration (but see below for clarification of what is meant by 'stability').

Such a bifurcation to alternative stable states at critical values of plant nitrogen concentration appear to at least provide partial underlying unification to the apparent differences between grazing systems (represented by the Serengeti) and browsing systems (represented by Isle Royale). Evidence for these divergent responses of browsing and grazing ecosystems has recently been presented by Singer and Schoenecker (2003), who compared the effects of grazing elk in Yellowstone National Park grasslands with those of browsing elk in willow communities in nearby Rocky Mountain National Park, USA. By using exclosures, Singer and Schoenecker 2003 show that grazing increases net primary productivity, soil nitrogen mineralization rate, above-ground plant nitrogen pools and plant nitrogen concentrations in the grasslands of Yellowstone National Park, but decreased pools of nitrogen-rich forage species, net primary productivity and nitrogen mineralization rates in Rocky Mountain National Park. These responses are all consistent with our proposed feedbacks, and the results are not confounded by comparing responses of ecosystems with different herbivores (such as our comparison of the Serengeti with Isle Royale, which initially motivated our proposed model). Unfortunately, Singer and Schoenecker (2003) do not give complete enough data on nitrogen concentrations in all plant species to determine whether Rocky Mountain National Park and Yellowstone National Park fall on opposite sides of our proposed critical plant nitrogen concentration.

But some important questions remain unanswered. First, the role of herbivore biomass density in influencing nutrient cycling must be separated from other secondary effects of changes in plant community composition. Herbivore population densities in the Serengeti (and grazing systems in general) are usually orders of magnitude higher than those in browsing systems. Could the Serengeti herbivores increase rates of nitrogen cycling were their densities as low as browsers in the boreal forest?

Moreover, the results of Singer and Schoenecker (2003) reported above are an exception to the generally higher herbivore biomass in grazing systems. Elk density in the browsing systems of Rocky Mountain National Park, where nitrogen mineralization was depressed by elk, was double that in the grazing systems of Yellowstone National Park, where nitrogen mineralization was enhanced. Can these higher densities be maintained in the face of their depressions of nitrogen cycling, net primary productivity and preferred forage production or are they transient? This also raises the question of how fluctuations in herbivore densities affect soil nitrogen pools, which may respond on longer time scales. For example, fluctuations of herbivore densities in the Serengeti occur seasonally whereas those in boreal forests occur on decadal time scales. There are few data on how fluctuations in herbivore biomass or population density affect nitrogen cycling. Sirotnak and Huntly (2000) present some intriguing evidence that nitrogen mineralization rates are temporarily enhanced during a peak in vole populations because of the deposition of larger amounts of urine and faeces, but decline during vole population lows as the plant community changes to dominance by unpalatable and slowly decaying species. Indeed, this shift in forage quality which depresses nitrogen availability may also have been responsible for the decline in vole density.

Not only must the effects of herbivore biomass density be sorted out from secondary effects on nutrient cycling via forage selection, but differences in soil nitrogen density must also be accounted for. The total amount of nitrogen in the soils of grazing/grassland systems are generally greater than those in browsing/forest systems (compare data in Pastor *et al.* 1993 with those in McNaughton *et al.* 1997). Would we still see differences between the two systems if the total amount of nitrogen in the soil were the same?

The role of herbivores in importing or exporting nitrogen to and from ecosystems through migration (de Mazancourt *et al.* 1998) also needs to be experimentally addressed. Singer and Schoenecker (2003) found that elk import a net of 0.49 g N/m^2 per year in Yellowstone grasslands, where nitrogen mineralization rate was enhanced, but exported a net of 2.01 g N/m^2 per year from the willow communities in Rocky Mountain National Park, where nitrogen mineralization rate declined. Experiments are needed where the import/export of nitrogen in ecosystems by herbivores is more precisely measured or even controlled in some way through temporary exclosures or by partially excluding some herbivores.

Thus far, we have focused exclusively on browsers and grazers because their effects on nutrient cycles have been especially well-documented in the past several decades. These two groups comprise most of the world's large mammal biomass (see Chapter 8). But we have ignored most of the world's species of large mammalian herbivores, namely the frugivores that inhabit mainly tropical ecosystems (see Chapter 8). Thus, while Table 10.1 and Figs. 10.1–10.3 apply to the majority of large mammalian biomass, they do not apply to the majority of the world's large mammalian species. Frugivores consume the parts of plants that have the highest nutrient concentrations but the amount of nutrients diverted through their biomass is virtually unknown. Perhaps more importantly, frugivores disperse seeds, which in a very real sense contain the genetic code for particular rates of nutrient cycling insofar as individual plant species affect nutrient cycling through uptake and decay rates. By dispersing these seeds, frugivores may determine where particular rates of nutrient cycling take place and thus the spatial patterns of nutrient cycling across some landscapes. This is an untapped area of research and perhaps one of the most important areas to be explored for making progress in our understanding of herbivore-ecosystem interactions.

IMPLICATIONS FOR EVOLUTION

Traditionally, both evolutionary and ecosystem ecologists have made simplifying assumptions that allow each subdiscipline to approach problems without considering the processes studied by the other. Each subdiscipline assumes to be constant (or at least slowly changing) those properties which the other subdiscipline has shown are dynamic. It is no longer desirable or even possible for these two subdisciplines to ignore the findings of the other. On the one hand, evolutionary ecologists have implicitly assumed that potential primary productivity is constant and stable, and determined extrinsically by abiotic processes such as (ultimately) sunlight. This has allowed evolutionary ecologists to investigate coevolution between herbivores and plant defences without considering how the plant defences affect the supply of materials required for the plant to compensate for loss of consumed parts (Stamp 2003). Thus, potential plant productivity (the underpinnings of 'carrying capacity') is assumed to form a stable platform for Hutchinson's ecological theatre upon which the evolutionary play is performed and so almost all evolutionary population models have an underlying basis in logistic and Lotka-Volterra equations.

On the other hand, ecosystem ecologists have treated the properties of the plants that control nutrient cycling (such as plant chemistry) to be fixed within a given species. This has allowed them to focus on how changes in species composition induced by selective foraging affect nutrient cycling rates without considering how selection pressure by the herbivore changes the chemistry of each plant species. These assumptions have allowed ecosystem ecologists to simplify their experiments by focusing on large-scale differences between plant species rather than differences between individuals within a species; it has also facilitated the finding of analytical solutions to ecosystem models of mass balance of nutrient flows (DeAngelis 1992, Loreau 1995, Pastor & Cohen 1997).

Recent experimental results show that these assumptions are probably untenable for both ecosystem and evolutionary ecology. Uriarte (2000) showed that chrysomelid beetles selectively forage on *Solidago* individuals with higher nitrogen concentrations, thereby increasing the representation of genotypes with lower nitrogen concentration; this shift in genotypic proportions also depressed soil nitrogen availability through litter feedbacks. Other studies have also shown that nitrogen availability changes relatively rapidly – within several generations – upon excluding the herbivores from a plot of land (Pastor *et al.* 1993, McNaughton *et al.* 1997, Ritchie *et al.* 1998). Different plant species or genotypes within a species affect nitrogen availability in soils within several years (Wedin & Tilman 1990, Wedin & Pastor 1993, Uriarte 2000) because much, if not most, of the nitrogen in litter is released relatively rapidly from labile compounds in the early years of decay. Thus, changes in plant species composition or genotypic proportions within a population due to selective foraging are rather quickly manifested in changes in soil nitrogen availability, which in turn controls forage production and quality. Add to this the well-documented (but still poorly understood) correlations between plant chemistry, plant palatability, digestibility and decomposability (Grime *et al.* 1996) and it is easy to see the strong potential for how changes in nutrient cycles exert selection pressure on herbivores and their forage, and how coevolution between herbivores and their forage affect nutrient cycles within at least the lifetime of an herbivore's F1 and F2 generations, if not their own lifetimes.

Recent theoretical studies have shed some light on how feedbacks between herbivores, plants and decomposers, and evolution of these trophic levels, affect stability of models and perhaps of real ecosystems (Pastor & Cohen 1997, Cohen *et al.* 2000). Pastor and Cohen (1997) present and analyse a model of nutrient flow through an ecosystem in which a herbivore preferentially consumes a species with rapid nutrient uptake and decay rates, and avoids a species with slow nutrient uptake. In this model, stable coexistence between the herbivore and the two plant species was achieved only at the expense of a lower rate of nutrient cycling, compared with a system in which the herbivore was absent. In other words, if the herbivore chooses a plant species with rapid rates of nutrient uptake, as in the boreal forest, then plant species coexistence and stability to disturbances near equilibrium (such as harvesting one or more of the species, for example) comes at the expense of lower cycling rates and lower productivity. Pastor and Cohen (1997) show that herbivores can increase rates of nutrient cycling only by consuming plants in proportion to their abundance, and thereby not changing plant species composition, which appears to correspond to the situation in the Serengeti.

In the model analysis of Pastor and Cohen (1997), the parameters are held constant. Each of these parameters represents some measured value of a particular trait (such as uptake, consumption or decay rates, for example). But evolution changes traits (represented by parameter values in a model) by mutation, selection, immigration/emigration or drift. If parameters in the model are allowed to change (evolve), then ecological stability in the restricted sense used above no longer applies and we must consider stability in an evolutionary sense. This gets us to the idea of evolutionary stable strategies, first proposed by Maynard Smith and Price (1973). An evolutionary stable strategy is a set of parameter values (values of traits) for all species in the system such that no other combination of parameter values can do better (in some specific sense such as productivity) in the long run. Thus, ecological stability refers to recovery of a system with a set of fixed parameter values after disturbances to the size of its compartments, while evolutionary stability refers to the resistance of a system to invasion by a species with a different set of parameter values (a 'mutant'). The two may be related but are not the same.

Cohen et al. (2000) analysed the same model for evolutionary stable strategies when parameters were allowed to evolve. In this case, evolutionary stability was associated with higher rates of nutrient cycling. To see what this means, consider a system composed of a number of plant species that form a 'gradient' of digestibility and decomposability without a herbivore and with some particular rate of nutrient cycling. We now introduce a herbivore that feeds selectively on the most digestible plant species that cycles nutrients most rapidly. This causes the rate of nutrient cycling to decline as the abundance of this preferred species declines relative to that of the less preferred species with lower decomposability. This has apparently been the situation on Isle Royale in the past century since moose arrived on the island (Pastor et al. 1993). In order for another herbivore (a 'mutant') to successfully invade this system by avoiding competition with the first herbivore, it must forage on the next plant species with a slower nutrient cycling rate that was avoided by the first herbivore. But if it decreases the rate of nitrogen cycling further, it will decrease forage production. It can avoid this by converting this plant material with a slow turnover and decay rate to urine and faeces with a faster decay rate. By increasing the rate of cycling of the limiting nutrient, it also increases total forage production. This benefits both the first herbivore and the invading mutant. Any subsequent mutant can successfully invade only by foraging on the next less preferred species and converting its biomass with slow turnover into urea and faeces with faster turnover. The limit of 'invasibility' is set when all plant material is consumed in proportion to its abundance amongst species, but at every step of the way the rate of nutrient cycling has increased. It is then not possible for another herbivore to invade. Therefore, an evolutionarily stable system with herbivores is one with a diversity of herbivores partitioning their foraging such that each consumes a particular plant species, but in total the herbivore trophic level consumes all plant biomass in proportion to its distribution amongst all plant species, and converts plant nitrogen into urine and faeces with a higher turnover rate. This appears to resemble the Serengeti.

Thus, the two case studies described here may represent two different sorts of stable systems. The browsing system in which the herbivore forages selectively and decreases rates of nutrient cycling may appear to be stable ecologically over extended periods so long as the parameter values of the constituent species are not changing (evolving) very rapidly. It is perhaps not a coincidence that boreal forests are ecologically quite young (less than 10 000 years since the last glaciation when the current assemblage of boreal species came together) (see Larsen 1980) and so perhaps there has not been sufficient time for evolution of an 'invader' which can offset the effect of the browsers (although spruce budworm may be a possibility). In contrast, the Serengeti grasslands (including their herbivores) are orders of magnitude older than the boreal forests. The Serengeti and similar grassland ecosystems that have persisted through glaciations could be examples of evolutionarily stable ecosystems with a high diversity of herbivores that increase rates of nitrogen cycling (or at least they may be systems close to an evolutionary stable strategy).

Another difference between browsing and grazing systems lies in the social structures of the herbivore species. Browsers are almost always solitary, although they may form loose, small groups during breeding seasons. Grazers, in contrast, are noted for the large, dense herds, and the migrations of these herds in the Serengeti, the American Great Plains and the tundra may be among the most spectacular ecological phenomena known. McNaughton (1984) suggests that the ability of grazers to increase rates of nutrient cycling and forage production may be a selective factor allowing or even favouring the formation of herding social behaviour in large mammals. Concentrating populations in herds increases the probability of the formation of large patches with higher productivity and nutritional quality, which makes it easier to locate food next time. Furthermore, the pattern of foraging in successive waves of different herbivores facilitates the maintenance of large 'grazing lawns' and mitigates against unpreferred species becoming dominant, so long as the herds are allowed to migrate and are not confined to a small portion of the landscape. Moreover, the concentration of grazers in herds appears to be a strong selection pressure for some rather simple genetic changes that control plant form and chemistry in grasses (Kemp 1937, McNaughton 1979, Detling & Painter 1983). Thus, 'the high rates of energy and nutrient flow... in the Serengeti region are strongly regulated by the adaptive properties of both the animals and plants resulting from their interactions and consequent evolution over long time periods' (McNaughton 1984). There is, therefore, some limited behavioural and genetic evidence for the suggestion made by Cohen et al. (2000) that an evolutionary stable strategy in an ecosystem context must have the properties associated with the Serengeti.

Similar sorts of arguments could be made for the solitary social structure of most browsers. If browsers feed selectively and change plant community composition towards species with even slower nutrient cycling rates, then it would seem to be a reasonable hypothesis that herding behaviour would be selected against in order to disperse the effect of the browser across the landscape and to avoid concentrating a negative effect in one spot. Put another way, the genes for herding behaviour would be selected against because of the negative effect of herding behaviour on soil fertility and forage production. Therefore, in contrast to grazing systems, there is the fascinating possibility of selection against herding behaviour in browsers so that their deleterious effects on ecosystem properties are dispersed across the landscape.

IMPLICATIONS FOR CONSERVATION OF LARGE HERBIVORES

Traditionally, conservation biology has made great advances by concentrating on individual species in danger of extinction. It has drawn its theoretical basis almost entirely from population biology. A central tenet of population biology is 'carrying capacity', or the equilibrium population size obtained by a species in the absence of environmental change.

The simple concept of asymptotic and constant carrying capacity is no longer tenable for species such as large herbivores because they affect the ability of the environment to support them through the flow of limiting nutrients up the food chain (Pastor *et al.* 1997). In a very real sense, what needs to be sustained or 'conserved' is not simply a particular population, but an entire ecosystem through which nutrients circulate at characteristic rates and in which large mammalian herbivores play an essential role. These nutrient cycles are the real underpinning of sustainability and they are affected by the species that are the primary 'targets' of conservation policy. These are new concepts to conservation biology and it will take some time to sort out the full implications of what this means and how to incorporate them into management decisions.

Nevertheless, we can offer a few general observations. The positive feedbacks in Figs. 10.2 and 10.3 all have delays which virtually guarantee that herbivore populations, their forage species and the nutrient cycles through them will undergo oscillations. In fact, the model of Pastor and Cohen (1997) discussed above exhibits damped oscillations during recovery from disturbances near equilibrium. Furthermore, the large migrations in the Serengeti are simply population oscillations in a spatial as well as temporal context. By overly focusing on asymptotic carrying capacity, both conservation biology and wildlife management have ignored what is likely to be more fundamental cyclic behaviours of interacting populations and ecosystem properties. Herbivores have different effects on ecosystems at different extremes of their cycles. Conservation biologists and managers should consider that the large mammalian herbivores they wish to conserve sometimes must undergo population declines as part of their cycles in order to allow recovery of other desired and essential ecosystem properties from previously high herbivore densities. Conversely, plant populations may undergo considerable so-called 'damage' when large mammalian herbivore populations are high. These changes are the inevitable result of population cycles. So long as the cycle falls within natural ranges of amplitude and period, which have resulted from coevolution of herbivores and plants in an ecosystem context, then the target population to be conserved and the ecosystem supporting it may be 'healthy'.

Perhaps what need to be conserved are the characteristic periods, amplitude and spatial extent of oscillations of large mammalian herbivores, and the other species of the ecosystems to which they belong. One implication of this is that conservation reserves need to be large enough to sustain these oscillations and migrations. But until we understand how the periods, amplitudes and spatial extent of oscillations relate to nutrient cycles and productivity, we cannot make any predictions about how large these reserves need to be. Thus, the argument of 'many small or few large reserves' may be premature. Nonetheless, as the studies in the Serengeti have clearly shown, these reserves may need to be especially large.

Migrating animals do not respect political boundaries so confining populations of large mammalian herbivores to landscapes or reserves that are too small could result in negative effects of the herbivores on nutrient cycles and productivity. This appears to have been the result when elephants in East Africa were confined to remnant forest reserves in order to foster settlement and farming outside the reserves (Laws *et al.* 1975, Caughley 1975). Sometimes, confinement is also the inadvertent result of otherwise well-intentioned conservation efforts. For example, permanent watering holes were established in much of East Africa in order to support declining mammalian populations during a prolonged drought (Weir 1971). However, when the animals became resident for longer periods around water holes, they greatly decreased water-holding capacity of the soil and nutrient cycling rates by trampling and overgrazing/overbrowsing (du Toit 1991). Inevitably, the confined populations were affected more through their feedbacks with ecosystem properties, than directly by the management practice itself.

Native human societies have learned ways to both hunt large wild mammals and herd domestic mammals, apparently without greatly reducing nutrient cycling rates or productivity. These management traditions often involve mimicking the migration behaviours of the herbivores themselves (see Chapter 9). It would be fascinating to learn how nutrient cycling rates and productivity are affected by herbivore confinement and how they differ between Western and native management traditions. Such a study could go a long way to providing some sound scientific underpinnings for designing conservation practices that do not cause deleterious effects to ecosystem properties, and local human economies and societies.

Figures 10.2 and 10.3, as well as other modelling studies (Walker *et al.* 1981), also indicate that there may be alternative stable states of herbivore-plant-soil systems, caused largely by feedbacks between herbivores and the flow of nutrients or water. These alternative stable states are separated by critical values of certain parameters, such as plant nitrogen concentration in Figs. 10.2 and 10.3. The critical parameter values control when the system bifurcates into two or more stable states or from one stable state to another. A key feature of these bifurcations is that once a system crosses such critical values, feedbacks then repel the system from that state towards a very different stable state, often quite unlike the original one. Without recognition of these critical values and the bifurcations they cause, conservation practices may inadvertently push the system across them, resulting in rapid, unintended and unanticipated changes in population density. Given that many, if not most, conservation efforts are under serious scrutiny from a public that expects tight control over populations or successful re-establishment of endangered species, such rapid changes can precipitate serious political and public relations problems. Bifurcations in herbivore-plant-soil systems are not simply of academic interest, fascinating though these theoretical questions are.

Finally, we wish to call attention to the conservation problem arising from the introduction of mammals into ecosystems where they have not coevolved with the other constituents (Wardle & Bardgett 2004). It has long been recognized that introduced mammals can have adverse effects on native vegetation (recall the well-known example of the introduction of rabbits into Australia). But the situation may be worse than previously realized: Wardle *et al.* (2001, 2002) and Wardle and Bardgett (2004), using data from 30 exclosures in New Zealand (which had no native mammals), show that introduced mammals consistently reduced diversity and density of under-storey plant species in all sites, reduced productivity and caused increased dominance of unpalatable plant species with poor litter quality. However, microbial biomass and other aspects of decomposer communities (and by inference nitrogen mineralization) did not decline at all sites as expected from the decreased litter quality, although the responses of the soil nitrogen pool may be delayed in some cases because of slow turnover rates. Nevertheless, these results should make managers pause regarding species introduction for the purposes of providing game populations or promoting tourism. This again points to the need to reorient conservation biology towards not just conserving species but also considering the roles that species play in the ecosystem processes which sustain their populations, and those of other species.

CONCLUSIONS

Large mammalian herbivores can both increase and decrease nutrient cycling rates by a variety of processes and feedbacks with vegetation and soils. These processes include defecation and urination, and changes in plant species composition due to selective foraging. Responses of plants such as compensatory growth, changes in morphology and changes in tissue chemistry may offset or amplify these direct effects. Defecation, urination, plant growth responses and changes in plant community composition affect nutrient supply in the soil, which in turn determines future forage production. These processes operate simultaneously in all ecosystems but at different temporal and spatial scales. So the effects of the herbivores are contingent on the scales of the processes. Plant tissue chemistry may be one of the most fundamental properties determining the magnitude and direction of herbivore-driven feedbacks. Moreover, there may be a critical plant nitrogen concentration, above which feedbacks between herbivores, plants and soils increase rates of nitrogen cycling, and below which such feedbacks decrease rates of nitrogen cycling. These feedbacks may result in alternative stable states of ecosystems and herbivore populations. When these herbivore-driven feedbacks are considered, a very dynamic picture emerges of ecosystems and their constituent herbivores. The dynamic nature of these systems poses serious problems for conservation biology, most especially about the fundamental nature of just what it is that conservation policies seek to conserve.

ACKNOWLEDGEMENTS

The US National Science Foundation has supported most of the previous research by us upon which this paper is based. The continued assistance of this agency is greatly appreciated. We thank Peter Högberg, Robin Gill and Angela Hodgson for helpful comments.

REFERENCES

Adler, P.B., Raff, D.A. & Laurenroth, W.K. (2001). The effect of grazing on the spatial heterogeneity of vegetation. *Oecologia*, **128**, 465–79.
Belovsky, G.E. (1978). Diet optimization in a generalist herbivore: the moose. *Theoretical Population Biology*, **14**, 105–34.
Bell, R.H.V. (1971). A grazing ecosystem in the Serengeti. *Scientific American*, **225**, 86–93.
Bell, R.H.V. (1982). The effect of soil nutrient availability on community structure in African ecosystems. In *Ecology of Tropical Savannas*, ed. B.J. Huntly & B.H. Walker. Heidelberg: Springer-Verlag, pp. 193–216.
Bergström, R. (1984). Rebrowsing on birch *Betula pendula* and *B. pubescens* stems by moose. *Alces*, **12**, 870–96.
Bergström, R. & Danell, K. (1987). Effects of simulated winter browsing by moose on morphology and biomass of two birch species. *Journal of Ecology*, **75**, 533–44.
Biondini, M.E., Patten, B.D. & Nyren, P.E. (1998). Grazing intensity and ecosystem processes in a northern mixed-grass prairie, USA. *Ecological Applications*, **8**, 469–79.

Brandner, T.A., Peterson, R.O. & Risenhoover, K. (1990). Balsam fir on Isle Royale: effects of moose herbivory and population density. *Ecology*, **7**, 155–64.

Bryant, J.P. & Chapin, F.S., III (1986). Browsing – woody plant interactions during boreal forest plant succession. In *Forest Ecosystems in the Alaskan Taiga*, ed. K. Van Cleve, F.S. Chapin, III, P.W. Flanagan, L.A. Viereck & C.T. Dyrness. New York, Springer-Verlag, pp. 213–25.

Bryant, J.P. & Kuropat, P.J. (1980). Selection of winter forage by subarctic browsing vertebrates: the role of plant chemistry. *Annual Review of Ecology and Systematics*, **11**, 261–85.

Bryant, J.P., Tahvanainen, J., Sulkinoja, M. *et al.* (1989). Biogeographic evidence for the evolution of chemical defense by boreal birch and willow against mammalian browsing. *American Naturalist*, **134**, 20–34.

Bryant, J.P., Provenza, F.D., Pastor, J., Reichardt, P.B., Clausen, T.P. & du Toit, J.T. (1991). Interactions between woody plants and browsing mammals mediated by secondary metabolites. *Annual Review of Ecology and Systematics*, **22**, 431–46.

Bryant, J.P., Reichardt, P.B. & Clausen, T.P. (1992). Chemically mediated interactions between woody plants and browsing mammals. *Journal of Range Management*, **45**, 18–24.

Bråthen, K.A. & Oksanen, J. (2001). Reindeer reduce biomass of preferred species. *Journal of Vegetation Science*, **12**, 473–80.

Caughley, G. (1975). The elephant problem, an alternative hypothesis. *East African Wildlife Journal*, **14**, 265–83.

Caughley, G. (1976). Plant-herbivore systems. In *Theoretical Ecology*, ed. R. May. Oxford: Blackwell, pp. 94–113.

Cohen, Y., Pastor, J. & Vincent, T. (2000). Nutrient cycling in evolutionary stable ecosystems. *Evolutionary Ecology Research*, **6**, 719–43.

Coley, P.D., Bryant, J.P. & Chapin, F.S., III (1985). Resource availability and plant herbivore defense. *Science*, **230**, 895–9.

Coughenour, M.B. (1991). Biomass and nitrogen responses to grazing of upland steppe on Yellowstone's northern winter range. *Journal of Applied Ecology*, **28**, 71–82.

Danell, K. & Huss-Danell, K. (1985). Feeding by insects and hares on birches earlier affected by moose browsing. *Oikos*, **44**, 75–81.

Danell, K., Huss-Danell, K. & Bergström, R. (1985). Fractions between browsing moose and two species of birch in Sweden. *Ecology*, **66**, 1867–78.

Danell, K., Berteaux, D. & Bråthen, K.A. (2002). Effects of muskox carcasses on nitrogen concentration in tundra vegetation. *Arctic*, **55**, 389–92.

Danell, K., Bergström, R., Edenius, L. & Ericsson, G. (2003). Ungulates as drivers of tree population dynamics at module and genet levels. *Forest Ecology and Management*, **181**, 67–76.

DeAngelis, D.L. (1992). *Dynamics of Nutrient Cycling and Food Webs*. New York: Kluwer Academic Publishing.

de Mazancourt, C., Loreau, M. & Abbadie, L. (1998). Grazing optimization and nutrient cycling: when do herbivores enhance plant production? *Ecology*, **79**, 2242–52.

Detling, J.K. & Painter, E.L. (1983). Defoliation responses of western wheatgrass population with diverse histories of prairie dog grazing. *Oecologia*, **57**, 65–71.

Doak, B.W. (1952). Some chemical changes in the nitrogenous constituents of urine when voided on pasture. *Journal of Agricultural Science*, **42**, 162–71.

du Toit, J.T. (1991). Introduction of artificial waterpoints: potential impacts on nutrient cycling. In *Management of the Hwange Ecosystem*, ed. M. Jones & R. Martin. Harare, Zimbabwe: USAID/Zimbabwe Department of National Parks and Wildlife Management.

Edenius, L., Danell, K. & Nyquist, H. (1995). Effects of simulated moose browsing on growth, mortality, and fecundity in Scots pine: relations to plant productivity. *Canadian Journal of Forest Research*, **25**, 529–35.

Flanagan, P.W. & Van Cleve, K. (1983). Nutrient cycling in relation to decomposition and organic-matter quality in taiga ecosystems. *Canadian Journal of Forest Research*, **13**, 795–817.

Floate, M.J.S. (1970). Mineralization of N and P from organic material of plant origin and animal origin and its significance in the nutrient cycle in grazed upland hill soils. *Journal of the British Grassland Society*, **25**, 295–302.

Frank, D.A. & Evans, R.D. (1997). Effects of native grazers on N cycling in a north temperate grassland ecosystem: Yellowstone National Park. *Ecology*, **78**, 2238–49.

Frank, D.A., Groffman, P.M., Evans, R.D. & Tracy, B.F. (2000). Ungulate stimulation of nitrogen cycling and retention in Yellowstone Park grasslands. *Oecologia*, **123**, 116–21.

Georgiadis, N.J., Ruess, R.W., McNaughton, S.J. & Western, D. (1989). Ecological conditions that determine when grazing stimulates grass production. *Oecologia*, **81**, 316–22.

Grellmann, D. (2002). Plant responses to fertilization and exclusion of grazers on an arctic tundra heath. *Oikos*, **98**, 190–204.

Grime, J.P., Cornelissen, J.H.C., Thompson, K. & Hodgson, J.G. (1996). Evidence of a causal connection between anti-herbivore defence and the decomposition rate of leaves. *Oikos*, **77**, 489–94.

Gross, J.E., Shipley, L.A., Hobbs, N.T., Spalinger, D.E. & Wunder, B.A. (1993). Functional response of herbivores in food-concentrated patches: tests of a mechanistic model. *Ecology*, **74**, 778–91.

Hairston, N.G., Smith, F.E. & Slobodkin, L.B. (1960). Community structure, population control, and competition. *American Naturalist*, **879**, 421–5.

Heinen, J.T. & Sharik T.L. (1990). The influence of mammalian browsing on tree growth and mortality in the Pigeon River State Forest, Michigan. *American Midland Naturalist*, **123**, 202–6.

Hjältén, J., Danell, K. & Ericson, L. (1993). Effects of simulated herbivory and intraspecific competition on the compensatory ability of birches. *Ecology*, **74**, 1136–42.

Hobbie, S.E. (1996). Temperature and plant species control over litter decomposition in Alaskan tundra. *Ecological Monographs*, **66**, 503–22.

Hobbs, N.T. (1996). Modification of ecosystems by ungulates. *Journal of Wildlife Management*, **60**, 695–713.

Hobbs, N.T., Schimel, D.S., Owensby, C.E. & Ojima, D.J. (1991). Fire and grazing in the tallgrass prairie, contingent effects on nitrogen budgets. *Ecology*, **72**, 1374–82.

Holland, E.A., Parton, W.J., Detling, J.K. & Coppock, D.L. (1992). Physiological responses of plant populations to herbivory and their consequences for ecosystem nutrient flow. *American Naturalist*, **140**, 685–796.

Huntly, N. (1991). Herbivores and the dynamics of communities and ecosystems. *Annual Review of Ecology and Systematics*, **22**, 477–503.

Irons, J.G., III, Bryant, J.P. & Oswood, M.W. (1991). Effects of moose browsing on decomposition rates of birch leaf litter in a subarctic stream. *Canadian Journal of Fisheries and Aquatic Sciences*, **48**, 442–4.

Jefferies, R.L., Klein, D.R. & Shaver, G.R. (1994). Vertebrate herbivores and northern plant communities: reciprocal influences and responses. *Oikos*, **71**, 193–206.

Kemp, W.B. (1937). Natural selection within plant species as exemplified in a permanent pasture. *Journal of Heredity*, **28**, 329–33.

Kielland, K. & Bryant, J.P. (1998). Moose herbivory in taiga: effects on biogeochemistry and vegetation dynamics in primary succession. *Oikos*, **82**, 377–83.

Kingdon, J. (1982). *East African Mammals. An Atlas of Evolution in Africa.* Chicago, Illinois: University of Chicago Press.

Kitchell, J.F., O'Neill, R.V., Webb, D. *et al.* (1979). Consumer regulation of nutrient cycling. *BioScience*, **29**, 28–34.

Krefting, L.W. (1974). *The Ecology of the Isle Royale Moose with Special Reference to the Habitat.* Technical Bulletin 297-1974, Forestry Series 15. St. Paul, MN, Agricultural Experiment Station, University of Minnesota.

Larcher, W. (1995). *Physiological Plant Ecology*, 3rd edn. New York: Springer-Verlag.

Larsen, J.A. (1980). *The Boreal Ecosystem.* New York: Academic Press.

Laws, R.M., Parker, I.C.S. & Johnstone, R.C.B. (1975). *Elephants and their Habitats.* Oxford: Clarendon Press.

Loreau, M. (1995). Consumers as maximizers of energy and material flow in ecosystems. *American Naturalist*, **145**, 22–42.

Macfadyen, A. (1964). Energy flow in ecosystems and its exploitation by grazing. In *Grazing in Terrestrial and Marine Environments*, ed. D.J. Crisp. Oxford: Blackwell, pp. 3–20.

Mattson, W.J. & Addy, N.D. (1975). Phytophagous insects as regulators of forest primary production. *Science*, **190**, 515–22.

Maynard Smith, J. & Price, G.R. (1973). The logic of animal conflict. *Nature*, **246**, 15–18.

McInnes, P.F., Naiman, R.J., Pastor, J. & Cohen, Y. (1992). Effects of moose browsing on vegetation and litterfall of the boreal forest, Isle Royale, Michigan, USA. *Ecology*, **73**, 2059–75.

McKendrick, J.D., Batzli, G.O., Everett, K.R. & Swanson, J.C. (1980). Some effects of mammalian herbivores and fertilization on tundra soils and vegetation. *Arctic and Alpine Research*, **12**, 565–78.

McNaughton, S.J. (1979). Grazing as an optimization process: grass-ungulate relationships in the Serengeti. *American Naturalist*, **113**, 691–703.

McNaughton, S.J. (1983). Compensatory plant growth as a response to herbivory. *Oikos*, **40**, 329–36.

McNaughton, S.J. (1984). Grazing lawns: animals in herds, plant form, and coevolution. *American Naturalist*, **124**, 863–86.

McNaughton, S.J. (1985). Ecology of a grazing ecosystem: the Serengeti. *Ecological Monographs*, **55**, 259–94.

McNaughton, S.J. & Georgiadis, N.J. (1986). Ecology of African grazing and browsing mammals. *Annual Review of Ecology and Systematics*, **17**, 39–65.

McNaughton, S.J., Banyikwa, F.F. & McNaughton, M.M. (1997). Promotion of diet-enhancing nutrients by African grazers. *Science*, **278**, 1798–800.

Melillo, J.M., Aber, J.D. & Muratore, R.F. (1983). Nitrogen and lignin control of hardwood leaf litter dynamics. *Ecology*, **63**, 621–6.

Moen, R., Cohen, Y. & Pastor, J. (1998). Evaluating foraging strategies with a moose energetics model. *Ecosystems*, **1**, 52–63.

Mould, E.D. & Robbins, C.T. (1981). Nitrogen metabolism in elk. *Journal of Wildlife Management*, **45**, 323–34.

Oksanen, L. (1983). Trophic exploitation and arctic phytomass patterns. *American Naturalist*, **122**, 45–52.

Oksanen, L. (1988). Ecosystem organization: mutualism and cybernetics or plain Darwinian struggle for existence? *American Naturalist*, **131**, 424–44.

Oksanen, L., Fretwell, S.D., Arruda, J. & Niemelä, P. (1981). Exploitation ecosystems in gradients of primary productivity. *American Naturalist*, **118**, 240–62.

Olofsson, J. & Oksanen, L. (2002). Role of litter decomposition for the increased primary production in areas of heavy grazing by reindeer: a litterbag experiment. *Oikos*, **96**, 507–15.

Olofsson, J., Kitti, H., Rautainen, P., Stark, S. & Oksanen, L. (2001). Effects of summer grazing by reindeer on composition of vegetation, productivity and nitrogen cycling. *Ecography*, **24**, 13–24.

Pastor, J. & Cohen, Y. (1997). Herbivores, the functional diversity of plants species, and the cycling of nutrients in ecosystems. *Theoretical Population Biology*, **51**, 165–79.

Pastor, J. & Danell, K. (2003). Moose-vegetation-soils: a dynamic system. *Alces*, **39**, 177–92.

Pastor, J. & Naiman, R.J. (1992). Selective foraging and ecosystem processes in boreal forests. *American Naturalist*, **139**, 690–705.

Pastor, J., Dewey, B., Naiman, R.J., McInnes, P.F. & Cohen, Y. (1993). Moose browsing and soil fertility in the boreal forests of Isle Royale National Park. *Ecology*, **74**, 467–80.

Pastor, J., Dewey, B. & Christian, D. (1996). Carbon and nutrient mineralization and fungal spore composition of vole fecal pellets in Minnesota. *Ecography*, **19**, 52–61.

Pastor, J., Moen, R. & Cohen, Y. (1997). Spatial heterogeneities, carrying capacity, and feedbacks in animal-landscape interactions. *Journal of Mammalogy*, **78**, 1040–52.

Pastor, J., Dewey, B., Moen, R. *et al.* (1998). Spatial patterns in the moose-forest-soil ecosystem on Isle Royale, Michigan, USA. *Ecological Applications*, **8**, 411–24.

Pastor, J., Cohen, Y. & Moen, R. (1999a). The generation of spatial patterns in boreal landscapes. *Ecosystems*, **2**, 439–50.

Pastor, J., Standke, K., Farnsworth, K., Moen, R. & Cohen, Y. (1999b). Further development of the Spalinger-Hobbs mechanistic foraging model for free-ranging moose. *Canadian Journal of Zoology*, **77**, 1505–12.

Renecker, L.A. & Schwartz, C.C. (1998). Food habits and feeding behavior. In *Ecology and Management of the North American Moose*, ed. A.W. Franzmann & C.C. Schwarz. Washington, DC: Smithsonian Institution Press, pp. 403–40.

Risenhoover, K.L. (1987). Winter foraging strategies of moose in subarctic and boreal forest habitats. Ph.D. dissertation, Houghton, MI, Michigan Technological University.

Risenhoover, K.L. & Maass, S.A. (1987). The influence of moose on the composition and structure of Isle Royale forests. *Canadian Journal of Forest Research*, **17**, 357–64.

Ritchie, M.E., Tilman, D. & Knops, J.M.H. (1998). Herbivore effects on plant and nitrogen dynamics in oak savanna. *Ecology*, **79**, 165–77.

Robbins, C.T. (1983). *Wildlife Feeding and Nutrition*. New York: Academic Press.

Robbins, C.T., Moen, A.N. & Reid, J.T. (1974). Body composition of white-tailed deer. *Journal of Animal Science*, **38**, 871–6.

Ruess, R.W. & McNaughton, S.J. (1987). Grazing and the dynamics of nutrient and energy regulated microbial processes in the Serengeti grasslands. *Oikos*, **49**, 101–10.

Ruess, R.W. & Seagle, S.W. (1994). Landscape patterns in soil microbial processes in the Serengeti National Park, Tanzania. *Ecology*, **75**, 892–904.

Schimel, D.S., Parton, W.J., Adamsen, F.J. *et al.* (1986). The role of cattle in the volatile loss of nitrogen from a shortgrass steppe. *Biogeochemistry*, **2**, 39–52.

Schultz, A.M. (1964). The nutrient recovery hypothesis for arctic microtine cycles. II. Ecosystem variables in relation to arctic microtine cycles. In *Grazing in Terrestrial and Marine Environments*, ed. D.J. Crisp. Oxford: Blackwell, pp. 57–68.

Seagle, S.W., McNaughton, S.J. & Ruess, R.W. (1992). Simulated effects of grazing on soil nitrogen and mineralization in contrasting Serengeti grasslands. *Ecology*, **73**, 1105–23.

Senn, J. & Haukioja, E. (1994). Reactions of the mountain birch to bud removal: effects of severity and timing, and implications for herbivores. *Ecology*, **75**, 494–501.

Shariff, A.R., Biondini, M.E. & Grygiel, C.E. (1994). Grazing intensity effects on litter decomposition and soil nitrogen mineralization. *Journal of Range Management*, **47**, 444–9.

Shipley, L.A., Blomquist, S. & Danell, K. (1998). Diet choices made by free-ranging moose in northern Sweden in relation to plant distribution, chemistry, and morphology. *Canadian Journal of Zoology*, **76**, 1722–33.

Sinclair, A.R.E. & Norton-Griffiths, M. (1979). *Serengeti: Dynamics of an Ecosystem*. Chicago, Illinois: University of Chicago Press.

Singer, F.J. & Schoenecker, K.A. (2003). Do ungulates accelerate or decelerate nitrogen cycling? *Forest Ecology and Management*, **181**, 189–204.

Sirotnak, J.M. & Huntly, N.J. (2000). Direct and indirect effects of herbivores on nitrogen dynamics: voles in riparian areas. *Ecology*, **81**, 78–87.

Snyder, J.D. & Janke, R.A. (1976). Impact of moose browsing on boreal-type forests of Isle Royale National Park. *American Midland Naturalist*, **95**, 79–92.

Spalinger, D.E. & Hobbs, N.T. (1992). Mechanisms of foraging in mammalian herbivores: new models of functional response. *American Naturalist*, **140**, 325–48.

Stamp, N. (2003). Out of the quagmire of plant defense hypotheses. *Quarterly Review of Biology*, **78**, 23–55.

Stark, S., Wardle, D.A., Ohtonen, R., Helle, T. & Yeates, G.W. (2000). The effect of reindeer grazing on decomposition, mineralization, and soil biota in a dry oligotrophic Scots pine forest. *Oikos*, **90**, 301–10.

Stark, S. & Grellmann, D. (2002). Soil microbial responses to herbivory in an arctic tundra heath at two levels of nutrient availability. *Ecology*, **83**, 2736–44.

Stark, S., Tuomi, J., Strömmer, R. & Helle, T. (2003). Non-parallel changes in soil microbial carbon and nitrogen dynamics due to reindeer grazing in northern boreal forests. *Ecography*, **26**, 51–9.

Sterner, R.W. & Elser, J.J. (2002). *Ecological Stoichiometry: The Biology of Elements from Molecules to the Biosphere*. Princeton, NJ: Princeton University Press.

Thompson, I.D. & Curran, W.J. (1993). A reexamination of moose damage to balsam fir – white birch forests in central Newfoundland: 27 years later. *Canadian Journal of Forest Research*, **23**, 1388–95.

Thompson, I.D., Curran, W.J., Hancock, J.A. & Butler, C.E. (1992). Influence of moose browsing on successional forest growth on black spruce sites in Newfoundland. *Forest Ecology and Management*, **47**, 29–37.

Trottier, G.C. (1981). Beaked hazelnut – a key browse species for moose in the boreal forest region of western Canada. *Alces*, **17**, 257–81.

Uriarte, M. (2000). Interactions between goldenrod (*Solidago altissima* L.) and its insect herbivore (*Trirhabda virgata*) over the course of succession. *Oecologia*, **122**, 521–8.

Väre, H., Ohtonen, R. & Mikkola, K. (1996). The effect and extent of heavy grazing by reindeer in oligotrophic pine heaths in northeastern Fennoscandia. *Ecography*, **19**, 245–53.

Vivås, H.J. & Saether, B.-E. (1987). Interactions between a generalist herbivore, the moose (*Alces alces*) and its food resources: An experimental study of winter foraging behavior in relation to browse availability. *Journal of Animal Ecology*, **56**, 509–20.

Walker, B.H., Ludwig, D., Holling, C.S. & Peterman, R.M. (1981). Stability of semi-arid savanna grazing systems. *Journal of Ecology*, **69**, 473–98.

Wardle, D.A. & Bardgett, R.D. (2004). Human-induced changes in large herbivorous mammal density: the consequences for decomposers. *Frontiers in Ecology and the Environment*, **2**, 145–53.

Wardle, D.A., Barker, G.M., Yeates, G.W., Bonner, K.I. & Ghani, A. (2001). Introduced browsing mammals in natural New Zealand forests: aboveground and belowground consequences. *Ecological Monographs*, **71**, 587–614.

Wardle, D.A., Bonner, K.I. & Barker, G.M. (2002). Linkages between plant litter decomposition, litter quality, and vegetation responses to herbivores. *Functional Ecology*, **16**, 585–95.

Wedin, D.A. & Tilman, D. (1990). Species effects on nitrogen cycling: a test with perennial grasses. *Oecologia*, **84**, 433–41.

Wedin, D.A. & Pastor, J. (1993). Nitrogen mineralization dynamics in grass monocultures. *Oecologia*, **96**, 186–92.

Weir, J.S. (1971). The effect of creating additional water supplies in a Central African National Park. In *The Scientific Management of Animal and Plant Communities for Conservation*, ed. E. Duffey & A.S. Watt. Oxford: Blackwell, pp. 367–85.

White, T.C.R. (1993). *The Inadequate Environment: Nitrogen and the Abundance of Animals*, New York: Springer-Verlag.

Wiener, J.G. (1975). Nutrient cycles, nutrient limitation and vertebrate populations. *The Biologist*, **57**, 104–24.

Large herbivores in heterogeneous grassland ecosystems

DOUGLAS A. FRANK

INTRODUCTION

Satisfying energetic and nutritional requirements is a difficult challenge for herbivores in grassland. Grass is a relatively abrasive, low-quality forage (Van Soest 1982, Robbins 1983, McDowell 1985) whose nutritional content varies over complex spatial and temporal scales (Houston 1982, Hudson & White 1985, McNaughton 1985, Laca & Dement 1986, Senft *et al.* 1987, Demment & Greenwood 1988, Hobbs 1989, Singer *et al.* 1989). Ungulates, the principal large herbivores of grassland, are well suited for the dietary rigours of their habitat by possessing three important adaptations: (1) high-crowned, hypsodontic dentition that resists wear and increases the capacity for long-lived organisms to grind plant tissue; (2) a multichambered digestive tract that functions as a fermentation vat to efficiently extract energy from high cellulose ingesta; and (3) an elongation of limbs, reduction of digits and the development of a massive, hardened nail, the hoof, that provides for efficient and injury-resistant travel over open terrain in search of food (Van Soest 1982, McNaughton 1989, 1991). This suite of adaptations facilitates energy and nutrient extraction from forage, and is testimony to the severe resource-limiting conditions that ungulates face in a grassland habitat.

There has been considerable recent interest in factors controlling the development and maintenance of a spatial pattern in landscapes, and the flows of energy and material among landscape patches (Levin 1992, Pickett & Cadenasso 1995, Turner *et al.* 2001). In this chapter I will focus

Large Herbivore Ecology, Ecosystem Dynamics and Conservation, ed. K. Danell, P. Duncan, R. Bergström & J. Pastor. Published by Cambridge University Press. © Cambridge University Press 2006.

on how ungulates interact with and, in part, are responsible for an immense degree of spatial and temporal complexity in a grassland habitat. Because forage in grassland is generally of low quality and spatio-temporally variable, where herbivores choose to feed and what plant species they select to graze will have a significant impact on whether or not dietary requirements are met. Furthermore, food in grassland is heterogeneous at many different scales. Thus large herbivores must make a series of important hierarchically organized feeding decisions that include: what range to move to seasonally; which portions of a landscape to graze each day; and what plant or plant part to bite each fraction of a second (Senft *et al.* 1987).

Understanding the response of ungulates to a heterogeneous habitat has been an important priority of ungulate biology, starting with its emergence as a modern science (Leopold 1933) and continuing right up to the present (Festa-Bianchet 1988, Fryxell & Sinclair 1988, Coughenour 1991, Turner *et al.* 1994, Illius & O'Connor 2000). However, in addition to *responding* to the spatial variability of their habitat, large herbivores also may be important *determinants* of that variability. For example, herbivores collect nutrients that are diffusely distributed and concentrate them in urine and faecal patches (McNaughton *et al.* 1988, Hobbs 1996). This process can affect spatial heterogeneity at a range of scales: microsites within a community where animals graze, urinate and defecate; the landscape, where animals concentrate on selected topographic positions; and the region, where annual herd movements lead to herd weight gain and weight loss on distinct seasonal ranges (Hobbs 1996). Furthermore, grazing preferences exhibited by herbivores at scales ranging from plant species to positions on landscapes can influence the spatial pattern of plant performance and species composition, which, in turn, may feed back on the patchiness of soil processes (Wedin & Tilman 1990, Moen *et al.* 1997, Pastor *et al.* 1998).

Compared to how large herbivores respond to habitat variability, the role that herbivores play in creating heterogeneity has received little attention. In a survey of papers published 1995–2003 in three leading journals, *Ecology, Landscape Ecology* and *The Wildlife Bulletin*, representing ecological subdisciplines with overlapping interests in plant-animal interactions, I found 57 studies on large herbivore-habitat interactions. Some 54 of these studies examined the *response* of herbivores to habitat heterogeneity and only three (5%) investigated how herbivores *influenced* habitat variability. Two of the latter papers examined the effects of urine patches on heterogeneity. Although this analysis represents a subsample of all the papers published on herbivore-habitat relationships during these eight years, it clearly indicates the comparatively few studies that have examined consumer effects on spatial heterogeneity, reflecting a limited understanding of the phenomenon.

The objective of this chapter is to discuss how free-roaming wild ungulates respond to and determine grassland heterogeneity. Heterogeneity in this discussion is defined as the degree that forage abundance, quality and/ or plant resources are dissimilar among different spatial elements in an ecosystem. I will use the temperate grassland ecosystem of Yellowstone National Park, where I have studied ungulate-grassland interactions since 1988, as a case study, and supplement with information from other ecosystems where available. Grazer-grassland interactions will be discussed at three spatial scales, regional (ungulate seasonal ranges), landscape (topo-edaphic gradient) and within community (within a relatively homogenous grassland at a single topographic position). These results indicate: large, ecologically relevant variability in forage quality and availability; the patchy use of the environment by herbivores that base feeding decisions on forage properties; and an important role of herbivores in increasing the spatial heterogeneity of ecological processes at a range of spatial scales that are likely to feedback positively on large herbivores in Yellowstone Park.

REGIONAL HETEROGENEITY

The response of large herbivores to regional heterogeneity

The semi-nomadic migrations of large herds of ungulates are among the most spectacular phenomena in nature. These synchronized, en masse movements by tens to hundreds of thousands of animals reflect behavioural responses of herds to the spatio-temporal variability of their environment, particularly forage, across large spatial scales (Klein 1965, Fryxell et al. 1988, Fryxell & Sinclair 1988, McNaughton 1990).

In Yellowstone National Park, the annual migration of herds of elk (*Cervus elaphus*), bison (*Bison bison*) and pronghorn (*Antilocapra americana*) from low elevation, winter range to high elevation, summer range is closely associated with the isocline of high quality forage sweeping up the elevation gradient through the plant growing season (Frank & McNaughton 1992, Frank et al. 1998). Chemical analyses of dominant grass species on winter, transitional and summer range grassland indicate that concentrations of several important minerals for ungulates decline through the growing season (Frank 1998). For example, forage nitrogen (N), phosphorus (P) and sodium (Na) concentrations were significantly higher during the first month after snowmelt and potassium (K) was significantly higher during the first two months after snowmelt in grassland. Ungulates generally graze sites within the first two months of the growing season, which is precisely when concentrations of several important minerals are highest (Frank & McNaughton 1992). Therefore the migration from winter to summer range promotes a high-quality diet as a consequence of ungulates feeding on phenologically young and nutrient-rich forage during the growing season.

A similar relationship between forage quality and long distance ungulate migration has been observed in other ecosystems. Morgantini and Hudson (1988) found that the upslope spring and summer migration of elk in the Canadian Rocky Mountains also was associated with animals following a wave of high nutrient vegetation moving up the elevation gradient through the season. Likewise, in the tropical Serengeti ecosystem of East Africa, the onset of the wet season triggers the migration of large numbers of wildebeest (*Connochaetes taurinus*), zebra (*Equus burchelli*) and eland (*Taurotragus oryx*) from areas supporting nutrient-poor vegetation in the northwest corner of the Serengeti to a region of nutrient-rich vegetation on the southeast plains (McNaughton 1979, 1990, Ben-Shahar & Coe 1992).

In addition to affecting diet quality, foraging decisions can also influence feeding efficiency. Herbivores need to balance time spent filling their rumens with time devoted to other essential activities, such as rumination, rest, travel, predator vigilance and reproduction (McNaughton 1984, Spalinger & Hobbs 1992). Thus the less time herbivores need to ingest sufficient food, the more time the animals can budget to other important activities. In Yellowstone, the spring-summer ungulate migration also appears to promote feeding efficiency. The concentration of forage biomass in Yellowstone grassland, i.e. the amount of plant biomass within a volume of grassland canopy, declines through the growing season (Frank & McNaughton 1992). Forage concentration is associated with the amount of plant biomass obtained per bite, a form of feeding efficiency, for cattle (Ludlow *et al.* 1982) and African water buffalo (*Syncerus caffer*) (Prins 1996). Thus during their upslope migration, Yellowstone ungulates graze sites when their yield per bite should be highest, in the first 1–2 months of the growing season. Consequently, by migrating from low-elevation winter range to high-elevation summer range, Yellowstone grazers are likely to increase their feeding efficiency, while simultaneously enhancing diet quality.

The effect of large herbivores on regional heterogeneity

Herds of seasonally migrating ungulates may move large amounts of nutrients across an ecosystem from one region where they gain mass to another region where they lose mass (Hobbs 1996). To explore if the quantity of nutrients being transported in this way could be ecologically significant, I approximated the net N transported to the northern winter range annually by herds of Yellowstone elk and bison. Assuming Yellowstone northern range elk and bison populations of 23000 and 500, respectively (Singer & Mack 1993), mean weights of 230 kg (elk) (Houston 1982) and 430 kg (bison) (Meagher 1973), and a 30% loss in dressed weight while on the winter range, estimated as 67% of total body mass (Mitchell *et al.* 1976), elk and bison transport 1.88×10^5 kg of N from high elevation range to low elevation, winter range each year. The figure also assumes 100% of the dressed weight loss is due to protein catabolism, with an estimated protein N content of 17% (Sterner & Elsner 2002). Assuming a core winter range of 100 000 ha (Houston 1982), this rough estimate is equivalent to an average rate of 1.9 kg N ha^{-1} yr^{-1} transported to the winter range, if the faeces and urine were spread evenly. Such a flux is ecologically significant when comparing it to annual wet N deposition for Yellowstone (2 kg N ha^{-1} yr^{-1}) (Swank 1984) or the pools of above-ground plant N at peak biomass, ranging from 3 kg N ha^{-1} to 14 kg N ha^{-1}, at sites along a hilltop to slope-bottom catena on the northern winter range (Frank *et al.* 1994). However, this uniform N application on the winter range probably distorts its ecological impact for two reasons. First, its effect on the winter range probably will increase over time as N accumulates. Second, a homogeneous application of N is not realistic because of the heterogeneous use of the northern winter landscape by ungulates (Wallace *et al.* 1995). Because Yellowstone ungulates tend to excrete nutrients where they graze (Frank & McNaughton 1992), herbivores are likely to pinpoint their fertilization at positions on the landscape that are most critical for providing them with forage during the winter, the food-limiting part of the year.

Comparing forage nutrition from grazed sites on winter, transitional and summer ranges supports the notion that ungulates transport an ecologically important amount of nutrients to the winter range. Nitrogen and P content of graminoid forage species collected at one month intervals after snowmelt from the three seasonal ranges is provided in Fig. 11.1. Concentrations of both N and P declined over time, reflecting the general decline in forage quality during the growing season, as discussed above. In

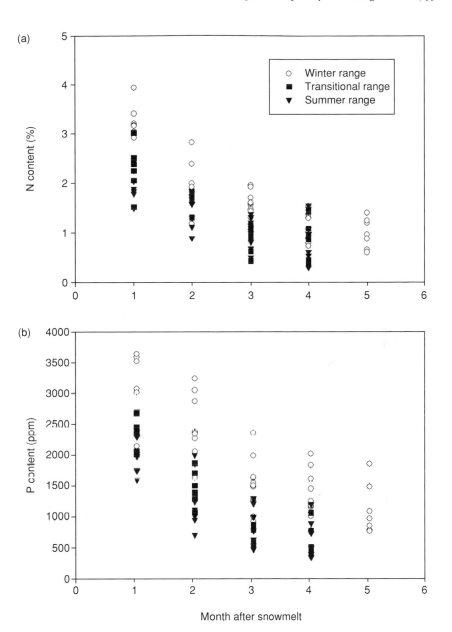

Figure 11.1. Nitrogen (a) and phosphorus (b) content of grass forage species collected from winter, transitional and summer ranges 1–5 months after snowmelt.

Table 11.1. *The N and P contents of two grasses collected from winter range and one higher elevation range during months 1–4 after snowmelt*

	Phleum pratense				Festuca idahoensis			
	Nitrogen (%)		Phosphorus (ppm)		Nitrogen (%)		Phosphorus (ppm)	
Month	winter range	transitional range	winter range	transitional range	winter range	summer range	winter range	summer range
1	3.9	2.4	3599	2358	3.0	2.4	3650	1990
2	2.4	1.7	3063	1717	1.9	1.9	2388	1408
3	1.3	1.1	1633	872	1.6	1.4	1644	1307
4	1.0	0.8	1164	1070	1.6	1.4	1842	1210

addition though, forage N and P were significantly higher ($P < 0.05$, Fisher's LSD) on the winter range for all months of the growing season, except for N content in month 2, when N content on the winter range was not different from that of the transitional range, and month 4, when there were no significant differences in forage N among ranges. For two winter range forage species, *Phleum pratense* and *Festuca idaohensis*, that also were collected from a second higher elevation range, N and P concentrations for both species were greater on the winter range, except for N content of *F. idahoensis* in month 2 after snowmelt (Table 11.1). These results support the hypothesis that migrating ungulates transport ecologically important quantities of nutrients that improve the nutritional condition and, thereby, the physiological status of plants growing on Yellowstone's winter range. Clearly, a caveat for interpreting these findings is that these plant nutrient data do not account for potentially confounding differences among seasonal ranges, unrelated to ungulates, e.g. differences in parent rock composition or climate, that may have influenced plant nutritional condition. An exclosure study combining fertilization and clipping treatments would help disentangle consumer influences versus climate and edaphic effects on plant nutrient status. However, until such work is performed, I believe that the combination of (1) the magnitude of estimated nutrients transported to the northern winter range by ungulates, and (2) higher nutrient levels of winter range plants compared to those of plants on higher ranges, suggest that the movement of nutrients across regions by large herbivores is a significant large-scale influence of consumers on Yellowstone processes.

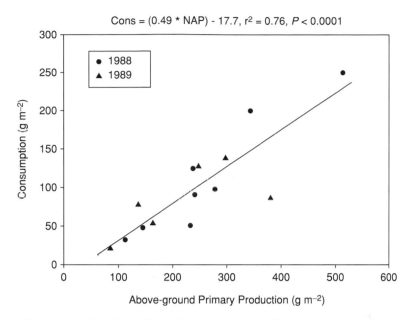

Figure 11.2. The relationship of ungulate consumption to above-ground production for Yellowstone grassland.

The importance of the seasonal segregation of consumption, leading to forage conservation for ungulate herds during periods of limited food intake has been discussed previously (Sinclair & Norton-Griffiths 1979, Morgantini & Hudson 1988, Frank & McNaughton 1992). What is not well understood and, in my estimation, requires further examination, is how the seasonal net transport of nutrients by herbivores may facilitate processes during the food-limiting season in grazed grassland and potentially enhance ungulate consumption rates, diet quality and, concomitantly, population density.

LANDSCAPE HETEROGENEITY

The response of large herbivores to landscape heterogeneity

Once arriving on a seasonal range, herbivores must decide where to graze on the landscape. Plant biomass can vary markedly across a landscape, generally declining from the base to the top of slopes (Schimel *et al.* 1985, Knapp *et al.* 1998) corresponding to declining soil moisture up these topo-edaphic gradients (Jenny 1980, Schimel *et al.* 1985, Burke 1989).

In Yellowstone Park, grazers behave in this patchy environment by increasing the amount they consume as above-ground production of a patch increases (Fig. 11.2). These data show what appears to be a production threshold (34 g/m^2) in Yellowstone, below which sites are not grazed. Furthermore, such a threshold, combined with the linear nature of the function, means that the intensity at which ungulates graze sites (i.e. the proportion of above-ground productivity removed) increases with plant production. For example, grassland that supports 50 g m^{-2} versus 400 g m^{-2} of plant growth, on average, experiences grazing intensities of 14% and 45%, respectively. Similar linear relationships between consumption and production show increasing grazing intensities with plant productivity in tropical savanna ecosystems occupied by large herds of ungulates (McNaughton 1985, Augustine et al. 2003). These suggest that the spatial concordance of forage production and grazing in Yellowstone may be a robust characteristic of grassland landscapes that support abundant ungulates.

The effect of large herbivores on landscape heterogeneity

The fact that grazers exhibit strong preferences on landscapes for sites with high plant production suggests that herbivores can potentially intensify or reduce heterogeneity, depending on whether their indirect effects on processes, including primary productivity, are facilitating or inhibiting. In Yellowstone, where herbivores facilitate biogeochemical processes, ungulates increase the spatial variability of a number of key grassland properties.

Yellowstone grassland, like most terrestrial ecosystems (Vitousek & Howarth 1991), is N limited, meaning that increasing the availability of N to plants enhances plant production. Thus N mineralization, or the conversion of N in organic material to inorganic forms that are readily available to plants, is a key process that limits plant growth. A comparison of annual rates of N mineralization inside and outside 45-year-old exclosures, i.e. 'park exclosures', at seven topographically diverse sites on Yellowstone's northern winter range revealed that grazers significantly increased mineralization and the rate of N available to plants (Frank & Groffman 1998). More pertinent to the topic of this chapter, however, grazers also increased the range (range$_{grazed}$ = 6.5 g N m^{-2}, range$_{ungrazed}$ = 2.2 g N m^{-2}) and standard deviation (1 SD$_{grazed}$ = 2.2, 1 SD$_{ungrazed}$ = 0.85) of N mineralization rates across the seven sites. Such findings indicate that ungulates enhanced the spatial variability of microbial processes and the availability of a plant-limiting nutrient in Yellowstone grassland.

The spatial pattern across which dung is deposited on Yellowstone landscapes corroborates the notion that grazers increase the heterogeneity of plant-available nutrients. The amount of dung deposited at a site is positively correlated with above-ground grassland production in Yellowstone (Frank & McNaughton 1992). If one assumes that the flux of dung deposited in a community is an index of nutrients that flow from ungulates to the soil in dung and urine combined (Frank et al. 1994), the rate that ungulates fertilize sites along topographic gradients is associated with plant production along those gradients. Because nutrients in dung and urine are sometimes in forms more available to plants and microbes (Frank et al. 2004, but see Pastor et al. 1993), compared to the forms in senescing plant tissue, ungulates should relax nutrient limitation of plants more in productive sites compared to less productive sites, and thus increase the spatial variability of plant production.

To examine this prediction, I compared production in grazed and paired ungrazed (fenced) vegetation across a range of grassland. Previously (Frank & McNaughton 1993, Frank et al. 2002), Yellowstone ungulates have been shown to facilitate above-ground production. Plotting the amount that grazers stimulated shoot growth against the rate of above-ground production of ungrazed grassland revealed that stimulation was positively associated with fenced plant productivity (Fig. 11.3). Thus grazers increased plant growth in high productive sites more than in low productive sites, indicating that ungulates enhanced the heterogeneity of above-ground grassland production in Yellowstone. These findings also highlight a spatial component of the positive feedback that grazers have on their forage: forage is stimulated more at sites that are most intensively grazed by ungulates. Therefore the greatest positive effect on forage production occurs at sites on the landscape where herbivores can benefit the most.

HETEROGENEITY WITHIN A PLANT COMMUNITY

The response of herbivores to heterogeneity within communities

It is clear from the chemical analyses of forage from different grassland ecosystems that some minerals are more difficult to acquire in sufficient quantities than others (McDowell 1985). In a study of forages in Yellowstone, for example, the average concentrations of minerals in grasses during the first month after snowmelt satisfied estimated requirements for domesticated grazers, except for copper (Cu) and Na (McDowell 1985, Taylor & Murray 1987). Grasses were deficient in P and zinc (Zn) by the

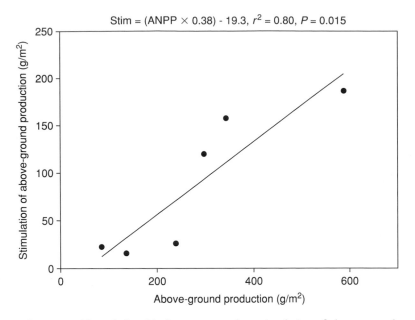

Figure 11.3. The relationship between ungulate stimulation of above-ground production and above-ground production for Yellowstone grassland. Stimulation was calculated as the difference between production in grazed grassland minus that in fenced, ungrazed grassland.

second month, and N in the third month. There were season-long deficiencies for Cu, magnesium (Mg), Na and Zn for lactating cows that required higher concentrations of some minerals (Frank 1998). Thus by grazing sites early in the growing season, which occurs in Yellowstone during the spring-summer migration, herbivores avoided deficiencies for most, but probably not all of their essential nutrients.

One way that herbivores can reduce deficiencies in minerals that are difficult to obtain is by feeding selectively among forage species that have high concentrations of specific nutrients (Senft *et al.* 1987). For species growing on moderately productive grassland in Yellowstone Park, for instance, the coefficient of variation of concentrations of the six limiting elements (Cu, Mg, N, Na, P, Zn), ranged from 33% for N to 99% for P (Fig. 11.4). Much of this variation was due to the general decline in mineral levels from the first to the second month, and differences between lower nutrient graminoid versus higher nutrient dicot species. Forage species offering the highest levels of limiting nutrients tended to be relatively uncommon or rare in the community, underscoring the need for herbivores

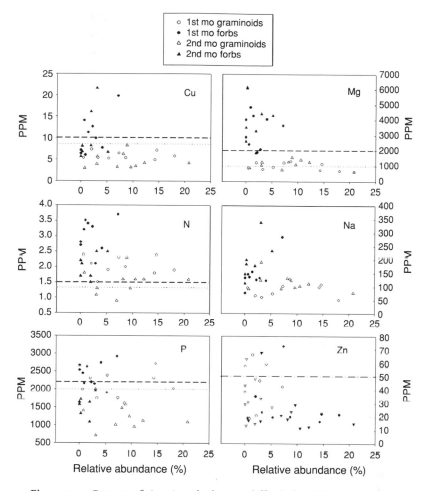

Figure 11.4. Content of six minerals that are difficult for Yellowstone ungulates to obtain in sufficient quantities. Each data point represents graminoid (open symbol) or dicot (filled symbol), and a species collected at a summer range site one (circle) or two (triangle) months after snowmelt. Nutrient content is plotted against the relative abundance of each of the forage species. Dashed and dotted lines denote suggested requirements for lactating cows and beef cattle, respectively (McDowell 1985). Sodium requirements (1800 ppm for lactating cows and 800 ppm for beef cattle) are well beyond the Na levels found in forage. Zinc requirements for the two types of livestock are the same.

to feed selectively and have a broad diet to meet nutritional requirements. Thus comparing the mineral content of forages with the nutritional requirements for ruminants in this way highlights the importance of a feeding strategy for herbivores that incorporates (1) migrating with and feeding on phenologically young vegetation, and (2) selectively consuming nutrient-rich species within the plant community that they graze. Sodium is required at far greater concentrations than provided by any forage species, and in Yellowstone, like in most grasslands, is supplemented heavily by geophagy in local hot-spots such as mineral springs (Jones & Hanson 1985, Tracy & McNaughton 1995).

The effect of large herbivores on variability within the community
The creation of localized nutrient-rich patches of urine and dung is thought to be the principal mechanism for herbivores increasing within community heterogeneity (McNaughton *et al.* 1988, Hobbs 1996, Steinauer & Collins 2001). The amount of N delivered to the soil in a single urine patch is quite high, estimated at about 50 g N m^{-2} (Stillwell 1983), which is many times greater than annual rates of mineralization measured in a variety of grasslands (McNaughton *et al.* 1997, Johnson & Machett 2001), including Yellowstone (Frank & Groffman 1998). Because of the large quantity of readily available N, areas that are recently urinated upon develop bright green vegetation, which is clearly distinguishable from unaffected areas. The size of these patches is quite small. In Yellowstone grassland, we found that the mean of 15 sampled patches in upland and lowland grassland was 0.18 m^2 and ranged 0.11–0.25 m^2.

In addition to increasing patchiness of plant and soil processes, urine patches also can promote the heterogeneity of grazing within a community. Both native (Day & Detling 1990) and domesticated (Jaramillo & Detling 1992) ruminants have been shown to graze urine patches at higher rates than the surrounding grassland. Using ^{15}N to track the short-term flows of N from simulated urine to plant and soil pools in Yellowstone grassland revealed that foliage within a urine patch directly absorbed N that had been volatilized as ammonia from simulated urine (Frank *et al.* 2004). Most of the N absorbtion by shoots occurred within three days after urine was added to the soil, indicating that a portion of N lost by ungulates was rapidly made re-available to herbivores. The results from the ^{15}N study, along with evidence indicating that urine patches are microsites of intensive grazing, suggest that these patches also represent areas where N lost by ungulates in urine is recycled to herbivores at unusually rapid rates, compared to the surrounding community.

The areal extent of grassland influenced by urine can vary depending on herbivore density (Augustine & Frank 2001). In rangeland supporting high densities of livestock (3 animals/ha) for extended periods (200 days), the coverage of urine patches may be as much as 27% (Afzal & Adams 1992). However, urine patches in Yellowstone, with much lower densities of grazers, cover a much smaller percentage of grassland, probably <3% (Augustine & Frank 2001). Indeed, during a season-long study of *in situ* N mineralization rates at seven grazed grassland sites on the northern winter range of Yellowstone Park, only two soil samples out of 420 collected across seven grassland sites exhibited an unusually high level of inorganic N characteristic of a urination event (Afzal & Adam 1992). Therefore, although the formation of intensely nutrient-enriched patches by herbivores undoubtedly increases spatial variability within a community, the preponderance of the surface area of most grasslands is unaffected by urine.

So, an important question I now will consider is: how do grazers influence the spatial variability of processes outside of urine patches, which represents the majority of grazed grassland? To address this question I re-examined the variability in potential rates of N mineralization and soil microbial respiration from a long-term laboratory incubation experiment that was reported previously (Frank & Groffman 1998), using only the soil samples that were unaffected by recent deposits of urine or dung. Potential rates of N mineralization and microbial respiration were determined on soil in the laboratory, with microclimatic conditions optimized (e.g. warm and moist) for microbial activity. Consequently, microbes during the experiment were limited only by the quality of organic material that was metabolized. I calculated the variation in potential rates on nine replicate soil samples per plot collected inside and outside the park exclosures at seven grassland sites in Yellowstone. It was previously reported that grazers increased rates of N mineralization and CO_2 respiration in soil incubated for two weeks (Frank & Groffman 1989). This reanalysis showed that, in addition, herbivores had no effect ($P > 0.10$) on the standard deviation or the coefficient of variation for either flux. These findings indicate that Yellowstone ungulates did not change the amount of total variation of potential rates of soil processes and organic matter quality in areas unaffected by ungulate dung or urine. Future studies would need to address if grazers influence the variation of other plant or soil processes.

An alternative way that herbivores may affect the variability of plant and soil properties is by changing the spatial structure of variability (Robertson 1987). Geostatistical analysis is a technique that estimates the amount of autocorrelation in samples. Autocorrelation occurs if samples near each other tend to be more similar than samples collected far apart. If autocorrelation is present, the variability in a data set is said to have spatial structure. Geostatistical methods are based on collecting samples from known locations, usually at points within grids, so the exact distances between samples can be calculated and the presence of spatial structure in the variation of a property detected.

To examine the effect of grazers on the spatial structure of soil processes, soil cores were collected every 10 cm within a 4×4 m grid located inside and outside the park exclosures on three upland grasslands (Augustine & Frank 2001). Grazers increased the fine-scale ($<$10 cm) variation in soil N content and potential N mineralization. This spatial scale is far finer than the size of urine patches measured in Yellowstone grassland (average $= 0.18$ m^2), thus some unknown mechanism(s) other than urine deposition must have increased fine-grained heterogeneity in grazed grassland. One potential mechanism is if herbivores indirectly influenced soil processes within the rhizospheres of grazed plants. Several species of grass have been shown in the laboratory to increase the rate that they exude carbon (C) from their roots after they are clipped (Bokari & Singh 1974, Bokari 1977, Holland et al. 1996). The same was reported for a common species of Yellowstone grass, Poa pratensis, which, when grown in pots, increased rates of root exudation and rhizospheric rates of net N mineralization in response to clipping (Hamilton & Frank 2001). These grazer-induced changes in rhizospheric processes could explain the fine-scale heterogeneity observed in Yellowstone grassland if the spatial scale of grazing is equivalently small. However, it still remains to be determined if herbivores induce exudation of C in the field.

Alternatively, a herbivore-induced increase in small-scale species richness may be a second mechanism for herbivores promoting fine-scale soil variability. Plant species richness in 20×20 cm quadrats was found to be greater in grazed compared to fenced grassland at the same grids used to examine the structure of soil N variation (Augustine & Frank 2001). Because different species can, over time, cause the properties of rhizospheric soils to diverge (Wedin & Tilman 1990), the higher number of co-occurring plant species in grazed grassland may feed back on soils to produce fine-grain soil heterogeneity. However, cause and effect of the fine-scale plant and soil properties is unclear. Thus, it remains unresolved whether herbivores increased numbers of co-occurring species that, subsequently, produced fine-grain variability in soil, or herbivores first enhanced soil fine-grain variability that resulted in high small-scale plant richness.

EFFECTS OF HERBIVORES ON HETEROGENEITY AND ASSOCIATED FEEDBACKS

I have presented evidence that grazers are an important determinant of habitat variability. In this section I wish to argue two points. First, grazers in Yellowstone increase habitat patchiness across all spatial scales. Second, ungulates increase spatial heterogeneity in a way that feeds back positively on themselves.

The long-distance seasonal migrations of large herds of ungulates occupying grassland is a function of the spatial separation of habitat supporting the most nutrient-rich forage during the growing season versus habitat that offers the most ameliorating conditions during the food-limiting portion of the year, i.e. highest precipitation during tropical dry season (McNaughton 1985) or warmest and least snowfall during temperate winter (Meagher 1973, Houston 1982). The physiological cycle of weight gain on one range and weight loss on the other should result in a net import of nutrients to the range that supports herds during the leanest period of the year. Significant quantities of nutrients are likely to be transported by ungulates across seasonal ranges in Yellowstone based on estimates of the biomass and nutrients that animals lose while on the winter range. A long-term net flux of nutrients to the winter range should facilitate plant processes there, which is corroborated by results in Yellowstone indicating that winter range forages are nutritionally richer than forages on higher elevation range. Thus migrating herds of Yellowstone ungulates appear to increase regional variation in a way that should benefit them at precisely the time of the year that they are most stressed.

At the landscape scale, a positive relationship between ungulate grazing intensity and shoot production has been reported for a number of ecosystems (McNaughton 1985, Frank & McNaughton 1992, Augustine et al. 2003). Furthermore, in Yellowstone, the rate that nutrients flow from ungulates to the soil, and the amount that herbivores stimulate plant productivity, also is associated with plant production. Thus, not only do ungulates increase the patchiness of soil processes and shoot production across landscapes in Yellowstone, herbivores stimulate processes most in precisely the patches that they prefer to graze.

Within communities, ungulate urine patches increase the spatial variability of soil and plant processes (Day & Detling 1990, Jaramillo & Detling 1992, Frank et al. 2004). Mineral-rich forage is concentrated within these patches, which are more intensively grazed than the surrounding vegetation (Day & Detling 1990, Jaramillo & Detling 1992). Furthermore, geostatistical results indicate that grazers increase the fine-scale, <10 cm, variability of soil N content and mineralization in areas unaffected by urine and dung, which is associated with grazers increasing the number of co-occurring plant species at a similar small spatial scale (Augustine & Frank 2001). A greater mix of such co-occurring species may facilitate a nutritionally balanced diet for herbivores, if species with relatively high mineral contents are better represented in swards that ungulates graze.

Thus findings in Yellowstone indicate that herbivores increase the patchiness of several important ecosystem processes at regional, landscape, and community scales. Moreover, the manner that consumers alter spatial heterogeneity of ecological processes in Yellowstone should feed back positively on large herbivores.

Grassland is a difficult habitat for ungulates to meet energetic and nutrient requirements. The hierarchical feeding decisions that large herbivores make across scales are important in determining their physiological condition. Work in Yellowstone indicates that herbivores both respond to forage heterogeneity and play an important role in creating that heterogeneity. Furthermore herds of Yellowstone ungulates appear to alter the spatial properties of the environment in a way that is likely to enhance their ability to extract energy and nutrients from their habitat and satisfy dietary requirements.

CONCLUSIONS

Yellowstone ungulates respond to habitat heterogeneity at several different spatial scales. Ungulates track nutrient-rich and highly concentrated forage during their regional, spring-summer migration from low elevation to high elevation range. At the landscape scale, grazing is positively and linearly related to above-ground grassland productivity. Within communities, herbivores probably feed selectively on rare and uncommon nutrient-rich plants to overcome deficiencies of some difficult to obtain minerals.

Yellowstone ungulates also create heterogeneity. At the regional scale, grazers transport an ecologically significant amount of nutrients to the winter range that may improve the physiological status of plants growing there. In addition, herbivores increase the spatial variability of plant production in landscapes by stimulating plant growth more in high productive compared to less productive grassland communities. Within communities, large herbivores increase fine-scale (<10 cm) variability of soil properties. This grazer-induced enhancement of spatial heterogeneity across several spatial scales should feed back positively on the capacity of herbivores to meet energetic and nutritional requirements.

ACKNOWLEDGEMENTS

I thank Ben Tracy for help measuring urine patch size, and M. Anderson and A. Risch for comments on an earlier draft. The NSF and National Park Service provided funding for this research.

REFERENCES

Afzal, M. & Adams, W.A. (1992). Heterogeneity of soil mineral nitrogen in pasture grazed by cattle. *Soil Science Society of America Journal*, **56**, 1160–66.

Augustine, D.J. & Frank, D.A. (2001). Effects of migratory grazers on spatial heterogeneity of soil nitrogen properties in a grassland ecosystem. *Ecology*, **82**, 3149–62.

Augustine, D.J., McNaughton, S.J. & Frank, D.A. (2003). Feedbacks between soil nutrients and large herbivores in a managed savanna ecosystem: bottom up is top down. *Ecological Applications*, **13**, 1325–37.

Ben-Shahar, R. & Coe, M.J. (1992). The relationships between soil factors, grass nutrients and the foraging behaviour of wildebeest and zebra. *Oecologia*, **90**, 422–8.

Bokhari, U.G. (1977). Regrowth of western wheatgrass utilizing ^{14}C-labeled assimilates stored in belowground parts. *Plant Soil*, **48**, 115–27.

Bokhari, U.G. & Singh, J.S. (1974). Effects of temperature and clipping on growth, carbohydrate reserves, and root exudation of western wheatgrass in hydroponic culture. *Crop Science*, **14**, 790–4.

Burke, I.C. (1989). Control of nitrogen mineralization in a sagebrush steppe landscape. *Ecology*, **70**, 1115–26.

Coughenour, M.B. (1991). Spatial components of plant-herbivore interactions in pastoral, ranching, and native ungulate ecosystems. *Journal of Range Management*, **44**, 530–42.

Day, T.A. & Detling, J.K. (1990). Grassland patch dynamics and herbivore grazing preference following urine deposition. *Ecology*, **71**, 180–8.

Demment, M.W. & Greenwood, G.B. (1988). Forage ingestion: effects of sward characteristics and body size. *Journal of Animal Science*, **66**, 2380–92.

Frank D.A. (1998). Ungulate regulation of ecosystem processes in Yellowstone National Park: direct and feedback effects. *Wildlife Society Bulletin*, **26**, 410–18.

Frank, D.A. & Groffman, P.M. (1998). Ungulate vs landscape control of soil C and N processes in grasslands of Yellowstone National Park. *Ecology*, **79**, 2229–41.

Frank, D.A. & McNaughton, S.J. (1992). The ecology of plants, large mammalian herbivores, and drought in Yellowstone National Park. *Ecology*, **73**, 2043–58.

Frank, D.A. & McNaughton, S.J. (1993). Evidence for the promotion of aboveground grassland production by native large herbivores in Yellowstone National Park. *Oecologia*, **96**, 157–61.

Frank, D.A., Inouye, R.S., Huntly, N., Minshall, G.W. & Anderson, J.E. (1994). The biogeochemistry of a north-temperate grassland with native ungulates: nitrogen dynamics in Yellowstone National Park. *Biogeochemistry*, **26**, 163–88.

Frank, D.A., McNaughton, S.J. & Tracy, B.F. (1998). The ecology of the earth's grazing ecosystems. *Bioscience*, **48**, 513–21.

Frank, D.A., Kuns, M.M. & Guido, D.R. (2002). Consumer control of grassland plant production. *Ecology*, **83**, 602–6.

Frank, D.A., Evans, R.D. & Tracy, B.F. (2004). The role of ammonia volatilization in controlling the natural ^{15}N abundance of a grazed grassland. *Biogeochemistry*, **68**, 169–78.

Festa-Bianchet, M. (1988). Seasonal range selection in bighorn sheep: conflicts between forage quality, forage quantity, and predator avoidance. *Oecologia*, **75**, 580–6.

Fryxell, J.M. & Sinclair, A.R.E. (1988). Causes and consequences of migration by large herbivores. *Trends in Ecology and Evolution*, **3**, 237–41.

Fryxell, J.M., Greever, J. & Sinclair, A.R.E. (1988). Why are migratory ungulates so abundant? *American Naturalist*, **131**, 781–98.

Hamilton E.W. & Frank, D.A. (2001). Can plants stimulate soil microbes and their own nutrient supply? Evidence from a grazing tolerant grass. *Ecology*, **82**, 2397–402.

Hobbs, N.T. (1989). Linking energy balance to survival in mule deer: development and test of a simulation model. *Wildlife Monographs*, No. 101, Bethesda, MD: The Wildlife Society.

Hobbs, N.T. (1996). Modification of ecosystems by ungulates. *Journal of Wildlife Management*, **60**, 695–713.

Holland, J.N., Cheng, W. & Crossley, D.A. (1996). Herbivore-induced changes in plant carbon allocation: assessment of below-ground C fluxes using carbon-14. *Oecologia*, **107**, 87–94.

Houston, D.B. (1982). *The Northern Yellowstone Elk: Ecology and Management*. New York, NY: Macmillan.

Hudson, R.J. & White, R.G. (eds.) (1985). *Bioenergetics of Wild Herbivores*. Boca Raton, FL: CRC Press.

Illius, A.W. & O'Connor, T.G. (2000). Resource heterogeneity and ungulate population dynamics. *Oikos*, **89**, 283–94.

Jaramillo, V.J. & Detling, J.K. (1992). Small-scale heterogeneity in a semi-arid North American grassland. I. Tillering, N uptake and retranslocation in simulated urine patches. *Journal of Applied Ecology*, **29**, 1–8.

Jenny, H. (1980). *The Soil Resource: Origin and Behavior*. Ecological Studies, vol. 37. New York: Springer-Verlag.

Johnson, L.C. & Machett, J.R. (2001). Fire and grazing regulate belowground processes in tallgrass prairie. *Ecology*, **82**, 3377–89.

Jones, R.L. & Hanson, H.C. (1985). *Mineral Licks, Geophagy, and Biogeochemistry of North American Ungulates*. Ames, IA: Iowa State University Press.

Klein, D.R. (1965). Ecology of deer range in Alaska. *Ecological Monographs*, **35**, 259–84.

Knapp, A.K., Briggs, J.M., Blair, J.M. & Turner, C.L. (1998). Patterns and controls of aboveground net primary production in tallgrass prairie. In *Grassland Dynamics: Long-term Ecological Research in Tallgrass Prairie*, ed. A.K. Knapp, J.M. Briggs, D.C. Hartnett & S.L. Collins. Oxford: Oxford University Press, pp. 193–221.

Laca, E.A. & Demment, M.W. (1986). The feeding behavior of a grazing herbivore: harvesting limitations. *Proceedings of the International Congress of Ecology*, **4**, 209.

Leopold, A. (1933). *Game Management*. Madison, Wisconsin: University of Wisconsin Press.

Levin, S.A. (1992). The problem of pattern and scale in ecology. *Ecology*, **73**, 1943–83.

Ludlow, M.M., Stobbs, T.H., Davis, R. & Charles-Edwards, D.A. (1982). Effect of sward structure of two tropical grasses with contrasting canopies on light distribution, net photosynthesis and size of bite harvested by grazing cattle. *Australian Journal of Agricultural Research*, **33**, 187–201.

McDowell, L.R. (1985). *Nutrition of Grazing Ruminants in Warm Climates*. New York: Academic Press.

McNaughton, S.J. (1979). Grassland-herbivore dynamics. In *Serengeti: Dynamics of an Ecosystem*, ed. A.R.E. Sinclair & M. Norton-Griffiths. Chicago: University of Chicago, pp. 46–81.

McNaughton, S.J. (1984). Grazing lawns: animals in herds, plant form, and coevolution. *American Naturalist*, **124**, 863–86.

McNaughton, S.J. (1985). Ecology of a grazing ecosystem: the Serengeti. *Ecological Monographs*, **55**, 259–95.

McNaughton, S.J. (1989). Interactions of plants of the field layer with large herbivores. *Symposia of the Zoological Society of London*, **61**, 15–29.

McNaughton, S.J. (1990). Mineral nutrition and seasonal movements of African migratory ungulates. *Nature*, **345**, 613–15.

McNaughton, S.J. (1991). Evolutionary ecology of large tropical herbivores. In *Plant-Animal Interactions: Evolutionary Ecology in Tropical and Temperate Regions*, ed. P.W. Price, T.M. Lewinsohn, G.W. Fernandes & W.W. Benson. New York: John Wiley & Sons, Inc., pp. 509–22.

McNaughton, S.J., Ruess, R.W. & Seagle, S.W. (1988). Large mammals and process dynamics in African ecosystems. *Bioscience*, **38**, 794–800.

McNaughton, S.J., Banyikawa, F.F. & McNaughton, M.M. (1997). Promotion of the cycling of diet-enhancing nutrients by African grazers. *Science*, **278**, 1798–800.

Meagher, M.M. (1973). *The Bison of Yellowstone National Park*. NPS Scientific Monograph Series Number 1. Washington, DC: United States Department of Interior.

Mitchell, B., McCowan, D. & Nicholson, I.A. (1976). Annual cycles of body weight and condition in Scottish red deer, *Cervus elaphus*. *Journal of Zoology (London)*, **180**, 107–27.

Moen, R., Pastor, J. & Cohen, Y. (1997). A spatially explicit model of moose foraging and energetics. *Ecology*, **78**, 505–21.

Morgantini, L.E. & Hudson, R.J. (1988). Migratory patterns of the wapati, *Cervus elaphus*, in Banff National Park, Alberta. *Canadian Field Naturalist*, **102**, 12–19.

Pastor, J., Dewey, B., Naiman, R.J., McInnes, P.F. & Cohen, Y. (1993). Moose browsing and soil fertility in the boreal forests of Isle Royale National Park. *Ecology*, **74**, 467–80.

Pastor, J., Dewey, B., Moen, R. *et al.* (1998). Spatial patterns in the moose-forest-soil Ecosystem on Isle Royale, Michigan, USA. *Ecological Applications*, **8**, 411–24.

Pickett, S.T.A. & Cadenasso, M.L. (1995). Landscape ecology: spatial heterogeneity in ecological systems. *Science*, **269**, 331–4.

Prins, H.H.T. (1996). *Ecology and Behavior of the African Buffalo: Social Inequality and Decision Making*. London: Chapman & Hall.

Robertson, G.P. (1987). Geostatistics in ecology: interpolating with known variance. *Ecology*, **68**, 744–8.

Robbins, C.T. (1983). *Wildlife Feeding and Nutrition*. New York: Academic Press.

Schimel D.S., Stillwell, M.A. & Woodmansee, R.G. (1985). Biogeochemistry of C, N, and P on a catena of the shortgrass steppe. *Ecology*, **66**, 276–82.

Senft, R.L., Coughenhour, M.B., Bailey, D.W. *et al.* (1987). Large herbivore foraging and ecological hierarchies. *Bioscience*, **37**M, 789–99.

Sinclair, A.R.E. & Norton-Griffiths, M. (1979). *Serengeti: Dynamics of an Ecosystem*. Chicago: University of Chicago Press.

Singer, F.J., Schreier, W., Oppenheim, J. & Garton, E.O. (1989). Drought, fires, and large mammals. *Bioscience*, **39**, 716–22.

Singer, F.J. & Mack, J.A. (1993). Potential ungulate prey for gray wolves. In *Ecological Issues on Reintroducing Wolves into Yellowstone National Park*. ed. R.S. Cook. United States Department of Interior. Scientific Monograph no. NPS/NRYELL/NRSM-93/22, pp. 75–117.

Spalinger, D.E. & Hobbs, N.T. (1992). Mechanisms of foraging in mammalian herbivores: new models of functional response. *American Naturalist*, **140**, 325–48.

Steinauer, E.M. & Collins, S.L. (2001). Spatial cascades in community structure following urine deposition in tallgrass prairie. *Ecology*, **82**, 1319–29.

Sterner, R.W. & Elser, J.J. (2002). *Ecological Stoichiometry*. Princeton, NJ: Princeton University Press.

Stillwell, M.A. (1983). Effects of bovine urinary nitrogen on the nitrogen cycle of a shortgrass prairie. Dissertation, Colorado State University, Fort Collins, CO.

Swank, W.T. (1984). Atmospheric contributions to forest nutrient cycling. *Water Resources Bulletin*, **20**, 313–21.

Taylor, St. C.S. & Murray, J.I. (1987). Genetic aspects of mammalian survival and growth in relation to body size. In *The Nutrition of Herbivores*, ed. J.B. Hacker & J.H. Ternouth. New York: Academic Press, pp. 487–533.

Tracy, B.F. & McNaughton, S.J. (1995). Elemental analysis of mineral lick soils from Serengeti National Park, the Konza Prairie, and Yellowstone National Park. *Ecography*, **18**, 91–4.

Turner, M.G., Wu, Y., Wallace, L.L., Romme, W.H. & Brenkert, A. (1994). Simulating winter interactions among ungulates, vegetation, and fire in northern Yellowstone Park. *Ecological Applications*, **4**, 472–96.

Turner, M.G., Gardner, R.H. & O'Neill, R.V. (2001). *Landscape Ecology in Theory and Practice*. New York: Springer-Verlag.

Van Soest, P.J. (1982). *Nutritional Ecology of the Ruminant*. Corvallis, OR: O & B Books.

Vitousek, P.M. & Howarth, R.W. (1991). Nitrogen limitation on land and in the sea: how can it occur? *Biogeochemistry*, **13**, 87–115.

Wallace, L.L., Turner, M.G., Romme, W.H., O'Neill, R.V. & Wu, Y. (1995). Scale of heterogeneity of forage production and winter foraging by elk and bison. *Landscape Ecology*, **10**, 75–83.

Wedin, D.A. & Tilman, D. (1990). Species effects on nitrogen cycling: a test with perennial grasses. *Oecologia*, **84**, 433–41.

12

Modelling of large herbivore–vegetation interactions in a landscape context

PETER J. WEISBERG, MICHAEL B. COUGHENOUR
AND HARALD BUGMANN

INTRODUCTION

There is growing appreciation of the important role large herbivores can play in vegetation, ecosystem and landscape dynamics (Hobbs 1996, Danell *et al.* 2003, Rooney & Waller 2003, and earlier chapters of this volume). In turn, there has been an improved understanding of the importance of landscape pattern for large herbivore dynamics (Turner *et al.* 1994, Illius & O'Connor 2000, Walters 2001), and research into patterns of animal movement through landscapes (Gross *et al.* 1995, Schaefer *et al.* 2000, Johnson *et al.* 2002). At landscape scales, the large herbivore-vegetation interaction can be quite complex, involving many interacting factors such as plant competition, landscape pattern, climate, disturbance regimes and biogeochemical cycles. The earlier chapters of this volume demonstrate the complexity of such relationships, and the difficulty in establishing simple generalizations.

Simulation modelling has proved a useful tool for disentangling some of this complexity, and for integrating information across multiple scales. There are numerous modelling approaches, at varying levels of complexity, developed to satisfy different research objectives, for simulating the impacts of large herbivores upon vegetation or vice versa. However, few represent key interactions between the two ecosystem components in a balanced manner.

In this chapter, we review the different modelling approaches for representing large herbivore-landscape interactions in an integrated way.

Large Herbivore Ecology, Ecosystem Dynamics and Conservation, ed. K. Danell, P. Duncan, R. Bergström & J. Pastor. Published by Cambridge University Press. © Cambridge University Press 2006.

By integrated models, we refer to modelling approaches that consider vegetation and animal dynamics with similar levels of complexity, bridging the two key components through the ecological process of herbivory. Integrated grazing models have been used to address a number of ecological questions that consider sufficiently long time scales for feedbacks between large herbivores and vegetation to become important. Due to our emphasis on the landscape context, we will focus on spatially explicit models. The major challenges inherent in such modelling approaches are discussed, particularly problems related to scale and constructing models of use for management and conservation. It is not our goal to provide solutions to all of these difficulties, but rather to synthesize the scope of the problem, and to briefly summarize how these challenges are or are not addressed by the current generation of integrated large herbivore-vegetation models. We hope that by describing the current limitations for such models, we identify critical gaps in our knowledge of how large herbivores and vegetation interact in complex landscape systems.

MODELLING APPROACHES

Three general approaches to modelling large herbivore-vegetation processes can be characterized: animal-focused, plant-focused, and integrated (Fig. 12.1). We briefly discuss the former two approaches, focusing the remainder of our chapter on the latter.

Approaches focusing on large herbivore dynamics

When the questions of interest focus on animal physiology or population dynamics, vegetation may be portrayed as a single input variable for available forage or, if foraging ecology is irrelevant for the model, available energy (Fig. 12.1a). Forage or energy intake is balanced against the large herbivore's energetic requirements (basal metabolism, thermal metabolism, requirements for travel, foraging and lactation), often using a simple 'input-output' energy budget approach. The energetic state of the animal typically influences reproductive success through population parameters determining mortality and fecundity. Populations may then be distributed over some larger area either through explicit simulation of their movement patterns, or using a 'fly and sit' approach where habitat selection functions are related to landscape pattern as represented by a spatial database. Distribution determines the local population density, which in turn influences future intake rates for each simulated patch.

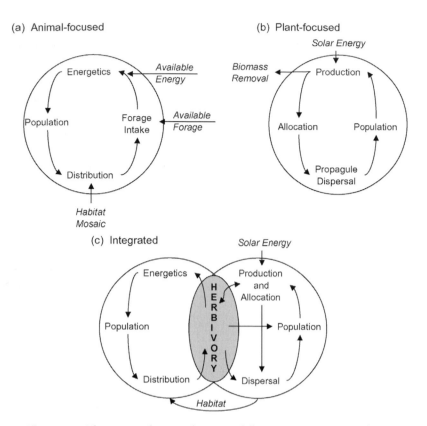

Figure 12.1. Three general approaches to modelling interactions among large herbivores and vegetation: (a) animal-focused, (b) plant-focused, and (c) integrated.

Such animal-focused models will generally require two inputs that relate to vegetation: (1) the amount and quality of available forage, and (2) the mosaic pattern and availability of suitable habitat. In some cases, the models use the spatial pattern of forage availability itself as the habitat map (e.g. Moen *et al.* 1997). Plant production, which varies seasonally and with the weather, represents the critical driving variable, but there is little or no feedback of herbivory to plant productivity. A single forage quantity representing vegetation at each patch may be decremented due to browsing and decomposition, but plant responses to browsing (e.g. compensatory growth, structural and compositional changes) are not represented. By varying the forage input seasonally, annually or according to scenarios of vegetation change, such a model can be used to describe the influence of variation in forage resources on large herbivore dynamics (Turner *et al.*

1994, Illius & O'Connor 2000). Similarly, animal distribution or movement patterns can be made to vary with landscape patterns that vary over time (e.g. Loza *et al.* 1992). However, such models do not describe the influences of large herbivore effects on plant production or landscape pattern, and so do not represent potentially important feedbacks between plant and animal processes (e.g. resource depletion, stimulation of compensatory growth, nutrient relocation, competitive influences, trophic cascades). Therefore, although models of the type shown in Fig. 12.1a may prove theoretically interesting, they are unlikely to provide realistic results for actual landscapes over time periods sufficiently long for plant-animal feedbacks to become important. Regardless, most carrying capacity models, foraging models and animal population models fall into the strictly animal-focused category (e.g. Hobbs & Swift 1985, Loza *et al.* 1992, Xie *et al.* 1999). We advocate the utility of more integrated modelling approaches for estimating carrying capacity and appropriate large herbivore population objectives in the context of spatio-temporal variation and long time periods (e.g. Weisberg *et al.* 2002).

Approaches focusing on vegetation dynamics

Another approach to modelling large herbivore-vegetation processes emphasizes the vegetation side (Fig. 12.1b). Where the focus has been on production or population dynamics of vegetation, herbivory has most often been represented simply as the removal of biomass or individual plants. Plant-focused models of herbivory generally take one of two forms: (1) biomass-based production models with grazing as a driving variable, and (2) forest gap models with a browsing effect on tree regeneration. In neither case are feedbacks of altered vegetation composition, spatial pattern or forage availability upon the herbivores explicitly incorporated.

Biomass-based models of plant productivity are usually applied to grasslands and other vegetation types dominated by grazers and herbaceous vegetation, where population dynamics at the level of individual plants are neither important nor feasible to consider. These types of models can represent the effects of herbivory without modelling actual animals associating reductions in plant biomass with particular grazing intensities (Fig. 12.1b). Forage biomass may influence simulated grazing intensity, where large herbivore intake rate is reduced at low biomass levels (representing inefficiency of foraging in resource-poor patches, or animal decisions to forage in more resource-rich patches). However, there is no long-term feedback on grazing intensity due to reductions in large herbivore condition or population levels, or shifts in spatial allocation of foraging effort, as a result of resource depletion. Jeltsch *et al.* (1997) used such a model to explore the relative influences of cattle grazing and precipitation on shrub encroachment processes in the South African savanna. In their model, production is determined empirically from the amount of plant-available soil moisture on a given patch. Functional plant types (i.e. shrubs, perennial herbaceous, annual grasses) compete for soil moisture on patches where root systems overlap. Removal of herbaceous biomass due to grazing, which influences competition among plant types, is calculated from patch-specific livestock stocking rates.

The widely used forest gap models simulate the population dynamics (establishment, growth and mortality) of individual trees on small patches as functions of competition and environmental factors (reviewed in Bugmann 2001). Gap models have represented browsing effects on forest succession in different ways. In some models, browsing is treated as just another stochastic environmental variable influencing the probability with which small trees of a given species might establish in a particular time step (e.g. Bugmann 1996a). Such models can explore the effects of particular browsing intensities on long-term forest dynamics in a manner that is very general, empirically based and time-invariant. Important interactive influences for forest regeneration, such as the importance of light availability or site productivity for influencing species-specific responses to a given browsing level (Edenius *et al.* 1995, Saunders & Puettmann 1999), cannot be represented.

Other gap modelling applications go one step further and incorporate the process of browsing into an explicit representation of sapling growth and mortality (Jorritsma *et al.* 1999, Kienast *et al.* 1999, Seagle & Liang 2001). This requires certain modifications to the basic gap model structure, since most gap models regenerate new trees at 1.2–2.5 cm diameter at breast height, and do not explicitly represent seedlings or saplings. Tree seedlings and saplings may be included by simply lowering the minimum tree size for inclusion in the model to a near-zero value (Kienast *et al.* 1999, Seagle & Liang 2001), or by considering height or age cohorts of saplings (Jorritsma *et al.* 1999). Browsing regimes are determined in such models by: (1) treating browsing intensity as a random variable with site- and species-specific mean and variance (Kienast *et al.* 1999), (2) introducing a density dependence between stem density and browsing probability, along with a species-specific diet preference factor (Seagle & Liang 2001), or (3) explicitly modelling herbivore biomass and energetic demand, coupled with a diet selection submodel (Jorritsma *et al.* 1999). The first approach implies that browsing intensity is stationary over time, and cannot change in response to directional environmental variability, or feedbacks from changes in the forage base. The second represents forage selection as a hierarchical process where animals first select high-density forage patches, and then select individual stems within patches according to their species-specific diet preferences. This allows for feedbacks between browsing intensity and the forage base. The third approach truly integrates vegetation with animal processes in a single model, which brings us to our third class of large herbivore–vegetation models.

Integrated approaches

As discussed above, the process of mammalian herbivory has typically been represented by models in a non-integrated way. Both classes of models described above (Fig. 12.1a,b) have contributed greatly to our understanding of large herbivore-vegetation interactions. However, they do not represent plant and animal systems at similar levels of complexity, being heavily skewed toward one side of the interaction or the other. An appropriate level of complexity for forecasting the responses to novel environmental and management-related conditions is therefore not available at the present time.

Where modelling objectives require forecasting such responses to novel conditions, we propose there is great value in adopting an integrated approach, where balanced animal and plant submodels are linked through the process of herbivory (Fig. 12.1c). The level of herbivory is influenced by plant production, biomass allocation and animal distribution (density on a patch), and in turn influences animal energetics and further plant production. Such integrated approaches become particularly valuable where research questions involve long time scales over which feedbacks between plant and animal components cannot reasonably be ignored. Note that any of the three approaches (Fig. 12.1) may either consider spatial heterogeneity of the environment or vegetation pattern (i.e. spatially explicit models), or assume spatial homogeneity (i.e. point models). Spatially explicit models are essential for capturing long-term interactions between large herbivores and vegetation dynamics, since over long time periods large herbivore populations or individuals are likely to move to more favourable patches during periods of resource scarcity, or even to alter the spatial patterns of the utilized landscapes (Pastor *et al.* 1999a). Representing the critical, long-term interactions between large herbivores and vegetation requires that vegetation pattern and dynamics be linked to actual landscape variability. Integrated models of large herbivore-vegetation interactions (Fig. 12.1c) are exemplified by the

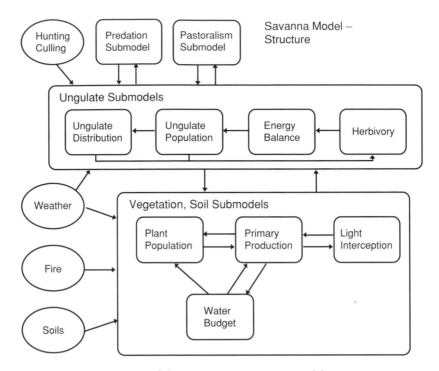

Figure 12.2. Structure of the SAVANNA ecosystem model.

SAVANNA model. SAVANNA is a spatially explicit, process-oriented model of grassland, shrubland, savanna and forested ecosystems. The first versions were developed to study a nomadic pastoral ecosystem in Kenya (Coughenour 1992), while subsequent versions were developed for other ecosystems in North America (Coughenour & Singer 1996, Coughenour 2002, Weisberg *et al.* 2002, Weisberg & Coughenour 2003), Australia (Liedloff *et al.* 2001, Ludwig *et al.* 2001), Africa (Kiker 1998, Boone *et al.* 2002) and Asia (Christensen *et al.* 2003). The model is composed of site water balance, plant biomass production, plant population dynamics, litter decomposition and nitrogen cycling, ungulate herbivory, ungulate spatial distribution, ungulate energy balance, and ungulate population dynamics submodels (Fig. 12.2). SAVANNA simulates processes at landscape through regional spatial scales over annual to decadal time scales. The time-step of the model is one week.

Savanna has a hierarchical spatial structure. It is spatially explicit at the landscape scale but is spatially inexplicit at patch scales. The mosaic of grid-cells covers landscapes or regional-scale ecosystems. Within each grid-cell the model simulates three vegetation patch types or 'facets'. These are defined by the fractional covers of herbaceous plants, shrubs and trees. Since shrub and tree cover are simulated variables, facet cover is a dynamic outcome of vegetation growth and mortality.

While the SAVANNA model has been successfully applied to scientific and management problems in a great variety of biome and ecosystem types, it has clear limitations. For example, animals are distributed each time-step according to a habitat suitability model, but since simulated herds of animals do not actually move from patch to patch, the importance of landscape connectivity or anthropogenic barriers such as roads cannot be represented. In addition, forest dynamics are summarized using 'representative trees' within six age/size classes, which is often insufficient for modelling the effects of herbivore browsing on long-term tree population dynamics (but see Weisberg & Coughenour 2003). This model will be discussed further in later sections of this chapter in the context of how it addresses several key challenges in integrating large herbivore-vegetation processes.

That relatively few other truly integrated models of large herbivore-vegetation interactions have been developed besides SAVANNA reflects the complexity underlying this approach. We call attention to three other integrated models, summarized in Table 12.1. Other models reported in the literature may be considered to integrate plant and animal processes. We do not discuss these because in some cases they are not spatially explicit and so do not fit into the 'landscape context' of our chapter (e.g. Hacker et al. 1991, Jorritsma et al. 1999), while in other cases they are entirely empirical and do not represent large herbivore-vegetation interactions at a process level (e.g. Armstrong et al. 1997a,b, Blatt et al. 2001). We realize that even within our fairly narrow criteria for what constitutes a landscape-level, integrated model, we may have inadvertently omitted some.

While the models shown in Table 12.1 differ in a number of ways, they have several features in common (Table 12.1). All have a sub-annual time-step, since seasonal effects are important for understanding ungulate-vegetation processes. Individual plant responses vary with seasonality of browsing relative to plant phenology and species-specific traits for carbon and nutrient allocation (Millard et al. 2001, see also Chapter 4). At landscape scales, the strength of the coupling between large herbivores and their resource base may vary seasonally. This can result in quite different large herbivore-vegetation dynamics between seasons of resource abundance and scarcity, with implications for system resilience to grazing pressure,

Table 12.1. *Representative, integrated models of interactions among large herbivores and vegetation at a landscape scale. The table summarizes key features for each model including representation of time and space, biome applicability, and the degree of complexity with which each broad category of animal or vegetation process, shown in Fig. 12.1, is represented. The number of plus signs indicates the level of process complexity, while a minus sign indicates that the process is not represented*

Model	Temporal Grain / Extent**	Spatial Grain / Extent††	Biomes Applied	Animal Energetics	Animal Pop Dynamics	Animal Distrib	Plant Production	Plant Pop Dynamics	Plant Dispersal
Van Oene*	1 day / 25 yr	4–500 ha / 10^2–10^3 ha	Temperate Wetlands	+[a]	−	+[f]	++[j]	−[l]	−[o]
SAVANNA†	1 week / 10–150 yr	1–100 ha / 10^3–10^5 ha	Savannas, Grasslands, Woodlands, Temperate and Boreal Forests	+[a] ++[b] +++[c]	+++[e]	++[g]	+++[k]	++[n]	−[p]
FORSPACE‡	1 month / 100 yr	0.04 ha/ 10^4 ha	Temperate Deciduous Forest	++[b]	+[d]	+[f]	++[j]	+[m]	+[q]
EASE§	1 hour / 1–100 yr	10^{-4} ha / 8.1 ha	Boreal Forest	+++[c]	+++[e]	+++[h]	+[i]	−	−

Key model references:
* *van Oene et al. 1999b.*
† *Coughenour 2002.*
‡ *Kramer et al. 2001, 2003.*
§ *Moen et al. 1997, 1998.*
Key to Process Abbreviations:
Animal Energetics
[a] *Simple energy balance – fixed energy costs per unit body weight per unit time.*

b Simple energy balance plus travel and lactation/gestation costs.

c Physiological model differentiating costs of activity, growth, thermoregulation, gestation and lactation.

Animal Population Dynamics

d 2-cohort, single-sex population model (juveniles and adults).

e Age-sex class model (annual classes), with fecundity and survivorship influenced by animal energetic state.

Animal Distribution

f 'Fly and Sit' – landscape-level optimal foraging.

g 'Fly and Sit' with habitat suitability model (including forage availability), and minima/maxima for animal density.

h Individual-based animal movement model allowing for different foraging strategies.

Plant Production

i Empirically derived intrinsic growth rate.

j Radiation use efficiency with environmental modifiers.

k Net photosynthesis linked to transpiration and water use efficiency, including calculation of stomatal conductance (Ball et al. 1987), nitrogen and temperature dependent maintenance respiration.

Plant Population Dynamics

l Neither individual plants nor cohorts of individuals represented, but tracks biomass pools by plant organ.

m A single cohort represents the presence of a given species in each of the following layers: herb, shrub, tree.

n Woody plants tracked in six age/size classes; herbaceous vegetation represented as an index of basal cover.

o Plant Dispersal. Assumes a continuous, universal seed pool at each spatial unit. Environmental filters used to control establishment.

p As above, but separated into endogenous vs. exogenous seed rain.

q Represents seed dispersal between patches using a Gaussian distribution. Environmental filters used to control establishment.

Other Footnotes:

** Temporal extent is variable; shown is a range of values used in published applications. If multiple time steps are present in the model, the finest time step is given in the table.

†† Spatial extent is variable; shown is a range of values used in published applications. If multiple spatial resolutions are present in the model, the finest cell size is given in the table.

climate variability and environmental change (Illius & O'Connor 1999). Most integrated models are designed to run for multiple decades, allowing consideration of long-term dynamics. All have components for representing the energetics of large herbivores, although in some cases this is a simple energy balance with fixed costs per unit animal mass (van Oene *et al.* 1999b), while in other cases a detailed physiological model is applied differentiating the costs of travel, growth, thermoregulation, gestation and lactation (Moen *et al.* 1997). Some simulate animal population dynamics, allowing a feedback loop where herbivore-induced degradation of the forage base can lead to an herbivore population decline, which in turn might have positive effects on the ability of vegetation to recover, and so on. All represent animal distribution, although that may be an artefact of our having selected only those models relevant at the landscape scale. Large herbivore selectivity for particular patch types is a key to understanding large herbivore interactions with landscape dynamics. All represent dynamic plant production, although over varying levels of complexity. Only two of the four models represent plant population dynamics, while only FORSPACE explicitly considers plant dispersal.

There is no simple recipe for modelling large herbivore–vegetation interactions, and the four models shown in Table 12.1 vary widely in how they do or do not represent the abiotic environment ('landscape template'), climate, flows of water and nutrients, and the plant-soil system. Some include plant processes such as phenology, carbon reserve dynamics, water uptake, nutrient uptake and allocation, senescence of plant parts, and shading (Coughenour 2002). Others represent primary production as simple functions of available light (van Oene *et al.* 1999b, Kramer *et al.* 2001) or as an intrinsic growth rate (Moen *et al.* 1998). Depending on their objectives and underlying assumptions, integrated models elaborate certain processes with a high level of mechanistic complexity, while treating others quite empirically (Table 12.1).

Large herbivores are extremely mobile organisms, yet are highly selective about their movements. Therefore, it is useful for integrated models to consider the environmental (climate, topography) and resource availability (forage, habitat) factors that influence large herbivore movement and distribution. This often requires that dynamic climatic variables, which may act as important model drivers, be interpolated over a heterogeneous landscape. In cold systems, forage availability, energetic limitations for large herbivore movement, and hence large herbivore distribution are greatly influenced by snow patterns (Sweeney & Sweeney 1984). In temperate grasslands, deserts and savannas, the spatial and temporal variability of soil moisture becomes most important for understanding patterns of forage availability (see Chapter 5). Where integrated models of herbivory attempt to forecast large herbivore effects or responses to vegetation change for actual landscapes (e.g. Weisberg *et al.* 2002, Kramer *et al.* 2003), they must incorporate linkages to an underlying Geographic Information Systems (GIS) database describing landscape heterogeneity of vegetation, soils, topography and possibly other physical features.

CHALLENGES OF INTEGRATED LARGE HERBIVORE-VEGETATION MODELS IN A LANDSCAPE CONTEXT

Based on this review and our experiences with developing and applying this type of model, we identify several challenges that need to be overcome before we can move substantially forward. These are summarized as follows:

1. Including important interactions among multiple plant and animal species.
2. Representing the effects of cultural features and land use change.
3. Representing interactions among large herbivores and disturbances.
4. Incorporating potentially important, landscape-scale effects other than herbivory, such as plant propagule dispersal and nutrient redistribution.
5. Incorporating multiple scales of processes and interactions.

The first four topics on this list are briefly discussed below. The last challenge is quite involved, however, and is discussed in the next section.

At least four classes of interspecific interactions are relevant for landscape-level large herbivore-vegetation models: interactions between predator and large herbivore species; interactions among large herbivore species; interactions among plant species; and interactions between large herbivore and plant species. The latter interaction type is generally the focus of such models. However, the former three classes of interactions are often of great importance.

Predator-large herbivore interactions

The influences of predators on large herbivore population and community dynamics have been reviewed in Chapter 14. Andersen *et al.* (Chapter 14) review both numerical and behavioural influences of predators on large herbivore individuals and populations. Recent work with wolf–elk–aspen trophic systems in the western United States suggests that behavioural responses to predation may be quite important for influencing landscape-scale effects of large herbivores on vegetation (Ripple & Larsen 2000, Ripple et al. 2001, White et al. 2003). Predation risk factors condition the spatial distribution of large herbivores, often mitigating the intensity of herbivory on critical areas where ungulate herds would congregate for long time periods in the absence of predators. Areas near predator travel routes and denning sites are often avoided (e.g. White et al. 2003).

Despite the importance of predation for understanding carrying capacity, animal distribution and landscape-level large herbivore effects, surprisingly few integrated herbivory models consider more than two trophic levels. Of the four models described in Table 12.1, only SAVANNA considers predation. It considers only numerical effects of predation on large herbivore population numbers, not behavioural effects on large herbivore distribution and foraging behaviour. Simulation of herbivore behavioural responses to predators in SAVANNA would require a more detailed representation of predator spatial distributions. Currently, the model represents pack ranges, but not distributions within ranges. It is difficult to incorporate such behavioural effects in a landscape-level model, although the approach of DeAngelis et al. (1998) shows promise, where individual-based models of panther and deer reproduction, growth, mortality and movements are incorporated within a spatially explicit model of vegetation and hydrology.

Interactions among large herbivore species

Interactions among large herbivore species are significant and may exert a strong influence upon landscape use and foraging impacts (Latham 1999). There are numerous examples of facilitative interactions (Sinclair & Norton-Griffiths 1982, Gordon 1988, Abrams & Matsuda 1996). On rangelands in western North America, elk consumption of standing dead grass in winter may increase the live/dead ratio of perennial bunch-grasses in spring, enhancing forage quality for cattle (Hobbs et al. 1996a). In turn, cattle have been known to facilitate elk foraging. On the Isle of Rhum in Scotland, winter cattle grazing enhances spring grazing conditions for red deer (Gordon 1988). Large herbivore browsers can reduce shrub competition with grasses for water and nutrients, thus increasing available forage for grazers.

Despite the many examples of facilitative interactions, competitive influences tend to dominate where large herbivore population levels are high or available forage resources are low. In many cases large herbivore species compete for limited resources, as manifested by decreased production, fecundity or survivorship in the presence of competitors (e.g. Hobbs *et al.* 1996b). Habitat use may shift markedly in the presence of superior competitors. Similarly, where competing species must share the same or similar habitat, diet composition may shift.

The ability of integrated models to represent such interspecific relationships among large herbivore species at the landscape scale depends upon the level of detail with which feedbacks between resource quantity and use are represented. For example, large herbivore species may compete for forage resources at the scale of the patch, and then again when selecting plants or plant parts to consume within patches. Models that represent differential patch selection according to species-specific preferences and tolerances (e.g. SAVANNA, FORSPACE) (van Oene *et al.* 1999b) are capable of representing the dynamics of niche partitioning at the patch scale. Similarly, models of diet selection that consider species-specific forage preferences in combination with the relative availabilities of forage species (e.g. Ellis *et al.* 1976) are well-suited for representing shifts in diet that result from competition. The four models considered in Table 12.1 vary in their ability to simulate large herbivore competition in an ecosystem context. EASE has not been applied to large herbivore species assemblages, the focus being on moose energetics and landscape patterning effects. The van Oene *et al.* (1999b) model would, in principle, represent distributional and energetic effects of interspecific competition for large herbivores, since animal distribution is determined by the quantity of preferred forage in each patch, and resources consumed by one species would not be available to another. However, the one published application of this model to plant-herbivore interactions considers a single large herbivore species (domestic cattle). The SAVANNA and FORSPACE models are well-suited for representing those interspecific interactions resulting from changes in the quantity or quality of forage. Applying SAVANNA to the problem of elk-cattle competition in northern Colorado, Weisberg *et al.* (2002) found that the balance of elk effects for cattle forage and condition was likely to be negative (at high elk densities) as a result of significant spring forage reduction, despite a facilitative influence of improved forage quality.

Interspecific competition occurs when one species pre-empts the resources of another, as discussed above. However, interspecific competition may also occur due to behavioural responses to the presence of other large herbivore species. Such behavioural responses can be difficult to capture in ecosystem models, which focus on flows of carbon and nutrients among ecosystem components or trophic layers. None of the integrated models highlighted in this chapter includes such behavioural responses. As a result, competition effects between large herbivore species are likely to be under-represented.

Interactions among plant species

Interspecific interactions within the plant community may transmit the direct effects of selective herbivory on a target species to additional 'receiver' species, resulting in indirect effects that permeate entire communities and ecosystems (reviewed in Rooney & Waller 2003). Competition may amplify the direct effects of selective herbivory, as the increased net production of unpalatable species allows them to control more resources than palatable ones when browsing pressure is intense. However, herbivory may also promote the dominance of more palatable species, where compensatory growth responses are prevalent (McNaughton 1979, Coughenour 1985). Additionally, facilitative interactions among plant species may dampen the influence of selective herbivory on vegetation and landscape dynamics. For example, unpalatable 'nurse shrubs' may protect palatable herbaceous species or allow tree seedlings to persist even on sites with high large herbivore densities (e.g. Kuiters & Slim 2003).

A potential limitation of landscape-level models is that they generally operate over too coarse a scale for modelling of the plant community at an individual species level. Vegetation communities may contain a great many important species and multiple community types are likely to occur on a given landscape. As a result, plant interspecific interactions may be only coarsely represented at the level of plant functional types (PFTs) (e.g. deciduous trees, coniferous trees, shrubs, perennial bunchgrasses, annual grasses). This level of classification may be sufficient for detecting major shifts in vegetation structure, such as the ability of grazers to promote shrub encroachment on African savannas (Jeltsch *et al.* 1997). Plant functional type approaches are less adequate for detecting and modelling more subtle vegetation changes, and are completely inadequate for modelling large herbivore effects on plant biodiversity.

Competition between plant functional types is likely to be captured by the models where plant growth is sufficiently mechanistic so as to involve a co-option of resources, which are then no longer available to a competing functional group. Some examples of this are shading of under-storey vegetation (shrubs, small trees) by the forest over-storey, or the uptake of water from a soil layer where another functional group also has roots. FORSPACE considers shading of lower height layers and so includes competition for light. The van Oene *et al.* (1999b) model not only considers shading, but also considers competition for nitrogen, based on the relative root length of a given species. SAVANNA considers competition for light, nitrogen and soil moisture (Coughenour 2002).

An important problem of landscape-level models that seek to integrate large herbivore and vegetation processes, therefore, is how to identify plant functional types. This is by no means a trivial task. Usually, models focusing on herbivore effects will use criteria of palatability to differentiate plant functional types (e.g. palatable upland shrubs, unpalatable upland shrubs), since this approach can capture the long-term effects of large herbivore diet selectivity for vegetation change. The palatability distinction can be greatly complicated where multiple large herbivore species differ in their diet preferences, so that it is no longer clear which species to consider 'palatable' or not. Furthermore, plant species of similar palatability may differ in terms of physiological or life history parameters. If these differences are not captured, models are less capable of faithfully simulating interactive effects between herbivory and other key influences on the plant community, such as the environment (water availability, shading, temperature) or natural disturbances. Since herbivory processes can seldom be understood in isolation from other ecosystem and landscape processes (Weisberg & Bugmann 2003), there is a trade-off between creating plant functional types that represent different assumptions about large herbivore dietary preference, vs. those that capture differences in plant form or function. Fortunately, the two categories often overlap. For example, foliage palatability of tree species in New Zealand appears to be related to similar plant traits as litter decomposability, such that species preferred by (and hence, reduced by) large herbivore browsers tend to accelerate litter decomposition rates (Wardle *et al.* 2002).

The problem of deciding which attributes to use for differentiating plant functional types in a modelling context may merit further consideration than is usually given. These attributes determine how well and which interspecific interactions are included in the models. Those that are best suited for capturing the large herbivore-vegetation interaction (i.e. palatability scores) may not be best for capturing plant-plant interactions, which in turn might strongly condition community- or landscape-level responses to herbivory. Noble and Gitay (1996) have proposed a functional classification of 13 plant functional types that is designed to predict the dynamics of plant communities subject to natural disturbances. Bugmann (1996b) demonstrated that a plant functional type approach can be used for modelling long-term forest succession.

Therefore, we are confident that a systematic approach to assigning plant functional types appropriate for modelling plant responses to herbivory and other environmental influences that interact with herbivory, should prove valuable.

Cultural features and land use change

Given the prevalence of anthropogenic influences on the vast majority of landscapes, integrated large herbivore-vegetation models must often include cultural features and land use change. Large herbivore species may avoid features such as urban environments, grazed pastures, human transportation routes or points of access for hunters. Alternatively, large herbivores may favour cultural environments where they are protected from predation or where abundant, high-quality forage resources are available year-round. For example, white-tailed deer in the eastern United States may concentrate in suburban neighbourhoods at the rural-urban interface, to the frustration of gardeners. Elk in the Canadian Rocky Mountains prefer to concentrate along valley bottom transportation routes where heavy human use deters wolves (White *et al.* 2003). Near Rocky Mountain National Park, the winter energy requirements for a large elk herd are partially provided by the ready availability of perennially green golf courses (Coughenour 2002).

Landscape-level large herbivore models are well-suited for capturing such influences, provided they represent different habitat types at a sufficiently fine spatial resolution. For example, the SAVANNA model has been used to forecast the potential influences of increased agricultural activity in the Ngorongoro conservation area for domestic and wild large herbivore species (Boone *et al.* 2002). Risenhoover *et al.* (1997) have developed a spatially explicit modelling software for evaluating deer population and distributional responses to wildlife management treatments.

It is relatively simple, from an implementational point of view, for a spatially explicit model of large herbivore distribution to assign a habitat preference to a cultural feature or land use category. In this way it can describe the influence of land use change or urbanization on large herbivore landscape use and, ultimately, the landscape-level influences of large herbivores on vegetation. The difficulty lies in a lack of empirical data describing how large herbivore landscape use is influenced by human land uses, settlements, transportation networks and physical structures. We know little about the lag effects of land use change on large herbivore-vegetation interactions, where historical land use patterns may continue to be important. Large herbivores such as red deer and wild ponies have been observed to preferentially graze former agricultural fields, even decades after agricultural use of the land had ceased (Kuiters & Slim 2003, Schütz et al. 2003).

The application of integrated models of large herbivore-landscape interactions to problems of land use change will be likely to increase in future, as such issues become increasingly important. For example, in the foothills of the Swiss Alps, foresters blame high deer populations for a perceived lack of forest regeneration (Ott 1989). In turn, wildlife managers blame land use changes, such as expanded urban development and transportation corridors, for concentrating deer in less accessible areas where their effects on forest dynamics soon become apparent.

Interactions with disturbances

Although large herbivores can be considered agents of disturbance themselves, they may strongly interact with other disturbance agents (reviewed in Hobbs 1996, see also Chapter 9). In particular, grazing and fire regimes interact to influence mosaic structures of forests and more open vegetation types. Large herbivores influence fire regimes by consuming fine fuels, shifting vegetation composition more toward woody or herbaceous species, fostering or impeding development of 'ladder' fuels such as shrubs and small trees, or maintaining post-fire vegetation in an open state for longer time periods (Hobbs 1996). Fire regimes influence large herbivores by modifying the landscape mosaic of habitat and forage patches.

The latter influence (fire effects on large herbivores) is, in principle, not difficult to implement in landscape-level large herbivore models. Initially, fire may reduce forage supply and so negatively influence large herbivore populations. Over the longer-term, fire may create a favourable or unfavourable habitat for large herbivores. Turner et al. (1994) explored the effects of different fire patterns and total amounts of area burned, simply by imposing fire patches upon a landscape and using a generalized model of elk energetics, distribution and population dynamics to predict the implications for elk winter survival. Liedloff et al. (2001) used SAVANNA to investigate interactions between fire and grazing in a tropical savanna of northern Australia. Maintenance of such savannas requires the use of fire to prevent woody encroachment. However, overuse of fire leads to a reduction in herbaceous biomass. Model results showed that grazing and fire interact in complex ways to alter the balance of grass and woody biomass, which might similarly alter the balance between browser and grazer large herbivores.

More sophisticated approaches (e.g. FORSPACE model) simulate actual fire spread in response to the quantity and spatial arrangement of fuels. Such approaches allow exploration of large herbivore influences on fire regimes, since large herbivore impacts on vegetation influence the fuel mosaic. Based on an application of the FORSPACE model to a forest-heathland-grassland mosaic in the Netherlands, Kramer *et al.* (2003) suggest that fires may shift the producer-consumer system to a different stable state. While ungulate grazing can help to maintain the system in its new state, fire is required to initiate the conversion from forest to grassland. In addition, they found that simulated large herbivore grazing reduced fire frequency due to the removal of fine fuels.

We conclude that there is value in integrated large herbivore-landscape models that include a process representation of fire spread, allowing for interactions and feedbacks between large herbivores and fire regimes. In some cases, the direct influences of herbivory on the plant community may pale in comparison to the indirect influences on long-term landscape change as manifested through large herbivore-fire interactions.

Herbivore effects other than herbivory

Integrated large herbivore-vegetation models (Table 12.1) are essentially ecosystem models, representing flows of matter and energy among system components that include trophic levels. Hence, the interaction among large herbivores (consumers) and vegetation (producers) is represented mainly through the process of herbivory itself. Plant biomass is removed from the producer, with possible implications for producer population dynamics, and converted into energy for the consumer. This approach may be overly simplified, since many important effects of large herbivores on vegetation dynamics do not involve herbivory. These have been reviewed in Chapters 4 and 9 of this volume, and include nutrient effects by the addition of dung, urine and carcasses, seed dispersal effects, physical alteration of the environment, and influences on disturbance regimes (discussed above).

Large herbivores may play a key role in nutrient cycling over patch to landscape scales, as reviewed in Chapter 10. At the patch level, Seagle *et al.* (1992) linked a mechanistic model of grassland productivity (Coughenour *et al.* 1984) with a decomposition submodel to explore the effects of grazing on nitrogen cycling and below-ground processes in the Serengeti. Their model predicted that grazing should exert significant influences upon soil mineral nitrogen, but that response curves differed for tallgrass vs. shortgrass vegetation types. On shortgrass, soil mineral nitrogen levels were greatest at moderate grazing intensities. On tallgrass, soil mineral nitrogen increased continuously with grazing intensity due to lower foliage decomposition rates, resulting in net nitrogen immobilization.

Over landscape scales, the spatial effects of large herbivores on nutrient cycling become important. Such influences are created by diet selectivity for species of different chemical composition, and by subsequent nutrient redistribution through faecal and urinary outputs. Selective foraging by large herbivores may create spatial mosaics of patches characterized by different nitrogen cycling rates, as for moose in the boreal forest (Pastor et al. 1998). Or, large herbivores may move nutrients from one patch type (e.g. willow carr) to another (e.g. coniferous forest) simply by eating and excreting in different places, as has been suggested for elk in Rocky Mountain National Park (Singer & Schoenecker 2003).

Simulation modelling of large herbivore effects at within-patch scales, as in Seagle et al. (1992), requires detailed representation of biogeochemical cycling and decomposition processes. The van Oene et al. (1999b) model includes a relatively detailed submodel for nitrogen and carbon cycling that has been used to analyse the effects of elevated CO_2 and nitrogen deposition on vegetation development in a nutrient-poor sand dunes ecosystem (van Oene et al. 1999a). However, the interaction between herbivory and nutrient cycling has not yet been explored using this model. None of the other integrated models in Table 12.1 includes sufficiently detailed biogeochemical routines to explore such effects, although SAVANNA has been linked with the CENTURY model (Parton et al. 1988) for this purpose.

Nutrient redistribution effects can be simulated where animal distributions change over time, faecal and urinary outputs are modelled, and a separation is maintained between animal habitats used for foraging or for other purposes, such as thermal cover in winter. Only the first criterion is met by EASE, FORSPACE and the van Oene et al. (1999b) model, which do not simulate excretion. SAVANNA meets the first two criteria but does not separate foraging from other habitats in a spatially explicit manner, which would require a sub-daily time-step. Therefore, nutrient redistribution effects are not simulated by any of the models described in Table 12.1.

Large herbivores may play an important role as seed dispersal vectors for many plant species, transporting intact seeds on fur, or excreting viable seeds that have passed through the alimentary tract. The importance of this role for influencing vegetation composition and structure at the landscape scale is little known, but would be interesting to explore using spatially explicit models. For example, FORSPACE includes a distance-dependent seed dispersal routine (Table 12.1). An additional seed dispersal routine might be incorporated that tracks large herbivore movements from seed sources to potential germination sites during times of the year when seeds are available, and generates probability distributions for seed dispersal based upon animal mass (as a proxy for available surface area). To our knowledge, the potential influence of large herbivores for dispersing plant propagules has not been explored using any simulation model.

Additional large herbivore effects such as physical alteration of the environment (e.g. wallows, trampling, trails) may be important in certain situations (see Chapter 9). The influence of trampling for destroying seedlings or reducing herbaceous biomass is sometimes modelled as a constant wastage fraction or proportion associated with forage off-take (van Oene et al. 1999b, Coughenour 2002). This is probably sufficient for understanding trampling effects at landscape scales. However, the potentially positive effects of trampling for creating new germination sites occur over too fine scales to be included in landscape models. Other physical effects of large herbivores such as antler-rubbing and bark removal may be locally quite important, but are not generally considered.

It is clear that many potential large herbivore effects other than herbivory are poorly represented, if at all, in the current generation of integrated large herbivore-landscape models. It is difficult to say whether this is a major limitation or rather an appropriate simplification, since the empirical basis for many of these effects remains limited, particularly at landscape scales. One value of large herbivore-landscape models would be to evaluate the potential importance of such effects for real or artificial landscapes, using scenarios that explore the outcomes of various assumptions concerning nutrient effects, seed dispersal and physical alteration of the environment. This approach is exemplified by the use of LINKAGES and EASE to explore how seed dispersal and selective herbivore foraging might interact to create spatial patterns on artificial landscapes representing the boreal forest (Pastor et al. 1999a).

APPROACHES FOR MODELLING ACROSS SCALES

Multiple scales and scale mismatches

A multi-scale understanding is essential to link large herbivore movements, habitat use and ultimately population dynamics with landscape pattern (Senft et al. 1987, Apps et al. 2001). We propose that there is a fundamental mismatch (from the modelling perspective) between the scales at which herbivore and vegetation processes influence each other. Large herbivores influence vegetation proximately over very fine spatio-temporal scales, although ultimately their effects may become amplified over large areas and long time periods. Vegetation dynamics, however,

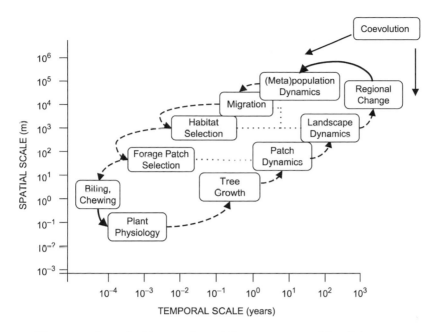

Figure 12.3. Large herbivore and vegetation processes, and key linkages between them, in the context of spatial and temporal scales. Effects of large herbivores on vegetation occur primarily at fine scales and then are amplified over time and space. Effects of vegetation on large herbivores may occur over coarser scales (dashed arrows), but serve to constrain finer scale large herbivore processes.

directly influence large herbivores over a broad range of scales. Figure 12.3 shows large herbivore and vegetation processes, and key linkages between them, in a space-time scaling diagram. Herbivore processes are shown to be constrained by other processes at coarser scales (dashed arrows) (Senft *et al.* 1987). For example, regional population levels influence animal dispersal and potentially the timing and magnitude of seasonal migrations. Seasonal migration patterns constrain which portions of landscape are utilized by ungulates, within which specific habitats are selected. Within habitats, forage patches are selected at a sub-daily time scale. Finally, individual plant species and parts are selected within forage patches at sub-hourly time intervals. The key proximate influences of large herbivores on vegetation are exerted at these fine spatial and temporal scales through the process of forage intake, at the level of individual bites, within small patches. Except for the more extreme cases such as elephants in the East African savanna or immense herds of bison on the pre-settlement

American prairies, herbivores do not usually influence vegetation at landscape scales directly.

The immediate effects of browsing or grazing on the plant are physiological; individual plants respond to losses of structural and chemical elements in various ways to mitigate impacts on growth and survivorship. Over time and with repeated herbivory, these effects may amplify over space to patch, landscape and regional scales (dashed arrows on the vegetation side of Fig. 12.3). Long time periods are generally required for understanding the full implications of ungulate herbivory for vegetation change, particularly where vegetation is composed of long-lived functional types such as tree species. Since the time periods involved generally exceed those for which historical records are available, simulation models of long-term large herbivore effects on vegetation prove invaluable.

Feedbacks from browsed or grazed vegetation back to large herbivores may be slow or fast, expressed at the level of individual plant organs, or as large-scale shifts in landscape structure (Fig. 12.3). As landscapes change, large herbivore browsers and grazers adjust their habitat use accordingly. There may be population-level changes, or even shifts in large herbivore community composition, if habitat or forage resources become significantly altered. Changes in large herbivore population numbers or age-sex structures may result in altered migration patterns, changes in habitat and forage patch selection, and ultimately altered herbivore impacts on individual plants.

It is apparent from Fig. 12.3 that integrated large herbivore-landscape models need to consider both animal and plant processes operating over multiple scales. Models need to include effects of large herbivores on vegetation that occur primarily at fine scales and then are amplified over time and space, as well as effects of vegetation on large herbivores that may occur over coarser scales, but serve to constrain finer-scale large herbivore processes. For example, selective foraging by large herbivores occurs one bite at a time, but can eventually convert a grassland community into a shrub savanna. At some point, the altered habitat mosaic (shrub-dominated instead of herbaceous patches) would influence large herbivore dynamics over large scales, perhaps causing herds to forage on different landscapes, or a population crash.

Example: Scaling forage intake from bite to landscape

Even landscape-level integrated models need to consider forage intake at fine scales, whether implicitly or explicitly (Fig. 12.3). This is fundamental for understanding large herbivore effects on vegetation. Our predictive ability for understanding the relationship between large herbivore intake rates and fine-scale forage characteristics is relatively high (Spalinger & Hobbs 1992, Gordon 2003). The series of functional response models originated by Spalinger and Hobbs (1992) appear to faithfully describe intake rates for a wide range of browsers and grazers spanning orders of magnitude of body size (Gross *et al.* 1993). Forage intake rate is represented as a mathematical function of bite size, bite processing rate and time required to crop a single bite (i.e. handling time):

$$I = \frac{R_{MAX} S}{R_{MAX} h + S} \tag{12.1}$$

where: I = intake rate, R_{MAX} = maximum processing rate of chewing, h = average handling time, and S = average bite size. Numerous researchers have modified this basic model: to accommodate fixed and variable handling costs (Ginnet & Demment 1995); to allow for overlap of searching and handling (Farnsworth & Illius 1996); to predict diet choice (Farnsworth & Illius 1998); and to incorporate the effects of bite-sequence length on bite rate (Pastor *et al.* 1999b). Note the short time scales involved; the latter modification extends the foraging model to entire moose feeding bouts of 1–2 hours. All variants on the Spalinger and Hobbs (1992) model describe foraging activities within a single, homogeneous vegetation patch.

Unfortunately, despite all of the attention this promising mathematical model has received, the methods for scaling the functional response to landscape scales and longer time periods are not well developed. Integrated large herbivore-landscape models must scale forage intake from leaf to landscape, yet few models explicitly span the full range of scales, from cm to km.

In the context of forest succession modelling, Bugmann *et al.* (2000) propose that scaling in models takes place through either implicit or explicit modes. In the case of implicit scaling, model equations and parameters incorporate scale transitions. Bugmann *et al.* (2000) suggest that most scaling is done implicitly in models, but that this is often not acknowledged explicitly. Sometimes, the modeller is not even aware that a scale transition has been made. Explicit scaling uses numerical or analytical methods to scale up (as discussed in King 1991). This can be accomplished within a single model framework, or by linking nested models at different levels of resolution.

The application of these ideas to the example of scaling up large herbivore forage intake (reviewed also in Coughenour 2000) is described in Fig. 12.4. Forage intake is discretized at the scales of individual bites,

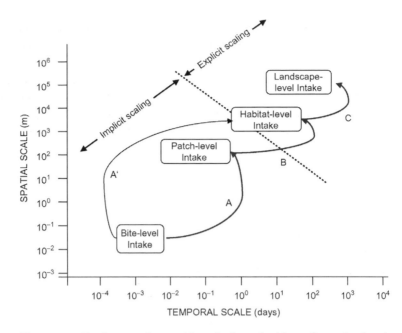

Figure 12.4. Pertinent scale transitions for large herbivore forage intake, that must be bridged either implicitly (aggregated model equations or parameters) or explicitly (numerical methods or nested models). Transition A′ represents implicit scaling, while transitions A, B and C represent explicit scaling. In practice, most landscape-level models in large herbivore-vegetation processes scale implicitly to the habitat (or grid-cell) level (transition A′), and then scale explicitly to the landscape level using spatially distributed simulation (transition C). See text for further explanation.

small forage patches, individual habitats that would represent grid-cells in most spatially explicit landscape models, and entire landscapes. Bite-level intake is difficult to scale up explicitly, since the functional response models used to describe this process are designed for homogeneous units of vegetation and short time scales. For example, the bite size parameter of such a model changes with changing shoot height, leaf size, canopy density and other structural characteristics (Stuth 1991, Hobbs 1999). Bite processing rates and handling times are likely to vary with plant species for plant morphological and chemical traits, particularly digestibility and plant defences. Explicit scaling of the functional response model would therefore require an extensive database of plant traits, as well as a very detailed map of vegetation patch structure at the level of individual species (Coughenour 2000). Spatial information at such a high resolution is not generally available at landscape scales.

The EASE model (Moen *et al.* 1997) represents transitions A and B (Fig. 12.4) explicitly by nesting within-patch and among-patch foraging. The limitation of this approach is that only small landscapes (e.g. 8 ha) can be simulated due to computational limitations, and simulations cannot be run for real landscapes, for which the necessary spatial data would not be available at a 1-m resolution. Therefore, this model is suitable for exploring theoretical implications of moose herbivory in boreal forests, but not for drawing inferences specific to actual, 'on the ground' landscapes.

The other three integrated models (Table 12.1) bypass transitions A and B entirely, and use implicit scaling (transition A') to infer intake rate at the level of a habitat patch (or grid-cell). The fine-scale process of intake rate as a function of bite size, handling time and bite processing rate is not represented explicitly, but is subsumed in the parameterization of supposedly more general algorithms. In SAVANNA, weekly forage intake rate varies with available forage biomass according to a flexible, user-defined function, and then is modified according to snow depth and the level of animal satiation. A similar approach is taken in FORSPACE, although forage digestibility (but neither snow depth nor animal satiation) is included as a modifier on intake rate. The van Oene *et al.* (1999b) model simply calculates daily intake rate according to a fixed target requirement per unit animal mass. Turner *et al.* (1994) represent daily forage intake rate, at a spatial resolution of 1 ha, using a hyperbolic biomass feedback function where forage intake is reduced at lower values of forage biomass, and a non-linear snow feedback function that takes into account snow depth and density.

Thus, the typical scaling pathway for integrated large herbivore-landscape models is to represent patch-level forage intake through implicit scaling, and then to explicitly scale from habitat patches to the landscape scale (transition C on Fig. 12.4). The latter is accomplished simply by aggregating grid-cells through summation to achieve landscape-level estimates, or producing maps that represent the spatial heterogeneity of forage intake across a landscape. This approach is necessary because methods are not yet available for applying mechanistic patch foraging models to real landscapes. One problem with this approach is that the theoretical basis for estimating forage intake in landscape models may be weakly developed. Despite the current trend toward increasing mechanistic complexity of foraging models, it might be most useful to develop aggregated foraging models for application over broader spatial and temporal scales (Coughenour 2000). However, the behaviours of the aggregated models need to be consistent with those of the more detailed models on which they are based. This is a fundamental problem, which has not yet received the attention it deserves.

MODELS FOR MANAGEMENT AND CONSERVATION

Sage *et al.* (2003) make the case for integrated models of large herbivore-vegetation management by comparing ungulate populations to an aircraft in flight. Both can be managed only by considering multiple interacting factors. Both require training tools designed to deal with the management of holistic systems, or simultaneous manipulation of multiple buttons and monitoring of multiple gauges. In the case of an aircraft, the relevant training tool is the flight simulator. For ungulate managers, the relevant tool may be the ecosystem simulation model. Regardless of whether this colourful analogy is an apt one, integrated simulation models can certainly prove a useful tool for the natural resource manager. However, not all integrated large herbivore-vegetation models are useful for addressing management questions, and many of those that can are not useful as decision support systems.

Models that are useful for addressing management questions should: (1) maintain strong connections to real-world data; and (2) include management activities as driving variables. Of the models considered in Table 12.1, only SAVANNA and FORSPACE are strongly connected to real-world data in the sense of representing landscape patterns of vegetation, topography and climate as they occur on the ground. The other two models are designed more for theoretical inquiries, and so are of less direct utility for management applications. Management models of landscape-level large herbivore-vegetation interactions not only need to represent actual landscape heterogeneity (e.g. through interfaces with underlying Geographic Information System layers), but should be capable of calibration and validation using readily collected field or remote sensing data. Model inputs, parameters and outputs should be measurable quantities, as far as this is possible, to reduce the probability that managers will make substantial 'translation errors' (Bunnell & Boyland 2003) between the simulation model and the real world. For example, managers will be able to better assess the outcomes of particular model scenarios for rangeland conditions if outputs are expressed as percent basal area cover of herbaceous vegetation, rather than as herbaceous root biomass.

Although it seems obvious that management models must include management activities as driving variables, this can be difficult to accomplish. Models will be most useful where model drivers represent particular treatments such as hunting and culling, silvicultural manipulations, supplemental feeding, fencing, prescribed fire, grazing or fertilization. The difficulty lies, again, in the translation process (Bunnell & Boyland 2003). Does hunting as implemented in the model simply represent a reduction in large herbivore numbers, or does it also lead to distributional, behavioural and energetic responses? Is supplemental feeding applied evenly to an entire population, or is the spatial distribution of feeding stations taken into account? Does fertilization simply increase forage production, or is the quality of forage also affected? No model can represent any given management treatment with 100% fidelity, and none should be expected to. What is important is that the differences between modelled and real-world management treatments be explored and communicated, so that the connection between the model and the real world can be maintained. This may be a key difference between models intended for addressing theoretical issues vs. those designed for management questions.

Management models are not likely to be decision support systems unless they are accessible and transparent, and are developed with stakeholder and end-user interaction. Only if these conditions are true are managers themselves likely to use the models appropriately, since the analysis and use of simulation results require knowledge about the inner workings of a model. In this regard, none of the models discussed in this chapter are examples of decision support systems. Perhaps scientists need to go to greater lengths to make their models accessible, and include managers in the model-building process. In turn, managers may need to become more willing to accept complexity and uncertainty, if they are to interact with such models. It is paradoxical that management models often require more mechanistic complexity than theoretical ones, since they are required to make time-and-place-specific forecasts that are as accurate as possible. Yet as a result of integrating multiple animal and plant components at the landscape scale such models can become overly complex, increasing the likelihood that they will not be understood or trusted by managers and policymakers.

CONCLUSIONS

We have identified several difficulties for modelling interactions among large herbivores and vegetation at landscape scales. Interspecific interactions such as predation, competition and facilitation are quite incompletely incorporated into the current generation of such models, if at all. Landscape-scale models often gloss over the details of plant community interactions, concentrating instead on plant functional types reflecting different herbivore dietary preferences. Such models may be suitable for investigating competition and facilitation within the herbivore community, but typically fail to account for behavioural responses. Animal behaviour is difficult to incorporate into system-based models that are structured according to flow, conversion and storage of matter and energy. Where modelling objectives require explicit accounting of large herbivore behavioural responses, individual-based models may show promise (e.g. Dumont & Hill 2001).

Models could improve their representation of large herbivore effects other than herbivory, including physical effects such as trampling, biogeochemical effects such as nutrient redistribution, and effects on plant dispersal. There is relatively little empirical data on this topic, particularly for wild large herbivore species. Hobbs (Chapter 9) uses allometric relationships to develop simple mathematical models of trampling and nutrient redistribution effects. Models such as these, once tested and refined using empirical data, might be incorporated into the class of integrated models described here.

It is most important that landscape-level, large herbivore-vegetation models represent anthropogenic features and land use change, if they are to realistically predict dynamics of today's highly cultural landscapes. More research is needed concerning how large herbivores respond to such anthropogenic factors at the urban-rural interface, and how wild and domestic large herbivores interact in agricultural areas. Linking such large herbivore-landscape models to models of land use change is especially important because human settlement patterns often coincide with the same habitat types that many large herbivore species rely upon for critical-season range.

Perhaps most importantly, modellers need to exert great care in how they extrapolate an understanding of fine-scale processes to coarser scales. We do not yet have a quantitative understanding of how many large herbivore processes and effects operate over coarse scales. So we represent them at fine scales in our models, sometimes in an inappropriate way, and often with a great degree of mechanistic detail. There is a need for more aggregated models, whose behaviour is consistent with that of more detailed models with a firmer empirical basis.

Despite these difficulties, models that integrate large herbivore-vegetation processes at landscape scales have yielded high rewards both for increasing our level of scientific understanding, and for allowing managers to evaluate potential outcomes of their activities. In particular, they have shown promise for linking effects of herbivory to those of other disturbance types, for elucidating how large herbivores may influence the spatial structure of vegetation and nutrients, and for estimating carrying capacity in a dynamic sense over meaningfully large areas and long time periods. These efforts need to continue, but with improved linkages to empirical research, particularly long-term studies that consider multiple scales, including coarser ones. Conceptual integration of large herbivore-vegetation processes at landscape scales may be advanced most rapidly when modelling is conducted with real-world model applications in mind, linking model processes to on-the-ground geographic information, and incorporating enough realism so that results can be meaningfully compared with empirical data.

ACKNOWLEDGEMENTS

Special thanks to K. Danell, R. Bergström and J. Pastor for organizing the Large Herbivore Workshop in Umeå, which provided the initial impetus for preparing our chapter. J. Pastor and two anonymous reviewers provided useful comments. T. Rooke edited the manuscript. This research was funded through the Swiss Agency for the Environment, Forests and Landscape (BUWAL), project no. WT-03/00.

REFERENCES

Abrams, P.A. & Matsuda, H. (1996). Positive indirect effects between prey species that share predators. *Ecology*, 77, 610–16.

Apps, C.D., McLellan, B.N., Kinley, T.A. & Flaa, J.P. (2001). Scale-dependent habitat selection by mountain caribou, Columbia Mountains, British Columbia. *Journal of Wildlife Management*, 65, 65–77.

Armstrong, H., Gordon, I.J., Grant, S.A. *et al.* (1997a). A model of the grazing of hill vegetation by sheep in the UK. I. The prediction of vegetation biomass. *Journal of Applied Ecology*, 34, 166–85.

Armstrong, H., Gordon, I.J., Hutchings, N.J. *et al.* (1997b). A model of the grazing of hill vegetation by sheep in the UK. II. The prediction of offtake by sheep. *Journal of Applied Ecology*, 34, 186–207.

Ball, J.T., Woodrow, I.E. & Berry, J.A. (1987). A model predicting stomatal conductance and its contribution to the control of photosynthesis under different environmental conditions. In *Progress in Photosynthesis Research*, Vol. IV, ed. I. Biggins. Dordrecht: Martinees Nijhof, pp. 221–4.

Blatt, S.E., Janmaat, J.A. & Harmsen, R. (2001). Modelling succession to include a herbivore effect. *Ecological Modelling*, 139, 123–36.

Boone, R.B., Coughenour, M.B., Galvin, K.A. & Ellis, J.E. (2002). Addressing management questions for Ngorongoro conservation area, Tanzania, using the savanna modeling system. *African Journal of Ecology*, 40, 138–50.

Bugmann, H. (1996a). A simplified forest model to study species composition along climate gradients. *Ecology*, 77, 2055–74.

Bugmann, H. (1996b). Functional types of trees in temperate and boreal forests: classification and testing. *Journal of Vegetation Science*, 7, 359–70.

Bugmann, H. (2001). A review of forest gap models. *Climatic Change*, 51, 259–305.

Bugmann, H., Lindner, M., Lasch, P. et al. (2000). Scaling issues in forest succession modelling. *Climatic Change*, 44, 265–89.

Bunnell, F. L. & Boyland, B. (2003). Decision-support systems: it's the question not the model. *Journal for Nature Conservation*, 10, 269–79.

Christensen, L., Coughenour, M., Ellis, J. & Chen, Z. (2003). Sustainability of the typical steppe: model assessment of grazing on ecosystem state. *Journal of Range Management*, 56, 319–27.

Coughenour, M. B. (1985). Graminoid responses to grazing by large herbivores: adaptations, exaptations, and interacting processes. *Annals of the Missouri Botanical Gardens*, 72, 852–63.

Coughenour, M. B. (1992). Spatial modeling and landscape characterization of an African pastoral ecosystem: a prototype model and its potential use for monitoring droughts. In *Ecological Indicators*, Volume I, ed. D. H. McKenzie, D. E. Hyatt & V. J. McDonald. New York: Elsevier Applied Science, pp. 787–810.

Coughenour, M. B. (2000). Ungulates and grassland interactions: integrating across scales with models. *Proceedings of the British Grassland Society 6th Research Conference*, 9/11/2000, Aberdeen, Scotland. British Grassland Society, University of Reading, UK, pp. 1–21.

Coughenour, M. B. (2002). *Elk in the Rocky Mountain National Park Ecosystem – a model-based assessment*. Final Report, US Geological Survey Biological Resources Division and US National Park Service, Rocky Mountain National Park.

Coughenour, M. B. & Singer, F. J. (1996). Yellowstone elk population responses to fire – a comparison of landscape carrying capacity and spatial-dynamic ecosystem modeling approaches. In *The Ecological Implications of Fire in Greater Yellowstone*, ed. J. Greenlee. Fairfield, WA: International Association of Wildland Fire, pp. 169–80.

Coughenour, M. B., McNaughton, S. J. & Wallace, L. L. (1984). Simulation study of east-African perennial graminoid responses to defoliation. *Ecological Modelling*, 26, 177–201.

Danell, K., Bergström, R., Edenius, L. & Ericsson, G. (2003). Ungulates as drivers of tree population dynamics at module and genet levels. *Forest Ecology and Management*, 181, 67–76.

DeAngelis, D. L., Gross, L. J., Huston, M. A. et al. (1998). Landscape modeling for Everglades ecosystem restoration. *Ecosystems*, 1, 64–75.

Dumont, B. & Hill, D. R. C. (2001). Multi-agent simulation of group foraging in sheep: effects of spatial memory, conspecific attraction and plot size. *Ecological Modelling*, 141, 201–15.

Edenius, L., Danell, K. & Nyquist, H. (1995). Effects of simulated moose browsing on growth, mortality, and fecundity in Scots pine: relations to plant productivity. *Canadian Journal of Forest Research*, 25, 529–35.

Ellis, J.E., Wiens, J.A., Rodell, C.F. & Anway, J.C. (1976). A conceptual model of diet selection as an ecosystem process. *Journal of Theoretical Biology*, **60**, 93–108.

Farnsworth, K.D. & Illius, A.W. (1996). Large grazers back in the fold: generalizing the prey model to incorporate mammalian herbivores. *Functional Ecology*, **10**, 678–80.

Farnsworth, K.D. & Illius, A.W. (1998). Optimal diet choice for large herbivores: an extended contingency model. *Functional Ecology*, **12**, 74–81.

Ginnett, T.F. & Demment, M.W. (1995). The functional response of herbivores: analysis and test of a simple mechanistic model. *Functional Ecology*, **9**, 376–84.

Gordon, I.J. (1988). Facilitation of red deer grazing by cattle and its impact on red deer performance. *Journal of Applied Ecology*, **25**, 1–10.

Gordon, I.J. (2003). Browsing and grazing ruminants: are they different beasts? *Forest Ecology and Management*, **181**, 13–22.

Gross, J.E., Shipley, L.A., Hobbs, N.T., Spalinger, D.E. & Wunder, B.A. (1993). Functional response of herbivores in food-concentrated patches: tests of a mechanistic model. *Ecology*, **74**, 778–91.

Gross, J.E., Zank, C., Hobbs, N.T. & Spalinger, D.E. (1995). Movement rules for herbivores in spatially heterogeneous environments: responses to small scale pattern. *Landscape Ecology*, **10**, 209–17.

Hacker, R.B., Wang, K.M., Richmond, G.S. & Lindner, R.K. (1991). IMAGES: an integrated model of an arid grazing ecological system. *Agricultural Systems*, **37**, 119–63.

Hobbs, N.T. (1996). Modification of ecosystems by ungulates. *Journal of Wildlife Management*, **60**, 695–713.

Hobbs, N.T. (1999). Responses of large herbivores to spatial heterogeneity in ecosystems. In *Nutritional Ecology of Herbivores*, ed. H.G. Jung & G.C. Fahey. Proceeding of the Fifth International Symposium on the Nutrition of Herbivores. Savory, Illinois: American Society of Animal Sciences, pp. 97–129.

Hobbs, N.T. & Swift, D.M. (1985). Estimates of habitat carrying capacity incorporating explicit nutritional constraints. *Journal of Wildlife Management*, **49**, 814–22.

Hobbs, N.T., Baker, D.L., Bear, G.D. & Bowden, D.C. (1996a). Ungulate grazing in sagebrush grassland: mechanisms of resource competition. *Ecological Applications*, **6**, 200–217.

Hobbs, N.T., Baker, D.L., Bear, G.D. & Bowden, D.C. (1996b). Ungulate grazing in sagebrush grassland: effects of resource competition on secondary production. *Ecological Applications*, **6**, 218–77.

Illius, A.W. & O'Connor, T.G. (1999). On the relevance of nonequilibrium concepts to arid and semiarid grazing systems. *Ecological Applications*, **9**, 798–813.

Illius, A.W. & O'Connor, T.G. (2000). Resource heterogeneity and ungulate population dynamics. *Oikos*, **89**, 283–94.

Jeltsch, F., Milton, S.J., Dean, W.R.J. & van Rooyen, N. (1997). Analysing shrub encroachment in the southern Kalahari: a grid-based modelling approach. *Journal of Applied Ecology*, **34**, 1497–1508.

Johnson, C.J., Parker, K.L., Heard, D.C. & Gillingham, M.P. (2002). Movement parameters of ungulates and scale-specific responses to the environment. *Journal of Animal Ecology*, **71**, 225–35.

Jorritsma, I.T.M., van Hees, A.F.M. & Mohren, G.M.J. (1999). Forest development in relation to ungulate grazing: a modeling approach. *Forest Ecology and Management*, **120**, 23–34.

Kienast, F., Fritschi, J., Bissegger, M. & Abderhalden, W. (1999). Modeling successional patterns of high-elevation forests under changing herbivore pressure – responses at the landscape level. *Forest Ecology and Management*, **120**, 35–46.

Kiker, G.A. (1998). Development and comparison of savanna ecosystem models to explore the concept of carrying capacity. Ph.D. thesis, Cornell University, Ithaca, New York.

King, A.W. (1991). Translating models across scales in the landscape. In *Quantitative Methods in Landscape Ecology: The Analysis and Interpretation of Landscape Heterogeneity*, ed. M.G. Turner & R.H. Gardner. New York: Springer-Verlag, pp. 479–517.

Kramer, K., Baveco, H., Bijlsma, R.J. *et al.* (2001). *Landscape Forming Processes and Diversity of Forested Landscapes: Description and Application of the Model FORSPACE.* Wageningen: Alterra, Green World Research.

Kramer, K., Groen, T.A. & van Wieren, S.E. (2003). The interacting effects of ungulates and fire on forest dynamics: an analysis using the model FORSPACE. *Forest Ecology and Management*, **181**, 205–22.

Kuiters, A.T. & Slim, P.A. (2003). Tree colonisation of abandoned arable land after 27 years of horse-grazing: the role of bramble as a facilitator of oak wood regeneration. *Forest Ecology and Management*, **181**, 239–52.

Latham, J. (1999). Interspecific interactions of ungulates in European forests: an overview. *Forest Ecology and Management*, **120**, 13–21.

Liedloff, A.C., Coughenour, M.B., Ludwig, J.A. & Dyer, R. (2001). Modelling the trade-off between fire and grazing in a tropical savanna landscape, northern Australia. *Environment International*, **27**, 173–80.

Loza, H.J., Grant, W.E., Stuth, J.W. & Forbes, T.D.A. (1992). Physiologically based landscape use model for large herbivores. *Ecological Modelling*, **61**, 227–52.

Ludwig, J.A., Coughenour, M.B., Liedloff, A.C. & Dyer, R. (2001). Modelling the resilience of Australian savanna systems to grazing impacts. *Environment International*, **27**, 167–72.

McNaughton, S.J. (1979). Grazing as an optimization process: grass-ungulate relationships in the Serengeti. *American Naturalist*, **113**, 691–703.

Millard, P., Hester, A.J., Wendler, R. & Baillie, G. (2001). Interspecific defoliation responses of trees depend on sites of winter nitrogen storage. *Functional Ecology*, **15**, 535–43.

Moen, R.A., Pastor, J. & Cohen, Y. (1997). A spatially explicit model of moose foraging and energetics. *Ecology*, **78**, 505–21.

Moen, R.A., Pastor, J. & Cohen, Y. (1998). Linking moose population and plant growth models with a moose energetics model. *Ecosystems*, **1**, 52–63.

Noble, I.R. & Gitay, H. (1996). A functional classification for predicting the dynamics of landscapes. *Journal of Vegetation Science*, **7**, 329–36.

Ott, E. (1989). Verjüngungsprobleme in hochstaudenreichen Gebirgsnadelwäldern. *Schweizerische Zeitschrift für Forstwesen*, **140**, 23–42.

Parton, W.J., Stewart, J.W.B. & Cole, C.V. (1988). Dynamics of C, N, P and S in grassland soils: a model. *Biogeochemistry*, **5**, 109–31.

Pastor, J., Dewey, B., Moen, R. *et al.* (1998). Spatial patterns in the moose-forest-soil ecosystem on Isle Royale, Michigan, USA. *Ecological Applications*, **8**, 411–24.

Pastor, J., Cohen, Y. & Moen, R. (1999a). Generation of spatial patterns in boreal forest landscapes. *Ecosystems*, **2**, 439–50.

Pastor, J., Standke, K., Farnsworth, K., Moen, R. & Cohen, Y. (1999b). Further development of the Spalinger-Hobbs mechanistic foraging model for free-ranging moose. *Canadian Journal of Zoology*, **77**, 1505–12.

Ripple, W.J. & Larsen, E.J. (2000). Historic aspen recruitment, elk, and wolves in northern Yellowstone National Park, USA. *Biological Conservation*, **95**, 361–70.

Ripple, W.J., Larsen, E.J, Renkin, R.A. & Smith, D.W. (2001). Trophic cascades among wolves, elk and aspen on Yellowstone National Park's northern range. *Biological Conservation*, **102**, 227–34.

Risenhoover, K.L., Underwood, H.B, Yan, W. & Cooke, J.L. (1997). A spatially explicit modeling environment for evaluating deer management strategies. In *The Science of Overabundance: Deer Ecology and Population Management*, ed. W.J. McShea, H.B. Underwood & J.H. Rappole. Washington, DC: Smithsonian Institute, pp. 366–79.

Rooney, T.P. & Waller, D.M. (2003). Direct and indirect effects of white-tailed deer in forest ecosystems. *Forest Ecology and Management*, **181**, 165–76.

Sage, R.W., Patten, B.C. & Salmon, P.A. (2003). Flying the North American adirondack whitetail on instruments: a multi-parameter modeling approach to ecosystem-based wildlife management. *Journal for Nature Conservation*, **10**, 280–94.

Saunders, M.R. & Puettmann, K.J. (1999). Effects of overstory and understory competition and simulated herbivory on growth and survival of white pine seedlings. *Canadian Journal of Forest Research*, **29**, 536–46.

Schaefer, J.A., Bergman, C.M. & Luttich, S.N. (2000). Site fidelity of female caribou at multiple spatial scales. *Landscape Ecology*, **15**, 731–9.

Schütz, M., Risch, A.C., Leuzinger, E., Krüsi, B.O. & Achermann, G. (2003). Impact of herbivory by red deer (*Cervus elaphus* L.) on patterns and processes in subalpine grasslands in the Swiss National Park. *Forest Ecology and Management* **181**, 177–88.

Seagle, S.W. & Liang, S.-Y. (2001). Application of a forest gap model for prediction of browsing effects on riparian forest succession. *Ecological Modelling*, **144**, 213–29.

Seagle, S.W., McNaughton, S.J. & Ruess, R.W. (1992). Simulated effects of grazing on soil nitrogen and mineralization in contrasting Serengeti grasslands. *Ecology*, **73**, 1105–23.

Senft, R.L., Coughenour, M.B., Bailey, D.W. *et al.* (1987). Large herbivore foraging and ecological hierarchies. *BioScience*, **37**, 789–99.

Sinclair, A.R.E. & Norton-Griffiths, M. (1982). Does competition or facilitation regulate migrant ungulate populations in the Serengeti? A test of hypothesis. *Oecologia*, **53**, 364–9.

Singer, F.J. & Schoenecker, K.A. (2003). Do ungulates accelerate or decelerate nitrogen cycling? *Forest Ecology and Management*, **181**, 189–204.

Spalinger, D.E. & Hobbs, N.T. (1992). Mechanisms of foraging in mammalian herbivores: new models of functional response. *American Naturalist*, **140**, 325–48.

Stuth, J.W. (1991). Foraging behavior. In *Grazing Management: An Ecological Perspective*, ed. R.K. Heitschmidt & J.W. Stuth. Portland: Timber Press, pp. 65–82.

Sweeney, J.M. & Sweeney, J.R. (1984). Snow depths influencing winter movements of elk. *Journal of Mammalogy*, **65**, 524–6.

Turner, M.G., Wu, Y., Wallace, L.L., Romme, W.H. & Brenkert, A. (1994). Simulating winter interactions among ungulates, vegetation, and fire in northern Yellowstone Park. *Ecological Applications*, **4**, 472–96.

van Oene, H., Berendse, F. & de Kovel, C.G.F. (1999a). Model analysis of the effects of historic CO_2 levels and nitrogen inputs on vegetation succession. *Ecological Applications*, **9**, 920–35.

van Oene, H., van Deursen, E.J.M. & Berendse, F. (1999b). Plant-herbivore interaction and its consequences for succession in wetland ecosystems: a modeling approach. *Ecosystems*, **2**, 122–138.

Walters, S. (2001). Landscape pattern and productivity effects on source-sink dynamics of deer populations. *Ecological Modelling*, **143**, 17–32.

Wardle, D.A., Bonner, K.I. & Barker, G.M. (2002). Linkages between plant litter decomposition, litter quality, and vegetation responses to herbivores. *Functional Ecology*, **16**, 585–95.

Weisberg, P.J. & Bugmann, H. (2003). Forest dynamics and ungulate herbivory: from leaf to landscape. *Forest Ecology and Management*, **181**, 1–12.

Weisberg, P.J. & Coughenour, M.B. (2003). Model-based assessment of aspen responses to elk herbivory in Rocky Mountain National Park, USA. *Environmental Management*, **32**, 152–69.

Weisberg, P.J., Hobbs, N.T., Ellis, J.E. & Coughenour, M.B. (2002). An ecosystem approach to population management of ungulates. *Journal of Environmental Management*, **65**, 181–97.

White, C.A., Feller, M.C. & Bayley, S. (2003). Predation risk and the functional response of elk-aspen herbivory. *Forest Ecology and Management*, **181**, 77–98.

Xie, J., Hill, H.R., Winterstein, S.R. *et al.* (1999). White-tailed deer management options model (DeerMOM): design, quantification, and application. *Ecological Modelling*, **124**, 121–30.

13

Effects of large herbivores on other fauna

OTSO SUOMINEN AND KJELL DANELL

INTRODUCTION

Here we will describe and discuss the effects of large herbivores on animal community composition, diversity and abundance, using examples from different taxonomic and functional groups in different habitats. The main focus is the effect of wild ungulates in natural or semi-natural habitats, but when relevant we will also cover the effects of domestic grazers in agricultural systems. Less attention will be given to the effects of large herbivores on groups which recently have been reviewed (e.g. birds) (McShea & Rappole 1997, Van Wieren 1998, Fuller 2001), less studied groups (e.g. reptiles and aquatic communities) (but see e.g. Strand & Merritt 1999) and on the consequences following the transfer of forests into grasslands by large herbivores (e.g. Van Wieren 1998, see also Chapter 7).

Our focus will be on ecological processes affecting animal communities, e.g. impacts of competition for food with other herbivores, and indirect impacts via changes in habitat structure on seemingly unrelated taxa. The possible differences between introduced and native wild herbivores as well as between wild and domestic grazers will be discussed; parasitism and the role of dung will only briefly be mentioned. By impacts, or effects, we mean observed changes in animal community composition, or abundance in response to changes in presence, density or species composition of large herbivores. The last part of the chapter summarizes the observed impacts on other biota, and discusses some theoretical and practical issues associated with the effects of large herbivores on other animals.

Large Herbivore Ecology, Ecosystem Dynamics and Conservation, ed. K. Danell, P. Duncan, R. Bergström & J. Pastor. Published by Cambridge University Press. © Cambridge University Press 2006.

METHODOLOGICAL ISSUES

For smaller animals, data are often gathered from studies of paired plots where large herbivores have access to one plot, but are excluded from another plot. Exclosures are often built when large herbivores are exceptionally abundant and expected to threaten some important component of the ecosystem. The fact that the areas have already been affected before the exclosures were set up often reduces their value for studies of natural ecosystem processes. Further, comparisons of unnaturally high grazing pressures with no grazing at all have low relevance for management because both situations are often abnormal. Studies of the impacts on larger and more mobile animals, such as birds, require areas that are too large to permit experimental manipulation of grazing by wild large herbivores. Instead, areas with different herbivore densities are compared, but are confounded by other factors (e.g. geography and management differences) which are difficult to control and may co-vary with grazing.

In addition, proper spatial and temporal scales are difficult issues. Large herbivores can potentially affect the ecosystem during all phases of succession, and the strength as well as the direction of their impacts can differ markedly during the different successional phases (e.g. Kielland & Bryant 1998, Suominen & Olofsson 2000). Engelmark *et al.* (1998) demonstrated that more than 200 years after a forest fire, reindeer (*Rangifer tarandus*) grazing affected successional dynamics in a Swedish pine forest. Most exclosure studies are of relatively short duration compared to succession. Also, the impacts of grazing on animal assemblages can vary between seasons and years (e.g. Gonzáles-Megías *et al.* 2004), which means that the duration of sampling may affect the results.

Another problem is the variety of ways in which richness or diversity of different taxa are reported. Surprisingly large numbers of studies use only the number of species, without any scaling to the number of individuals in the sample (e.g. rarefaction), as a measure of biodiversity even though the number of individuals in the sample differs greatly. Similarly, most diversity indices are sensitive to the observed number of species (Magurran 1988). Thus one should be cautious when uncorrected richness/diversity values follow the pattern of substantial differences in abundance.

The results presented here should be read with care due to this long array of confounding factors, the scarcity of research in this area, and the difficulties connected with studies of complex, indirect community impacts (Wootton 1994).

THE POTENTIAL MECHANISMS HOW LARGE HERBIVORES CAN AFFECT OTHER BIOTA

Large herbivores as resources

Large herbivores are consumers of resources, but they also produce food for other consumers. Because of their size and abundance they can be particularly important resources for other organisms. When they die, large numbers of fungi, invertebrates and vertebrates use the carrion. Faeces and urine of large mammalian herbivores are important and abundant resources for many specialized fungi and invertebrates (e.g. Nyberg & Persson 2002) as well as for less specialized animals which feed occasionally on dung. By short- and large-scale movements, large herbivores can transfer nutrients between habitats if they feed and defecate in different habitats, e.g. hippopotami (*Hippopotamus amphibius*) grazing on land and defecating in water. In nutrient-poor waters, hippo dung can be a major resource base for the whole aquatic community (Palm 1993).

Large mammalian species host a large number of species of endo- and ectoparasites with various degrees of host specialization, and thus contribute substantially to the total biodiversity, but they also transmit parasites to humans and domestic livestock.

Large herbivores as 'predators'

Sometimes large herbivores also act as predators. This is most evident for omnivores, e.g. wild boar (*Sus scrofa*), but also occurs among more herbivorous species when the diet does not satisfy their nutritional needs. For example, red deer (*Cervus elaphus*) and sheep (*Ovis aries*) have been observed eating ground-nesting seabirds and their nestlings on islands with low forage quality (Furness 1988), and cattle on poor soils can feed on dead rabbits (WallisDeVries 1998).

Herbivores also ingest animals and fungi when feeding on plants (e.g. Tscharntke 1997). This incidental omnivory (Polis *et al.* 1989) can affect invertebrate populations. For example, ungulates (sheep and ibex, *Capra pyrenaica*) ingested 60%–80% of a specialist weevil (*Ceutorhynchus* sp.) population living in flowers of the shrub *Hormatophylla spinosa* in Spain (Gómez & Gonzáles-Megías 2002). Large herbivores caused higher mortality among the beetles than true predators or parasites. An indication of the importance of incidental omnivory is the fact that the whole life cycle of many endoparasites is based on the herbivore host accidentally ingesting a carrier of their larva, i.e. a snail.

The indirect effects of large herbivores

The removal of plant tissues by herbivores changes the morphology and chemistry of the remaining and regrowing tissues above and below ground (see Chapter 4). These changes can have negative or positive effects on other herbivore species feeding on the plants, and corresponding changes in the quality of the leaf litter may affect the decomposer food web (Bardgett *et al.* 1998). Above-ground herbivory also affects the growth and chemical composition of roots and thus herbivory, as well as other processes below ground.

Plant reproductive organs, flowers, fruits and seeds, are often strongly affected by large herbivores (see Chapter 4). The impacts of large herbivores on these organs are often larger than impacts on biomass or cover of a plant species (e.g. Tscharntke 1997, Cooper & Wookey 2003). A large number of animals are either heavily dependent on these plant parts (e.g. pollinators, frugivores and granivores), or these parts are at least seasonally important resources for them (see Chapter 8).

Other herbivores and decomposers using the same plants as large herbivores are potentially affected by the reduction of plant biomass (competition) as well as many other organisms in the same food webs (trophic effects) (e.g. Tscharntke 1997). By changing the vegetation, large herbivores can have a substantial effect on habitat structure. The herbivores, such as moose (*Alces alces*), using preferably the early stages of forest succession can affect both the speed and course of the succession (e.g. Bryant & Chapin 1986, Kielland & Bryant 1998, see also Chapter 4). Large herbivore feeding tends to decrease litter accumulation in forests and grasslands, and may thus change the ratio of detrivores to herbivores in the food webs (e.g. Andresen *et al.* 1990, Van Wieren 1998).

Large herbivores will affect the physical properties of habitats since the plants themselves are major controllers of light penetration, temperature, wind, humidity, soil moisture, nutrient cycling and hydrology (e.g. Jones *et al.* 1994, 1997), and further, they will affect their physical environments by trampling and rooting (see Chapter 9). Large herbivores can act as keystone modifiers (Mills *et al.* 1993), or ecosystem engineers (Jones *et al.* 1994, 1997) when they change the physical environment in a way that affects other organisms.

IMPACTS ON VERTEBRATES

Small mammals

Flowerdew & Ellwood (2001) reviewed the potential impacts of high deer (*Cervus, Capreolus, Dama, Muntiacus*) densities on small mammals in temperate woodlands. However, the number of actual studies on this subject is quite modest. In temperate forests (Fig. 13.1a,b), both the population density index and species richness of rodents were, without exception, considerably higher in the absence of large herbivores than when they were present. In England (Putman *et al.* 1989) and Japan (M. Koganezawa, K. Suda, O. Kurashima & T. Takashima, unpublished data), only one rodent species was found in the (heavily) grazed plots. Despite the small number of studies, it seems likely that large mammalian herbivores may substantially reduce both the abundance and species richness of rodents in forested habitats, and may even cause local extinction of some rodent species when large herbivore densities are extraordinarily high.

In temperate grasslands, the negative impact of large herbivores on rodents seems to be similar, but less dramatic compared with the forests (Fig. 13.1c,d), and some rodent species seem to benefit from grazing. In American temperate grasslands, rodents were often more abundant and had higher species richness in ungrazed exclosures than in grazed areas. The study of Matlack *et al.* (2001) is an exception because the pooled abundance of small mammals was greater in grazed plots. The only common small mammal species, and the one that responded positively to grazing, was the deer mouse (*Peromyscus maniculatus*), which has been reported to be favoured by grazing and fire in other studies as well (Grant *et al.* 1982). *Peromyscus* responded more strongly to bison than to cattle grazing (Matlack *et al.* 2001); bison create larger patches with shorter plants as well as more patches of bare ground. In general, grazing-induced reduction in plant cover changed the rodent communities (Grant *et al.* 1982) from a dominance of herbivorous, litter-dwelling species to granivorous/insectivorous species preferring short, open vegetation. In Kenya, abundance of the dominant rodent (*Saccostomus mearnsi*; 75% of captures) increased significantly after two years of ungulate exclusion, but there was no consistent change in species diversity in the savanna habitat (Keesing 1998).

There are several non-mutually exclusive mechanisms proposed to explain the impact of large herbivores on small mammal communities. Changes in vegetation composition and biomass are stressed in all studies

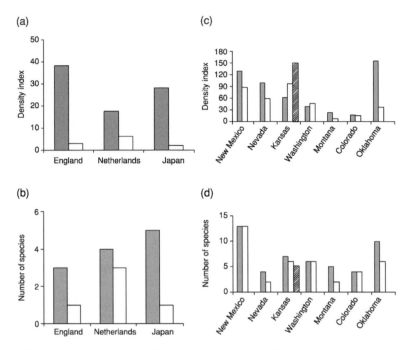

Figure 13.1. Abundance and species richness of small mammal communities in exclosure studies in Eurasian temperate forests (a, b) and American temperate grasslands (c, d). Grey bars = ungrazed exclosures, open bars = grazed plots (in burned tallgrass open bar = cattle grazed, hatched bar = bison grazed). Richness is given as the number of species without correcting for the differences in the number of individuals in samples.
Sites: England (temperate forest, deer grazing) (Putman *et al.* 1989); the Netherlands (temperate forest, deer and wild boar) (Hazebroek *et al.* 1994); Japan (temperate forest, deer) (M. Koganezawa, K. Suda, O. Kurashima and T. Takashima unpublished data); New Mexico (desert wetland, livestock) (Hayward *et al.* 1997); Nevada (montane meadow, feral horse) (Beever & Brussard 2000); Kansas (tallgrass, burned prairie, cattle or bison) (Matlack *et al.* 2001); Washington (bunchgrass), Montana (montane), Colorado (shortgrass) and Oklahoma (tallgrass) (all four sites, cattle grazed prairies) (Grant *et al.* 1982).

(Grant *et al.* 1982, Putman *et al.* 1989, Hazebroek *et al.* 1994, Hayward *et al.* 1997, Keesing 1998, Beever & Brussard 2000, Matlack *et al.* 2001, M. Koganezawa, K. Suda, O. Kurashima & T. Takashima unpublished data) because they can affect the quality and quantity of food plants as well as habitat structure. As a consequence, exploitative competition can take place between different herbivore groups, and due to large differences in body size the competition could be expected to be highly asymmetric;

small species are probably more affected. However, at high densities small mammals may influence vegetation composition and plant biomass in some habitats more than large herbivores at normal densities. For example, Olofsson et al. (2004) showed that voles and lemmings had a stronger impact on ground vegetation at the Arctic tree line than reindeer. Large herbivores tend to reduce cover, height and complexity of the forest under-storey, and the field layer mainly used by small mammals. The increased exposure to predation due to more open vegetation is most likely to affect behaviour and habitat choice of small mammals. The impact on litter by large herbivore grazing possibly affects small litter-dwelling mammals. Changes in fruit and seed abundance are very important to frugivorous or granivorous rodents. Focardi et al. (2000) concluded that wild boars can, by exploiting acorns hoarded by small mammals, increase their own survival, but reduce the rodent populations. Large herbivores can have a substantial impact on invertebrate abundance (see below), and because many small mammals, e.g. shrews and some rodents, are at least partly insectivorous they can be affected (Putman et al. 1989, Milchunas et al. 1998). The impact of soil compaction is regarded as one partial reason for the negative impact of heavy mammals on small burrowing animals (Grant et al. 1982, Hayward et al. 1997, Keesing 1998, Beever & Brussard 2000).

Hazebroek et al. (1994) measured several attributes of the vegetation in a temperate forest in the Netherlands where they sampled small mammals. The small mammal abundance was correlated with the functional diversity and height of vegetation as well as shrub species diversity; the species diversity of small mammals was correlated with shrub species diversity and forest successional stage. Grant et al. (1982) concluded that their study of small mammals in grasslands 'support the hypothesis that the composition of small mammal communities is determined by structural attributes of the habitat'. Thus, the impact of large herbivores on the vegetation structure, and food availability are probably the main reasons for the observed changes in rodent assemblages both in grasslands and forested habitats.

It seems evident that large mammalian herbivores can have a strong (order of magnitude) impact on small mammal abundance. Small mammals are important prey for a large number of vertebrate predators, and a substantial reduction in small mammal prey density will affect the predators (Putman et al. 1989, Hayward et al. 1997, Flowerdew & Ellwood 2001). From a conservation point-of-view, these effects might be more interesting than the impacts on small mammals themselves, because some of the predators are endangered species (Hayward et al. 1997).

Birds

Effects on the avifauna have been studied mainly in temperate forests and grasslands (e.g. reviews by: McShea & Rappole 1997, Van Wieren 1998, Fuller 2001) (Table 13.1). However, agricultural habitats with domestic animals have been more widely studied (e.g. Van Wieren 1998).

Birds depending upon forest undergrowth, the sapling layer and the intermediate canopy tend to suffer when large herbivores are abundant (Casey & Hein 1983, deCalesta 1994, McShea & Rappole 2000, Berger *et al.* 2001, Fuller 2001). These birds form a major part of the avifauna in temperate forests (e.g. 61% of British woodland breeding birds) (Fuller 2001). For Finland, one major cause suggested for the increase in the number of breeding forest birds during the twentieth century has been the cessation of extensive cattle grazing in forests, and the following increase in deciduous under-storey (von Haartman 1978, Järvinen & Väisänen 1978). The few species favoured by large herbivore grazing are usually open under-storey species (McShea & Rappole 2000), bark-foraging species (e.g. woodpeckers, tree-creepers) and some hole-nesters (Casey & Hein 1983, Perrins & Overall 2001).

As for small mammals, the three-dimensional vegetation structure, rather than the plant species composition, is considered to be important for the bird community composition (e.g. MacArthur & MacArthur 1961, Lack 1968, Wiens 1989, Scott *et al.* 2003). The structural changes in vegetation caused by large herbivores (usually more open and less layered habitats), have been suggested as the main cause of changes in forest bird assemblages in all studies (Casey & Hein 1983, deCalesta 1994, McShea & Rappole 2000, Popotkin & Giuliano 2000, Berger *et al.* 2001, Fuller 2001, Scott *et al.* 2003).

Large herbivores might improve habitat conditions for predatory birds by opening vegetation and reducing cover for small mammals (Flowerdew & Ellwood 2001). deCalesta (1994) suggests that the direct trampling effects on birds are probably negligible and found no impact of high white-tailed deer (*Odocoileus virginianus*) density on ground-nesting birds. On the other hand, McShea & Rappole (2000) reported that birds nesting/ feeding on the ground were negatively affected by deer, but that this was due to changes in vegetation. The negative impacts of high moose density (winter browsing) on species richness and density of migratory birds in riparian habitats in Wyoming, were stronger for birds nesting above ground than for birds nesting near the ground, where the vegetation was protected from heavy browsing by snow cover (Berger *et al.* 2001).

Table 13.1. *The relative magnitude of the impact of grazing on birds in different studies*

Biome	Habitat	Grazer/browser	Density or abundance Grazing intensity					Richness or diversity Grazing intensity				
			Ungr.	Graz.	Low	Interm.	High	Ungr.	Graz.	Low	Interm.	High
Temperate grassland, USA[*]		Cattle			90	75	100			100	90	70
Temperate forest, USA[†]		Deer										
	Ground nesting				100	100	90 (ns)			100	100	80 (ns)
	Intermediate canopy				100	75	60			100	65	70
	Upper canopy				85	100	85 (ns)			100	75	80 (ns)
Boreal, riparian, USA[‡]		Moose										
	Near-ground nesting				100		75					
	Above-ground nesting				100		58					
	All breeding birds				100		60					
Temperate, riparian, USA[§]		Cattle										
	Individuals		100	67				100	63			
	Nests		100	52								

Values are expressed as % of the treatment with highest value in each case. In some cases data were extracted from published diagrams and then rounded to the nearest 5%. For richness or diversity, if several indices were used, the measure that had greatest response to grazing is given.
[*] Milchunas *et al.* 1998 and references therein
[†] deCalesta 1994.
[‡] Berger *et al.* 2001.
[§] Popotkin & Giuliano 2000.

In wetlands, grazing (cattle) reduces reedbeds and increases the area of open water. This has a positive impact on waterfowl (e.g. ducks, coots, grebes), but a negative effect on birds (mainly passerine) living among the reeds (e.g. von Haartman 1975, Soikkeli & Salo 1979, Gordon *et al.* 1990). In temperate grasslands, the bird diversity declined with increasing grazing (cattle) intensity and the dominant passerine species differed between lightly grazed and heavily grazed treatments (Giezentanner 1970, Milchunas *et al.* 1998). From a conservation perspective it should be stressed that some native bird species are adapted to environments with native grazers and prefer heavily grazed areas; thus grazing-related decline in the number of species as such, is not necessarily negative (Milchunas *et al.* 1998, Fuhlendorf & Engle 2001). Beck and Mitchell (2000) and Fuhlendorf and Engle (2001) noted that the vegetation structure of nesting, feeding and courtship habitats is important for prairie birds, and that the impact of grazing on these habitats may be opposite. For example, ungrazed high and dense vegetation gives good cover and is a preferred nesting habitat, but lightly grazed areas may be better feeding habitats for sage grouse (*Centrocercus urophasianus*) (Beck & Mitchell 2000). Structural attributes and heterogeneity of the vegetation, at several spatial scales (Fuhlendorf & Engle 2001) should thus be considered when evaluating the impact of large herbivores.

Reduced fruit and seed production as a consequence of large herbivore grazing is also important for birds; granivores are often negatively affected by ungulates (Donald *et al.* 1997, Fuller 2001). Decline in invertebrate abundance in foliage due to large herbivore grazing has been suggested as a potential cause for the decline in numbers of insectivorous birds inhabiting grazed forests (Baines *et al.* 1994, Fuller 2001). Bailey and Whitham (2003) found that bird predation on galling sawflies living on aspen (*Populus tremuloides*) was higher on unbrowsed ramets than on ramets browsed by deer (*Cervus canadensis*) due to the higher abundance of galls in the unbrowsed area.

IMPACTS ON INVERTEBRATES

Impacts on macro-invertebrates

Invertebrates are sensitive to small changes in microclimate (e.g. temperature, humidity) (e.g. Wallis De Vries & Raemakers 2001), and are thus indirectly affected, through physical habitat modification, by large herbivores (e.g. Bromham *et al.* 1999, Suominen 1999a, Wardle *et al.* 2001). Soil compaction due to trampling can affect burrowing invertebrates

(Bromham *et al.* 1999, Wardle *et al.* 2001), and decreased litter accumulation due to herbivory may reduce the size and affect the structure of the detrivore community (e.g. Andresen *et al.* 1990, Van Wieren 1998, Bromham *et al.* 1999).

Impacts of large herbivores on the structural diversity and heterogeneity of plant communities are important for invertebrates living in the vegetation (e.g. Dennis *et al.* 1998, Rambo & Faeth 1999, Hartley *et al.* 2003) and on the ground (Putman *et al.* 1989, Dennis *et al.* 1997, Bromham *et al.* 1999, Suominen *et al.* 1999a,b; but see Gonzáles-Megías *et al.* 2004). For example, in a Japanese forest Miyashita *et al.* (2004) showed that the negative impact of deer on web spider abundance and species richness did not correlate with the availability of prey, but with the availability of web sites, i.e. vegetation height structure. Spiders that hunt among the vegetation using a web (e.g. Linyphiidae) are also less abundant in grazed Scottish grasslands and forests in Sweden and Finland, that are grazed or browsed by domestic herbivores, moose and reindeer, respectively, than in habitats without herbivores (Table 13.2, 13.3). The impact of large herbivores can be more favourable for ground-dwelling species adapted to open habitat than for species living in the vegetation. This pattern may partly explain contrasting results based on pitfall catches versus samples of arthropods taken from the vegetation (e.g. Kruess & Tscharntke 2002a,b, Gonzáles-Megías *et al.* 2004). Insect species differ often in microhabitat choice, as well as in the resource requirements between adult and larval stages, and some species may need two or more different habitat types for development (Stewart 2001).

A well-known mechanism through which large herbivores affect invertebrate herbivores is through induced chemical and morphological changes in eaten plants. Leaf beetles (*Chrysomela confluens*) on resprouting leaves from beaver-cut cottonwood (*Populus fremontii* × *P. angustifolia*) are even able to use the induced plant defence substances for their own defence against predators, in addition to the benefits of the better nutritional quality of these types of leaves (Martinsen *et al.* 1998). Many studies have found more insect herbivores on previously browsed trees/shoots, i.e. positive effects (e.g. Danell & Huss-Danell 1985, Roininen *et al.* 1997, Olofsson & Strengbom 2000), whereas some studies have reported more insect herbivory on unbrowsed trees (Bailey & Whitham 2003, den Herder 2003). It has been suggested that the contrasting results might be linked to the vigour of the browsed trees (e.g. Bailey & Whitham 2003).

The impact of large herbivores on plant biomass and food availability for invertebrate herbivores may also affect invertebrates. A negative effect

Table 13.2. *The relative magnitude of the impact of grazing on ground-dwelling invertebrates (pitfall traps) in different studies*

Biome	Taxon	Grazer/browser	Density or abundance Grazing intensity				Richness or diversity Grazing intensity	
			Ungr.	Graz.	Interm.	High	Ungr.	Graz.
Semi-natural grassland, Scotland[*]								
	Carabidae	Sheep	31		81	100		
	Carabidae	Sheep, cattle	51		100	47		
	Staphylinidae	Sheep	100		75	85		
	Staphylinidae	Sheep–cattle	100		89	50		
Woodland, Australia[†]								
	All arthropods		53	100				
	Formicidae		38	100			100	96
	Araneae		100	93				
	Coleoptera		69	100				
	Insect orders						100	80
Temperate forest, England[‡]		Wild & domestic ungulates						
	Carabidae		100	85				
	Staphylinidae		22	100				
	Formicidae		36	100				
	Araneae		35	100				
	Opiliones		100	53				
Mixed boreal forest, Sweden[§]		Moose, deer						
	All arthropods		100	73				
	Coleoptera		100	77			100	91
	Carabidae		100	87				
	Staphylinidae		100	78				

Taxon					Large herbivore
Formicidae	60	100			
Araneae	98	100			
Lycosidae	92	100			
Linyphiidae	98	100			
Opiliones	100	68			
Gastropoda	100	84	85	100	Moose, deer
Boreal pine forest, Sweden§					
All arthropods	48	100	100	77	
Coleoptera	93	100	100	67	
Carabidae	100	70			
Staphylinidae	77	100			
Formicidae	18	100			
Araneae	100	88			
Lycosidae	54	100			
Linyphiidae	100	66			
Opiliones	100	23			
Gastropoda	100	79			
Boreal riparian, Alaska**					Moose, hare
Orthoptera+Coleoptera	91	100	88	100	
Orthoptera	88	100			
Carabidae	77	100			
Staphylinidae	94	100			
Curculionidae	100	70			
Boreal pine & birch, Finland†† >40% lichen cover					Reindeer, moose
All arthropods	77	100	78	100	
Formicidae	37	100		100	
Carabidae	45	100	81	100	
Staphylinidae	95	100		100	

Biome	Taxon	Grazer/browser	Density or abundance Grazing intensity				Richness or diversity Grazing intensity	
			Ungr.	Graz.	Interm.	High	Ungr.	Graz.
	Curculionidae		64	100			51	100
	Araneae		100	93			89	100
	Lycosidae		71	100				
	Linyphiidae		100	56				
	Gastropoda		100	43				
Boreal birch, Finland††		Reindeer, moose						
<25% lichen cover								
	All arthropods		76	100			95	100
	Formicidae		51	100				
	Carabidae		83	100			82	100
	Staphylinidae		81	100				
	Curculionidae		100	53			47	100
	Araneae		86	100			100	97
	Lycosidae		80	100				
	Linyphiidae		100	91				
	Gastropoda		100	90			100	74

Values are expressed as % of the treatment with highest value in each case. In some cases values were extracted from published diagrams and then rounded to the nearest 5 %. For richness or diversity, if several indices were used the measure that had greatest response to grazing is given. It is notable that in several studies richness was given as only the number of species (or other taxa) without scaling to the differences in the number of individuals in samples.

* Dennis et al. 1997.
† Bromham et al. 1999.
‡ Putman et al. 1989.
§ Suominen 1999a.b, Suominen et al. 1999a.
** Suominen et al. 1999b.
†† Suominen 1999a.b, Suominen et al. 2003.

Table 13.3. *The relative magnitude of the impact of grazing on litter and soil dwelling invertebrates in different studies*

Biome	Taxon	Grazer	Density or abundance — Grazing intensity					Richness or diversity — Grazing intensity				
			Ungr.	Graz.	Low	Interm.	High	Ungr.	Graz.	Low	Interm.	High
Temp. grassland, USA[*]	Nematoda	Cattle	100			15		100			100	
Temp. grassland, USA[†]	Nematoda, under *Festuca*	Wild ungulates	70	100								
Temp. forest, New Zealand[‡]	Nematoda	Introduced wild ungulates	ns	ns				ns	ns			
	litter microarthropods		+	−								
	Coleoptera		+	−				91	100			
	Staphylinidae		+	−				91	100			
	Araneida		+	−								
	Opiliones		+	−								
	Chilopoda		+	−								
	Diplopoda		+	−				100	94			
	Gastropoda		+	−				100	87			
Boreal forest, Finland[§]	Nematoda, lichen layer	Reindeer						78	100			
	Bact. feeding		30	100								
	Fungal feeding		25	100								
	Pred+omnivor		28	100								
	Herbivorous		100	25								

Values expressed as % of the treatment with highest value in each case. In one case only symbols for treatment with significantly higher (+) and lower (−) value are given. In some cases values were extracted from published diagrams and then rounded to the nearest 5%. For richness or diversity, if several indices were used the measure that had greatest response to grazing is given. It is notable that in several studies richness was given as the plain number of species (or other taxa) without scaling to the differences in the number of individuals in samples.

[*] Milchunas *et al.* 1998 and references therein.
[†] Merrill *et al.* 1994.
[‡] Wardle *et al.* 2001.
[§] Stark *et al.* 2000.

on smaller herbivores sharing the same food plants through exploitative competition has been found in several studies (e.g. Baines *et al.* 1994, Gómez & Gonzáles-Megías 2002, Hartley *et al.* 2003, Suominen *et al.* 2003). Usually this competition has been considered to be higly asymmetric due to the huge size difference (e.g. Gómez & Gonzáles-Megías 2002). However, phytophagous insects can have a higher biomass and consumption per unit area in some habitats than mammalian herbivores (e.g. Tscharntke 1997). For example, outbreaks of autumnal moth (*Epirrita autumnata*) in mountain birch (*Betula pubescens*) forests can significantly reduce availability of deciduous trees (e.g. Kallio & Lehtonen 1975), an important summer forage for reindeer (Haukioja & Heino 1974).

Most of the studies on the impact of large herbivores on invertebrate assemblages are from different types of grasslands, and temperate and boreal forests (Tables 13.3, 13.4). However, it is difficult to make generalizations due to the small number of studies that have used different methods, habitats and herbivores. Even within a single study, the responses of invertebrates can differ depending on habitat, taxon, year or season (e.g. Suominen *et al.* 1999a, Gonzáles-Megías *et al.* 2004).

There is no consistent pattern on how large herbivores affect the abundance of ground-dwelling invertebrates in forests (Table 13.2). Both sheep grazing in Australian woodlands (Bromham *et al.* 1999) and reindeer grazing in Finnish Lapland (Suominen 1999b) resulted in higher pooled invertebrate abundance in grazed plots, but heavy ungulate grazing in England decreased the total invertebrate catch (Putman *et al.* 1989). Moose browsing has either negative or positive impact on invertebrate abundance depending on the habitat and taxonomic/functional groups (Suominen *et al.* 1999a,b). However, the abundance of some invertebrate groups tends to respond consistently to grazing in most studies, and species richness is often higher in grazed sites (Tables 13.2, 13.3). Mobile ground-dwelling predators, e.g. lycosid spiders and ants, are more common in grazed than in ungrazed sites (Table 13.2) (Putman *et al.* 1989, Bromham *et al.* 1999, Suominen 1999b, Suominen *et al.* 1999a), probably due to the more open vegetation and higher temperature. Ants are considered as keystone species by having an impact on other invertebrates. If large herbivores affect ants there can be complex indirect effects on the whole invertebrate assemblage.

Coprophagous species using dung of large herbivores are more abundant where the herbivores are abundant (Stewart 2001). Reduction of plant litter and vegetation by large herbivores tends to decrease humidity and raise temperature extremes (Suominen *et al.* 1999a, Bromham *et al.*

Table 13.4. *The relative magnitude of the impact of grazing on invertebrates in vegetation*

Biome	Taxon	Grazer	Density or abundance Grazing intensity					Richness or diversity Grazing intensity				
			Ungr.	Graz.	Low	Interm.	High	Ungr.	Graz.	Low	Interm.	High
Temperate pine-grassland, USA*	Insecta	Deer & cattle	100	18				100	27			
Boreal forest, Scotland†	Lepidoptera, larva	Deer	100	30								
	Coleoptera		100	55								
	Araneae		100	50								
	Diptera		100	55								
	Hymenoptera		100	40								
Temperate grassland, Argentina‡	Insects (family)	Cattle			100		64			100		50
	Coleoptera (species)				100		63			100		55
Temperate pasture, Germany§	Phytophagous insects	Cattle	100		55		38	100		73		48
	Predatory insects		100		68		40	100		75		49
	Saltatoria		100					100		95		43
	Lepidoptera, adult		100		30		5	100		82		59
	Coleoptera		100		53		21	100		92		49
	Heteroptera		100		65		26	100		76		39

Table 13.4. (*cont.*)

Biome	Taxon	Grazer	Density or abundance Grazing intensity					Richness or diversity Grazing intensity				
			Ungr.	Graz.	Low	Interm.	High	Ungr.	Graz.	Low	Interm.	High
Savanna, South Africa**	Orthoptera	Wild/domestic ungulates			100		60			100		56
Temperate grassland, USA††	Macroarthropods	Cattle	95		100	85	70	30		85	100	60

Values are expressed as % of the treatment with highest value in each case. In some cases values were extracted from published diagrams and then rounded to the nearest 5%. For richness or diversity, if several indices were used the measure that had greatest response to grazing is given. It is notable that in several studies richness was given as only the number of species (or other taxa) without scaling to the differences in the number of individuals in samples.

* Rambo & Faeth 1999.
† Baines *et al.* 1994.
‡ Cagnolo *et al.* 2002.
§ Kruess & Tscharntke 2002a,b.
** Samways & Kreuzinger 2001.
†† Milchunas *et al.* 1998 and references therein.

1999). Moist microclimate and thick litter layer are important for terrestrial gastropods and harvestmen (Opiliones), and their population density and species richness are higher in the absence of large herbivores, both in the boreal forests of Fennoscandia and in the deciduous forests of New Zealand (Suominen 1999a, Wardle et al. 2001) (Tables 13.2, 13.3).

The total abundance of arthropods in the vegetation layer of forests tends to be higher in ungrazed or lightly grazed areas (Table 13.4). This holds for several phytophagous insect groups, e.g. larvae of Lepidoptera (Baines et al. 1994), or herbivorous weevils sharing the same food plants as large herbivores (Suominen et al. 1999b, Goméz & Gónzales-Megías 2002, Suominen et al. 2003), and in grasslands, e.g. for hemipterans (Kruess & Tscharntke 2002b, Hartley et al. 2003). In forests and grasslands, responses of plant-living invertebrates seem to be more consistent than the ground-dwelling ones. Dennis et al. (1998) found by suction sampling that the abundance of most of the studied arthropod groups and species were highest in the ungrazed tall vegetation, and that ground-dwelling beetles caught by pitfall traps had more divergent responses to grazing treatments (Dennis et al. 1997). Dense large herbivore populations tend to create lower and structurally less complex vegetation, supporting less rich and sparser invertebrate fauna than more complex vegetation (e.g. Tscharntke 1997, Dennis et al. 1998). Low grazing intensity, on the other hand, may maximize height variation of the vegetation (Dennis et al. 1998). According to Samways and Kreuzinger (2001), grasshopper density and species richness were higher in lightly grazed areas than in heavily grazed ones in South African grasslands.

At the landscape scale, low or moderate grazing/browsing intensity helps to create and maintain open patches within forests (Van Wieren 1998), which are important for several invertebrates (e.g. butterflies) (Stewart 2001, Wallis De Vries & Raemakers 2001) during some stages of their life cycle. Grazing by domestic and wild large herbivores has been used, or suggested, as a management tool for conservation of some forest habitats (e.g. Van Wieren 1998).

Grazing intensity and response of invertebrate fauna

In shortgrass steppes in Colorado (Lavigne et al. 1972, Lloyd et al. 1973, Milchunas et al. 1998), the abundance of invertebrates in the vegetation and below ground increased with light grazing, but decreased with moderate or heavy grazing compared to ungrazed areas. Diversity of invertebrates in vegetation was highest in moderately grazed areas and lowest in ungrazed areas. However, there were only small differences in the abundance or diversity of micro-invertebrates in soil and litter (Leetham & Milchunas 1985, Milchunas et al. 1998).

In the succulent Karoo in South Africa, ground-dwelling invertebrates were more abundant in areas heavily grazed by cattle, but diversity was higher in a moderately grazed area (Seymour & Dean 1999).

In Scottish semi-natural grasslands, most of the carabid and staphylinid beetles (pitfall traps) responding to differing grazing treatments, were most common in ungrazed or moderately sheep-grazed plots, but some species were most common in intensely grazed plots with short vegetation (Dennis et al. 1997). Kruess and Tscharntke (2002a,b) found that the abundance and species richness of vegetation-living insect groups increased consistently and monotonically from intensively to extensively grazed to ungrazed pastures (Table 13.4). Insect diversity and abundance were related to vegetation heterogeneity and/or height, but vegetation characteristics did not differ significantly between extensively and intensively grazed pastures even though insect assemblages differed. In Scottish grasslands (Dennis et al. 1998), there was a negative linear relationship between grazing intensity and invertebrate abundance in suction samples. Small-scale heterogeneity of vegetation structure and height promoted abundance and species richness of invertebrates living in the vegetation, and these variables were maximized by low grazing intensities. The time scale of the study/treatment should be noted here; the above-mentioned studies were conducted only after a few years of treatment. Vegetation height and height variation are most probably linked to the time since the cessation of grazing or the beginning of grazing treatment, as well as to grazing intensity.

In contrast to the Scottish grasslands, most of the carabid species in the forests of Finnish Lapland seem to be favoured by quite high reindeer-grazing intensity (Suominen et al. 2003). The impact of grazing on the abundance of several ground-dwelling taxa (all invertebrates pooled, spiders, ants) and carabid diversity was related to the magnitude of the impact on vegetation, with the highest positive effect of reindeer at an intermediate level of grazing impact on vegetation (Suominen 1999b, Suominen et al. 2003).

In deciduous temperate forests of New Zealand, the abundance of most litter-dwelling invertebrate groups was higher in unbrowsed exclosures, but there was no general trend in the impact of introduced browsers on the diversity of most groups (Wardle et al. 2001). Beetle family diversity was higher in browsed plots, and the abundance and diversity of gastropods and harvestmen were higher in unbrowsed plots. The impact of ungulates on macro-invertebrate abundance and diversity was unrelated to magnitude of the impact on vegetation, and the impact of browsers on gastropods and diplopods was positively related to the impact on leaf-litter diversity.

Impacts on soil microfauna

There are very few studies on the impacts of large herbivores on soil micro-invertebrates outside agricultural systems. Plant-parasitic nematodes, bacterial-feeding nematodes and fungal-feeding nematodes were all more abundant under grasses grazed by native ungulates in Yellowstone (Merrill et al. 1994), probably due to changes in plant chemistry and increased root mortality after spring grazing. Stark et al. (2000) studied nematodes in a reindeer exclosure and a grazed reference plot in a Finnish pine forest, and observed that grazing increased the abundance of all trophic groups of nematodes and their diversity. Proposed causes were changes in litter quality and quantity as well as soil microclimate due to grazing. Stark et al. (2000) also showed that experimental removal of ground lichens (simulating reindeer impact) had a similar impact as reindeer grazing and trampling.

Browsers in New Zealand forests (Wardle et al. 2001) had significant effects on nematodes in many sites, but there was no consistent pattern over the 30 different exclosure sites. The effect on the diversity of nematodes in the humus layer was related to the effect of browsers on vegetation diversity; no such pattern was found in any other invertebrate group. Wardle et al. (2001) suggest that, in general, there is no consistent relationship between plant species richness and richness or diversity of the soil fauna. Loss of plant species from a community can either increase or decrease the diversity of the soil fauna depending on the special attributes of each plant species (Wardle et al. 1999, Wardle et al. 2001). Wardle et al. (2001) give support to earlier findings (e.g. Sulkava & Huhta 1998) that soil and litter faunal diversity are affected by microhabitat diversity in the soil and litter layers.

CONCLUSIONS

It is not surprising that herbivore-induced changes in the vegetation are often proposed as the main cause for changes in animal assemblages. There are, however, a few studies where large herbivores affected other animals without any substantial effect on the vegetation (e.g. Kruess & Tscharntke 2002a,b, Suominen, unpublished data). Disturbances by large herbivores as such may have an impact on trophic interactions and thus induce changes in animal assemblages (e.g. Tscharntke 1997, Holt *et al.* 1999). When vegetational changes are considered to be the driving force, the impacts on structural attributes of the vegetation, at different scales, are often considered most important (e.g. Dennis *et al.* 1998, Fuller 2001, Wardle *et al.* 2001, Hartley *et al.* 2003). Also the impacts on plant biomass or specific plant parts (seeds, nectar) are important for some organisms. A clear conclusion from this review is that large herbivores tend to decrease the abundance of other herbivores feeding upon the same plants. Alteration of litter quality and quantity by large herbivores seems to be another important mechanism for the effects of large herbivores on other animals (e.g. Suominen *et al.* 1999a,b, Wardle *et al.* 2001), and it also includes both microhabitat alteration and trophic effects.

Several authors have suggested (explicitly or implicitly) a 'moderate grazing hypothesis' (cf. intermediate disturbance hypothesis), i.e. that moderate grazing intensity maximizes animal diversity (e.g. Van Wieren 1998). However, moderate grazing is a relative concept. Intuitively, it would be an intensity that supports maximal habitat heterogeneity, and it would probably be different for different taxonomic and functional groups. A few studies have found a humped (unimodal) response of taxonomic richness to grazing intensity for some groups (e.g. Milchunas *et al.* 1998, Suominen *et al.* 2003). Some studies have not found (e.g. Wardle *et al.* 2001), or tested, any relationship between the impact of herbivores on diversity and grazing intensity, while some have found a monotonic relationship (usually negative impact of grazing intensity on diversity) (e.g. Dennis *et al.* 1998, Kruess & Tscharntke 2002a,b). Some groups seem to be almost invariably negatively affected (e.g. small mammals, passerine birds, terrestrial gastropods, web spiders) and, for them, the negative impact will probably be stronger when grazing intensity increases. For the groups that respond positively to a low or moderate level of grazing, it seems intuitively obvious that increasing grazing intensity will eventually reach a point when the impact becomes negative. The role of herbivore density also incorporates differences between wild and domestic large herbivores; livestock density and grazing intensity are usually higher. The importance of heterogeneity (both spatial and temporal) of the natural grazing process versus livestock management is often emphasized (e.g. Strand & Merritt 1999, Suominen & Olofsson 2000, Fuhlendorf & Engle 2001, WallisDeVries & Raemakers 2001), but not really studied.

The importance of the 'evolutionary history' of the community and the differences in the impacts of native versus introduced large herbivores have been discussed (e.g. Milchunas *et al.* 1988, Vázquez 2002). For example, Fuhlendorf and Engle (2001) suggest that if (!) cattle and bison graze similarly, their effects are quite similar. They argue that many native prairie birds occur at the highest densities in cattle-grazed landscapes because they have evolved with bison grazing. Samways and Kreuzinger (2001) stress that diversity of African savanna grasshoppers, which have evolved with native large mammals, is higher with cattle grazing than without cattle in areas from which the natural wild mammalian grazers are gone. Reindeer grazing is a natural part of the ecosystems in Lapland, and it has predominantly positive effects on the abundance and diversity of plants, soil nematodes and ground-dwelling invertebrates (Väre et al. 1996, Suominen & Olofsson 2000, Stark et al. 2000, Suominen et al. 2003), despite the often presumed 'overgrazing' by semi-domesticated reindeer. Wardle et al. (2001) argue that the predominantly negative effects of introduced browsers on invertebrate abundance and plant diversity in New Zealand habitats might be partly explained by their evolutionary history without large mammalian herbivores.

'Overgrazing' by large herbivores has been seen as an environmental problem, mainly due to the effects on vegetation, but also due to the drastic impacts on animal communities (see above, and Chapter 14). Possible reasons for the 'overabundance' and factors that regulate herbivore density are discussed in Chapter 14. For most of the animal groups or species, there are not enough data to assess the possible threat at present herbivore densities, and even less to judge what would be the optimal grazing intensity. It seems likely that dense wild ungulate populations are capable of causing local extinction of some animals. Population decline of some specialist invertebrate herbivores feeding on preferred forage species of large herbivores have been linked to the high abundance of ungulate grazers (e.g. Miller et al. 1992, Feber et al. 2001). The focus of studies and concerns of managers and conservation agencies has usually been the visible impacts of large herbivores on plant communities, while the more indirect and less conspicuous changes in other community elements have not been recognized. However, there has recently been great concern over the negative impacts of high deer density on birds – a visible and popular animal group – in Great Britain (e.g. http://www.nationalgeografic.com, March 2003). The impacts have often not been studied directly but rather deduced from the knowledge of the impacts on vegetation and the ecology of the animal species (e.g. Feber et al. 2001). On the other hand, large herbivore grazing is regarded as a management tool for nature conservation (e.g. Van Wieren 1998 and references therein). For example, grazing at low intensity (usually by livestock), has been used to create open habitats for butterflies and other invertebrates (e.g. Pykälä 2000, Feber *et al.* 2001, Wallis De Vries & Raemakers 2001, Ellis 2003).

Studies on the indirect impacts of large herbivores on other biota have been few, but they are now increasing in number. However, there is still a great need for research on the impacts of large herbivores on almost any group of animals, and there are several habitats without any data at all. Assessment of the impacts of different grazing intensities and different herbivore species are needed for practical management recommendations. At present, a major part of the evidence of large herbivore impacts comes from exclosure studies commonly comparing high grazing intensity with no grazing at all. In most cases, it means that two unnatural and undesirable extreme situations are compared. Also, the different interacting mechanisms behind the observed faunal changes should be studied experimentally. The possibility of threshold densities in the responses of other biota to grazing intensity proposed by e.g. deCalesta (1994), is one area of research that would have both scientific and practical values. Most studies on the impacts of large herbivores on other biota have studied 'overabundant' wild herbivores or domestic grazers. This skewed choice of study systems might also give a skewed picture of how large herbivores shape community structures. One might either exaggerate the impact of large herbivores or get a view that large herbivores have a substantial impact on other animals only when grazing intensity is exceptionally high. One fruitful approach has been used by Persson (2003), who tested experimentally the impacts of four different moose densities by simulating feeding (clipping, leaf-stripping), and the addition of faeces and urine, and studied the following responses of e.g. shoot and litter production.

The impacts of grazing at different spatial and temporal scales are also poorly studied; most studies so far have explored the local scale and short time scales. In short, there is still need for more research, theoretical as well as applied, on the roles of large herbivores as modifiers of assemblages of other animals.

ACKNOWLEDGEMENTS

We would like to express our sincere thanks to M. Koganezawa, K. Suda, O. Kurashima and T. Takashima for letting us use their unpublished data here, and R. Andersen for his kind tip of interesting literature. Comments by D. Ward and an anonymous reviewer have greatly improved the manuscript. We are also grateful for the financial support given to Otso Suominen by Kone Foundation and Maj and Thor Nessling Foundation and to Kjell Danell by the Swedish Environmental Protection Board, The Swedish Research Council for Environment, Agricultural Sciences and Spatial Planning (Formas) and the Swedish Research Council (VR).

REFERENCES

Andresen, H., Bakker, J.P., Brongers, M., Heydemann, B. & Irmler, U. (1990). Long-term changes of salt marsh communities by cattle grazing. *Vegetatio*, **89**, 137–48.

Bailey, J.K. & Whitham, T.G. (2003). Interactions among elk, aspen, galling sawflies and insectivorous birds. *Oikos*, **101**, 127–34.

Baines, D., Sage, R.B. & Baines, M.M. (1994). The implications of red deer grazing to ground vegetation and invertebrate communities of Scottish native pinewoods. *Journal of Applied Ecology*, **31**, 776–83.

Bardgett, R.D., Wardle, D.A. & Yeates, G.W. (1998). Linking above-ground and below ground interactions: how plant responses to foliar herbivory influence soil organisms. *Soil Biology and Biochemistry*, **30**, 1867–78.

Beck, J.L. & Mitchell, D.L. (2000). Influences of livestock grazing on sage grouse habitat. *Wildlife Society Bulletin*, **28**, 993–1002.

Beever, E.A. & Brussard, F. (2000). Examining ecological consequences of feral horse grazing using exclosures. *Western North American Naturalist*, **60**, 236–54.

Berger, J., Stacey, P.B., Bellis, L. & Johnson, M.P. (2001). A mammalian predator-prey imbalance: grizzly bear and wolf extinction affect avian neotropical migrants. *Ecological Applications*, **11**, 947–60.

Bromham, L., Cardillo, M., Bennett, A.F. & Elgar, M.A. (1999). Effects of stock grazing on the ground invertebrate fauna of woodland remnants. *Australian Journal of Ecology*, **24**, 1999–2007.

Bryant, J.P. & Chapin, F.S., III (1986). Browsing-woody plant interactions during boreal forest plant succession. In *Forest Ecosystems in the Alaskan Taiga*, ed. K. Van Kleve, F.S. Chapin, III, P.W. Flanagan, L.A. Viereck & C.T. Dyrness. New York: Springer, pp. 213–25.

Cagnolo, L., Molina, S.I. & Valladares, G.R. (2002). Diversity and guild structure of insect assemblages under grazing and exclusion regimes in a montane grassland from Central Argentina. *Biodiversity and Conservation*, **11**, 407–20.

Casey, D. & Hein, D. (1983). Effects of heavy browsing on a bird community in deciduous forest. *Journal of Wildlife Management*, **47**, 829–36.

Cooper, E.J. & Wookey, P.A. (2003). Floral herbivory of *Dryas octopetala* by Svalbard reindeer. *Arctic, Antarctic and Alpine Research*, **35**, 369–76.

Danell, K. & Huss-Danell, K. (1985). Feeding by insects and hares on birches earlier affected by moose browsing. *Oikos*, **44**, 75–81.

deCalesta, D. (1994). Effect of white-tailed deer on songbirds within managed forests in Pennsylvania. *Journal of Wildlife Management*, **58**, 711–18.

den Herder, M. (2003). Impacts of ungulates in boreal forest and subarctic tundra ecosystems in Finland. D.Sc. thesis, Faculty of Forestry, University of Joensuu, Finland.

Dennis, P., Young, M.R., Howard, C.L. & Gordon, I.J. (1997). The response of epigeal beetles (Col.: Carabidae, Staphylinidae) to varied grazing regimes on upland *Nardus stricta* grasslands. *Journal of Applied Ecology*, **34**, 433–43.

Dennis, P., Young, M.R. & Gordon, I.J. (1998). Distribution and abundance of small insects and arachnids in relation to structural heterogeneity of grazed, indigenous grasslands. *Ecological Entomology*, **23**, 253–64.

Donald, P.F., Haycock, D. & Fuller, R.J. (1997). Winter bird communities in forest plantations in western England and their response to vegetation growth stage and grazing. *Bird Study*, **44**, 206–19.

Ellis, S. (2003). Habitat quality and management for the northern brown argus butterfly *Aricia artaxerxes* (Lepidoptera, Lycaenidae) in North East England. *Biological Conservation*, **113**, 285–94.

Engelmark, O., Hofgaard, A. & Arnborg, T. (1998). Successional trends 219 years after fire in an old *Pinus sylvestris* stand in northern Sweden. *Journal of Vegetation Science*, **9**, 583–92.

Feber, R.E., Brereton, T.M., Warren, M.S. & Oates, M. (2001). The impact of deer on woodland butterflies: the good, the bad and the complex. *Forestry*, **74**, 271–6.

Flowerdew, J.R. & Ellwood, S.A. (2001). Impacts of woodland deer on small mammal ecology. *Forestry*, **74**, 277–87.

Focardi, S., Capizzi, D. & Monetti, D. (2000). Competition for acorns among wild boar (*Sus scrofa*) and small mammals in a Mediterranean woodland. *Journal of Zoology*, **250**, 329–34.

Fuhlendorf, S.D. & Engle, D.M. (2001). Restoring heterogeneity on rangelands: ecosystem management based on evolutionary grazing patterns. *BioScience*, **51**, 625–32.

Fuller, R.J. (2001). Responses of woodland birds to increasing numbers of deer: a review of evidence and mechanisms. *Forestry*, **74**, 289–98.

Furness, R.W. (1988). Predation on ground-nesting seabirds by island populations of red deer *Cervus elaphus* and sheep *Ovis*. *Journal of Zoology*, **216**, 565–73.

Giezentanner, J.B. (1970). *Avian Distribution and Population Fluctuations on the Shortgrass Prairie of North Central Colorado*. USIBP-Grassland Biome Technical Report No. 62, Natural Resource Ecology Laboratory, Fort. Collins, CO.

Gómez, J.M. & González-Megías, A. (2002). Asymmetrical interactions between ungulates and phytophagous insects: being different matters. *Ecology*, **83**, 203–11.

Gonzáles-Megías, A., Gómez, J.M. & Sánches-Piñero, F. (2004). Effects of ungulates on epigeal arthropods in Sierra Nevada National Park (southeast Spain). *Biodiversity and Conservation*, **13**, 733–52.

Gordon, I.J., Duncan, P., Grillas, P. & Lecomte, T. (1990). The use of domestic herbivores in the conservation of the biological richness of European wetlands. *Bulletin Ecologique*, **21**, 49–60.

Grant, W.E., Birney, E.C., French, N.R. & Swift, D.M. (1982). Structure and productivity of grassland small mammal communities related to grazing-induced changes in vegetative cover. *Journal of Mammalogy*, **63**, 248–60.

Hartley, S.E., Gardner, S.M. & Mitchell, R.J. (2003). Indirect effects of grazing and nutrient addition on the hemipteran community of heather moorlands. *Journal of Applied Ecology*, **40**, 793–803.

Haukioja, E. & Heino, J. (1974) Birch consumption by reindeer (*Rangifer tarandus*) in Finnish Lapland. *Reports from the Kevo Subarctic Research Station*, **11**, 22–5.

Hayward, B., Heske, E.J. & Painter, C.W. (1997). Effects of livestock grazing on small mammals at a desert cienaga. *Journal of Wildlife Management*, **61**, 123–9.

Hazebroek, E., Groot Bruiderink, G.W.T.A. & Van Biezen, J.B. (1994). Changes in the occurrence of small mammals following the exclusion of red deer, roe deer and wild boar. *Lutra*, **38**, 50–9. (In Dutch with an English abstract.)

Holt, R.D., Lawton, J.H., Polis, G.A. & Martinez, N.D. (1999). Trophic rank and species-area relationship. *Ecology*, **80**, 1495 504.

Järvinen, O. & Väisänen, R.A. (1978). Long-term population changes of the most abundant south Finnish forest birds during the past 50 years. *Journal of Ornithology*, **119**, 441–9.

Jones, C.G., Lawton, J.H. & Shachak, M. (1994). Organisms as ecosystem engineers. *Oikos*, **69**, 373–86.

Jones, C.G., Lawton, J.H. & Shachak, M. (1997). Positive and negative effects of organisms as physical ecosystem engineers. *Ecology*, **78**, 1946–57.

Kallio, P. & Lehtonen, J. (1975). On the ecocatastrophe of birch forests caused by *Oporinia autumnata* (Bkh.) and the problem of reforestation. In *Fennoscandian Tundra Ecosystems, Part 2*, ed. F.E. Wielgolaski Ecological Studies 17. Berlin, Heidelberg, New York: Springer Verlag, pp. 174–80.

Keesing, F. (1998). Impacts of ungulates on the demography and diversity of small mammals in central Kenya. *Oecologia*, **116**, 381–9.

Kielland, K. & Bryant, J.P. (1998). Moose herbivory in taiga: effects on biogeochemistry and vegetation dynamics in primary succession. *Oikos*, **82**, 377–83.

Kruess, A. & Tscharntke, T. (2002a). Grazing intensity and the diversity of grasshoppers, butterflies, and trap nesting bees and wasps. *Conservation Biology*, **16**, 1570–80.

Kruess, A. & Tscharntke, T. (2002b). Contrasting responses of plant and insect diversity to variation in grazing intensity. *Biological Conservation*, **106**, 293–302.

Lack, D. (1968). *Ecological Adaptations for Breeding Birds*. London, UK: Methuen.

Lavigne R.J., Kumar, R., Leetham, J.W. & Keith, V. (1972). *Population Densities and Biomass of Arthropods under Various Grazing and Environmental Stress Treatments on Pawnee Site, 1971*. USIBP-Grassland Biome Technical Report No. 204, Natural Resource Ecology Laboratory, Fort Collins, CO.

Leetham, J.W. & Milchunas, D.G. (1985). The composition and distribution of soil microarthropods in the shortgrass steppe in relation to the soil water, root biomass, and grazing by cattle. *Pedobiologia*, **28**, 311–25.

Lloyd, J.E. et al. (1973). *Abundance and Biomass of Soil Macroinvertebrates of the Pawnee Site Collected from Pastures Subjected to Different Grazing Pressures, Irrigation and/or Water Fertilization, 1970–1971*. USIBP-Grassland Biome Technical Report No. 239, Natural Resource Ecology Laboratory, Fort Collins, CO.

MacArthur, R.H. & MacArthur, J.W. (1961). On bird species diversity. *Ecology*, **42**, 594–8.

Magurran, A.E. (1988). *Ecological Diversity and its Measurement*. Princeton, USA: Princeton University Press.

Martinsen, G.D., Driebe, E.M. & Whitham, T. (1998). Indirect interactions mediated by changing plant chemistry: beaver browsing benefits beetles. *Ecology*, **79**, 192–200.

Matlack, R.S., Kaufman, D.W. & Kaufman, G.A. (2001). Influence of grazing by bison and cattle on deer mice in burned tallgrass prairie. *American Midland Naturalist*, **146**, 361–8.

McShea, W.J. & Rappole, J.H. (1997). Herbivores and the ecology of forest understory birds. In *The Science of Overabundance: Deer Ecology and Population Management*, ed. W. J. McShea, H. B. Underwood & J. H. Rappole. Washington: Smithsonian Institution Press, pp. 298–309.

McShea, W.J. & Rappole, J.H. (2000). Managing the abundance and diversity of breeding bird populations through manipulation of deer populations. *Conservation Biology*, **14**, 1161–70.

Merrill, E.H., Stanton, N.I. & Hak, J.C. (1994). Responses of bluebunch wheatgrass, *Idaho fescue*, and nematodes to ungulate grazing in Yellowstone National Park. *Oikos*, **69**, 231–40.

Milchunas, D.G., Sala, O.E. & Lauenroth, W.K. (1988). A generalized model of the effects of grazing by large herbivores on grassland community structure. *American Naturalist*, **132**, 87–106.

Milchunas, D.G., Lauenroth, W.K. & Burke, I.C. (1998). Livestock grazing: animal and plant biodiversity of shortgrass steppe and the relationship to ecosystem function. *Oikos*, **83**, 65–74.

Miller, S.G., Bratton, S.P. & Hadidian, J. (1992). Impacts of white-tailed deer on endangered plants. *Natural Areas Journal*, **12**, 67–74.

Mills, L.S., Soulé, M.E. & Doak, D.F. (1993). The keystone-species concept in ecology and conservation. *BioScience*, **43**, 219–24.

Miyashita, T., Takada, M. & Shimazaki, A. (2004). Indirect effects of herbivory by deer reduce abundance and species richness of web spiders. *Ecoscience*, **11**, 74–9.

Nyberg, Å. & Persson, I.-L. (2002). Habitat differences of coprophilous fungi on moose dung. *Mycological Research*, **106**, 1360–6.

Olofsson, J. & Strengbom, J. (2000). Response of galling invertebrates on *Salix lanata* to reindeer herbivory. *Oikos*, **91**, 493–8.

Olofsson, J., Hulme, P.E., Oksanen, L. & Suominen, O. (2004). Importance of large and small mammalian herbivores for the plant community structure in the forest tundra ecotone. *Oikos*, **106**, 324–34.

Palm, A. (1993). Den fyrbenta valen. *Fauna och Flora*, **88**, 37–9. (In Swedish.)

Perrins, C.M. & Overall, R. (2001). Effect of increasing numbers of deer on bird populations in Wytham Woods, central England. *Forestry*, **74**, 299–309.

Persson, I.-P. (2003). Moose population density and habitat productivity as drivers of ecosystem processes in northern boreal forests. Ph.D. thesis, Acta Universitatis Agriculturae Sueciae, Silvestria 272, Swedish University of Agricultural Sciences, Umeå, Sweden.

Polis, G.A., Myers, C.A. & Holt, R.D. (1989). The ecology and evolution of intraguild predation: potential competitors eat each other. *Annual Review of Ecology and Systematics*, **20**, 297–330.

Popotkin, G.J. & Giuliano, W.M. (2000). Response of birds to grazing of riparian zones. *Journal of Wildlife Management*, **64**, 976–82.

Putman, R.J., Edwards, P.J., Mann, J.C.E, How, R.C. & Hill, S.D. (1989). Vegetational and faunal changes in an area of heavily grazed woodland following relief of grazing. *Biological Conservation*, **47**, 487–90.

Pykälä, J. (2000). Mitigating human effects on European biodiversity through traditional animal husbandry. *Conservation Biology*, **14**, 705–12.

Rambo, J.L. & Faeth, S.H. (1999). Effect of vertebrate grazing on plant and insect community structure. *Conservation Biology*, **13**, 1047–54.

Roininen, H., Price, P.W. & Bryant, J.P. (1997). Response of galling insects to natural browsing by mammals in Alaska. *Oikos*, **80**, 481–6.

Samways, M.J. & Kreuzinger, K. (2001). Vegetation, ungulate and grasshopper interactions inside vs. outside an African savanna game park. *Biodiversity and Conservation*, **10**, 1963–81.

Scott, M.L., Skagen, S.K. & Merigliano, M.F. (2003). Relating geomorphic change and grazing to avian communities in riparian forests. *Conservation Biology*, **17**, 284–96.

Seymour, C.L. & Dean, W.R.J (1999). Effects of heavy grazing on invertebrate assemblage in the succulent Karoo, South Africa. *Journal of Arid Environments*, **43**, 267–86.

Soikkeli, M. & Salo, J. (1979). The bird fauna of abandoned shore pastures. *Ornis Fennica*, **56**, 124–32.

Stark, S., Wardle, D.A., Ohtonen, R., Helle, T. & Yeates, G.W. (2000). The effect of reindeer on decomposition, mineralization and soil biota in a dry oligotrophic Scots pine forest. *Oikos*, **90**, 301–10.

Stewart, A.J.A (2001). The impact of deer on lowland woodland invertebrates: a review of the evidence and priorities for future research. *Forestry*, **74**, 259–70.

Strand, M. & Merritt, R.W (1999). Impacts of livestock grazing activities on stream insect communities and the riverine environment. *American Entomologist*, **45**, 13–29.

Sulkava, P. & Huhta, V. (1998). Habitat patchiness affects decomposition and faunal diversity: a microcosm experiment on forest floor. *Oecologia*, **116**, 390–6.

Suominen, O. (1999a). Impact of cervid browsing and grazing on the terrestrial gastropod fauna in the boreal forests of Fennoscandia. *Ecography*, **22**, 651–8.

Suominen, O. (1999b). Mammalian herbivores, vegetation and invertebrate assemblages in boreal forests: feeding selectivity, ecosystem engineering and trophic effects. Ph.D. thesis, Annales Universitatis Turkuensis Ser. AII Tom. 122, University of Turku, Finland.

Suominen, O. & Olofsson, J. (2000). Impacts of semi-domesticated reindeer on structure of tundra and forest communities in Fennoscandia: a review. *Annales Zoologici Fennici*, **37**, 233–49.

Suominen, O., Danell, K. & Bergström, R. (1999a). Moose, trees, and ground-living invertebrates: indirect interactions in Swedish pine forests. *Oikos*, **84**, 215–26.

Suominen, O., Danell, K. & Bryant, J.P. (1999b). Indirect effects of mammalian browsers on vegetation and ground-dwelling insects in an Alaskan floodplain. *Ecoscience*, **6**, 505–10.

Suominen, O., Niemelä, J., Martikainen, P., Niemelä, P. & Kojola, I. (2003). Impact of reindeer on ground-dwelling Carabidae and Curculionidae assemblages in Lapland. *Ecography*, **26**, 503–13.

Tscharntke, T. (1997). Vertebrate effects on plant-invertebrate food-webs. In *Multitrophic Interactions in Terrestrial Ecosystems.*, ed. A.C. Gange & V. K. Brown. Oxford, UK: Proceedings of the 36th Symposium of the Brittish Ecological Society. Blackwell Science, pp. 277–297.

Van Wieren, S. E. (1998). Effects of large herbivores upon the animal community. In *Grazing and Conservation Management*, ed. M.F. Wallis De Vries, J.P. Bakker & S.E. Van Wieren. Dortdrecht: Kluwer Academic Publisher, pp. 185–214.

Väre, H., Ohtonen, R. & Mikkola, K. (1996). The effect of heavy grazing by reindeer in oligotrophic pine heats in northeastern Fennoscandia. *Ecography*, **19**, 245–53.

Vázquez, D.P. (2002). Multiple effects of introduced mammalian herbivores in a temperate forest. *Biological Invasions*, **4**, 175–91.

von Haartman, L. (1975). Changes in breeding bird fauna of coastal bays in southwestern Finland. *Ornis Fennica*, **52**, 57–67.

von Haartman, L. (1978). Changes in the bird fauna in Finland and their causes. *Fennia*, **150**, 25–32.

Wallis De Vries, M. F. (1998). Habitat quality and the performance of large herbivores. In *Grazing and Conservation Management*, ed. M.F. WallisDeVries, J.P. Bakker & S.E. Van Wieren. Dortdrecht: Kluwer Academic Publisher, pp. 275–320.

WallisDeVries, M.F. & Raemakers, I. (2001). Does extensive grazing benefit butterflies in coastal dunes? *Restoration Ecology*, **9**, 179–88.

Wardle, D.A., Bonner, K.I., Barker, G.M. *et al.* (1999). Plant removals on perennial grassland: vegetation dynamics, decomposers, soil biodiversity, and ecosystem properties. *Ecological Monographs*, **69**, 535–68.

Wardle, D.A., Barker, G.M., Yeates, G.W., Bonner, K.I. & Ghani, A. (2001). Introduced browsing mammals in New Zealand natural forests: aboveground and belowground consequences. *Ecological Monographs*, **71**, 587–614.

Wiens, J.A. (1989). *The Ecology of Bird Communities*. Cambridge, UK: Cambridge University Press.

Wootton, J.T. (1994). The nature and consequences of indirect effects in ecological communities. *Annual Reviews in Ecology and Systematics*, **25**, 443–66.

The future role of large carnivores in terrestrial trophic interactions: the northern temperate view

REIDAR ANDERSEN, JOHN D. C. LINNELL
AND ERLING J. SOLBERG

. . . I have lived to see state after state extirpate its wolves. I have watched the face of many new wolfless mountains, and seen the south-facing slopes wrinkle with a maze of new deer trails. I have seen every edible bush and seedling browsed, first to anemic desuetude, and then to death . . . I now suspect that just as a deer herd lives in mortal fear of its wolves, so does a mountain live in mortal fear of its deer. Aldo Leopold 1949.

INTRODUCTION

Central to any treatment of factors affecting the ecological role of large herbivores is a discussion about the factors influencing large herbivore population size and dynamics, and whether they are most influenced by top-down, or bottom-up, processes (Pace *et al.* 1999). The role of resource limitation (a bottom-up process) in herbivore dynamics is well-documented from many studies throughout the temperate zone (e.g. Fowler 1987, Gaillard *et al.* 2000). In contrast, the extent to which predation (a top-down process) influences herbivore dynamics is less clear, at least in part due to the fact that many of the most detailed long-term studies of herbivore population dynamics have been conducted in predator-free environments. The conceptual elegance of strong top-down effects on herbivores is clear in prosaic statements like Leopold's in the opening quotation, although the absence, or redundancy, of this effect has lain behind the philosophical adoption of the 'natural regulation' doctrine in

Large Herbivore Ecology, Ecosystem Dynamics and Conservation, ed. K. Danell, P. Duncan, R. Bergström & J. Pastor. Published by Cambridge University Press. © Cambridge University Press 2006.

US national parks. Similarly, the presumed role of large carnivores as top-down keystone species is very often used as an ecological justification for the restoration of large carnivores to areas from which they have been extirpated (Terborgh *et al.* 1999) in an attempt to reverse the effects of herbivore 'overabundance' (Alverson *et al.* 1988, McShea *et al.* 1997 and references therein).

However, in many cases this top-down role has been assumed rather than empirically tested. In addition, the future relevance of top-down effects has not been considered in the context of the highly modified and human-dominated landscapes where ecological processes now occur. It is the aim of this chapter to critically examine the potential impact that large carnivores can be expected to have on trophic interactions, both from the point of view of theory and empirical data. We shall first try to answer some vital questions about the effect of large carnivores on large herbivore numbers and stability. Furthermore, we will look at some of the more subtle non-lethal behavioural aspects of large carnivore-large herbivore interactions. Then we will contrast the community effects in studies with and without large carnivores, and conclude with a discussion about the future role that large carnivores can be expected to play in large herbivore dynamics. As far as possible we will draw on large carnivore/large herbivore examples from areas of their natural distribution, although to illustrate some points we will draw on examples from smaller species and some introduced species. Furthermore, our main focus is on northern temperate systems, but we shall flavour the chapter with some examples from other regions when appropriate.

WHAT RUNS THE WORLD – LITTLE THINGS OR BIG THINGS?

In the literature on large mammalian herbivores in grassland systems (e.g. Sinclair 1985) there has been a fundamental disagreement over whether bottom-up forces (e.g. nutrient availability) or top-down forces (e.g. predators) predominated in populations and communities. Or, in other words, whether little things (Wilson 1987) or big things (Terborgh 1988) run the world. Today, most ecologists agree that both top-down and bottom-up forces act on populations and communities simultaneously. The discussion is no longer about which occurs, but rather about what controls the strength and relative importance of the various forces under varying conditions, and what drives the feedback and interactions among multiple trophic levels (Matson & Hunter 1992). Hunter and Price (1992) suggested that ecologists should not ask, 'Do resources or predators regulate this population?', but rather 'What factors modulate resource limitation and predation in this system, determining when and where predators or resources will dominate in regulating populations?'

Top-down effects have been known to operate on communities in two fundamentally different ways. One is referred to as the 'Paine effect' after Paine (1966), where predators preferentially feed on a prey species that, in the absence of predation, is capable of competitively excluding other species that depend on a limiting resource. Thus, over an intermediate range of predation intensities, prey species diversity is increased in comparison to prey diversity in the overabundance or lack of predation (Terborgh et al. 1999). A more generalized form of this process is known as the intermediate disturbance model of species diversity (e.g. Sousa 1984). The second way predators influence their communities is through a cascade of interactions extending through successively lower trophic levels (Carpenter & Kitchel 1993).

Trophic cascades are regarded as important signals of top-down control of food web dynamics. Although there is clear evidence supporting the existence of trophic cascades, the mechanisms driving this important phenomenon are less clear (Schmiz et al. 1997). Tropic cascades could arise through direct population-level effects, in which predators prey on herbivores, thereby decreasing the abundance of herbivores that impact plant trophic level. Trophic cascades could also arise through indirect behavioural-level effects, in which herbivore prey shift their foraging behaviour in response to predation risk. Such behavioural shifts can result in reduced feeding time and increased starvation risk, again lowering the impact of herbivores on plants.

Hunter and Price (1992) argue that a true synthesis of the roles of top-down and bottom-up forces in terrestrial systems require a model that encompasses heterogeneity. Heterogeneity may be expressed as differences among species within a trophic level (e.g. Leibold 1989), differences in species interactions in a changing environment (e.g. Dobson & Travis 1991), and changes in population quality with population density (e.g. Rossiter 1991), including cohort effects (Lindstrøm & Kokko 2002). Consequently, individual species and environmental variation are as important determinants of population and community dynamics as are the number of levels in a food chain or the position of the system along a resource gradient. Consequently, it seems vital to have a broad overview of the ecology of the involved large carnivore and large herbivore species, and to know how large carnivore-large herbivore interactions are modulated by behavioural decisions made by both predators and prey. Let's start to introduce you to some of the species involved in the northern temperate region.

DRAMATIS PERSONAE

The last 300 to 400 years have seen dramatic changes in the landscapes of the northern temperate region. In western Europe and the continental United States wild herbivores and large carnivores were repeatedly hunted to regional extinction (Breitenmoser 1998, Woodroffe 2000), with only small remnant populations persisting. Despite the continuing modifications to landscapes that have occurred during the twentieth century, wild herbivores have recovered due to more restrictive hunting legislation and reintroduction to most of their former ranges, and now occur at densities that are probably higher than their original levels in many areas. Large carnivore recovery only really began in the 1970s, but they have demonstrated a surprising ability to survive in human-modified landscapes when given the chance. The result is that there are probably no areas left in the northern temperate region where populations of large carnivores or large herbivores persist that are not strongly influenced by man. As a result the present structure of large carnivore and large herbivore guilds and their communities is almost entirely a result of recent human influence rather than evolutionary biogeography.

Given this caveat, it is important to first obtain an overview of which species of herbivore and carnivore actually can interact with each other, and which age classes are vulnerable to predation by which predators (Table 14.1). Even with today's highly modified distributions, most herbivores have to face a wide range of carnivore species, with neonates being vulnerable to an even wider range of predators than adults, and most carnivores are able to prey on a range of herbivore species. The overview in Table 14.1 does not include exotic species, as sika deer, fallow deer, axis deer and mouflon have been introduced into many regions, and domestic livestock (mainly sheep, goats, horses and cattle) are also widely available in most ecosystems. Historically, few, if any, regions had single large carnivore-single large herbivore systems, and even today many regions have at least two large carnivores and two to three large herbivore species that interact. The most diverse of the northern temperate zone study areas is the Russian far east where the carnivore guild consists of tigers, leopards, Eurasian lynx, wolves, Asiatic black bear and red foxes, with wild

Table 14.1. *The potential predator/prey couplets within northern temperate large carnivore and large herbivore communities*

	Tiger	Leopard	Wolf	Puma	Lynx[a]	Brown bear	American black bear	Coyote	Bobcat	Red fox	Eagles
Bison			A N								
Moose			A N	n		a N	n				N
Reindeer / caribou			A N		n	N	N				
Red deer / elk[b]	A N		A N	A N	n	N					
Roe deer[b]	A N	A N	A N		A N					N	
Sika deer	A N	A N	A N								
Musk deer	A N	A N	A N								
White tail				A n				N	A N		
Mule deer			A N	A n				N	N		
Wild boar	A N		A N								
Chamois					A N						
Ibex											n
Bighorn sheep				A N							
Dall sheep			A N					N			
Rocky mt goat			A	A							
Pronghorn								N	N		

A = predation on adult sized animals (older than 6 months). N = predation on neonates only (younger than six months). Capital letter indicates that predation is common, a lower case letter indicates that predation has been documented, but is not a common event.

Literature used: Anderson 1983; Ballard *et al.* 2001; Husseman *et al.* 2003; Jedrzejewska & Jedrzejewski 1998; Jedrzejewski *et al.* 1993; Jobin *et al.* 2000; Kunkel *et al.* 1999; Linnell *et al.* 1995; Logan & Sweanor 2001; Makovkin 1999; Matyushkin & Vaisfeld 2003; Matyushkin 1998; Mech & Boitani 2003; Neale & Sacks 2001; Okarma 1995; Okarma *et al.* 1997; Patterson & Messier 2000; Swenson *et al.* 2001; Varley & Gunther 2002; Young & McCabe 1997.

[a] Refers to the Eurasian lynx, *Lynx lynx*, which has a large carnivore type ecology. Canadian lynx, *Lynx canadensis* has almost no interactions with large herbivores.

[b] Refers to both the European roe deer *Capreolus capreolus*, and the Siberian roe deer, *Capreolus pygargus*.

boar, moose, red deer, roe deer, musk deer and sika deer as available prey. This community complexity is just the first indication of the difficulties that lie ahead in predicting large carnivore impact on large herbivore dynamics, as we shall see later. A final factor that is important to consider is that many of these carnivores are able to exploit non-large herbivore prey for a substantial proportion of their diet if need be, for example, bears can survive without meat, and predators like lynx can subsist on lagomorphs and tetranoids.

PREDATOR–PREY INTERACTIONS

General problems

Even within a single large herbivore species, population densities may vary tremendously from one area to the other. Not surprisingly, numerous studies have tried to find the factors responsible for this variability, and large carnivore predation is often one of the factors that is considered. However, a decade ago a selective review of the literature could be interpreted to reinforce any perspective on predation (e.g. Messier & Crête 1985, Boutin 1992). One reason for this might be that although the interaction between natural mortality and population density is a central element in large herbivore population models (Caughley 1976), few studies have actually documented the relationship between major sources of mortality like food competition, predation and density-dependent changes in vital rates (Messier 1994). That is, as most studies are short-term in nature, it is difficult to take into account the fact that both bottom-up and top-down forces are affecting large herbivore population dynamics. A solution to this problem might be to contrast independent studies with comparable ecological conditions, but with varying large herbivore densities. Here we will first conceptualize the trophic interactions by using the four set of models of large herbivore regulation presented by Messier (1994, 1995), based on examinations of wolf-moose interactions over a broad spectrum of moose densities.

Theory

In discussions of large carnivore–large herbivore interactions, we often like to know under what circumstances large carnivores can maintain large herbivores at low densities. In order to answer such questions there has been a shift in focus from multi-factorial hypotheses to population models with clearly identified regulatory mechanisms (Messier 1994, Boutin 1992). This has forced the distinction between *density dependent factors* involved in population regulation, and *other limiting factors* that may influence the rate of increase in prey populations, although, without having any regulatory impact (Sinclair 1989, Messier 1994). Furthermore, it has been recognized that the presence of *one or more dynamic equilibria* must be linked to mechanisms of density dependence, while other limiting factors can influence the manifestation, location and stability of the equilibrium points (Sinclair 1989, Messier 1994). Another vital finding is that mortality sources can not be categorized as simply density-dependent or depensatory, but that we need to know the range of densities within which negative feedback mechanisms operate. For example, in most large herbivores food competition occurs at densities close to K (Caughley 1976), thus restricting its regulatory impact to relatively high densities (Messier 1994). On the other hand, large carnivore predation may change from being density-dependent at low large herbivore densities, to depensatory at medium to high densities.

Consequently, if we are able to answer the following four questions, we are closer to a unifying view of the effects of predation:

(1) Will a predator be able to suppress a large herbivore to a low stable density equilibrium?

(2) If such stable equilibria exist, what factors affect their stability/ instability?

(3) Can large herbivores be in a predator pit, thus increase in density after reduced predator pressure, and establish at a stable high-density equilibrium even after the return of large carnivores to former densities? Or asked in another way: do we have evidence for multiple stable states?

(4) Alternatively, can large carnivores drive large herbivores to extinction?

Also in the context of food chain dynamics, the answer to such questions will be vital. That is, will large carnivores be able to hold down large herbivores, which then in turn utilize only a fraction of available plant resources, or will large herbivores stabilize at high density and exert a strong regulatory control on plant productivity?

There are two vital interactive processes involved in large carnivore-large herbivore interactions; *the functional response*, that describes how the number of prey consumed per predator varies with prey density, and the *numerical response*, that summarizes changes in predator numbers caused by reproduction, immigration or emigration with prey density. The *total response*, which is the product of the functional and numerical response

(Seip 1992), gives an estimate of the predation rate, i.e. the proportion of the prey population subject to predation per unit time, when divided by prey numbers. We contrast the predation rate and large herbivore growth rate in the following models (Fig. 14.1).

(1) *The food model*
In the absence of large carnivores, large herbivores will be increasingly food-stressed as density increases, and establish a high density equilibrium around carrying capacity. That is, the population growth rate will increase monotonically if the density of large herbivores decreases.

(2) *The predation-food model (one-state)*
Here large carnivore predation reduces large herbivore population growth in a density-dependent manner at low densities. However, the predation rate is always lower than the large herbivore growth rate. That is, above a certain density, large carnivore predation is depensatory, and large herbivores will stabilise at a high density equilibrium, close to carrying capacity.

(3) *The predation-food model (two-state)*
Here large carnivore predation is also density-dependent at low large carnivore densities. However, the predation rate exceeds the growth rate of the large herbivore population at a certain point, K_4. If the large herbivores can increase in density to above K_u the predation rate will be inversely density-dependent, and large herbivores will stabilize at K_3 due to density-dependent food competition. The basic idea behind most predator-removal experiments in North America was that a relaxation of predation would enable large herbivore populations to escape the 'predator pit' between K_4 and K_u, and stabilize at high densities.

(4) *The predation model*
In this model there is no 'predator pit'. Large herbivore populations are maintained at low density equilibria due to density-dependent predation by an effective large carnivore.

THE PREDATION MODEL: CAN LARGE CARNIVORES SUPPRESS POPULATIONS OF LARGE HERBIVORES?

The number of large herbivores killed per large carnivore per unit time is a function of search time, i.e. the time required to find a suitable large herbivore, and handling time, the time associated with capture and feeding

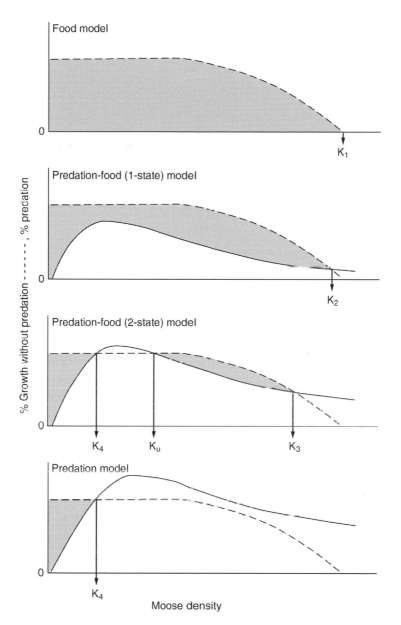

Figure 14.1. Four conceptual models of ungulate population regulation. The density relationship of wolf predation (solid line) and the growth rate of the prey without predation (dotted line) are illustrated. When the two lines cross an equilibrium condition is possible. K_1 to K_4 are stable equilibria, whereas K_u is dynamically unstable. The shaded area represents the net population growth rate after consideration of predation. After Messier (1994).

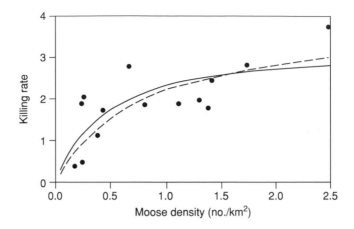

Figure 14.2. The functional response of wolves to changing moose density. Killing rate (number of moose killed per 100 days) was related to moose density with a hyperbolic Michaelis-Menten equation. The dashed line refers to an independent analysis after exclusion of the data obtained below 0.3 moose/km². After Messier (1994).

activities (Messier 1994). The handling time forces the functional response to reach a plateau, whereas the search time determines the speed at which this plateau is reached. This means that each large carnivore eats a decreasing proportion of large herbivores as large herbivore density increases. As large herbivore density increases, more large carnivores survive and reproduce, resulting in an increased large carnivore density, which in turn consumes more prey. In most cases where large carnivores are involved, territoriality or other interference behaviour cause the number of large carnivores to reach an asymptote. Because the functional and numerical responses reach a plateau as prey density increases, it is widely assumed that large carnivores will only be able to regulate large herbivores at low densities.

In accordance with this theory, Messier (1994) found by reviewing wolf-moose interactions over a broad spectrum of moose densities, that wolf predation was strongly density-dependent at the lower range of moose densities, up to about 0.65 moose/km². Above this density, predation rates gradually decreased, creating a depensatory destabilizing effect of predation (Fig. 14.2). At low moose densities, wolf numerical response contributed most to the density-dependent changes in predation rate, whereas the proportional effect of functional responses were more marked at higher moose densities (Fig. 14.3).

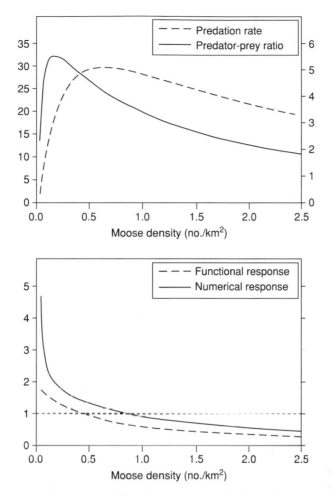

Figure 14.3. Changes in wolf predation rate (as calculated from the total response) with moose density showing a density-dependent response up to 0.65 moose km^{-2}, followed by an inversely density dependent response. The ratio of number of wolves per 100 moose (an index of predation rate) is also presented. The proportional effects of the functional and numerical responses on predation rate are presented in the lower panel. After Messier (1994).

There are very few systems where one predator feeds only on one prey, usually large carnivores operate in multi-prey systems. Here sigmoidal functional response curves of type three (c.f. Holling 1959) may occur where one or more large herbivore species have access to refuges at low densities, while other large herbivore species occur at higher densities or are easier prey for large carnivores. At higher densities of the first species, large carnivores may switch to this species, i.e. creating a situation where the proportion of prey eaten increases with prey density. However, at increasing densities of prey, the handling time constitutes an increasing proportion of available time for foraging activities, i.e. forcing the functional response to reach a level like in the type two curves.

Van Ballenberghe (1987) reviewed the existing literature and concluded that two-predator/single-prey systems were more likely to be stable at low densities than were one-predator/one-prey systems. It is quite clear that, for example, wolf predation alone can limit prey density (Peterson *et al.* 1984a,b, Ballard *et al.* 1987, Larsen *et al.* 1989). However, the presence of a second predator like the brown bear, would favour a low-density equilibrium for prey. Including bear-induced moose calf mortality in his models, Messier (1994) found that the low-density equilibrium moved from 0.65 moose km^{-2} to 0.2–0.4 moose km^{-2}.

CAN LARGE CARNIVORES DRIVE LARGE HERBIVORES TO LOCAL EXTINCTION?

So far we have taken for granted that there is density dependency involved in both functional and numerical responses, i.e. predation has a regulatory effect. Do we find cases where the numerical response of large carnivores is not affected by large herbivore density, i.e.; cases where large carnivores can drive large herbivores to extinction? Such a situation may occur when there is no switching (i.e. large carnivores prefer one single large herbivore species irrespective of its density), large herbivores have no refuge areas at low densities, and large carnivores have an alternative prey source that maintains large carnivore density even when their preferred prey occur at low densities.

Most large carnivores have the ability to prey upon several different species of large herbivore (Table. 14.1), and can even sustain themselves on medium sized and small herbivores. In Scandinavia, Eurasian lynx maintained high densities without having access to roe deer and reindeer, which compose up to 80% of their diet within the present ranges of lynx. However, as pointed out by Messier (1994) the existence of alternative prey may cause at least two opposite effects. First, an increase in alternative prey may lower the predation rate on primary prey, especially if the alternative prey have a higher vulnerability to predation. Studies of wolf predation in areas where moose are sympatric with white-tailed deer and wapiti, strongly indicate a diluting effect on moose predation, as moose are found at higher densities than expected (Pimlott *et al.* 1969, Carbyn 1983, Potvin 1988). Second, the presence of an alternative prey may lead to an increased predation rate on the primary prey by promoting a high numerical response in large carnivores, i.e., large carnivore numerical responses may not pass through the origin. Assuming a functional response type two and a numerical response with a positive y-intercept, i.e. the predator is able to survive and reproduce given access to alternate prey, this will have a profound influence on the total response. In a multi-prey system with wolves, Seip (1992) concluded that wolves may eliminate some caribou herds in southern British Columbia because moose sustained the wolf population when the caribou herd declined. A similar situation may have occurred within the Mackenzie bison sanctuary (Larter *et al.* 1994), where bison (*Bison bison athabascae*) numbers have increased and moose numbers appear to have decreased. Moose made up a significantly greater proportion of the wolf diet than expected, and wolf predation may therefore be destabilizing and exacerbating the decline in the moose populations.

The bighorn sheep can be found from the high alpine of the Rocky Mountains to the arid, rocky peaks of the southwestern deserts. Although each subspecies of bighorn sheep is uniquely suited to survive in the climates in which it is found (Festa-Bianchet 1991), the bighorn sheep's range is nowhere near its historical size. The once vast numbers of bighorn sheep, and especially the desert bighorn sheep, have been severely reduced, and several isolated populations are at the brink of extinction. Within several bighorn populations cougar predation is believed to be the proximate factor threatening the populations (Wehausen 1996), and e.g. in New Mexico the Game Commission approved a cougar killing programme promoted by the Department of Game and Fish in order to ostensibly protect New Mexico's endangered bighorn sheep population. However, in most cases the bighorn populations are affected by: habitat loss and fragmentation due to urban development; grazing domestic sheep; goats and llamas potentially transferring diseases to the bighorn; fire suppression causing forest encroachment on grasslands; and increased human activity in general (Habitat Atlas for Species at Risk 2003). Although predation may drive bighorns to local extinction, there are still a lot of unknowns about the effect of cougar predation on bighorn sheep populations under more natural conditions.

THE PREDATION–FOOD MODEL (TWO-STAGE): DO PREDATOR PITS EXIST?

During the first half of the twentieth century, the goal of predator control in Alaska and the rest of North America was primarily to increase large herbivore populations for human harvest. In the second half of the twentieth century the government conducted a series of control programmes, where wolves and brown bears were systematically killed. The rationale behind this activity was to allow prey to recover following overharvest, severe winters and high predation pressure. By reducing the number of large carnivores for a certain period of time, large herbivores were expected to escape the predator pit, and stabilize at a high-density equilibrium closer to the carrying capacity. A cessation in large carnivore control was expected to enable large carnivores to return to pre-control densities, but at this stage, being only able to have limiting effects on the density of large herbivores. As public attitudes shifted during the 1960s and 1970s, predator control programmes were increasingly questioned. As a consequence, the results from all predator control experiments were analysed (National Research Council 1997).

The conclusion was that the predator control experiments provided no evidence for the existence of a predator pit. Only two experiments were monitored for long enough time to test for the existence of a stable high-density equilibrium, and the results from those studies were at best equivocal. Consequently, there was no basis for the assumption that a short period of large carnivore control results in a long-term change in large herbivore population densities. The critical elements to generate predator pits are a rapidly increasing predation rate at extremely low large herbivore densities, and relaxation of predation at elevated large herbivore densities (Messier 1994). In areas where one species of large herbivore overlaps with at least two large carnivores, or inhabiting poor habitats, the weak depensatory nature of large carnivore predation, as is indicated for the moose-wolf interactions (Fig. 14.4, Messier 1994), will preclude the formation of a high-density equilibrium.

Considering that most large herbivore populations, like the moose in North America, are found in areas with at least two large carnivore species, it is not surprising to observe that even lightly exploited large herbivore populations are found at low densities compared to the carrying capacity. A review of geographical patterns of ungulate densities in North America performed by Crête (1999) support the hypothesis that high-density

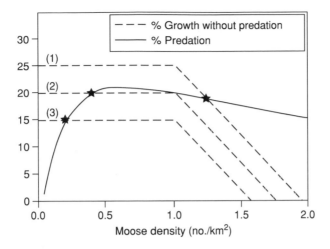

Figure 14.4. Empirical model of moose–wolf dynamics as derived from field data on wolf predation rate (solid line) and moose population growth without wolf predation (dotted lines). Models 1, 2 and 3 illustrate the possible states when the productivity of moose populations are reduced by either deteriorating habitat quality or bear-induced calf mortality. After Messier (1994).

equilibria do not exist. The hypothesis of exploitation ecosystems (EEH) (Oksanen & Oksanen 2000) predicts that, along a productivity gradient in terrestrial environments, predators will regulate herbivores at a relatively constant density whenever the primary productivity exceeds 700 g m² year⁻¹. Under this threshold, or if predators are absent, forage production determines herbivore density. Crête (1999) tested the EEH and found that cervid biomass increased from the high Arctic to the north of the boreal forest and remained in the same range southward within the grey wolf range. For the same latitude, cervid biomass increased by a factor of five in the absence of wolves. South of the wolf range, there was a clear relationship between actual evapotranspiration, which reflects primary productivity, and cervid biomass. Crête (1999) claims that the observed pattern supports the EEH and suggests that the removal of large predators in southern North America have imposed an unprecedented pressure on plants eaten by cervids. In areas where full re-establishment of large carnivores is allowed, large herbivores are therefore expected to be driven to the same low level, with less than 100 kg biomass per km², as found in the Canadian taiga.

The moose-wolf-balsam fir studies on Isle Royale

Among the very best studied large mammal predator-prey systems that also include the interaction with primary producers, is the long-term study of wolves, moose and balsam fir on Isle Royale, USA (McLaren & Peterson 1994, Post *et al.* 1999). Following the colonization of the island by moose (between 1905 and 1913, Murie 1934) and wolves (1948) in the first half of the twentieth century, these dynamics have been studied intensively since 1958 (Peterson 1995a,b). Despite the relatively simple ecosystem with only one large predator (the wolf) and few alternative prey species (hares and beavers), the analyses have revealed quite complex dynamics.

The general picture that emerges after more than 40 years of study is a strong interaction between wolves and moose, and density dependence acting within species (Post *et al.* 2002). In addition, there is a strong impact of annual variation in snow depth on both moose body condition and survival, as well as wolf pack size and kill rate (leading to increasing predation rate) (Post *et al.* 1999). The moose population increases in density during years of low wolf density, followed by a time delayed increase in wolf abundance (Peterson 1999, Post *et al.* 2002). Further increase in moose density is then halted, and finally reversed, by a combination of density-dependent and density-independent food limitation, and predation (Peterson 1999, Post *et al.* 1999, 2002). Following the decline in moose density, the wolf population density declines, probably because of increasing intraspecific competition (increasing adult mortality) and reduced pup production during years of few calves and old moose available in the moose population (Post *et al.* 1999).

Besides being the main food of wolves, moose also have a strong impact on the vegetation on the island. During periods of high moose density on Isle Royale there is heavy browsing on balsam fir, their primary winter forage (McLaren & Peterson 1994, Post *et al.* 1999). This negatively affects fir seedling establishment (McLaren & Janke 1996), sapling recruitment (Brandner *et al.* 1990) and growth rate (McLaren & Peterson 1994). Conversely, balsam fir is released from heavy browsing and responds by increasing growth rate (McLaren & Peterson 1994, Post *et al.* 1999) as the moose density decreases.

Although largely dominated by top-down control, the system on Isle Royale also involves facets of bottom-up effects, mainly working through density-dependent food limitation in the moose population. During periods of high moose density, the predation rate does not increase sufficiently to halt the moose population increase unless accompanied by density-dependent and density-independent (climatic) effects on the moose population growth rate. Moreover, because of the negative impact of snow depth on the vulnerability of balsam fir to browsing (Post et al. 1999), there is a potential effect on the moose dynamics caused by stochastic variation in the environmental conditions. Thus, following the strong impact of predation on the moose fluctuations, there is a direct link between the variation in predation rates and variation in fir growth rate, although variation in climate (snow) at times may moderate this dynamics.

Oksanen et al. (2001) have questioned the long-held assumption that the interaction between large predators and ungulate prey may occur at two alternative equilibria; one where predation regulates prey at a low equilibrium, and one where prey densities are regulated by food limitation close to carrying capacity. In their view the empirical arguments for the assumption regarding the numerical responses (Boutin 1992, Messier 1994, Eberhardt & Peterson 1999, Marshal & Boutin 1999, Eberhardt 2000, Hayes et al. 2000, Messier & Joly 2000), should be derived from observations of density combinations of predator and prey, accompanied by data on rates of change in predator density (Oksanen et al. 2001).

Using data from Isle Royale (Peterson & Page 1983, McLaren & Peterson 1994), Oksanen et al. (2001) found no indication for strong direct density dependence in wolves, which is a prerequisite for the existence of two alternative equilibria. In fact, they found that the moose density at which the numerical trend in wolves changed its sign, was similar in the top and bottom phases of the wolf cycle.

CAN WE EXPECT STABILITY IN PREDATOR-PREY SYSTEMS?

Classic ecological theory predicts that most interactions between large carnivores and large herbivores should be highly unstable or cyclic (Rosenzweig 1971, May 1973). However, this is not consistent with the current knowledge. With the possible exception of Isle Royale, cycles do not seem to dominate in ecological communities involving large carnivores and large herbivores. Are there general features of large carnivore-large herbivore interactions that tend to stabilize interactions? If so, will large herbivores in areas lacking large carnivores stabilize at a certain density, or will they grow beyond their carrying capacity, overgraze their food resources and create highly unstable dynamics with large temporal variation in numbers? In such a case, will the reintroduction of large carnivores be able to create stable systems?

One major conclusion from analysis of several long-term individual based population studies of large herbivores, is that the population dynamics of large herbivores in predator-free environments are strongly influenced by a combination of stochastic variation in the environment, and population density (Sæther 1997). Both factors operate through changes in life history traits which generates delays in the response of the population to changes in the environment. Accordingly Sæther (1997) claimed that in the absence of predation, a stable equilibrium between a large herbivore population and its food resources is therefore unlikely to exist. Then, what factors are able to stabilize large carnivore-large herbivore interactions?

Several different factors have been suggested. These are predator search images, spatial segregation of different prey in the environment, risk avoidance by foragers or optimal patterns of foraging effort. In all cases, a sigmoid functional response will be formed, meaning that in the region of positive density-dependence, this will potentially counteract or compensate for perturbations away from population equilibria (Abrams 1987, Fryxell & Lundberg 1994).

(1) *Interference*
Many theoretical models of trophic interactions assume that predator and prey populations have overlapping spatial distributions and that predator dynamics are dictated solely by prey abundance (Fryxell & Lundberg 1998). Although this can be true in some cases, the norm is rather that predators show various forms of interference. Interference with other predators may reduce the efficiency of the predator, i.e. crowding may cause the searching efficiency to drop, hence lowering the functional response. All theoretical interference models (e.g. Fryxell & Lundberg 1998, Ruxton *et al.* 1992) have found that such systems have a stabilizing effect on trophic interactions. However, it is still not clear whether the cost of interference (i.e. lowering the functional response) at population densities found in most large carnivore-large herbivore systems in nature would be sufficient to be stabilizing.

(2) *Territoriality*
Like most other forms of social behaviour, territoriality has a strong stabilizing effect on trophic interactions. Optimal territory formation is strongly stabilizing because it protects prey from intense predation

rates, and because it affects the predator's numerical response (Fryxell & Lundberg 1998).

(3) *Prey defence*

Theoretically, a predator-prey system where prey allocate their time optimally between eating and hiding is more stable than a system with constant prey foraging activity. Here optimal time allocation creates a pronounced prey refuge at high prey densities, causing a positive density-dependent predation (Fryxell & Lundberg 1998).

(4) *Facultative diet selection/switching behaviour*

Both of these behavioural mechanisms induce density-dependent effects on prey mortality, which sometimes are sufficient to stabilize community interactions (Fryxell & Lundberg 1994).

In fact, it could be that natural selection tends to favour stabilizing mechanisms that counteract the intrinsic tendency of most trophic models for instability (Fryxell & Lundberg 1998). Given that behaviour is central to the question of who eats how much of whom, let us take a closer look at some of the behavioural interactions between large carnivores and large herbivores.

BEHAVIOURAL ASPECTS

Effects of prey migration

By considering the dynamics of intact ecosystems comprising migratory herbivores and grasslands, Fryxell et al. (1988) examined three hypotheses that might explain why migratory ungulates are more abundant than resident. Comparing resident (Ngorogoro crater) and migratory (Serengeti) wildebeest, they found that resident wildebeest suffer a 10% loss due to predation, whereas the same figure for migratory is less than 1% (Schaller 1972, Elliot & Cowan 1978). For several years during the 1970s, dry-season rainfall was above average, leading to higher grassland production. This in turn resulted in a substantial increase in migratory wildebeest, whereas resident species like kongoni, topi and impala were apparently unaffected (Sinclair 1979). These empirical observations suggest that migratory wildebeest in the Serengeti ecosystem are regulated by food abundance, whereas non-migratory populations are regulated by predators (Fryxell et al. 1988). The explanation for this escape from predator regulation is that predators, with slow growing, altricial young have to stay within a restricted area to give birth and lactate, whereas some large herbivores have precocial young that can follow their mother shortly after birth. A similar escape from predation is suggested for several migrating caribou herds: the George River herd (Messier *et al.* 1988); the barren ground caribou; (Heard & Williams 1992); and the Wells Gray Park mountain caribou (Seip 1991).

Effects of prey defence

The variation in potential defence strategies among large herbivores is large, and the exact nature of the behavioural interaction between large carnivores and large herbivores is crucial for understanding the evolution and dynamic implications of anti-predator adaptations. Large herbivores can reduce detection by large carnivores in many ways. Many large herbivores (e.g. roe deer, red deer) have cryptic neonates, some large herbivores form larger groups (e.g. reindeer, muskox), which increases the risk of detection of the entire group but decreases the risk of individual capture. Large herbivores may also adjust the time they are exposed to large carnivores. Often such a strategy also affects the rate of energy gain, i.e. large herbivore impact on the environment may also change.

Although there is substantial evidence for a trade-off between energy gain from foraging and the risk of predation, few examples are found within large herbivores (see Lima & Dill 1990, Lima 2002). In general, the behavioural response to predation risk involves adjustments of foraging speed, instantaneous intake rate (Lima 1985, Lima 2002 and references therein), diet choice, patch use (Brown 1988) and reproductive decisions (Korpimäki *et al.* 1994). Accordingly, White and Berger (2001) contrasted data from behavioural observations of female moose that differed in parity, calf activity and habitat use at a site in south-central Alaska. They found that females with active juveniles were more vigilant (and as a consequence spent less time feeding) than those with inactive young. Furthermore, distance to apparent protective refugia (e.g. vegetative cover) was positively related to vigilance for all calf-status categories, but lactating females spent more time closer to thick vegetation than did non-lactating females. White and Berger (2001) conclude that maternal trade-offs can be highly labile and that mothers are able to adjust rapidly to environment-specific situations.

Effects of naïve prey

The post-Pleistocene extinctions of a large part of the megafauna (MacPhee 1999) have been attributed primarily to human overkill as hunters encountered naïve prey – the blitzkrieg hypothesis (Mosimann &

Martin 1975) – and/or to climate change (Martin & Klein 1984). If as a consequence of today's lack of large carnivores over large areas, large herbivores have lost their knowledge about how to behave towards predators, the current expansion of large carnivores into formerly depopulated ecosystems can bring them in contact with naïve prey, and potentially cause local extinctions of large herbivores.

Some large herbivores may retain predator recognition capabilities ('ghost effect') for thousands of years even after predation as a selective force has been relaxed (Byers 1997). However, in a series of papers Joel Berger and co-workers have shown how the absence of large carnivores has consequences for subtle, but important, ecological patterns involving behaviour and interspecific ecological interactions. For example, Berger (1999) found that moose monitored scavengers as a method to detect large carnivores. However, this behaviour was labile and was dropped from the behavioural repertoire when predation was no longer a significant risk.

Current results indicate that offspring loss to predators may cause maternal hypersensitivity, and contribute to increased survival in large herbivores (Berger et al. 2001a,b). What is evident is that naïve prey have the capacity to process information about predators rapidly – in the case of moose, in one generation. If predation affects both young and adults, the potential for learning will decrease and consequently increase the possibilities for local extinction. Because large carnivores are currently being reintroduced to parts of Africa, Europe and North America, these findings have relevance for conservation. In extant prey, rapid learning may prevent a complete blitzkrieg, and should negate fears about localized prey extinction (Berger et al. 2001a,b).

Changes in predator behaviour

It is obvious that non-lethal interactions between predators and their prey are important components of predator-prey interactions in general. However, as most studies have been focused on prey behaviour, the behaviour of predators is often forgotten (Lima 2002). Normally predators have been treated as unresponsive participants in behavioural interactions. However, predators can do more than just move around in patches searching for prey. In a model of the temporal activity of predator and prey (Brown et al. 2001), a top predator feeds on a prey species that consumes a depleting resource. As both predator and prey are allowed to be active at any time, predator activity tends to mirror the level of the resource of the prey, while the proportion of prey being active remains constant (Lima 2002). So far, studies involving large carnivores and large herbivores have assumed a predator behaviour, which will not detect the effects of such behaviour.

COMMUNITY EFFECTS

The 'evidence' for the cascading effects of large carnivore depredation comes from various field experiments. In most cases the effect of lack of predators is discussed, assuming that the presence of a predator would have had dramatic effect on the prey population growth. Such assumptions are easy to make knowing the results from the famous dingo-red kangaroo example (Caughley *et al.* 1980). The largest carnivore in Australia, the dingo, was fenced out from sheep grazing areas by a 9660 km long fence. A spectacular increase in the abundance of red kangaroos resulted when the dingoes were eliminated; densities being 166 times higher in dingo-free areas in New South Wales compared to South Australia.

From a conservation perspective we may be concerned about the destabilizing forces that can operate in ecosystems that lack large carnivores. There are clear consequences of removing large carnivores from an ecosystem, but what are these consequences and how severe are they? A set of predator-free islands created by a hydroelectric impoundment in Venezuela allowed Terborgh *et al.* (2001) to monitor the community effects. On islands where predators like jaguar, puma and harpy eagle were absent, densities of rodents, monkeys, iguanas and leaf-cutter ants were 10 to 100 times higher than on the neighbouring mainland. The densities of seedlings and saplings of canopy trees were severely affected, providing evidence of a trophic cascade, 'unleashed in the absence of top-down regulation' (Terborgh *et al.* 2001). However, the results of these studies may also be confounded by the effect of working on islands which hinders the potential for dispersal and migration.

When gravel pits change mammal community structure

Several scientists have questioned the long-held fact that the concepts of temperate-zone ecology derived from studies in Europe and North America, also were appropriate in southern Africa. In a study in Etosha National park (nicely presented by Jared M. Diamond in *Nature* 1986) gravel pits excavated during road construction, a seemingly modest disturbance, caused crashes in the wildebeest and zebra populations, declines in cheetah, brown hyena and eland, and increases in lions, spotted hyenas, jackal and springbok. The reconstruction of the causal sequence of these changes showed that rainwater standing in the alkaline gravel pits became a reservoir for anthrax bacteria. Wildebeest and zebras are especially susceptible to anthrax, and the resulting abundance of sick or dead prey more than offset the decline in healthy prey, causing a population surge of the two dominant and largest large carnivores, the lion and the spotted hyena, which are immune to anthrax. The lions reduced the population of eland, which suffered little from anthrax but are the favourite alternative prey of lions. The lions and spotted hyenas competitively suppressed the cheetah and brown hyena. Release from competition from the two latter species, in addition to high abundance of carcasses, caused the next-largest carnivore/scavenger, the black-backed jackal, to increase. The same kind of competitive release was also seen among large herbivores; the wildebeest and zebra crashes, in addition to the decline in cheetah numbers, permitted the smaller and more anthrax-resistant springbok to increase. As Diamond (1986) points out, ecologists will never be allowed to kill 25 000 wildebeest out of curiosity. However, the same result caused by anthrax clearly illustrates how predation and competition controls population sizes and community structure of large carnivores and large herbivores.

Large carnivore-large herbivore interactions in Yellowstone National Park

The Paine effect in northern boreal forests?

In the book *Carnivores in Ecosystems: The Yellowstone Experience*, Clark *et al.* (1999) speculate about the effect the reintroduction of wolves will have on the ungulate guild in this system. Put shortly, they predicted that:

(1) Wolf reintroduction will lead to coyote decline, which means that the neonatal mortality on elk calves will decrease. At the same time pronghorn antelope may increase due to the same effect.

(2) The total population of large herbivores will increase following wolf restoration, because the main prey of wolves, the elk, have suppressed populations of moose, bison, pronghorn antelope, mule deer and bighorn sheep.

The elk-wolf-aspen interaction

The decrease in biomass of quaking aspen (*Populus tremuloides*) in Yellowstone National Park in the past century is often explained by heavy browsing pressure from an increasing elk population. Monitoring of aspen stands within and outside established wolf pack territories, indicated that wolves might have an indirect effect on aspen regeneration by altering elk movements, browsing patterns and foraging behaviour (Ripple *et al.* 2001). Indexes of elk habitat use and the browsing pressure on aspen stands was closely related to wolf distribution, which supports the assumption of reintroduced wolves causing a trophic cascade through predation risk effects in elk. Investigations of the level of vigilance on elk and bison also indicated that the reintroduction of wolves to Yellowstone National Park have re-established a 'landscape of fear' (Laundre *et al.* 2001). While male elk and bison, which are not easily accessible prey for wolves, did not change their vigilance level in areas with wolves, vigilance levels more than doubled in female elk and bison. Such behavioural responses to the presence of wolves may have more far-reaching consequences for the ecology of elk and bison than the actual killing of individuals (Laundre *et al.* 2001).

Grizzly bear and wolf extinctions affect avian neotropical migrants
Berger *et al.* (2001a,b) have demonstrated a trophic cascade that was triggered by the extinction of grizzly bears and wolves from the southern greater Yellowstone ecosystem. The eruption of moose lead to a subsequent alteration of riparian willow vegetation structure and density by ungulate herbivory, which again affected the avian neotropical migrants. By contrasting hydrologically and ecologically similar sites in Grand Teton National Park, Wyoming, USA, with varying moose densities due to differences in predation and hunting pressure, it was found that avian species richness and nesting density varied inversely with moose abundance. In fact two riparian specialists, gray catbirds (*Dumetella carolinensis*) and MacGillivray's warblers (*Oporornis tolmiei*), were absent from park riparian systems where moose densities were high. The findings certainly offer empirical support for the top-down effect of large carnivores in terrestrial communities, and provide a scientific rationale for restoration options to conserve biological diversity. Consequently, 'to predict future impacts, whether overt or subtle, of past management, and to restore biodiversity, more must be known about ecological interactions, including the role of large carnivores' (Berger *et al.* 2001a,b).

The Glacier National Park
In the Glacier National Park area, wolves, cougars, bears, coyotes and humans prey upon white-tailed deer, elk and moose. In this multi-predator-multi-prey system Kunkel and Pletscher (1999) examined population trends and female survival rates in the prey species. All age-classes of white-tailed deer were equally vulnerable to predators, while young and old moose and elk were most vulnerable. Obviously the moose benefited from the predator's access to alternative prey, as moose survival rates were significantly higher in areas with white-tailed deer present. This lead to a

relatively stable population density of moose, whereas predation appeared to be the primary factor limiting deer and elk populations.

The Silent Spring – The Rachel Carson revival

First published in 1962, the American writer Rachel Carson's book *The Silent Spring* alerted a large audience to the environmental dangers of indiscriminate use of pesticides, spurring revolutionary changes in the laws affecting our air, land and water. Some 40 years later, leading British ornithologists are claiming that the British woods are losing their spring chorus of birdsong. The chief suspect this time is not pesticides – but the deer. Lacking both large predators and a public interest in deer culling, both native (roe deer and red deer) and introduced deer like fallow, sika, muntjac and Chinese water deer, have reached extremely high densities in many areas. The increased grazing pressure within woodland have affected the species composition of bird communities, through a reduction in low foliage density (Fuller 2001), leading to a nearly 80% decrease in numbers of selected bird species in some areas (http://www./nationalgeographic. com, March 2003). The lack of large carnivores might also have lead to a mesopredator increase, which can further reduce the breeding success of ground nesting bird species (see also Chapter 13).

The mesopredator release effect

The extirpation of dominant large carnivores in large parts of North America has lead to a 'mesopredator release' (e.g. Crooks & Soulé 1999). Medium-sized predators (mesopredators) like foxes, skunks, raccoons, opossums, and feral and domestic cats have been released from intra-guild predation by large carnivores, and have started to act as surrogate top predators. This has created large changes in the community structure by decreasing the number of ground nesting birds and other small vertebrates from a variety of terrestrial ecosystems (see references in Terborgh *et al.* 1999). As nearly 100 intra-guild interactions have been registered among terrestrial predators (Palomares & Caro 1999), it is most likely that meso-predator release effects could be operating in large parts of Europe as well.

HUMANS ARE THE MAIN KEYSTONE

In most parts of the world humans have exerted very different impacts on large carnivores and large herbivores. While large carnivore eradication has been the norm rather than the exception, humans have modified the environment in such a way that large herbivores can reach very high densities. At the same time, large predators as a group have developed several traits allowing a high degree of self-regulation through various interference behaviours, territoriality and prey-switching, while for large herbivores strong density-dependent factors operate very close to the carrying capacity, often leading to a dramatic overshooting of the environment's carrying capacity. If we agree that herbivores above a certain critical level will cause shifts in community functioning by altering plant and animal composition, and nutrient and energy flow patterns (Flueck 2000), we need to actively replace missing factors in the system (see also Chapters 4, 10 and 13). In many places such a factor will be predation.

In some parts of the world carnivore populations are clearly limited by access to prey. For example, the high levels of wolf-human interactions in several parts of India, causing the registered deaths of several hundred children (Linnell & Bjerke 2002), reflects a lack of natural prey to wolves. However, in many parts of the world the problem is rather over-abundance of prey (e.g. McShea et al. 1997), from kangaroos in Australia (Caughley et al. 1987), elephants and other large ungulates in savanna Africa (Owen-Smith 1988), rabbits, roe deer, sika deer and red deer in many parts of Europe (e.g. Putman 1996) to white-tailed deer in North America (McCabe & McCabe 1997). In Scandinavia the increase in the cervid populations in the last few decades has been exceptional. In 40 years the number of ungulates harvested in Norway (moose, roe deer, red deer and reindeer) increased from 14000 to 106500. Adding the numbers of moose and roe deer harvested in Sweden, Scandinavian hunters were able to shoot nearly 500000 cervids in 1997. Clearly, in such areas lack of prey is not the most important factor influencing the numerical response of large carnivores.

Large carnivores are especially sensitive to human activity, because their requirements often conflict with those of people, and as a consequence large carnivores have been actively persecuted all over the world. We will argue that 'competition' with man is the single most important factor affecting the numerical response of large carnivores, and hence their potential effect on large herbivores and large herbivore environment.

Many studies show that large carnivores living outside protected areas are limited by human persecution (e.g. Fuller 1989, Wielgus & Bunnell 1994). There are strong associations between human density and the loss of carnivore populations in general (Woodroffe 2000), and at high human densities large carnivores may be completely extirpated (Woodroffe &

Ginsberg 1998). However, it is not the human density *per se* that is important, but more the influence of local culture, government policy and international trade that influence human attitudes to predators (Linnell *et al.* 2001). This means that even inside protected areas large carnivores may suffer high levels of human-related mortality. In a review Woodroffe (2000) summarized 16 studies of large carnivore inhabiting protected areas, and recorded adult large carnivore mortality directly attributable to humans. A remarkably high number of human-induced deaths were recorded (Woodroffe & Ginsberg 2000); of 616 large carnivore deaths, 455 (74%) were caused by humans. For the eight species included in Woodroffe's review, she found that human activity was the major cause of mortality for seven of them.

So, not surprisingly, large carnivores need large areas. Where do we find such areas? Or, where do we find areas where large carnivore numerical responses are dependent on large herbivore density only? Let's face it, there are very few such areas around.

CONCLUSIONS

Large carnivore effects on large herbivore numbers

As we have seen, the effect a large carnivore will have on a particular large herbivore population is highly situation dependent and depends on: (i) the presence of other predators; (ii) availability of alternative prey; (iii) the impact of food competition on the prey species; (iv) degree of human harvest of both prey and predators; and (v) the mobility of the prey. The empirical evidence for the impact of predator control of northern boreal large herbivores has been mixed, but it is widely recognized that most large carnivores are able to strongly affect their large herbivore prey. Although the dichotomy of top-down vs. bottom-up regulation is too simplistic, it is now widely accepted that it is the interaction of both these processes that shapes population dynamics.

Because of fairly flat functional response curves (i.e. rapid increase up to a certain level), and a strong human and intraspecific impact on the large carnivore numerical response, the impact of large carnivores will depend mainly on large herbivore density. Therefore, the return of large carnivores to e.g. Scotland/Germany (where roe deer, sika deer and red deer occur at very high densities) will do little to influence the dramatic impact of large herbivores on vegetation. Exceptions could be found in areas with mouflon and forest dwelling chamois. Here large carnivores like wolves and lynx have the potential to exterminate mouflon, due to naïve animals lacking escape terrain, and by causing dramatic changes in habitat use for chamois from forest to mountain areas.

In multi-use landscapes, the extent to which large carnivores will influence large herbivore-habitat relationships may be strong locally, but weak in general. However, this reflects the artifically high densities (overabundance) of the large herbivores in these multi-use landscapes (due to fragmentation, resource subsidy, harvest strategies, etc). In contrast, in 'natural' systems or those with low productivity, we expect that large carnivores will maintain a keystone role in limiting ungulate population densities and therefore their impact on the habitat. Humans now dominate both the top-down and bottom-up processes – often for the benefit of ungulates (at least in western Europe and North America). While fundamental research in 'pristine' areas is interesting we really need to start to view human influence in an ecological context – therefore more focus on multi-use landscapes will be desirable.

'The enemy of my enemy is my friend'

In its simplest form a trophic cascade is an ecological variant of this basic truism. Although trophic cascades in principle occur throughout the food web, there has been most focus on indirect carnivore impacts on plants via shifts in herbivore abundance and activity (Pace *et al.* 1999, Persson 1999, Schmitz *et al.* 2000). This focus reflects the fundamental question often put forward by ecologists: do we have to pay attention to the food webs to understand the forces that control plant community composition and dynamics? If trophic cascades are large in magnitude, the obvious answer is 'yes' (Holt 2000).

There are today several studies in terrestrial ecosystems indicating that the removal of large carnivores (and cessation of human hunting) have led to dramatic increases in herbivore densities, which in turn have cause concern about the long-term forest dynamics (Miller *et al.* 1992, Terborgh *et al.* 1997, Terborgh 1999). Furthermore, if removal of a large carnivore causes an increase in a generalist herbivore, some plants might be vulnerable to exclusion via apparent competition, while this will not be the case if removal of a large carnivore causes a specialist herbivore to increase (Holt 2000). Clearly, there is a wide spectrum of studies that have to be carried out. As many ecologists in the years to come will work with trophic interactions and search for cascading effects, it will be vital to distinguish between species-level and community-level cascades (Polis 1999), and to use a proper time scale for studying such cascades (Holt 2000). If we have species-level cascades, altering predator numbers will only influence one or a few species, whereas in community-level cascades, a substantial impact on plant biomass for entire communities will be found. Long-term projects will be needed. In a recent review by Schmitz *et al.* (2000), 81% of the studies involved measurements taken within a single annual growing season. It is obvious that for a fair test of trophic cascades studies need to be carried out over multiple plant generations (Holt 2000).

ACKNOWLEDGEMENTS

We would like to thank the Directorate for Nature Management and The Norwegian Research Council for supporting a variety of projects related to large carnivore ecology, predator-prey relationships and management of large carnivores.

REFERENCES

Abrams, P.A. (1987). Indirect interactions between species that share a common predator: varieties in indirect effects. In *Predation: Direct and Indirect Impacts on Aquatic Communities*, ed. W.C. Kerfoot & A. Sih. Dartmouth, NH: University Of New England Press, pp. 38–54.

Alverson, W.S., Waller, D.M. & Solheim, S.I. (1988). Forest too deer: edge effects in northern Wisconsin. *Conservation Biology*, **2**, 348–58.

Anderson, A.E. (1983). *A Critical Review of Literature on Puma (Felis concolor)*. *Colorado Division of Wildlife Research Section, Special Report Number 54*.

Ballard, W.B., Whitman, J.S. & Gardner, C.L. (1987). Ecology of an exploited wolf population in south-central Alaska. *Wildlife Monographs*, **98**, 1–54.

Ballard, W.B., Lutz, D., Keegan, T.W., Carpenter, L.H. & de Vos, J.C. (2001). Deer-predator relationships: a review of recent North American studies with emphasis on mule and black-tailed deer. *Wildlife Society Bulletin*, **29**, 99–115.

Berger, J. (1999). Anthropogenic extinction of top carnivores and interspecific animal behaviour: implications for the rapid decoupling of a web involving wolves, bears, moose and ravens. *Proceedings of the Royal Society of London, Series B, Biological Sciences*, **266**, 2261–7.

Berger, J., Stacey, P.B., Bellis, L. & Johnson, M.P. (2001a). A mammalian predator-prey imbalance: grizzly bear and wolf extinction affect avian neotropical migrants. *Ecological Applications*, **11**, 947–60.

Berger, J., Swenson, J.E. & Persson, I-L. (2001b). Recolonizing carnivores and naive prey: Conservation lessons from pleistocene extinctions. *Science*, **291**, 1036–9.

Boutin, S. (1992). Predation and moose population dynamics: a critique. *Journal of Wildlife Management*, **56**, 116–27.

Brandner, T.A., Peterson, R.O. & Risenhoover, K.L. (1990). Balsam fir on Isle Royale: effects of moose herbivory and population density. *Ecology*, **71**, 155–64.

Breitenmoser, U. (1998). Large predators in the Alps: the fall and rise of man's competitors. *Biological Conservation*, **83**, 279–89.

Brown, J.S. (1988). Patch use as an indicator of habitat preference, predation risk, and competition. *Behavioral Ecology and Sociobiology*, **22**, 37–47.

Brown, J.S., Kotler, B.P. & Bouskila, A. (2001). Ecology of fear: foraging games between predators and prey with pulsed resources. *Annales Zoologici Fennici*, **38**, 71–87.

Byers, J.A. (1997). *American Pronghorn: Social Adaptations and the Ghosts of Predators Past*. Chicago: University of Chicago Press.

Carbyn, L.N. (1983). Wolf predation on elk in Riding Mountain National Park, Manitoba. *Journal of Wildlife Management*, **47**, 963–76.

Carpenter, S.R. & Kitchel, J.F. (1993). *The Trophic Cascade in Lake Ecosystems*. Cambridge, UK: Cambridge University Press.

Carson, R. (1962). *The Silent Spring*. Harmondsworth: Penguin.

Caughley, G. (1976). Wildlife management and the dynamics of ungulate populations. In *Applied Biology*, Vol. 1, ed. T.H. Coaker. New York: Academic Press, pp. 183–246.

Caughley, G., Grigg, G.G., Caughley, J. & Hill, G.J.E. (1980). Does dingo predation control the densities of kangaroos and emus? *Australian Wildlife Research*, **7**, 1–12.

Caughley, G., Sheperd, N. & Short, J. (1987). *Kangaroos: Their Ecology and Management in the Sheep Rangelands of Australia*. Cambridge, UK: Cambridge University Press.

Clark, T.W., Curlee, A.P. Minta, S.C. & Kareiva, P.M. (1999). *Carnivores in Ecosystems: The Yellowstone Experience*. New Haven: Yale University Press.

Crete, M. (1999). Distribution of deer biomass supports the hypothesis of exploitation ecosystems. *Ecology Letters*, **2**, 223–7.

Crooks, K.R. & Soulé, M.E. (1999). Mesopredator release and avifaunal extinctions in a fragmented system. *Nature*, **400**, 563–6.

Diamond, J.M. (1986). Carnivore dominance and herbivore coexistence in Africa. *Nature*, **320**, 112.

Dunson, W.A. & Travis, J. (1991). The role of abiotic factors in community organisation. *American Naturalist*, **138**, 1067–91.

Eberhardt, L.L. (2000). Reply: predator-prey ratio dependence and regulation of moose populations. *Canadian Journal of Zoology*, **78**, 511–13.

Eberhardt, L.L. & Peterson, R.O. (1999). Predicting the wolf-prey equilibrium point. *Canadian Journal of Zoology*, **77**, 494–8.

Festa-Bianchet, M. (1991). The social system of bighorn sheep: grouping patterns, kinship and female dominance rank. *Animal Behaviour*, **42**, 71–82.

Flueck, W.T. (2000). Population regulation in large northern herbivores: evolution, thermodynamics, and large predators. *Zeitschrift für Jagdwissenschaft*, **46**, 139–66.

Fowler, C.W. (1987). A review of density dependence in populations of large mammals. In *Current Mammalogy*, Vol. 1, ed. H.H. Genoways. New York, USA: Plenum, pp. 401–41.

Fryxell, J.M. & Lundberg, P. (1994). Diet choice and predator-prey dynamics. *Evolutionary Ecology*, **7**, 379–93.

Fryxell, J.M. & Lundberg, P. (1998). *Individual Behavior and Community Dynamics*. Population and Community Biology Series 20. London: Chapman & Hall.

Fryxell, J.M., Greever, J. & Sinclair, A.R.E. (1988). Why are migratory ungulates so abundant? *American Naturalist*, **131**, 781–98.

Fuller, R.J. (2001). Responses of woodland birds to increasing numbers of deer: a review of evidence and mechanisms. *Forestry*, **74**, 289–98.

Fuller, T.K. (1989). Population dynamics of wolves in north-central Minnesota. *Wildlife Monographs*, **105**, 1–41.

Gaillard, J.-M., Festa-Bianchet, M., Yoccoz, N.G., Loison, A. & Toïgo, C. (2000). Temporal variation in fitness components and population dynamics of large herbivores. *Annual Review of Ecology and Systematics*, **31**, 367–93.

Habitat atlas for species at risk (2003). http://wlapwww.gov.bc.ca/sir/fwh/wld/atlas/species/bighorn.html

Hayes, R.D., Baer, A.M., Wotschikowsky, U. & Harestad, A.S. (2000). Kill rate by wolves on moose in the Yukon. *Canadian Journal of Zoology*, **78**, 49–59.

Heard, D.C. & Williams, T.M. (1992). Distribution of wolf dens on migratory caribou ranges in the Northwest Territories, Canada. *Canadian Journal of Zoology*, **70**, 1504–10.

Holling, C.S. (1959). Some characteristics of simple types of predation and parasitism. *The Canadian Entomologist*, **91**, 385–98.

Holt, R.D. (2000). Trophic cascades in terrestrial ecosystems. Reflections on Polis *et al. Trends in Ecology and Evolution*, **15**, 444–5.

Hunter, M.D. & Price, P.W. (1992). Playing chutes and ladders: heterogeneity and the relative roles of bottom-up and top-down forces in natural communities. *Ecology*, **73**, 724–32.

Husseman, J.S., Murray, D.L. & Power, G. (2003). Assessing differential prey selection patterns between two sympatric large carnivores. *Oikos*, **101**, 591–601.

Korpimäki, E., Norrdahl, K. & Valkama, J. (1994). Reproductive investment under fluctuating predation risk: microtine rodents and small mustelids. *Evolutionary Ecology*, **8**, 357–68.

Kunkel, K. & Pletscher, D.H. (1999). Species specific population dynamics of cervids in a multipredator ecosystem. *Journal of Wildlife Management*, **63**, 1082–93.

Jedrzejewska, B. & Jedrzejewski, W. (1998). *Predation in Vertebrate Communities: the Bialowieza Primeval Forest as a Case Study*. Berlin: Springer.

Jedrzejewski, W., Schmidt, K., Milkowski, L., Jedrzejewska, B. & Okarma, H. (1993). Foraging by lynx and its role in ungulate mortality: the local (Bialowieza Forest) and the Palaearctic viewpoint. *Acta Theriologica*, **38**, 385–403.

Jobin, A., Molinari, P. & Breitenmoser, U. (2000). Prey spectrum, prey preference and consumption rates of Eurasian lynx in the Swiss Jura Mountains. *Acta Theriologica*, **45**, 243–52.

Kunkel, K.E., Ruth, T.K., Pletscher, D.H. & Hornocker, M.G. (1999). Winter prey selection by wolves and cougars in and near Glacier National Park, Montana. *Journal of Wildlife Management*, **63**, 901–10.

Larsen, D.G., Gauthier, D.A. & Markel, R.L. (1989). Causes and rate of moose mortality in the southwest Yukon. *Journal of Wildlife Management*, **53**, 548–57.

Larter, N.C., Sinclair, A.R.E. & Gates, C.C. (1994). The response of predators to an erupting bison, *Bison bison athabascae*, population. *Canadian Field Naturalist*, **108**, 318–27.

Laundre, J.W., Lucina, H. & Altendorf, K.B. (2001). Wolves, elk, and bison: Reestablishing the 'landscape of fear' in Yellowstone National Park, U.S.A. *Canadian Journal of Zoology*, **79**, 1401–9.

Leibold, M.A. (1989). Resource edibility and the effects of predators and productivity on the outcome of trophic interactions. *American Naturalist*, **134**, 922–49.

Leopold, A. (1949). *A Sand County Almanac and Sketches from Here and There.* Oxford: Oxford University Press.

Lima, S.L. (1985). Maximizing feeding efficiency and minimizing time exposed to predators: a trade-off in the black-capped chicadee. *Oecologia*, **66**, 60–7.

Lima, S.L. (2002). Putting predators back into behavioural predator-prey interactions. *Trends in Ecology and Evolution*, **17**, 70–5.

Lima, S.L. & Dill, L.M. (1990). Behavioral decisions made under the risk of predation: a review and prospectus. *Canadian Journal of Zoology*, **68**, 619–40.

Linnell, J.D.C. & Bjerke, T. (2002). The fear of wolves: a review of wolf attacks on humans. *NINA-Oppdragsmelding*, **731**, 1–65.

Linnell, J.D.C., Aanes, R. & Andersen, R. (1995). Who killed Bambi? The role of predation in the neonatal mortality of temperate ungulates. *Wildlife Biology*, **1**, 209–24.

Linnell, J.D.C., Swenson, J.E. & Andersen, R. (2001). Predators and people: conservation of large carnivores is possible at high human densities if management policy is favourable. *Animal Conservation*, **4**, 345–50.

Logan, K.A. & Sweanor, L.L. (2001). *Desert Puma: Evolutionary Ecology and Conservation of an Enduring Carnivore.* London: Island Press.

MacPhee, R.D.E. (1999). *Extinctions in Near Time: Causes, Contexts, and Consequences.* New York: Kluwer Academic/Plenum Publishers.

Makovkin, L.I. (1999). *The Sika Deer of Lazovsky Reserve and Surrounding Areas of the Russian Far East.* Vladivostok: Almanac Russki Ostrov.

Marshal, J.P. & Boutin, S. (1999). Power analysis of wolf-moose functional responses. *Journal of Wildlife Management*, **63**, 396–402.

Martin, P.S. & Klein, R.G. (eds.) (1984). *Quaternary Extinctions: A Prehistoric Revolution.* Tuscon: University of Arizona Press.

Matson, P.A. & Hunter, M.D. (1992). The relative contributions of top-down and bottom-up forces in population and community ecology. *Ecology*, **73**, 723–23.

Matyushkin, E.N. (1998). *The Amur Tiger in Russia: an Annotated Bibliography 1925–1997.* Moscow.

Matyushkin, E.N. & Vaisfeld, M.A. (eds.) (2003). *The Lynx: Regional Features of Use, Ecology, and Protection.* Moscow: Nauka.

May, R. (1973). *Stability and Complexity in Model Ecosystems.* Princeton, NJ: Princeton University Press.

McCabe, T. R. & McCabe, R. E. (1997). Recounting whitetails past. In *The Science of Overabundance: Deer Ecology and Population Management*. Washington & London: Smithsonian Institution Press, pp. 11–26.

McLaren, B. E. & Janke, R. A. (1996). Seedbed and canopy cover effects on balsam fir seedling establishment in Isle Royale National Park. *Canadian Journal of Forest Research*, 26, 782–96.

McLaren, B. E. & Peterson, R. O. (1994). Wolves, moose, and tree rings on Isle Royale. *Science*, 266, 1555–8.

McShea, W. J., Underwood, H. B. & Rappole, J. H. (1997). *The Science of Overabundance: Deer Ecology and Population Management*. Washington DC: Smithsonian Institution Press.

Mech, L. D. & Boitani, L. (eds.) (2003). *Wolves: Behavior, Ecology, and Conservation*. Chicago: University of Chicago Press.

Messier, F. (1994). Ungulate population models with predation: a case study with North American moose. *Ecology*, 75, 478–88.

Messier, F. (1995). Trophic interactions in two northern wolf-ungulate systems. *Wildlife Research*, 22, 131–46.

Messier, F. & Crête, M. (1985). Moose-wolf dynamics and the natural regulation of moose populations. *Oecologia*, 65, 503–12.

Messier, F. & Joly, D. O. (2000). Regulation of moose populations by wolf predation. *Canadian Journal of Zoology*, 78, 506–10.

Messier, F., Huot, J., Le Henaff, D. & Luttich, S. (1988). Demography of the George River caribou herd: evidence of population regulation by forage exploitation and range expansion. *Artic*, 41, 279–87.

Miller, S. G., Bratton, S. P. & Hadidian, J. (1992). Impacts of white-tailed deer on endangered and threatened vascular plants. *Natural Areas Journal*, 12, 67–74.

Mosimann, J. E. & Martin, P. S. (1975). Simulating overkill by paleoindians. *American Scientist*, 63, 304–13.

Murie, A. (1934). *The Moose of Isle Royale*. University of Michigan, Museum of Zoology, Miscellaneous Publication 25.

National Research Council (1997). *Wolves, Bears, and their Prey in Alaska: Biological and Social Challenges of Wildlife Management*. Washington, DC: National Academy Press.

Neale, J. C. C. & Sacks, B. N. (2001). Resource utilization and interspecific relations of sympatric bobcats and coyotes. *Oikos*, 94, 236–49.

Okarma, H. (1995). The trophic ecology of wolves and their predatory role in ungulate communities of forest ecosystems in Europe. *Acta Theriologica*, 40, 335–86.

Okarma, H., Jedrzejewski, W., Schmidt, K., Kowalczk, R. & Jedrzejewska, B. (1997). Predation of Eurasian lynx on roe deer *Capreolus capreolus* and red deer *Cervus elaphus* in Bialowieza Primeval Forest, Poland. *Acta Theriologica*, 42, 203–24.

Oksanen, L. & Oksanen, T. (2000). The logic and realism of the hypothesis of exploitation ecosystems (EEH). *American Naturalist*, 155, 703–23.

Oksanen, T., Oksanen, L., Schneider, M. & Aunapuu, M. (2001). Regulation, cycles and stability in northern carnivore-herbivore systems: back to first principles. *Oikos*, 94, 101–17.

Owen-Smith, N. (1988). *Megaherbivores: the Influence of Very Large Body Size on Ecology*. Cambridge: Cambridge University Press.

Pace, M.L., Cole, J.J., Carpenter, S.R. & Kitchell, J.F. (1999). Trophic cascades revealed in diverse ecosystems. *Trends in Ecology and Evolution*, **14**, 483–8.

Paine, R. (1966). Food web complexity and species diversity. *American Naturalist*, **100**, 65–75.

Palomares, F., Gaona, P., Ferreras, P. & Debiles, M. (1995). Positive effects on game species of top predators by controlling smaller predator populations: an example with lynx, mongooses, and rabbits. *Conservation Biology*, **9**, 295–305.

Patterson, B.R. & Messier, F. (2000). Factors influencing killing rates of white-tailed deer by coyotes in eastern Canada. *Journal of Wildlife Management*, **64**, 721–32.

Persson, L. (1999). Trophic cascades: abiding heterogeneity and the trophic level concept at the end of the road. *Oikos*, **85**, 385–97.

Peterson, R.O. (1977). *Wolf Ecology and Prey Relationships on Isle Royale*. Natl. Park Serv. Sci. Monogr. Ser. 11. 210 pp.

Peterson, R.O. & Page, R.E. (1983). Wolf-moose fluctuations at Isle Royale National Park, Michigan, USA. *Acta Zoologica Fennica*, **174**, 251–3.

Peterson, R.O. & Page, R.E. (1988). The rise and fall of Isle Royale wolves 1975–1986. *Journal of Mammalogy*, **69**, 89–99.

Peterson, R.O. & Vucetich, J.A. (2002). *Ecological Studies of Wolves on Isle Royale*. Annual report 2001–2002. School of Forestry and Wood Products, Michigan Technological Univeristy, Houghton, Michigan, USA.

Peterson, R.O. (1995a). Wolves as interspecific competitors in canid ecology. In *Ecology and Conservation of Wolves in a Changing World*, ed. L.N. Carbyn, S. H. Fritts & D.R. Seip. Alberta, Canada, pp. 315–24.

Peterson, R.O. (1995b). *The wolves of Isle Royale: A Broken Balance*. Minocqua, Wisconsin: Willow Creek Press.

Peterson, R.O. (1999). Wolf-moose interaction on Isle Royale: the end of natural regulation. *Ecological Applications*, **9**, 10–16.

Peterson, R.O., Woolington, J.D. & Bailey, T.N. (1984a). Wolves of the Kenai Peninsula, Alaska. *Wildlife Monographs*, **88**, 1–52.

Peterson, R.O., Page, R.E. & Dodge, K.M. (1984b). Wolves, moose and the allometry of population cycles. *Science*, **224**, 1350–2.

Pimlott, D.H., Shannon, J.A. & Kolenosky, G.B. (1969). *The Ecology of the Timber Wolf in Algonquin Provincial Park*. Ontario Department of Lands and Forests, Report 87. Toronto, Ontario, Canada.

Polis, G.A. (1999). Why are parts of the world green? Multiple factors control productivity and the distribution of biomass. *Oikos*, **86**, 3–15.

Post, E. & Forchhammer, M.C. (2001). Pervasive influence of large-scale climate in the dynamics of a terrestrial vertebrate community. *BMC Ecology* **1**, 5.

Post, E., Stenseth, N.C., Peterson, R.O., Vucetich, J.A. & Ellis, A.M. (2002). Phase dependence and population cycles in a large-mammal predator-prey system. *Ecology*, **83**, 2997–3002.

Post, E., Peterson, R.O., Stenseth, N.C. & McLaren, B.E. (2002). Ecosystem consequences of wolf behavioural response to climate. *Nature* **401**, 905–7.

Potvin, F. (1988). Wolf movements and population dynamics in Papineau-Labelle reserve, Québec. *Canadian Journal of Zoology*, **66**, 1266–73.

Putman, R.J. (1996). Ungulates in temperate forest ecosystems: perspectives and recommendations for future research. *Forest Ecology and Management*, **88**, 205–14.

Ripple, W.J., Larsen, E., Renkin, R.A. & Smith, D.W. (2001). Trophic cascades among wolves, elk and aspen on Yellowstone National Park's northern range. *Biological Conservation*, **102**, 227–34.

Rosenzweig, M.L. (1971). Paradox of enrichment: destabilization of exploitation ecosystems in ecological time. *Science*, **171**, 385–7.

Rossiter, M.C. (1991). Environmentally-based maternal effects a hidden force in insect population dynamics. *Oecologia*, **87**, 288–94.

Ruxton, G.D., Gurney, W.S.C. & deRoos, A.M. (1992). Interference and generation cycles. *Theoretical Population Biology*, **42**, 235–53.

Sæther, B.-E. (1997). Environmental stochasticity and population dynamics of large herbivores: a search for mechanisms. *Trends in Ecology and Evolution*, **12**, 143–9.

Schmitz, O.J., Beckerman, A.P. & O'Brien, (1997). Behaviorally-mediated trophic cascades: the effects of predation risk on food web interactions. *Ecology*, **78**, 1388–99.

Schmitz, O.J., Hamback, P.A. & Beckerman, A.P. (2000). Trophic cascades in terrestrial ecosystems: a review of the effects of carnivore removals on plants. *American Naturalist*, **155**, 141–53.

Schaller, G.B. (1972). *The Serengeti Lion: A Study of Predator-Prey Relations.* Chicago: University of Chicago Press.

Seip, D.R. (1991). Predation and caribou populations. *Rangifer*, Special Issue No. 7, 46–52.

Seip, D.R. (1992). Factors limiting woodland caribou populations and their interrelationships with wolves and moose in southeastern British Columbia. *Canadian Journal of Zoology*, 70, 1494–503.

Sinclair, A.R.E. (1979). The eruption of ruminants. In *Serengeti: Dynamics of an Ecosystem*, ed. A.R.E. Sinclair & M. Norton-Griffiths Chicago: University of Chicago Press, pp. 31–45.

Sinclair, A.R.E. (1985). Does interspecific competition or predation shape the African ungulate community? *Journal of Animal Ecology*, **54**, 899–918.

Sinclair, A.R.E. (1989). Population regulation in animals. In *Ecological Concepts*, ed. J.M. Cherrett. British Ecology Society Symposium 26. Oxford: Blackwell, pp. 197–241.

Sousa, W.P. (1984). The role of disturbance in natural communities. *Annual Review of Ecology and Systematics*, **15**, 353–41.

Swenson, J.E., Dahle, B. & Sandegren, F. (2001). Brown bear predation on moose [Bjørnens predasjon på elg]. *Norwegian Institute for Nature Research (NINA), Fagrapport*, **48**, 1–22.

Terborgh, J. (1988). The big things that run the world – a sequel to E.O. Wilson. *Conservation Biology*, **2**, 402–3.

Terborgh, J., Lopez, L., Tello, J., Yu, D. & Bruni, A.R. (1997). Transitory states in relaxing land bridge islands. In *Tropical Forest Remnants: Ecology, Management, and Conservation of Fragmented Communities*, ed. W.F. Laurance & R.O. Bierregaard, Jr. Chicago: University of Chicago Press.

Terborgh, J., Estes, J.A., Paquet, P. *et al.* (1999). The role of top carnivores in regulating terrestrial ecosystems. In *Continental Conservation*, ed. M.E. Soulé & J. Terborgh. Washington DC: Scientific Foundations of Regional Reserve Networks, Island Press.

Terborgh, J., Lopez, L., Nuñes, P. *et al.* (2001). Ecological meltdown in predator-free forest fragments. *Science*, **294**, 1923–6.

Van Ballenberghe, V. (1987). Effects of predation on moose numbers: a review of recent North American studies. *Swedish Wildlife Research*, Supplement **1**, 431–60.

Varley, N. & Gunther, K.A. (2002). Grizzly bear predation on a bison calf in Yellowstone National Park. *Ursus*, **13**, 377–81.

Wehausen, J.D. (1996). Effects of mountain lion predation on bighorn sheep in Sierra Nevada and Granite Mountains of California. *Wildlife Society Bulletin*, **24**, 471–9.

White, K.S. & Berger, J. (2001). Antipredator strategies of Alaskan moose: are maternal trade-offs influenced by offspring activity? *Canadian Journal of Zoology*, **79**, 2055–62.

Wielgus, R.B. & Bunnell, F.L. (1994). Dynamics of small, hunted brown bear *Ursus arctos* population in southwestern Alberta, Canada. *Biological Conservation*, **67**, 161–6.

Wilson, E.O. (1987). The little things that run the world – the importance and conservation of invertebrates. *Conservation Biology*, **1**, 344–6.

Woodroffe, R. (2000). Predators and people: using human densities to interpret decline of large carnivores. *Animal Conservation*, **3**, 165–73.

Woodroffe, R. & Ginsberg, J.R. (1998). Edge effects and the extinction of populations inside protected areas. *Science*, **280**, 2126–8.

Young, D.D. & McCabe, T.R. (1997). Grizzly bear predation rates on caribou calves in northeastern Alaska. *Journal of Wildlife Management*, **61**, 1056–66.

15

Restoring the functions of grazed ecosystems

IAIN J. GORDON

INTRODUCTION

Since the Neolithic, human populations have expanded across the globe, changing the landscape through fire, forest clearance, hunting and the grazing of domestic stock (Van Wieren 1995, see also Chapter 7). As a consequence the majority of the terrestrial ecosystems of the globe are man made, dominated by large herbivores, be they domestic or wild. Today, over 50% of the global land surface is managed for livestock grazing and other large expanses supporting wild herbivores, with up to 20% of the land area put over to nature conservation in some countries (e.g. Cumming 1998, Olff *et al.* 2002). Large herbivores are major drivers of the shape and function of terrestrial ecosystems modifying nutrient cycles, soil properties, net primary production and fire regimes. Whilst these impacts can be positive for ecosystem function, if grazing pressure is high, in the long-term, changes in ecosystem structure and its effects on ecosystem function (e.g. accepting, storing and recycling water, nutrients and energy) can lead to a reduction in the ability of the ecosystem to provide goods and services, in which case the land is degraded. If degraded ecosystems are to fulfil their potential in the economic, aesthetic and cultural landscape there is a need to restore their functioning through changes in management and land use. Some of these changes may be minor, e.g. changes in the densities of herbivores, others may be more dramatic, for example, restoration of predators or reductions in soil nutrient levels, through the removal of topsoil.

Large Herbivore Ecology, Ecosystem Dynamics and Conservation, ed. K. Danell, P. Duncan, R. Bergström & J. Pastor. Published by Cambridge University Press. © Cambridge University Press 2006.

The previous chapters in this book clearly demonstrate that a great deal is known about the ways in which herbivores affect the structure and function of terrestrial ecosystems. In this chapter, I will discuss how this understanding could be used to restore and/or maintain the functioning of ecosystems, and the goods and services they provide. First, I will discuss the issue of ecosystem health, second, I will cover the ways in which ecosystems can become degraded, by which I mean that they lose the ability to provide goods and services to us. Third, I will discuss how managers may use the understanding of the role of herbivores in affecting ecosystem function to restore the functioning of degraded ecosystems. I will concentrate on two examples of using scientific information to manage ecosystems, first, the restoration of hydrological function in degraded semi-arid savanna systems, second, the restoration of woodland in degraded European conservation areas, specifically Caledonian pine forest. It is clear that managers cannot do this without the consent of the people affected by these restoration efforts since, at the very least, people will be affected by, for example, changes in water quality or changes in the number of animals available to hunt, or the public may be expected to foot the bill for any changes in management. Finally, I go back to the previous chapters in the book and assess what further research is needed for scientists to be able to support practical management for the restoration of grazed ecosystems.

The extent to which ecological knowledge, described in previous chapters in this book, is being used for restoration management is pitiful. For example, in a Web of Science review of all publications since 1986 including 'restoration AND herbivore' in the title, abstract or keywords, only ten articles referred to the large mammalian herbivores and none of these looked at the restoration of ecological function other than vegetation cover or species composition. This is not to say that research on the relationship between large herbivores and soil/vegetation/biodiversity is not being used for ecosystem restoration; however, it does not appear to be couched in these terms. With over 50% of the global land surface being shaped by the management of large herbivores, and much of it being degraded, there is likely to be to an increasing requirement to use the theoretical and empirical research outlined in the earlier chapters in this book, to develop protocols for grazing land restoration. Why then do ecologists not present their work in ways that link to the restoration of degraded grazing landscapes? Gone are the days when we could sit back and say that it is the fault of the manager for not seeking our advice. The ball is now firmly in our court to ensure that our research meets the needs for restoration of grazing ecosystem function and is provided to the managers in a way that is useful to them.

HOW DO WE DEFINE A HEALTHY ECOSYSTEM?

With the realization that extensive areas of the globe are degraded, or becoming so, there has been increasing interest in the science and management of restoring ecosystem health. The broadest definition of ecosystem health is that it:

(1) Maintains basic functions, including nutrient cycling, water capture, provision of food and shelter for animals, at the full ecosystem potential and at a range of spatial scales.
(2) Maintains viable populations of native species of plants and animals at appropriate spatial and temporal scales.
(3) Reliably meets the long-term needs (material, aesthetic and spiritual) of people with an ongoing interest in the landscape.

This definition is basically anthropocentric and incorporates attributes and indicators which are specific to particular uses of the landscape (pastoral, conservation, social, harvesting) and at different scales (paddock, property, catchment, landscape). There are also much more limited definitions which only take into account the biophysical measures of ecosystem health (e.g. Pyke *et al.* 2002).

Much work has gone into developing methods for monitoring indicators of ecosystem health, and determining ways in which to manage for the indicators of ecosystem health. For grazed ecosystems the indicators are generally based on soil stability, hydrological function, biotic integrity, land fragmentation and networks, pasture condition, and invasive species trends (Pyke *et al.* 2002). Given the degree of knowledge imparted in this book it is clear that more sophisticated indicators can be defined which relate directly to ecosystem function and its relationship with the provision of goods and services. For example, the majority of chapters in this book demonstrate the importance of heterogeneity in ecosystem structure for biological processes, such as the role that heterogeneity in vegetation structure plays in determining faunal biodiversity (see Chapter 13). Future indices of ecosystem health should include, not only the quantity of a parameter but also its variance within a system at a range of spatial scales, or some other index of the spatial structuring of the landscape.

DEGRADATION IN GRAZED ECOSYSTEMS

Between one-third and one-half of the land surface has been transformed by human action; currently more atmospheric nitrogen is fixed by humanity than by all natural terrestrial sources combined and more than one-half of all accessible surface fresh water is put to use by humanity (Vitousek *et al.* 1997). Much of the land, nitrogen and water are used for agricultural production, specifically the production of livestock for the provision of meat, fibre and milk. The majority of livestock production occurs on transformed landscapes where substantial inputs of capital and resources have created highly productive and responsive systems. However, in many regions of the world the beef industry relies on extensive grazing of marginal vegetation resources in ecosystems which are highly vulnerable to overexploitation. For example, in semi-arid systems heavy stocking levels and periodic droughts have lead to substantial degradation of vegetation cover, soil surface condition, soil erosion, biodiversity, etc. Wild large herbivores can also have a negative impact on biodiversity if managed in a way which allows their numbers to increase beyond a certain threshold because of, for example, reduced predation, or culling or the provision of water. For example, in many areas of the eastern seaboard of the USA where hunting has ceased and predators extirpated, deer numbers have increased to levels that are thought to be even higher than pre-European times, with a resultant impact on biodiversity (Garrott *et al.* 1993, McShea *et al.* 1997, Peek & Stahl, 1997, Crête 1999). On the other hand, because of their role as keystone species (Thompson *et al.* 1995, Pickup *et al.* 1998, Wallis de Vries *et al.* 1998), removal of large herbivores from ecosystems can lead to domination of the landscape with monocultures of plant species which are susceptible to grazing (Wallis de Vries *et al.* 1998). This domination by a single or a few species can also reduce vegetation structural heterogeneity, nutrient cycling rates and biodiversity.

THE ROLE OF HERBIVORES IN ECOSYSTEM FUNCTION

As has been described in detail in earlier chapters in this book, large herbivores play a vital role in the functioning of healthy ecosystems. Through their grazing, trampling, defecation, urination and seed transport they tend to increase the productivity of grazed ecosystems (Hobbs 1996). The life cycle of plants is one where young plants produce high levels of new vegetative material, but as the plant matures more energy is used for storage and reproduction. Though removal of plant tissue, herbivory can maintain plants in an early phenological state which is associated with the increased production of new vegetative material. However, if grazing/browsing is too heavy then the plant will have reduced growth and may even die (see Chapter 4). At the level of the vegetation community, earlier successional stages are more productive than later successional stages because more of the carbon is used for growth instead of being locked up in structural or storage forms. In some circumstances grazing/browsing can change the plant species composition to one of an earlier successional stage which tends to be of higher productivity than later successional stages, however, in certain systems (e.g. northern/ temperate forests) browsing can remove fast growing, early successional species leading to dominance of slow growing, chemically defended, late-successional stage species (Augustine & McNaughton 1998, Skarpe *et al.* 2004) and reduce nutrient cycling rates (Pastor & Naiman 1992).

The grazing/browsing, defecation and urination behaviour of large herbivores affects the spatial and temporal dynamics of nutrients in grazed ecosystems. As described above the selective grazing and browsing behaviour of large herbivores can maintain vegetation in early phenological and successional stages, which reduces the amount of nutrients tied up in structural material, increasing the readily available nutrients for soil microbes to degrade and provides for further absorption by the plants. However, in other circumstances where grazing/browsing kills plants or stops them regenerating, herbivores can drive succession towards slow growing, well-defended species which have their nutrients locked in wood or secondary compounds, reducing nutrient availability and nutrient cycling rates (see Chapter 10). Through digestion, defeication and urination, vegetation is transformed into compounds that are more easily degraded into nutrients which can be recycled by the plants. Defecation and urination also redistributed nutrients across the landscape, creating nutrient hot-spots where animals preferentially defecate and urinate, and reducing the nutrient levels in the vegetation where herbivores selectively forage. This increases the heterogeneity of nutrients in the landscape, particularly in nutrient-poor systems, and in turn increases the diversity of vegetation (i.e. some plant species thrive in nutrient-rich patches whilst others are able to cope in nutrient-poor patches) and the associated fauna (Wallis de Vries *et al.* 1998).

The intermediate grazing hypothesis, a variant of the intermediate disturbance hypothesis (Grime 1973, Connell 1979) proposes that species diversity in grazed ecosystems is highest when an ecosystem is grazed at intermediate levels. This is because intermediate levels of defoliation lead to greatest structural complexity in the vegetation allowing species of different autoecological niches to survive in the landscape. For example, web building spiders require sites on which to build their webs and therefore require, trees/shrubs/tussocks, whereas rove beetles need open areas of grassland in which to pursue their prey. Birds may require different habitats for nesting and feeding, for example, the meadow pipit nests in tussocks in grassland but feeds on leather-jackets in the open grassland areas.

Generally, the intermediate grazing hypothesis is based on a spatial frame-work; however, I would argue that there is an opportunity to develop this hypothesis on a temporal basis. Natural grazing systems are typified by dynamic herbivore populations (Sæther 1997, Clutton-Brock & Pemberton 2004) and, as such, the present management ethos which commonly manages herbivore populations for stability (du Toit *et al.* 2003), often at levels well below the carrying capacity, is 'unnatural'. For example, for over 50 years the management of the Kruger National Park in South Africa was predicated on the basis of using culling to manage large herbivore populations at set predetermined levels. This management strategy does not reflect the natural dynamics of this semi-arid grazing system where, climatic variability, predator/prey cycles and disease would have meant that there were dramatic annual, decadal and centurial fluctuations in the numbers of large herbivores in the region (Owen-Smith & Ogutu 2003). This would have lead to increased diversity of vegetation in the park reflecting periods of low grazing pressure when tree recruitment, for example, would have been high, and periods of high grazing pressure when trees and shrubs would be been rare in the system and grasslands dominated (e.g. Prins & Van der Jeugd 1993, see also Chapter 10). In an area the size of the Kruger National Park it should be possible to restore this temporal variation in herbivore grazing pressure by using spatially variable population management policies; however, in many other national parks, especially in Europe, this management opportunity does not exist. I would advocate that management of large herbivore populations in the European context will require cooperative management policies which link groups of national parks together allowing the build up of large herbivore densities in some parks whilst reducing densities in others. This situation could be reversed over time to allow ecosystem dynamics to mimic natural boom and bust cycles, with movement of animals between parks maintaining genetic integrity of the metapopulation (Hanski & Gilpin 1997). Whilst this strategy would require human intervention, it mimics the natural cycles of interactions between plants and herbivores, allowing plants and animals adapted to both severe and lax grazing pressure to coexist.

Large herbivores are also major prey of top predators within ecosystems. Healthy herbivore populations are required to maintain viable large carnivore populations. Since the carnivore and scavenger guilds are determined by the interaction between top predators (Carbone *et al.* 1997), a truly functional multi-trophic ecosystem requires healthy herbivore populations. Whilst carnivores rarely control large herbivore populations in a top-down fashion (see Chapter 14), their role as part of healthy ecosystems cannot be denied, through, for example, affecting the distribution of prey in the landscape at a range of scales (Frid & Dill 2002) with consequent effects for environmental heterogeneity. For this reason, ecosystems in which large carnivores have been extirpated would benefit from their reintroduction, or where this cannot take place because of the human impact of predation/ predator threat, then human hunting should mimic natural predation and be used as a mechanism for changing herbivore distribution patterns.

RESTORING ECOSYSTEM FUNCTION

Restoring hydrological function in degraded rangelands

Globally, rangeland systems are degraded or are degrading fast. This is primarily because the stocking levels of livestock in rangelands have increased in the past, although climate driven droughts may also play a part. Degradation is manifested by loss of vegetation cover, bush encroachment, soil erosion and nutrient loss. Ultimately, this leads to a loss of animal production and an impoverishment of the livelihoods of pastoralists.

In Northern Australia, extended droughts over the past two decades, combined with changed cattle production systems have placed increasing pressure on the native grass savannas. The resultant increase in grazing pressure has caused substantial degradation in pasture biomass, vegetation cover and species composition, with knock on effects for soils and animal production. Apart from the negative effects of soil loss for pasture productivity, there is increasing concern that erosion and nutrient run-off will lead to reduced water quality downstream in rivers, estuaries and off-shore reefs. This is precipitating the development of government policy for changes in grazing practices to meet both on-site and off-site water quality objectives.

Large areas of the catchments draining into the Great Barrier Reef Lagoon along Australia's north-east Queensland coast are used for extensive beef production. There is evidence that heavy grazing pressure over the past decades has lead to land degradation in some of these catchments (Tothill & Gillies 1992, Ash et al. 1997). It has also led to increased discharge of nutrients and sediments into the Great Barrier Reef Lagoon, with an estimated four- to five-fold increase in the sediment (Brodie et al. 2001, Neil et al. 2002, McCulloch et al. 2003) and nutrient (Furnas 2003) delivery since the Europeans started grazing their sheep (*Ovis aries*) and cattle (*Bos indicus*) in the area in the 1860s.

The grazing lands of north-eastern Queensland are dominated by native pasture underlying eucalypt woodland. These systems cover approximately 15 million hectares and support almost one million head of cattle. The rangelands of Queensland's dry tropics are characterized by variable wet season and dry seasons with a mean rainfall of approximately 650 mm per annum but a range from 150 mm to 1600 mm per annum (over the past 120 years). The rainfall is captured by the system through infiltration or lost from the system through run-off. The soil structure determines the extent to which water infiltrates or runs off, whilst vegetation cover acts as a trap for water which runs overland allowing it to infiltrate. To date, although there has been very little research linking grazing to hydrological function in rangelands, the conceptual framework linking vegetation cover to infiltration and run-off has been well developed (Ludwig et al. 2000).

Since grazing affects vegetation cover, grazing management can have a major effect on the proportion of rain which infiltrates rather than running off. In rangelands, heavy grazing leads to a reduction in the cover of perennial grasses and an increase in the proportion of annual species in the system (Fensham et al. 1999). It also reduces vegetation height (favouring prostrate species) and vegetation cover. When rainfall events do occur a greater proportion of the rain leaves the system as run-off than enters the system as infiltration (Ludwig et al. 2000). The run-off takes with it sediments and nutrients degrading soil health and reducing the nutrient content of these already nutrient-poor systems. As a consequence there is a reduction in the soil organic matter, soil nutrient levels, soil porosity and soil respiration rates. The latter is, in part, a consequence of the reduction in soil micro- and macro-fauna. In order to restore the functioning of these ecosystems there is a need to increase the organic matter content of the soils. This happens when vegetation cover increases, not only contributing to the availability of organic matter through litterfall, but also acting as a barrier to overland water flow, increasing infiltration, reducing soil surface hardness and allowing the soil organisms to recolonize the site, all of which increase soil porosity.

In order to allow vegetation cover to increase there has to be a reduction in grazing pressure at critical times of the year. Rangeland systems are characterized by ground cover of annual and perennial grasses. Annual grasses become more dominant under intense grazing whereas the perennial species tend to decrease, because they are preferred by livestock during the extended dry season. Long periods of intense grazing reduce the root stores of the perennial grasses and lead to the death of perennial plants, whereas the annual grasses survive over the dry season, or drought, as seeds. If intense grazing continues then even the abundance of annual grasses declines, leaving very low vegetation cover. Australian rangelands do not appear to be invaded by shrub species under intense grazing pressure in the way that African rangelands are.

Recent evidence suggests that the vegetation cover at the end of the dry season is the most important contributor to water retention and soil stability, so a heavily grazed system, dominated by annuals does not provide the vegetation cover necessary to protect the landscape from rainfall events (McIvor *et al.* 1995, Scanlon *et al.* 1996, Roth 2004). Grazing management strategies are, therefore, required which allow the perennial grasses to re-establish, recuperate their root stores and not suffer excessive dry season/drought defoliation. In the semi-arid rangelands of north-east Australia this can happen if the land is utilized at relatively low stocking densities, such that only 25% of the current wet season's standing biomass is consumed by the end of the dry season, under continuous (i.e. year-round) grazing; or where degraded pastures are destocked during the wet season, allowing the perennial grasses to re-establish and restore their reserves (Ash *et al.* 2001). The mechanism involved is that structures in the landscape, be they live tree or shrubs, fallen trees or ground vegetation cover, act as traps for vegetation litter. When this litter becomes incorporated into the soil it increases the soil's moisture holding capacity. Increased moisture holding capacity allows annual grasses to establish followed by re-establishment of the perennial grasses. Soil macro-invertebrates play a major role in savanna systems, through increasing the amount of macropores in the soil, turning over the soil, reducing the crust on the surface layer and incorporating litter into the soil (Holt *et al.* 1996). In degraded savanna systems, an increase in vegetation cover may not initially increase vegetation production, only when the macro-invertebrates colonize the system will productivity increase.

Financial analysis suggests that reducing stock levels and wet season spelling can be done without affecting the long-term cash flows because economic returns from degraded pastures are more variable and there are more years in which financial losses occur (Ash *et al.* 2001). Hence, in degraded pastures the risk of not being able to carry the herd through drought years is greater. Improvement in grazing practice will not only improve the productivity of the rangeland, increasing profit for the landholder, it will also decrease year-to-year risk of herd failure. In addition, improved grazing practices have other indirect benefits, such as reducing the run-off of nutrients and sediments into the Great Barrier Reef Lagoon.

Through a science-based understanding of the relationship between landscape structure, at a range of scales, researchers have been able to provide practical advice on grazing management to improve the hydrological functioning of degraded rangelands. This example demonstrates the importance of restoration of grazed ecosystems, not only for improving the health of the managed system but also for the downstream effects on other ecosystems of conservation and economic importance.

Restoring the conservation value of Scottish Caledonian forest

The original Caledonian forest which covered most of Scotland has dwindled to only about 1% of its original cover today. Much of the last remaining forest has been lost in the last 40 years due to a combination of commercial afforestation, and heavy grazing by sheep and red deer (*Cervus elaphus*). The Scots pine (*Pinus sylvestris*) which characterizes the Caledonian forest is a keystone species upon which many other species depend. Within the UK the Caledonian forest has high conservation value because a number of rare plants are particularly associated with the pinewoods including twinflower (*Linnaea borealis*), one-flowered wintergreen (*Moneses uniflora*) and orchids, such as creeping ladies tresses (*Goodyera repens*) and lesser twayblade (*Listera cordata*). There are also characteristic insects such as the pine weevil (*Hylobius abietis*), pine looper moth (*Bupalus piniaria*) and wood ants (*Formica aquilonia*); and birds like the siskin (*Carduelis spinus*), Scottish crossbill (*Loxia scotica*), black grouse (*Tetrao tetrix*) and capercaillie (*Tetrao urogallus*). Finally, mammals typical of the Caledonian forest include the red squirrel (*Sciurus vulgaris*), pine marten (*Martes martes*), wild cat (*Felis silvestris*), badger (*Meles meles*), fox (*Vulpes vulpes*), roe deer (*Capreolus capreolus*) and red deer.

Both roe and red deer browse on Scots pine seedlings, eating the needles and leader shoots of young trees, and the heavy browsing from their increased numbers in the last 70 years has prevented the natural regeneration of the native pinewoods throughout the highlands. Red deer also damage or kill sapling Scots pines by de-barking or thrashing them with their antlers, particularly in late spring when the new season's antlers are shedding their velvet. In a natural, healthy forest ecosystem, the deer numbers would be such that they allow regeneration of trees in the forest, but the present-day imbalance in Scottish pinewoods has created a 'generation gap' in the Scots pines, with no trees younger than 150 years in most locations. For example, Nixon and Cameron (1994) used dendrochronology to demonstrate that heavy grazing by deer over the past 100 years has stopped recruitment in Caledonian forests on the east coast of Scotland.

Long-term analysis of vegetation trends suggested that heavy grazing pressure affects not only the Scots pine itself, but also the ground vegetation, with the forest moving to acid grassland if heavily grazed over a period of time. As such it has been recommended that grazing be removed to allow the regeneration of the forest and the associated ground vegetation. Grazing exclosures were established in order to prevent grazing by large herbivores. These exclosures demonstrate the benefits to vegetation and the associated fauna from grazing removal (Baines et al. 1994). However, deer are a natural part of the Caledonian forest ecosystem, so if grazing is removed for long periods there would be an increase in the biomass of the ground layer and shading of tree seedlings thereby reducing their opportunity to become established. This would create an homogeneous vegetation which reduces the niches available for species more typical of open areas within the woodland. Whilst there is no clear evidence from Caledonian forest, several controlled studies suggest that there is an intermediate grazing pressure (between heavy stocking and no stocking), which would maximize the conservation value of grazed ecosystems (Wallis de Vries et al. 1998). For the Caledonian forest this would require the managers to cull the deer herd to densities at which Scots pine regeneration could occur. Broadly, this is assumed to be about 6 deer km^{-2} (Scottish Natural Heritage 1994), but this is likely to be related to distance from seed source, soil type, climate, other grazers and alternate vegetation resources (Scott et al. 2000). Where this has been tried it has been demonstrated that deer can coexist with native woodland and sapling establishment can take place in the presence of deer browsing (Fig. 15.1, for birch woodland see Stewart 1996). Similarly, recruitment increased near a chairlift in the Scottish cairngorms (Beaumont et al. 1995) because disturbance decreased the deer use of areas adjacent to the chairlift (Miller et al. 1998).

In the longer term, however, it may be necessary to instigate a means by which grazing pressure can be varied in time by creating a network of cooperating management units where grazing pressure, in this case deer density, is managed over the whole of the cooperative to maintain population cycles at local scales while maintaining a steady harvest at larger regional scales. This would require that populations in different places fluctuate out of phase with one another. In Scotland this is happening with the development of a network of deer management groups (http://www.deer-management. co.uk/) which come up with a cooperative management plan for deer roaming across their holdings. Cooperative management groups have been set up in other countries, in recognition that resource management has to be implemented at a spatial scale relevant to the resource being managed (Prins et al. 2000).

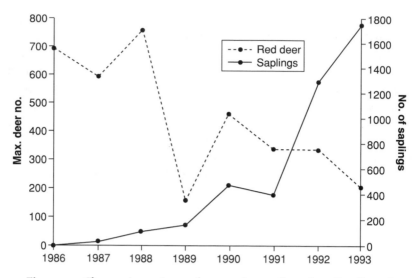

Figure 15.1. Changes in maximum deer numbers and number of saplings above ground vegetation height at Craig Meagaidh National Nature Reserve, Scotland. Data from Nature Conservancy Council (1989) and Stewart (1996).

INVOLVING PEOPLE IN MANAGING FOR RESTORATION

Cooperative management groups are necessary because wild herbivores range over areas much larger than traditional individual management units. Therefore, the management of one management unit affects what happens at another. For example, Scottish red deer have home ranges which range across a number of estates. There has been a long debate amongst deer managers that heavy culling of deer in one part of their range, to meet conservation objectives, will have a negative effect on the availability of trophy animals in another estate, which forms part of the population's range where sport hunting is the main objective. A recent empirical and modelling study clearly demonstrated that emigration of male red deer from natal areas increases with female density (Clutton-Brock *et al.* 2002). The authors incorporated this information into an economic model, to assess optimal culling strategies on Scottish estates, taking account of deer numbers on neighbouring estates. They concluded that managers hoping to maximize their economic returns from hunting stags should reduce female densities on their land to around 50% of the ecological carrying capacity, to reduce emigration and possibly encourage immigration from neighbouring populations. However, the conclusions should be treated with caution as stags often move large distances in search of hinds during the mating season. Since this coincides with the hunting season in Scotland, stags are likely to be shot by landowners on whose land they do not spend most of their lives (Sibbald *et al.* 2001). Large-scale male movements during the rut also demonstrate that biological processes often occur at a much larger scale than that affected by individual management plans. Hence, there is great value in the co-operation between different resource managers to ensure that their management targets are not jeopardized by the activities of others.

Whilst cooperation is necessary for the development of common, co-herent management strategies for wild herbivore populations, it can also be used to help manage the conservation value of the ecosystem by providing the opportunity for linked management units (parks, reserves or hunting areas) to manage fluctuations in herbivore population density. In general terms, in nature, and in natural grazed ecosystems in particular, there is no such thing as a stable herbivore population or grazing pressure. For example, many grazed ecosystems are characterized by severe dynamics with peaks and troughs in population density driven by climate, disease and predation (Coulson *et al.* 2000, Owen-Smith 2000, Messier 1994). This results in periods over which vegetation is heavily impacted and lightly impacted. During the latter there are opportunities for trees to regenerate (e.g. Prins & Van der Jeugd 1993, Pastor *et al.* 1997). Given that most grazed systems are mosaics of heavily and lightly grazed areas, and that species characteristic of grazed systems are associated with specific features of the grazed system, it would be expected that varied grazing pressure would allow a greater number of species to survive.

As has been shown throughout this book there is a great deal of excellent research on the relationship between herbivores, the soil, vegetation, fauna and predators. However, the future management of large mammalian herbivores will require biologists, sociologists, economists, politicians and the public to come together to ensure that local communities are involved in the management of natural resources to provide public benefits from wildlife through sustainable use. Whilst this holistic approach to wildlife management is necessary, recent publications (e.g. Adams & Hulme 2001, Hulme & Murphree 2001) demonstrate that the current emphasis on the community conservation approach is predominantly driven by the benefits for the livelihoods of the communities/households involved, and not the benefits for species conservation or the conservation of whole ecosystems. This appears to reflect an over-emphasis on funding for research on the socio-economic, as opposed to the ecology/ wildlife biology component, of the community conservation paradigm because of the involvement of humans in all aspects of wildlife policy development and implementation. In fact, socio-economists have not been particularly interested in the wildlife conservation part of the relationship, particularly the ecosystem consequences of certain management actions to enhance economically desirable species. This has provoked some recent debate on the relative benefits to biodiversity of traditional protectionist versus community-based approaches (e.g. Walker 1999, Attwell & Cotterill 2000, Wilshusen *et al.* 2002). Ecological research is invaluable in highlighting the issues concerned with the management of natural resources and coming up with practical tools for effecting the management on the ground. In the end, however, there is a pressing need for ecologists/ wildlife biologists to work with socio-economists and local communities to develop truly sustainable approaches to wildlife management.

CONCLUSIONS

Each of the chapters in this book highlight the future areas of research needed to address the issues they raise. Most call for long-term studies of the role of large herbivores within ecosystems highlighting that without these our understanding of the dynamics of the system will be poor. However, whilst I agree that long-term studies are needed for understanding, managers need the knowledge we have now and if they are to start restoring grazed ecosystem health. This will require scientists and managers to enter into collaboration where management is an adaptive process, taking the knowledge scientists have now and implementing this in models which allow managers to assess the consequences of different management actions for ecosystem provision of goods and services. Establishing a monitoring programme which assesses the impacts of management on system response, will allow scientists and managers to use this information to inform the further development of models that support adaptive management decisions (Fig. 15.2).

The types of models described in Chapter 12 then become part of a long-term scientific development rather than an end-point for handing over to managers (the usual fate of decision support systems). One of the problems with most ecosystem models (e.g. SAVANNA) is that they are incredibly parameterized, and require a great deal of information to run and generate scenarios. For many situations it will be necessary for scientists to say that they only have limited information on system

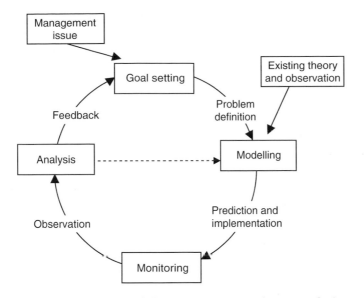

Figure 15.2. Collaboration cycle between managers and scientists for long-term, science-based adaptive management.

function, and will have to develop soft system models in the first instance using expert systems and Bayesian belief networks to utilize grey knowledge (Starfield *et al.* 1993). This will mean that scientists have to enter into a dialogue with the managers, informing them of the limitations, uncertainties and likely errors in predictions, but demonstrating that the models producing are 'to the best of our knowledge' as good predictions as can be produced at the current time. It is to be hoped that the adaptive interactions between scientists and managers will lead to further improvements in these models.

As I mentioned at the beginning of the chapter, whilst there has been some effort to link an understanding of the relationship between herbivore grazing and the restoration of vegetation biomass and composition, there has been little research on how to restore herbivore communities into areas where they have been extirpated. To date, much of the research and management of herbivores within grazed ecosystems has focused on the management of individual species (Gordon *et al.* 2004). For example, the majority of reintroductions have been single species (Gordon 1991) whereas in many ecosystems, communities of herbivore species have been lost from the system. Given the different roles played by herbivores of different size and feeding strategy in ecosystem function it is unlikely that there will be a truly functioning ecosystem reinstated unless the community is reconstituted. Within natural large herbivore communities competition and facilitation play important roles in shaping habitat use, population dynamics and vegetation structure. In general, herbivores of small body size are facilitated by large herbivores when the latter reduce the biomass of poor quality vegetation, and return the structure of the vegetation to an earlier phenological and successional state. This would mean that where herbivory is being restored into an ungrazed system the reintroduction of large herbivores should precede that of the smaller herbivores. Only when the vegetation has been transformed into a mosaic of low and high quality resources should smaller species be reintroduced. Once these smaller species are established they are likely to out-compete the larger bodied species for the high quality, but scarce, resources, thus limiting the populations of the larger species to the poorer quality habitats.

This book demonstrates the extensive knowledge science has accumulated on the role of herbivores in driving the structure and function of grazed ecosystems. To date, much of this knowledge is not being used for ecosystem management, be it to meet economical, social or conservation objectives (Gordon et al. 2004). In this chapter I have attempted to demonstrate how this knowledge can be used in an adaptive science-based ecosystem management approach. The future of many grazed ecosystems will depend upon scientists and practitioners forming a partnership in which scientists can investigate hypotheses at the landscape scale whilst managers can gain from the knowledge to provide guidance to management in the collaborative cycle for adaptive management (Fig. 15.2).

ACKNOWLEDGEMENTS

Firstly I would like to thank Kjell Danell for inviting me to the workshop on large herbivore ecology held in Kronlund, Sweden, 22–26 May 2002. It was an excellent opportunity to get scientists from a range of backgrounds together to discuss issues close to their hearts, that is the role of herbivores in driving ecosystem structure and function. Patrick Duncan, John Pastor and Kjell gave extremely valuable comments on an early draft of this manuscript, although they are not to be held accountable for the final product. Finally, I would like to thank the Scottish Executive Environment and Rural Affairs Department, and CSIRO for supporting my research over the past 20 years.

REFERENCES

Ash, A.J., McIvor, J.G., Mott, J.J. & Andrews, M.H. (1997). Building grass castles: integrating ecology and management of Australia's tropical tall grasslands. *The Rangelands Journal*, 19, 123–44.

Ash, A., Corfield, J. & Ksiksi, T. (2001). *The Ecograze Project: Developing Guidelines to Better Manage Grazing Country*. Australia: CSIRO.

Augustine, D.J. & McNaughton, S.J. (1998). Ungulate effects on the functional species composition of plant communities: herbivore selectivity and plant tolerance. *Journal of Wildlife Management*, 62, 1165–83.

Baines, D., Sage, R.B. & Baines, M. (1994). The implications of red deer grazing to ground vegetation and invertebrate communities of Scottish native pinewoods. *Journal of Applied Ecology*, 31, 776–83.

Brodie, J., Furnas, M., Ghonim, S. *et al.* (2001). *Great Barrier Reef Water Quality Action Plan*. Townsville, Australia: Great Barrier Reef Marine Park Authority. [http://www.gbrmpa.gov.au/corp_site/key_issues/water_quality/action_plan]

Carbone, C., du Toit, J.T. & Gordon, I.J. (1997). Feeding success in African wild dogs: does kleptoparasitism by spotted hyaenas influence pack size? *Journal of Animal Ecology*, 66, 318–26.

Connell, J.H. (1979). Tropical rainforests and coral reefs as open non-equilibrium systems. In *Population Dynamics: 20th Symposium of the BES*, ed. R.M. Anderson, B.D. Turner & L.R. Taylor. Oxford: Blackwell Scientific Publications, pp. 141–63.

Clutton-Brock, T.H. & Pemberton, J.M. (eds.) (2004). *Soay Sheep. Dynamics and Selection in an Island Population*. Cambridge: Cambridge University Press.

Coulson, T., Milner-Gulland, E.J. & Clutton-Block, T.H. (2000). The relative roles of density and climatic variation on population dynamics and fecundity rates in three contrasting ungulate species. *Proceedings of the Royal Society of London, Series B*, 267, 1771–9.

Crête, M. (1999). The distribution of deer in North America supports the hypothesis of exploitation ecosystems. *Ecology Letters*, 2, 223–7.

Cumming, D.H.M. (1998). Can the use of big game help to conserve biodiversity in southern African savannas? *South African Journal of Animal Science*, 94, 362.

du Toit, J.T., Biggs, H.C. & Rogers, H.K. (eds.) (2003). *The Kruger Experience: Ecology and Management Of Savanna Heterogeneity*. Washington DC: Island Press.

Fensham, R.J., Holman, J.E. & Cox, M.J. (1999). Plant species responses along a grazing disturbance gradient in Australian grassland. *Journal of Vegetation Science*, 10, 77–86.

Frid, A. & Dill, L. (2002). Human-caused disturbance stimuli as a form of predation risk. *Conservation Ecology*, 6 (1).

Furnas, M.J. (2003). *Catchment and Corals: Terrestrial Runoff to the Great Barrier Reef*. Townsville, Australia: AIMS and Reef CRC.

Garrott, R.A., White, P.J. & White, C.V.A. (1993). Overabundance: an issue for conservation biologists? *Conservation Biology*, 7, 946–9.

Gordon, I.J. (1991). Ungulate reintroductions: the case of the scimitar-horned oryx. *Symposium of the Zoological Society of London*, **62**, 217–40.

Grime, J.P. (1973). Competitive exclusion in herbaceous vegetation. *Nature*, **242**, 344–7.

Hanski, I.A. & Gilpin, M.E. (eds.) (1997). *Metapopulation Biology: Ecology, Genetics and Evolution*. New York: Academic Press.

Hobbs, N.T. (1996). Modification of ecosystems by ungulates. *Journal of Wildlife Management*, **60**, 695–713.

Holt, J.A., Bristow, K.L. & McIvor, J. (1996). The effects of grazing pressure on soil animals and the hydraulic properties of two soils in semi-arid tropical Queensland. *Australian Journal of Soil Research*, **34**, 69–79.

Ludwig, J.A., Wiens, J.A. & Tongway, D.J. (2000). A scaling rule for landscape patches and how it applies to conserving soil resources in savannas. *Ecosystems*, **3**, 84–97.

McCulloch, M.T., Fallon, S., Wyndham, T. *et al.* (2003). Coral record of increased sediment influx to the inner Great Barrier Reef of Australia since European settlement. *Nature*, **421**, 727–30.

McIvor, J.G., Williams, J. & Gardiner, C.J. (1995). Pasture management influences runoff and soil movement in the semi-arid tropics. *Australian Journal of Experimental Agriculture*, **35**, 55–65.

McShea, W.J., Underwood, H.B. & Rappole, J.H. (eds.). (1997). *The Science of Overabundance. Deer Ecology and Population Management*. Washington: Smithsonian Institution Press.

Messier, F. (1994). Ungulate population models with predation: a case study with the North American moose. *Ecology*, **75**, 478–88.

Nature Conservancy Council (1989). *Craig Meagaidh National Nature Reserve, First Management Plan 1989–93*. Edinburgh: Nature Conservancy Council.

Neil, D.T., Orpin, A.R., Ridd, P.V. & Yu, B. (2002). Sediment yield and impacts on river catchments to the Great Barrier Reef Lagoon. *Marine and Freshwater Research*, **53**, 733–52.

Olff, H., Ritchie, M.E. & Prins, H.H.T. (2002). Global environmental controls of diversity in large herbivores. *Nature*, **415**, 901–4.

Owen-Smith, N. (2000). Modeling the population dynamics of a subtropical ungulate in a variable environment: rain, cold and predators. *Natural Resource Modelling*, **13**, 57–87.

Owen-Smith, N. & Ogutu, J. (2003). Rainfall influences on ungulate population dynamics. In *The Kruger Experience: Ecology and Management of Savanna Heterogeneity*, ed. J.T. duToit, H.C. Biggs & H.K. Rogers. Washington DC: Island Press, pp. 310–31.

Pastor, J. & Naiman, R.J. (1992). Selective foraging and ecosystem processes in boreal forests. *American Naturalist*, **139**, 305–705.

Pastor, J., Moen, R. & Cohen, Y. (1997). Spatial heterogeneities, carrying capacity, and feedbacks in animal-landscape interactions. *Journal of Mammalogy*, **78**, 1040–52.

Peek, L.J. & Stahl, J.F. (1997). Deer management techniques employed by the Colombus and Franklin County Park District, Ohio. *Wildlife Society Bulletin*, **25**, 440–2.

Pickup, G., Bastin, G.N. & Chewings, V.H. (1998). Identifying trends in land degradation in non-equilibrium rangelands. *Journal of Applied Ecology*, **35**, 365–77.

Prins, H.H.T. & Van der Jeugd, H.P. (1993). Herbivore population crashes and woodland structure in East Africa. *Journal of Ecology*, **81**, 305–14.

Prins, H.H.T., Geu Grootenhuis, J. & Dolan, T.T. (2000). *Wildlife Conservation by Sustainable Use*. Dordrecht: Kluwer Academic Publishers.

Pyke, D.A., Herrick, J.E., Shaver, P. & Pellant, M. (2002). Rangeland health attributes and indicators for qualitative assessment. *Journal of Range Management*, **55**, 584–97.

Roth, C.H. (2004). A framework relating soil surface condition to infiltration and sediment and nutrient mobilization in grazed rangelands of northeastern Queensland, Australia. *Earth Surface Processes and Landforms*, **29**, 1093–104.

Sæther, B.E. (1997). Environmental stochasticity and population dynamics of large herbivores: A search for mechanisms. *Trends in Ecology and Evolution*, **12**, 143–9.

Scott, D., Welch, D., Thurlow, M. & Elston, D.A. (2000). Regeneration of *Pinus sylvestris* in a natural pinewood in NE Scotland following reduction in grazing by *Cervus elaphus*. *Forest Ecology and Management*, **130**, 199–211.

Skarpe, C., Aarrestad, P.A., Andreassen, H.P. *et al.* (2004). The return of the giants: ecological effects of an increasing elephant population. *Ambio*, **33**, 276–82.

Starfield, A.M., Cumming, D.H.M., Taylor, R.D. & Quadling, M.S. (1993). A frame-based paradigm for dynamic ecosystem models. *AI Applications*, **7**, 1–13.

Stewart, F. (1996). The effects of red deer (*Cervus elaphus*) on the regeneration of birch (*Betula pubescens*) woodlands in the Scottish Highlands. Unpublished Ph.D. thesis, University of Aberdeen.

Thompson, D.B.A., Hester, A.J. & Usher, M.B. (eds.) (1995). *Heaths and Moorland: Cultural Landscapes*. Edinburgh: HMSO.

Tohill, J.C. & Gillies, C. (1992). The pasture lands of northern Australia. Their condition, productivity and sustainability. *Tropical Grasslands Society of Australia. Occasional Paper No. 5.*

Van Wieren, S.E. (1995). The potential role of large herbivores in nature conservation and extensive land use in Europe. *Biological Journal of the Linnean Society*, **56**, 11–23.

Wallis de Vries, M.F., Bakker, J.P. & Van Wieren, S.E. (1998). *Grazing and Conservation Management. Conservation Biology Series*. Dordrecht: Kluwer Academic Publishers.

16

Themes and future directions in herbivore-ecosystem interactions and conservation

JOHN PASTOR, KJELL DANELL,
ROGER BERGSTRÖM AND PATRICK DUNCAN

Some 50 years ago, *Nature* made the following observation on the issue of management of large game animals, mainly herbivores, in Africa: 'The presence of enormous herds of game animals is quite incompatible with the economic exploitation of the country. . .the game must go and there can be no hope of its survival outside the National Parks. . .As yet, however, there is practically no information available on the biology of these mammals, information that is essential for successfully managing such parks and reserves.' (reprinted in *Nature*, **431**, 638, 7 October 2004). Twenty-five years later, the first comprehensive analysis on the interaction of large herbivorous mammals and ecosystems was published (Sinclair & Norton-Griffiths 1979). This seminal volume summarized over a decade of research by Sinclair, Norton-Griffiths, Bell, McNaughton and their colleagues on the ecology of large mammals in the Serengeti, initiated partly in response to the situation developing in Africa that prompted *Nature* to make the earlier observation.

As the papers in the present volume show, current research on how large mammalian herbivores affect ecosystem properties and on the problems of their conservation extends far beyond Africa to every biome and on every continent except Antarctica. In the past 25 years since the publication of the Serengeti volume, new effects of herbivores, and new mechanisms of response of plants and ecosystems have been discovered. New

Large Herbivore Ecology, Ecosystem Dynamics and Conservation, ed. K. Danell, P. Duncan, R. Bergström & J. Pastor. Published by Cambridge University Press. © Cambridge University Press 2006.

mathematical theories of functional responses and herbivore-ecosystem interactions have also been developed. The study of large mammal-ecosystem interactions has come a long way in the past 50 years. These new discoveries and theories have formed the basis of this book.

In this summary chapter, we wish to point out four major synthetic themes that run through these chapters. It is our hope that these themes may suggest directions for future research. Two of these themes (body size and plant tissue chemistry) pertain to problems faced by large mammalian herbivores in securing enough food to survive and reproduce. The other two themes (the responses of individual plants to grazing or browsing and the altered plant community composition) pertain to the effects of herbivores on ecosystems and other members of food webs. Together, these themes form a framework for understanding the richness of herbivore-ecosystem interactions described throughout this book.

THEME 1: THE IMPORTANCE OF BODY SIZE

Virtually every chapter in this book mentions body size as an important factor determining the impact of herbivores on ecosystems. Indeed, the title of this book implicitly recognizes the importance of herbivores with 'large' body size. In several chapters, especially Chapters 1 and 9, body size is a central organizing principle.

Most (but not all) physiological and ecological processes of large herbivores scale allometrically instead of proportionally to body mass. In allometric scaling, the rates of processes scale to mass raised to a power that is not equal to 1 and is usually around 0.75, rather than simply increasing or decreasing in a constant proportion to mass. This allometric scaling is well-known (e.g., Peters 1983, Schmidt-Neilson 1984) and derives from the fact that resources and waste products are used and produced throughout the animal's volume (proportional to a linear dimension cubed), but taken in and expelled through the animal's surface area (proportional to a linear dimension squared). The allometric scaling relationships determine virtually every step in the passage of food through the animal, including: food requirements and consumption rates (see Chapter 4); bite force and the ability to physically exploit tough foods such as seeds (see Chapter 6); maximum chewing rate (see Chapters 3 and 9); digestion time, food retention time, and the ability to break down cell walls (see Chapters 6 and 8); metabolic rate (see Chapter 2); and return of nitrogen to the soil via defecation and urination (see Chapters 9 and 10). Allometric scaling of physiological processes are therefore powerful tools which we can use to integrate herbivore-ecosystem interactions across a wide diversity of species and biomes.

While many processes scale allometrically to body mass, they do not all scale at the same rate. Consequently, the differences between, for example, metabolic rate, digestion time and excretion rate do not remain constant with body mass because they do not increase with body mass in parallel. The differences in these rates determine the input-output balance of materials through the animal and therefore its control over ecosystem processes. Because the differences in rates are not constant with increasing body mass, nutrient input-output balances of an herbivore also differ greatly with body mass. Consequently, larger-bodied animals will have different effects on ecosystem processes than smaller-bodied animals (see Chapters 9 and 10). It seems clear that we do not yet fully understand the origin and implications of differences in herbivore body mass. The values of allometric scaling relationships with body mass are well-documented in the literature. What is required now is a comprehensive analysis of what these different values mean for the energy and nutrient balance of large herbivores with body masses ranging across several orders of magnitude as well as how these differences underlie the different magnitudes and directions of ecosystem effects of large mammalian herbivores.

THEME 2: TISSUE CHEMISTRY

Every herbivore faces a problem in converting plant material to body tissues because plant foods contain nutrients in stoichiometric ratios that are usually very different from what a herbivore requires (Sterner & Elser 2002). Some nutrients are present in a herbivore's food in excess of its tissue requirements, while other nutrients in a herbivore's food are deficient with respect to its tissue requirements. These deficient nutrients are likely to be limiting to the animal's growth and development, including its reproductive potential. Overcoming these stoichiometric problems is implicit in such behaviours as selecting a diet, allocating time and energy to different behaviours such as travelling, handling, and processing, and defending or sharing resources from and with competitors.

Most large mammalian herbivores try to partly overcome a stoichiometric imbalance of their foods by having a mixed diet, such that the stoichiometry of the mixed diet approximates that of the herbivore's body. Because of the stoichiometric differences between their body chemistry and that of their plant food, large mammalian herbivores must forage selectively on different plant parts and plant species (see Chapters 4, 6, 8 and 10). Furthermore, because herbivores occupy an intermediate position in food chains, a stoichiometric imbalance between plant and herbivores also determines how efficiently energy and nutrients are transferred from plants to higher trophic levels (Sterner & Elser 2002).

The nutrients which are overabundant in plants relative to herbivore requirements must be rapidly expelled in urine to prevent toxic accumulation in the herbivore's body. Conversely, other nutrients which are deficient must be conserved in the digestive tract and herbivore body (see Chapters 9, 10 and 11) and are usually excreted in faecal material. The nitrogen in urine is made available to plants more quickly than that in faecal material but also volatizes more quickly (see Chapters 9 and 10). Therefore, the stoichiometric imbalance between plants and herbivores determines the pathway of nutrient excretion from an herbivore and consequently the rates of nutrient cycling and productivity of ecosystems (see Chapters 9, 10 and 11).

The stoichiometric needs of herbivores also vary allometrically with body mass because of the different proportions of skeletal to soft tissues in large compared with small mammals. Large mammals (in the order of 1000 kg body mass) require a higher proportion of their mass in skeletal tissues (greater than 20%) to support their weight compared with small mammals (in the order of 1–10 kg body mass requiring 5% of that mass to be in skeletal tissues). Because skeletal tissues contain high concentrations of phosphorus (P) compared with soft tissues, the proportion of P in the bodies of large mammals relative to other elements is double that of small mammals (Sterner & Elser 2002). Presumably the same applies to calcium (Ca), another element with high concentrations in skeletal tissues. In ungulates, annual production and shedding of antlers increases P and Ca requirements even further (Moen & Pastor 1998). These greater P and Ca needs of large mammals might mean that they have to search for food high in Ca and P. Bark, especially that of species in the Salicaceae and Populaceae, is relatively high in Ca and P. This may explain why the Salicaceae and Populaceae are preferred foods amongst many large mammalian herbivores across many orders and in several biomes. How do changes in stoichiometry with body mass affect dietary changes for an individual animal as it grows as well as the dietary differences between different taxa of different body sizes? Does the ability of an ecosystem to supply P and Ca keep pace with the increasing skeletal burden of P and Ca in larger mammals? If not, does the rate of cycling of these nutrients set mass balance constraints on body size and survival (Moen *et al.* 1999)? The relationship of plant tissue chemistry to the nutrient requirements of herbivores, especially in relation to body mass, is a problem rich with potential for future research.

THEME 3: PHYSIOLOGICAL RESPONSES OF PLANTS TO HERBIVORES

Herbivores affect plants in many ways, including stripping leaves, grazing, browsing shoots, trampling shoots and roots, and eating and dispersing seeds and fruits (see Chapters 4, 8 and 9). Many hundreds of experiments have shown that the plants respond to herbivores with a bewildering variety of physiological changes, ranging from changes in tissue chemistry, through changes in allocation of new growth, to changes in growth form (Chapter 4).

Such experiments have been valuable in developing the database needed to understand plant-herbivore interactions. While the results of each experiment are understandable within their own limited context, generalizations about how plants respond to herbivore impact have proven far more difficult to make, partly because of the great variety and specificity of the many plant responses observed. Although the diversity of plant responses to herbivory may be one of the salient features of herbivore-ecosystem interactions, a general theory of plant responses is still sorely needed.

Such a general theory must distinguish between the plasticity of responses by an individual plant to herbivory from the long-term adaptive responses of a population. Short-term plastic responses of individuals involve reallocation of internal resources to allow the plant to continue to photosynthesize and accumulate biomass in spite of temporary loss of some tissues. Short-term plastic responses of grazed or browsed individuals are tightly constrained by mass balances of carbon, nutrients and other internal resources. Long-term adaptive responses, however, involve the spread of genes or alleles which control the phenotypic responses through a population; these genes spread only if individuals possessing them have greater reproductive fitness, or greater representation in the next generation compared with individuals that do not possess them. Short-term plastic responses are physiological and constrained by resource availability. Long-term adaptive responses are evolutionary and constrained by net increases in reproductive fitness. Failure to distinguish between plastic and adaptive responses has in the past led to much confusion (see McNaughton 1983 vs. Belsky et al. 1993 for an example involving compensatory growth of plants to herbivory).

There is a great need now for general theories of herbivore-plant interactions that can account for the plasticity of individual plant responses and the adaptive responses of populations. A general theory accounting for plastic responses has to provide mechanisms for certain phenomena (compensatory regrowth, changes in tissue chemistry, etc.) given the constraints of resource availability and allocation on plant growth. A general theory for adaptive responses must explain how the genes controlling them spread through populations and how this further affects evolution of the herbivores themselves. These are two different theories which are not necessarily mutually exclusive. Ideally we want one theory unifying both, but this may be far into the future.

The carbon-nutrient balance hypothesis (Bryant et al. 1983) was an early attempt at a general theory of the plasticity of plant responses to herbivory subject to the constraints of limited supplies of carbon or nutrients. Unfortunately, this hypothesis has not withstood every experimental test expected of it (Hamilton et al. 2001). Some of the criticism seems to be based on its failure to provide an evolutionary frame-work for plant responses to herbivory (Nitao et al. 2002). However, this criticism did not recognize that the carbon-nutrient balance hypothesis was an attempt at providing a physiological frame-work for understanding short-term plastic responses of individual plants, not the spread of adaptations through populations (Lerdau & Coley 2002). Nevertheless, no general theory of plant physiological and evolutionary responses to herbivory has been developed since the carbon-nutrient balance hypothesis was proposed. The next large step in understanding plant-herbivore interactions will probably not come from one more experiment, no matter how well designed. It will almost certainly come from someone taking a comprehensive look at the myriad of experiments on plant responses to herbivory that have already been done (reviewed in Chapters 4, 8 and 9) and proposing a new testable theory that attempts to unify this bewildering variety of responses within a simple framework.

THEME 4: CHANGES IN PLANT COMMUNITIES AND ECOSYSTEM PROPERTIES

The effects of herbivores, whether through selective consumption of particular plant species or plant parts, through redistributing nutrients in carcasses, faeces and urine, or through physical disturbance such as trampling, are not randomly distributed across all plant species, nor are the responses of each plant species the same for the same herbivore impact. This biased effect of large mammalian herbivores on resource distribution, plant consumption, and the divergence of plant responses to herbivory, necessarily results in changes in plant communities that often persist for long periods of time, often as much as several generations of herbivores. Therefore, herbivores and their descendents must contend with the changes they have wrought through their selective foraging decisions, their non-random trampling impacts, and the variety of plant responses to them (see Chapters 4, 5, 6, 7, 8, 9, 10 and 11).

Different plant species within a community have different nutrient uptake rates and different litter chemistries, properties which together determine rates of nutrient cycling and productivity. It is intriguing that the same chemical properties of green tissues and woody meristems which determine the degree of selection or avoidance by herbivores, such as nitrogen and lignin concentrations or concentrations of secondary 'defensive' metabolites, are also the very same properties which determine leaf and twig litter decay rates in the soils. Therefore, the initial changes in productivity upon browsing or grazing are amplified over time, because of concomitant changes in the chemistry of the litter entering the soil and subsequent changes in soil nutrient availability (see Chapters 9, 10 and 11). And so, herbivore-induced changes in plant community composition cannot be separated from the changes in productivity and nutrient cycling rates.

Changes in plant community composition also affect the microclimate because of changes in the plant canopy, penetration of sunlight, and evapotranspiration. These changes in microclimate then impact other animals, especially invertebrate herbivores and detritivores, something which has only recently been recognized (see Chapter 13). Through their non-random impacts on plant communities, large mammalian herbivores therefore affect many higher members of food webs, even species with whom they are not in direct competition.

A major new mechanism of how herbivores may affect plant community dynamics, explored especially in Chapters 6 and 8, concerns the consumption and dispersal of seeds and fruits. Most of the world's large mammalian herbivores are specialized as browsers or grazers, but most also supplement their traditional diets with seeds when they can, such as oak acorn consumption by deer (see Chapter 6) and fruit consumption by ungulates, especially in the tropical forests (see Chapter 8). Although consumption and dispersal of seeds is a minor, perhaps even negligible portion of the nutrient flow in most ecosystems (except perhaps for tropical forests), the seed contains within itself the DNA determining future nutrient uptake rates and tissue chemistry of the plants – through genetic control of properties such as tissue chemistry, the DNA in the seeds ultimately determines the nutrient cycling rate of an ecosystem. Therefore, by moving the DNA for a particular species around in the landscape, large mammalian herbivores may have a much greater and longer lasting effect on the distribution of ecosystem properties than their direct browsing/grazing of existing plants in any one spot. But we currently know very little about distances of seed dispersal by large mammalian herbivores, germination rates of consumed seeds, and survival rates of seedlings germinated from seeds that are consumed compared with seeds that are not. This area of research represents perhaps the largest current deficiency in our understanding of herbivore-plant community interactions.

The impact of large herbivores on ecosystem dynamics and functioning ('cascade effects') clearly depends on many factors, perhaps the most important being the density of the herbivores. Many of the ungulate populations in the northern hemisphere are increasing rapidly (see chapter 6) and the processes which limit these populations are clearly of central importance. Because large herbivores affect nutrient cycling through their effects on plant communities as well as serving as conduits of energy and nutrient flow to predators, both 'top-down' and 'bottom-up' forces operate simultaneously in all ecosystems. Population dynamics of large mammalian herbivores are complicated because of their influence on plant communities and energy/nutrient flow through food webs. The search for a single mechanism regulating mammalian herbivore populations (a major theme of the Third European Mammalogy Conference as recently as 1999, for example) is therefore no longer a tenable research problem. Rather, we must begin to understand how these complicated population dynamics emerge from the changes in plant communities and associated changes in nutrient cycling and energy flow up food chains to the predators. The information available suggests that herbivore populations are limited by interactions between bottom-up and top-down processes which are highly dependent on the rate of energy and nutrient flow through food webs and ecosystems, in particular, (i) the presence of predators; (ii) availability of alternative prey; (iii) the impact of food competition on the prey species; (iv) degree of human harvest of both prey and predators; and (v) the mobility of the prey (see Chapter 14). Unfortunately there are very few studies where the limiting processes are well documented over adequate time periods and across multiple trophic levels. Classical studies of ungulate population dynamics measured population sizes and vital rates in the target population, and perhaps also either in their predators or in their food supply. If we are to understand the ecological process driving the dynamics of herbivore populations, it will be necessary to measure the interactions between the herbivores and their predators, food, and the underlying nutrient supply processes in the soil. For the resource–herbivore interactions, the concept of 'key resources' clearly provides a promising approach (see Chapter 3).

CONCLUSIONS

It will not be possible to integrate these four themes into a comprehensive view of herbivore-ecosystem interactions without building and analysing models of specific processes (see Chapters 3 and 12). The intertwining of body size, tissue chemistry, plant physiology and community/ecosystem interactions with herbivores is too complicated to be sorted out by experiments alone. Increasingly, hypotheses will need to be encapsulated into equations representing different types of possible responses: the per capita functional responses that describe the behavioural decisions of individual herbivores (see Chapter 3); the numerical responses of aggregate populations (see Chapter 3); the changes in nutrient cycles as they are constrained by mass balance (see Chapters 9, 10 and 11); and the changes in spatial distribution of food and other required resources across the landscape (see Chapters 9, 11 and 12). To accomplish these goals, modellers need experiments designed to distinguish between different functional responses of the herbivore and numerical responses of their populations to the plants, as well as the different responses of plants and ecosystems to individual behavioural decisions, and aggregate herbivory by entire populations and trophic levels. All of these responses may differ along gradients of climate, soil fertility, herbivore population density, or both per capita and aggregate population consumption rates. In addition, because of the large home range size and long lives of many large mammalian herbivores, many of their effects and the problems they pose for conservation are on very large spatial and very long temporal scales, which virtually preclude any manipulative experiment. The origin and dynamics of spatial patterns in herbivore-dominated landscapes (see Chapter 11), can for all practical purposes be addressed only through a combination of modelling and observational field studies, not by direct manipulation of herbivores over large landscapes (see Chapter 12). Solving these problems will require greater communication between modellers, experimentalists and field naturalists than many will be comfortable with at present. It will require an appreciation of the problems of each approach – not all the experiments that modellers might desire can be done and not all the data that experimenters collect will prove useful to the modellers.

Some 50 years ago, the typical management tool used to conserve populations of large mammalian herbivores was either to try to contain them in large reserves where their populations could reach a stable carrying capacity and/or hunt the population outside the reserves to maintain it at a level lower than the carrying capacity and lower than acceptable 'damage' to crops. Five decades of experience have shown that establishing reserves and controlling populations through hunting, while still useful, have more limited success than originally realized (see Chapter 15). One reason why their success has been so limited is because herbivore-ecosystem interactions are much more complicated than simply being determined by some vaguely defined 'carrying capacity' (Pastor *et al.* 1997). We are on the verge of some exciting new ideas about how management techniques affect the interactions of herbivores with ecosystems (see Chapter 15). Such new ideas must go beyond the standard views of single populations constrained by 'carrying capacity'. It is likely that the new ideas that emerge from addressing management problems will also shed new light on fundamental scientific problems of how ecosystems work.

We hope that this book provides a scientific foundation for herbivore-ecosystem interactions that will assist in helping their conservation worldwide. After all, it would be a shame if, despite all our recent gains in knowledge, the world's populations of large mammalian herbivores, perhaps the most extraordinary product of evolution, were to continue to decline towards extinction or to increase to densities which impedes the ability of ecosystems to sustain them.

REFERENCES

Belsky, A. J., Carson, W. P., Jensen, C. L. & Fox, G. A. (1993). Overcompensation by plants: herbivore optimisation or red herring? *Evolutionary Ecology*, 7, 109–21.

Bryant, J., Chapin, F. S., III & Klein, D. (1983). Carbon/nutrient balance of boreal plants in relation to vertebrate herbivory. *Oikos*, 40, 357–68.

Hamilton, J., Zangerl, A., DeLucia, E. & Berenbaum, M. (2001). The carbon-nutrient balance hypothesis: its rise and fall. *Ecology Letters*, 4, 86–95.

Lerdau, M. & Coley, P. D. (2002). Benefits of the carbon-nutrient balance hypothesis. *Oikos*, 98, 534–6.

McNaughton, S. J. (1983). Compensatory plant growth as a response to herbivory. *Oikos*, **40**, 329–36.

Moen, R. & Pastor, J. (1998). Simulating antler growth and energy, nitrogen, calcium, and phosphorus metabolism in caribou. *Rangifer*, Special Issue No. 10, 85–97.

Moen, R., Pastor, J. & Cohen, Y. (1999). Antler growth and extinction of the Irish elk. *Evolutionary Ecology Research*, **1**, 235–49.

Nitao, J. K., Zangerl, A. R., Berenbaum, M., Hamilton, J. G. & Delucia, E. H. (2002). CNB: requiescat in pace? *Oikos*, **98**, 540–6.

Pastor, J., Moen, R. & Cohen, Y. (1997). Spatial heterogeneities, carrying capacity, and feedbacks in animal-landscape interactions. *Journal of Mammalogy*, **78**, 1040–52.

Peters, R. H. (1983). *The Ecological Implications of Body Size*. Cambridge, UK: Cambridge University Press.

Schmidt-Nielsen, K. (1984). *Scaling: Why is Animal Size So Important?* Cambridge, UK: Cambridge University Press.

Sinclair, A. R. E. & Norton-Griffiths, M. (1979). *Serengeti: Dynamics of an Ecosystem*. Chicago, Illinois: University of Chicago Press.

Sterner, R. W. & Elser, J. J. (2002). *Ecological Stoichiometry: The Biology of Elements from Molecules to the Biosphere*. Princeton, NJ, USA: Princeton University Press.

Index

Page numbers in *italics* refer to figures and tables.